Instant Vortex Air Fryer

Cookbook for Beginners

Simple and Fast Air Fryer Recipes
for Beginners and Advanced Users

Stacy Blaine

Table of Contents

Snacks and Appetizers 35

Vegetable and Sides 86

Poultry Recipes 109

Introduction

The Instant Vortex Plus Air Fryer is a unique and latest cooking appliance. It is a multifunctional cooking appliance that comes with six cooking programs. Instant Vortex Plus Air Fryer is used for cooking food with hot air circulation technology. It blows very hot air in the chamber to cook food fast and evenly from all sides. The best thing about this appliance is that it is enough for your big family because it has a large capacity to cook food for the whole family. It comes with a touch control panel that shows cooking time and temperature. It comes with useful accessories like an air fryer basket, cooking tray, and cooking chamber.

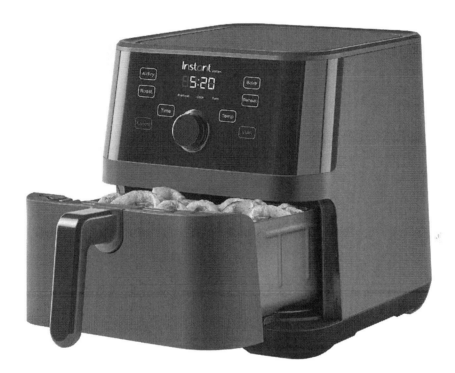

The cleaning process of this appliance is simple and easy to understand. It has six cooking functions: Air Fry, Bake, Broil, Dehydrate, Roast, and Reheat. You can select the "Air Fry" cooking function, prepare chicken wings, thighs, and mixed vegetables, and make it crispy by broiling it. You didn't need a regular oven to bake the cakes, muffins, cupcakes, and brownies. The Instant Vortex Plus Air Fryer has a Bake option. Dehydrate the meats, fruits, and vegetables and preserve them in the jar. This cookbook has delicious recipes for your Instant Vortex Plus Air Fryer. Finally, with one appliance, you can cook healthy, easy, and quick food for your friends and family.

Fundamentals of Instant Vortex Air Fryer

What Is Instant Vortex Air Fryer?

The multi-functional Instant Vortex Air Fryer is designed for you to make your cooking easier. It has six cooking functions; Air fry, Roast, Dehydrate, Bake, Broil, and Reheat.

It has a touch control panel with user-friendly operating buttons; Time display, Temperature display, cooking status, smart programs, dial, start button and cancel button. It has useful accessories and parts; Air vent, Control panel, Dial, Air fryer basket, Air fryer basket handle, Power cord, cooking chamber, and cooking tray.

The Instant Vortex Air Fryer is a time and money-saving appliance. You didn't need to stand in the kitchen for a long time. You will get delicious and healthy food using this appliance because you don't need oil to cook food with an air fryer basket. If you have leftover foods, don't worry because this appliance has a "reheat" cooking function.

Benefits of Using Instant Vortex Air Fryer

The Instant Vortex Air Fryer comes with various benefits some of them are following:

Multi-Tasking Cooking Functions:
You will get six cooking functions; Air fry, bake, dehydrate, broil, reheat, and roast. You didn't need to get another appliance for cooking food because you will get all the useful cooking functions in one appliance. Bake your favorite cake, muffins, and brownies. Roast the beef, chicken, and seafood. Fry your main dishes and dinner meals using the air fry cooking function. Dehydrate the meats, fruits, and vegetables. To get crispy food, use the broil cooking function. Reheat your leftover foods.

Cook Healthy Food in Less Fat and Oil:
The best thing about this appliance is that it takes little to no oil to cook food. You didn't worry about your health because if you are cooking in an air fryer basket, you didn't need to add oil to cook food. You will get healthy food in very little time. It is the perfect appliance for your kitchen.

Time-Saving Cooking Appliance:
This unique appliance is perfect for those who are busy in their life and have no time to cook healthy food in very little time. This cooking appliance cooks food in very time. You will get delicious and healthy food with Instant Vortex Air Fryer appliance.

User-Friendly Features and Buttons:
The Instant Vortex Air Fryer has easy-to-use operating buttons. If you read this book, you will use this appliance.

Cleaning Process:
The cleaning process of this appliance is simple. This book will get details about the cleaning process of Instant Vortex Air Fryer cooking appliance.

Safe to Use:
The Instant Vortex Air Fryer is a safe appliance than other appliances. There is no risk of the splatter of oil on your skin.

Initial Use

When you purchase this appliance, you should understand its initial use. It takes a few times to understand.
Stage: 1
Connect the power cord to the power source. The Instant Vortex Air Fryer is in standby mode, and the display shows "OFF" onto the screen.
Remove the air fryer basket from the cooking chamber. Place cooking tray onto the middle of air fryer basket.
Insert the air fryer basket into the cooking chamber. Then, touch "Air Fry" onto the display screen. Then, touch "Temp" and turn the dial to adjust the temperature to 205ºC/ 400ºF.
Then, touch the "START" button to begin! The display shows "On" on the screen. The cooking status shows "Preheat" on the screen.

When the unit is hot, the display shows "Add Food" onto the screen. Do not add food to the basket for the initial test because it is just a test.

Remove and again insert the air fryer basket. The display shows the temperature and cooking time, and the cooking status shows "Cook" onto the screen.

Partway through cooking, the display shows "turn Food". Remove and re-insert the air fryer basket to pause and resume the program manually.

When one minute is left, the display shows counting in seconds. When the cooking time is completed, the display shows "End" onto the screen, and the fan blows for a while to cool the unit. Touch "Cancel" to return to standby mode and start cooking for real.

Main Functions of Instant Vortex Air Fryer

These six cooking functions are unique on the Instant Vortex Air Fryer. All you need to do is press your favorite function, and the unit will cook different foods perfectly. You need to adjust the cooking time and temperature onto the touch display.

1. Air Fry:

Air fry is a versatile cooking appliance. This cooking function allows you to cook food with less to no oil. Using this cooking appliance, you can cook French fries, chicken nuggets, chicken wings, cauliflower wings, and many more. This cooking function gives you crisp food from the outside and tender from the inside. You can prepare your favorite meals on any occasion using this cooking function.

How to use:
• Press the dial to TURN ON the appliance.
• Touch the smart program "Air Fry" onto the display screen.
• Then, touch the "Temp" to adjust the cooking temperature according to the recipe instructions.
• Touch the "Time" to adjust the cooking time according to the recipe instructions.
• Touch the "Start" button to start. Smarts program automatically saves temperature and cooking time when you touch the "Start" button.
• The display shows "On," and the cooking status shows "Preheat" onto the screen.
• When the display shows "Add Food" onto the screen. Remove the air fryer basket from the unit and place food inside the hot cooking chamber.
• Again insert the air fryer basket. The display shows the cooking time and temperature onto the screen. The cooking status shows "Cook" onto the screen.
• During cooking, the display shows "turn Food" onto the screen.
• If your food doesn't need to be flipped, wait ten seconds for the cooking function to resume automatically.
• When the display shows "End" onto the screen, remove food from the basket. Serve and eat!

Smart program	Time range	Temperature range
Air fry	1 minute to 1 hour	82 to 205°C/180 to 400°F

2. Roast:

You can roast chicken, beef, seafood, and vegetables with roast cooking function and serve on the dining table at dinner or lunchtime. Using this cooking function, you can prepare your favorite dishes like roasted chicken, roasted cauliflower, bell pepper, asparagus, green beans, beef, and many more.

Smart program	Time range	Temperature range
Roast	1 minute to 1 hour	82 to 205°C/180 to 400°F

How to use:
• Press the dial to TURN ON the appliance.
• Touch the smart program "Roast" onto the display screen.
• Then, touch the "Temp" to adjust the cooking temperature according to the recipe instructions.
• Touch the "Time" to adjust the cooking time according to the recipe instructions.
• Touch the "Start" button to start. Smarts program automatically saves temperature and cooking time when you touch the "Start" button.
• The display shows "On," and the cooking status shows "Preheat" onto the screen.
• When the display shows "Add Food" onto the screen. Remove the air fryer basket from the unit and place food inside the hot cooking chamber.
• Again insert the air fryer basket. The display shows the cooking time and temperature onto the screen. The cooking status shows "Cook" onto the screen.
• During cooking, the display shows "turn Food" onto the screen.
• If your food doesn't need to be flipped, wait ten seconds for the cooking function to resume automatically.
• When the display shows "End" onto the screen, remove food from the basket. Serve and eat!

3. Bake:

You didn't need an oven to bake different dishes like desserts, cakes, cookies, muffins, cupcakes, brownies, and many more. The Instant Vortex Air Fryer cooking appliances offer "BAKE." Thanks to vortex because it fulfills all cooking needs.

Smart program	Time range	Temperature range
Bake	1 minute to 1 hour	82 to 205°C 180 to 400°F

How to use:
• Press the dial to TURN ON the appliance.
• Touch the smart program "Bake" onto the display screen.
• Then, touch the "Temp" to adjust the cooking temperature according to the recipe instructions.
• Touch the "Time" to adjust the cooking time according to the recipe instructions.
• Touch the "Start" button to start. Smarts program automatically saves temperature and cooking time when you touch the "Start" button.
• The display shows "ON," and the cooking status shows "Preheat" onto the screen.
• When the display shows "Add Food" onto the screen. Remove the air fryer basket from the unit and place food inside the hot cooking chamber.
• Again insert the air fryer basket. The display shows the cooking time and temperature onto the screen. The cooking status shows "Cook" onto the screen.
• The bake cooking option does not need to flip food.
• When the display shows "End" onto the screen, remove food from the basket. Serve and eat!

4. Broil:

With broil cooking function, you will get crispy and delicious food. You can broil meats, vegetables, and many more. It is used to melt cheese on the top of the nachos, casseroles, pizza, etc.

Smart program	Time range	Temperature range
Broil	1 minute to 40 minutes	Not adjustable

How to use:
• Press the dial to TURN ON the appliance.
• Touch the smart program "Broil" onto the display screen.
• Then, touch the "Temp" to adjust the cooking temperature according to the recipe instructions.
• Touch the "Time" to adjust the cooking time according to the recipe instructions.
• Touch the "Start" button to start. Smarts program automatically saves temperature and cooking time when you touch the "Start" button.
• The display shows "On," and the cooking status shows "Preheat" onto the screen.
• When the display shows "Add Food" onto the screen. Remove the air fryer basket from the unit and place food inside the hot cooking chamber.
• Again insert the air fryer basket. The display shows the cooking time and temperature onto the screen. The cooking status shows "Cook" onto the screen.
• The broil cooking option does not need to flip food.
• When the display shows "End" onto the screen, remove food from the basket. Serve!

5. Dehydrate:

Dehydrate cooking function is used to preserve the food. This cooking function dehydrates meats, fruits, and vegetables. It takes a long to cook, but you will get delicious meals.

How to use:
• Press the dial to TURN ON the appliance.
• Touch smart program "Dehydrate" onto the display screen.
• Then, touch the "Temp" to adjust the cooking temperature according to the recipe instructions.
• Touch the "Time" to adjust the cooking time according to the recipe instructions.
• Touch the "Start" button to start. Smarts program automatically saves temperature and cooking time when you touch the "Start" button. Place food into the air fryer basket.
• The display shows the cooking time and temperature onto the screen. The cooking status shows "Cook" onto the screen.
• When the display shows "End" onto the screen, remove food from the basket. Serve.

6. Reheat:

You didn't worry about leftover foods. The Instant Vortex Air Fryer cooking appliance offers a "Reheat" cooking function. You will get crispy and fresh food after reheating it.

How to use:
• Press the dial to TURN ON the appliance.
• Touch smart program "Reheat" onto the display screen.
• Then, touch the "Temp" to adjust the cooking temperature according to the recipe instructions.

• Touch the "Time" to adjust the cooking time according to the recipe instructions.
• Touch the "Start" button to start. Smarts program automatically saves temperature and cooking time when you touch the "START" button. Place food into the air fryer basket.
• The display shows the cooking time and temperature onto the screen. The cooking status shows "COOK" onto the screen.
• When the display shows "End" onto the screen, remove food from the basket.

Buttons and User Guide of Instant Vortex Air Fryer

The Instant Vortex Air Fryer has user-friendly buttons. There are eight keys on the display of the appliance.

Time/Temperature Display:
The display shows temperature and cooking time onto the screen while cooking.

Time:
Touch on "Time" to adjust the cooking time for your food according to recipe instructions.

Temperature:
Touch on "Temp" to adjust the temperature for your food according to recipe instructions.

Smart Programs:
Touch on corresponding buttons and adjust the cooking functions: Air Fry, Roast, Bake, Reheat, Dehydrate, Broil.

Dial:
Rotate to adjust the cooking time and temperature and press to wake the display screen.

Start:
Press Start to start the smart cooking programs.

Cancel:
Press Cancel to stop the selected cooking function at any time and go back to standby.

Cooking Status:
OFF:
The display shows "OFF" when the unit is in standby mode.

ON:
The display shows "ON" when the smart program is in the PREHEAT stage.

Add Food:
This status shows when the unit reaches the desired cooking temperature, and the display shows "Add Food" to the air fryer basket.
Note: It is not valid for dehydrate or reheat cooking functions.

00:15:
The display shows cooking time in seconds.

400F:
The display shows to adjust the temperature onto the screen.

turn Food:
When is ready to flip or tossed according to recipe instructions.
Note: It is only valid for air fry and roast cooking functions.

End:
When cooking time is completed, the display shows "END" onto the screen.

Accessories of Instant Vortex Air Fryer

The Instant Vortex Air Fryer comes with a cooking chamber and air fryer basket.

Control Panel:
The Instant Vortex Air Fryer comes with a touch control panel. You can touch to adjust the time, temperature, functions, etc.

Cooking Chamber:
The cooking chamber is an essential accessory and it is interior.

Air Fryer Basket:
The air fryer basket is the main accessory in the appliance. It is applicable for all cooking functions.

Cooking Tray:
This accessory is used to storage the food. When the display shows "Add Food" status onto the screen, you should place the cooking tray in the air fryer basket.

Troubleshooting

Problem 1: Black smoke is coming from the unit

Possible reason:
• May be food residue on the cooking chamber, heating coil, or on accessories
• Using an oil with a low smoke point
• May be there is a fault in the circuit or heating element

Solution:
• Touch "Cancel," unplug the unit, and allow it to cool. Clean the cooking chamber or accessories.
• Touch "Cancel," unplug the unit, and allow it to cool. Use neutral oil with high smoke points such as bran, rice, safflower, canola, avocado, canola, soybean oil, etc.
• Touch "Cancel," unplug the unit, and allow it to cool. Contact customer care for this problem.

Problem 2: White smoke is coming from the unit

Possible reason:
• May be you are cooking high-fat foods such as bacon, hamburger or sausage, etc.
• May be water is vaporizing and producing thick steam
• You sprinkle the seasoning on the food it has blown into the element

Solution:
• Don't air frying foods with high-fat content. Remove excess oil from the basket.
• Pat dry moist ingredients before air frying and don't add water or liquid into the cooking chamber when using the air fryer cooking method.
• Spray the vegetables and meats with oil before seasoning the food. It will help to stick the seasoning onto the meat or vegetables.

Problem 3: The unit is plugged in but will not turn on

Possible reason:
• The unit is properly plugged in.
• May be outlet is not be powered.
• May be you didn't insert the air fryer basket into the cooking chamber accurately.

Solution:
• Make sure that the power cord is in good condition.
• Plug unit in another outlet.
• Ensure that the air fryer basket is properly inserted into the cooking chamber.

How to Clean & Maintain the Instant Vortex Air Fryer

You should clean the unit and accessories after every use. The cleaning process of this appliance is pretty simple.
• Unplug the unit from the outlet. Let cool it at room temperature before cleaning.
• Don't use harsh chemical detergents to clean the unit or accessories.
• Remove all accessories from the main unit.
• Clean the air fryer basket with a soft cloth and warm soapy water. Then, rinse well. Make sure that the grease and leftover food is not present on the surface of the basket.
• Do not immerse the air fryer basket into the water or liquid.
• Clean the cooking tray with a damp cloth and warm water soapy water and rinse well. The cooking tray is made of a non-stick coating. Don't use metal cleaning utensils.
• Clean the cooking chamber with a soft or sponge cloth, warm, and soapy water.
• To remove the grease from the cooking chamber, spray with a mixture of vinegar and baking soda and clean it with a damp cloth.
• For stubborn grease, allow the mixture to sit onto the surface of the cooking chamber for several minutes.
• Clean the heating coil with a damp cloth.
• Make sure that the heating coil is completely dry before the next use.
• Clean the main unit with a soft and damp cloth. Do not immerse the main unit in the water.
• Clean the exterior part of the unit with a damp and soft cloth.
• Allow the accessories to dry before returning to the unit.

Breakfast Recipes

Egg Tofu Omelet

Prep time: 15 minutes| Cook time: 10 minutes| Serves: 4

1 teaspoon arrowroot starch	Ground black pepper, to taste
2 teaspoons water	1 teaspoon olive oil
3 eggs	8 ounces' silken tofu, pressed
2 teaspoons fish sauce	and sliced

In a large bowl, dissolve arrowroot starch in water. Add the eggs, fish sauce, oil and black pepper and beat well. Place tofu in the bottom of a greased cooking tray and top with the egg mixture. Select the "Air Fry" mode on your Air Fryer. Press Temp button and then turn the dial to adjust the cooking temperature to 390 degrees F. Press Time button and then turn the dial to adjust the cooking time to 10 minutes. Press the Start button to initiate preheating. Transfer the cooking tray to the air fryer basket of the Air Fryer when the screen displays "Add Food." Close its door, and let the machine do the cooking. Cut into equal-sized wedges and serve hot.
Per serving: Calories 192; Fat 12g; Sodium 597 mg; Carbs 4.6g; Fiber 0.2g; Sugar 2.2g; Protein 16.4 g

Eggs, Tofu and Mushroom Omelet

Prep time: 15 minutes| Cook time: 35 minutes| Serves: 4

2 teaspoons canola oil	3½ ounces fresh mushrooms,
¼ of onion, chopped	sliced
8 ounces silken tofu, pressed	1 garlic clove, minced
and sliced	Salt and ground black pepper,
3 eggs, beaten	as needed

In a skillet, heat the oil over medium heat and sauté the onion, and garlic for about 4-5 minutes. Add the mushrooms and cook for about 4-5 minutes. Remove from the heat and stir in the tofu, salt and black pepper. Place the tofu mixture into the cooking tray and top with the beaten eggs. Select the "Air Fry" mode on your Air Fryer. Press Temp button and then turn the dial to adjust the cooking temperature to 355 degrees F. Press Time button and then turn the dial to adjust the cooking time to 25 minutes. Press the Start button to initiate preheating. Transfer the cooking tray to the air fryer basket of the Air Fryer when the screen displays "Add Food." Close its door, and let the machine do the cooking. Cut into equal-sized wedges and serve hot.
Per serving: Calories 224; Fat 14.5g; Sodium 214 mg; Carbs 6.6g; Fiber 0.9g; Sugar 3.4g; Protein 17.9 g

Mini Mushroom Frittatas

Prep time: 15 minutes| Cook time: 17 minutes| Serves: 3

2 cups button mushrooms,	1 tablespoon olive oil
sliced	3 tablespoons feta cheese,
½ of onion, sliced thinly	crumbled
Salt and ground black pepper,	3 eggs
to taste	

In a frying pan, heat the oil over medium heat and cook the onion and mushroom for about 5 minutes. Remove from the heat and set aside to cool slightly. Meanwhile, in a small bowl, add the eggs, salt and black pepper and beat well. Divide the beaten eggs in 2 greased ramekins evenly and top with the mushroom mixture. Select the "Air Fry" mode on your Air Fryer. Press Temp button and then turn the dial to adjust the cooking temperature to 330 degrees F. Press Time button and then turn the dial to adjust the cooking time to 12 minutes. Press the Start button to initiate preheating. Transfer the ramekins to the air fryer basket of the Air Fryer when the screen displays "Add Food." Close its door, and let the machine do the cooking. Serve hot.
Per serving: Calories 218; Fat 16.8g; Sodium 332 mg; Carbs 6g; Fiber 1.3g; Sugar 3.5g; Protein 12.8 g

Tomato Frittata

Prep time: 10 minutes| Cook time: 30 minutes| Serves: 4

4 eggs	½ cup milk
¼ cup onion, chopped	1 cup Gouda cheese, shredded
½ cup tomatoes, chopped	Salt, to taste

In a small baking pan, add all the ingredients and mix well. Select the "Air Fry" mode on your Air Fryer. Press Temp button and then turn the dial to adjust the cooking temperature to 340 degrees F. Press Time button and then turn the dial to adjust the cooking time to 30 minutes. Press the Start button to initiate preheating. Transfer the baking pan to the air fryer basket of the Air Fryer when the screen displays "Add Food." Close its door, and let the machine do the cooking. Cut into 2 wedges and serve.
Per serving: Calories 247; Fat 16.1g; Sodium 417 mg; Carbs 7.3g; Fiber 0.9g; Sugar 5.2g; Protein 18.6 g

Broccoli Frittata

Prep time: 15 minutes| Cook time: 36 minutes| Serves: 4

½ teaspoon fresh dill, minced	¼ teaspoon red pepper flakes,
1 shallot, sliced thinly	crushed
4 cups broccoli, cut into florets	6 large eggs
2 garlic cloves, minced	Salt and ground black pepper,
½ cup cream cheese, softened	to taste
2 tablespoons olive oil	

In a skillet, heat the oil over medium heat and cook the shallot, broccoli and garlic for about 5-6 minutes, stirring frequently. Remove from the heat and transfer the broccoli mixture into a bowl. In another bowl, add the eggs, red pepper flakes, salt and black peppers and beat well. Add the mushroom mixture and stir to combine. Place the egg mixture into a greased cooking tray and sprinkle with the dill. Spread cream cheese over egg mixture evenly. Select the "Air Fry" mode on your Air Fryer. Press Temp button and then turn the dial to adjust the cooking temperature to 330 degrees F. Press Time button and then turn the dial to adjust the cooking time to 30 minutes. Press the Start button to initiate preheating. Transfer the cooking tray to the air fryer basket of the Air Fryer when the screen displays "Add Food." Close its door, and let the machine do the cooking. Cut into equal-sized wedges and serve
Per serving: Calories 290; Fat 24.8g; Sodium 236 mg; Carbs 5g; Fiber 0.8g; Sugar 1.9g; Protein 14.1 g

Mixed Veggies Frittata

Prep time: 15 minutes| Cook time: 21 minutes| Serves: 4

4 fresh mushrooms, sliced	4 tablespoons fresh spinach, chopped
½ teaspoon olive oil	
3 tablespoons heavy cream	Salt, to taste
1 scallion, sliced	3 grape tomatoes, halved
4 tablespoons Cheddar cheese, grated	2 tablespoons fresh mixed herbs, chopped
4 eggs	

In a skillet, heat the oil over medium heat and cook the mushrooms for about 5-6 minutes, stirring frequently. Remove from the heat and transfer the mushroom into a bowl. In a bowl, add the eggs, cream and salt and beat well. Add the mushroom and remaining ingredients and stir to combine. Place the mixture into a greased cooking tray evenly. Select the "Air Fry" mode on your Air Fryer. Press Temp button and then turn the dial to adjust the cooking temperature to 350 degrees F. Press Time button and then turn the dial to adjust the cooking time to 15 minutes. Press the Start button to initiate preheating. Transfer the cooking tray to the air fryer basket of the Air Fryer when the screen displays "Add Food." Close its door, and let the machine do the cooking. Cut into equal-sized wedges and serve.
Per serving: Calories 159; Fat 11.7g; Sodium 156 mg; Carbs 5.6g; Fiber 1.7g; Sugar 3.2g; Protein 9.1 g

Pancetta and Spinach Frittata

Prep time: 15 minutes| Cook time: 16 minutes| Serves: 4

¼ cup fresh baby spinach	½ of tomato, cubed
3 eggs	¼ cup Parmesan cheese, grated
Salt and ground black pepper, to taste	¼ cup pancetta

Heat a nonstick skillet over medium heat and cook the pancetta for about 5 minutes. Add the tomato and spinach cook for about 2-3 minutes. Remove from the heat and drain the grease from skillet. Set aside to cool slightly. Meanwhile, in a small bowl, add the eggs, salt and black pepper and beat well. In the bottom of a greased cooking tray, place the pancetta mixture and top with the eggs, followed by the cheese. Select the "Air Fry" mode on your Air Fryer. Press Temp button and then turn the dial to adjust the cooking temperature to 355 degrees F. Press Time button and then turn the dial to adjust the cooking time to 8 minutes. Press the Start button to initiate preheating. Transfer the cooking tray to the air fryer basket of the Air Fryer when the screen displays "Add Food." Close its door, and let the machine do the cooking. Cut into equal-sized wedges and serve.
Per serving: Calories 287; Fat 20.8g; Sodium 915 mg; Carbs 1.7g; Fiber 0.3g; Sugar 0.9g; Protein 23.1 g

Bacon, Mushroom and Tomato Frittata

Prep time: 15 minutes| Cook time: 16 minutes| Serves: 4

1 cooked bacon slice, chopped	¼ cup Parmesan cheese, grated
6 cherry tomatoes, halved	
1 tablespoon fresh parsley, chopped	6 fresh mushrooms, sliced
3 eggs	Salt and ground black pepper, to taste

In a cooking tray, add the bacon, tomatoes, mushrooms, salt, and black pepper and mix well. Select the "Air Fry" mode on your Air Fryer. Press Temp button and then turn the dial to adjust the cooking temperature to 320 degrees F. Press Time button and then turn the dial to adjust the cooking time to 16 minutes. Press the Start button to initiate preheating. Transfer the cooking tray to the air fryer basket of the Air Fryer when the screen displays "Add Food." Close its door, and let the machine do the cooking. Meanwhile, in a bowl, add the eggs and beat well. Add the parsley and cheese and mix well. After 6 minutes of cooking, top the bacon mixture with egg mixture evenly. Cut into equal-sized wedges and serve.
Per serving: Calories 228, Fat 15.5g; Sodium 608 mg; Carbs 3.5g; Fiber 0.9g; Sugar 2.1g; Protein 19.8 g

Sausage, Spinach and Broccoli Frittata

Prep time: 15 minutes| Cook time: 30 minutes| Serves: 4

1 teaspoon butter	small pieces
6 eggs	1 cup broccoli florets, cut into small pieces
2 tablespoons half-and-half	
⅛ teaspoon hot sauce	½ cup fresh spinach, chopped up
¾ cup Cheddar cheese, shredded	
⅛ teaspoon garlic salt	Salt and ground black pepper, to taste
6 turkey sausage links, cut into	

In a skillet, melt the butter over medium heat and cook the sausage for about 7-8 minutes or until browned. Add the broccoli and cook for about 3-4 minutes. Add the spinach and cook for about 2-3 minutes. Remove from the heat and set aside to cool slightly. Meanwhile, in a bowl, add the eggs, half-and-half, hot sauce, garlic salt, salt and black pepper and beat until well combined. Add the cheese and stir to combine. In the bottom of a lightly greased cooking tray, place the broccoli mixture and to with the egg mixture. Select the "Air Fry" mode on your Air Fryer. Press Temp button and then turn the dial to adjust the cooking temperature to 400 degrees F. Press Time button and then turn the dial to adjust the cooking time to 15 minutes. Press the Start button to initiate preheating. Transfer the cooking tray to the air fryer basket of the Air Fryer when the screen displays "Add Food." Close its door, and let the machine do the cooking. Cut into equal-sized wedges and serve hot.
Per serving: Calories 339; Fat 27.4g; Sodium 596 mg; Carbs 3.7g; Fiber 0.7g; Sugar 1.5g; Protein 19.6 g

Sausage and Scallion Frittata

Prep time: 15 minutes| Cook time: 20 minutes| Serves: 4

½ cup Cheddar cheese, shredded	Pinch of cayenne pepper
4 eggs, beaten lightly	¼ lb. cooked breakfast sausage, crumbled
2 scallions, chopped	

In a bowl, add the sausage, cheese, eggs, scallion and cayenne and mix until well combined. Place the mixture into a greased cooking tray. Select the "Air Fry" mode on your Air Fryer. Press Temp button and then turn the dial to adjust the cooking temperature to 360 degrees F. Press Time button and then turn the dial to adjust the cooking time to 20 minutes. Press the Start button to initiate preheating. Transfer the cooking tray to the air fryer basket of the Air Fryer when the screen displays "Add Food." Close its door, and let the machine do the cooking. Cut into equal-sized wedges and serve hot.
Per serving: Calories 437; Fat 32.4g; Sodium 726 mg; Carbs 2.2g; Fiber 0.4g; Sugar 1.2g; Protein 29.4 g

Trout Frittata

Prep time: 15 minutes| Cook time: 25 minutes| Serves: 6

¼ cup fresh dill, chopped
1 tablespoon olive oil
½ tablespoon horseradish sauce
1 onion, sliced
2 tablespoons crème fraiche
6 eggs
2 hot-smoked trout fillets, chopped

In a skillet, heat the oil over medium heat and cook the onion for about 4-5 minutes. Remove from the heat and set aside. Meanwhile, in a bowl, add the eggs, horseradish sauce, and crème fraiche and mix well. In the bottom of a cooking tray, place the cooked onion and top with the egg mixture, followed by trout. Select the "Air Fry" mode on your Air Fryer. Press Temp button and then turn the dial to adjust the cooking temperature to 320 degrees F. Press Time button and then turn the dial to adjust the cooking time to 20 minutes. Press the Start button to initiate preheating. Transfer the cooking tray to the air fryer basket of the Air Fryer when the screen displays "Add Food." Close its door, and let the machine do the cooking. Cut into equal-sized wedges and serve with the garnishing of dill.

Per serving: Calories 258; Fat 15.7g; Sodium 141 mg; Carbs 5.1g; Fiber 1g; Sugar 1.8g; Protein 24.4 g

Mini Macaroni Quiches

Prep time: 15 minutes| Cook time: 20 minutes| Serves: 4

1 short crust pastry
1 teaspoon garlic puree
½ cup leftover macaroni n' cheese
2 large eggs
2 tablespoons plain Greek yogurt
11 ounce milk
2 tablespoons Parmesan cheese, grated

Dust 4 ramekins with a little flour. Line the bottom of prepared ramekins with short crust pastry. In a bowl, mix together macaroni, yogurt and garlic. Transfer the macaroni mixture between ramekins about ¾ full. In a small bowl, add the milk and eggs and beat well. Place the egg mixture over the macaroni mixture and top with the cheese evenly. Select the "Air Fry" mode on your Air Fryer. Press Temp button and then turn the dial to adjust the cooking temperature to 355 degrees F. Press Time button and then turn the dial to adjust the cooking time to 20 minutes. Press the Start button to initiate preheating. Transfer the ramekins to the air fryer basket of the Air Fryer when the screen displays "Add Food." Close its door, and let the machine do the cooking. Serve hot.

Per serving: Calories 209; Fat 10.4g; Sodium 135 mg; Carbs 19.1g; Fiber 0.6g; Sugar 4.6g; Protein 9.6 g

Tomato Quiche

Prep time: 15 minutes| Cook time: 30 minutes| Serves: 4

¼ cup onion, chopped
Salt, to taste
½ cup tomatoes, chopped
½ cup milk
1 cup Gouda cheese, shredded
4 eggs

In a small baking pan, add all the ingredients and mix well. Select the "Air Fry" mode on your Air Fryer. Press Temp button and then turn the dial to adjust the cooking temperature to 340 degrees F. Press Time button and then turn the dial to adjust the cooking time to 30 minutes. Press the Start button to initiate preheating. Transfer the baking pan to the air fryer basket of the Air Fryer when the screen displays "Add Food." Close its door, and let the machine do the cooking. Cut into equal-sized wedges and serve.

Per serving: Calories 247; Fat 16.1g; Sodium 417 mg; Carbs 7.3g; Fiber 0.9g; Sugar 5.2g; Protein 18.6 g

Chicken Broccoli Quiche

Prep time: 15 minutes| Cook time: 12 minutes| Serves: 4

½ of frozen ready-made pie crust
¼ tablespoon olive oil
3 tablespoons cheddar cheese, grated
1 small egg
1½ tablespoons whipping
cream
Salt and black pepper, as needed
3 tablespoons boiled broccoli, chopped
2 tablespoons cooked chicken, chopped

Cut 1 (5-inch) round from the pie crust. Arrange the pie crust round in a small pie pan and gently, press in the bottom and sides. In a bowl, mix together the egg, cheese, cream, salt, and black pepper. Pour the egg mixture over dough base and top with the broccoli and chicken. Select the "Air Fry" mode on your Air Fryer. Press Temp button and then turn the dial to adjust the cooking temperature to 390 degrees F. Press Time button and then turn the dial to adjust the cooking time to 12 minutes. Press the Start button to initiate preheating. Transfer the pie pan to the air fryer basket of the Air Fryer when the screen displays "Add Food." Close its door, and let the machine do the cooking. Cut into equal-sized wedges and serve.

Per serving: Calories 197; Fat 15g; Sodium 184 mg; Carbs 7.4g; Fiber 0.4g; Sugar 0.9g; Protein 8.6 g

Salmon Quiche

Prep time: 15 minutes| Cook time: 20 minutes| Serves: 4

½ tablespoon fresh lemon juice
1 egg yolk
3½ tablespoons chilled butter
⅔ cup flour
1 tablespoon cold water
2 eggs
3 tablespoons whipping cream
1 scallion, chopped
5½ ounces salmon fillet, chopped
Salt and ground black pepper, to taste

In a bowl, mix together the salmon fillet, salt, black pepper and lemon juice. In another bowl, add the egg yolk, butter, flour and water and mix until a dough forms. Place the dough onto a floured smooth surface and roll into about 7-inch round. Place the dough in a quiche pan and press firmly in the bottom and along the edges. Trim the excess edges. In a small bowl, add the eggs, cream, salt and black pepper and beat until well combined. Place the cream mixture over crust evenly and top with the salmon mixture, followed by the scallion. Select the "Air Fry" mode on your Air Fryer. Press Temp button and then turn the dial to adjust the cooking temperature to 355 degrees F. Press Time button and then turn the dial to adjust the cooking time to 20 minutes. Press the Start button to initiate preheating. Transfer the pan to the air fryer basket of the Air Fryer when the screen displays "Add Food." Close its door, and let the machine do the cooking. Cut into equal-sized wedges and serve.

Per serving: Calories 592; Fat 39g; Sodium 331 mg; Carbs 33.8g; Fiber 1.4g; Sugar 0.8g; Protein 27.2 g

Bacon Spinach Quiche

Prep time: 15 minutes| Cook time: 10 minutes| Serves: 4

½ cup fresh spinach, chopped
2 dashes Tabasco sauce
½ cup Parmesan cheese, shredded
2 tablespoons milk
2 cooked bacon slices, chopped
¼ cup mozzarella cheese,

shredded   to taste
Salt and ground black pepper,

In a bowl, add all ingredients and mix well. Transfer the mixture into the cooking tray. Select the "Air Fry" mode on your Air Fryer. Press Temp button and then turn the dial to adjust the cooking temperature to 320 degrees F. Press Time button and then turn the dial to adjust the cooking time to 10 minutes. Press the Start button to initiate preheating. Transfer the cooking tray to the air fryer basket of the Air Fryer when the screen displays "Add Food." Close its door, and let the machine do the cooking. Cut into equal-sized wedges and serve hot.
Per serving: Calories 130; Fat 9.3g; Sodium 561 mg; Carbs 1.1g; Fiber 0.1g; Sugar 0.4g; Protein 10 g

Sausage and Mushroom Casserole

Prep time: 15 minutes| Cook time: 19 minutes| Serves: 8

½ lb. spicy ground sausage
1 tablespoon olive oil
¾ cup yellow onion, chopped
½ teaspoon garlic salt
5 fresh mushrooms, sliced

8 eggs, beaten
¼ cup Alfredo sauce
¾ cup Cheddar cheese, shredded and divided

In a skillet, heat the oil over medium heat and cook the sausage and onions for about 4-5 minutes. Add the mushrooms and cook for about 6-7 minutes. Remove from the oven and drain the grease from skillet. In a bowl, add the sausage mixture, beaten eggs, garlic salt, ½ cup of cheese and Alfredo sauce and stir to combine. Place the sausage mixture into the cooking tray. Select the "Air Fry" mode on your Air Fryer. Press Temp button and then turn the dial to adjust the cooking temperature to 390 degrees F. Press Time button and then turn the dial to adjust the cooking time to 12 minutes. Press the Start button to initiate preheating. Transfer the cooking tray to the air fryer basket of the Air Fryer when the screen displays "Add Food." Close its door, and let the machine do the cooking. After 6 minutes of cooking, stir the sausage mixture well. Cut into equal-sized wedges and serve with the topping of remaining cheese.
Per serving: Calories 319; Fat 24.5g; Sodium 698 mg; Carbs 5g; Fiber 0.5g; Sugar 1.5g; Protein 19.7 g

Sausage and Bell Pepper Casserole

Prep time: 15 minutes| Cook time: 25 minutes| Serves: 8

1 lb. ground sausage
¼ cup onion, chopped
8 eggs, beaten
1 teaspoon fennel seed
1 teaspoon olive oil

½ teaspoon garlic salt
½ cup Colby Jack cheese, shredded
1 green bell pepper, seeded and chopped

In a skillet, heat the oil over medium heat and cook the sausage for about 4-5 minutes. Add the bell pepper and onion and cook for about 4-5 minutes. Remove from the heat and transfer the sausage mixture into a bowl to cool slightly. In the cooking tray, place the sausage mixture and top with the cheese, followed by the beaten eggs, fennel seed and garlic salt. Select the "Air Fry" mode on your Air Fryer. Press Temp button and then turn the dial to adjust the cooking temperature to 390 degrees F. Press Time button and then turn the dial to adjust the cooking time to 15 minutes. Press the Start button to initiate preheating. Transfer the cooking tray to the air fryer basket of the Air Fryer when the screen displays "Add Food." Close its door, and let the machine do the cooking. Cut into equal-sized wedges and serve hot.
Per serving: Calories 394; Fat 1.1g; Sodium 709 mg; Carbs 3.1g; Fiber 0.5g; Sugar 1.7g; Protein 24.4 g

Turkey Yogurt Casserole

Prep time: 10 minutes| Cook time: 25 minutes| Serves: 6

½ cup plain Greek yogurt
6 eggs
½ cup cooked turkey meat, chopped

Salt and ground black pepper, to taste
½ cup sharp Cheddar cheese, shredded

In a bowl, add the egg and yogurt and beat well. Add the remaining ingredients and stir to combine. In the greased cooking tray, place the egg mixture. Select the "Air Fry" mode on your Air Fryer. Press Temp button and then turn the dial to adjust the cooking temperature to 375 degrees F. Press Time button and then turn the dial to adjust the cooking time to 25 minutes. Press the Start button to initiate preheating. Transfer the cooking tray to the air fryer basket of the Air Fryer when the screen displays "Add Food." Close its door, and let the machine do the cooking. Cut into equal-sized wedges and serve.
Per serving: Calories 203; Fat 12.5g; Sodium 253 mg; Carbs 2.9g; Fiber 0g; Sugar 0.4g; Protein 18.7 g

Ham Hashbrown Casserole

Prep time: 15 minutes| Cook time: 37 minutes| Serves: 6

¼ cup Cheddar cheese, shredded
2 tablespoons milk
½ of large onion, chopped
½ lb. ham, chopped

24 ounces frozen hashbrowns
3 eggs
Salt and ground black pepper, to taste
1½ tablespoons olive oil

In a skillet, heat the oil over medium heat and sauté the onion for about 4-5 minutes. Remove from the heat and transfer the onion into a bowl. Add the hashbrowns and mix well. Place the mixture into the cooking tray. Select the "Air Fry" mode on your Air Fryer. Press Temp button and then turn the dial to adjust the cooking temperature to 350 degrees F. Press Time button and then turn the dial to adjust the cooking time to 32 minutes. Press the Start button to initiate preheating. Transfer the cooking tray to the air fryer basket of the Air Fryer when the screen displays "Add Food." Close its door, and let the machine do the cooking. Meanwhile, in a bowl, add the eggs, milk, salt and black pepper and beat well. After 15 minutes of cooking, place the egg mixture over hashbrown mixture evenly and top with the ham. After 30 minutes of cooking, sprinkle the casserole with the cheese. Cut into equal-sized wedges and serve.
Per serving: Calories 540; Fat 29.8g; Sodium 1110 mg; Carbs 51.5g; Fiber 5.3g; Sugar 3.2g; Protein 16.7 g

Eggs with Ham

Prep time: 15 minutes| Cook time: 13 minutes| Serves: 4

2 ounces ham, sliced thinly
4 large eggs
Salt and ground black pepper, to taste
2 tablespoons heavy cream
⅛ teaspoon smoked paprika

3 tablespoons Parmesan cheese, grated
2 teaspoons fresh chives, minced
2 teaspoons unsalted butter, softened

In the bottom of the cooking tray, spread butter. Arrange the ham slices over the butter. In a bowl, add 1egg, salt, black pepper and cream and beat until smooth. Place the egg mixture over the ham slices evenly. Carefully, crack the remaining eggs on top and sprinkle with paprika, salt, black pepper, cheese and chives evenly. Select the "Air Fry" mode on your Air Fryer. Press Temp button and then turn the dial to adjust the cooking temperature to 320 degrees F. Press Time button and then turn the dial to adjust the cooking time to 13 minutes. Press the Start button to initiate preheating. Transfer the cooking tray to the air fryer basket of the Air Fryer when the screen displays "Add Food." Close its door, and let the machine do the cooking. Cut into equal-sized wedges and serve.

Per serving: Calories 302; Fat 23.62g; Sodium 685 mg; Carbs 2.4g; Fiber 0.5g; Sugar 0.8g; Protein 20.7 g

Eggs with Turkey Spinach

Prep time: 15 minutes| Cook time: 23 minutes| Serves: 4

1 lb. fresh baby spinach	4 teaspoons milk
4 eggs	1 tablespoon unsalted butter
7 ounces cooked turkey, chopped	Salt and ground black pepper, to taste

In a skillet, melt the butter over medium heat and cook the spinach for about 2-3 minutes or until just wilted. Remove from the heat and transfer the spinach into a bowl. Set aside to cool slightly. Divide the spinach into 4 greased ramekins, followed by the turkey. Crack 1 egg into each ramekin and drizzle with milk. Sprinkle with salt and black pepper. Select the "Air Fry" mode on your Air Fryer. Press Temp button and then turn the dial to adjust the cooking temperature to 355 degrees F. Press Time button and then turn the dial to adjust the cooking time to 20 minutes. Press the Start button to initiate preheating. Transfer the ramekins to the air fryer basket of the Air Fryer when the screen displays "Add Food." Close its door, and let the machine do the cooking. Serve hot.

Per serving: Calories 201; Fat 10.3g; Sodium 248 mg; Carbs 4.7g; Fiber 2.5g; Sugar 1.1g; Protein 23.5 g

Eggs with Ham Veggies

Prep time: 15 minutes| Cook time: 15 minutes| Serves: 4

6 cherry tomatoes, halved	2 eggs
4 slices shaved ham	6 small button mushroom, quartered
2 tablespoons spinach, chopped	1 tablespoon fresh rosemary, chopped
1 teaspoon olive oil	Salt and ground black pepper, to taste
1 cup cheddar cheese, shredded	

In a skillet, heat the oil over medium heat and cook the mushrooms for about 6-7 minutes. Remove from the heat and set aside to cool slightly. In a bowl, mix together the mushrooms, tomatoes, ham and greens. Place half of the vegetable mixture in the greased cooking tray and top with half of the cheese. Repeat the layers once. Make 2 wells in the mixture. Select the "Air Fry" mode on your Air Fryer. Press Temp button and then turn the dial to adjust the cooking temperature to 390 degrees F. Press Time button and then turn the dial to adjust the cooking time to 8 minutes. Press the Start button to initiate preheating. Transfer the cooking tray to the air fryer basket of the Air Fryer when the screen displays "Add Food." Close its door, and let the machine do the cooking. Serve hot.

Per serving: Calories 424; Fat 30.7g; Sodium 1140 mg; Carbs 7g; Fiber 2.3g; Sugar 2.2g; Protein 31 g

Egg Cheese Roll-Ups

Prep time: 10 minutes| Cook time: 23 minutes| Serves: 4

1 cup shredded sharp cheddar cheese.	12 slices sugar-free bacon.
6 large eggs.	2 tablespoons unsalted butter.
½ cup mild salsa, for dipping	¼ cup chopped onion
	½ medium green bell pepper;

seeded and chopped

In a medium skillet over medium heat, melt butter. Add onion and pepper to the skillet and sauté until fragrant and onions are translucent about 3 minutes. Whisk eggs in a small bowl and pour into skillet. Scramble eggs with onions and peppers until fluffy and fully cooked, about 5 minutes. Remove from heat and set aside. On the work surface, place 3 slices of bacon side by side, overlapping about ¼-inch. Place ¼ cup scrambled eggs in a heap on the side closest to you and sprinkle ¼ cup cheese on top of the eggs. Tightly roll the bacon around the eggs and secure the seam with a toothpick if necessary. Place each roll into a suitable baking pan. Select the "Air Fry" mode on your Air Fryer. Press Temp button and then turn the dial to adjust the cooking temperature to 350 degrees F. Press Time button and then turn the dial to adjust the cooking time to 15 minutes. Press the Start button to initiate preheating. Transfer the baking pan to the air fryer basket of the Air Fryer when the screen displays "Add Food." Close its door, and let the machine do the cooking. Rotate the rolls halfway through the cooking time. Serve immediately with salsa for dipping.

Per serving: Calories 460; Fat 31,7 g; Sodium 643 mg; Carbs 6.1g; Fiber 0.8g; Sugar 1.3g; Protein 28.2 g

Eggs in Bread and Sausage Cups

Prep time: 10 minutes| Cook time: 22 minutes| Serves: 4

¼ cup cream	2 cooked sausages, sliced
3 eggs	¼ cup mozzarella cheese,
1 bread slice, cut into sticks	grated

In a bowl, add the cream and eggs and beat well. Transfer the egg mixture into ramekins. Place the sausage slices and bread sticks around the edges and gently push them in the egg mixture. Sprinkle with the cheese evenly. Select the "Air Fry" mode on your Air Fryer. Press Temp button and then turn the dial to adjust the cooking temperature to 355 degrees F. Press Time button and then turn the dial to adjust the cooking time to 22 minutes. Press the Start button to initiate preheating. Transfer the ramekins to the air fryer basket of the Air Fryer when the screen displays "Add Food." Close its door, and let the machine do the cooking. Serve warm.

Per serving: Calories 229; Fat 18,6g; Sodium 360 mg; Carbs 3.9g; Fiber 0.1g; Sugar 1.3g; Protein 15.2 g

Eggs in Bread and Bacon Cups

Prep time: 10 minutes| Cook time: 15 minutes| Serves: 4

4 bacon slices	seeded and chopped
4 bread slices	1½ tablespoons mayonnaise
1 scallion, chopped	4 eggs
2 tablespoons bell pepper,	

Grease 6 cups muffin tin with cooking spray. Line the sides of each prepared muffin cup with 1 bacon slice.
Cut bread slices with round cookie cutter. Arrange the bread slice in the bottom of each muffin cup. Top with, scallion, bell pepper and mayonnaise evenly. Carefully, crack 1 egg in each muffin cup. Select the "Air Fry" mode on your Air Fryer. Press Temp button and then turn the dial to adjust the cooking temperature to 375 degrees F. Press Time button and then turn the dial to adjust the cooking time to 15 minutes. Press the Start button to initiate preheating. Transfer the muffin pan to the air fryer basket of the Air Fryer when the screen displays "Add Food." Close its door, and let the machine do the cooking. Serve warm.

Per serving: Calories 298; Fat 20.7g; Sodium 829 mg; Carbs 10.1g; Fiber 1.1g; Sugar 3.8g; Protein 17.6 g

Spinach and Mozzarella Muffins

Prep time: 10 minutes| Cook time: 10 minutes| Serves: 2

2 tablespoons half-and-half	4 teaspoons mozzarella
2 large eggs	cheese, grated
2 tablespoons frozen spinach, thawed	Salt and ground black pepper, to taste

Grease 2 ramekins. In each prepared ramekin, crack 1 egg. Divide the half-and-half, spinach, cheese, salt and black pepper and each ramekin and gently stir to combine, without breaking the yolks. Select the "Air Fry" mode on your Air Fryer. Press Temp button and then turn the dial to adjust the cooking temperature to 330 degrees F. Press Time button and then turn the dial to adjust the cooking time to 10 minutes. Press the Start button to initiate preheating. Transfer the ramekins to the air fryer basket of the Air Fryer when the screen displays "Add Food." Close its door, and let the machine do the cooking. Serve warm.

Per serving: Calories 251; Fat 16.7g; Sodium 495 mg; Carbs 3.1g; Fiber 0g; Sugar 0.4g; Protein 22.8 g

Bacon and Spinach Muffins

Prep time: 10 minutes| Cook time: 17 minutes| Serves: 6

1 cup fresh spinach, chopped	½ cup milk
6 eggs	Salt and ground black pepper,
4 cooked bacon slices, crumbled	to taste

In a bowl, add the eggs, milk, salt and black pepper and beat until well combined. Add the spinach and stir to combine. Divide the spinach mixture into 6 greased cups of an egg bite mold evenly. Select the "Air Fry" mode on your Air Fryer. Press Temp button and then turn the dial to adjust the cooking temperature to 325 degrees F. Press Time button and then turn the dial to adjust the cooking time to 17 minutes. Press the Start button to initiate preheating. Transfer the cups to the air fryer basket of the Air Fryer when the screen displays "Add Food." Close its door, and let the machine do the cooking. Top with bacon pieces and serve warm.

Per serving: Calories 179; Fat 12.9g; Sodium 549 mg; Carbs 1.8g; Fiber 0.1g; Sugar 1.3g; Protein 13.5 g

Bacon Muffins

Prep time: 10 minutes| Cook time: 18 minutes| Serves: 6

6 bacon slices	6 eggs
6 tablespoons cream	3 tablespoon mozzarella
¼ teaspoon dried basil, crushed	cheese, shredded

Lightly, grease 6 cups of a silicone muffin tin. Line each prepared muffin cup with 1 bacon slice. Crack 1 egg into each muffin cup and top with cream. Sprinkle with cheese and basil. Select the "Air Fry" mode on your Air Fryer. Press Temp button and then turn the dial to adjust the cooking temperature to 350 degrees F. Press Time button and then turn the dial to adjust the cooking time to 18 minutes. Press the Start button to initiate preheating. Transfer the muffin pan to the air fryer basket of the Air Fryer when the screen displays "Add Food." Close its door, and let the machine do the cooking. Serve warm.

Per serving: Calories 156; Fat 10g; Sodium 516 mg; Carbs 2.3g; Fiber 0.4g; Sugar 0.6g; Protein 14.3 g

Savory Carrot Muffins

Prep time: 15 minutes| Cook time: 7 minutes| Serves: 6

For Muffins:	3 tablespoons cottage cheese,
¼ cup whole-wheat flour	grated
¼ cup all-purpose flour	1 teaspoon vinegar
½ teaspoon baking powder	1 carrot, peeled and grated
⅛ teaspoon baking soda	2-4 tablespoons water
½ teaspoon dried parsley, crushed	For Topping:
½ teaspoon salt	7 ounces Parmesan cheese, grated
1 tablespoon vegetable oil	¼ cup walnuts, chopped
½ cup plain yogurt	

For muffin: in a large bowl, mix together the flours, baking powder, baking soda, parsley, and salt. In another large bowl, mix well the yogurt, and vinegar. Add the remaining ingredients except water and beat them well. Make a well in the center of the yogurt mixture. Slowly, add the flour mixture in the well and mix until well combined. Place the mixture into lightly greased muffin molds evenly and top with the Parmesan cheese and walnuts. Select the "Air Fry" mode on your Air Fryer. Press Temp button and then turn the dial to adjust the cooking temperature to 355 degrees F. Press Time button and then turn the dial to adjust the cooking time to 7 minutes. Press the Start button to initiate preheating. Transfer the muffin pan to the air fryer basket of the Air Fryer when the screen displays "Add Food." Close its door, and let the machine do the cooking. Serve.

Per serving: Calories 292; Fat 13.1g; Sodium 579 mg; Carbs 27.2g; Fiber 1.5g; Sugar 2g; Protein 17.7 g

Potato and Bell Pepper Hash

Prep time: 15 minutes| Cook time: 25 minutes| Serves: 4

¼ teaspoon garlic powder	½ of onion, chopped
2 cups water	5 russet potatoes, peeled and
¼ teaspoon ground cumin	cubed
½ of jalapeño, chopped	1 green bell pepper, seeded
¼ teaspoon red chili powder	and chopped
½ tablespoon olive oil	¼ teaspoon dried oregano,
Salt and black pepper, as needed	crushed

In a large bowl, add the water and potatoes and set aside for about 30 minutes. Drain well and pat dry with the paper towels. In a bowl, add the potatoes and oil and toss to coat well. Select the "Air Fry" mode. Press the Time button and again turn the dial to set the cooking time to 5 minutes. Now push the Temp button and rotate the dial to set the temperature at 330 degrees F. Press "Start" button to start. When the unit beeps to show that it is preheated, open the lid. Arrange the potato cubes in "Air Fry Basket" and insert in the oven. Transfer the potatoes onto a plate. In a bowl, add the potatoes and remaining ingredients and toss to coat well. Arrange the veggie mixture in the cooking tray. Select the "Air Fry" mode on your Air Fryer. Press Temp button and then turn the dial to adjust the cooking temperature to 390 degrees F. Press Time button and then turn the dial to adjust the cooking time to 20 minutes. Press the Start button to initiate preheating. Transfer the cooking tray to the air fryer basket of the Air Fryer when the screen displays "Add Food." Close its door, and let the machine do the cooking. Serve hot.

Per serving: Calories 216; Fat 2.2g; Sodium 58 mg; Carbs 45.7g; Fiber 7.2g; Sugar 5.2g; Protein 5 g

Aromatic Baked Eggs

Prep time: 10 minutes. | Cook time: 13 minutes. | Serves: 2

4 eggs	2 teaspoons olive oil

1 teaspoon rosemary
1 teaspoon basil
½ teaspoon garlic powder

Sea salt and ground black pepper, to taste

Brush two ramekins with olive oil. Then crack two eggs into each ramekin. Season the eggs with rosemary, basil, garlic powder, salt, and pepper. Place the ramekins on the cooking tray in the center position. Select the "Air Fry" mode on your Air Fryer. Press Temp button and then turn the dial to adjust the cooking temperature to 350 degrees F. Press Time button and then turn the dial to adjust the cooking time to 13 minutes.
Press the Start button to initiate preheating. Transfer the cooking tray to the air fryer basket of the Air Fryer when the screen displays "Add Food." Close its door, and let the machine do the cooking. Serve warm.
Per serving: Calories 169; Fat 12g; Sodium 430mg; Carbs 1.2g; Sugar 0.6g; Fiber 0.7g; Protein 11.2g

Classic Blueberry Muffins

Prep time: 10 minutes. | Cook time: 20 minutes. | Serves: 6

1 cup all-purpose flour
1 cup coconut flour
1 teaspoon baking powder
¼ teaspoon salt
1 cup granulated; Sugar
½ cup coconut oil, at room temperature

2 large eggs, whisked
½ teaspoon cinnamon powder
1 teaspoon vanilla paste
½ cup milk
2 cups fresh or frozen blueberries

In a mixing bowl, stir together the dry ingredients. Then, in a separate bowl, thoroughly combine the wet ingredients. Add the wet mixture to the dry ingredients and stir just until moistened. Gently fold in the blueberries. Spoon the batter into a parchment-lined muffin tin. Select the "Air Fry" mode on your Air Fryer. Press Temp button and then turn the dial to adjust the cooking temperature to 330 degrees F. Press Time button and then turn the dial to adjust the cooking time to 20 minutes. Press the Start button to initiate preheating. Transfer the muffin pan to the air fryer basket of the Air Fryer when the screen displays "Add Food." Close its door, and let the machine do the cooking. Serve.
Per serving: Calories 410; Fat 25.2g; Sodium 384mg; Carbs 42.2g; Sugar 0.8g; Fiber 0.7g; Protein 5.5g

Bacon and Cheese Toasted Sandwich

Prep time: 10 minutes. | Cook time: 9 minutes. | Serves: 1

2 (1-inch thick) slices bread
1 (1-ounce) slice cheese

1 (1-ounce) slice bacon

Place the bacon on the cooking tray. Select the "Air Fry" mode on your Air Fryer. Press Temp button and then turn the dial to adjust the cooking temperature to 390 degrees F. Press Time button and then turn the dial to adjust the cooking time to 6 minutes. Press the Start button to initiate preheating. Transfer the cooking tray to the air fryer basket of the Air Fryer when the screen displays "Add Food." Close its door, and let the machine do the cooking. Place the fried bacon on a paper towel and reserve. Assemble your sandwich with the cheese and reserved bacon; you can use a toothpick to keep the sandwich together. Select the "Bake" function and press the "Start" key. Bake the sandwich for about 3 minutes or until crispy and golden brown

on top. Serve immediately.
Per serving: Calories 301; Fat 18.2g; Sodium 502mg; Carbs 22.5g; Sugar 1.2g; Fiber 0.7g; Protein 11.5g

Classic Hot Dogs

Prep time: 10 minutes. | Cook time: 15 minutes. | Serves: 2

2 beef sausages
2 hot dog buns

2 tablespoons tomato ketchup
2 tablespoons Dijon mustard

Place the sausage on the cooking tray. Select the "Air Fry" mode on your Air Fryer. Press Temp button and then turn the dial to adjust the cooking temperature to 360 degrees F. Press Time button and then turn the dial to adjust the cooking time to 15 minutes. Press the Start button to initiate preheating. Transfer the cooking tray to the air fryer basket of the Air Fryer when the screen displays "Add Food." Close its door, and let the machine do the cooking. Serve the warm sausages on hot dog buns, garnished with ketchup and mustard. Enjoy!
Per serving: Calories 521; Fat 33.9g; Sodium 502mg; Carbs 33.1g; Sugar 1.1g; Fiber 0.7g; Protein 20.6g

Salt and Black Pepper African Shakshuka

Prep time: 10 minutes. | Cook time: 15 minutes. | Serves: 4

2 teaspoons olive oil
6 eggs
1 small onion, peeled, halved and sliced
½ teaspoon fresh garlic, pressed
1 bell pepper, deseeded and sliced

1 chili pepper, deseeded and sliced
1 medium tomato, chopped
½ cup tomato soup
Sea salt and ground black pepper, to taste
1 teaspoon saffron (optional)

Grease the cooking tray with olive oil and set it aside. Whisk the eggs in a large mixing bowl until frothy. Stir in the remaining ingredients. Pour the egg mixture into the prepared cooking tray. Select the "Air Fry" mode on your Air Fryer. Press Temp button and then turn the dial to adjust the cooking temperature to 350 degrees F. Press Time button and then turn the dial to adjust the cooking time to 15 minutes. Press the Start button to initiate preheating. Transfer the cooking tray to the air fryer basket of the Air Fryer when the screen displays "Add Food." Close its door, and let the machine do the cooking. Serve.
Per serving: Calories 150; Fat 8.7g; Sodium 427mg; Carbs 7.4g; Sugar 1.4g; Fiber 0.7g; Protein 9.6g

Mini Pizzas with Smoked Sausage

Prep time: 10 minutes. | Cook time: 5 minutes. | Serves: 4

1 teaspoon olive oil
½ can (13.8-ounce) refrigerated pizza crust
1 cup tomato sauce
4 ounces smoked sausage,

sliced
8 ounces parmesan cheese, grated
1 teaspoon dried oregano

Grease a cooking tray with olive oil. Unroll refrigerated dough on a work surface and press it into a rectangle. With a round cutter, cut dough into four rounds then spread on the cooking tray. Top each pizza crust with tomato sauce, sausage, parmesan, and oregano. Select the "Air Fry" mode on your Air Fryer. Press Temp button and then turn the dial to adjust the cooking temperature to 390 degrees F. Press Time button and then turn the dial to adjust the cooking time to 5 minutes. Press the Start

button to initiate preheating. Transfer the cooking tray to the air fryer basket of the Air Fryer when the screen displays "Add Food." Close its door, and let the machine do the cooking. Serve.
Per serving: 527 Calories; 24.5g; Fat; 48g; Sodium 502mg; Carbs; 26g; Sugar 0.6g; Fiber 0.7g; Protein

Classic Cinnamon Fritters

Prep time: 10 minutes. | Cook time: 14 minutes. | Serves: 4

6 ounces canned refrigerated buttermilk biscuits	½ cup granulated Sugar
5 tablespoons butter, melted	1 teaspoon ground cinnamon

Separate the dough into 6 rolls. Place the rolls on a parchment-lined cooking tray. Bake the rolls for about 7 minutes at 350 degrees F or until done. In a mixing bowl, thoroughly combine the butter, sugar, and cinnamon. Press the warm rolls into the cinnamon mixture until well coated on all sides. Select the "Air Fry" mode on your Air Fryer. Press Temp button and then turn the dial to adjust the cooking temperature to 350 degrees F. Press Time button and then turn the dial to adjust the cooking time to 7 minutes. Press the Start button to initiate preheating. Transfer the cooking tray to the air fryer basket of the Air Fryer when the screen displays "Add Food." Close its door, and let the machine do the cooking. Serve.
Per serving: Calories 317; Fat 19.1g; Sodium 437mg; Carbs 33.8g; Sugar 1.2g; Fiber 0.7g; Protein 3.1g

Vegetable and Sausage Frittata

Prep time: 10 minutes. | Cook time: 15 minutes. | Serves: 4

1 teaspoon olive oil	chopped
½ pound cooked breakfast sausage, crumbled	1 small red onion, chopped
6 eggs, beaten	1 teaspoon garlic, pressed
½ cup cheddar cheese, shredded	Sea salt and ground black pepper, to taste
1 chili pepper, seeded and	1 teaspoon paprika

Grease a cooking tray with olive oil and set it aside. In a mixing bowl, thoroughly combine all the ingredients. Pour the mixture into the prepared cooking tray. Select the "Air Fry" mode on your Air Fryer. Press Temp button and then turn the dial to adjust the cooking temperature to 330 degrees F. Press Time button and then turn the dial to adjust the cooking time to 15 minutes. Press the Start button to initiate preheating. Transfer the cooking tray to the air fryer basket of the Air Fryer when the screen displays "Add Food." Close its door, and let the machine do the cooking. Serve.
Per serving: Calories 367; Fat 28.6g; Sodium 502mg; Carbs 6.4g; Sugar 1.2g; Fiber 0.7g; Protein 19.1g

Soft Zucchini Galettes

Prep time: 10 minutes. | Cook time: 10 minutes. | Serves: 4

1 teaspoon butter, melted	drained
1 pound zucchini, grated and squeezed	2 eggs, whisked
1 cup feta cheese, crumbled	1 cup all-purpose flour
1 cup canned green peas,	1 teaspoon dried oregano

Grease the cooking tray with melted butter and set it aside. In a mixing bowl, thoroughly combine the remaining ingredients. Shape the mixture into equal patties. Place them on the prepared cooking tray. Select the "Air Fry" mode on your Air Fryer. Press Temp button and then turn the dial to adjust the cooking temperature to 350 degrees F. Press Time button and then turn

the dial to adjust the cooking time to 10 minutes. Press the Start button to initiate preheating. Transfer the cooking tray to the air fryer basket of the Air Fryer when the screen displays "Add Food." Close its door, and let the machine do the cooking. Serve.
Per serving: Calories 309; Fat 12.2g; Sodium 383mg; Carbs 34.2g; Sugar 1.2g; Fiber 0.7g; Protein 16.5g

Spinach and Feta Baked Eggs

Prep time: 10 minutes. | Cook time: 13 minutes. | Serves: 4

2 teaspoons olive oil	torn into pieces
4 large eggs	1 teaspoon dried rosemary
2 ounces feta cheese, crumbled	1 teaspoon dried parsley flakes
2 tablespoons fresh scallions, sliced	1 teaspoon dried basil
2 cups fresh baby spinach,	Coarse sea salt and ground black pepper, to taste

Brush two ramekins with olive oil. Then crack two eggs into each ramekin. Add in the remaining ingredients. Place the ramekins on the cooking tray in the center position. Select the "Bake" mode on your Air Fryer. Press Temp button and then turn the dial to adjust the cooking temperature to 350 degrees F. Press Time button and then turn the dial to adjust the cooking time to 13 minutes. Press the Start button to initiate preheating. Transfer the cooking tray to the air fryer basket of the Air Fryer when the screen displays "Add Food." Close its door, and let the machine do the cooking. Enjoy.
Per serving: Calories 277; Fat 20.2g; Sodium 309mg; Carbs 5.8g; Sugar 0.1g; Fiber 0.7g; Protein 18.2g

Pigs in a Blanket

Prep time: 10 minutes. | Cook time: 8 minutes. | Serves: 6

6 ounces canned crescent rolls	2 tablespoons butter, melted
1 tablespoon Dijon mustard	12 mini cocktail sausages

Line a cooking tray with parchment paper. Unroll the dough and separate into 4 triangles. Then, cut each triangle lengthwise into 3 triangles. Spread each triangle with mustard and butter. Place 1 sausage on the shortest side of each triangle; roll them up. Place the rolls on the cooking tray. Select the "Air Fry" mode on your Air Fryer. Press Temp button and then turn the dial to adjust the cooking temperature to 390 degrees F. Press Time button and then turn the dial to adjust the cooking time to 8 minutes. Press the Start button to initiate preheating. Transfer the tray to the air fryer basket of the Air Fryer when the screen displays "Add Food." Close its door, and let the machine do the cooking. Bake your rolls for about 8 minutes at 350 degrees F. Serve.
Per serving: Calories 197; Fat 11.8g; Sodium 427mg; Carbs 15.8g; Sugar 0.6g; Fiber 0.7g; Protein 5.5g

Breakfast Muffins with Almonds

Prep time: 10 minutes. | Cook time: 20 minutes. | Serves: 6

½ cup almond flour	½ teaspoon ground cinnamon
1 cup all-purpose flour	2 eggs, whisked
¾ cup granulated; Sugar	½ cup full-fat milk
1 teaspoon baking powder	¼ cup butter, at room temperature
A pinch of ground nutmeg	
A pinch of sea salt	½ cup almonds, slivered

In a mixing bowl, stir together the dry ingredients. Then, in a separate bowl, thoroughly combine all the wet ingredients. Add the wet mixture to the dry ingredients and stir just until moistened. Gently fold in the almonds. Spoon the batter into a parchment-lined muffin tin. Select the "Bake" mode on your

Air Fryer. Press Temp button and then turn the dial to adjust the cooking temperature to 330 degrees F. Press Time button and then turn the dial to adjust the cooking time to 20 minutes. Press the Start button to initiate preheating. Transfer the muffin pan to the air fryer basket of the Air Fryer when the screen displays "Add Food." Close its door, and let the machine do the cooking. Enjoy!

Per serving: Calories 334; Fat 14.2g; Sodium 502mg; Carbs 46g; Sugar 1.4g; Fiber 0.7g; Protein 6.7g

Easy Grilled Breakfast Sausages

Prep time: 10 minutes. | Cook time: 15 minutes. | Serves: 4

1 pound breakfast sausage links

4 hot dog buns
4 teaspoons Dijon mustard

Arrange the breakfast sausage on the cooking tray. Select the "Air Fry" mode on your Air Fryer. Press Temp button and then turn the dial to adjust the cooking temperature to 360 degrees F. Press Time button and then turn the dial to adjust the cooking time to 15 minutes. Press the Start button to initiate preheating. Transfer the sausage to the air fryer basket of the Air Fryer when the screen displays "Add Food." Close its door, and let the machine do the cooking. Place the warm sausages on hot dog buns and serve with mustard. Enjoy.

Per serving: Calories 355; Fat 21.7g; Sodium 369mg; Carbs 17g; Sugar 1.1g; Fiber 0.7g; Protein 20.4g

Classic Banana Beignets

Prep time: 10 minutes. | Cook time: 10 minutes. | Serves: 4

2 large ripe bananas
1 teaspoon vanilla essence
½ teaspoon cinnamon powder
½ teaspoon ground cloves

4 tablespoons brown sugar
A pinch of kosher salt
1 cup all-purpose flour

Line the cooking tray with parchment paper and set it aside. In a mixing bowl, thoroughly combine all the ingredients. Shape the mixture into equal balls and place them on the prepared cooking tray. Select the "Air Fry" mode on your Air Fryer. Press Temp button and then turn the dial to adjust the cooking temperature to 360 degrees F. Press Time button and then turn the dial to adjust the cooking time to 10 minutes. Press the Start button to initiate preheating. Transfer the cooking tray to the air fryer basket of the Air Fryer when the screen displays "Add Food." Close its door, and let the machine do the cooking. Serve.

Per serving: Calories 205; Fat 0.5g; Sodium 369mg; Carbs 45.7g; Sugar 0.4g; Fiber 0.7g; Protein 3.8g

Peppery Breakfast Quiche

Prep time: 10 minutes. | Cook time: 15 minutes. | Serves: 6

1 tablespoon olive oil
5 large eggs
1 red bell pepper, seeded and diced
1 green bell pepper, seeded and diced
2 tablespoons scallions, sliced

4 ounces brown mushrooms, sliced
1 teaspoon paprika
Sea salt and ground black pepper, to taste
¼ cup cream cheese, at room temperature

Grease a cooking tray with olive oil and set it aside. In a mixing bowl, thoroughly combine all the ingredients. Pour the mixture into the prepared cooking tray. Select the "Air Fry" mode on your Air Fryer. Press Temp button and then turn the dial to adjust the cooking temperature to 330 degrees F. Press Time button and then turn the dial to adjust the cooking time to 15 minutes. Press

the Start button to initiate preheating. Transfer the cooking tray to the air fryer basket of the Air Fryer when the screen displays "Add Food." Close its door, and let the machine do the cooking. Serve.

Per serving: Calories 365; Fat 19.7g; Sodium 472mg; Carbs 34.7g; Sugar 0.5g; Fiber 0.7g; Protein 17.8g

Russian Sweet Cheese Blintzes

Prep time: 10 minutes. | Cook time: 9 minutes. | Serves: 4

1 (13-ounce) package frozen sweet cheese blintzes

2 tablespoons confectioners' sugar

Grease a cooking tray with butter and add the cheese blintzes and then drizzle the sugar on top. Select the "Air Fry" mode on your Air Fryer. Press Temp button and then turn the dial to adjust the cooking temperature to 340 degrees F. Press Time button and then turn the dial to adjust the cooking time to 9 minutes. Press the Start button to initiate preheating. Transfer the cooking tray to the air fryer basket of the Air Fryer when the screen displays "Add Food." Close its door, and let the machine do the cooking. Serve.

Per serving: Calories 187; Fat 7.1g; Sodium 430mg; Carbs 22.5g; Sugar 1.2g; Fiber 0.7g; Protein 8.3g

Cinnamon Biscuit Donuts

Prep time: 10 minutes. | Cook time: 15 minutes. | Serves: 4

8 ounces refrigerated buttermilk biscuits
2 tablespoons butter, unsalted and melted

¼ teaspoon grated nutmeg
1 teaspoon cinnamon powder
4 tablespoons powdered sugar

Separate the biscuits and cut holes out of the center of each biscuit using a 1-inch round biscuit cutter; place them on parchment paper. Brush them with melted butter. Lower your biscuits into the cooking tray. Select the "Air Fry" mode on your Air Fryer. Press Temp button and then turn the dial to adjust the cooking temperature to 350 degrees F. Press Time button and then turn the dial to adjust the cooking time to 15 minutes. Press the Start button to initiate preheating. Transfer the cooking tray to the air fryer basket of the Air Fryer when the screen displays "Add Food." Close its door, and let the machine do the cooking. Mix the nutmeg, cinnamon, and powdered sugar. Roll the warm donuts onto the cinnamon sugar until well-coated on all sides. Serve.

Per serving: Calories 257; Fat 8.7g; Sodium 387mg; Carbs 40g; Sugar 0.8g; Fiber 0.7g; Protein 4.5g

Italian-Style Crepes

Prep time: 10 minutes. | Cook time: 13 minutes. | Serves: 3

1 teaspoon coconut oil
½ cup all-purpose flour
½ teaspoon sea salt

1 tablespoon brown sugar
2 large eggs
½ cup milk

Grease a cooking tray with coconut oil and set it aside. In a mixing bowl, thoroughly combine all the ingredients. Spoon the mixture into the prepared cooking tray. Select the "Air Fry" mode on your Air Fryer. Press Temp button and then turn the dial to adjust the cooking temperature to 360 degrees F. Press Time button and then turn the dial to adjust the cooking time to 13 minutes. Press the Start button to initiate preheating. Transfer the cooking tray to the air fryer basket of the Air Fryer when the screen displays "Add Food." Close its door, and let the machine do the cooking. Serve.

Per serving: Calories 177; Fat 6.2g; Sodium 413mg; Carbs 20.7g; Sugar 0.6g; Fiber 0.7g; Protein 8.3g

Naan Pizza with Bacon

Prep time: 10 minutes. | Cook time: 5 minutes. | Serves: 1

1 mini naan	cheese, shredded
3 tablespoons marinara sauce	1 (1-ounce) slices bacon, diced
3 tablespoons Mozzarella	

Grease a cooking tray with olive oil and spread naan on top. Top your naan with marinara sauce, cheese, and bacon. Select the "Air Fry" mode on your Air Fryer. Press Temp button and then turn the dial to adjust the cooking temperature to 390 degrees F. Press Time button and then turn the dial to adjust the cooking time to 5 minutes. Press the Start button to initiate preheating. Transfer the cooking tray to the air fryer basket of the Air Fryer when the screen displays "Add Food." Close its door, and let the machine do the cooking. Serve.

Per serving: Calories 525; Fat 26.1g; Sodium 383mg; Carbs 53.3g; Sugar 1.2g; Fiber 0.7g; Protein 20.4g

Cheesy Egg Cups

Prep time: 10 minutes. | Cook time: 13 minutes. | Serves: 2

2 teaspoons olive oil	grated
2 large egg	Sea salt and ground black
2 tablespoons sour cream	pepper, to taste
2 tablespoons cheddar cheese,	

Brush two silicone muffin cups with olive oil. Mix all the ingredients until well combined. Divide the mixture between the muffin cups. Select the "Bake" mode on your Air Fryer. Press Temp button and then turn the dial to adjust the cooking temperature to 350 degrees F. Press Time button and then turn the dial to adjust the cooking time to 13 minutes. Press the Start button to initiate preheating. Transfer the muffin cups to the air fryer basket of the Air Fryer when the screen displays "Add Food." Close its door, and let the machine do the cooking. Enjoy!

Per serving: Calories 277; Fat 20.2g; Sodium 384mg; Carbs 5.8g; Sugar 1.1g; Fiber 0.7g; Protein 18.2g

Breakfast Buttermilk Biscuits

Prep time: 10 minutes. | Cook time: 7 minutes. | Serves: 4

8 ounces refrigerated buttermilk biscuits	4 ounces cheddar cheese, cut into ten ¾-inch cubes
2 teaspoons mustard	1 tablespoon butter, melted
4 slices bacon, diced	

Separate the dough into 4 biscuits. Then, separate each biscuit into 2 layers and press them into rounds. Top them with mustard, bacon, and cheese. Gently stretch the biscuit over the filling, pressing and firmly sealing around the edges of the biscuit. Brush the biscuits with melted butter. Place the biscuits on a parchment-lined cooking tray. Select the "Air Fry" mode on your Air Fryer. Press Temp button and then turn the dial to adjust the cooking temperature to 350 degrees F. Press Time button and then turn the dial to adjust the cooking time to 7 minutes. Press the Start button to initiate preheating. Transfer the cooking tray to the air fryer basket of the Air Fryer when the screen displays "Add Food." Close its door, and let the machine do the cooking. Serve.

Per serving: Calories 367; Fat 22.1g; Sodium 502mg; Carbs 31.2g; Sugar 0.4g; Fiber 0.7g; Protein 11.2g

Italian-Style Spring Frittata

Prep time: 10 minutes. | Cook time: 15 minutes. | Serves: 4

6 eggs, whisked	1 cup cherry tomatoes, halved
3 ounces mozzarella cheese, shredded	1 pound baby spinach
	2 stalks spring onions, sliced

Grease the cooking tray with cooking oil and set it aside. In a mixing bowl, thoroughly combine all the ingredients. Pour the mixture into the prepared cooking tray. Select the "Air Fry" mode on your Air Fryer. Press Temp button and then turn the dial to adjust the cooking temperature to 330 degrees F. Press Time button and then turn the dial to adjust the cooking time to 15 minutes. Press the Start button to initiate preheating. Transfer the cooking tray to the air fryer basket of the Air Fryer when the screen displays "Add Food." Close its door, and let the machine do the cooking. Serve.

Per serving: Calories 167; Fat 6.8g; Sodium 369mg; Carbs 7.3g; Sugar 1.4g; Fiber 0.7g; Protein 18.7g

Classic Breakfast Pancakes

Prep time: 10 minutes. | Cook time: 13 minutes. | Serves: 4

1 cup all-purpose flour	1 cup milk
2 teaspoons baking powder	1 medium egg
1 teaspoon baking soda	2 tablespoons coconut oil, melted
½ teaspoon salt	
1 teaspoon granulated; Sugar	

In a mixing bowl, thoroughly combine the dry ingredients. In another bowl, whisk the wet ingredients. Add the wet mixture to the dry ingredients, and mix to combine well. Grease a cooking tray with nonstick cooking oil and stir in cooking tray. Select the "Air Fry" mode on your Air Fryer. Press Temp button and then turn the dial to adjust the cooking temperature to 350 degrees F. Press Time button and then turn the dial to adjust the cooking time to 13 minutes. Press the Start button to initiate preheating. Transfer the cooking tray to the air fryer basket of the Air Fryer when the screen displays "Add Food." Close its door, and let the machine do the cooking. Enjoy.

Per serving: Calories 227; Fat 10.1g; Sodium 427mg; Carbs 27.3g; Sugar 0.1g; Fiber 0.7g; Protein 6.5g

Corn and Zucchini Fritters

Prep time: 10 minutes. | Cook time: 10 minutes. | Serves: 4

1 teaspoon olive oil	2 tablespoons fresh cilantro
1 pound zucchini, peeled and grated (and squeezed)	Kosher salt and black pepper, to taste
1 cup corn kernels, canned or frozen	1 teaspoon dried oregano
¼ cup cheddar cheese, grated	2 eggs, beaten
2 scallion stalks, sliced	¼ cup corn flour
2 cloves garlic, minced	½ cup all-purpose flour
	1 teaspoon baking powder

Grease the cooking tray with olive oil and set it aside. In a mixing bowl, thoroughly combine the remaining ingredients. Shape the mixture into equal patties and place them on the prepared cooking tray. Select the "Air Fry" mode on your Air Fryer. Use the timer (+ / − Time) arrow keys to adjust cooking time to 10 minutes. Adjust its cooking temperature to 350 degrees F, using the temp (+/- Temp) arrow keys. Press the Start button to initiate preheating. Transfer the cooking tray to the air fryer basket of the Air Fryer when the screen displays "Add Food." Close its door, and let the machine do the cooking. Serve.

Per serving: Calories 259; Fat 10.1g; Sodium 502mg; Carbs 31.5g; Sugar 1.2g; Fiber 0.7g; Protein 14.2g

Banana and Almond Muffins

Prep time: 10 minutes. | Cook time: 20 minutes. | Serves: 6

2 carrots, shredded	1 teaspoon baking powder
2 bananas, mashed	½ cup packed brown sugar
¼ cup coconut oil	¼ teaspoon grated nutmeg
½ cup yogurt	¼ teaspoon grated cardamom
1 cup all-purpose flour	½ teaspoon cinnamon powder
½ cup rolled oats	1 cup almonds, chopped

In a mixing bowl, stir together the dry ingredients. Then, in a separate bowl, thoroughly combine all the wet ingredients. Add the wet mixture to the dry ingredients and stir just until moistened. Gently fold in the almonds. Spoon the batter into a parchment-lined muffin tin. Select the "Air Fry" mode on your Air Fryer. Press Temp button and then turn the dial to adjust the cooking temperature to 330 degrees F. Press Time button and then turn the dial to adjust the cooking time to 20 minutes. Press the Start button to initiate preheating. Transfer the muffin pan to the air fryer basket of the Air Fryer when the screen displays "Add Food." Close its door, and let the machine do the cooking. Enjoy.

Per serving: Calories 397; Fat 20.6g; Sodium 437mg; Carbs 49.2g; Sugar 1.2g; Fiber 0.7g; Protein 9.5g

Spaghetti Squash Croquettes

Prep time: 10 minutes. | Cook time: 10 minutes. | Serves: 4

1 pound spaghetti squash	2 tablespoons fresh parsley
2 medium eggs, whisked	leaves, chopped
½ cup all-purpose flour	2 tablespoons fresh cilantro,
2 scallion stalks, sliced	chopped
1 garlic clove, pressed	Sea salt and ground black
1 tablespoon olive oil	pepper, to taste

Line the cooking tray with parchment paper and set it aside. In a mixing bowl, thoroughly combine all the ingredients. Shape the mixture into equal balls and arrange them on the prepared cooking tray. Select the "Air Fry" mode on your Air Fryer. Press Temp button and then turn the dial to adjust the cooking temperature to 360 degrees F. Press Time button and then turn the dial to adjust the cooking time to 10 minutes. Press the Start button to initiate preheating. Transfer the cooking tray to the air fryer basket of the Air Fryer when the screen displays "Add Food." Close its door, and let the machine do the cooking. Serve.

Per serving: Calories 186; Fat 5.9g; Sodium 383mg; Carbs 28.3g; Sugar 0.6g; Fiber 0.7g; Protein 7.3g

Salt and black Pepper Indian Thalipith

Prep time: 10 minutes. | Cook time: 13 minutes. | Serves: 4

1 tablespoon ghee, melted	A few dashes of hot sauce
½ cup all-purpose flour	Sea salt and ground black
½ cup chickpea flour	pepper, to taste
½ cup rice flour	½ teaspoon curry powder

Grease the cooking tray with melted ghee and set it aside. In a mixing bowl, thoroughly combine the dry ingredients. In another bowl, whisk the wet ingredients. Add the wet mixture to the dry ingredients; mix to combine well. Now, spoon the batter into the prepared tray. Gently shake the tray to make sure that the batter is evenly spread. Select the "Air Fry" mode on your Air Fryer. Press Temp button and then turn the dial to adjust the cooking temperature to 350 degrees F. Press Time button and then turn the dial to adjust the cooking time to 13 minutes. Press the Start button to initiate preheating. Transfer the cooking tray to the air fryer basket of the Air Fryer when the screen displays "Add Food." Close its door, and let the machine do the cooking. Cut the thalipith into equal squares and serve warm. Enjoy!

Per serving: Calories 206; Fat 4.1g; Sodium 309mg; Carbs 35.6g; Sugar 1.1g; Fiber 0.7g; Protein 5.6g

Sweet Corn Muffins

Prep time: 10 minutes. | Cook time: 13 minutes. | Serves: 6

1 cup flour	1 cup buttermilk
1 cup yellow cornmeal	¼ cup water
½ teaspoon salt	2 large eggs
1 teaspoon baking powder	½ cup brown sugar
1 teaspoon baking soda	¼ cup butter, melted

In a mixing bowl, stir together the dry ingredients. Then, in a separate bowl, thoroughly combine all the wet ingredients. Add the wet mixture to the dry ingredients and stir just until moistened. Spoon the batter into a parchment-lined muffin tin. Select the "Air Fry" mode on your Air Fryer. Press Temp button and then turn the dial to adjust the cooking temperature to 330 degrees F. Press Time button and then turn the dial to adjust the cooking time to 13 minutes. Press the Start button to initiate preheating. Transfer the muffin pan to the air fryer basket of the Air Fryer when the screen displays "Add Food." Close its door, and let the machine do the cooking. Serve.

Per serving: Calories 315; Fat 10.2g; Sodium 409mg; Carbs 47g; Sugar 0.5g; Fiber 0.7g; Protein 7.6g

Breakfast German Kartoffelpuffer

Prep time: 10 minutes. | Cook time: 20 minutes. | Serves: 4

1 tablespoon olive oil	Kosher salt and ground black
1 pound potatoes, peeled and	pepper, to taste
grated	2 large eggs, whisked
1 small shallot, chopped	1 cup applesauce
½ teaspoon garlic powder	

Grease the cooking tray with olive oil and set it aside. In a mixing bowl, combine grated potatoes, shallot, garlic powder, salt, black pepper, and eggs. Now, spoon the batter into the prepared pan. Gently shake the pan to make sure that the batter is evenly spread. Select the "Air Fry" mode on your Air Fryer. Press Temp button and then turn the dial to adjust the cooking temperature to 350 degrees F. Press Time button and then turn the dial to adjust the cooking time to 20 minutes. Press the Start button to initiate preheating. Transfer the cooking tray to the air fryer basket of the Air Fryer when the screen displays "Add Food." Close its door, and let the machine do the cooking. Cut the potato cake into equal squares and serve warm with applesauce. Enjoy.

Per serving: Calories 186; Fat 5.9g; Sodium 472mg; Carbs 28.6g; Sugar 0.1g; Fiber 0.7g; Protein 5.9g

Sausage and Egg Cups

Prep time: 10 minutes. | Cook time: 15 minutes. | Serves: 3

6 large eggs	1 pork sausage, chopped
Sea salt and ground black	1 bell pepper, chopped
pepper, to taste	2 ounces cheddar cheese,
1 medium tomato, chopped	shredded

Brush 3 silicone muffin cups with olive oil. Mix all the ingredients until well combined. Divide the mixture between the muffin cups. Select the "Bake" mode on your Air Fryer. Press Temp button and then turn the dial to adjust the cooking temperature to 350 degrees F. Press Time button and then turn the dial to adjust the cooking time to 15 minutes. Press the Start button to initiate preheating. Transfer the muffin cups to the air fryer basket of the Air Fryer when the screen displays "Add Food." Close its door, and let the machine do the cooking. Serve.
Per serving: Calories 327; Fat 23.3g; Sodium 369mg; Carbs 7.1g; Sugar 1.2g; Fiber 0.7g; Protein 21.2g

Old-Fashioned Donuts

Prep time: 10 minutes. | Cook time: 15 minutes. | Serves: 6

2 cups all-purpose flour	½ teaspoon kosher salt
½ cup milk	1 egg, whisked
2 teaspoons active dry yeast	¼ cup butter, melted
2 tablespoons granulated; Sugar	1 cup powdered sugar

Mix all the ingredients, except for the powdered sugar, until a smooth and elastic dough forms. Cover your dough with plastic wrap and allow it to rise in a warm place until doubled. Drop spoonful of the batter onto the greased cooking tray. Select the "Air Fry" mode on your Air Fryer. Press Temp button and then turn the dial to adjust the cooking temperature to 360 degrees F. Press Time button and then turn the dial to adjust the cooking time to 15 minutes. Press the Start button to initiate preheating. Transfer the cooking tray to the air fryer basket of the Air Fryer when the screen displays "Add Food." Close its door, and let the machine do the cooking. Dust warm donuts with powdered sugar. Serve.
Per serving: Calories 319; Fat 9.4g; Sodium 502mg; Carbs 52.1g; Sugar 0.8g; Fiber 0.7g; Protein 5.9g

Eggplant Bacon

Prep time: 10 minutes. | Cook time: 20 minutes. | Serves: 4

8 (1-inch) slices of eggplant

Select the "Air Fry" mode on your Air Fryer. Press Temp button and then turn the dial to adjust the cooking temperature to 400 degrees F. Press Time button and then turn the dial to adjust the cooking time to 20 minutes. Press the Start button to initiate preheating. Transfer the eggplant slices to the air fryer basket of the Air Fryer when the screen displays "Add Food." Close its door, and let the machine do the cooking. Serve.
Per serving: Calories 231; Fat 22.4g; Sodium 391mg; Carbs 0.4g; Sugar 1.4g; Fiber 0.7g; Protein 7.2g

Spanish-Style Cheese Sandwich

Prep time: 10 minutes. | Cook time: 5 minutes. | Serves: 1

2 (1-inch) pieces of bread	1 tablespoon butter
2 (1-inch) slices of cheddar cheese	1 teaspoon paprika

Assemble your sandwich with cheese, butter, and paprika; you can use a toothpick to keep the sandwich together. Select the "Bake" mode on your Air Fryer. Press Temp button and then turn the dial to adjust the cooking temperature to 350 degrees F. Press Time button and then turn the dial to adjust the cooking time to 5 minutes. Press the Start button to initiate preheating. Transfer the sandwich to the air fryer basket of the Air Fryer when the screen displays "Add Food." Close its door, and let the machine do the cooking. Serve immediately.
Per serving: Calories 343; Fat 18.1g; Sodium 309mg; Carbs 32.2g; Sugar 1.1g; Fiber 0.7g; Protein 14.1g

Biscuits with Smoked Sausage

Prep time: 10 minutes. | Cook time: 10 minutes. | Serves: 4

8 ounces refrigerated crescent dinner rolls	chopped
½ pound smoked sausage,	1 cups cheddar cheese, shredded

Separate the dough into 4 biscuits. Unroll the crescent dough on a work surface and cut it into bite-sized pieces. Mix the crescent dough pieces with sausage and cheese. Mix to combine and roll the mixture into balls. Select the "Air Fry" mode on your Air Fryer. Press Temp button and then turn the dial to adjust the cooking temperature to 350 degrees F. Press Time button and then turn the dial to adjust the cooking time to 10 minutes. Press the Start button to initiate preheating. Transfer the balls to the air fryer basket of the Air Fryer when the screen displays "Add Food." Close its door, and let the machine do the cooking. Serve.
Per serving: Calories 415; Fat 23.4g; Sodium 387mg; Carbs 32g; Sugar 1.2g; Fiber 0.7g; Protein 22.1g

Mediterranean-Style Mini Pizza

Prep time: 10 minutes. | Cook time: 5 minutes. | Serves: 1

1 naan bread	grated
1 tablespoon olive oil	1 teaspoon Mediterranean seasoning blend
2 tablespoons pesto	
2 ounces provoll cheese,	

Grease a cooking tray with olive oil and place the naan on it. Top your naan with pesto sauce, cheese, and seasoning blend. Select the "Air Fry" mode on your Air Fryer. Press Temp button and then turn the dial to adjust the cooking temperature to 390 degrees F. Press Time button and then turn the dial to adjust the cooking time to 5 minutes. Press the Start button to initiate preheating. Transfer the cooking tray to the air fryer basket of the Air Fryer when the screen displays "Add Food." Close its door, and let the machine do the cooking. Serve.
Per serving: Calories 576; Fat 46.1g; Sodium 467mg; Carbs 19.7g; Sugar 0.6g; Fiber 0.7g; Protein 20.2g

Vanilla Pear Beignets

Prep time: 10 minutes. | Cook time: 10 minutes. | Serves: 4

2 large pears, cored and diced	¼ teaspoon ground cloves
2 cups all-purpose flour	¾ cup apple juice
½ cup brown sugar	2 eggs
2 teaspoons baking powder	2 tablespoons butter, melted
½ teaspoon salt	1 teaspoon vanilla
1 teaspoon cinnamon powder	

Line the cooking tray with parchment paper and set it aside. In a mixing bowl, thoroughly combine all the ingredients. Shape the mixture into equal balls and place them on the prepared cooking tray. Select the "Air Fry" mode on your Air Fryer. Press Temp button and then turn the dial to adjust the cooking temperature to 360 degrees F. Press Time button and then turn the dial to adjust the cooking time to 10 minutes. Press the Start button to initiate preheating. Transfer the cooking tray to the air fryer basket of the Air Fryer when the screen displays "Add Food." Close its door, and let the machine do the cooking. Dust your beignets

with confectioners' sugar, if desired. Serve.
Per serving: Calories 450; Fat 8.6g; Sodium 399mg; Carbs 83.7g; Sugar 0.5g; Fiber 0.7g; Protein 9.7g

Bacon Mini Quiche

Prep time: 10 minutes. | Cook time: 13 minutes. | Serves: 4

6 large eggs
½ cup sour cream
Sea salt and black pepper
4 ounces smoked bacon,

chopped
4 ounces feta cheese, crumbled
2 tablespoons fresh cilantro, chopped

Brush two silicone muffin trays with olive oil. Mix all the ingredients until well combined. Divide the mixture between muffin cups. Select the "Bake" mode on your Air Fryer. Press Temp button and then turn the dial to adjust the cooking temperature to 350 degrees F. Press Time button and then turn the dial to adjust the cooking time to 13 minutes. Press the Start button to initiate preheating. Transfer the muffin trays to the air fryer basket of the Air Fryer when the screen displays "Add Food." Close its door, and let the machine do the cooking. Enjoy!
Per serving: Calories 338; Fat 27.3g; Sodium 384mg; Carbs 3.9g; Sugar 1.4g; Fiber 0.7g; Protein 18.1g

Salt and black Pepper Polish Naleśniki

Prep time: 10 minutes. | Cook time: 13 minutes. | Serves: 4

1 cup all-purpose flour
½ teaspoon granulated; Sugar
½ teaspoon salt
1 cup milk
2 large eggs, whisked

2 tablespoons butter, melted
4 ounces cottage cheese
½ cup raisins, soaked for 15 minutes

In a mixing bowl, thoroughly combine the flour, sugar, and salt. Gradually add in the milk, eggs, and butter; mix to combine well. Grease the cooking tray with nonstick cooking oil and set it aside. Select the "Air Fry" mode on your Air Fryer. Press Temp button and then turn the dial to adjust the cooking temperature to 350 degrees F. Press Time button and then turn the dial to adjust the cooking time to 13 minutes. Press the Start button to initiate preheating. Transfer the cooking tray to the air fryer basket of the Air Fryer when the screen displays "Add Food." Close its door, and let the machine do the cooking. Enjoy!
Per serving: Calories 268; Fat 11.6g; Sodium 502mg; Carbs 28.2g; Sugar 1.2g; Fiber 0.7g; Protein 11.5g

Classic Breakfast Frittata

Prep time: 10 minutes. | Cook time: 15 minutes. | Serves: 4

1 tablespoon olive oil
6 eggs
1 shallot, peeled and chopped
6 tablespoons sour cream
1 cup Monetary-Jack cheese,

shredded
½ teaspoon cayenne pepper
Coarse sea salt and ground black pepper, to taste

Grease a cooking tray with nonstick cooking oil and set it aside. In a mixing bowl, thoroughly combine all the ingredients. Pour the mixture into the prepared cooking tray. Select the "Air Fry" mode on your Air Fryer. Press Temp button and then turn the dial to adjust the cooking temperature to 330 degrees F. Press Time button and then turn the dial to adjust the cooking time to 15 minutes. Press the Start button to initiate preheating. Transfer the cooking tray to the air fryer basket of the Air Fryer when the

screen displays "Add Food." Close its door, and let the machine do the cooking. Serve.
Per serving: Calories 265; Fat 20.5g; Sodium 502mg; Carbs 3.8g; Sugar 1.1g; Fiber 0.7g; Protein 16.1g

Cheesy Omelet with Scallions

Prep time: 10 minutes. | Cook time: 15 minutes. | Serves: 4

8 medium eggs
½ cup half-and-half
2 scallion stalks, chopped
2 ounces cream cheese, at room temperature

Sea salt and ground black pepper, to taste
2 ounces cheddar cheese, shredded

In the meantime, whisk the eggs with half-and-half. Add in the scallions, cheese, salt, and black pepper. Pour the mixture into a lightly oiled cooking tray. Select the "Air Fry" mode on your Air Fryer. Press Temp button and then turn the dial to adjust the cooking temperature to 350 degrees F. Press Time button and then turn the dial to adjust the cooking time to 10 minutes. Press the Start button to initiate preheating. Transfer the cooking tray to the air fryer basket of the Air Fryer when the screen displays "Add Food." Close its door, and let the machine do the cooking. When the time is up, top your omelet with cheddar cheese and Bake for 5 minutes at 350 degrees F or until the cheese melted. Serve.
Per serving: Calories 237; Fat 14.3g; Sodium 437mg; Carbs 9.3g; Sugar 1.2g; Fiber 0.7g; Protein 16.6g

Salt and black Pepper Greek Tiganite

Prep time: 10 minutes. | Cook time: 13 minutes. | Serves: 5

1-½ cups all-purpose flour
1 teaspoon baking powder
½ baking soda
½ teaspoon kosher salt
1 teaspoon granulated; Sugar

1 cup lukewarm water
½ cup Greek-style yogurt
1 large egg, whisked
Topping:
½ cup honey

In a mixing bowl, thoroughly combine the dry ingredients. In another bowl, whisk the wet ingredients. Add the wet mixture to the dry ingredients, and mix to combine well. Grease a cooking tray with nonstick cooking oil and set it aside. Select the "Air Fry" mode on your Air Fryer. Press Temp button and then turn the dial to adjust the cooking temperature to 350 degrees F. Press Time button and then turn the dial to adjust the cooking time to 13 minutes. Press the Start button to initiate preheating. Transfer the cooking tray to the air fryer basket of the Air Fryer when the screen displays "Add Food." Close its door, and let the machine do the cooking. Enjoy
Per serving: Calories 222; Fat 1.3g; Sodium 309mg; Carbs 47.3g; Sugar 0.1g; Fiber 0.7g; Protein 5.2g

Favorite Pizza Sandwich

Prep time: 10 minutes. | Cook time: 6 minutes. | Serves: 2

4 (¾ inch thick) slices bread
2 tablespoons tomato paste

4 slices mozzarella cheese
16 slices pepperoni

Assemble two sandwiches with the bread slices, tomato paste, cheese, and pepperoni; you can use a toothpick to keep the sandwich together. Select the "Air Fry" mode on your Air Fryer. Press Temp button and then turn the dial to adjust the cooking temperature to 350 degrees F. Press Time button and then turn the dial to adjust the cooking time to 3 minutes. Press the Start button to initiate preheating. Transfer the sandwich to the air fryer basket of the Air Fryer when the screen displays "Add Food." Close its door, and let the machine do the cooking. When the time is up, bake the sandwich for about 3 minutes more at 350 degrees F. Serve.

Per serving: Calories 357; Fat 17.9g; Sodium 383mg; Carbs 24.3g; Sugar 1.2g; Fiber 0.7g; Protein 23.3g

Double Cheese Breakfast Casserole

Prep time: 10 minutes. | Cook time: 10 minutes. | Serves: 4

1 teaspoon olive oil	1 bell pepper, chopped
½ pound smoked sausage, crumbled	6 eggs, beaten
1 small onion, chopped	½ cup cream cheese, crumbled
1 teaspoon garlic, pressed	½ cup cheddar cheese, shredded

Grease the sides and bottom of the cooking tray with olive oil. Arrange sausage, onion, garlic, and peppers in the prepared cooking tray. Then, whisk the eggs and cream cheese until well combined. Pour the mixture into the cooking tray. Select the "Bake" mode on your Air Fryer. Press Temp button and then turn the dial to adjust the cooking temperature to 360 degrees F. Press Time button and then turn the dial to adjust the cooking time to 5 minutes. Press the Start button to initiate preheating. Transfer the cooking tray to the air fryer basket of the Air Fryer when the screen displays "Add Food." Close its door, and let the machine do the cooking. When the time is up, top your casserole with cheddar cheese and bake for about 5 minutes or until the cheese melted. Serve.

Per serving: Calories 353; Fat 25.7g; Sodium 369mg; Carbs 7.3g; Sugar 0.6g; Fiber 0.7g; Protein 22.8g

Mediterranean-Style Cornbread Muffins

Prep time: 10 minutes. | Cook time: 13 minutes. | Serves: 6

1 cup yellow cornmeal	1 cup buttermilk
1 cup all-purpose flour	½ cup water
1 tablespoon honey	2 eggs, beaten
1 teaspoon baking powder	2 tablespoons olives, pitted and sliced
1 teaspoon baking soda	
½ teaspoon kosher salt	6 tablespoons olive oil

In a mixing bowl, stir together the dry ingredients. Then, in a separate bowl, thoroughly combine all the wet ingredients. Add the wet mixture to the dry ingredients and stir just until moistened. Fold in the olives. Spoon the batter into a parchment-lined muffin tin. Select the "Bake" mode on your Air Fryer. Press Temp button and then turn the dial to adjust the cooking temperature to 390 degrees F. Press Time button and then turn the dial to adjust the cooking time to 13 minutes. Press the Start button to initiate preheating. Transfer the muffin pan to the air fryer basket of the Air Fryer when the screen displays "Add Food." Close its door, and let the machine do the cooking. Serve.

Per serving: Calories 348; Fat 16.7g; Sodium 387mg; Carbs 41.8g; Sugar 0.5g; Fiber 0.7g; Protein 7.3g

Giant Dutch Pancake (Pannekoek)

Prep time: 10 minutes. | Cook time: 13 minutes. | Serves: 4

1 tablespoon butter	½ teaspoon kosher salt
1 cup all-purpose flour	1 teaspoon granulated; Sugar

2 eggs	1 large apple, cored and sliced
1 cup milk	1 teaspoon cinnamon powder
2 ounces cream cheese	

Grease the cooking tray with melted butter and set it aside. In a mixing bowl, thoroughly combine the flour, salt, and sugar. Add in the eggs and milk; mix to combine well. Now, spoon the batter onto the prepared pan. Gently shake the pan to make sure that the batter is evenly spread. Select the "Air Fry" mode on your Air Fryer. Press Temp button and then turn the dial to adjust the cooking temperature to 350 degrees F. Press Time button and then turn the dial to adjust the cooking time to 13 minutes. Press the Start button to initiate preheating. Transfer the cooking tray to the air fryer basket of the Air Fryer when the screen displays "Add Food." Close its door, and let the machine do the cooking. Cut the pancake into equal squares and serve warm with cream cheese, apple, and cinnamon. Enjoy!

Per serving: Calories 282; Fat 11.3g; Sodium 427mg; Carbs 36.3g; Sugar 1.4g; Fiber 0.7g; Protein 9.2g

Loaded Hash Browns

Prep time: 10 minutes. | Cook time: 15 minutes. | Serves: 4

1 tablespoon olive oil	chopped
16 ounces hash browns, shredded	7 eggs, whisked
	1 cup full-fat milk
½ pound ham, diced	1 teaspoon paprika
2 garlic cloves, minced	1 teaspoon dried rosemary, chopped
1 small onion, chopped	
1 bell pepper, seeded and diced	Sea salt and ground black pepper, to taste
1 jalapeno pepper, seeded and	1 cup Colby cheese, shredded

Grease the sides and bottom of a suitable casserole dish with olive oil. Place the hash browns, ham, garlic, onion, and peppers in the prepared casserole dish. Then, whisk the eggs, milk, and spices until everything is well incorporated. Spoon the topping over the hash browns; top with cheese. Select the "Air Fry" mode on your Air Fryer. Press Temp button and then turn the dial to adjust the cooking temperature to 380 degrees F. Press Time button and then turn the dial to adjust the cooking time to 15 minutes. Press the Start button to initiate preheating. Transfer the casserole dish to the air fryer basket of the Air Fryer when the screen displays "Add Food." Close its door, and let the machine do the cooking. Serve.

Per serving: Calories 448; Fat 23.3g; Sodium 387mg; Carbs 29.4g; Sugar 1.1g; Fiber 0.7g; Protein 31.3g

Baked Pita Bread

Prep time: 10 minutes. | Cook time: 5 minutes. | Serves: 2

2 (6 ½-inch) pita breads	½ teaspoon dried oregano
1 teaspoon Dijon mustard	1 medium tomato, sliced
2 ounces mozzarella cheese slices	2 ounces Kalamata olives, pitted and sliced

Assemble pita breads with the other ingredients; you can use a toothpick to secure your pitas. Select the "Bake" mode on your Air Fryer. Press Temp button and then turn the dial to adjust the cooking temperature to 350 degrees F. Press Time button and then turn the dial to adjust the cooking time to 5 minutes. Press the Start button to initiate preheating. Transfer the cooking tray to the air fryer basket of the Air Fryer when the screen displays "Add Food." Close its door, and let the machine do the cooking. Enjoy!

Per serving: Calories 289; Fat 10.1g; Sodium 472mg; Carbs 36g; Sugar 0.8g; Fiber 0.7g; Protein 13.7g

Classic Indian Malpua

2 teaspoons ghee
1 cup all-purpose flour
1 cup semolina flour

2 cups milk
A pinch of sea salt

Grease the cooking tray with melted ghee and set it aside. In a mixing bowl, thoroughly combine the dry ingredients. In another bowl, whisk the wet ingredients. Add the wet mixture to the dry ingredients; mix to combine well. Now, spoon the batter onto the prepared pan. Gently shake the pan to make sure that the batter is evenly spread. Select the "Air Fry" mode on your Air Fryer. Press Temp button and then turn the dial to adjust the cooking temperature to 350 degrees F. Press Time button and then turn the dial to adjust the cooking time to 13 minutes. Press the Start button to initiate preheating. Transfer the cooking tray to the air fryer basket of the Air Fryer when the screen displays "Add Food." Close its door, and let the machine do the cooking. Cut the malpua into equal squares. Serve warm.
Per serving: Calories 284; Fat 5.3g; Sodium 437mg; Carbs 48g; Sugar 1.2g; Fiber 0.7g; Protein 9.9g

Easy Bacon Cup

4 slices smoked bacon, sliced in half
4 thin slices tomato

4 eggs
Sea salt and ground black pepper, to taste

Put 1 slice of bacon and 1 slice of tomato in a muffin cup of a mini muffin tray. Crack 1 egg on top of each tomato slice. Select the "Air Fry" mode on your Air Fryer. Press Temp button and then turn the dial to adjust the cooking temperature to 370 degrees F. Press Time button and then turn the dial to adjust the cooking time to 18 minutes. Press the Start button to initiate preheating. Transfer the muffin pan to the air fryer basket of the Air Fryer when the screen displays "Add Food." Close its door, and let the machine do the cooking. Sprinkle with sea salt and ground black pepper on top of the ramekins. Serve.
Per serving: Calories 177; Fat 14.4g; Sodium 428mg; Carbs 1.2g; Sugar 0.4g; Fiber 0.7g; Protein 8.9g

Scotch Eggs with Sausage

4 medium eggs
½ cup all-purpose flour
½ cup tortilla chips, crushed

Sea salt and ground black pepper, to taste
8 ounces breakfast sausage

Place the eggs in a small saucepan and cover them with cold water. Bring to a boil; remove from the heat, cover, and let them sit for 3 minutes. Next, fill the saucepan with cold water to cool the eggs. After that, carefully peel the eggs under cold running water. Keep the eggs chilled. Mix the flour, crushed corn tortillas, salt, and black pepper in a shallow bowl. Divide the sausage into 4 equal portions and form them into thin patties. Place 1 boiled egg on top of each sausage patty and wrap them around the boiled eggs. Select the "Air Fry" mode on your Air Fryer. Press Temp button and then turn the dial to adjust the cooking temperature to 400 degrees F. Press Time button and then turn the dial to adjust the cooking time to 2 minutes. Press the Start button to initiate preheating. Transfer the sausages to the air fryer basket of the Air Fryer when the screen displays "Add Food." Close its door, and let the machine do the cooking. Serve immediately and enjoy!
Per serving: Calories 333; Fat 22.4g; Sodium 409mg; Carbs

15.6g; Sugar 0.6g; Fiber 0.7g; Protein 15.6g

Mustard Cheese Sandwich

4 large slices crusty bread
2 teaspoons Dijon mustard

4 ounces Colby cheese, sliced
2 tablespoons chives, chopped

Assemble your sandwich with mustard, cheese, and chives, you can use a toothpick to keep the sandwich together. Select the "Bake" mode on your Air Fryer. Press Temp button and then turn the dial to adjust the cooking temperature to 350 degrees F. Press Time button and then turn the dial to adjust the cooking time to 5 minutes. Press the Start button to initiate preheating. Transfer the cooking tray to the air fryer basket of the Air Fryer when the screen displays "Add Food." Close its door, and let the machine do the cooking. Serve immediately.
Per serving: Calories 385; Fat 20.4g; Sodium 502mg; Carbs 31.5g; Sugar 1.2g; Fiber 0.7g; Protein 19.1g

Mom's Cheesy Biscuits

2 cups self-rising flour
1 tablespoon; Sugar
⅓ cup butter
½ cup Colby cheese, grated

1 cup buttermilk
1 cup all-purpose flour, for shaping

Line the cooking tray with parchment paper. Thoroughly combine self-rising flour and sugar. Add in butter, cheese, and buttermilk; stir to combine well. Spread the all-purpose on a work surface. Then, scoop 6 balls of dough into the flour, coating them with flour and shaking off any excess flour. Place the floured dough balls in the prepared cooking tray. Select the "Air Fry" mode on your Air Fryer. Press Temp button and then turn the dial to adjust the cooking temperature to 390 degrees F. Press Time button and then turn the dial to adjust the cooking time to 20 minutes. Press the Start button to initiate preheating. Transfer the cooking tray to the air fryer basket of the Air Fryer when the screen displays "Add Food." Close its door, and let the machine do the cooking. Serve.
Per serving: Calories 377; Fat 14.6g; Sodium 384mg; Carbs 50.2g; Sugar 0.5g; Fiber 0.7g; Protein 10.3g

Colorful Mini Frittatas

1 tablespoon olive oil
7 medium eggs
¼ cup full-fat milk
2 ounces sour cream
2 ounces cheddar cheese shredded
1 small shallot, chopped

2 garlic cloves, pressed
½ teaspoon Dijon mustard
½ cup cherry tomatoes, quartered
Sea salt and black pepper, to taste
1 cup spinach leaves, chopped

Brush silicone muffin cups with olive oil. Mix all the ingredients until well combined. Divide the mixture between the muffin cups of a muffin tray. Select the "Bake" mode on your Air Fryer. Press Temp button and then turn the dial to adjust the cooking temperature to 350 degrees F. Press Time button and then turn the dial to adjust the cooking time to 13 minutes. Press the Start button to initiate preheating. Transfer the muffin tray to the air fryer basket of the Air Fryer when the screen displays "Add Food." Close its door, and let the machine do the cooking. Serve warm.
Per serving: Calories 237; Fat 17.6g; Sodium 369mg; Carbs

3.7g; Sugar 1.2g; Fiber 0.7g; Protein 14.3g

Fall Pumpkin Pancakes

Prep time: 10 minutes. | Cook time: 13 minutes. | Serves: 4

1 teaspoon coconut oil	2 eggs
1 cup pumpkin puree	1 teaspoon pumpkin pie spice
½ cup brown sugar	1 teaspoon baking powder
⅔ cup peanut butter	

Grease the cooking tray with coconut oil and set it aside. In a mixing bowl, thoroughly combine all the ingredients; mix to combine well. Spoon your batter onto the cooking tray. Select the "Air Fry" mode on your Air Fryer. Press Temp button and then turn the dial to adjust the cooking temperature to 350 degrees F. Press Time button and then turn the dial to adjust the cooking time to 13 minutes. Press the Start button to initiate preheating. Transfer the cooking tray to the air fryer basket of the Air Fryer when the screen displays "Add Food." Close its door, and let the machine do the cooking. Serve.
Per serving: Calories 440; Fat 25.5g; Sodium 309mg; Carbs 42.3g; Sugar 1.4g; Fiber 0.7g; Protein 14.7g

Chocolate Orange Muffins

Prep time: 10 minutes. | Cook time: 20 minutes. | Serves: 6

1 cup all-purpose flour	½ cup brown sugar
1 cup coconut flakes	½ cup milk
1 teaspoon baking powder	½ cup orange juice
½ teaspoon salt	1 teaspoon coconut extract
½ cup chocolate chips	¼ cup coconut oil
2 eggs	

In a mixing bowl, stir together the dry ingredients. Then, in a separate bowl, thoroughly combine all the wet ingredients. Add the wet mixture to the dry ingredients and stir just until moistened. Spoon the batter into a parchment-lined muffin pan. Select the "Bake" mode on your Air Fryer. Press Temp button and then turn the dial to adjust the cooking temperature to 330 degrees F. Press Time button and then turn the dial to adjust the cooking time to 20 minutes. Press the Start button to initiate preheating. Transfer the muffin pan to the air fryer basket of the Air Fryer when the screen displays "Add Food." Close its door, and let the machine do the cooking. Serve.
Per serving: Calories 365; Fat 15.5g; Sodium 502mg; Carbs 51.3g; Sugar 1.1g; Fiber 0.7g; Protein 5.7g

Cheese Egg in a Hole

Prep time: 10 minutes. | Cook time: 6 minutes. | Serves: 2

4 slices bread	2 eggs
2 teaspoons butter	Kosher salt and black pepper,
2 slices Colby cheese	to taste

Use a sharp paring knife to scoop a circle in the middle of two slices of bread. Spread the butter on the other two slices of bread. Top them with cheese. Top them with the bread slices with circles. Crack the eggs into the center of the bread; season with kosher salt and black pepper. Place the bread with eggs on the cooking tray. Select the "Air Fry" mode on your Air Fryer. Press Temp button and then turn the dial to adjust the cooking temperature to 380 degrees F. Press Time button and then turn the dial to adjust the cooking time to 6 minutes. Press the Start button to initiate preheating. Transfer the tray to the air fryer basket of the Air Fryer when the screen displays "Add Food." Close its door, and let the machine do the cooking. Serve.

Per serving: Calories 315; Fat 18.3g; Sodium 430mg; Carbs 20.3g; Sugar 1.2g; Fiber 0.7g; Protein 15.7g

Greek-Style Pita Pizza

Prep time: 10 minutes. | Cook time: 5 minutes. | Serves: 2

1 teaspoon olive oil	4 ounces feta cheese, crumbled
2 medium pita breads	1 tablespoon Greek seasoning
4 tablespoons tomato sauce	mix

Grease the cooking tray with olive oil and spread pita bread on it. Top your pita with tomato sauce, cheese, and seasoning mix. Select the "Air Fry" mode on your Air Fryer. Press Temp button and then turn the dial to adjust the cooking temperature to 390 degrees F. Press Time button and then turn the dial to adjust the cooking time to 5 minutes. Press the Start button to initiate preheating. Transfer the cooking tray to the air fryer basket of the Air Fryer when the screen displays "Add Food." Close its door, and let the machine do the cooking. Serve.
Per serving: Calories 300; Fat 15.3g; Sodium 484mg; Carbs 26.6g; Sugar 0.8g; Fiber 0.7g; Protein 11.7g

Grandma's Apple Fritters

Prep time: 10 minutes. | Cook time: 10 minutes. | Serves: 4

¼ cup plus 1 teaspoon coconut oil, melted	¼ teaspoon kosher salt
1 cup all-purpose flour	½ cup full-fat milk
¼ cup brown sugar	2 eggs, whisked
1 teaspoon baking powder	1 teaspoon vanilla paste
1 teaspoon ground cinnamon	2 medium apples, peeled and grated
½ teaspoon ground cloves	1 cup confectioners' sugar

Grease the cooking tray with 1 teaspoon of coconut oil and set it aside. In a mixing bowl, thoroughly combine the flour, brown sugar, baking powder, spices, milk, eggs, vanilla, apples, and ¼ cup of coconut oil. Shape the mixture into equal patties and place them on the prepared cooking tray. Select the "Air Fry" mode on your Air Fryer. Press Temp button and then turn the dial to adjust the cooking temperature to 360 degrees F. Press Time button and then turn the dial to adjust the cooking time to 10 minutes. Press the Start button to initiate preheating. Transfer the cooking tray to the air fryer basket of the Air Fryer when the screen displays "Add Food." Close its door, and let the machine do the cooking. Dust your fritters with confectioners' sugar. Serve.
Per serving: Calories 451; Fat 16.3g; Sodium 383mg; Carbs 69.6g; Sugar 1.4g; Fiber 0.7g; Protein 7.2g

Mexican-Style Quiche

Prep time: 10 minutes. | Cook time: 15 minutes. | Serves: 3

1 tablespoon butter, melted	chopped
5 eggs	1 cup Mexican cheese blend, grated
2 bell peppers, seeded and diced	1 tablespoon Mexican oregano
1 habanero pepper, seeded and chopped	Sea salt and ground black pepper, to taste
1 cup baby spinach leaves,	

Grease the cooking tray with melted butter and set it aside. In a mixing bowl, thoroughly combine all the ingredients. Pour the mixture into the prepared cooking tray. Select the "Air Fry" mode on your Air Fryer. Press Temp button and then turn the dial to adjust the cooking temperature to 330 degrees F. Press Time button and then turn the dial to adjust the cooking time to

15 minutes. Press the Start button to initiate preheating. Transfer the cooking tray to the air fryer basket of the Air Fryer when the screen displays "Add Food." Close its door, and let the machine do the cooking. Serve.

Per serving: Calories 314; Fat 21.3g; Sodium 430mg; Carbs 9.1g; Sugar 0.6g; Fiber 0.7g; Protein 21.2g

Classic Breakfast Cups with Pesto

Prep time: 10 minutes. | Cook time: 15 minutes. | Serves: 2

4 eggs	1 tablespoon pesto sauce
2 ounces ham, diced	Sea salt and ground black
2 tablespoons yellow onion,	pepper, to taste
chopped	½ teaspoon garlic powder
A few dashes of hot sauce	2 ounces feta cheese, crumbled

Line a cupcake tin with parchment paper. Mix all the ingredients until well combined. Divide the mixture between muffin cups. Select the "Bake" mode on your Air Fryer. Press Temp button and then turn the dial to adjust the cooking temperature to 350 degrees F. Press Time button and then turn the dial to adjust the cooking time to 15 minutes. Press the Start button to initiate preheating. Transfer the muffin pan to the air fryer basket of the Air Fryer when the screen displays "Add Food." Close its door, and let the machine do the cooking. Serve.

Per serving: Calories 252; Fat 15.4g; Sodium 384mg; Carbs 6.3g; Sugar 1.2g; Fiber 0.7g; Protein 20.7g

Nuts and Seeds Granola

Prep time: 15 minutes| Cook time: 15 minutes| Serves: 8

⅓ cup olive oil	shelled
¼ cup maple syrup	1 tablespoon flax seed
2 tablespoons honey	2 tablespoons pecans, chopped
½ teaspoon vanilla extract	2 tablespoons hazelnuts,
2 cups rolled oats	chopped
½ cup wheat germ, toasted	2 tablespoons almonds,
¼ cup dried cherries	chopped
¼ cup dried blueberries	2 tablespoons walnuts,
2 tablespoons dried cranberries	chopped
2 tablespoons sunflower seeds	½ teaspoon ground cinnamon
2 tablespoons pumpkin seeds,	⅛ t teaspoon ground cloves

In a small bowl, add the oil and maple syrup and mix well. In a large bowl, add the remaining ingredients and mix well. Add the oil mixture and mix until well combined. Place the mixture into a baking dish that will fit in the Air Fryer. Select the "Air Fry" mode on your Air Fryer. Press Temp button and then turn the dial to adjust the cooking temperature to 350 degrees F. Press Time button and then turn the dial to adjust the cooking time to 15 minutes. Press the Start button to initiate preheating. Transfer the cooking tray to the air fryer basket of the Air Fryer when the screen displays "Add Food." Close its door, and let the machine do the cooking. When cooking time is complete, remove the cooking tray from oven. Set the granola side to cool completely before serving.

Per serving: Calories 302; Fat 16.1g; Sodium 4 mg; Carbs 35.1g; Fiber 5.7g; Sugar 14g; Protein 6.9 g

Simple Bagels

Prep time: 1 minutes| Cook time: 12 minutes| Serves: 4

1 cup all-purpose flour	1 egg, beaten
2 teaspoons baking powder	1 tablespoon water
Salt, to taste	1 tablespoon sesame seeds
1 cup plain Greek yogurt	1 teaspoon coarse salt

In a large bowl, mix together the flour, baking powder and salt. Add the yogurt and mix until a dough ball form. Place the dough onto a lightly floured surface and then, cut into 4 equal-sized balls. Roll each ball into a 7-8-inch rope and then join ends to shape a bagel. Place 2 bagels onto the cooking tray. In a small bowl, add egg and water and mix well. Brush the bagels with egg mixture evenly. Sprinkle the top with sesame seeds and salt, pressing lightly. Select the "Air Fry" mode on your Air Fryer. Press Temp button and then turn the dial to adjust the cooking temperature to 330 degrees F. Press Time button and then turn the dial to adjust the cooking time to 12 minutes. Press the Start button to initiate preheating. Transfer the bagels to the air fryer basket of the Air Fryer when the screen displays "Add Food." Close its door, and let the machine do the cooking. Serve with your favorite topping.

Per serving: Calories 188; Fat 3.3g; Sodium 580mg; Carbs 29.9g; Fiber 1.2g; Sugar 4.5g; Protein 8.5 g

Eggs and Cheese Puffs

Prep time: 1 minutes| Cook time: 15 minutes| Serves: 4

1 (8-ounce) frozen puff pastry	4 large eggs
sheet, thawed	1 tablespoon fresh chives,
¾ cup Monterey Jack cheese,	minced
shredded and divided	

Unfold the puff pastry and arrange onto a lightly floured surface. Cut pastry into 2 equal-sized squares. Arrange 2 squares onto the cooking tray. Select the "Air Fry" mode on your Air Fryer. Press Temp button and then turn the dial to adjust the cooking temperature to 390 degrees F. Press Time button and then turn the dial to adjust the cooking time to 10 minutes. Press the Start button to initiate preheating. Transfer the cooking tray to the air fryer basket of the Air Fryer when the screen displays "Add Food." Close its door, and let the machine do the cooking. With a metal spoon, press down the center of each pastry to make a nest. Place ¼ of the cheese into each nest and carefully, push it to the sides. Carefully crack an egg into each nest and cook for 5 minutes more. Repeat with the remaining pastry squares, cheese and eggs. Garnish with chives and serve warm.

Per serving: Calories 398; Fat 27.6g; Sodium 234 mg; Carbs 26.2g; Fiber 0.9g; Sugar 0.8g; Protein 11.3 g

Egg, Bacon and Cheese Puffs

Prep time: 15 minutes| Cook time: 15 minutes| Serves: 4

1 (8-ounce) frozen puff pastry	crumbled
sheet, thawed	4 eggs
⅔ cup cheddar cheese,	1 tablespoon fresh parsley,
shredded	chopped
4 cooked bacon slices,	

Unfold the puff pastry and arrange onto a lightly floured surface. Cut pastry into 2 equal-sized squares. Arrange 2 squares onto the cooking tray. Select the "Air Fry" mode on your Air Fryer. Press Temp button and then turn the dial to adjust the cooking temperature to 390 degrees F. Press Time button and then turn the dial to adjust the cooking time to 10 minutes. Press the Start button to initiate preheating. Transfer the pastries to the air fryer basket of the Air Fryer when the screen displays "Add Food." Close its door, and let the machine do the cooking. With a metal spoon, press down the center of each pastry to make a nest. Place ¼ of the cheese into each nest and carefully, push it to the sides. Now, place ¼ of the bacon around the edges of the nest. Carefully crack an egg into each nest and cook for 5 minutes. Repeat with the remaining pastry squares, cheese, bacon and eggs. Garnish with parsley and serve warm.

Per serving: Calories 608; Fat 44.3g; Sodium 990 mg; Carbs

26.6g; Fiber 0g; Sugar 0.9g; Protein 25.1 g

Breakfast Egg Rolls

Prep time: 20 minutes| Cook time: 20 minutes| Serves: 12

½ pound bulk pork sausage	1 tablespoon 2% milk
½ cup cheddar cheese, shredded	Salt and ground black pepper, to taste
½ cup Monterrey Jack cheese, shredded	1 tablespoon butter
1 tablespoon scallion, chopped	12 egg roll wrappers
4 large eggs	Olive oil cooking spray

Heat a small nonstick skillet over medium heat and cook the sausage for about 5-6 minutes, breaking into crumbles. Drain the grease from skillet. Stir in the cheeses and scallion and transfer the mixture into a bowl. In a small bowl, add the eggs, milk, salt and black pepper and beat until well combined. In another small skillet, melt the butter over medium heat. Add the egg mixture and cook for about 2-3 minutes, stirring continuously. Remove from the heat and stir with the sausage mixture. Arrange 1 egg roll wrapper onto a smooth surface. Place ¼ cup of filling over 1 corner of a wrapper, just below the center. Fold the bottom corner over filling. With wet fingers, moisten the remaining wrapper edges. Fold side corners toward center over filling. Roll egg roll up tightly and with your fingers, press at tip to seal. Repeat with the remaining wrappers and filling. Arrange the 6 rolls onto a cooking tray and spray with the cooking spray. Select the "Air Fry" mode on your Air Fryer. Press Temp button and then turn the dial to adjust the cooking temperature to 400 degrees F. Press Time button and then turn the dial to adjust the cooking time to 8 minutes. Press the Start button to initiate preheating. Transfer the rolls to the air fryer basket of the Air Fryer when the screen displays "Add Food." Close its door, and let the machine do the cooking. Repeat with the remaining wrappers ad filling. Serve warm.
Per serving: Calories 212; Fat 10.3g; Sodium 401 mg; Carbs 18.9g; Fiber 0.6g; Sugar 0.2g; Protein 10.3 g

Veggies Frittata

Prep time: 15 minutes| Cook time: 15 minutes| Serves: 4

4 eggs	4 tablespoons fresh spinach, chopped
3 tablespoons heavy cream	3 grape tomatoes, halved
Salt, to taste	2 tablespoons fresh mixed herbs, chopped
4 tablespoons Cheddar cheese, grated	1 scallion, sliced
4 fresh mushrooms, sliced	

In a bowl, add the eggs, cream and salt and beat well. Add the remaining ingredients and stir to combine. Place the mixture into a greased pan evenly. Select the "Air Fry" mode on your Air Fryer. Press Temp button and then turn the dial to adjust the cooking temperature to 350 degrees F. Press Time button and then turn the dial to adjust the cooking time to 15 minutes. Press the Start button to initiate preheating. Transfer the cooking tray to the air fryer basket of the Air Fryer when the screen displays "Add Food." Close its door, and let the machine do the cooking. Serve warm.
Per serving: Calories 139; Fat 11g; Sodium 152 mg; Carbs 2.4g; Fiber 0.7g; Sugar 1g; Protein 8.4 g

Eggs in Bread Hole

Prep time: 10 minutes| Cook time: 6 minutes| Serves: 2

2 whole-wheat bread slices	Salt and ground black pepper, to taste
2 large eggs	

With a cookie cutter, cut a hole in the center of each bread slice. Arrange the bread slices in the cooking tray. Crack 1 egg in the hole of each bread slice. Select the "Air Fry" mode on your Air Fryer. Press Temp button and then turn the dial to adjust the cooking temperature to 320 degrees F. Press Time button and then turn the dial to adjust the cooking time to 6 minutes. Press the Start button to initiate preheating. Transfer the cooking tray to the air fryer basket of the Air Fryer when the screen displays "Add Food." Close its door, and let the machine do the cooking. Sprinkle the top of egg with salt and black pepper and serve.
Per serving: Calories 141; Fat 5.9g; Sodium 280 mg; Carbs 12g; Fiber 1.9g; Sugar 2g; Protein 9.9 g

Sausage and Bacon Omelet

Prep time: 10 minutes| Cook time: 10 minutes| Serves: 2

4 eggs	1 onion, chopped
Ground black pepper, to taste	1 teaspoon fresh parsley, minced
1 bacon slice, chopped	
2 sausages, chopped	

In a bowl, crack the eggs and black pepper and beat well. Add the remaining ingredients and gently, stir to combine. Place the mixture into the cooking tray. Select the "Air Fry" mode on your Air Fryer. Press Temp button and then turn the dial to adjust the cooking temperature to 320 degrees F. Press Time button and then turn the dial to adjust the cooking time to 10 minutes. Press the Start button to initiate preheating. Transfer the cooking tray to the air fryer basket of the Air Fryer when the screen displays "Add Food." Close its door, and let the machine do the cooking. Serve warm.
Per serving: Calories 508; Fat 38.4g; Sodium 1000 mg; Carbs 6.1g; Fiber 1.2g; Sugar 3g; Protein 33.2 g

Sausage with Eggs

Prep time: 10 minutes| Cook time: 6 minutes| Serves: 2

4 breakfast sausage	1 avocado, peeled, pitted and sliced
2 hard-boiled eggs, peeled	

Select the "Roast" mode on your Air Fryer. Press Temp button and then turn the dial to adjust the cooking temperature to 375 degrees F. Press Time button and then turn the dial to adjust the cooking time to 6 minutes. Press the Start button to initiate preheating. Transfer the sausage to the air fryer basket of the Air Fryer when the screen displays "Add Food." Close its door, and let the machine do the cooking. Remove from the Air Fryer and place the sausages onto serving plates. Divide eggs and avocado slices onto each plate and serve.
Per serving: Calories 322; Fat 28.5g; Sodium 187 mg; Carbs 9g; Sugar 0.8g; Fiber 0.7g; Protein 10.6 g

Churros Fingers with Chocolate Dipping Sauce

Prep time: 8 minutes| Cook time: 10 minutes| Serves: 4

5 teaspoon butter, unsalted	⅛ teaspoon salt
1 tsp. sugar	⅛ teaspoon nutmeg
1-cup water	1-cup dark chocolate, chopped into small cubes
1-cup flour, all-purpose type	
2 medium eggs	

In a saucepan, heat up water, butter and sugar. Make sure to put it on high until the sugar is melted completely. Stir the butter until it melts. Add the flour and stir quickly to make a paste. Put the heat to low. It will take longer and it will be hot, but you can reduce the heat. Stir the food a lot while it is cooking until it starts to come away from the sides of your pan. Remove the mixture from heat and let it cool for 10 minutes. Then beat in the eggs and salt. Mixture should be smooth and glossy. Transfer the mixture from the bowl to a pastry bag with a star shaped nozzle. Then, pipe the mixture into any shape you want on the cooking tray. Select the "Air Fry" mode on your Air Fryer. Press Temp button and then turn the dial to adjust the cooking temperature to 390 degrees F. Press Time button and then turn the dial to adjust the cooking time to 6 minutes. Press the Start button to initiate preheating. Transfer the cooking tray to the air fryer basket of the Air Fryer when the screen displays "Add Food." Close its door, and let the machine do the cooking. Cook until crisp and golden brown. Repeat with remaining batter. Put chocolate, water and sugar in a double boiler. Let them sit until they have completely melted. Stir it occasionally while you wait. When the mixture is melted, stir in butter. Keep cooking until it's all mixed together. Serve with churros.

Per serving: Calories 645; Fat 37g; Sodium 502mg; Carbs 68g; Sugar 1.2g; Fiber 0.7g; Protein 12g

Biscuits Donuts

Prep time: 7 minutes| Cook time: 5 minutes| Serves: 4

Coconut oil
1 can of biscuit dough, pre-made
½ cup of white sugar

½ cup of powdered sugar
2 tablespoons of melted butter
2 teaspoons of cinnamon

Cut the biscuit dough with a biscuit cutter. Then brush the cooking tray with coconut oil. Add biscuit and the remaining ingredients and stir well. Select the "Air Fry" mode on your Air Fryer. Press Temp button and then turn the dial to adjust the cooking temperature to 350 degrees F. Press Time button and then turn the dial to adjust the cooking time to 5 minutes. Press the Start button to initiate preheating. Transfer the biscuits to the air fryer basket of the Air Fryer when the screen displays "Add Food." Close its door, and let the machine do the cooking. Serve while warm!

Per serving: Calories 305; Fat 33.2g; Sodium 437mg; Carbs 27g; Sugar 0.5g; Fiber 0.7g; Protein 8.9g

French Toast with Cranberry Jam

Prep time: 12 minutes| Cook time: 8 minutes| Serves: 2

½ cup cranberry jam
4 slices of bread
⅛ cup skimmed milk
3 eggs

1 teaspoon ground cinnamon
1 tablespoon brown Sugar
Salt, to taste

In a low and wide dish break the eggs, add a pinch of salt and begin to beat them, without stopping, add the milk and then add the cinnamon and sugar. Mix again and set aside for a moment. Soak bread in the mixture and place on rack. Let the rack sit over the plate to drain a little. Select the "Air Fry" mode on your Air Fryer. Press Temp button and then turn the dial to adjust the cooking temperature to 350 degrees F. Press Time button and then turn the dial to adjust the cooking time to 8 minutes. Press the Start button to initiate preheating. Transfer the rack to the air fryer basket of the Air Fryer when the screen displays "Add Food." Close its door, and let the machine do the cooking. Serve hot with cranberry jam and a cup of tea.

Per serving: Calories 248; Fat 2.3g; Sodium 413mg; Carbs 27.2g; Sugar 1.4g; Fiber 0.7g; Protein 7.5g

Scrambled Eggs

Prep time: 12 minutes| Cook time: 10 minutes| Serves: 2

1 tablespoon of butter
8 grape tomatoes out
½ cup of parmesan cheese, grated

¾ cup of milk
Salt
4 eggs

Mix the eggs with milk, salt and butter. Pour the mixture into the cooking tray. Add grape tomatoes and cheese to it. Select the "Air Fry" mode on your Air Fryer. Press Temp button and then turn the dial to adjust the cooking temperature to 360 degrees F. Press Time button and then turn the dial to adjust the cooking time to 10 minutes. Press the Start button to initiate preheating. Transfer the tray to the air fryer basket of the Air Fryer when the screen displays "Add Food." Close its door, and let the machine do the cooking. Serve warm.

Per serving: Calories 351; Fat 22g; Sodium 502mg; Carbs 25.2g; Sugar 1.1g; Fiber 0.7g; Protein 26.4g

Waffles with Turkey breast

Prep time: 10 minutes| Cook time: 20 minutes| Serves: 4

Chicken seasoning, to taste
Salt and black pepper
½ cup all-purpose flour
1 lb. boneless turkey breast, diced

1 teaspoon garlic powder
Cooking oil
8 frozen waffles
Maple syrup (optional)

In a medium bowl, mix the garlic powder and chicken seasoning with some salt and pepper. Put the turkey breast in a bag and add flour. Shake to make sure that all of the turkey is covered. Sprinkle the turkey with cooking oil. Select the "Air Fry" mode on your Air Fryer. Press Temp button and then turn the dial to adjust the cooking temperature to 370 degrees F. Press Time button and then turn the dial to adjust the cooking time to 20 minutes. Press the Start button to initiate preheating. Transfer the turkey to the air fryer basket of the Air Fryer when the screen displays "Add Food." Close its door, and let the machine do the cooking. Transfer the turkey to a plate Put the waffles in the Air Fryer. Then cook for 9 minutes more at the same mode. Serve the turkey with waffles, you can also serve with some maple syrup if desired.

Per serving: Calories 465; Fat 24; Sodium 309mg; Carbs 45g; Sugar 0.4g; Fiber 0.7g; Protein 28g

Sweet Waffles

Prep time: 10 minutes| Cook time: 6 minutes| Serves: 2-3

6 frozen waffles
Maple Syrup or Honey

Butter

Put 2 frozen waffles on the cooking tray. Select the "Air Fry" mode on your Air Fryer. Press Temp button and then turn the dial to adjust the cooking temperature to 360 degrees F. Press Time button and then turn the dial to adjust the cooking time to 6 minutes. Press the Start button to initiate preheating. Transfer the tray to the air fryer basket of the Air Fryer when the screen displays "Add Food." Close its door, and let the machine do the cooking. Serve immediately with butter and syrup or honey.

Per serving: Calories 325; Fat 24; Sodium 472mg; Carbs 15g; Sugar 0.1g; Fiber 0.7g; Protein 15g

Sausage Appetizer in Egg Pond

Prep time: 25 minutes| Cook time: 20-25 minutes| Serves: 4

½ cup of bread cut into cubes	grated
3 eggs	¼ cup of cream
½ lb. sausages, sliced	¼ cup of mozzarella cheese,
¼ cup of parmesan cheese,	grated

Mix the eggs with cream in a bowl. Pour the egg mixture into the ramekins. Put sausage and bread slices in the ramekins. Select the "Air Fry" mode on your Air Fryer. Press Temp button and then turn the dial to adjust the cooking temperature to 365 degrees F. Press Time button and then turn the dial to adjust the cooking time to 20 minutes. Press the Start button to initiate preheating. Transfer the ramekins to the air fryer basket of the Air Fryer when the screen displays "Add Food." Close its door, and let the machine do the cooking. When the time is up, top with the cheese and cook for a few minutes more until the cheeses are melted. Serve.
Per serving: Calories 261; Sugar 0.8g; Fiber 1.3g; Protein 18.3g; Sodium 387mg; Carbs 4.2g; Fat 18.8g

Sausage Treat

Prep time: 5 minutes| Cook time: 11 minutes| Serves: 4

12 ounces chicken breakfast sausage	1 can of biscuits, 6 ounces
	⅛ cup pf cream cheese

Form the sausage into 5 small patties. Select the "Air Fry" mode on your Air Fryer. Press Temp button and then turn the dial to adjust the cooking temperature to 390 degrees F. Press Time button and then turn the dial to adjust the cooking time to 6 minutes. Press the Start button to initiate preheating. Transfer the sausages to the air fryer basket of the Air Fryer when the screen displays "Add Food." Close its door, and let the machine do the cooking. Separate the biscuit dough into 5 biscuits. Put the biscuits in the air fryer and cook for 3 minutes. First, open the air fryer. Flip the biscuits. Cook an additional 2 minutes in the air fryer and remove them when they are done cooking after 2 minutes. Split each biscuit in half with a knife. Spread 1 teaspoon of cream cheese on the bottom of each biscuit. Top with a sausage patty and put the other half of the biscuit on top. Serve.
Per serving: Calories 22g; Fat 13g; Sodium 427mg; Carbs 20g; Sugar 0.5g; Fiber 0.8g; Protein 9g

Crispy Ham Cups

Prep time: 5 minutes| Cook time: 12 minutes| Serves: 4

4 large eggs.	pepper.
4: 1-ounces slices deli ham	2 tablespoon diced white
½ cup shredded medium cheddar cheese.	onion.
¼ cup diced green bell pepper.	2 tablespoons full-fat sour cream.
2 tablespoon diced red bell	

Place 1 slice of ham on the bottom of four suitable baking cups. Take a large bowl, whisk eggs with sour cream. Stir in green pepper, red pepper and onion. Pour the egg mixture into ham-lined baking cups. Top with Cheddar. Select the "Air Fry" mode on your Air Fryer. Press Temp button and then turn the dial to adjust the cooking temperature to 320 degrees F. Press Time button and then turn the dial to adjust the cooking time to 12 minutes. Press the Start button to initiate preheating. Transfer the baking cups to the air fryer basket of the Air Fryer when the screen displays "Add Food." Close its door, and let the machine

do the cooking. Serve warm.
Per serving: Calories 382; Fat 23.6g; Sodium 761mg; Carbs 6.0g: Fiber 0.7g; Protein 29.4g

Potato Hash

Prep time: 15 minutes| Cook time: 32 minutes| Serves: 4

5 eggs, beaten	½ green bell pepper, seeded and chopped
1 medium onion, chopped	
½ teaspoon of thyme leaves, crushed	½ pound russet potatoes, peeled and cubed
2 teaspoons of butter, melted	½ teaspoon dried savory, crushed
Salt and black pepper to taste	

Put the onion, bell pepper, thyme, potatoes, savory, salt and black pepper in a cooking tray. Select the "Air Fry" mode on your Air Fryer. Press Temp button and then turn the dial to adjust the cooking temperature to 390 degrees F. Press Time button and then turn the dial to adjust the cooking time to 30 minutes. Press the Start button to initiate preheating. Transfer the cooking tray to the air fryer basket of the Air Fryer when the screen displays "Add Food." Close its door, and let the machine do the cooking. Add butter and eggs to a pan. Whisk them together while they cook. Cook the egg pieces for about 1 minute each side. Put them on a cooking tray. Serve and enjoy.
Per serving: Calories 230; Sugar 1.3g; Fiber 0.6g; Protein 10.3g; Sodium 430mg; Carbs 30.8g; Fat 7.6g

Veggie Egg Cups

Prep time: 15 minutes| Cook time: 15 minutes| Serves: 4

4 eggs	shredded
1 tablespoon cilantro chopped	1-cup vegetables, diced
4 tablespoon half and half	Salt and black pepper
1 cup of cheddar cheese,	

To make egg cups, first put on four ramekins on the cooking tray. Then add eggs, cilantro, half and half, vegetables, ½ cup of cheese, pepper, and salt to a bowl. Pour the mixture into the ramekins that you sprayed with cooking spray Select the "Air Fry" mode on your Air Fryer. Press Temp button and then turn the dial to adjust the cooking temperature to 300 degrees F. Press Time button and then turn the dial to adjust the cooking time to 12 minutes. Press the Start button to initiate preheating. Transfer the ramekins to the air fryer basket of the Air Fryer when the screen displays "Add Food." Close its door, and let the machine do the cooking. Spread remaining cheese making sure to cover it and cook for 3 minutes more. Enjoy!
Per serving: calories 202; Fat 10g; Sodium 502mg; Carbs 6g; Sugar 0.4g; Fiber 0.3g; Protein 12g;

Muffins with Bacon

Prep time: 7 minutes| Cook time: 15 minutes| Serves: 4

Two eggs	For cooked and bacon slices:
Parsley	1 shredded onions
1-cup and half of all-purpose flour	½ cup of shredded cheddar cheese
2 teaspoons baking powder	½ teaspoon of onion powder
½ cup of milk	Salt and black pepper

Stir the ingredients in a bowl until they mix well. Add some grease to the muffin cups and then add the batter. Select the "Air Fry" mode on your Air Fryer. Press Temp button and then turn the dial to adjust the cooking temperature to 360 degrees F. Press Time button and then turn the dial to adjust the cooking time to 15 minutes. Press the Start button to initiate preheating. Transfer the baking muffin pan to the air fryer basket of the Air Fryer when the screen displays "Add Food." Close its door, and let the machine do the cooking. Take it out of oven, let it cool down. Serve.

Per serving: Calories 180; Fat 18g; Sodium 384mg; Carbs 17g; Sugar 0.5g; Fiber 0.8g; Protein 14g

English Breakfast

Prep time: 5 minutes| Cook time: 12 minutes| Serves: 2

4 sausages
4 bacon slices
2 eggs

1 can of baked beans
4 slices toast

Select the "Air Fry" mode on your Air Fryer. Press Temp button and then turn the dial to adjust the cooking temperature to 320 degrees F. Press Time button and then turn the dial to adjust the cooking time to 10 minutes. Press the Start button to initiate preheating. Add the sausages and bacon to the air fryer basket of the Air Fryer when the screen displays "Add Food." Close its door, and let the machine do the cooking. Add baking beans and whisk eggs in a ramekin and cook for 2 minutes more. Serve with the toast slices.

Per serving: Calories 364; Fat 27; Sodium 391mg; Carbs 6g; Sugar 0.8g; Fiber 1.3g; Protein 24

Tomatoes Swiss Chard Bake

Prep time: 5 minutes| Cook time: 15 minutes| Serves: 4

4 eggs; whisked
3 ounces' Swiss chard; chopped

1 cup tomatoes; cubed
1 teaspoon olive oil
Salt and black pepper to taste

Take a bowl and mix the eggs with the rest of the ingredients, except for the oil and whisk well. Grease the cooking tray that fits the fryer with the oil pour the Swiss chard mix on top. Select the "Air Fry" mode on your Air Fryer. Press Temp button and then turn the dial to adjust the cooking temperature to 360 degrees F. Press Time button and then turn the dial to adjust the cooking time to 15 minutes. Press the Start button to initiate preheating. Transfer the cooking tray to the rack of the Air Fryer when the screen displays "Add Food." Close its door, and let the machine do the cooking. Divide between plates and serve.

Per serving: Calories 202; Fat 14g; Sodium 441mg; Carbs 5g; Fiber 3g; Sugars 1.3g; Protein 12g

English Bacon Eggs

Prep time: 5 minutes| Cook time: 7 minutes| Serves: 2

2 large eggs
2 tablespoon half and half

Black pepper and salt, to taste

Beat eggs with half and half, cheese, salt and black pepper in a bowl. Divide the eggs in 2 ramekins. Select the "Air Fry" mode on your Air Fryer. Press Temp button and then turn the dial to adjust the cooking temperature to 335 degrees F. Press Time button and then turn the dial to adjust the cooking time to 7 minutes. Press the Start button to initiate preheating. Transfer the ramekins to the air fryer basket of the Air Fryer when the screen displays "Add Food." Close its door, and let the machine do the cooking. Serve.

Per serving: Calories 185; Fat 17g; Sodium 383mg; Carbs 15g; Sugar 0.5g; Fiber 0.7g; Protein 14g

Olive Bread

Prep time: 10 minutes| Cook time: 15 minutes| Serves: 2

3 bread slices
2 tablespoons of Cheddar cheese
1 tablespoon of Olives
1 tablespoon of mustard

1 tablespoon of paprika
2 eggs, white and yolks, separated
1 tablespoon of chives

Select the "Air Fry" mode on your Air Fryer. Press Temp button and then turn the dial to adjust the cooking temperature to 360 degrees F. Press Time button and then turn the dial to adjust the cooking time to 5 minutes.
Press the Start button to initiate preheating. Transfer the bread to the air fryer basket of the Air Fryer when the screen displays "Add Food." Close its door, and let the machine do the cooking. Mix the egg whites and yolks with the olives, cheese, paprika, chives and mustard. Put the mixture on the slices of bread. Cook in an Air Fryer at 350 degrees F for 10 minutes on Bake mode. Serve.

Per serving: Calories 165; Fat 9g; Sodium 437mg; Carbs 13g; Sugar 0.8g; Fiber 1.3g; Protein 13g

Cheddar Omelet

Prep time: 10 minutes| Cook time: 5 minutes| Serves: 2

1 large onion, sliced
4 eggs
Ground black pepper
1/8 cup of cheddar cheese,

grated
1/8 cup of mozzarella cheese, grated
1/4 teaspoon of soy sauce

Cook the onions in a pan. Add eggs, ground black pepper, and soy sauce. Mix it up. Place the onion on the cooking tray and put the egg mixture on top of that and then put cheeses on top of that. Select the "Air Fry" mode on your Air Fryer. Press Temp button and then turn the dial to adjust the cooking temperature to 360 degrees F. Press Time button and then turn the dial to adjust the cooking time to 5 minutes. Press the Start button to initiate preheating. Transfer the tray to the air fryer basket of the Air Fryer when the screen displays "Add Food." Close its door, and let the machine do the cooking. Serve warm.

Per serving: Calories 214; Fat 13.5g; Sodium 408mg; Carbs 7.9g; Sugar 0.5g; Fiber 0.8g; Protein 14.5g

Sausage Breakfast

Prep time: 5 minutes| Cook time: 20 minutes| Serves: 4

8 sausages
8 bacon slices
4 eggs

1 (16-ounce) can of baked beans
8 slices of toast

Using a ramekin or heat-safe bowl, add the baked beans, then place another ramekin and add the eggs and whisk. Select the "Air Fry" mode on your Air Fryer. Press Temp button and then turn the dial to adjust the cooking temperature to 320 degrees F. Press Time button and then turn the dial to adjust the cooking time to 10 minutes. Press the Start button to initiate preheating. Add the sausages and bacon slices to the air fryer basket of the Air Fryer when the screen displays "Add Food." Close its door, and let the machine do the cooking. Place the ramekins inside your oven and cook it for an additional 10 minutes. When done, serve with the toast slices.

Per serving: Calories 850; Fat 40g; Sodium 502mg; Carbs 20g; Sugar 1.3g; Fiber 0.6g; Protein 48g

Strawberry Cobbler

Prep time: 5 minutes| Cook time: 15 minutes| Serves: 4

⅓ cup whole-wheat pastry flour
¾ teaspoon baking powder
Dash sea salt
½ cup fresh strawberries
¼ cup Granola, or plain store-

bought granola
½ cup 2% milk
2 tablespoons pure maple syrup
½ teaspoon vanilla extract
Cooking oil spray

In a medium bowl, whisk the baking powder, flour, and salt. Add the milk, maple syrup, and vanilla and gently whisk, just until thoroughly combined. Spray the cooking tray with cooking oil and pour the batter into the tray. Top evenly with the strawberries and granola. Select the "Bake" mode on your Air Fryer. Press Temp button and then turn the dial to adjust the cooking temperature to 350 degrees F. Press Time button and then turn the dial to adjust the cooking time to 15 minutes. Press the Start button to initiate preheating. Transfer the cooking tray to the air fryer basket of the Air Fryer when the screen displays "Add Food." Close its door, and let the machine do the cooking. Enjoy with a little vanilla yogurt on top if desired.
Per serving: Calories 112; Fat 1g; Sodium 428mg; Carbs 23g; Sugar 0.4g; Fiber 0.3g; Protein 3g

Scramble Casserole

Prep time: 20 minutes| Cook time: 15 minutes| Serves: 4

6 slices bacon
6 eggs
Cooking oil
½ cup chopped red bell pepper
½ cup chopped green bell pepper

½ cup chopped onion
¾ cup shredded Cheddar cheese
Salt, to taste
Pepper, to taste

In a pan, over medium-high heat, cook the bacon for 5 to 7 minutes, flipping regularly to evenly crisp. Dry out on paper towels, crumble, and set aside. In a bowl, whisk the eggs. Add salt and black pepper. Spray a barrel pan with cooking oil. Make sure to cover the bottom and sides of the pan. Add the beaten eggs, crumbled bacon, red bell pepper, green bell pepper, and onion to the pan. Select the "Air Fry" mode on your Air Fryer. Press Temp button and then turn the dial to adjust the cooking temperature to 390 degrees F. Press Time button and then turn the dial to adjust the cooking time to 6 minutes. Press the Start button to initiate preheating. Transfer the cooking tray to the air fryer basket of the Air Fryer when the screen displays "Add Food." Close its door, and let the machine do the cooking. Open the Air Fryer and sprinkle the cheese over the casserole. Cook for an additional 2 minutes. Serve.
Per serving: Calories 348; Fat 26g; Sodium 387mg; Carbs 4g; Sugar 1.3g; Fiber 0.6g; Protein 25g

Chocolate-Filled Doughnuts

Prep time: 10 minutes| Cook time: 12 minutes| Serves: 12

1 (8-count) can refrigerated biscuits
Cooking oil spray
Forty-8 semisweet chocolate

chips
3 tablespoons melted unsalted butter
¼ cup confectioners' sugar

Separate the biscuits and cut each biscuit into thirds, for twenty-four pieces. Flatten each biscuit piece slightly and put two chocolate chips in the center. Wrap the dough around the chocolate and seal the edges. Brush each doughnut hole with a bit of the butter and place them in a suitable baking sheet.

Select the "Air Fry" mode on your Air Fryer. Press Temp button and then turn the dial to adjust the cooking temperature to 330 degrees F. Press Time button and then turn the dial to adjust the cooking time to 12 minutes. Press the Start button to initiate preheating. Transfer the baking sheet to the air fryer basket of the Air Fryer when the screen displays "Add Food." Close its door, and let the machine do the cooking. Place the doughnut holes on a plate and dust with the confectioners' sugar. Serve.
Per serving: Calories 393; Fat 17g; Sodium 309mg; Carbs 55g; Sugar 0.5g; Fiber 0.8g; Protein 5g

Paprika Hash Browns

Prep time: 15 minutes| Cook time: 20 minutes| Serves: 4

4 russet potatoes
1 teaspoon paprika
Salt, to taste

Pepper, to taste
Cooking oil

Peel the potatoes. Using a cheese grater shred the potatoes. If your grater has different-size holes, use the area of the tool with the largest holes. Put the shredded potatoes in a large bowl of cold water. Let the potatoes sit for 5 minutes. Cold water helps remove excess starch from the potatoes. Toss to help dissolve the starch. Dry out the potatoes and dry with paper towels. Make sure the potatoes are completely dry. Season the potatoes with the paprika, salt and black pepper. Spray the potatoes with cooking oil. Select the "Air Fry" mode on your Air Fryer. Press Temp button and then turn the dial to adjust the cooking temperature to 330 degrees F. Press Time button and then turn the dial to adjust the cooking time to 20 minutes. Press the Start button to initiate preheating. Transfer the potatoes to the air fryer basket of the Air Fryer when the screen displays "Add Food." Close its door, and let the machine do the cooking. Serve.
Per serving: Calories 150; Sodium 387mg; Carbs 34g; Sugar 0.4g; Fiber 0.3g; Protein 4g

Cheese Ham Soufflé

Prep time: 5 minutes| Cook time: 8 minutes| Serves: 4

6 eggs
⅓ of cup of milk
½ cup of shredded mozzarella cheese
1 tablespoon of freshly

chopped parsley
½ cup of chopped ham
½ teaspoon of garlic powder
1 teaspoon of salt
1 teaspoon of pepper

Grease 4 ramekins with a nonstick cooking spray. Using a bowl, add and mix all the ingredients properly Pour the egg mixture into the greased ramekins. Select the "Air Fry" mode on your Air Fryer. Press Temp button and then turn the dial to adjust the cooking temperature to 350 degrees F. Press Time button and then turn the dial to adjust the cooking time to 8 minutes. Press the Start button to initiate preheating. Transfer the ramekins to the air fryer basket of the Air Fryer when the screen displays "Add Food." Close its door, and let the machine do the cooking. Serve.
Per serving: Calories 195; Fat 15g; Sodium 472mg; Carbs 6g; Sugar 1.5g; Fiber 1.2g; Protein 9g

Yogurt Bagels

Prep time: 10 minutes| Cook time: 10 minutes| Serves: 2

1 egg
½ cup self-rising flour
½ cup plain Greek yogurt
1 tablespoon water

4 teaspoons everything bagel spice mix
Cooking oil spray
1 tablespoon butter, melted

In a bowl, using a wooden spoon, mix together the flour and yogurt until a tacky dough forms. Transfer the dough to a lightly floured work surface and roll the dough into a ball. Cut the dough into two pieces and roll each piece into a log. Form each log into a bagel shape, pinching the ends together. In a small bowl, whisk the water and egg. Brush the egg wash on the bagels. Sprinkle 2 teaspoons of the spice mix on each bagel and press it into the dough. Select the "Bake" mode on your Air Fryer. Press Temp button and then turn the dial to adjust the cooking temperature to 330 degrees F. Press Time button and then turn the dial to adjust the cooking time to 10 minutes. Press the Start button to initiate preheating. Drizzle with the bagels with the butter and place them on the sprayed cooking tray. Transfer the cooking tray to the air fryer basket of the Air Fryer when the screen displays "Add Food." Close its door, and let the machine do the cooking. Serve.
Per serving: Calories 271; Fat 13g; Sodium 384mg; Carbs 28g; Sugar 11g; Fiber 0.3g; Protein 10g

Fried Zucchini

Prep time: 5 minutes| Cook time: 24 minutes| Serves: 4

3 large zucchini	1 cup chopped red bell pepper
1 tablespoon canola oil	1 cup chopped green bell
1 tablespoon olive oil	pepper
1 teaspoon paprika	Salt, to taste
1 cup chopped onion	Black pepper, to taste

Cut the zucchini into ½-inch cubes. Place the zucchini in a bowl of cold water and allow them to soak for at least 30 minutes. Dry out the zucchini and wipe thoroughly with paper towels. Return them to the empty bowl. Add the canola and paprika, olive oils, salt and black pepper to flavor. Stir to fully coat the zucchini. Select the "Air Fry" mode on your Air Fryer. Use the timer (+ / − Time) arrow keys to adjust cooking time to 20 minutes. Adjust its cooking temperature to 390 degrees F, using the temp (+/- Temp) arrow keys. Press the Start button to initiate preheating. Transfer the potatoes to the air fryer basket of the Air Fryer when the screen displays "Add Food." Close its door, and let the machine do the cooking. Put the onion and peppers to the zucchini. Air Fry for additional 3 to 4 minutes more. Serve.
Per serving: Calories 279; Fat 8g; Sodium 369mg; Carbs 50g; Sugar 2.4g; Fiber 0.3g; Protein 9.1g

Cherry Tarts

Prep time: 15 minutes| Cook time: 10 minutes| Serves: 6

For the tarts:	For the frosting:
2 refrigerated piecrusts	½ cup vanilla yogurt
⅓ Cup cherry preserves	1-ounce cream cheese
1 teaspoon cornstarch	1 teaspoon stevia
Cooking oil	Rainbow sprinkles

Place the piecrusts on a flat surface. Make use of a knife or pizza cutter, cut each piecrust into 3 rectangles, for 6 in total. In a bowl, combine the preserves and cornstarch. Stir well. Scoop 1 tablespoon of the preserve mixture onto the top half of each piece of piecrust. Fold the bottom of each piece up to close the tart. Press along the edges of each tart to seal using the back of a fork. Select the "Air Fry" mode on your Air Fryer. Press Temp button and then turn the dial to adjust the cooking temperature to 390 degrees F. Press Time button and then turn the dial to adjust the cooking time to 10 minutes. Press the Start button to initiate preheating. Sprinkle the breakfast tarts with cooking oil. Transfer the tarts to the air fryer basket of the Air Fryer when the screen displays "Add Food." Close its door, and let the machine do the cooking. Allow the breakfast tarts to cool fully before removing from the air fryer. If needed, repeat steps 5 and 6 for the remaining breakfast tarts.

To make the frosting: In a bowl, mix the cream cheese, yogurt, and stevia. Mix well. Spread the breakfast tarts with frosting and top with sprinkles.
Per serving: Calories 119; Fat 4g; Sodium 409mg; Carbs 19g; Sugar 8g; Fiber 1.7g; Protein 11g

Strawberry Tarts

Prep time: 15 minutes| Cook time: 10 minutes| Serves: 6

2 refrigerated piecrusts	temperature
½ cup strawberry preserves	3 tablespoons confectioners'
1 teaspoon cornstarch	sugar
Cooking oil spray	Rainbow sprinkles, for
½ cup low-fat vanilla yogurt	decorating
1-ounce cream cheese, at room	

Place the piecrusts on a flat surface. Cut each piecrust into 3 rectangles using a knife or pizza cutter, for 6 in total. Discard any unused dough from the piecrust edges. In a small bowl, mix the preserves and cornstarch. Ensuring there are no lumps of cornstarch remaining. Scoop 1 tablespoon of the strawberry mixture onto the top half of each piece of piecrust. Fold the bottom of each piece up to enclose the filling. Press along the edges of each tart to seal using the back of a fork. Select the "Air Fry" mode on your Air Fryer. Press Temp button and then turn the dial to adjust the cooking temperature to 375 degrees F. Press Time button and then turn the dial to adjust the cooking time to 10 minutes. Press the Start button to initiate preheating. spray the breakfast tarts with cooking oil and place them in the cooking tray in a single layer. Transfer the cooking tray to the air fryer basket of the Air Fryer when the screen displays "Add Food." Close its door, and let the machine do the cooking. In a bowl, mix together the cream cheese, yogurt, and confectioners' sugar. Spread the breakfast tarts with the frosting and top with sprinkles. Serve.
Per serving: Calories 408; Fat 20.5g; Sodium 437mg; Carbs 56g; Sugar 7.4g; Fiber 1.3g; Protein 11g

Jalapeno Muffins

Prep time: 10 minutes| Cook time: 15 minutes| Serves: 8

5 eggs	milk
⅓ cup coconut oil, melted	⅔ cup coconut flour
2 teaspoons baking powder	3 tablespoons jalapenos, sliced
3 tablespoons erythritol	¾ teaspoon sea salt
¼ cup unsweetened coconut	

In a large bowl, stir coconut flour, erythritol, baking powder, and sea salt. Mix eggs, jalapenos, coconut milk, and coconut oil until well-combined. Pour batter into the silicone muffin molds. Select the "Air Fry" mode on your Air Fryer. Press Temp button and then turn the dial to adjust the cooking temperature to 325 degrees F. Press Time button and then turn the dial to adjust the cooking time to 15 minutes. Press the Start button to initiate preheating. Transfer the muffin pan to the air fryer basket of the Air Fryer when the screen displays "Add Food." Close its door, and let the machine do the cooking. Serve.
Per serving: Calories 125; Fat 12g; Sodium 399mg; Carbs 7 g; Sugar 1.1g; Fiber 0.3g; Protein 22g

Mushrooms Frittata

Prep time: 10 minutes| Cook time: 13 minutes| Serves: 1

1 cup egg whites	2 tablespoons parmesan
1 cup spinach, chopped	cheese, grated
Two mushrooms, sliced	Salt, to taste

Sprinkle pan with cooking spray and heat over medium heat. Add mushrooms and sauté for 2-3 minutes Add spinach and cook for 1-2 minutes or until wilted. Transfer mushroom spinach mixture into a pan. Beat egg whites in a mixing bowl until frothy. Season it with a pinch of salt. Pour egg white mixture into the spinach and mushroom mixture and sprinkle with parmesan. Select the "Air Fry" mode on your Air Fryer. Press Temp button and then turn the dial to adjust the cooking temperature to 350 degrees F. Press Time button and then turn the dial to adjust the cooking time to 8 minutes. Press the Start button to initiate preheating. Transfer the cooking tray to the air fryer basket of the Air Fryer when the screen displays "Add Food." Close its door, and let the machine do the cooking.
Per serving: Calories 176; Fat 3g; Sodium 387mg; Carbs 4 g; Sugar 1.3g; Fiber 2.1g; Protein 16g

Omelet

Prep time: 10 minutes| Cook time: 16 minutes| Serves: 3

3 eggs, lightly beaten	¼ small onion, chopped
2 tablespoon cheddar cheese, shredded	¼ bell pepper, diced
	Black pepper, to taste
2 tablespoon heavy cream	Salt, to taste
2 mushrooms, sliced	

In a medium bowl, whisk eggs with cream, vegetables, pepper, and salt. Pour egg mixture into the cooking tray.
Select the "Air Fry" mode on your Air Fryer. Press Temp button and then turn the dial to adjust the cooking temperature to 400 degrees F. Press Time button and then turn the dial to adjust the cooking time to 15 minutes. Press the Start button to initiate preheating. Transfer the cooking tray to the air fryer basket of the Air Fryer when the screen displays "Add Food." Close its door, and let the machine do the cooking. Add shredded cheese on top of the frittata and cook for 1 minute more. Serve warm.
Per serving: Calories 160; Fat 10g; Sodium 427mg; Carbs 4 g; Sugar 1.1g; Fiber 0.6g; Protein 27g

Sausage and Egg Burrito

Prep time: 5 minutes| Cook time: 18 minutes| Serves: 6

6 eggs	8 ounces ground chicken sausage
Salt, to taste	
Black pepper, to taste	½ cup salsa
Cooking oil	6 medium (8-inch) flour tortillas
½ cup chopped red bell pepper	
½ cup chopped green bell pepper	½ cup shredded Cheddar cheese

In a medium bowl, whisk the eggs. Add salt and black pepper. Place a skillet on medium-high heat. Spray with cooking oil. Add the eggs. Scramble for 2 to 3 minutes, until the eggs are fluffy. Remove the eggs from the skillet and set aside. If needed, spray the skillet with more oil. Add the chopped red and green bell peppers. Cook for 2 to 3 minutes, once the peppers are soft. Add the ground sausage to the skillet. Break the sausage into smaller pieces using a spatula or spoon. Cook for 3 to 4 minutes, until the sausage is brown. Add the salsa and scrambled eggs. Stir to combine. Remove the skillet from heat. Spoon the mixture evenly onto the tortillas. To form the burritos, fold the sides of each tortilla in toward the middle and then roll up from the bottom. You can secure each burrito with a toothpick. Select the "Air Fry" mode on your Air Fryer. Press Temp button and then turn the dial to adjust the cooking temperature to 390 degrees F. Press Time button and then turn the dial to adjust the cooking time to 8 minutes. Press the Start button to initiate preheating. Transfer the burritos to the air fryer basket of the Air Fryer when the screen displays "Add Food." Close its door, and let the machine do the cooking. Sprinkle the cheddar over the burritos. Serve.
Per serving: Calories 236; Fat 13g; Sodium 502mg; Carbs 16g; Sugar 0.8g; Fiber 1.1g; Protein 31g

Cheese and Bacon Muffins

Prep time: 5 minutes| Cook time: 15 minutes| Serves: 4

1 ½ cup of all-purpose flour	chopped
2 teaspoons of baking powder	1 onion, chopped
½ cup of milk	½ cup of cheddar cheese, shredded
2 eggs	
1 tablespoon of freshly chopped parsley	½ teaspoon of onion powder
	1 teaspoon of salt
4 bacon slices, cooked and	1 teaspoon of black pepper

Using a large bowl, add and mix all the ingredients until it mixes properly. Then grease the muffin cups with a nonstick cooking spray or line it with a parchment paper. Pour the batter proportionally into each muffin cup. Select the "Air Fry" mode on your Air Fryer. Press Temp button and then turn the dial to adjust the cooking temperature to 360 degrees F. Press Time button and then turn the dial to adjust the cooking time to 15 minutes. Press the Start button to initiate preheating. Transfer the muffin pan to the air fryer basket of the Air Fryer when the screen displays "Add Food." Close its door, and let the machine do the cooking. Serve.
Per serving: Calories 180; Fat 18g; Sodium 430mg; Carbs 16g; Sugar 0.4g; Fiber 0.3g; Protein 4g

Spinach Frittata

Prep time: 5 minutes| Cook time: 8 minutes| Serves: 4

3 eggs	2 tablespoon mozzarella cheese, grated
1 cup spinach, chopped	
1 small onion, minced	Salt and black pepper, to taste

Spray air fryer pan with cooking spray. In a bowl, whisk eggs with remaining ingredients until well combined. Pour egg mixture into the prepared pan. Select the "Air Fry" mode on your Air Fryer. Press Temp button and then turn the dial to adjust the cooking temperature to 350 degrees F. Press Time button and then turn the dial to adjust the cooking time to 8 minutes. Press the Start button to initiate preheating. Transfer the cooking tray to the air fryer basket of the Air Fryer when the screen displays "Add Food." Close its door, and let the machine do the cooking. Serve warm.
Per serving: Calories 384; Fat 23.3g; Sodium 413mg; Carbs 10.7 g Sugar 1.2g; fiber 0.2g; Protein 1.2g

Italian Frittata

Prep time: 5 minutes| Cook time: 10 minutes| Serves: 6

6 eggs	½ cup of a grated feta cheese
⅓ cup of milk	1 chopped zucchini
4-ounces of Italian sausage, chopped	1 tablespoon of freshly chopped basil
3 cups of stemmed and chopped kale	1 teaspoon of garlic powder
	1 teaspoon of onion powder
1 red deseeded and chopped bell pepper	1 teaspoon of salt
	1 teaspoon of black pepper

Grease the cooking tray with a nonstick cooking spray. Add the Italian sausage to the tray. Select the "Air Fry" mode on your Air Fryer. Press Temp button and then turn the dial to adjust the cooking temperature to 350 degrees F. Press Time button and then turn the dial to adjust the cooking time to 5 minutes. Press the Start button to initiate preheating. Transfer the cooking tray to the air fryer basket of the Air Fryer when the screen displays "Add Food." Close its door, and let the machine do the cooking. While doing that, add and toss in the remaining ingredients until it mixes properly. Add the egg mixture to the tray and allow it to cook inside your Air Fryer for 5 minutes more. Serve.

Per serving: Calories 225; Fat 14g; Sodium 309mg; Carbs 22g; Sugar 0.4g; Fiber 0.3g; Proteins 4.5g

Cheese Ham Omelet

Prep time: 10 minutes| Cook time: 25 minutes| Serves: 6

8 eggs	shredded
1 cup ham chopped	⅓ cup milk
1 cup cheddar cheese,	Black pepper and Salt, to taste

Spray a suitable baking dish with cooking spray and set aside. In a large bowl, whisk eggs with milk, pepper, and salt. Stir in ham and cheese. Pour egg mixture into the prepared baking dish. Select the "Air Fry" mode on your Air Fryer. Press Temp button and then turn the dial to adjust the cooking temperature to 390 degrees F. Press Time button and then turn the dial to adjust the cooking time to 25 minutes. Press the Start button to initiate preheating. Transfer the baking dish to the air fryer basket of the Air Fryer when the screen displays "Add Food." Close its door, and let the machine do the cooking. Slice and serve.

Per serving: Calories 203; Fat 14.3g; Sodium 384mg; Carbs 2.2g; Sugar 0.8g; Fiber 1.3g; Protein 16.3g

Squash Oat Muffins

Prep time: 10 minutes| Cook time: 20 minutes| Serves: 12

2 eggs	1 teaspoon vanilla
1 tablespoon pumpkin pie spice	⅓ cup olive oil
2 teaspoon baking powder	½ cup yogurt
1 cup oats	½ cup maple syrup
1 cup all-purpose flour	1 cup butternut squash puree
	½ teaspoon sea salt

Line 12 cups muffin pan with cupcake liners. In a large bowl, whisk together eggs, vanilla, oil, yogurt, maple syrup, and squash puree. In a small bowl, mix together flour, pumpkin pie spice, baking powder, oats, and salt. Add flour mixture into the wet mixture and stir to combine. Scoop the batter to the prepared muffin pan.
Select the "Air Fry" mode on your Air Fryer. Press Temp button and then turn the dial to adjust the cooking temperature to 390 degrees F. Press Time button and then turn the dial to adjust the cooking time to 20 minutes. Press the Start button to initiate preheating. Transfer the muffin pan to the air fryer basket of the Air Fryer when the screen displays "Add Food." Close its door, and let the machine do the cooking. Serve and enjoy.

Per serving: Calories 171; Fat 7.1g; Sodium 427mg; Carbs 23.8g; Sugar 9.4g; Fiber 0.7g; Protein 3.6g

Perfect Brunch Baked Eggs

Prep time: 10 minutes| Cook time: 20 minutes| Serves: 4

4 eggs	2 cups marinara sauce
½ cup parmesan cheese grated	Black pepper and salt, to taste

Spray 4 shallow baking dishes with cooking spray and set aside. Divide marinara sauce into four baking dishes. Break the egg into each baking dish. Sprinkle cheese, pepper and salt on top of eggs. Select the "Air Fry" mode on your Air Fryer Press Temp button and then turn the dial to adjust the cooking temperature to

390 degrees F. Press Time button and then turn the dial to adjust the cooking time to 20 minutes. Press the Start button to initiate preheating. Transfer the baking dishes to the air fryer basket of the Air Fryer when the screen displays "Add Food." Close its door, and let the machine do the cooking. Serve and enjoy.

Per serving: Calories 208; Fat 10.1g; Sodium 369mg; Carbs 18g; Sugar 11.4g; Fiber 0.7g; Protein 11.4g

Peanut Butter and Banana Sandwich

Prep time: 4 minutes| Cook time: 6 minutes| Serves: 1

2 slices whole-wheat bread	1 sliced banana
1 teaspoon sugar-free maple syrup	2 tablespoons peanut butter

Evenly coat each side of the sliced bread with peanut butter. Add the sliced banana and drizzle with some sugar-free maple syrup then place them in a cooking tray. Select the "Air Fry" mode on your Air Fryer. Press Temp button and then turn the dial to adjust the cooking temperature to 330 degrees F. Press Time button and then turn the dial to adjust the cooking time to 6 minutes. Press the Start button to initiate preheating. Transfer the cooking tray to the air fryer basket of the Air Fryer when the screen displays "Add Food." Close its door, and let the machine do the cooking. Serve.

Per serving: Calories 211; Fat 8.2g; Sodium 437mg; Carbs 6.3g; Sugar 0.5g; Fiber 0.8g; Protein 11.2g

Classic Corned Beef Hash and Eggs

Prep time: 10 minutes| Cook time: 35 minutes| Serves: 4

2 medium Yukon Gold potatoes, peeled, cubed	½ teaspoon salt
1 medium onion, chopped	½ teaspoon black pepper
⅓ cup diced red bell pepper	¾ pound corned beef, cut into
3 tablespoons vegetable oil	¼-inch pieces
½ teaspoon dried thyme	4 large eggs

In a large bowl, mix the potatoes, onion, red pepper, oil, thyme, ¼ teaspoon of salt, and ¼ teaspoon of pepper. Spread the vegetables on the suitable sheet pan in an even layer. Select the "Roast" mode on your Air Fryer. Press Temp button and then turn the dial to adjust the cooking temperature to 375 degrees F. Press Time button and then turn the dial to adjust the cooking time to 25 minutes. Press the Start button to initiate preheating. Transfer the sheet pan to the air fryer basket of the Air Fryer when the screen displays "Add Food." Close its door, and let the machine do the cooking. Remove the pan from the oven and add the corned beef. Stir the mixture to incorporate the corned beef. Return the pan to the Air Fryer and continue cooking for 5 minutes. Using a large spoon, create 4 circles in the hash to hold the eggs. Gently crack an egg into each circle; season eggs with remaining ¼ teaspoon of salt and ¼ teaspoon of pepper. Return the sheet pan to the oven. Continue cooking for 3 to 8 minutes more. Serve immediately

Per serving: Calories 397; Fat 26g; Sodium 777mg; Carbs 21g; Sugar 0.5g; Fiber 0.7g; Protein 20g

Buttery Chocolate Toast

Prep time: 5 minutes| Cook time: 5 minutes| Serves: 1

2 Whole wheat bread slices	1 tablespoon pure maple syrup
1 tablespoon coconut oil	1 teaspoon cacao powder

Spread coconut oil over the bread slices. Drizzle maple syrup in lines over the bread slices. Select the "Bake" mode on your Air Fryer. Press Temp button and then turn the dial to adjust the cooking temperature to 350 degrees F. Press Time button and then turn the dial to adjust the cooking time to 5 minutes. Press the Start button to initiate preheating. Transfer the bread slices to the air fryer basket of the Air Fryer when the screen displays "Add Food." Close its door, and let the machine do the cooking. Sprinkle cacao powder and serve.

Per serving: Calories 101; Fat 3.5g; Sodium 383mg; Carbs 14.8g; Sugar 1.3g; Fiber 0.6g; Protein 4.0g

Ham and Cheese Sandwiches

Prep time: 5 minutes| Cook time: 5 minutes| Serves: 2

2 bagels	4 slices ham
4 teaspoons honey mustard	4 slices Swiss cheese

Spread honey mustard on each half of the bagel. Add ham and cheese and close the bagel. Select the "Air Fry" mode on your Air Fryer. Press Temp button and then turn the dial to adjust the cooking temperature to 400 degrees F. Press Time button and then turn the dial to adjust the cooking time to 5 minutes. Press the Start button to initiate preheating. Transfer the bagel sandwich to the air fryer basket of the Air Fryer when the screen displays "Add Food." Close its door, and let the machine do the cooking. Serve warm.

Per serving: Calories 588; Fat 20.1g; Sodium 387mg; Carbs 62.9g; Sugar 0.4g; Fiber 0.3g; Protein 38.4g

Avocado Spinach with Poached Eggs

Prep time: 7 minutes| Cook time: 12 minutes| Serves: 1

2 eggs	1 bunch spinach
½ avocado	Pinch of salt
2 slices bread	Pinch of black pepper

Bring a pan of water to a rolling boil. Once the water is boiling, whisk it around in a circle until it creates a vortex. Drop 1 egg in the hole and turn the heat to low, and then poach for 2 minutes. Place bread on the cooking tray. Select the "Air Fry" mode on your Air Fryer. Press Temp button and then turn the dial to adjust the cooking temperature to 400 degrees F. Press Time button and then turn the dial to adjust the cooking time to 10 minutes. Press the Start button to initiate preheating. Transfer the cooking tray to the air fryer basket of the Air Fryer when the screen displays "Add Food." Close its door, and let the machine do the cooking. Mash avocado and spread it over the toast while the eggs poach. Add the eggs to the toast and top with spinach

Per serving: Calories 409; Fat 29.7g; Sodium 502mg; Carbs 21.7g; Sugar 0.4g; Fiber 0.3g; Protein 22.7g

Tomato Spinach Frittata

Prep time: 15 minutes| Cook time: 30 minutes| Serves: 4

3 tablespoons olive oil	1 (5-ounce) bag baby spinach
10 large eggs	1 pint grape tomatoes
2 teaspoons salt	4 scallions
½ teaspoon black pepper	8 ounces feta cheese

Halve tomatoes and slice scallions into thin pieces. Grease a suitable oven-safe pan with cooking oil. Combine the eggs, salt and pepper in a medium mixing bowl and whisk together for a minute. Add spinach, tomatoes, and scallions to the bowl and

mix together until even. Crumble feta cheese into the bowl and mix together gently. Pour in the egg mixture, mix and add to the cooking tray. Select the "Air Fry" mode on your Air Fryer. Press Temp button and then turn the dial to adjust the cooking temperature to 350 degrees F. Press Time button and then turn the dial to adjust the cooking time to 30 minutes. Press the Start button to initiate preheating. Transfer the cooking tray to the air fryer basket of the Air Fryer when the screen displays "Add Food." Close its door, and let the machine do the cooking. Serve.

Per serving: Calories 448; Fat 35.4g; Sodium 502mg; Carbs 9.3g; Sugar 1.2g; Fiber 0.7g; Protein 25.9g

Breakfast Sausage Sandwich

Prep time: 5 minutes| Cook time: 7 minutes| Serves: 2

2 English muffins	2 large spicy pork sausage
2 eggs	patties
2 slices cheddar	Softened butter

Add sausages and muffins to the cooking tray. Select the "Air Fry" mode on your Air Fryer. Press Temp button and then turn the dial to adjust the cooking temperature to 390 degrees F. Press Time button and then turn the dial to adjust the cooking time to 7 minutes. Press the Start button to initiate preheating. Transfer the cooking tray to the air fryer basket of the Air Fryer when the screen displays "Add Food." Close its door, and let the machine do the cooking. Set the sausages aside and add eggs to the skillet. Let the whites set, then carefully flip the eggs to keep the yolks intact. Turn off the heat and add cheese and sausage to the top of the eggs. This will allow everything to melt together but leave the yolks with the perfect consistency. Add the mixture to the muffin and enjoy the breakfast.

Per serving: Calories 332; Fat 14.9g; Sodium 484mg; Carbs 26.1g; Sugar 0.5g; Fiber 0.8g; Protein 22.7g

Wheat and Seed Bread

Prep time: 40 minutes| Cook time: 18 minutes| Serves: 1

3 ½ ounces of flour	3 ½ ounces of wheat flour
1 teaspoon of yeast	¼ cup of pumpkin seeds
1 teaspoon of salt	¾ cup lukewarm water

Mix the wheat flour, yeast, salt, seeds and the plain flour in a large bowl. Stir in ¾ cup of lukewarm water and keep stirring until dough becomes soft. Knead for another 5 minutes until the dough becomes elastic and smooth. Form a ball and cover with a plastic bag. Set aside for 30 minutes for it to rise. Transfer the dough into a small pizza pan. Select the "Air Fry" mode on your Air Fryer. Press Temp button and then turn the dial to adjust the cooking temperature to 390 degrees F. Press Time button and then turn the dial to adjust the cooking time to 18 minutes. Press the Start button to initiate preheating. Transfer the pan to the air fryer basket of the Air Fryer when the screen displays "Add Food." Close its door, and let the machine do the cooking. Remove the dough and then place it on a wire rack to cool Serve.

Per serving: Calories 154; Fat 0.5g; Sodium 467mg; Carbs 40.2g; Sugar 0.8g; Fiber 1.3g; Protein 1.5g

Raspberry Scones

Prep time: 10 minutes| Cook time: 15 minutes| Serves: 6

Olive oil spray	¼ teaspoon salt
2½ tablespoons cubed cold butter	1 cup all-purpose flour
	½ cup milk
1½ tsps. baking powder	½ cup fresh raspberries

1 tablespoon granulated sugar

Place a parchment liner in the cooking tray. Combine the sugar, flour, baking powder, cold butter, and salt in a mixing bowl. Work the ingredients together with clean hands until the mixture is crumbly. Create a hole in the center of the mixture, and pour in the milk. Knead the combination with your hands until it forms thick dough. Transfer to a well-floured, flat work surface. Add the raspberries, and gently work them throughout the dough, taking care to not squash the berries. Mold the dough into a ball and flatten out slightly, making sure to not crush the berries. Cut into 6 wedges, and place on the sprayed cooking tray. Select the "Air Fry" mode on your Air Fryer. Press Temp button and then turn the dial to adjust the cooking temperature to 400 degrees F. Press Time button and then turn the dial to adjust the cooking time to 10 minutes. Press the Start button to initiate preheating. Transfer the cooking tray to the air fryer basket of the Air Fryer when the screen displays "Add Food." Close its door, and let the machine do the cooking. Flip the scones over, and cook for a final 5 minutes. Serve warm

Per serving: Calories 152; Fat 6g; Sodium 384mg; Carbs 22g; Sugar 1.3g; Fiber 0.6g; Protein 3g

Cinnamon Honey Pancakes

Prep time: 5 minutes| Cook time: 5 minutes| Serves: 2

2 tablespoons honey	¼ teaspoon cinnamon powder
½ cup coconut milk	Salt, to taste
¼ teaspoon baking soda	1 cup whole wheat flour
4 tablespoons brown sugar	1 teaspoon baking powder
2 whisked eggs	½ cup almond flour

In a large bowl, add wheat flour, almond flour, cinnamon powder, salt, baking powder, baking soda and brown sugar, mix well. Now add eggs and milk, whisk a little with a fork for 1-2 minutes. Grease a cooking tray with some oil. Transfer half of the batter into the pan. Select the "Air Fry" mode on your Air Fryer. Press Temp button and then turn the dial to adjust the cooking temperature to 400 degrees F. Press Time button and then turn the dial to adjust the cooking time to 5 minutes. Press the Start button to initiate preheating. Transfer the cooking tray to the air fryer basket of the Air Fryer when the screen displays "Add Food." Close its door, and let the machine do the cooking. Make another pancake with the same method. When done transfer to serving platter and drizzle honey on top. Serve with berries

Per serving: Calories 447; Fat 20.15g; Sodium 309mg; Carbs 57.93g; Sugar 1.3g; Fiber 0.6g; Protein 14.92g

Cream Frittata

Prep time: 10 minutes| Cook time: 6 minutes| Serves: 2

3 eggs, beaten	2 mushrooms, sliced
2 tablespoon cheddar cheese, shredded	¼ small onion, chopped
2 tablespoons heavy cream	¼ bell pepper, diced
	Black pepper and salt, to taste

In a bowl, whisk eggs with cream, vegetables, black pepper and salt. Pour egg mixture into a cooking tray. Select the "Air Fry" mode on your Air Fryer. Press Temp button and then turn the dial to adjust the cooking temperature to 400 degrees F. Press Time button and then turn the dial to adjust the cooking time to 5 minutes. Press the Start button to initiate preheating. Transfer the cooking tray to the air fryer basket of the Air Fryer when the screen displays "Add Food." Close its door, and let the machine do the cooking. Add shredded cheese on top of the frittata and cook for 1 minute more. Serve and enjoy

Per serving: Calories 160; Fat 10g; Sodium 409mg; Carbs 4g; Sugar 2g; Sugar 0.6g; Fiber 0.7g; Protein 12g

Ham Breakfast

Prep time: 5 minutes| Cook time: 20 minutes| Serves: 4

8 turkey sausages	1 (16-ounce) can of baked
8 ham slices	beans
4 eggs	8 slices of toast

Select the "Air Fry" mode on your Air Fryer. Press Temp button and then turn the dial to adjust the cooking temperature to 320 degrees F. Press Time button and then turn the dial to adjust the cooking time to 10 minutes. Press the Start button to initiate preheating. Transfer the ham and turkey sausage to the air fryer basket of the Air Fryer when the screen displays "Add Food." Close its door, and let the machine do the cooking. Add the baked beans to 1 ramekin, and then add the eggs to another ramekin. Drizzle the bacon and sausage on top of the eggs and beans, and then Bake the ramekins for 10 minutes at the same temperature. Serve with the toast slices and enjoy!

Per serving: Calories 850; Fat 40g; Sodium 369mg; Carbs 20g; Sugar 0.5g; Fiber 0.7g; Protein 48g

Seasoned Sweet Potatoes

Prep time: 5 minutes| Cook time: 40 minutes| Serves: 2

2 sweet potatoes, scrubbed	blend seasoning
½ tablespoon Butter, melted	½ teaspoon garlic powder
½ teaspoon garlic and herb	Salt

In a bowl, mix all of the spices and salt. With a fork, prick the potatoes. Coat the potatoes with butter and sprinkle with spice mixture. Arrange the potatoes onto the cooking rack. Select the "Air Fry" mode on your Air Fryer. Press Temp button and then turn the dial to adjust the cooking temperature to 400 degrees F. Press Time button and then turn the dial to adjust the cooking time to 40 minutes. Press the Start button to initiate preheating. Transfer the potatoes to the air fryer basket of the Air Fryer when the screen displays "Add Food." Close its door, and let the machine do the cooking. Serve hot.

Per serving: Calories 176; Sodium 437mg; Carbs 34.2g; Fat 2.1g; Sugar 0.5g; Fiber 0.8g; Protein 3.8g

Peppers and Lettuce Salad

Prep time: 10 minutes. | Cook time: 10 minutes. | Serves: 10

2 ounces rocket leaves	1 tablespoon lime juice
4 red bell peppers	3 tablespoon heavy cream
1 lettuce head; torn	Salt and black pepper to taste
2 tablespoon olive oil	

Arrange the bell pepper to the cooking tray. Select the "Air Fry" mode on your Air Fryer. Press Temp button and then turn the dial to adjust the cooking temperature to 400 degrees F. Press Time button and then turn the dial to adjust the cooking time to 10 minutes. Press the Start button to initiate preheating. Transfer the tray to the air fryer basket of the Air Fryer when the screen displays "Add Food." Close its door, and let the machine do the cooking. Remove the peppers, peel, cut them into strips and put them in a bowl. Add all remaining ingredients, toss and serve.

Per serving: Calories 255; Sodium 427mg; Carbs 1g; Fat 20g; Sugar 0.4g; Fiber 0.3g; Protein 4.

Artichoke Omelet

Prep time: 10 minutes. | Cook time: 15 minutes. | Serves: 4

3 artichoke hearts; canned,	drained and chopped

6 eggs; whisked
2 tablespoon avocado oil
½ teaspoon oregano; dried
Salt and black pepper to taste

In a bowl, mix all ingredients except the oil; stir well. Grease the cooking tray with reserved oil and add the egg mixture. Select the "Air Fry" mode on your Air Fryer. Press Temp button and then turn the dial to adjust the cooking temperature to 320 degrees F. Press Time button and then turn the dial to adjust the cooking time to 15 minutes. Press the Start button to initiate preheating. Transfer the cooking tray to the air fryer basket of the Air Fryer when the screen displays "Add Food." Close its door, and let the machine do the cooking. Serve warm.
Per serving: Calories 250; Sodium 502mg; Carbs 11g; Fat 21g; Sugar 0.8g; Fiber 1.3g; Protein 14g

Chicken Burrito

Prep time: 10 minutes. | Cook time: 13 minutes. | Serves: 2
---

4 chicken breast slices; cooked and shredded
2 tortillas
1 avocado; peeled, pitted and sliced
1 green bell pepper; sliced

2 eggs; whisked
2 tablespoon mild salsa
2 tablespoon cheddar cheese; grated
Salt and black pepper to taste

In a bowl, whisk the eggs with the salt and black pepper and pour them into the cooking tray. Select the "Air Fry" mode on your Air Fryer. Press Temp button and then turn the dial to adjust the cooking temperature to 400 degrees F. Press Time button and then turn the dial to adjust the cooking time to 9 minutes. Press the Start button to initiate preheating. Transfer the cooking tray to the air fryer basket of the Air Fryer when the screen displays "Add Food." Close its door, and let the machine do the cooking. Transfer the mix to a plate. Place the tortillas on a working surface and between them divide the eggs, chicken, bell peppers, avocado and the cheese; roll the burritos Line your air fryer with tin foil, add the burritos and cook them at for 3-4 minutes. Serve for breakfast-or lunch, or dinner!
Per serving: Calories 324; Sodium 502mg; Carbs 21g; Fat 16g; Sugar 0.4g; Fiber 0.3g; Protein 22g

Tarragon Omelet

Prep time: 10 minutes. | Cook time: 15 minutes. | Serves: 6
---

6 eggs; whisked
2 tablespoon parmesan cheese; grated
4 tablespoon heavy cream

1 tablespoon parsley; chopped
1 tablespoon tarragon; chopped
2 tablespoon chives; chopped
Salt and black pepper to taste

In a bowl, mix all ingredients except for the parmesan and whisk well. Pour this into the cooking tray. Select the "Air Fry" mode on your Air Fryer. Press Temp button and then turn the dial to adjust the cooking temperature to 350 degrees F. Press Time button and then turn the dial to adjust the cooking time to 15 minutes. Press the Start button to initiate preheating. Transfer the cooking tray to the air fryer basket of the Air Fryer when the screen displays "Add Food." Close its door, and let the machine do the cooking. Divide the omelet between plates and serve with the parmesan sprinkled on top. Serve warm.
Per serving: Calories 220; Sodium 472mg; Carbs 3.6g; Fat 13g; Sugar 0.5g; Fiber 0.7g; Protein 19g

Carrots and Cauliflower Mix

Prep time: 10 minutes. | Cook time: 20 minutes. | Serves: 4
---

1 cauliflower head; stems

removed, florets and steamed

2 ounces milk
2 ounces cheddar cheese; grated
3 carrots; chopped and

steamed
3 eggs
2 teaspoon cilantros; chopped
Salt and black pepper to taste

In a bowl, mix the eggs with the milk, parsley, salt and black pepper. Put the cauliflower and the carrots in a cooking tray; add the egg mixture and spread. Then sprinkle the cheese on top. Select the "Air Fry" mode on your Air Fryer. Press Temp button and then turn the dial to adjust the cooking temperature to 350 degrees F. Press Time button and then turn the dial to adjust the cooking time to 20 minutes. Press the Start button to initiate preheating. Transfer the cooking tray to the air fryer basket of the Air Fryer when the screen displays "Add Food." Close its door, and let the machine do the cooking. Serve warm with the chopped cilantros.
Per serving: Calories 507; Sodium 383mg; Carbs 1g; Fat 32g; Sugar 1.2g; Fiber 0.7g; Protein 11g

Fish Tacos Breakfast

Prep time: 10 minutes. | Cook time: 20 minutes. | Serves: 10
---

4 big tortillas
1 yellow onion; chopped
1 cup corn
1 red bell pepper; chopped
½ cup salsa

4 white fish fillets; skinless and boneless
1handful mixed romaine lettuce; spinach and radicchio
4 tablespoon parmesan; grated

Arrange the fish fillets to the cooking tray. Select the "Air Fry" mode on your Air Fryer. Press Temp button and then turn the dial to adjust the cooking temperature to 350 degrees F. Press Time button and then turn the dial to adjust the cooking time to 6 minutes. Press the Start button to initiate preheating. Transfer the tray to the air fryer basket of the Air Fryer when the screen displays "Add Food." Close its door, and let the machine do the cooking. Meanwhile; heat up a pan over medium high heat, add bell pepper, onion and corn; stir and cook for 1 to 2 minutes. Arrange tortillas on a working surface, divide fish fillets, spread salsa over them; divide mixed veggies and mixed greens and spread parmesan on each at the end. Roll your tacos and place them in the Air Fryer and cook for 6 minutes more. Divide fish tacos on plates and serve for breakfast
Per serving: Calories 232; Sodium 413mg; Carbs 17g; Fat 3.5g; Sugar 1.3g; Fiber 0.6g; Protein 27g

Olives Kale Frittata

Prep time: 5 minutes| Cook time: 20 minutes| Serves: 4
---

4 eggs; whisked
1 cup kale; chopped.
½ cup black olives, pitted and sliced

2 tablespoon cheddar; grated
Cooking spray
A pinch of salt and black pepper

Take a bowl, mix the eggs with the rest of the ingredients, except for the cooking spray, and whisk well. Now, take a pan that fits in your air fryer and grease it with the cooking spray, pour the olives mixture inside, spread. Select the "Air Fry" mode on your Air Fryer. Press Temp button and then turn the dial to adjust the cooking temperature to 360 degrees F. Press Time button and then turn the dial to adjust the cooking time to 20 minutes.
Press the start button to initiate preheating. Transfer the baking pan to the air fryer basket when the screen displays "Add Food." Close its door, and let the machine do the cooking. Serve.
Per serving: Calories 220; Fat 13g; Sodium 424mg; Carbs 6g; Fiber 4g; Sugars 1.3g; Protein 12g

Snacks and Appetizers

Roasted Almond Garlic Cauliflower Chunks

Prep time: 10 minutes| Cook time: 15 minutes | Serves: 4

1 cauliflower head, diced into chunks
½ cup unsweetened almond milk
1 tbsp. mayo
¼ cup all-purpose flour
¾ cup almond meal
¼ cup almond meal
1 tsp. onion powder
1 tsp. garlic powder
1 tsp. of sea salt
½ tsp. paprika
Pinch of black pepper
Cooking oil spray

In a mixing Bowl, toss the cauliflower with the remaining ingredients, then put to the air fryer cooking tray. Using frying oil, coat them. Using the display panel, select Roast, then adjust the temperature to 400 degrees F and the time to 15 minutes; touch the Start button to initiate preheating. When the display indicates "Add Food", place the cooking tray in the air fryer basket. When the time is up, carefully remove them from the cooking tray. Once done, serve and enjoy.
Per Serving: Calories 180; Fat 11g; Sodium 517mg; Carbs 15.7g; Fiber 4.7g; Sugar 3.3g; Protein 7.4g

Garlic Lemon Tofu Popcorns

Prep time: 15 minutes| Cook time: 15 minutes | Serves: 4

2 cups tofu, diced
3-¾ cups vegetable broth, divided
2 garlic cloves, mashed
1 tsp. salt
1-inch cube ginger, grated
½ cup all-purpose flour
½ cup of corn starch
1 cup panko breadcrumbs
1 tbsp. garlic powder
1 tbsp. lemon pepper
½ tsp.. salt

In a large mixing bowl, combine tofu, ginger, salt, and garlic. Soak for 20 minutes with 3 cups of broth. In a mixing bowl, whisk together wheat flour, cornstarch, and ¾ cup broth until smooth. Toss the tofu cubes in the flour batter after removing them from the milk. Arrange tofu cubes into cooking tray of air fryer. Using the display panel, select Air Fry,, then adjust the temperature to 390 degrees F and the time to 15 minutes; touch the Start button to initiate preheating. When the display indicates "Add Food", place the cooking tray in the air fryer basket. When the display indicates "turn Food", turn the food When the time is up, carefully remove them from the cooking tray. Once done, serve and enjoy.
Per Serving: Calories 335; Fat 7.3g; Sodium 1450mg; Carbs 51.7g; Fiber 4.7g; Sugar 2.5g; Protein 19.4g

Coconut Parsley Cauliflower Tater Tots

Prep time: 15 minutes| Cook time: 10 minutes | Serves: 6

2 pound fresh cauliflower, cut into chunks
1.5 tbsp. Cheddar cheese
1 cup Panko breadcrumbs
1 tsp. desiccated coconut
1 tsp. Oats
1 egg, beaten
2 tbsp. onion, chopped

1 tsp. garlic puree
1 tsp. parsley
1 tsp. chives
1 tsp. oregano
Salt and pepper to taste

Fresh cauliflower florets should be cooked for 10 minutes in salted water until tender, then drained. In a mixing bowl, mash the cauliflower and add salt, black pepper, garlic, parsley, chives, and oregano. Mix thoroughly, then form little tater tots from the mixture. In a tray, combine breadcrumbs, oats, and coconut shreds. After dipping the tater tots in the egg, coat them with the crumb mixture. Arrange the tater tots into cooking tray of air fryer. Using the display panel, select Air Fry,, then adjust the temperature to 360 degrees F and the time to 10 minutes; touch the Start button to initiate preheating. When the display indicates "Add Food", place the cooking tray in the air fryer basket. When the display indicates "turn Food", turn the food. When the time is up, carefully remove them from the cooking tray. Once done, serve and enjoy.
Per Serving: Calories 140; Fat 5.3g; Sodium 150mg; Carbs 20g; Fiber 6.2g; Sugar 4.5g; Protein 6.2g

Turmeric Parsley Cauliflower Patties

Prep time: 10 minutes| Cook time: 20 minutes | Serves: 4

3 large eggs
3 cups cauliflower florets
½ cup all-purpose flour
3 tbsp. wheat flour
1 tsp. coconut oil (melted)
½ tsp. garlic powder
½ tsp. turmeric
½ tsp. parsley
Salt & pepper to taste
Cooking oil spray

In a food processor, grate the cauliflower, then add the parsley, turmeric, garlic powder, and wheat flour. Mix thoroughly after whisking in the eggs and coconut oil. This cauliflower mixture should yield 4 patties. Arrange patties into cooking tray of air fryer. Using the display panel, select Air Fry,, then adjust the temperature to 375 degrees F and the time to 20 minutes; touch the Start button to initiate preheating. When the display indicates "Add Food", place the cooking tray in the air fryer basket. When the display indicates "turn Food", turn the food When the time is up, carefully remove them from the cooking tray. Once done, serve and enjoy.
Per Serving: Calories 150; Fat 5.3g; Sodium 76mg; Carbs 18.7g; Fiber 2.7g; Sugar 2.2g; Protein 8.1g

Tilapia Fish Sticks

Prep time: 10 minutes| Cook time: 15 minutes | Serves: 4

4 frozen tilapia fillets, cut into sticks
1 cup all-purpose flour
2 large eggs, beaten
1 ½ cups seasoned panko breadcrumbs
1 tbsp. kosher salt
For Serving:
1 lemon, cut in wedges
Tartar sauce
Ketchup

Dredge the tilapia sticks in flour with salt, then dip them in the egg, and finally coat them with the crumb mixture. In the air fryer cooking tray, place the coated sticks. Using the display panel, select Air Fry, then adjust the temperature to 390 degrees F and the time to 12 minutes; touch the Start button to initiate

preheating. When the display indicates "Add Food", place the cooking tray in the air fryer basket. When the display indicates "turn Food", turn the food When the time is up, carefully remove them from the cooking tray. Once done, serve and enjoy.
Per Serving: Calories 415; Fat 10.6g; Sodium 2350mg; Carbs 49.7g; Fiber 2.3g; Sugar 0.2g; Protein 30.4g

Bacon-Wrapped Scallops with Mayo

Prep time: 10 minutes| Cook time: 12 minutes | Serves: 9

½ cup mayonnaise
2 tbsp. Sriracha sauce
1 pound bay scallops
1 pinch coarse salt

1 pinch freshly cracked black pepper
4 slices bacon, cut into three pieces
Olive oil cooking; Spray

Set aside a bowl containing Sriracha sauce and mayonnaise. Place the scallops on a work surface and dry them. Season with salt and black pepper, then wrap a third of a bacon slice around each scallop and fasten with a toothpick. Arrange scallops into cooking tray of air fryer. Using the display panel, select Air Fry, then adjust the temperature to 390 degrees F and the time to 7 minutes; touch the Start button to initiate preheating. When the display indicates "Add Food", place the cooking tray in the air fryer basket. When the display indicates "turn Food", turn the food When the time is up, carefully remove them from the cooking tray. Once done, serve and enjoy.
Per Serving: Calories 177; Fat 12.3g; Sodium 422mg; Carbs 4.7g; Fiber 0g; Sugar 1.1g; Protein 11.4g

Honey Coconut Almond Graham Crackers

Prep time: 10 minutes| Cook time: 45 minutes | Serves: 8

2 Cups self-rising; Flour
1 Cup almond flour
1 Teaspoon baking; Powder
½ Cup butter, softened

½ Cup packed brown sugar
⅓ Cup honey
1 Teaspoon vanilla extract
½ Cup coconut milk

Separately sieve self-rising flour, almond flour, baking powder, and baking powder. Butter, brown sugar, and honey in a medium container, mix softly and loosely. Alternate adding the sifted ingredients with the milk and vanilla extract. Cover the dough and set it aside to chill overnight. Make quarters out of the cold dough. Quarterly, roll out the dough into a 5 x 15-inch rectangle on a well-floured board. Using a knife, cut the dough into rectangles. Place rectangles on baking sheets that haven't been greased. Draw a line in the center and use a fork to click it. Sprinkle a mixture of sugar and cinnamon on the biscuits before baking for a cinnamon biscuit. Arrange cinnamon biscuit to the cooking tray of air fryer Using the display panel, select Bake, then adjust the temperature to 350 degrees F and the time to 15 minutes; touch the Start button to initiate preheating. When the display indicates "Add Food", place the cooking tray in the air fryer basket. When the time is up, carefully remove them from the cooking tray. Once done, serve and enjoy.
Per Serving: Calories 396; Fat 22.1g; Sodium 127mg; Carbs 40.7g; Fiber 8.7g; Sugar 22.5g; Protein 3.4g

Garlic Chicken with Italian Seasoning

Prep time: 10 minutes| Cook time: 15 minutes | Serves: 4

4 ounces garlic and herb   cream cheese

Salt and pepper to taste
2 teaspoons dried Italian seasoning

Olive oil as needed
2 chicken breast fillets

Brush the chicken with oil and set aside. Salt, pepper, and Italian seasoning are used to season them. Cream cheese with garlic and herbs on top Carefully roll up the chicken. Arrange chicken into cooking tray of air fryer. Using the display panel, select Roast, then adjust the temperature to 370 degrees F and the time to 7 minutes; touch the Start button to initiate preheating. When the display indicates "Add Food", place the cooking tray in the air fryer basket. When the display indicates "turn Food", turn the food. When the time is up, carefully remove them from the cooking tray. Once done, serve and enjoy.
Per Serving: Calories 170; Fat 9.4g; Sodium 61mg; Carbs 0.3g; Fiber 0g; Sugar 0.2g; Protein 20.4g

Tasty Bratwursts

Prep time: 10 minutes| Cook time: 12 minutes | Serves: 4

1 pack bratwursts

Arrange bratwursts into cooking tray of air fryer Using the display panel, select Roast, then adjust the temperature to 350 degrees F and the time to 10 minutes; touch the Start button to initiate preheating. When the display indicates "Add Food", place the cooking tray in the air fryer basket. When the time is up, carefully remove them from the cooking tray. Once done, serve and enjoy.
Per Serving: Calories 71; Fat 6.3g; Sodium 180mg; Carbs 0.7g; Fiber 0g; Sugar 0g; Protein 2.9g

Delicious Taco Beef Cups

Prep time: 10 minutes| Cook time: 10 minutes | Serves: 4

1 cup cheddar cheese, shredded
2 tablespoons taco seasoning

½ cup tomatoes, chopped
1 pound ground beef, cooked
Wonton wrappers

Firmly press the wrappers into the muffin tray. Add ground meat and tomatoes to the top. Season the food with taco seasoning and cheese. Arrange wonton wrappers into cooking tray of air fryer. Using the display panel, select Air Fry, then adjust the temperature to 350 degrees F and the time to 15 minutes; touch the Start button to initiate preheating. When the display indicates "Add Food", place the cooking tray in the air fryer basket. When the display indicates "turn Food", turn the food. When the time is up, carefully remove them from the cooking tray. Once done, serve and enjoy.
Per Serving: Calories 537; Fat 26.9g; Sodium 698mg; Carbs 19.2g; Fiber 0.4g; Sugar 0.7g; Protein 52.4g

Honey Dijon and Veggie

Prep time: 10 minutes| Cook time: 30 minutes | Serves: 4

Vinaigrette
½ cup olive oil
½ cup avocado oil
¼ teaspoon pepper
1 teaspoon salt
2 tablespoons honey
½ cup red wine vinegar

2 tablespoons Dijon Mustard
Veggies
4 zucchinis, halved
4 sweet onion, quartered
4 red pepper, seeded and halved
2 bunch green onions, trimmed
4 yellow squash, cut in half

Whisk together mustard, honey, vinegar, salt, and pepper in a small basin. Mix with the oil thoroughly. Arrange veggies into cooking tray of air fryer. Using the display panel, select Roast, then adjust the temperature to 350 degrees F and the time to 15 minutes; touch the Start button to initiate preheating. When the display indicates "Add Food", place the cooking tray in the air fryer basket. When the time is up, carefully remove them from the cooking tray. Serve with a side of mustard vinaigrette.

Per Serving: Calories 415; Fat 29.3g; Sodium 793mg; Carbs 37g; Fiber 7.6g; Sugar 23.1g; Protein 5.4g

Paprika Cumin Chickpeas

Prep time: 05 minutes| Cook time: 10 minutes | Serves: 4

1 (15-oz.) can chickpeas rinsed and Dry-out
1 tablespoon olive oil
½ teaspoon ground cumin
½ teaspoon cayenne pepper
½ teaspoon smoked paprika
Salt, as required

In a bowl, add all the ingredients and toss to coat well. Place the drip pan in the bottom of the cooking chamber. Using the display panel, select Air Fry, then adjust the temperature to 390 degrees F and the time to 10 minutes, then touch Start button to initiate preheating. When the display indicates "Add Food", place the cooking tray in the air fryer basket. When the display indicates "turn Food", turn the food. When the time up carefully remove them from the cooking tray Serve warm.

Per Serving: Calories 159; Fat 4.8g; Sodium 357mg; Carbs 24.4g; Fiber 4.9g; Sugar 0.1g; Protein 5.4 g

Crispy Sausage Patties

Prep time: 10 minutes| Cook time: 10 minutes | Serves: 2

1 pack sausage patties

Transfer the sausages to into cooking tray Place the cooking tray in the air fryer basket of your air fryer. Using the display panel, select Roast, then adjust the temperature to 400 degrees F and the time to 10 minutes; touch the Start button to initiate preheating. When the display indicates "Add Food", place the cooking tray in the air fryer basket. When the time is up, carefully remove them from the cooking tray. Once done, serve and enjoy.

Per Serving: Calories 100; Fat 0.4g; Sodium 350mg; Carbs 5.5g; Fiber 0g; Sugar 0g; Protein 8.4g

Tasty Crunchy Peanuts

Prep time: 05 minutes| Cook time: 14 minutes | Serves: 6

1½ cups raw peanuts
Nonstick cooking spray

Arrange the peanuts in cooking tray of air fryer. Spray the peanuts with cooking Spray. Using the display panel, select Air Fry, then adjust the temperature to 320 degrees F and the time to 15 minutes, then touch Start button to initiate preheating. When the display indicates "Add Food", place the cooking tray in the air fryer basket. When the display indicates "turn Food", turn the food and spray the peanuts with cooking spray. When the time is up, carefully remove them from the cooking tray. Serve warm.

Per Serving: Calories 207; Fat 18g; Sodium 7mg; Carbs 5.9g; Fiber 3.1g; Sugar 1.5g; Protein 9.4g

Parsley Garlic Bread

Prep time: 10 minutes| Cook time: 5 minutes | Serves: 4

Salt to taste
1 Italian loaf of bread
1 tablespoon fresh parsley, chopped

½ cup butter, melted
4 garlic cloves, chopped

Take a bowl and add parsley, butter, and garlic Spread the mixture on the bread slices Arrange bread slices into cooking tray of air fryer. Using the display panel, select Air Fry, then adjust the temperature to 400 degrees F and the time to 3 minutes; touch the Start button to initiate preheating. When the display indicates "Add Food", place the cooking tray in the air fryer basket. When the display indicates "turn Food", turn the food. When the time is up, carefully remove them from the cooking tray. Once done, serve and enjoy.

Per Serving: Calories 236; Fat 23.3g; Sodium 271mg; Carbs 6.6g; Fiber 0.3g; Sugar 0.6g; Protein 1.5g

Creole Almond Crispy Tomatoes

Prep time: 10 minutes| Cook time: 5 minutes | Serves: 4

Bread crumbs as needed
½ cup buttermilk
¼ cup almond flour
Salt and pepper to taste
¼ tablespoon Creole seasoning
1green tomato

Take a plate and put flour on it, then take another plate and put buttermilk on it. Season tomatoes with salt and pepper after cutting them up. Combine creole seasoning and breadcrumbs in a bowl. Cover a tomato slice in flour, dip it in buttermilk, and then roll it in crumbs. Make the remaining tomatoes with the same steps. Arrange tomatoes into cooking tray of air fryer. Using the display panel, select Air Fry, then adjust the temperature to 350 degrees F and the time to 5 minutes; touch the Start button to initiate preheating. When the display indicates "Add Food", place the cooking tray in the air fryer basket. When the display indicates "turn Food", turn the food. When the time is up, carefully remove them from the cooking tray. Once done, serve and enjoy.

Per Serving: Calories 87; Fat 4.3g; Sodium 292mg; Carbs 9.7g; Fiber 1.4g; Sugar 3.4g; Protein 3.8g

Vanilla Yogurt Blueberry Muffins

Prep time: 10 minutes| Cook time: 10 minutes | Serves: 10

2 teaspoons vanilla extract
1 cup blueberries
½ teaspoon salt
1 cup yogurt
1-½ cups cake flour
½ cup sugar
2 teaspoons baking Powder
⅓ cup vegetable oil
1 egg

Coat 10 muffin tins in a little coating of cooking oil or spray. Combine the flour, sugar, baking powder, and salt in a medium mixing basin. Combine the yoghurt, oil, egg, and vanilla extract in a medium mixing bowl. Combine the contents of both bowls. Place the chocolate chips on top. Pour the batter evenly into the muffin tins. Arrange muffins into cooking tray of air fryer. Using the display panel, select Bake, then adjust the temperature to 355degrees F and the time to 10 minutes; touch the Start button to initiate preheating. When the display indicates "Add Food", place the cooking tray in the air fryer basket. When the time is up, carefully remove them from the cooking tray. Once done, serve and enjoy.

Per Serving: Calories 204; Fat 8.3g; Sodium 140mg; Carbs 28.7g; Fiber 0.9g; Sugar 13.4g; Protein 4g

Paprika Shrimp with Bacon Bites

Prep time: 10 minutes| Cook time: 8 minutes | Serves: 12

½ teaspoon red pepper flakes, crushed
1 tablespoon salt
1 teaspoon chili powder

1 ¼ pounds shrimp, peeled and deveined
1 teaspoon paprika
½ teaspoon black pepper,
ground
1 tablespoon shallot powder
¼ teaspoon cumin powder
1-¼ pounds thin bacon slices

In a medium-sized mixing dish, thoroughly combine the shrimp and seasoning until evenly coated. Wrap a piece of bacon around each shrimp, attach with a toothpick, and chill for 30 minutes. Arrange shrimps into cooking tray of air fryer. Using the display panel, select Air Fry, then adjust the temperature to 350 degrees F and the time to 15 minutes; touch the Start button to initiate preheating. When the display indicates "Add Food", place the cooking tray in the air fryer basket. When the display indicates "turn Food", turn the food. When the time is up, carefully remove them from the cooking tray. Once done, serve and enjoy.
Per Serving: Calories 314; Fat 20.6g; Sodium 1292mg; Carbs 1.7g; Fiber 0.2g; Sugar 0.1g; Protein 28.8g

Dijon Beef Quinoa Meatballs

Prep time: 10 minutes| Cook time: 15 minutes | Serves: 6

1 cup quinoa, cooked
1 beaten egg
½-pound pork, ground
½-pound beef, ground
2 scallions, chopped
½ teaspoon onion powder
1-½ tablespoons Dijon
mustard
1 tablespoon sesame oil
2 tablespoons tamari sauce
¾ cup ketchup
1 teaspoon ancho chili powder
¼ cup balsamic vinegar
2 tablespoons sugar

Mix the ingredients completely in a medium-sized mixing basin and form small meatballs from it. Arrange meatballs into cooking tray of air fryer. Using the display panel, select Air Fry, then adjust the temperature to 370 degrees F and the time to 05 minutes; touch the Start button to initiate preheating. When the display indicates "Add Food", place the cooking tray in the air fryer basket. When the display indicates "turn Food", turn the food. When the time is up, carefully remove them from the cooking tray. Once done, serve and enjoy.
Per Serving: Calories 307; Fat 8g; Sodium 768mg; Carbs 31.7g; Fiber 2.4g; Sugar 11.4g; Protein 27.8g

Raisins Apple Dumplings

Prep time: 10 minutes| Cook time: 15 minutes | Serves: 2

2 tablespoons raisins
2 apples, smallest possible size, peeled and cored
1 tablespoon brown sugar
2 tablespoon butter, melted
2 sheets puff pastry

Place the apples in the pastry sheets and fill the cores with the sugar and raisins. Fold the pastries one by one to make dumplings. Using a pastry brush, coat the dumplings in butter. Arrange dumplings into cooking tray of air fryer. Using the display panel, select Bake, then adjust the temperature to 350 degrees F and the time to 15 minutes; touch the Start button to initiate preheating. When the display indicates "Add Food", place the cooking tray in the air fryer basket. When the time is up, carefully remove them from the cooking tray. Once done, serve and enjoy.
Per Serving: Calories 482; Fat 27g; Sodium 506mg; Carbs 62.7g; Fiber 6.8g; Sugar 34g; Protein 4g

Roasted Squash Bites

Prep time: 10 minutes| Cook time: 15 minutes | Serves: 6

1 ½ pounds winter squash, peeled and make chunks
¼ cup dark brown sugar
2 tablespoons sage, chopped

Zest of 1 small-sized lemon
2 tablespoons coconut oil, melted
A coarse pinch salt
A pinch pepper
⅛ teaspoon allspice, ground

Except for the squash, thoroughly combine all of the ingredients in a medium-sized mixing bowl. Mixture should completely cover the squash chunks. Arrange squash into cooking tray of air fryer. Using the display panel, select Roast then adjust the temperature to 350 degrees F and the time to 15 minutes; touch the Start button to initiate preheating. When the display indicates "Add Food", place the cooking tray in the air fryer basket. When the time is up, carefully remove them from the cooking tray. Once done, serve and enjoy.
Per Serving: Calories 337; Fat 14.3g; Sodium 16mg; Carbs 57g; Fiber 6.4g; Sugar 13.4g; Protein 3.3g

Ham Cheese Potato Balls

Prep time: 10 minutes| Cook time: 5 minutes | Serves: 6

½ cup ham, chopped
½ cup Colby cheese, shredded
ounces soft cheese
3 cups potatoes, mashed
1 egg; Slightly beaten
2green onions, sliced
1 cup seasoned breadcrumbs
2 ½ tablespoons canola oil

Except for the breadcrumbs and canola oil, thoroughly combine the ingredients in a medium mixing bowl. Make little balls out of it. Arrange balls into cooking tray of air fryer. Using the display panel, select Air Fry, then adjust the temperature to 350 degrees F and the time to 15 minutes; touch the Start button to initiate preheating. When the display indicates "Add Food", place the cooking tray in the air fryer basket. When the display indicates "turn Food", turn the food. When the time is up, carefully remove them from the cooking tray. Once done, serve and enjoy.
Per Serving: Calories 249; Fat 13.3g; Sodium 465mg; Carbs 24.7g; Fiber 1.4g; Sugar 3.4g; Protein 3.8g

Bacon-Wrapped Garlic Jalapeño Poppers

Prep time: 15 minutes| Cook time: 12 minutes | Serves: 4

6 jalapeños (about 4" long each)
3 ounces full-fat cream cheese
⅓ cup shredded medium
Cheddar cheese
¼ teaspoon garlic powder
12 slices sugar-free bacon

Remove the tops of the jalapenos and cut them down the middle lengthwise into two pieces. Carefully remove the white membrane and seeds from peppers with a knife. Combine cream cheese, Cheddar, and garlic powder in a large microwave-safe container. Stir after 30 seconds in the microwave. Fill hollow jalapenos with cheese mixture. Wrap a slice of bacon over each jalapeno half, completely wrapping it; season with salt and pepper. Arrange jalapenos into cooking tray of air fryer. Using the display panel, select Air Fry, then adjust the temperature to 400 degrees F and the time to 12 minutes; touch the Start button to initiate preheating. When the display indicates "Add Food", place the cooking tray in the air fryer basket. When the display indicates "turn Food", turn the food. When the time is up, carefully remove them from the cooking tray. Once done, serve and enjoy.
Per Serving: Calories 73; Fat 4.1g; Sodium 215mg; Carbs 2.7g; Fiber 0.6g; Sugar 0.9g; Protein 6.2g

Pepper Potato Fries

Prep time: 15 minutes| Cook time: 16 minutes | Serves: 2

½ pound potatoes, peeled and
cut into ½-inch thick sticks

lengthwise
1 tablespoon olive oil

Salt and ground black pepper

Combine all of the ingredients in a large mixing bowl and toss well to combine. Arrange potatoes sticks into cooking tray of air fryer. Using the display panel, select Air Fry, then adjust the temperature to 400 degrees F and the time to 16 minutes; touch the Start button to initiate preheating. When the display indicates "Add Food", place the cooking tray in the air fryer basket. When the display indicates "turn Food", turn the food. When the time is up, carefully remove them from the cooking tray. Once done, serve and enjoy.
Per Serving: Calories 138; Fat 7.1g; Sodium 7mg; Carbs 17.6g; Fiber 2.7g; Sugar 1.6g; Protein 1.9g

Garlic Cayenne Pickle Slices

Prep time: 15 minutes| Cook time: 18 minutes | Serves: 8

16 dill pickle slices
¼ cup all-purpose flour
Salt, as required
2 small eggs, beaten lightly
1 tablespoon dill pickle juice

¼ teaspoon garlic powder
¼ teaspoon cayenne pepper
1 cup panko breadcrumbs
1 tablespoon fresh dill, minced
Cooking Spray

Place the pickle slices on paper towels for about 15 minutes, or until the liquid has been absorbed completely. Meanwhile, combine the flour and salt in a small dish. In a separate shallow dish, whisk together the eggs, pickle juice, garlic powder, and cayenne. Combine the panko and dill in a third shallow dish. Coat the pickle slices in flour, then dip them in the egg mixture, and finally in the panko mixture. Arrange pickle slices into cooking tray of air fryer. Using the display panel, select Air Fry, then adjust the temperature to 400 degrees F and the time to 18 minutes; touch the Start button to initiate preheating. When the display indicates "Add Food", place the cooking tray in the air fryer basket. When the display indicates "turn Food", turn the food. When the time is up, carefully remove them from the cooking tray. Once done, serve and enjoy.
Per Serving: Calories 67; Fat 1.3g; Sodium 476mg; Carbs 11.4g; Fiber 1.4g; Sugar 0.6g; Protein 2.8g

Tasty Vegetable Spring Rolls

Prep time: 10 minutes| Cook time: 13 minutes | Serves: 8

2 cups green cabbage, shredded
2 yellow onions, chopped.
1 carrot, grated
8 spring roll sheets
2 tbsp. corn flour
2 tbsp. water
½ chili pepper, minced

1 tbsp. ginger, grated
3 garlic cloves, minced
1 tsp.. sugar
1 tsp.. soy sauce
2 tbsp. olive oil
Salt and black pepper to the taste

Over medium heat, add the cabbage, onions, carrots, chili pepper, ginger, garlic, sugar, salt, pepper, and soy sauce to a skillet with the oil. Stir thoroughly, simmer for 2-3 minutes, then remove from heat and wait for a few minutes to cool. Cut the spring roll sheets into squares, divide the cabbage mixture among them, and roll them up. Combine corn flour and water in a mixing dish, stir well, and use this mixture to seal spring rolls. Arrange rolls into cooking tray of air fryer. Using the display panel, select Air Fry, then adjust the temperature to 360 degrees F and the time to 10 minutes; touch the Start button to initiate preheating. When the display indicates "Add Food", place the cooking tray in the air fryer basket. When the display indicates "turn Food", turn the food. When the time is up, carefully remove them from the cooking tray. Once done, serve and enjoy.
Per Serving: Calories 236; Fat 4.7g; Sodium 57mg; Carbs 44.6g; Fiber 2.7g; Sugar 3.6g; Protein 4.8g

Cajun Crab Sticks

Prep time: 10 minutes| Cook time: 12 minutes | Serves: 4

2 oz. Crab sticks, halved
2 tsp.. Cajun seasoning

2 tsp.. sesame oil

Toss crab sticks with sesame oil and Cajun seasoning in a bowl. Arrange crab sticks into cooking tray of air fryer. Using the display panel, select Air Fry, then adjust the temperature to 350 degrees F and the time to 12 minutes; touch the Start button to initiate preheating. When the display indicates "Add Food", place the cooking tray in the air fryer basket. When the display indicates "turn Food", turn the food. When the time is up, carefully remove them from the cooking tray. Once done, serve and enjoy.
Per Serving: Calories 67; Fat 4.5g; Sodium 50mg; Carbs 3.7g; Fiber 0; Sugar 0g; Protein 2.6g

Salmon Patties

Prep time: 15 minutes| Cook time: 22 minutes | Serves: 4

3 big Potatoes boiled, drained and mashed
1 egg
1 big Salmon fillet, skinless, boneless
2 tbsps. bread crumbs

2 tbsps. parsley, chopped
2 tbsps. dill, chopped
Salt and black pepper to the taste
Cooking Spray

Arrange salmon into cooking tray of air fryer Using the display panel, select Roast, then adjust the temperature to 360 degrees F and the time to 10 minutes; touch the Start button to initiate preheating. When the display indicates "Add Food", place the cooking tray in the air fryer basket. When the time is up, carefully remove them from the cooking tray. Place salmon in your air fryer's basket and cook for 10 minutes at 360 degrees F. Cool the salmon on a cutting board before flaking it and placing it in a bowl. Stir in the mashed potatoes, salt, pepper, dill, parsley, egg, and bread crumbs, and form 8 patties from the mixture. Arrange salmon patties into cooking tray of air fryer. Using the display panel, select Air Fry, then adjust the temperature to 350 degrees F and the time to 12 minutes; touch the Start button to initiate preheating. When the display indicates "Add Food", place the cooking tray in the air fryer basket. When the display indicates "turn Food", turn the food. When the time is up, carefully remove them from the cooking tray. Once done, serve and enjoy.
Per Serving: Calories 254; Fat 4.5g; Sodium 75mg; Carbs 48.6g; Fiber 4.5g; Sugar 2.2g; Protein 14.8g

Black Pepper Beef Slice

Prep time: 10 minutes| Cook time: 90 minutes | Serves: 6

2 tbsp. black peppercorns
2 cups soy sauce
2 tbsp. black pepper

2 lbs. beef round, sliced
½ cup Worcestershire sauce

Whisk together the soy sauce, black peppercorns, black pepper, and Worcestershire sauce in a mixing bowl. Add the beef slices, stir to coat, and refrigerate for 6 hours. Arrange beef into cooking tray of air fryer. Place the cooking tray in the air fryer basket. Using the display panel, select Dehydrate then adjust the temperature to 175 degrees F and the time to 90 minutes; touch the Start button to begin. When the time is up, carefully remove them from the cooking tray. Once done, serve and enjoy.
Per Serving: Calories 123; Fat 1.8g; Sodium 5031mg; Carbs 11.9g; Fiber 1.2g; Sugar 5.5g; Protein 14.2g

Spinach Chicken Breast with Mozzarella

Prep time: 10 minutes| Cook time: 17 minutes | Serves: 4

4 chicken breasts, boneless and skinless
1 cup sun dried tomatoes, chopped.
2 cups baby spinach

1-½ tbsp. Italian seasoning
4 mozzarella slices
A drizzle of olive oil
Salt and black pepper to the taste

Using a meat tenderizer, flatten the chicken breasts, divide the tomatoes, mozzarella, and spinach, season with salt, pepper, and Italian seasoning, then roll and seal them. Arrange chicken rolls into cooking tray of air fryer. Using the display panel, select Air Fry, then adjust the temperature to 375 degrees F and the time to 17 minutes; touch the Start button to initiate preheating. When the display indicates "Add Food", place the cooking tray in the air fryer basket. When the display indicates "turn Food", turn the food. When the time is up, carefully remove them from the cooking tray. Once done, serve and enjoy.
Per Serving: Calories 449; Fat 23.8g; Sodium 377mg; Carbs 8.3g; Fiber 1.9g; Sugar 0.4g; Protein 50.3g

Cheesy Broccoli Tots

Prep time: 10 minutes| Cook time: 15 minutes| Serves: 4

1-pound broccoli, grated
½ cup cheddar cheese, shredded
1 tablespoon extra-virgin olive oil

1 egg
½ cup panko breadcrumbs
2 cloves garlic, minced
Sea salt and freshly ground black pepper, to taste

Combine all of the ingredients thoroughly. Form the mixture into equal-sized balls and arrange them in a single layer in the cooking tray of the air fryer. Using the display panel, select Air fry then adjust the temperature to 390 degrees F and the time to 10 minutes, then touch START. When the display indicates "Add Food", place the cooking tray to the air fryer basket. When the display indicates "turn Food", turn the food. When the time up carefully remove them from the cooking tray Once done, serve and enjoy
Per Serving: Calories 179; Fat 9.9g; Sodium 209mg; Carbs 15.8g; Fiber 4g; Sugar 2.3g; Protein 9.2g

Basil Garlic Pesto Crackers

Prep time: 10 minutes| Cook time: 17 minutes | Serves: 6

½ tsp. baking Powder
¼ tsp. basil, dried
1-¼ cups flour
1garlic clove, minced

2 tbsp. basil pesto
3 tbsp. butter
Salt and black pepper to the taste

Combine salt, pepper, baking powder, flour, garlic, cayenne, basil, pesto, and butter in a mixing bowl and whisk until a dough form. This dough should be spread out into cooking tray of air fryer. Using the display panel, select Air Fry, then adjust the temperature to 325 degrees F and the time to 17 minutes; touch the Start button to initiate preheating. When the display indicates "Add Food", place the cooking tray in the air fryer basket. When the time is up, carefully remove them from the cooking tray. Allow to cool before cutting into crackers and serving as a snack.
Per Serving: Calories 128; Fat 6g; Sodium 207mg; Carbs 4.6g; Fiber 2g; Sugar 1.6g; Protein 1.8g

Garlic Italian Seasoning Mozzarella Sticks

Prep time: 1 hour and 05 minutes| Cook time: 10 minutes | Serves: 4

1 Tablespoon Italian Seasoning
1 Cup Parmesan Cheese

8 String cheeses, Diced
2 Eggs, Beaten
1 Clove Garlic, Minced

In a mixing bowl, combine the parmesan, garlic, and Italian seasoning. Dip your cheese into the egg and thoroughly mix it up. Roll it in your crumbled cheese, then press the crumbs into the cheese. Place them in the fridge for an hour, arrange the Mozzarella Sticks to the cooking tray of air fryer. Using the display panel, select Air Fry, then adjust the temperature to 375 degrees F and the time to 10 minutes, then touch Start button to initiate preheating. When the display indicates "Add Food", place the cooking tray in the air fryer basket. When the display indicates "turn Food" turn the food. When the Mozzarella Sticks are cooked, carefully remove them from the cooking tray
Per Serving: Calories 226; Fat 16.7g; Sodium 517mg; Carbs 3g; Fiber 0g; Sugar 0.5g; Protein 21.1 g

Turmeric and Chat Banana Chips

Prep time: 10 minutes| Cook time: 15 minutes | Serves: 4

½ tsp. turmeric powder
½ tsp. chat masala
1 tsp. olive oil

4 bananas, peeled and sliced
A pinch of salt

Combine banana slices, salt, turmeric, chat masala, and oil in a mixing basin and let aside for 10 minutes. Arrange banana slices into cooking tray of air fryer. Using the display panel, select Air Fry, then adjust the temperature to 360 degrees F and the time to 15 minutes; touch the Start button to initiate preheating. When the display indicates "Add Food", place the cooking tray in the air fryer basket. When the display indicates "turn Food", turn the food. When the time is up, carefully remove them from the cooking tray. Once done, serve and enjoy.
Per Serving: Calories 116; Fat 1.8g; Sodium 237mg; Carbs 28g; Fiber 3.1g; Sugar 14.6g; Protein 1.4g

Garlic Paprika Dill Pickles

Prep time: 15 minutes| Cook time: 12 minutes | Serves: 4

16 oz. jarred dill pickles
½ cup white flour
1 egg
¼ cup ranch sauce

¼ cup milk
½ tsp.. garlic powder
½ tsp.. sweet paprika
Cooking Spray

In a mixing dish, whisk together the milk and the egg. In a separate bowl, whisk together flour, salt, garlic powder, and paprika. Place pickles in the cooking tray after dipping them in flour, egg mix, then flour again. Cooking spray should be used to grease them. Using the display panel, select Air Fry, then adjust the temperature to 400 degrees F and the time to 15 minutes; touch the Start button to initiate preheating. When the display indicates "Add Food", place the cooking tray in the air fryer basket. When the display indicates "turn Food", turn the food. When the time is up, carefully remove them from the cooking tray. Once done, serve and enjoy.
Per Serving: Calories 105; Fat 2.7g; Sodium 1028mg; Carbs 16.2g; Fiber 1.8g; Sugar 2.6g; Protein 4.3g

Fried Tomatoes with Lots of Herbs

Prep time: 10 minutes| Cook time: 20 minutes | Serves: 2

2 tomatoes, halved	1 tsp. rosemary, dried
1 tsp. parsley, dried	Cooking; Spray
1 tsp. basil, dried	Salt and black pepper
1 tsp. oregano, dried	

Spray tomato halves with cooking oil, season with salt, pepper, parsley, basil, oregano and rosemary over them. Arrange tomato halves into cooking tray of air fryer. Using the display panel, select Air Fry, then adjust the temperature to 320 degrees F and the time to 20 minutes; touch the Start button to initiate preheating. When the display indicates "Add Food", place the cooking tray in the air fryer basket. When the display indicates "turn Food", turn the food. When the time is up, carefully remove them from the cooking tray. Once done, serve and enjoy.
Per Serving: Calories 27; Fat 0.4g; Sodium 7mg; Carbs 5.7g; Fiber 2.1g; Sugar 3.3g; Protein 1.2g

Cinnamon Salty Apple Slices

Prep time: 05 minutes| Cook time: 12 minutes | Serves: 1

1 apple, core and slice ¼-inch thick	¼ tsp. ground cinnamon
	Pinch of salt

Arrange apple slice into cooking tray of air fryer, season with the cinnamon and salt. Using the display panel, select Air Fry, then adjust the temperature to 350 degrees F and the time to 12 minutes; touch the Start button to initiate preheating. When the display indicates "Add Food", place the cooking tray in the air fryer basket. When the display indicates "turn Food", turn the food. When the time is up, carefully remove them from the cooking tray. Once done, serve and enjoy.
Per Serving: Calories 117; Fat 0.4g; Sodium 157mg; Carbs 31.3g; Fiber 5.7g; Sugar 23.2g; Protein 0.6g

Roasted Garlic Cumin Chickpeas

Prep time: 10 minutes| Cook time: 12 minutes | Serves: 4

2 oz. can chickpeas, drained and pat dry	1 tsp. garlic powder
1 ½ tsp. paprika	½ tbsp. cumin powder
	2 tbsp. olive oil

Chickpeas should be added to the mixing basin. Toss the other ingredients on top of the chickpeas until well coated. Arrange chickpeas into cooking tray of air fryer. Using the display panel, select Roast, then adjust the temperature to 375 degrees F and the time to 12 minutes; touch the Start button to initiate preheating. When the display indicates "Add Food", place the cooking tray in the air fryer basket. When the time is up, carefully remove them from the cooking tray. Once done, serve and enjoy.
Per Serving: Calories 84; Fat 7.5g; Sodium 44mg; Carbs 4.6g; Fiber 1.1g; Sugar 0.3g; Protein 1.1g

Garlic Paprika Baked Potato Wedges

Prep time: 10 minutes| Cook time: 12 minutes | Serves: 4

4 potatoes, cut into wedges	1 tbsp. garlic, minced
⅔ cup parmesan cheese, grated	¼ cup olive oil
1 tsp. paprika	Sea salt

Combine the cheese, paprika, garlic, oil, and salt in a mixing bowl. Toss the potato wedges in the basin until well coated. Arrange potatoes wedges into cooking tray of air fryer. Using the display panel, select Air Fry, then adjust the temperature to 400 degrees F and the time to 12 minutes; touch the Start button to initiate preheating. When the display indicates "Add Food", place the cooking tray in the air fryer basket. When the display indicates "turn Food", turn the food. When the time is up, carefully remove them from the cooking tray. Once done, serve and enjoy.
Per Serving: Calories 275; Fat 13.9g; Sodium 175mg; Carbs 38.6g; Fiber 5.4g; Sugar 2.5g; Protein 5.3g

Cheese Cumin Jalapeno Poppers

Prep time: 10 minutes| Cook time: 10 minutes | Serves: 4

4 jalapeno peppers, halved, remove seeds and stem	shredded
½ cup cheddar cheese, shredded	1 tsp. ground cumin
½ cup Monterey jack cheese,	2 oz. cream cheese, softened
	2 bacon slices, cut in half

Combine Monterey jack cheese, cumin, and cream cheese in a mixing bowl. Fill halved jalapeños with cheese mixture. Half a bacon slice should be wrapped around each jalapeno. Arrange jalapeños into cooking tray of air fryer. Using the display panel, select Air Fry, then adjust the temperature to 370 degrees F and the time to 10 minutes; touch the Start button to initiate preheating. When the display indicates "Add Food", place the cooking tray in the air fryer basket. When the display indicates "turn Food", turn the food. When the time is up, carefully remove them from the cooking tray. Once done, serve and enjoy.
Per Serving: Calories 193; Fat 16.2g; Sodium 684mg; Carbs 2g; Fiber 0.6g; Sugar 0.7g; Protein 10.1g

Butter Fried Pecans

Prep time: 10 minutes| Cook time: 6 minutes | Serves: 6

2 cups pecan halves	Salt
1 tbsp. butter, melted	

Toss the pecans, butter, and salt together in a mixing basin. Arrange Pecans into cooking tray of air fryer. Using the display panel, select Roast, then adjust the temperature to 350 degrees F and the time to 6 minutes; touch the Start button to initiate preheating. When the display indicates "Add Food", place the cooking tray in the air fryer basket. When the time is up, carefully remove them from the cooking tray. Once done, serve and enjoy.
Per Serving: Calories 307; Fat 31.5g; Sodium 41mg; Carbs 6g; Fiber 4.5g; Sugar 1.2g; Protein 4.8g

Basil Cheesy Pizza Toast

Prep time: 10 minutes| Cook time: 5 minutes | Serves: 4

4 Texas toast slices	½ jar pizza sauce
2 oz. mozzarella cheese, shredded	4 basil leaves

Arrange toast slices into cooking tray of air fryer. Using the display panel, select Roast, then adjust the temperature to 380 degrees F and the time to 2 minutes; touch the Start button to initiate preheating. When the display indicates "Add Food", place the cooking tray in the air fryer basket. When the time is up, carefully remove them from the cooking tray. After 2 minutes, remove the tray from the air fryer. Add pizza sauce, mozzarella cheese, and basil leaves on each toast slice. Return toast into cooking tray of air fryer. Using the display panel,

select Broil and set the time to 2 minutes, the default cooking temperature is 400 degrees F; touch the Start button to initiate preheating. When the display indicates "Add Food", place the cooking tray in the air fryer basket. Once done, serve and enjoy.
Per Serving: Calories 144; Fat 3.6g; Sodium 324mg; Carbs 20.6g; Fiber 1.1g; Sugar 2.3g; Protein 14.8g

Garlic Chili Sweet Potato Fries

Prep time: 10 minutes| Cook time: 10 minutes | Serves: 2

2 sweet potatoes, peeled and cut into fries shape
½ tsp. chili powder
¼ tsp. garlic powder
¼ tsp. onion powder
1 tbsp. olive oil
Salt

Combine the oil, chili powder, garlic powder, onion powder, and salt in a mixing bowl. Toss in the sweet potato fries until nicely coated. Arrange sweet potato fries into cooking tray of air fryer. Using the display panel, select Air Fry, then adjust the temperature to 380 degrees F and the time to 10 minutes; touch the Start button to initiate preheating. When the display indicates "Add Food", place the cooking tray in the air fryer basket. When the display indicates "turn Food", turn the food. When the time is up, carefully remove them from the cooking tray. Once done, serve and enjoy.
Per Serving: Calories 241; Fat 7.5g; Sodium 98mg; Carbs 42.6g; Fiber 6.5g; Sugar 1g; Protein 2.8g

Panko Chicken Tenders

Prep time: 10 minutes| Cook time: 10 minutes | Serves: 4

⅛ cup flour
Pepper and salt to taste
Olive spray
1 egg white
12 oz. chicken breasts
1-¼ oz. panko bread crumbs

Remove any excess fat from the chicken breast. Tenders should be cut into. Season the food with salt and pepper. The tenders should be floured first, then dipped in egg whites and bread crumbs. Arrange chicken tenders into cooking tray of air fryer. Using the display panel, select Air Fry, then adjust the temperature to 350 degrees F and the time to 10 minutes; touch the Start button to initiate preheating. When the display indicates "Add Food", place the cooking tray in the air fryer basket. When the display indicates "turn Food", turn the food and add the olive spray. When the time is up, carefully remove them from the cooking tray. Once done, serve and enjoy.
Per Serving: Calories 228; Fat 2.5g; Sodium 76mg; Carbs 36.8g; Fiber 1.5g; Sugar 0.5g; Protein 13.8g

Cheesy and Salty Zucchini Chips

Prep time: 15 minutes| Cook time: 10 minutes | Serves: 4

Salt to taste
3 medium zucchinis
1 cup grated Parmesan cheese

Slice the zucchinis very thinly using a mandolin slicer, season with salt, and coat well with Parmesan cheese. Arrange zucchini chips into cooking tray of air fryer. Using the display panel, select Air Fry, then adjust the temperature to 350 degrees F and the time to 10 minutes; touch the Start button to initiate preheating. When the display indicates "Add Food", place the cooking tray in the air fryer basket. When the display indicates "turn Food", turn the food. When the time is up, carefully remove them from the cooking tray. Once done, serve and enjoy.
Per Serving: Calories 46; Fat 1.8g; Sodium 118mg; Carbs 5.2g; Fiber 1.6g; Sugar 2.5g; Protein 4g

Ranch Butter Garlic Pretzels

Prep time: 10 minutes| Cook time: 15 minutes | Serves: 4

½ tsp. garlic powder
2 cups pretzels
1 ½ tsp. ranch dressing mix
1 tbsp. melted butter

In a medium mixing bowl, combine all of the ingredients and stir until well combined. Pour into pretzels Arrange pretzels into cooking tray of air fryer. Using the display panel, select Air Fry, then adjust the temperature to 350 degrees F and the time to 15 minutes; touch the Start button to initiate preheating. When the display indicates "Add Food", place the cooking tray in the air fryer basket. When the display indicates "turn Food", turn the food. When the time is up, carefully remove them from the cooking tray. Once done, serve and enjoy.
Per Serving: Calories 141; Fat 3.5g; Sodium 438mg; Carbs 24.6g; Fiber 0.9g; Sugar 1g; Protein 3.2g

Sweet Potato Chips with Mixed Herbs

Prep time: 10 minutes| Cook time: 15 minutes | Serves: 4

1 tsp. dried mixed herbs
2 medium sweet potatoes,
peeled
1 tbsp. olive oil

Thinly slice the sweet potatoes with a mandolin slicer, transfer to a medium bowl, and toss with the herbs and olive oil until completely coated. Arrange the sweet potatoes chips into cooking tray of air fryer Using the display panel, select Roast, then adjust the temperature to 350 degrees F and the time to 15 minutes; touch the Start button to initiate preheating. When the display indicates "Add Food", place the cooking tray in the air fryer basket. When the time is up, carefully remove them from the cooking tray. Once done, serve and enjoy.
Per Serving: Calories 119; Fat 3.6g; Sodium 7mg; Carbs 21g; Fiber 3.2g; Sugar 0.4g; Protein 1.2g

Crispy French Fries

Prep time: 10 minutes| Cook time: 1 hour | Serves: 4

2 tbsps. olive oil
6 peeled russet potatoes

Peel the potatoes and cut them into strips. Allow 30 minutes to soak in water. Using paper towels, absorb any excess moisture. Place them in a mixing basin and drizzle with oil. Toss until everything is evenly coated. Put the potato slices in the cooking tray. Using the display panel, select Air Fry, then adjust the temperature to 360 degrees F and the time to 30 minutes, then touch Start button to initiate preheating. When the display indicates "Add Food", place the cooking tray in the air fryer basket. When the display indicates "turn Food", turn the food. When the Sausages and Chorizos are cooked, carefully remove them from the cooking tray
Per Serving: Calories 165; Fat 7g; Sodium 75mg; Carbs 22.4g; Fiber 1.5g; Sugar 0g; Protein 3.1 g

Garlic Chili Cheese Toasts with Parsley

Prep time: 05 minutes| Cook time: 3 minutes | Serves: 4

1 tsp. garlic powder
1 tsp. red chili flakes

6 pieces sandwich bread	deseeded and minced
4 tablespoon butter	½ tsp. salt
1 cup grated cheddar cheese	1 tablespoon sliced fresh
2 little fresh red chilies,	parsley

Butter one side of each bread slice and place on a clean, level surface. Distribute the cheddar cheese on top, then layer the remaining ingredients on top. Arrange potatoes bread pieces cooking tray of air fryer. Using the display panel, select Broil, then adjust the time to 3 minutes; touch the Start button to initiate preheating. When the display indicates "Add Food", place the cooking tray in the air fryer basket. When the time is up, carefully remove them from the cooking tray. Once done, serve and enjoy.
Per Serving: Calories 323; Fat 22.5g; Sodium 1354mg; Carbs 21.6g; Fiber 0.5g; Sugar 3.3g; Protein 10.8g

Garlic Rosemary Cheese Sticks

Prep time: 10 minutes| Cook time: 15 minutes | Serves: 6

1 teaspoon garlic powder	1 cheese sticks
1 teaspoon of Italian spices	¼ cup parmesan cheese, grated
¼ teaspoon rosemary, ground	¼ cup whole-wheat flour
2 eggs	

Removes the cheese sticks from their packaging. Set aside for now. In a mixing dish, whisk together the eggs. In a separate bowl, combine the cheese, seasonings and flour. The sticks should now be dipped in the egg and then dipped in the batter. Apply a thick coat of paint. Arrange cheese sticks into cooking tray of air fryer. Using the display panel, select Bake, then adjust the temperature to 380 degrees F and the time to 15 minutes; touch the Start button to initiate preheating. When the display indicates "Add Food", place the cooking tray in the air fryer basket. When the time is up, carefully remove them from the cooking tray. Once done, serve and enjoy.
Per Serving: Calories 66; Fat 3.3g; Sodium 84mg; Carbs 4.6g; Fiber 0.2g; Sugar 0.3g; Protein 4g

Double-Baked Stuffed Potato with Cream

Prep time: 15 minutes| Cook time: 75 minutes | Serves: 2

2 large russet potatoes	¼ cup shredded cheddar
2 tbsps. butter	cheese
½ cup heavy whipping cream	2 slices cooked bacon, cut into
¼ teaspoon kosher salt	bits
¼ cup sour cream	1 green onion, sliced

Place the potatoes on the cooking tray Using the display panel, select Bake, then adjust the temperature to 350 degrees F and the time to 60 minutes, then touch Start button to initiate preheating. When the display indicates "Add Food", place the cooking tray in the air fryer basket. When the time up carefully remove them from the cooking tray Scoop the potatoes' insides into a large mixing basin. Mash together the butter, heavy whipping cream, and kosher salt in a mixing dish. Put the mashed potatoes into the potato skins into cooking tray Using the display panel, select Bake, then adjust the temperature to 350 degrees F and the time to 15 minutes, then touch Start button to initiate preheating. When the display indicates "Add Food", place the cooking tray in the air fryer basket. When the potatoes are cooked, carefully remove them from the cooking tray Remove potatoes and garnish with sour cream, cheddar cheese, bacon bits, and green onion.
Per Serving: Calories 684; Fat 41.7g; Sodium 949mg; Carbs 61.1g; Fiber 9.1g; Sugar 4.6g; Protein 18.6 g

Fried Hominy

Prep time: 05 minutes| Cook time: 60 minutes | Serves: 4

6 oz. dried hominy, soaked	2 tbsps. old bay seasoning
overnight	Salt to taste
3 tbsps. peanut oil	

Pat dry hominy and season with salt and old bay seasoning. Drizzle with oil and toss to coat. Spread in the air fryer cooking tray Using the display panel, select Air Fry, then adjust the temperature to 350 degrees F and the time to 60 minutes, then touch Start button to initiate preheating. When the display indicates "Add Food", place the cooking tray in the air fryer basket. When the display indicates "turn Food", turn the food. When the time up carefully remove them from the cooking tray Let cool and serve.
Per Serving: Calories 120; Fat 10.5g; Sodium 1088mg; Carbs 6.1g; Fiber 1.1g; Sugar 0.8g; Protein 0.6 g

Cheese Mushrooms with Walnuts and Parsley

Prep time: 05 minutes| Cook time: 10 minutes | Serves: 4

4 large Portobello mushroom	½ cup mozzarella cheese,
caps	shredded
⅓ cup walnuts, minced	2 tbsp. fresh parsley, chopped
1 tbsp. canola oil	

Grease the air fryer cooking tray with cooking spray. Fill the mushrooms with mozzarella cheese after rubbing them with canola oil. Place on the bottom of the greased air fryer cooking tray and top with minced walnuts. Using the display panel, select Bake, then adjust the temperature to 350 degrees F and the time to 60 minutes, then touch Start button to initiate preheating. When the display indicates "Add Food", place the cooking tray in the air fryer basket. When the time up carefully remove them from the cooking tray Let cool for a few minutes and sprinkle with freshly chopped parsley to serve.
Per Serving: Calories 128; Fat 10.5g; Sodium 28mg; Carbs 5.6g; Fiber 2.1g; Sugar 1.7g; Protein 5.7 g

Paprika Cumin Roasted Chickpeas

Prep time: 10 minutes| Cook time: 35 minutes | Serves: 4

¼ tsp. garlic powder	¼ tsp. chili pepper powder
1 (15 oz.) can chickpeas, Dry-	¼ tsp. curry powder
out pipes	¼ tsp. ground cumin
¼ tsp. ground coriander	¼ tsp. paprika
⅛ tsp. salt	Olive oil for spraying

Mix the chickpeas with all of the spices in a medium bowl until thoroughly combined, then pour into the rotisserie basket. Lightly grease the basket with olive oil, shake it, then close the seal. Arrange chickpeas into cooking tray of air fryer. Using the display panel, select Roast, then adjust the temperature to 375 degrees F and the time to 35 minutes; touch the Start button to initiate preheating. When the display indicates "Add Food", place the cooking tray in the air fryer basket. When the time is up, carefully remove them from the cooking tray. Once done, serve and enjoy.
Per Serving: Calories 419; Fat 10g; Sodium 26mg; Carbs 64.8g; Fiber 18.5g; Sugar 11.4g; Protein 20.8g

Tasty and Crunchy Corn Nuts

Prep time: 10 minutes| Cook time: 10 minutes | Serves: 8

3 tablespoons of vegetable oil   1-½ teaspoons salt
1 oz. white corn

In a bowl, cover the corn with water. Set aside for now. Allow the corn to air dry. Spread it out on a flat plate and pat it dry with paper towels. Using the display panel, select Roast and then adjust the temperature to 350 degrees F and the time to 10 minutes; touch the Start button to initiate preheating. When the display indicates "Add Food", place the cooking tray in the air fryer basket. When the time is up, carefully remove them from the cooking tray. Once done, serve and enjoy.
Per Serving: Calories 48; Fat 5.1g; Sodium 291mg; Carbs 0.6g; Fiber 0.1g; Sugar 0.1g; Protein 0.1g

Salty Roasted Potatoes

Prep time: 10 minutes| Cook time: 15 minutes | Serves: 2

½ teaspoon of coarse sea salt   2 large potatoes, scrubbed
1 tablespoon peanut oil

Brush your potatoes with peanut oil and season with salt. Arrange potatoes into cooking tray of air fryer. Using the display panel, select Roast and then adjust the temperature to 400 degrees F and the time to 15 minutes; touch the Start button to initiate preheating. When the display indicates "Add Food", place the cooking tray in the air fryer basket. When the time is up, carefully remove them from the cooking tray. Once done, serve and enjoy.
Per Serving: Calories 314; Fat 7.1g; Sodium 502mg; Carbs 58g; Fiber 8.9g; Sugar 4.2g; Protein 6.2g

Garlic Coconut Chicken Bites

Prep time: 10 minutes| Cook time: 15 minutes | Serves: 4

2 teaspoons garlic powder   ¾ cup panko bread crumbs
2 eggs   ¾ cup coconut, shredded
Salt and black pepper to the Cooking Spray
taste   8 chicken tenders

In a bucket, whisk together the pepper, salt, and eggs with the garlic powder. In a separate bowl, combine the coconut and panko and whisk thoroughly. The chicken tenders should be dipped in the egg mixture and then well coated in coconut. Cooking spray chicken bites. Arrange chicken bites into cooking tray of air fryer
Using the display panel, select Air Fry, then adjust the temperature to 350 degrees F and the time to 15 minutes; touch the Start button to initiate preheating. When the display indicates "Add Food", place the cooking tray in the air fryer basket. When the display indicates "turn Food", turn the food. When the time is up, carefully remove them from the cooking tray. Once done, serve and enjoy.
Per Serving: Calories 701; Fat 29g; Sodium 423mg; Carbs 18.6g; Fiber 2.4g; Sugar 2.7g; Protein 87.2g

Buffalo Panko Cauliflower

Prep time: 10 minutes| Cook time: 15 minutes | Serves: 4

4 cups cauliflower florets   ¼ cup butter, melted
1 cup panko bread crumbs   ¼ cup buffalo sauce

Mayonnaise for serving

Combine the buffalo sauce and butter in a mixing bowl and well combine. Soak cauliflower florets in this mixture and then breadcrumb to coat them. Arrange the coated cauliflower into cooking tray of air fryer.
Using the display panel, select Air Fry, then adjust the temperature to 350 degrees F and the time to 15 minutes; touch the Start button to initiate preheating. When the display indicates "Add Food", place the cooking tray in the air fryer basket. When the display indicates "turn Food", turn the food. When the time is up, carefully remove them from the cooking tray. Once done, serve with the Mayonnaise and enjoy
Per Serving: Calories 249; Fat 14.5g; Sodium 398mg; Carbs 25.6g; Fiber 3.5g; Sugar 4.3g; Protein 5.7g

Chocolate Banana Pups Crust

Prep time: 10 minutes| Cook time: 15 minutes | Serves: 4

16 baking Pups crust   1 banana, peeled and sliced
¼ cup peanut butter   into 16 pieces
¾ cup chocolate chips   1 tablespoon vegetable oil

In a small pot, melt chocolate chips over low heat, stirring constantly until completely melted. Remove from heat. Whisk together peanut butter and vegetable oil in a mixing basin. In a cup, put 1 teaspoon of chocolates mix, 1 banana slice, and 1 teaspoon of butter mix on top. Carry on with the rest of the cups in the same manner. Repeat with the rest of the cups. Arrange cups into cooking tray of air fryer. Using the display panel, select Bake, then adjust the temperature to 350 degrees F and the time to 15 minutes; touch the Start button to initiate preheating. When the display indicates "Add Food", place the cooking tray in the air fryer basket. When the time is up, carefully remove them from the cooking tray. Once done, serve and enjoy.
Per Serving: Calories 324; Fat 21g; Sodium 257mg; Carbs 32.6g; Fiber 1.7g; Sugar 12g; Protein 4.8g

Lemon Cumin Potato Spread

Prep time: 10 minutes| Cook time: 15 minutes | Serves: 10

19 ounces canned garbanzo   1 tablespoon olive oil
beans, Dried   5 garlic cloves, minced
1 cup sweet potatoes, peeled ½ teaspoon cumin, ground
and chopped   2 tablespoons water
¼ cup tahini   A pinch of salt and white
2 tablespoons lemon juice   pepper

Arrange potatoes into cooking tray of air fryer. Using the display panel, select roast then adjust the temperature to 350 degrees F and the time to 15 minutes; touch the Start button to initiate preheating. When the display indicates "Add Food", place the cooking tray in the air fryer basket. When the time is up, carefully remove them from the cooking tray. Cool them down, peel them, and pulse them in a food processor. In the food processor, combine sesame paste, garlic cloves, beans, lemon juice, cumin, water, and oil. Pulse until smooth. Season the mixture with salt and pepper, pulse them again, then divide into bowls and serve. Enjoy!
Per Serving: Calories 265; Fat 8g; Sodium 22mg; Carbs 38.6g; Fiber 10.5g; Sugar 6g; Protein 11.8g

Chocolate Lemon Apple Snack

Prep time: 10 minutes| Cook time: 15 minutes | Serves: 4

3 big apples, cored, peeled and   cubed

2 teaspoons lemon juice
¼ cup pecans, chopped
½ cup dark chocolate chips
½ cup clean caramel sauce

Combine apples and lemon juice in a mixing bowl and stir to combine. Arrange apple cubes into cooking tray of air fryer. Using the display panel, select Air Fry, then adjust the temperature to 350 degrees F and the time to 15 minutes; touch the Start button to initiate preheating. When the display indicates "Add Food", place the cooking tray in the air fryer basket. When the display indicates "turn Food", turn the food, and then add chocolate chips, pecans, drizzle with the caramel sauce. When the time is up, carefully remove them from the cooking tray. Once done, serve and enjoy.
Per Serving: Calories 172; Fat 5g; Sodium 2mg; Carbs 35.6g; Fiber 4.5g; Sugar 27.4g; Protein 1.8g

Cauliflower and Broccoli Dish

Prep time: 15 minutes| Cook time: 20 minutes | Serves: 4

1 and ½ cups broccoli, cut into 1-inch pieces
1 and ½ cups cauliflower, cut
into 1-inch pieces
1 tablespoon olive oil
Salt as needed

Take a bowl and add vegetables, oil, and salt. Toss well and coat them well Place into cooking tray Using the display panel, select Air Fry, then adjust the temperature to 375 degrees F and the time to 20 minutes, then touch Start button to initiate preheating. When the display indicates "Add Food", place the cooking tray in the air fryer basket. When the display indicates "turn Food", turn the food. When the time up carefully remove them from the cooking tray Let cool for a few minutes and sprinkle with freshly chopped parsley to serve Serve and enjoy!
Per Serving: Calories 107; Fat 4.1g; Sodium 121mg; Carbs 15.6g; Fiber 6.7g; Sugar 1.7g; Protein 5.7g

Hearty Lemon Green Beans

Prep time: 15 minutes| Cook time: 12 minutes | Serves: 4

1-pound green beans, trimmed
1 tablespoon butter, melted
1 tablespoon fresh lemon juice
¼ teaspoon garlic powder
Salt and pepper to taste
½ teaspoon lemon zest, grated

Add all of the specified ingredients, except the lemon zest, to a large mixing bowl. Toss and coat thoroughly. Using the display panel, select Air Fry, then adjust the temperature to 400 degrees F and the time to 12 minutes, then touch Start button to initiate preheating. When the display indicates "Add Food", place the cooking tray in the air fryer basket. When the display indicates "turn Food", turn the food. When the time up carefully remove them from the cooking tray Serve warm with a garnish with lemon zest! Serve and enjoy!
Per Serving: Calories 62; Fat 3.1g; Sodium 28mg; Carbs 8.4g; Fiber 3.9g, Sugar 1.7g; Protein 2.2g

Cheesy Cauliflower Bars with Italian Seasoning

Prep time: 10 minutes| Cook time: 20 minutes | Serves: 12

1 big Cauliflower head, florets separated
½ cup mozzarella, shredded
¼ cup egg whites
1 teaspoon Italian seasoning
Salt and black pepper to the taste

In a food processor, pulse cauliflower florets until smooth, then put on a baking sheet lined with parchment paper. Arrange the

baking sheet into cooking tray of air fryer. Using the display panel, select Air Fry, then adjust the temperature to 350 degrees F and the time to 15 minutes; touch the Start button to initiate preheating. When the display indicates "Add Food", place the cooking tray in the air fryer basket. When the display indicates "turn Food", turn the food. When the time is up, carefully remove them from the cooking tray. Once done, cut into 12 bars serve and enjoy
Per Serving: Calories 25; Fat 0.4g; Sodium 33mg; Carbs 3.8g; Fiber 1.5g; Sugar 1.8g; Protein 2.3g

Flax Nutmeg Pumpkin Muffins

Prep time: 10 minutes| Cook time: 15 minutes | Serves: 8

¼ cup butter
¾ cup pumpkin puree
2 tablespoons flaxseed meal
¼ cup flour
½ cup sugar
½ teaspoon nutmeg, ground
1 teaspoon cinnamon powder
½ teaspoon baking Soda
1 egg
½ teaspoon baking Powder

Add the butter, pumpkin puree, and egg in a mixing dish and well combine. Stir together flaxseed meal, flour, sugar, baking soda, baking powder, nutmeg, and cinnamon. Arrange muffins tin into cooking tray of air fryer. Using the display panel, select Bake, then adjust the temperature to 350 degrees F and the time to 15 minutes; touch the Start button to initiate preheating. When the display indicates "Add Food", place the cooking tray in the air fryer basket. When the time is up, carefully remove them from the cooking tray. Enjoy!
Per Serving: Calories 138; Fat 7g; Sodium 130mg; Carbs 36g; Fiber 1.5g; Sugar 13.4g; Protein 1.8g

Worcestershire Beef Jerky

Prep time: 40 minutes| Cook time: 30 minutes | Serves: 6

2 cups soy sauce
½ cup Worcestershire sauce
2 tablespoons black
peppercorns
2 tablespoons black pepper
2 pounds beef round, sliced

Whisk together the soy sauce, black peppercorns, black pepper, and Worcestershire sauce in a mixing bowl. Add the beef slices, toss to coat, and refrigerate them for 40 minutes. Arrange beef into cooking tray of air fryer. Using the display panel, select Roast, then adjust the temperature to 350 degrees F and the time to 30 minutes; touch the Start button to initiate preheating. When the display indicates "Add Food", place the cooking tray in the air fryer basket. When the time is up, carefully remove them from the cooking tray. Once done, serve and enjoy.
Per Serving: Calories 351; Fat 9.5g; Sodium 5112mg; Carbs 11.6g; Fiber 1.5g; Sugar 5.5g; Protein 51.8g

Honey Lime Chicken Wings

Prep time: 12 minutes| Cook time: 12 minutes | Serves: 8

16 chicken wings
2 tablespoons soy sauce
2 tablespoons of honey
Salt and black pepper taste to taste
2 tablespoons lime juice

Combine the wings, soy sauce, honey, salt, pepper, and lime juice in a bowl and toss well. Refrigerate the coated chicken wings for 10 minutes. Arrange chicken wings into cooking tray of air fryer. Using the display panel, select Air Fry, then adjust the temperature to 360 degrees F and the time to 12 minutes; touch the Start button to initiate preheating. When the display indicates "Add Food", place the cooking tray in the air fryer basket. When the display indicates "turn Food", turn the food.

When the time is up, carefully remove them from the cooking tray. Once done, serve and enjoy.

Per Serving: Calories 553; Fat 20.5g; Sodium 467mg; Carbs 5.6g; Fiber 0.1g; Sugar 4.6g; Protein 81.3g

Sesame Scallions Tofu Cubes

Prep time: 20 minutes| Cook time: 20 minutes| Serves: 2

8 oz. tofu	1 teaspoon rice vinegar
1 teaspoon cornstarch	1 teaspoon sesame oil
1 teaspoon scallions, chopped	1 teaspoon soy sauce

Cut the tofu into cubes. Toss the tofu cubes with the rice vinegar, sesame oil, and soy sauce in a mixing bowl. Shake the ingredients vigorously. Allow the tofu cubes to marinade for 10 minutes. Arrange the marinated tofu cubes into cooking tray of air fryer. Using the display panel, select Air Fry, then adjust the temperature to 370 degrees F and the time to 20 minutes; touch the Start button to initiate preheating. When the display indicates "Add Food", place the cooking tray in the air fryer basket. When the display indicates "turn Food", turn the food. When the time is up, carefully remove them from the cooking tray. Once done, serve and enjoy.

Per Serving: Calories 108; Fat 7g; Sodium 163mg; Carbs 3.6g; Fiber 1.1g; Sugar 0.8g; Protein 9.5g

Salty Thyme Tomatoes

Prep time: 10 minutes| Cook time: 10 minutes| Serves: 2

2 tomatoes	1 pinch salt
1 tablespoon thyme	1 teaspoon olive oil

Tomatoes should be sliced. After that, add the thyme and salt. Shake the ingredients vigorously. The thyme mixture should be sprinkled over the sliced tomatoes. Spray the sliced tomatoes with olive oil and then arrange into cooking tray of air fryer. Using the display panel, select Air Fry, then adjust the temperature to 350 degrees F and the time to 10 minutes; touch the Start button to initiate preheating. When the display indicates "Add Food", place the cooking tray in the air fryer basket. When the display indicates "turn Food", turn the food. When the time is up, carefully remove them from the cooking tray. Once done, serve and enjoy.

Per Serving: Calories 46; Fat 2.7g; Sodium 84mg; Carbs 5.6g; Fiber 2g; Sugar 3.3g; Protein 1.2g

Creamy Chicken Liver

Prep time: 10 minutes| Cook time: 10 minutes| Serves: 2

7 oz. chicken liver	1 tablespoon fresh dill, chopped
¼ cup water	
1 tablespoon butter	1 pinch salt
2 teaspoon cream	

Mix water, chicken liver, and salt in a bowl. Arrange the chicken liver into cooking tray of air fryer. Using the display panel, select Roast, then adjust the temperature to 390 degrees F and the time to 10 minutes; touch the Start button to initiate preheating. When the display indicates "Add Food", place the cooking tray in the air fryer basket. Then, into the bowl, add the cooked chicken liver. Pour in the cream and butter. Blend the mixture until it is completely smooth. After that, carefully whisk in the chopped fresh dill.

Per Serving: Calories 223; Fat 12.5g; Sodium 198mg; Carbs 1.9g; Fiber 0.2g; Sugar 0.1g; Protein 24.8g

Panko Catfish Sticks

Prep time: 10 minutes| Cook time: 10 minutes| Serves: 2

8 oz. catfish fillet	¼ cup panko breadcrumbs
½ teaspoon salt	1 egg
½ teaspoon ground black pepper	½ teaspoon olive oil

Catfish fillets should be cut into two medium-sized pieces (sticks). After that, season the catfish fillets with salt and black pepper. In a separate bowl, whisk the egg. Whisk the egg and dip the catfish fillets in it. Coat the fillets in panko breadcrumbs after that and then arrange them into cooking tray of air fryer. Using the display panel, select Air Fry, then adjust the temperature to 380 degrees F and the time to 10 minutes; touch the Start button to initiate preheating. When the display indicates "Add Food", place the cooking tray in the air fryer basket. When the display indicates "turn Food", turn the food. When the time is up, carefully remove them from the cooking tray. Once done, serve and enjoy.

Per Serving: Calories 231; Fat 12g; Sodium 698mg; Carbs 8g; Fiber 0.5g; Sugar 0.4g; Protein 21.8g

Pepper Honey Banana Chips

Prep time: 10 minutes| Cook time: 15 minutes| Serves: 2

2 bananas	1 pinch white pepper
1 teaspoon honey	½ teaspoon olive oil

Peel the bananas and cut them into chunks for the chips. Then add the honey and white pepper to the bananas. Spray the bananas with olive oil and gently mix them together with your hands. Arrange potatoes fries into cooking tray of air fryer. Using the display panel, select Air Fry, then adjust the temperature to 350 degrees F and the time to 15 minutes; touch the Start button to initiate preheating. When the display indicates "Add Food", place the cooking tray in the air fryer basket. When the display indicates "turn Food", turn the food. When the time is up, carefully remove them from the cooking tray. Once done, serve and enjoy.

Per Serving: Calories 241; Fat 7.5g; Sodium 98mg; Carbs 42.6g; Fiber 6.5g; Sugar 1g; Protein 2.8g

Apple Chips with Ginger

Prep time: 10 minutes| Cook time: 10 minutes| Serves: 2

½ teaspoon olive oil	1 pinch ground ginger
3 apples	

Peel the apples and remove the seeds. Slice the apples and sprinkle them with the ground ginger and olive oil. Arrange apple slice into cooking tray of air fryer. Using the display panel, select Roast. then adjust the temperature to 400 degrees F and the time to 10 minutes; touch the Start button to initiate preheating. When the display indicates "Add Food", place the cooking tray in the air fryer basket. When the time is up, carefully remove them from the cooking tray. Once done, serve and enjoy.

Per Serving: Calories 184; Fat 1.8g; Sodium 3mg; Carbs 46.3g; Fiber 8.1g; Sugar 34.8g; Protein 0.8g

Thyme Maple Carrot Fries

Prep time: 5 minutes| Cook time: 15 minutes| Serves: 2

1 cup baby carrot	¼ cup maple syrup

1 pinch salt	pepper
½ teaspoon thyme	1 teaspoon dried oregano
½ teaspoon ground black	1 tablespoon olive oil

Thyme, salt, ground black pepper, and dried oregano are sprinkled over the young carrots. Then spritz the baby carrot with olive oil and give it a good shake. Arrange carrot into cooking tray of air fryer. Using the display panel, select Air Fry, then adjust the temperature to 350 degrees F and the time to 15 minutes; touch the Start button to initiate preheating. When the display indicates "Add Food", place the cooking tray in the air fryer basket. When the display indicates "turn Food", turn the food. When the time is up, carefully remove them from the cooking tray. Once done, serve and enjoy.

Per Serving: Calories 170; Fat 7.2g; Sodium 87mg; Carbs 28g; Fiber 0.8g; Sugar 23.8g; Protein 0.2g

Onion Pepper Sweet Potato Fries

Prep time: 10 minutes| Cook time: 15 minutes| Serves: 2

2 sweet potatoes	½ teaspoon ground black
1 tablespoon coconut oil	pepper
⅓ teaspoon salt	½ teaspoon onion powder

Cut the sweet potatoes into fries after peeling them. Season the vegetables with salt, black pepper, and onion powder to taste. Sprinkle the coconut oil over the sweet potatoes and give them a good shake. Arrange potatoes fries into cooking tray of air fryer. Using the display panel, select Air Fry, then adjust the temperature to 350 degrees F and the time to 15 minutes; touch the Start button to initiate preheating. When the display indicates "Add Food", place the cooking tray in the air fryer basket. Every 5 minutes, give the sweet potato fries a good shake. When the time is up, carefully remove them from the cooking tray. Once done, serve and enjoy.

Per Serving: Calories 241; Fat 7.5g; Sodium 98mg; Carbs 42.6g; Fiber 6.5g; Sugar 1g; Protein 2.8g

Garlic Onion Squid Rings

Prep time: 10 minutes| Cook time: 10 minutes| Serves: 2

2 squid tubes	¼ teaspoon salt
2 eggs	½ teaspoon onion powder
⅓ cup flour	½ teaspoon garlic powder

Carefully wash and peel the squid cubes. After that, cut the squid cubes into rings. In a mixing dish, whisk together the eggs. The squid rings should then be dipped in the whisked eggs. Combine the flour, salt, onion powder, and garlic powder in a mixing bowl. Using a fork, stir the ingredients together. Then, using the flour mixture, coat the squid rings. Arrange squid into cooking tray of air fryer. Using the display panel, select Air Fry, then adjust the temperature to 400 degrees F and the time to 10 minutes; touch the Start button to initiate preheating. When the display indicates "Add Food", place the cooking tray in the air fryer basket. When the display indicates "turn Food", turn the food. When the time is up, carefully remove them from the cooking tray. Once done, serve and enjoy.

Per Serving: Calories 203; Fat 6.1g; Sodium 893mg; Carbs 17.2g; Fiber 0.7g; Sugar 0.8g; Protein 19.8g

Salty Crunchy Corn Okra Bites

Prep time: 10 minutes| Cook time: 10 minutes| Serves: 2

| 4 tablespoon corn flakes, crushed | 9 oz. okra |
| | 1 egg |

| ½ teaspoon salt | 1 teaspoon olive oil |

Roughly chop the okra. Combine the corn flakes and salt in a mixing bowl. In a mixing dish, crack the egg and whisk it. In a mixing bowl, toss the chopped okra with the whisked egg. Then sprinkle the corn flakes over the chopped okra. Arrange okra into cooking tray of air fryer and sprinkle with the olive oil. Using the display panel, select Air Fry, then adjust the temperature to 350 degrees F and the time to 10 minutes; touch the Start button to initiate preheating. When the display indicates "Add Food", place the cooking tray in the air fryer basket. When the display indicates "turn Food", turn the food. When the time is up, carefully remove them from the cooking tray. Once done, serve and enjoy.

Per Serving: Calories 115; Fat 4.8g; Sodium 654mg; Carbs 12.6g; Fiber 4.5g; Sugar 2.3g; Protein 5.5g

Crispy Potato Chips

Prep time: 10 minutes| Cook time: 19 minutes| Serves: 2

| 3 potatoes | ½ teaspoon salt |
| 1 tablespoon canola oil | |

Carefully wash the potatoes without peeling them. To make the chips, slice the potatoes into thin slices. Season the potato chips with salt and olive oil. Carefully combine the potatoes. Arrange potatoes chips into cooking tray of air fryer. Using the display panel, select Air Fry, then adjust the temperature to 400 degrees F and the time to 19 minutes; touch the Start button to initiate preheating. When the display indicates "Add Food", place the cooking tray in the air fryer basket. When the display indicates "turn Food", turn the food. When the time is up, carefully remove them from the cooking tray. Once done, serve and enjoy.

Per Serving: Calories 282; Fat 7.3g; Sodium 601mg; Carbs 50.2g; Fiber 7.7g; Sugar 3.7g; Protein 5.4g

Garlic Corn & Beans Fries

Prep time: 10 minutes| Cook time: 15 minutes| Serves: 2

¼ cup corn flakes crumbs	1 tablespoon canola oil
1 egg	½ teaspoon salt
10 oz. green beans	1 teaspoon garlic powder

Place the green beans in a mixing bowl. In a large mixing bowl, whisk together the egg and green beans until smooth. After that, season the green beans with salt and garlic powder. Gently shake the container. Then thoroughly coat the green beans in corn flakes crumbs. Arrange green beans into cooking tray of air fryer. Using the display panel, select Air Fry, then adjust the temperature to 400 degrees F and the time to 15 minutes; touch the Start button to initiate preheating. When the display indicates "Add Food", place the cooking tray in the air fryer basket. When the display indicates "turn Food", turn the food. When the time is up, carefully remove them from the cooking tray. Once done, serve and enjoy.

Per Serving: Calories 187; Fat 9.5g; Sodium 712mg; Carbs 22.6g; Fiber 5.1g; Sugar 3.6g; Protein 6.4g

Sweet Cinnamon Apple Fritters

Prep time: 10 minutes| Cook time: 15 minutes| Serves: 2

2 red apples	1 teaspoon lemon juice
1 teaspoon sugar	½ teaspoon ground cinnamon
1 tablespoon flour	1 teaspoon butter
1 tablespoon semolina	1 egg

Apples should be peeled and grated. Lemon juice should be sprinkled over the grated apples. Then add the sugar, flour, semolina, and cinnamon powder. Combine the ingredients and crack the egg. Carefully combine the apple mixture. Melt the butter and tossing it in there. Make the medium fritters from the apple mixture once the butter has melted. For this stage, you'll need two spoons. Arrange the fritters into cooking tray of air fryer. Using the display panel, select Air Fry, then adjust the temperature to 350 degrees F and the time to 15 minutes; touch the Start button to initiate preheating. When the display indicates "Add Food", place the cooking tray in the air fryer basket. When the display indicates "turn Food", turn the food. When the time is up, carefully remove them from the cooking tray. Once done, serve and enjoy.

Per Serving: Calories 207; Fat 4.6g; Sodium 47mg; Carbs 40.3g; Fiber 6g; Sugar 25.4g; Protein 4.8g

Salty Oregano Onion Rings

Prep time: 14 minutes| Cook time: 10 minutes| Serves: 2

1 tablespoon oregano	½ teaspoon salt
1 tablespoon flour	2 white onions, peeled
½ teaspoon cornstarch	1 tablespoon olive oil
1 egg	

In a mixing dish, crack the egg and whisk it. In a separate dish, whisk together the flour and cornstarch. Season with oregano and salt. Gently shake the ingredients. To make the "rings," peel and slice the onions.

The onion rings should then be dipped in the whisked egg. Coat the onion rings in the flour mixture after that. Arrange onion rings into cooking tray of air fryer. Using the display panel, select Air Fry, then adjust the temperature to 365 degrees F and the time to 10 minutes; touch the Start button to initiate preheating. When the display indicates "Add Food", place the cooking tray in the air fryer basket. When the display indicates "turn Food", turn the food. When the time is up, carefully remove them from the cooking tray. Once done, serve and enjoy.

Per Serving: Calories 159; Fat 9.6g; Sodium 617mg; Carbs 15.6g; Fiber 3.5g; Sugar 4.9g; Protein 4.8g

Sweet Cinnamon Mixed Nuts

Prep time: 5 minutes| Cook time: 10 minutes| Serves: 5

½ cup pecans	2 tbsps. sugar
½ cup walnuts	2 tbsps. egg whites
½ cup almonds	2 tsps. cinnamon
A pinch of cayenne pepper	

Add the pepper, sugar, and cinnamon to a bowl and mix them well; set aside. In another bowl, mix in the pecans, walnuts, almonds, and egg whites. Add the spice mixture to the nuts and give it a good mix. Arrange nut mix into cooking tray of air fryer. Using the display panel, select Roast, then adjust the temperature to 350 degrees F and the time to 10 minutes; touch the Start button to initiate preheating. When the display indicates "Add Food", place the cooking tray in the air fryer basket. When the time is up, carefully remove them from the cooking tray. Once done, serve and enjoy.

Per Serving: Calories 166; Fat 13.2g; Sodium 7mg; Carbs 9.1g; Fiber 2.5g; Sugar 5.5g; Protein 5.8g

Apple & Cinnamon Chips

Prep time: 15 minutes| Cook time: 15 minutes| Serves: 2

1 tsp. sugar	1 tsp. salt

1 whole apple, sliced
½ tsp. cinnamon

Confectioners' sugar for serving

Combine the cinnamon, salt, and sugar in a bowl; toss in the apple slices. Arrange apple slice into cooking tray of air fryer. Using the display panel, select Air Fry, then adjust the temperature to 350 degrees F and the time to 15 minutes; touch the Start button to initiate preheating. When the display indicates "Add Food", place the cooking tray in the air fryer basket. When the display indicates "turn Food", turn the food When the time is up, carefully remove them from the cooking tray. Once done, serve with the Confectioners' sugar and enjoy.

Per Serving: Calories 241; Fat 7.5g; Sodium 98mg; Carbs 42.6g; Fiber 6.5g; Sugar 1g; Protein 2.8g

Tasty Prawns Roll Wraps

Prep time: 32 minutes| Cook time: 25 minutes| Serves: 4

2 tbsps. vegetable oil	sauce
1 inch piece fresh ginger, grated	1 tbsp. sugar
1 tbsp. minced garlic	1 cup shredded Napa cabbage
1 carrot, cut into strips	1 tbsp. sesame oil
¼ cup chicken broth	8 cooked prawns, minced
2 tbsps. reduced-sodium soy	1 egg
	8 egg roll wrappers

Heat vegetable oil in a skillet over high heat and sauté ginger and garlic for 40 seconds, or until fragrant. Cook for another 2 minutes after adding the carrot. Bring the chicken stock, soy sauce and sugar to a boil. Add the cabbage and cook for 4 minutes, or until tender. Take off the heat and add the sesame oil. Allow 15 minutes for cooling. Strain the cabbage mixture and fold in the prawns, minced. In a small bowl, whisk together one egg. Fill each egg roll wrapper halfway with prawn mixture, placing the filling immediately below the wrapper's center. Tuck the bottom part under and fold it over the filling. Fold in both sides and roll up securely. To seal the wrapping, use the whisked egg. Arrange rolls into cooking tray of air fryer. Using the display panel, select Air Fry, then adjust the temperature to 350 degrees F and the time to 15 minutes; touch the Start button to initiate preheating. When the display indicates "Add Food", place the cooking tray in the air fryer basket. When the display indicates "turn Food", turn the food. When the time is up, carefully remove them from the cooking tray. Once done, serve and enjoy.

Per Serving: Calories 375; Fat 13.2g; Sodium 859mg; Carbs 44.6g; Fiber 1.8g; Sugar 4.3g; Protein 19g

Peppery Rosemary Potatoes

Prep time: 10 minutes| Cook time: 25 minutes| Serves: 2

2 pounds potatoes, halved	1 tsp. salt
2 tbsps. olive oil	¼ tsp. freshly ground black pepper
3 garlic cloves, grated	
1 tbsp. minced fresh rosemary	

Mix potatoes, olive oil, garlic, rosemary, salt, and pepper in a mixing bowl. Arrange the coated potatoes into cooking tray of air fryer. Using the display panel, select Air Fry, then adjust the temperature to 360 degrees F and the time to 25 minutes; touch the Start button to initiate preheating. When the display indicates "Add Food", place the cooking tray in the air fryer basket. When the display indicates "turn Food", turn the food. When the time is up, carefully remove them from the cooking tray. Once done, serve and enjoy.

Per Serving: Calories 446; Fat 14.5g; Sodium 1198mg; Carbs 74g; Fiber 11.5g; Sugar 5.3g; Protein 8g

Fried Thai Mozzarella Sticks

Prep time: 20 minutes| Cook time: 10 minutes| Serves: 12

12 mozzarella string cheese
2 cups breadcrumbs
3 eggs

1 cup sweet Thai sauce
4 tbsps. skimmed milk

Place the crumbs in a mixing dish. In a separate bowl, crack the eggs and whisk in the milk. Dip each cheese stick in the egg mixture, then in the crumbs, then in the egg mixture again, and finally in the crumbs. Freeze the coated cheese sticks for 10 to 20 minutes on a baking sheet. Arrange cheese sticks into cooking tray of air fryer. Using the display panel, select Air Fry, then adjust the temperature to 380 degrees F and the time to 8 minutes; touch the Start button to initiate preheating. When the display indicates "Add Food", place the cooking tray in the air fryer basket. When the display indicates "turn Food", turn the food. When the time is up, carefully remove them from the cooking tray. Once done, serve with a sweet Thai sauce

Per Serving: Calories 184; Fat 6.6g; Sodium 409mg; Carbs 18.5g; Fiber 0.8g; Sugar 6g; Protein 12.8g

Chili Salt Cheese Crisps

Prep time: 17 minutes| Cook time: 10 minutes| Serves: 3

4 tbsps. grated cheese + extra for rolling
1 cup flour + extra for kneading

¼ tsp. chili powder
½ tsp. baking Powder
3 tsp. butter
A pinch of salt

Combine the cheese, flour, baking powder, chili powder, butter, and salt in a mixing bowl. The mixture should have a crusty texture. To make dough, add a few drops of water and stir thoroughly. Place the dough on a flat surface to cool. Knead the dough for a few minutes with some extra flour in your palms and on the surface. Roll out the dough into a thin sheet with a rolling pin. Cut the dough into the form of the lings you want with a pastry cutter. Arrange Cheese Crisps into cooking tray of air fryer. Using the display panel, select Air Fry, then adjust the temperature to 350 degrees F and the time to 10 minutes; touch the Start button to initiate preheating. When the display indicates "Add Food", place the cooking tray in the air fryer basket. When the display indicates "turn Food", turn the food. When the time is up, carefully remove them from the cooking tray. Once done, serve and enjoy.

Per Serving: Calories 323; Fat 16.5g; Sodium 317mg; Carbs 29.5g; Fiber 5g; Sugar 0.2g; Protein 14.8g

Cheesy Fried Tomatoes

Prep time: 10 minutes| Cook time: 10 minutes| Serves: 4

1 cup grated mozzarella cheese
1 cup grated Parmesan cheese

½ cup chopped basil
Olive oil
4 tomatoes, halved

Spray a baking sheet with cooking spray; grease a baking sheet with cooking spray. Over the pan, place tomato halves and stuff with cheese and basil. Arrange tomatoes into cooking tray of air fryer. Using the display panel, select Bake then adjust the temperature to 400 degrees F and the time to 10 minutes; touch the Start button to initiate preheating. When the display indicates "Add Food", place the cooking tray in the air fryer basket. When the time is up, carefully remove them from the cooking tray. Once done, serve and enjoy.

Per Serving: Calories 95; Fat 6.5g; Sodium 114mg; Carbs 5.4g; Fiber 1.5g; Sugar 3.2g; Protein 5.4g

Tamarind Bacon Scallops

Prep time: 10 minutes| Cook time: 15 minutes| Serves: 4-6

6 very large sea scallops
¼ cup tamarind sauce
1 tablespoon dark brown sugar

6 slices bacon, cut in half crosswise
1 ½ teaspoons minced ginger

Combine the tamarind sauce, brown sugar, ginger, and scallops in a mixing bowl. Toss the items together to ensure that they are well combined. Allow 15-20 minutes for preparation. Wrap 2 bacon slices around each scallop. Toothpicks are a good way to keep things secure. Spray a suitable baking sheet with cooking spray. Place the scallops on top of the pan. Arrange the pan to cooking tray of air fryer. Using the display panel, select Air Fry, then adjust the temperature to 350 degrees F and the time to 15 minutes; touch the Start button to initiate preheating. When the display indicates "Add Food", place the cooking tray in the air fryer basket. When the display indicates "turn Food", turn the food. When the time is up, carefully remove them from the cooking tray. Once done, serve and enjoy.

Per Serving: Calories 227; Fat 9.5g; Sodium 664mg; Carbs 8.4g; Fiber 0.1g; Sugar 4.5g; Protein 28.1g

Baked Cheesy Bacon Russet Potatoes

Prep time: 5 minutes| Cook time: 15 minutes| Serves: 4

¼ cup chopped scallions
1 cup grated cheddar cheese
3 russet potatoes, cleaned and cut into 1-inch rounds

¼ cup butter
3 tablespoons bacon bits, cooked and crumbled

Using cooking spray, grease a baking pan. Brush the potato with butter and sprinkle with scallions and cheese on the pan. Arrange the baking pan into cooking tray of air fryer. Using the display panel, select Bake, then adjust the temperature to 350 degrees F and the time to 15 minutes; touch the Start button to initiate preheating. When the display indicates "Add Food", place the cooking tray in the air fryer basket. When the time is up, carefully remove them from the cooking tray. Once done, serve with the bacon bits and enjoy.

Per Serving: Calories 405; Fat 27g; Sodium 597mg; Carbs 26.1g; Fiber 4g; Sugar 2.2g; Protein 15.2g

Coconut Pepper Shrimps

Prep time: 10 minutes| Cook time: 15 minutes| Serves: 4

8 ounces coconut milk
½ cup panko breadcrumbs
8 large shrimp, peeled and deveined

Salt and ground black pepper, to taste
½ teaspoon cayenne pepper

Combine the salt, black pepper, and coconut milk in a mixing bowl. Toss the items together to ensure that they are well combined. Add breadcrumbs, cayenne pepper, ground black pepper, and salt to a separate bowl. Toss the items together to ensure that they are well combined. Coat the shrimps with the coconut mixture first, then the crumbs. Arrange shrimps into cooking tray of air fryer and spray with cooking spray. Using the display panel, select Air Fry, then adjust the temperature to 350 degrees F and the time to 15 minutes; touch the Start button to initiate preheating. When the display indicates "Add Food", place the cooking tray in the air fryer basket. When the display indicates "turn Food", turn the food. When the time is up, carefully remove them from the cooking tray. Once done, serve

and enjoy.
Per Serving: Calories 180; Fat 13.8g; Sodium 51mg; Carbs 10.9g; Fiber 1.5g; Sugar 2.2g; Protein 4.8g

Tortilla Chips with Guacamole

Prep time: 10 minutes| Cook time: 15 minutes| Serves: 4

Chips:	to taste
1 tablespoon cumin powder	Guacamole:
1 tablespoon paprika powder	1 small firm tomato, chopped
12 corn tortillas	1 large avocado, pitted, peeled
2 tablespoon olive oil	and mashed
Ground black pepper and salt	A pinch dried parsley

Combine all of the ingredients for the chips in a mixing basin. Toss the items together to ensure that they are well combined. Combine the ingredients for the guacamole in a separate bowl. Toss the items together to ensure that they are well combined. Arrange chips into cooking tray of air fryer. Using the display panel, select Air Fry, then adjust the temperature to 350 degrees F and the time to 15 minutes; touch the Start button to initiate preheating. When the display indicates "Add Food", place the cooking tray in the air fryer basket. When the display indicates "turn Food", turn the food When the time is up, carefully remove them from the cooking tray. Once done, serve and enjoy. Serve the chips with guacamole.
Per Serving: Calories 329; Fat 19.2g; Sodium 39mg; Carbs 38g; Fiber 8.3g; Sugar 1.5g; Protein 5.5g

Roasted Chickpeas with Herb

Prep time: 10 minutes| Cook time: 15 minutes| Serves: 12

1 (15 ounces) can chickpeas,	⅛ teaspoon salt
Dry outed	¼ teaspoon chili pepper
¼ teaspoon garlic powder	powder
¼ teaspoon ground cumin	¼ teaspoon paprika
¼ teaspoon ground coriander	Olive oil
¼ teaspoon curry powder	

Combine chickpeas and spices in a mixing bowl. Toss the items together to ensure that they are well combined. Arrange potatoes fries into cooking tray of air fryer. Using the display panel, select Roast, then adjust the temperature to 350 degrees F and the time to 15 minutes; touch the Start button to initiate preheating. When the display indicates "Add Food", place the cooking tray in the air fryer basket. When the time is up, carefully remove them from the cooking tray. Once done, serve and enjoy.
Per Serving: Calories 140; Fat 3.3g; Sodium 9mg; Carbs 21.6g; Fiber 6.2g; Sugar 3.8g; Protein 6.9g

Pepper Butter Cashews

Prep time: 5 minutes| Cook time: 15 minutes| Serves: 5-6

1 teaspoon butter, melted	Salt and black pepper to taste
1 ½ cups raw cashew nut	

Combine cashews and remaining ingredients in a mixing dish. Toss the items together to ensure that they are well combined. Spray some cooking oil on a baking pan. Cover the pan with cashews. Arrange baking pan into cooking tray of air fryer. Using the display panel, select Roast, then adjust the temperature to 350 degrees F and the time to 15 minutes; touch the Start button to initiate preheating. When the display indicates "Add Food", place the cooking tray in the air fryer basket. When the time is up, carefully remove them from the cooking tray. Once done, serve and enjoy.

Per Serving: Calories 202; Fat 16.5g; Sodium 10mg; Carbs 11.2g; Fiber 1g; Sugar 1.7g; Protein 5.3g

Tasty Salt and Sweet Carrot Fries

Prep time: 10 minutes| Cook time: 15 minutes| Serves: 6

1 lb. carrots, peeled and cut	1 teaspoon olive oil
into sticks	½ teaspoon ground cinnamon
1 teaspoon maple syrup	Salt, to taste

In a bowl, add all the ingredients and mix well. Arrange the carrot sticks into cooking tray of air fryer. Using the display panel, select Air Fry, then adjust the temperature to 350 degrees F and the time to 15 minutes; touch the Start button to initiate preheating. When the display indicates "Add Food", place the cooking tray in the air fryer basket. When the display indicates "turn Food", turn the food. When the time is up, carefully remove them from the cooking tray. Once done, serve and enjoy.
Per Serving: Calories 41; Fat 0.8g; Sodium 79mg; Carbs 8.3g; Fiber 2g; Sugar 4.4g; Protein 0.6g

Rosemary Potato Chips

Prep time: 15 minutes| Cook time: 30 minutes| Serves: 6

4 small russet potatoes, thinly	2 tablespoons fresh rosemary,
sliced	finely chopped
1 tablespoon olive oil	¼ teaspoon salt

In a large bowl of water, soak the potato slices for about 30 minutes, changing the water once halfway through. Drain the potato slices well and pat them dry with the paper towels. Arrange potatoes slices into cooking tray of air fryer. Using the display panel, select Air Fry, then adjust the temperature to 350 degrees F and the time to 25 minutes; touch the Start button to initiate preheating. When the display indicates "Add Food", place the cooking tray in the air fryer basket. When the display indicates "turn Food", turn the food. When the time is up, carefully remove them from the cooking tray. Once done, serve and enjoy.
Per Serving: Calories 102; Fat 2.5g; Sodium 104mg; Carbs 18.2g; Fiber 3.2g; Sugar 1.3g; Protein 2g

Bread Sticks

Prep time: 15 minutes| Cook time: 15 minutes| Serves: 6

1 egg	2 bread slices
⅛ teaspoon ground cinnamon	1 tablespoon butter, softened
Pinch of ground nutmeg	Nonstick cooking; Spray
Pinch of ground cloves	1 tablespoon icing; Sugar
Salt, to taste	

In a mixing basin, whisk together the eggs, cinnamon, nutmeg cloves, and salt until thoroughly blended. Evenly spread the butter on all sides of the slices. Cut each slice of bread into strips. Bread strips should be uniformly dipped in the egg mixture. Arrange bread slice into cooking tray of air fryer. Using the display panel, select Air Fry, then adjust the temperature to 355 degrees F and the time to 15 minutes; touch the Start button to initiate preheating. When the display indicates "Add Food", place the cooking tray in the air fryer basket. When the display indicates "turn Food", turn the food. When the time is up, carefully remove them from the cooking tray. Once done, serve immediately with the topping of icing sugar.
Per Serving: Calories 37; Fat 2.8g; Sodium 72mg; Carbs 1.9g; Fiber 0.3g; Sugar 0.2g; Protein 1.3g

Crispy Italian Eggplant Slices

Prep time: 15 minutes| Cook time: 10 minutes| Serves: 4

1 medium eggplant, peeled and cut into ½-inch round slices
Salt, as required
½ cup all-purpose flour

2 eggs, beaten
1 cup Italian-style breadcrumbs
¼ cup olive oil

In a mixing basin, whisk together the eggs, cinnamon, nutmeg cloves, and salt until thoroughly blended. Evenly spread the butter on all sides of the slices. Cut each slice of bread into strips. Bread strips should be uniformly dipped in the egg mixture. Coat each eggplant slice in flour, then in beaten eggs, and then in breadcrumbs. Arrange Eggplant fries into cooking tray of air fryer. Using the display panel, select Air Fry, then adjust the temperature to 390 degrees F and the time to 10 minutes; touch the Start button to initiate preheating. When the display indicates "Add Food", place the cooking tray in the air fryer basket. When the display indicates "turn Food", turn the food. When the time is up, carefully remove them from the cooking tray. Once done, serve and enjoy.
Per Serving: Calories 332; Fat 16.6g; Sodium 270mg; Carbs 38.3g; Fiber 5.7g; Sugar 5.3g; Protein 9.1g

Fried Pepper Cauliflower Poppers

Prep time: 10 minutes| Cook time: 15 minutes| Serves: 4

½ large head cauliflower, cut into bite-sized florets
1 tablespoon olive oil

Salt and ground black pepper, as required

Combine all of the ingredients in a mixing bowl and toss well to combine. Arrange Cauliflower Poppers into cooking tray of air fryer. Using the display panel, select Air Fry, then adjust the temperature to 350 degrees F and the time to 15 minutes; touch the Start button to initiate preheating. When the display indicates "Add Food", place the cooking tray in the air fryer basket. When the display indicates "turn Food", turn the food. When the time is up, carefully remove them from the cooking tray. Once done, serve and enjoy.
Per Serving: Calories 38; Fat 23.5g; Sodium 49mg; Carbs 1.8g; Fiber 0.8g; Sugar 0.7g; Protein 0.7g

Crispy Hot Sauce Cauliflower Poppers

Prep time: 10 minutes| Cook time: 20 minutes| Serves: 4

1 egg white
1½ tablespoons ketchup
1 tablespoon hot sauce

⅓ cup panko breadcrumbs
2 cups cauliflower florets

Combine the egg white, ketchup, and spicy sauce in a shallow bowl. Place the breadcrumbs in a separate bowl. After dipping the cauliflower florets in the ketchup mixture, coat them with breadcrumbs. Arrange cauliflower into cooking tray of air fryer. Using the display panel, select Air Fry, then adjust the temperature to 350 degrees F and the time to 20 minutes; touch the Start button to initiate preheating. When the display indicates "Add Food", place the cooking tray in the air fryer basket. When the time is up, carefully remove them from the cooking tray. Once done, serve and enjoy.
Per Serving: Calories 55; Fat 0.7g; Sodium 181mg; Carbs 5.6g; Fiber 1.3g; Sugar 2.7g; Protein 2.3g

Turmeric Broccoli Poppers

Prep time: 15 minutes| Cook time: 10 minutes| Serves: 4

2 tablespoons plain yogurt
½ teaspoon red chili powder
¼ teaspoon ground cumin
¼ teaspoon ground turmeric

Salt, to taste
1 lb. broccoli, cut into small florets
2 tablespoons chickpea flour

Combine the yoghurt and spices in a mixing dish. Add the broccoli florets and generously cover it with the marinade. Refrigerate the broccoli florets for about 20 minutes before serving. Arrange the broccoli florets into cooking tray of air fryer. Using the display panel, select Air Fry, then adjust the temperature to 400 degrees F and the time to 10 minutes; touch the Start button to initiate preheating. When the display indicates "Add Food", place the cooking tray in the air fryer basket. When the display indicates "turn Food", turn the food. When the time is up, carefully remove them from the cooking tray. Once done, serve and enjoy.
Per Serving: Calories 69; Fat 0.9g; Sodium 87mg; Carbs 12.2g; Fiber 4.2g; Sugar 3.2g; Protein 4.9g

Crunchy Mixed Veggie Balls

Prep time: 15 minutes| Cook time: 10 minutes| Serves: 5

¾ lb. fresh spinach, blanched, drained and chopped
¼ of onion, chopped
½ of carrot, peeled and chopped
1 garlic clove, minced
1 American cheese slice, cut

into tiny pieces
1 bread slice, toasted and processed into breadcrumbs
½ tablespoon corn flour
½ teaspoon red chili flakes
Salt, as required

Combine all of the ingredients, except the breadcrumbs, in a mixing bowl and stir until well blended. Toss in the breadcrumbs and mix lightly to incorporate. Make 10 balls of the mixture that are all the same size.
Arrange balls into cooking tray of air fryer. Using the display panel, select Air Fry, then adjust the temperature to 355 degrees F and the time to 10 minutes; touch the Start button to initiate preheating. When the display indicates "Add Food", place the cooking tray in the air fryer basket. When the display indicates "turn Food", turn the food. When the time is up, carefully remove them from the cooking tray. Once done, serve and enjoy.
Per Serving: Calories 43; Fat 1.4g; Sodium 155mg; Carbs 5.6g; Fiber 1.9g; Sugar 1.2g; Protein 3.1g

Cheesy Risotto Balls

Prep time: 15 minutes| Cook time: 10 minutes| Serves: 4

1½ cups cooked risotto
3 tablespoons Parmesan cheese, grated

½ egg, beaten
1½ oz. mozzarella cheese, cubed
⅓ cup breadcrumbs

Combine the risotto, Parmesan, and egg in a mixing bowl and stir until completely blended. Make 20 balls of the mixture that are all the same size. In the centre of each ball, place a mozzarella cube. Smooth the risotto mixture over the ball with your fingertips. Place the breadcrumbs in a small bowl. Evenly coat the balls in breadcrumbs and then arrange them to the cooking tray of air fryer. Using the display panel, select Air Fry, then adjust the temperature to 390 degrees F and the time to 10 minutes; touch the Start button to initiate preheating. When the display indicates "Add Food", place the cooking tray in the air fryer basket. When the display indicates "turn Food", turn the food. When the time is up, carefully remove them from the cooking tray. Once done, serve and enjoy.
Per Serving: Calories 340; Fat 4.3g; Sodium 173mg; Carbs 62.4g; Fiber 1.3g; Sugar 0.7g; Protein 11.3g

Berry Crumble

Prep time: 05 minutes| Cook time: 30 minutes | Serves: 6

12 oz. fresh strawberries
7 oz. fresh raspberries
5 oz. fresh blueberries
5 tablespoons cold butter
2 tablespoons lemon juice

1 cup flour
½ cup of sugar
1 tablespoon water
A pinch of salt

Gently mix the berries together, but leave some lumps. Combine the lemon juice and 2 tablespoons of sugar in a mixing bowl. Place the berry mixture in the bottom of a round cake that has been prepared. In a mixing dish, combine the flour, salt, and sugar. Pour in the water and knead the butter with your fingertips until it crumbles. Arrange the berries on top of the crisp batter and then transfer them to the cooking tray of air fryer. Using the display panel, select Bake, then adjust the temperature to 390 degrees F and the time to 20 minutes, then touch Start button to initiate preheating. When the display indicates "Add Food", place the cooking tray in the air fryer basket. When the time up carefully remove them from the cooking tray Serve chilled.
Per Serving: Calories 214; Fat 10.3g; Sodium 98mg; Carbs 28.4g; Fiber 4.4g; Sugar 7.5g; Protein 3.3g

Russet Potato Cheese Cutlet

Prep time: 15 minutes| Cook time: 30 minutes| Serves: 4

2 medium Russet potatoes, peeled and cubed
2 tablespoons all-purpose flour
½ cup Parmesan cheese, grated
1 egg yolk
2 tablespoons chives, minced

Pinch of ground nutmeg
Salt and freshly ground black pepper, as needed
2 eggs
½ cup breadcrumbs
2 tablespoons vegetable oil

Add the potatoes to a pan of boiling water and simmer for 15 minutes. Drain the potatoes thoroughly and place them in a large mixing dish. Mash the potatoes with a potato masher and let them to cool thoroughly.
Combine the flour, Parmesan cheese, egg yolk, chives, nutmeg, salt and black pepper in a mixing bowl with the mashed potatoes. Form the mixture into small, equal-sized balls. Make a cylinder out of each ball now.
Crack the eggs into a shallow bowl and thoroughly beat them. Combine the breadcrumbs and oil in a separate bowl. After dipping the balls in the egg mixture, coat them in the breadcrumbs mixture. Arrange the balls into cooking tray of air fryer. Using the display panel, select Air Fry, then adjust the temperature to 390 degrees F and the time to 15 minutes; touch the Start button to initiate preheating. When the display indicates "Add Food", place the cooking tray in the air fryer basket. When the display indicates "turn Food", turn the food When the time is up, carefully remove them from the cooking tray. Once done, serve and enjoy.
Per Serving: Calories 283; Fat 13.4g; Sodium 263mg; Carbs 29.9g; Fiber 3.3g; Sugar 2.3g; Protein 11.5g

Cheese Bacon Cutlet

Prep time: 15 minutes| Cook time: 8 minutes| Serves: 8

1-pound sharp cheddar cheese block
1-pound thin bacon slices
1 cup all-purpose flour

3 eggs
1 cup breadcrumbs
Salt, as required
¼ cup olive oil

Cut the block of cheese into 1-inch rectangles. Wrap 2 bacon pieces completely around 1 piece of cheddar cheese. Carry on with the rest of the bacon and cheese. Place the croquettes in a baking tray and place in the freezer for 5 minutes. Place the flour in a small dish. Crack the eggs into a second bowl and whisk them thoroughly. Combine the breadcrumbs, salt, and oil in a third dish. Coat the croquettes in flour, then dunk them in beaten eggs before coating them in the breadcrumbs mixture. Arrange the croquettes into cooking tray of air fryer. Using the display panel, select Air Fry, then adjust the temperature to 390 degrees F and the time to 8 minutes; touch the Start button to initiate preheating. When the display indicates "Add Food", place the cooking tray in the air fryer basket. When the display indicates "turn Food", turn the food. When the time is up, carefully remove them from the cooking tray. Once done, serve and enjoy.
Per Serving: Calories 723; Fat 51.3g; Sodium 1880mg; Carbs 23.3g; Fiber 1g; Sugar 1.3g; Protein 40.6g

Garlic Chicken & Vegetables Nuggets

Prep time: 20 minutes| Cook time: 15 minutes| Serves: 4

½ of zucchini, roughly chopped
½ of carrot, roughly chopped
8 oz. chicken breast, cut into chunks
½ tablespoon mustard powder
1 tablespoon garlic powder

1 tablespoon onion powder
Salt and freshly ground black pepper, as needed
1 cup all-purpose flour
2 tablespoons milk
1 egg
1 cup panko breadcrumbs

Pulse the zucchini and carrot in a food processor until finely minced. Pulse the chicken with the mustard powder, garlic powder, onion powder, salt, and black pepper until thoroughly incorporated. Place the flour in a small dish. Combine the milk and egg in a second bowl. Place the breadcrumbs in a third dish. Coat the nuggets in flour first, then in the egg mixture, and finally in breadcrumbs. Arrange nuggets into cooking tray of air fryer. Using the display panel, select Air Fry, then adjust the temperature to 350 degrees F and the time to 15 minutes; touch the Start button to initiate preheating. When the display indicates "Add Food", place the cooking tray in the air fryer basket. When the display indicates "turn Food", turn the food. When the time is up, carefully remove them from the cooking tray. Once done, serve and enjoy.
Per Serving: Calories 371; Fat 6.4g; Sodium 118mg; Carbs 33.4g; Fiber 1.9g; Sugar 2.6g; Protein 27.9g

Tasty Cod Nuggets

Prep time: 15 minutes| Cook time: 8 minutes| Serves: 5

1 cup all-purpose flour
2 eggs
¾ cup breadcrumbs
Pinch of salt

2 tablespoons olive oil
1 lb. cod, cut into 1x2½-inch strips

Place the flour in a small dish. In a separate dish, crack the eggs and whisk them thoroughly. Combine the breadcrumbs, salt, and oil in a third dish. Coat the nuggets in flour first, then in beaten eggs, and finally in breadcrumbs. Arrange nuggets into cooking tray of air fryer. Using the display panel, select Air Fry, then adjust the temperature to 390 degrees F and the time to 8 minutes; touch the Start button to initiate preheating. When the display indicates "Add Food", place the cooking tray in the air fryer basket. When the display indicates "turn Food", turn the food. When the time is up, carefully remove them from the cooking tray. Once done, serve and enjoy.
Per Serving: Calories 323; Fat 9.2g; Sodium 245mg; Carbs 30.9g; Fiber 1.4g; Sugar 1.2g; Protein 27.7g

Paprika Garlic Chicken Wings

Prep time: 15 minutes| Cook time: 19 minutes| Serves: 4

2 lbs. chicken wings	Salt and ground black pepper,
1 teaspoon olive oil	as required
1 teaspoon smoked paprika	¼ cup BBQ sauce
1 teaspoon garlic powder	

Combine the chicken wings, smoked paprika, garlic powder, oil, salt, and pepper in a large mixing basin and toss thoroughly. Arrange chicken wings into cooking tray of air fryer. Using the display panel, select Air Fry, then adjust the temperature to 360 degrees F and the time to 19 minutes; touch the Start button to initiate preheating. When the display indicates "Add Food", place the cooking tray in the air fryer basket. When the display indicates "turn Food", turn the food. When the time is up, carefully remove them from the cooking tray. Once done, serve and enjoy.
Per Serving: Calories 468; Fat 18.1g; Sodium 409mg; Carbs 6.5g; Fiber 0.4g; Sugar 4.3g; Protein 65.8g

Crispy Buffalo Chicken Wings

Prep time: 15 minutes| Cook time: 15 minutes| Serves: 5

2 lbs. frozen chicken wings,	½ teaspoon red pepper flakes,
drums and flats separated	crushed
2 tablespoons olive oil	Salt, as required
2 tablespoons Buffalo sauce	

Evenly coat the chicken wings in oil. Arrange chicken wings into cooking tray of air fryer. Using the display panel, select Air Fry, then adjust the temperature to 390 degrees F and the time to 15 minutes; touch the Start button to initiate preheating. When the display indicates "Add Food", place the cooking tray in the air fryer basket. When the display indicates "turn Food", turn the food. When the time is up, carefully remove them from the cooking tray. Meanwhile, combine Buffalo sauce, red pepper flakes, and salt in a large mixing basin. Toss the wings in the Buffalo sauce basin to thoroughly coat them. Serve and enjoy
Per Serving: Calories 394; Fat 19.1g; Sodium 339mg; Carbs 0.2g; Fiber 0.1g; Sugar 0.1g; Protein 52.5g

Crispy Prawns with Nacho Chips

Prep time: 15 minutes| Cook time: 8 minutes| Serves: 4

1 egg	prawns, peeled and deveined
½ pound nacho chips, crushed	

Beat the egg in a small dish. Place the crushed nacho chips in a separate shallow dish. Roll the prawns in nacho chips after coating them in egg. Arrange the prawn rolls into cooking tray of air fryer. Using the display panel, select Air Fry, then adjust the temperature to 355 degrees F and the time to 8 minutes; touch the Start button to initiate preheating. When the display indicates "Add Food", place the cooking tray in the air fryer basket. When the display indicates "turn Food", turn the food. When the time is up, carefully remove them from the cooking tray. Once done, serve and enjoy.
Per Serving: Calories 386; Fat 17g; Sodium 525mg; Carbs 36.1g; Fiber 2.6g; Sugar 2.2g; Protein 21g

Coconut Pepper Shrimp

Prep time: 20 minutes| Cook time: 12 minutes| Serves: 4

large shrimp, peeled and	deveined

Salt and ground black pepper, as required	½ cup panko breadcrumbs
ounces coconut milk	½ teaspoon cayenne pepper

Combine salt, black pepper, and coconut milk in a shallow bowl. Combine breadcrumbs, cayenne pepper, salt, and black pepper in another shallow dish. After dipping the shrimp in the coconut milk mixture, roll them in the breadcrumbs mixture. Arrange shrimp into cooking tray of air fryer. Using the display panel, select Air Fry, then adjust the temperature to 350 degrees F and the time to 12 minutes; touch the Start button to initiate preheating. When the display indicates "Add Food", place the cooking tray in the air fryer basket. When the display indicates "turn Food", turn the food. When the time is up, carefully remove them from the cooking tray. Once done, serve and enjoy.
Per Serving: Calories 193; Fat 14.7g; Sodium 74mg; Carbs 5.5g; Fiber 1.4g; Sugar 1.9g; Protein 4.2g

Tasty Bacon Wrapped Shrimp

Prep time: 15 minutes| Cook time: 7 minutes| Serves: 6

1 lb. bacon, sliced thinly	deveined
1 lb. shrimp, peeled and	

Wrap one slice of bacon fully around each shrimp. Refrigerate the shrimp for about 20 minutes after placing them in a baking dish. Arrange shrimp into cooking tray of air fryer. Using the display panel, select Air Fry, then adjust the temperature to 390 degrees F and the time to 6 minutes; touch the Start button to initiate preheating. When the display indicates "Add Food", place the cooking tray in the air fryer basket. When the display indicates "turn Food", turn the food. When the time is up, carefully remove them from the cooking tray. Once done, serve and enjoy.
Per Serving: Calories 499; Fat 32.9g; Sodium 1931mg; Carbs 2.2g; Fiber 0g; Sugar 0g; Protein 45.3g

Olive Feta Tater Tots

Prep time: 15 minutes| Cook time: 25 minutes| Serves: 6

2 lbs. frozen tater tots	¼ cup black olives, pitted and
½ cup feta cheese, crumbled	sliced
½ cup tomato, chopped	¼ cup red onion, chopped

Arrange tater tots into cooking tray of air fryer. Using the display panel, select Air Fry, then adjust the temperature to 350 degrees F and the time to 25 minutes; touch the Start button to initiate preheating. When the display indicates "Add Food", place the cooking tray in the air fryer basket. When the display indicates "turn Food", turn the food and add the feta cheese, tomatoes, olives and onion and toss to coat well. When the time is up, carefully remove them from the cooking tray. Serve warm.
Per Serving: Calories 332; Fat 17.7g; Sodium 784mg; Carbs 37.9g; Fiber 4.1g; Sugar 2g; Protein 5.5g

Buttermilk Biscuits

Prep time: 15 minutes| Cook time: 10 minutes| Serves: 8

½ cup cake flour	Salt, to taste
1¼ cups all-purpose flour	¼ cup cold unsalted butter, cut
¼ teaspoon baking; Soda	into cubes
½ teaspoon baking; Powder	¾ cup buttermilk
1 teaspoon granulated sugar	2 tablespoons butter, melted

Sift together flours, baking soda, baking powder, sugar, and salt in a large mixing basin. Cut cold butter with a pastry cutter and mix

until a coarse crumb form. Slowly drizzle in the buttermilk and continue to mix until a smooth dough form. Place the dough on a floured surface and press it into a 12 inch thickness using your hands. Cut the biscuits with a 1¾-inch round cookie cutter. Arrange the biscuits in a suitable baking sheet and brush with butter. Arrange baking sheet into cooking tray of air fryer. Using the display panel, select Bake, then adjust the temperature to 400 degrees F and the time to 10 minutes; touch the Start button to initiate preheating. When the display indicates "Add Food", place the cooking tray in the air fryer basket. When the time is up, carefully remove them from the cooking tray. Once done, serve and enjoy.
Per Serving: Calories 187; Fat 9.1g; Sodium 144mg; Carbs 22.6g; Fiber 0.8g; Sugar 1.7g; Protein 3.7g

Yummy Vanilla Lemon Biscuits

Prep time: 15 minutes| Cook time: 5 minutes| Serves: 10

8½ oz. self-rising; Flour	grated finely
3½ oz. caster sugar	2 tablespoons fresh lemon
3½ oz. cold butter	juice
1 small egg	1 teaspoon vanilla extract
1 teaspoon fresh lemon zest,	

Combine flour and sugar in a large mixing bowl. Cut cold butter with a pastry cutter and mix until a coarse crumb form. Mix in the egg, lemon zest, and lemon juice until you have a soft dough. Turn the dough out onto a floured board and roll it out. Make medium-sized biscuits out of the dough. Arrange the biscuits in a suitable baking sheet and brush with butter. Arrange the baking sheet into cooking tray of air fryer. Using the display panel, select Air Fry, then adjust the temperature to 355 degrees F and the time to 10 minutes; touch the Start button to initiate preheating. When the display indicates "Add Food", place the cooking tray in the air fryer basket. When the display indicates "turn Food", turn the food. When the time is up, carefully remove them from the cooking tray. Once done, serve and enjoy.
Per Serving: Calories 203; Fat 8.7g; Sodium 63mg; Carbs 28.5g; Fiber 0.7g; Sugar 10.2g; Protein 3.1g

Tasty Veggie and Shrimp Spring Rolls

Prep time: 20 minutes| Cook time: 5 minutes| Serves: 6

1 tablespoon vegetable oil, divided	cut into matchsticks
4 oz. fresh mushrooms, sliced	1 scallion (green part), chopped
½ oz. canned water chestnuts, sliced	½ tablespoon soy sauce
½ teaspoon fresh ginger, finely grated	½ teaspoon Chinese five-spice powder
½ oz. bean sprouts	1½ oz. cooked shrimps
½ of small carrot, peeled and	spring roll wrappers
	1 small egg, beaten

Heat the oil in a skillet over medium heat, sautés the mushrooms, water chestnuts, and ginger for 2-3 minutes. Sauté for 1 minute with the bean sprouts, carrot, scallion, soy sauce, and five-spice powder. Remove the shrimps from the fire and stir them in. Allow to cool before serving. Place the spring rolls on a smooth surface and arrange them. Distribute the vegetable mixture evenly among the spring rolls. Wrap the filling in the wrappers and seal with a beaten egg. Apply the remaining oil to each roll. Replace the slices, filling, and oil with the remaining slices, filling, and oil. Arrange the rolls into cooking tray of air fryer. Using the display panel, select Air Fry, then adjust the temperature to 390 degrees F and the time to 5 minutes; touch the Start button to initiate preheating. When the display indicates "Add Food", place the cooking tray in the air fryer basket. When the display indicates "turn Food", turn the food. When the time

is up, carefully remove them from the cooking tray. Once done, serve and enjoy.
Per Serving: Calories 153; Fat 3.7g; Sodium 292mg; Carbs 22.6g; Fiber 1.4g; Sugar 1.5g; Protein 7.9g

Spinach Cheese Rolls with Mint

Prep time: 20 minutes| Cook time: 4 minutes| Serves: 6

1 red onion, chopped	Salt and freshly ground black
1 cup fresh parsley, chopped	pepper, as needed
1 cup fresh mint leaves, chopped	1 package frozen phyllo
1 egg	dough, thawed
1 cup feta cheese, crumbled	1 (16-oz.) package frozen
½ cup Romano cheese, grated	spinach, thawed
¼ teaspoon ground cardamom	2 tablespoons olive oil

Pulse all of the ingredients in a food processor until smooth, excluding the phyllo dough and oil. Cut one phyllo sheet into three rectangular strips on the cutting board. Apply the oil to each strip. Along the short side of a strip, place roughly 1 spoonful of the spinach mixture. To keep the filling in place, roll the dough. Replace the phyllo sheets and spinach mixture with the remaining phyllo sheets and spinach mixture. Arrange rolls into cooking tray of air fryer. Using the display panel, select Air Fry, then adjust the temperature to 355 degrees F and the time to 4 minutes; touch the Start button to initiate preheating. When the display indicates "Add Food", place the cooking tray in the air fryer basket. When the display indicates "turn Food", turn the food. When the time is up, carefully remove them from the cooking tray. Once done, serve and enjoy.
Per Serving: Calories 206; Fat 13.8g; Sodium 512mg; Carbs 12.4g; Fiber 3.6g; Sugar 2.3g; Protein 11g

Cheese Scallion Pastries

Prep time: 15 minutes| Cook time: 10 minutes| Serves: 6

1 egg yolk	Salt and ground black pepper,
4 oz. feta cheese, crumbled	as needed
1 scallion, finely chopped	2 frozen phyllo pastry sheets,
2 tablespoons fresh parsley,	thawed
finely chopped	2 tablespoons olive oil

Add the egg yolk to a large mixing basin and whisk well. Mix in the feta cheese, onion, parsley, salt, and black pepper until thoroughly combined. Each pastry sheet should be cut into three strips. On the bottom of a strip, spread roughly 1 teaspoon of the feta mixture. To make a triangle, fold the sheet's tip over the filling in a zigzag pattern. Continue with the rest of the strips and fillings. Using a pastry brush, evenly coat each pastry with oil. Arrange pastry into cooking tray of air fryer. Using the display panel, select Air Fry, then adjust the temperature to 390 degrees F and the time to 10 minutes; touch the Start button to initiate preheating. When the display indicates "Add Food", place the cooking tray in the air fryer basket. When the display indicates "turn Food", turn the food. When the time is up, carefully remove them from the cooking tray. Once done, serve and enjoy.
Per Serving: Calories 128; Fat 10g; Sodium 286mg; Carbs 6g; Fiber 0.3g; Sugar 0.9g; Protein 3.9g

Onion Cheese Spinach Dip

Prep time: 15 minutes| Cook time: 35 minutes| Serves: 8

1 (8-oz.) package cream cheese, softened	1 cup frozen spinach, thawed and squeezed
1 cup mayonnaise	⅓ cup water chestnuts, drained
1 cup Parmesan cheese, grated	and chopped

½ cup onion, minced
¼ teaspoon garlic powder

Ground black pepper, as required

In a bowl, add all the ingredients and mix until well combined. Transfer the mixture into a suitable baking pan and spread in an even layer. Arrange the baking pan into cooking tray of air fryer. Using the display panel, select Air Fry, then adjust the temperature to 300 degrees F and the time to 35 minutes; touch the Start button to initiate preheating. When the display indicates "Add Food", place the cooking tray in the air fryer basket. When the time is up, carefully remove them from the cooking tray. Once done, serve and enjoy.
Per Serving: Calories 258; Fat 22.1g; Sodium 384mg; Carbs 9.4g; Fiber 0.3g; Sugar 2.3g; Protein 6.7g

Chili Cheese Dip

Prep time: 10 minutes| Cook time: 15 minutes| Serves: 8

1 (8-oz.) package cream cheese, softened
1 (16-oz.) can Hormel chili

without beans
1 (16-oz.) package mild cheddar cheese, shredded

Place the cream cheese in a suitable baking pan and spread it out evenly. Chili should be uniformly distributed on top, followed by the cheddar cheese. Arrange the baking pan into cooking tray of air fryer. Using the display panel, select Bake, then adjust the temperature to 375 degrees F and the time to 15 minutes; touch the Start button to initiate preheating. When the display indicates "Add Food", place the cooking tray in the air fryer basket. When the time is up, carefully remove them from the cooking tray. Once done, serve and enjoy.
Per Serving: Calories 388; Fat 31.3g; Sodium 674mg; Carbs 5.6g; Fiber 0.7g; Sugar 1.1g; Protein 21.1g

Cheese Onion Dip

Prep time: 10 minutes| Cook time: 45 minutes| Serves: 10

⅔ cup onion, chopped
1 cup cheddar jack cheese, shredded
½ cup Swiss cheese, shredded
¼ cup Parmesan cheese,

shredded
⅔ cup whipped salad dressing
½ cup milk
Salt, as required

Combine all of the ingredients in a large mixing basin and stir thoroughly. Fill a suitable baking pan halfway with the ingredients and smooth it out evenly. Arrange the baking pan into cooking tray of air fryer. Using the display panel, select Air Fry, then adjust the temperature to 375 degrees F and the time to 45 minutes; touch the Start button to initiate preheating. When the display indicates "Add Food", place the cooking tray in the air fryer basket. When the display indicates "turn Food", turn the food. When the time is up, carefully remove them from the cooking tray. Once done, serve and enjoy.
Per Serving: Calories 87; Fat 6g; Sodium 140mg; Carbs 2.3g; Fiber 0.3g; Sugar 1.1g; Protein 5.1g

Tasty Honey Baby Carrots

Prep time: 25 minutes| Cook time: 20 minutes| Serves: 4

1 pound baby carrots
2 tablespoons unsalted butter
2 tablespoons honey

1 teaspoon fresh dill
1 teaspoon parsley flakes

In a mixing dish, combine all of the ingredients. Arrange baby carrots into cooking tray of air fryer. Using the display panel,

select Air Fry, then adjust the temperature to 380 degrees F and the time to 20 minutes; touch the Start button to initiate preheating. When the display indicates "Add Food", place the cooking tray in the air fryer basket. When the display indicates "turn Food", turn the food. When the time is up, carefully remove them from the cooking tray. Once done, serve and enjoy.
Per Serving: Calories 123; Fat 5.9g; Sodium 130mg; Carbs 12.3g; Fiber 3.4g; Sugar 14g; Protein 0.9g

Crispy Paprika Vidalia Onion Rings

Prep time: 10 minutes| Cook time: 10 minutes| Serves: 4

2 large Vidalia onions, peeled and sliced
¾ cup all-purpose flour
2 eggs
2 tablespoons milk

1 cup seasoned breadcrumbs
1 teaspoon smoked paprika
Sea salt and ground black pepper, to taste
2 tablespoons olive oil

Place the onion rings in a bowl of very cold water and soak them for about 20 minutes. Drain and pat dry the onion rings. Incorporate flour, eggs, and milk in a small bowl and stir well to combine. Combine bread crumbs, paprika, salt, black pepper, and olive oil in a shallow basin. Dredge the onion rings in the breadcrumb mixture after dipping them in the flour/egg mixture. To uniformly coat them, roll them. Arrange breaded onion rings into cooking tray of air fryer. Using the display panel, select Air Fry, then adjust the temperature to 390 degrees F and the time to 10 minutes; touch the Start button to initiate preheating. When the display indicates "Add Food", place the cooking tray in the air fryer basket. When the display indicates "turn Food", turn the food. When the time is up, carefully remove them from the cooking tray. Once done, serve and enjoy.
Per Serving: Calories 322; Fat 13.2g; Sodium 388mg; Carbs 42.3g; Fiber 3.4g; Sugar 3.8g; Protein 9.4g

Parsley Parmesan Cocktail Meatballs

Prep time: 10 minutes| Cook time: 20 minutes| Serves: 6

1 pound ground pork
½ pound ground beef
1 cup breadcrumbs
¼ cup milk
4 cloves garlic, pressed or minced
2 eggs, beaten

1 cup Parmesan cheese, grated
¼ cup parsley, chopped
1 small onion, chopped
1 teaspoon dried oregano
1 teaspoon cayenne pepper
Sea salt and ground black pepper, to taste

Combine all of the ingredients in a mixing dish and stir thoroughly. Then, using a tiny scoop, place rounds of the mixture in a single layer onto the prepared pan. Arrange the pan into cooking tray of air fryer. Using the display panel, select Air Fry, then adjust the temperature to 350 degrees F and the time to 15 minutes; touch the Start button to initiate preheating. When the display indicates "Add Food", place the cooking tray in the air fryer basket. When the display indicates "turn Food", turn the food. When the time is up, carefully remove them from the cooking tray. Once done, serve and enjoy.
Per Serving: Calories 301; Fat 8.8g; Sodium 271mg; Carbs 16g; Fiber 1.3g; Sugar 2.3g; Protein 37.7g

Honey Garlic Chicken Wings

Prep time: 10 minutes| Cook time: 15 minutes| Serves: 5

1 pound chicken wings
¼ cup all-purpose flour
Kosher salt and ground black

pepper, to taste
2 teaspoons olive oil
¼ cup honey

2 tablespoons soy sauce

2 garlic cloves, crushed

1 teaspoon red chili flakes

¼ cup beer

Dry the chicken wings with a paper towel. Combine the remaining ingredients in a large mixing bowl and stir until thoroughly combined. Arrange the chicken wings into cooking tray of air fryer. Using the display panel, select Air Fry, then adjust the temperature to 375 degrees F and the time to 10 minutes; touch the Start button to initiate preheating. When the display indicates "Add Food", place the cooking tray in the air fryer basket. When the display indicates "turn Food", turn the food. When the time is up, carefully remove them from the cooking tray. Once done, serve and enjoy.

Per Serving: Calories 271; Fat 8.7g; Sodium 440mg; Carbs 19.7g; Fiber 0.3g; Sugar 14.1g; Protein 27.4g

Crunchy Italian Cheese Sticks

Prep time: 10 minutes| Cook time: 7 minutes| Serves: 6

2 medium eggs

1 teaspoon Italian seasoning

1 cup Italian breadcrumbs

(1-ounce) mozzarella sticks

Place a sheet of parchment paper in the air fryer oven pan. Whisk the eggs in a mixing bowl; then, add in the seasoning and breadcrumbs and mix to combine well. Dip each mozzarella stick into the egg mixture. Arrange the mozzarella sticks to the cooking tray and then place the tray into the air fryer basket. Air Fry your mozzarella sticks for 5 minutes at 390 degrees F; turn them over and continue to cook for a further 2 minutes or until they are golden brown and crispy. Bon appétit!

Per Serving: Calories 108; Fat 3.5g; Sodium 181mg; Carbs 13.3g; Fiber 0.8g; Sugar 1.3g; Protein 5.6g

Yummy Wonton Wraps with Sausage

Prep time: 10 minutes| Cook time: 15 minutes| Serves: 10

1 pound smoked sausage, crumbled

2 scallion stalks, chopped

2 tablespoons fish sauce

1 teaspoon ginger-garlic paste

1 package (12-ounce) wonton wrappers

1 egg

1 tablespoon olive oil

Combine crumbled sausage, scallions, fish sauce, and ginger-garlic paste in a mixing bowl. Fill wonton wrappers halfway with the mixture. Whisk together 1 tablespoon olive oil and 1 tablespoon water in a bowl. Fold the wonton in half and set aside. Bring the two ends of the wonton up and stick them together with the egg wash. Pinch the edges of each wonton and brush with egg wash. Arrange folded wontons into cooking tray of air fryer and make sure not to crowd them. Using the display panel, select Air Fry, then adjust the temperature to 380 degrees F and the time to 10 minutes; touch the Start button to initiate preheating. When the display indicates "Add Food", place the cooking tray in the air fryer basket. When the display indicates "turn Food", turn the food. When the time is up, carefully remove them from the cooking tray. Once done, serve and enjoy.

Per Serving: Calories 187; Fat 15g; Sodium 642mg; Carbs 2.2g; Fiber 0.1g; Sugar 0.2g; Protein 9.9g

Yummy Tasty Coconut Banana

Prep time: 10 minutes| Cook time: 15 minutes| Serves: 2

2 medium bananas, sliced

1 tablespoon avocado oil

2 tablespoons coconut flakes

Toss the banana with oil. Arrange banana slice into cooking tray of air fryer. Using the display panel, select Air Fry, then adjust the temperature to 350 degrees F and the time to 15 minutes; touch the Start button to initiate preheating. When the display indicates "Add Food", place the cooking tray in the air fryer basket. When the display indicates "turn Food", turn the food. When the time is up, carefully remove them from the cooking tray. Once done, sprinkle with the coconut flakes, serve and enjoy.

Per Serving: Calories 132; Fat 3g; Sodium 2mg; Carbs 28.3g; Fiber 3.8g; Sugar 14.1g; Protein 1.6g

Honey Cinnamon Apple Chips

Prep time: 10 minutes| Cook time: 15 minutes| Serves: 4

2 medium apples, cored and sliced

1 tablespoon coconut oil, melted

2 tablespoons honey

¼ teaspoon grated nutmeg

1 teaspoon ground cinnamon

Toss the apples with the remaining ingredients in a large mixing bowl. Arrange banana fies into cooking tray of air fryer. Using the display panel, select Air Fry, then adjust the temperature to 350 degrees F and the time to 15 minutes; touch the Start button to initiate preheating. When the display indicates "Add Food", place the cooking tray in the air fryer basket. When the display indicates "turn Food", turn the food. When the time is up, carefully remove them from the cooking tray. Once done, serve and enjoy.

Per Serving: Calories 121; Fat 3.6g; Sodium 2mg; Carbs 24.3g; Fiber 3.1g; Sugar 20.3g; Protein 0.4g

Garlic Parmesan Broccoli Florets

Prep time: 05 minutes| Cook time: 12 minutes | Serves: 2

2 tbsp. butter, melted

1 egg white

1 garlic clove, grated

¼ tsp salt

A pinch of black pepper

½ lb. broccoli florets

⅓ cup grated Parmesan cheese

In a bowl, whisk together the butter, egg, garlic, salt, and black pepper. Toss in broccoli to coat well. Top with Parmesan cheese and; toss to coat. Arrange broccoli in a single layer in the cooking tray, without overcrowding. Using the display panel, select Air Fry, then adjust the temperature to 340 degrees F and the time to 12 minutes, then touch Start button to initiate preheating. When the display indicates "Add Food", place the cooking tray in the air fryer basket. When the display indicates "turn Food", turn the food. When the time up carefully remove them from the cooking tray Remove to a serving; Plate and sprinkle with Parmesan cheese.

Per Serving: Calories 166; Fat 12.9g; Sodium 470mg; Carbs 8.4g; Fiber 3g; Sugar 2.1g; Protein 6.7 g

Garlic Onion Chicken Nuggets

Prep time: 10 minutes| Cook time: 20 minutes| Serves: 5

1 pound chicken breasts, sliced into bite-sized pieces

3 eggs

1 cup plain flour

1 teaspoon smoked paprika

1 teaspoon mustard powder

1 teaspoon garlic powder

1 teaspoon onion powder

Sea salt and ground black pepper, to taste

1 cup tortilla chips, crushed

Set the chicken aside after patting it dry. Whisk the egg in a shallow bowl until pale and foamy, then gradually add the flour and spices. Toss the chicken breasts in the bowl until they are thoroughly coated on both sides. Place the crushed tortilla chips in a separate shallow bowl. Roll the chicken breasts in crushed tortilla chips until completely covered. Coat the chicken breasts

with the remaining ingredients. Arrange the chicken breasts into cooking tray of air fryer. Using the display panel, select Air Fry, then adjust the temperature to 350 degrees F and the time to 15 minutes; touch the Start button to initiate preheating. When the display indicates "Add Food", insert one cooking tray in the air fryer basket. When the display indicates "turn Food", turn the food. When the time is up, carefully remove them from the cooking tray. Once done, serve and enjoy.
Per Serving: Calories 319; Fat 10g; Sodium 118mg; Carbs 22.3g; Fiber 1.3g; Sugar 0.1g; Protein 35.1g

Spicy Cheese Avocado Fritters

Prep time: 10 minutes| Cook time: 6 minutes| Serves: 4

2 large eggs	A few dashes of hot sauce
1 cup seasoned breadcrumbs	2 avocados, peeled, pitted and
½ cup parmesan cheese, grated	cut into wedges
Sea salt and ground black	2 teaspoon peanut oil (or
pepper, to taste	sesame oil)

Whisk the eggs in a small dish until foamy. Combine the breadcrumbs, cheese, salt, black pepper, and hot sauce in a mixing bowl. Using the breadcrumb mixture, coat the avocado wedges. Brush the avocado wedges on all sides with peanut oil. Arrange the avocado wedges into cooking tray of air fryer. Place the cooking tray in the air fryer basket of your air fryer. Using the display panel, select Air Fry, then adjust the temperature to 400 degrees F and the time to 6 minutes; touch the Start button to initiate preheating. When the display indicates "Add Food", place the cooking tray in the air fryer basket. When the display indicates "turn Food", turn the food. When the time is up, carefully remove them from the cooking tray. Once done, serve and enjoy.
Per Serving: Calories 382; Fat 28.6g; Sodium 455mg; Carbs 23g; Fiber 7.7g; Sugar 0.7g; Protein 9.1g

Paprika Rosemary Potato Wedges

Prep time: 10 minutes| Cook time: 35 minutes| Serves: 4

1 pound potatoes, peeled and	1 teaspoon garlic powder
cut into wedges	1 teaspoon yellow mustard
1 tablespoon dried rosemary,	Kosher salt and freshly ground
chopped	black pepper, to taste
1 teaspoon hot paprika	2 teaspoons olive oil

Toss the potato wedges with the remaining ingredients. Arrange potatoes wedges into cooking tray of air fryer. Using the display panel, select Air Fry, then adjust the temperature to 400 degrees F and the time to 35 minutes; touch the Start button to initiate preheating. When the display indicates "Add Food", place the cooking tray in the air fryer basket. When the display indicates "turn Food", turn the food. When the time is up, carefully remove them from the cooking tray. Once done, serve and enjoy.
Per Serving: Calories 107; Fat 2.6g; Sodium 88mg; Carbs19.3g; Fiber 3.3g; Sugar 1.7g; Protein 2.2g

Parsley Garlic French Bread

Prep time: 10 minutes| Cook time: 10 minutes| Serves: 4

1 loaf French bread, sliced	pepper, to taste
2 garlic cloves, minced	1 tablespoon dried parsley flakes
2 tablespoons olive oil	4 tablespoons Parmesan
Sea salt and ground black	cheese, grated

Toss the bread slices with the remaining ingredients in a large mixing bowl. Arrange the bread slices into cooking tray of air fryer. Using the display panel, select Air Fry, then adjust the

temperature to 350 degrees F and the time to 10 minutes; touch the Start button to initiate preheating. When the display indicates "Add Food", place the cooking tray in the air fryer basket. When the display indicates "turn Food", turn the food. When the time is up, carefully remove them from the cooking tray. Once done, serve and enjoy.
Per Serving: Calories 199; Fat 13.3g; Sodium 365mg; Carbs 10.6g; Fiber 0.4g; Sugar 0.4g; Protein 11g

Pepper Chicken Wings in BBQ Sauce

Prep time: 10 minutes| Cook time: 10 minutes| Serves: 5

1 ½ pounds chicken wings	Kosher salt and ground black
1 cup BBQ sauce	pepper, to taste
1 tablespoon olive oil	

Mix chicken wings with the remaining ingredients. Arrange the coated chicken wings into cooking tray of air fryer. Using the display panel, select Air Fry, then adjust the temperature to 350 degrees F and the time to 10 minutes; touch the Start button to initiate preheating. When the display indicates "Add Food", place the cooking tray in the air fryer basket. When the display indicates "turn Food", turn the food. When the time is up, carefully remove them from the cooking tray. Once done, serve and enjoy.
Per Serving: Calories 358; Fat 13g; Sodium 677mg; Carbs 18.1g; Fiber 0.3g; Sugar 13g; Protein 39.4g

Garlic Cheese Cauliflower Fritters

Prep time: 10 minutes| Cook time: 15 minutes| Serves: 4

1 pound cauliflower florets	2 spring onions, chopped
2 teaspoons olive oil	1garlic clove, minced
1 cup all-purpose flour	2 large eggs, whisked
1 cup cheddar cheese, grated	1 cup crushed crackers

Combine all of the ingredients thoroughly. Arrange the cauliflower fritters into cooking tray of air fryer. Using the display panel, select Air Fry, then adjust the temperature to 350 degrees F and the time to 15 minutes; touch the Start button to initiate preheating. When the display indicates "Add Food", place the cooking tray in the air fryer basket . When the display indicates "turn Food", turn the food. When the time is up, carefully remove them from the cooking tray. Once done, serve and enjoy.
Per Serving: Calories 345; Fat 16.1g; Sodium 291mg; Carbs 35g; Fiber 3.9g; Sugar 4.1g; Protein 15.1g

Baked Garlic Rosemary Pita Wedges

Prep time: 10 minutes| Cook time: 10 minutes| Serves: 4

4 small pitas, cut into triangles	1 teaspoon dried oregano
2 tablespoons extra-virgin	1 teaspoon dried rosemary
olive oil	Coarse sea salt and ground
1 teaspoon garlic powder	black pepper, to season

Mix pita triangles with the remaining ingredients. Arrange pita triangles into cooking tray of air fryer. Using the display panel, select Air Fry, then adjust the temperature to 330 degrees F and the time to 10 minutes; touch the Start button to initiate preheating. When the display indicates "Add Food", place the cooking tray in the air fryer basket . When the display indicates "turn Food", turn the food. When the time is up, carefully remove them from the cooking tray. Once done, serve and enjoy.

Garlicky Pepper Broccoli Florets

Prep time: 10 minutes| Cook time: 15 minutes| Serves: 4

1-pound broccoli florets
2 garlic cloves, crushed
1 teaspoon red pepper flakes

2 tablespoons olive oil
Sea salt and ground black pepper, to taste

Mix all the ingredients in a big bowl. Arrange the coated broccoli florets into cooking tray of air fryer. Using the display panel, select Air Fry, then adjust the temperature to 350 degrees F and the time to 15 minutes; touch the Start button to initiate preheating. Place the tray into the air fryer basket. When the display indicates "Add Food", place the cooking tray in the air fryer basket . When the display indicates "turn Food", turn the food. When the time is up, carefully remove them from the cooking tray. Once done, serve and enjoy.
Per Serving: Calories 102; Fat 7.5g; Sodium 38mg; Carbs 8.3g; Fiber 3.1g; Sugar 2g; Protein 3.3g

Ginger Garlic Cheese Shrimp Pot Stickers

Prep time: 10 minutes| Cook time: 10 minutes| Serves: 6

12 medium shrimp, peeled and chopped
1 teaspoon ginger-garlic paste
2 tablespoons cocktail sauce
4 tablespoons cream cheese,

room temperature
½ teaspoon red pepper flakes, crushed
1 (12-ounce) package wrappers
2 teaspoon olive oil

Combine the shrimp, ginger-garlic paste, cocktail sauce, cream cheese, and red pepper flakes in a mixing bowl. Fill wonton wrappers halfway with the mixture. Fold the wonton in half and set aside. Bring the two ends of the wonton together by bringing them up. Brush each wonton with olive oil after pinching the edges. Arrange the wonton wrappers into cooking tray of air fryer. Using the display panel, select Air Fry, then adjust the temperature to 380 degrees F and the time to 10 minutes; touch the Start button to initiate preheating. Place the tray into the air fryer basket. When the display indicates "Add Food", place the cooking tray in the air fryer basket . When the display indicates "turn Food", turn the food. When the time is up, carefully remove them from the cooking tray. Once done, serve and enjoy.
Per Serving: Calories 433; Fat 8.1g; Sodium 1040mg; Carbs 41.3g; Fiber 1.1g; Sugar 4.4g; Protein 44.1g

Balsamic Pepper Baby Carrots

Prep time: 10 minutes| Cook time: 25 minutes| Serves: 4

1 pound baby carrots
1 stick butter
3 tablespoons agave nectar

2 tablespoons balsamic vinegar
Sea salt and cayenne pepper, to taste

Mix all the ingredients in a mixing bowl. Arrange the baby carrots into cooking tray of air fryer. Using the display panel, select Air Fry, then adjust the temperature to 380 degrees F and the time to 20 minutes; touch the Start button to initiate preheating. When the display indicates "Add Food", place the cooking tray into the air fryer basket. When the display indicates "turn Food", turn the food. When the time is up, carefully remove them from the cooking tray. Once done, serve and enjoy.
Per Serving: Calories 287; Fat 23.1g; Sodium 252mg; Carbs 21.3g; Fiber 4g; Sugar 16.1g; Protein 1g

Almond Pepper Cheese Bites

Prep time: 10 minutes| Cook time: 15 minutes| Serves: 4

2 eggs
⅓ cup almond flour
¼ cup parmesan cheese grated
3 tablespoons mayonnaise
1 teaspoon cayenne pepper

½ teaspoon garlic powder
1 teaspoon Italian seasoning mix
(1-ounce) cheese sticks

In a mixing dish, whisk the eggs; then add the almond flour, cheese, mayonnaise, and spices; stir well to blend. Each cheese stick should be dipped in the egg/flour mixture. Arrange cheese stick into cooking tray of air fryer Using the display panel, select Air Fry, then adjust the temperature to 350 degrees F and the time to 15 minutes; touch the Start button to initiate preheating. When the display indicates "Add Food", place the cooking tray in the air fryer basket. When the display indicates "turn Food", turn the food. When the time is up, carefully remove them from the cooking tray. Once done, serve and enjoy.
Per Serving: Calories 199; Fat 13.1g; Sodium 253mg; Carbs 5.7g; Fiber 1.2g; Sugar 1.3g; Protein 7.3g

Mustard Onion Rings

Prep time: 10 minutes| Cook time: 15 minutes| Serves: 4

1 large onion, peeled and sliced
1 cup seasoned breadcrumbs
½ cup mayonnaise

1 teaspoon cumin powder
½ teaspoon mustard powder
Kosher salt and ground black pepper, to taste

Mix the onion rings with the other ingredients. Arrange onion rings into cooking tray of air fryer. Using the display panel, select Air Fry, then adjust the temperature to 350 degrees F and the time to 10 minutes; touch the Start button to initiate preheating. When the display indicates "Add Food", place the cooking tray in the air fryer basket. When the display indicates "turn Food", turn the food. When the time is up, carefully remove them from the cooking tray. Once done, serve and enjoy.
Per Serving: Calories 287; Fat 23.1g; Sodium 252mg; Carbs 21.3g; Fiber 4g; Sugar 16.1g; Protein 1g

Garlic Turkey Scallion Cheese Meatballs

Prep time: 10 minutes| Cook time: 10 minutes| Serves: 6

1 pound ground turkey
½ pound ground pork
¼ cup scallions, chopped
¼ cup fresh parsley leaves, chopped
2 cloves garlic, minced
1 cup breadcrumbs

½ cup cream of celery soup
2 eggs, beaten
½ cup Pecorino Romano cheese, grated
Sea salt and ground black pepper, to taste

Combine all of the ingredients in a mixing dish and stir well. Then, using a tiny scoop, place rounds of the mixture in a single layer onto the prepared pan. Arrange meatballs into cooking tray of air fryer. Using the display panel, select Air Fry, then adjust the temperature to 350 degrees F and the time to 10 minutes; touch the Start button to initiate preheating. When the display indicates "Add Food" insert one cooking tray in the in the top position. When the display indicates "turn Food", turn the food. When the time is up, carefully remove them from the cooking tray. Once done, serve and enjoy.

Per Serving: Calories 482; Fat 20.5g; Sodium 665mg; Carbs 23.1g; Fiber 1.7g; Sugar2.5g; Protein 54.11g

Montreal Chicken Wings

Prep time: 10 minutes| Cook time: 10 minutes| Serves: 6

2 pounds chicken wings	chopped
1 cup tomato sauce	1 tablespoon fresh parsley,
2 tablespoons olive oil	chopped
1 teaspoon Montreal seasoning mix	1 tablespoon fresh cilantro, chopped
1 tablespoon fresh basil,	

In the air fryer oven perforated pan, arrange the chicken wings in a single layer. Arrange chicken wings into cooking tray of air fryer Using the display panel, select Air Fry, then adjust the temperature to 350 degrees F and the time to 10 minutes; touch the Start button to initiate preheating. When the display indicates "Add Food", place the cooking tray in the air fryer basket. When the display indicates "turn Food", turn the food. When the time is up, carefully remove them from the cooking tray. Once done, serve and enjoy.
Per Serving: Calories 253; Fat 12g; Sodium 260mg; Carbs 1.7g; Fiber 0.5g; Sugar 1.3g; Protein 33.3g

Double Cheese Balls

Prep time: 10 minutes| Cook time: 15 minutes| Serves: 4

1 cup cheddar cheese, grated	Kosher salt and ground black
1 cup gruyere cheese, grated	pepper, to taste
1 egg	1 teaspoon olive oil
½ cup all-purpose flour	

Combine all of the ingredients thoroughly. Form the mixture into equal-sized balls and arrange them in a single layer in the cooking tray of the air fryer. Using the display panel, select Air Fry, then adjust the temperature to 350 degrees F and the time to 15 minutes; touch the Start button to initiate preheating. When the display indicates "Add Food", place the cooking tray in the air fryer basket. When the display indicates "turn Food", turn the food. When the time is up, carefully remove them from the cooking tray. Once done, serve and enjoy.
Per Serving: Calories 308; Fat 20.5g; Sodium 282mg; Carbs 12.5g; Fiber 0.4g; Sugar 0.4g; Protein 18.1g

Cheese Prawn Wontons

Prep time: 10 minutes| Cook time: 15 minutes| Serves: 4

2 ounces shrimp, peeled, deveined and chopped	2 cloves garlic, minced
4 ounces cream cheese, at room temperature	1 teaspoon Sriracha, optional
	Sea salt and ground black pepper, to taste
2 teaspoons sesame oil	4 wonton wrappers
2 tablespoons green olive, chopped	1 extra-large egg, well beaten with 1 tablespoon of water

All of the ingredients, except the wonton wrappers, should be properly combined in a mixing bowl. Distribute the filling among the wonton wrappers. Each wonton should be folded in half. Bring the two ends of the wonton up and stick them together with the egg wash. Pinch the edges of each wonton and brush with egg wash. Arrange wonton wrappers into cooking tray of air fryer. Using the display panel, select Air Fry, then adjust the temperature to 380 degrees F and the time to 10 minutes; touch the Start button to initiate preheating. When the display indicates "Add Food", place the cooking tray in the

air fryer basket. When the display indicates "turn Food", turn the food. When the time is up, carefully remove them from the cooking tray. Once done, serve and enjoy.
Per Serving: Calories 257; Fat 14.7g; Sodium 395mg; Carbs 20.3g; Fiber 0.8g; Sugar 0.2g; Protein 10.3g

Sugar Apple Pear Fritters

Prep time: 10 minutes| Cook time: 15 minutes| Serves: 4

2 large pears, cored and sliced	3 tablespoons butter, melted
1 cup plain flour	A pinch of kosher salt
½ cup granulated sugar	A pinch of grated nutmeg
1 tablespoon baking Powder	½ teaspoon cinnamon
½ cup apple juice	1 teaspoon vanilla
2 large eggs, whisked	

Combine all of the ingredients thoroughly. Form the mixture into equal-sized patties and arrange them in a single layer in the cooking tray of air fryer. Using the display panel, select Air Fry, then adjust the temperature to 380 degrees F and the time to 10 minutes; touch the Start button to initiate preheating. When the display indicates "Add Food", place the cooking tray in the air fryer basket. When the display indicates "turn Food", turn the food. When the time is up, carefully remove them from the cooking tray. Once done, serve and enjoy.
Per Serving: Calories 387; Fat 11.7g; Sodium 141mg; Carbs 67.3g; Fiber 3.7g; Sugar 36.1g; Protein 6.8g

Pepper Ranch Russet Potato Wedges

Prep time: 10 minutes| Cook time: 40 minutes| Serves: 5

1-pound russet potatoes, peeled and cut into wedges	1 teaspoon dry ranch seasoning
¼ cup olive oil	Kosher salt and cayenne pepper, to taste
½ teaspoon hot paprika	

Mix the potato wedges with the remaining ingredients. Arrange potato wedges into cooking tray of air fryer Using the display panel, select Air Fry, then adjust the temperature to 350 degrees F and the time to 35 minutes; touch the Start button to initiate preheating. When the display indicates "Add Food", place the cooking tray in the air fryer basket. When the display indicates "turn Food", turn the food. When the time is up, carefully remove them from the cooking tray. Once done, serve and enjoy.
Per Serving: Calories 152; Fat 10.2g; Sodium 77mg; Carbs 14.5g; Fiber 2.2g; Sugar 1.1g; Protein 1.6g

Roasted Black Pepper Cashews

Prep time: 05 minutes| Cook time: 5 minutes | Serves: 6

1½ cups raw cashew nuts	Salt and freshly ground black
1 teaspoon butter, melted	pepper, as needed

In a bowl, mix together all the ingredients. Arrange the cashews in cooking tray of air fryer. Using the display panel, select Air Fry, then adjust the temperature to 355 degrees F and the time to 5 minutes, then touch Start button to initiate preheating. When the display indicates "Add Food", place the cooking tray in the air fryer basket. When the display indicates "turn Food", turn the food. When the time up carefully remove them from the cooking tray. Shake the cashews once halfway through. Serve warm.
Per Serving: Calories 726; Fat 58.8g; Sodium 25mg; Carbs 41.1g; Fiber 3.8g; Sugar 6.3g; Protein 19.2g

Fish and Seafood Recipes

Cod and Tomatoes

Prep time: 15 minutes| Cook time: 15 minutes| Serves: 4

1 cup cherry tomatoes; halved
4 cod fillets, skinless and boneless
2 tablespoons olive oil

2 tablespoons Cilantro; chopped.
Salt
Pepper

Mix all the ingredients in the cooking tray, and mix gently. Select the "Air Fry" mode on your air fryer. Press Temp button and then turn the dial to adjust the cooking temperature to 370 degrees F. Press Time button and then turn the dial to adjust the cooking time to 15 minutes. Press the Start button to initiate preheating. When the screen displays "Add Food", transfer the cooking tray to the air fryer basket of your Air Fryer. Close its door, and let the machine do the cooking. Divide everything between plates and serve right away.
Per serving: Calories 285; Fat 9.8g; Sodium 639mg; Carbs 11.1g; Fiber 1.2g, Sugars 5.1g; Protein 27.8g

Crab Dip

Prep time: 15 minutes| Cook time: 8 minutes| Serves: 4

8 oz. full-fat cream cheese; softened.
2 (6-oz.) can lump crabmeat
¼ cup chopped pickled jalapeños.
¼ cup full-fat sour cream.

½ cup shredded Cheddar cheese
¼ cup full-fat mayo
1 tablespoon Lemon juice
¼ cup sliced green onion
½ teaspoon hot sauce

Place all ingredients into a suitable cup round baking pan and toss until thoroughly combined. Place dish into the baking pan Select the "Air Fry" mode on your air fryer. Press Temp button and then turn the dial to adjust the cooking temperature to 400 degrees F. Press Time button and then turn the dial to adjust the cooking time to 8 minutes. Press the Start button to initiate preheating. When the screen displays "Add Food", transfer the pan to the air fryer basket of you Air Fryer. Close its door, and let the machine do the cooking. When done, the dip will be bubbling and hot,
Per serving: Calories 336; Fat 17.3g; Sodium 281mg; Carbs 8.1g; Fiber 5.3g, Sugars 17.7g; Protein 32.3g

Crispy Paprika Fillets

Prep time: 15 minutes| Cook time: 15 minutes| Serves: 2

2 fish fillets halved
1egg, beaten
½ cup seasoned breadcrumbs
1 tablespoon balsamic vinegar
½ teaspoon seasoned salt

1 teaspoon paprika
½ teaspoon ground black pepper
1 teaspoon celery seed

In a bowl, add the breadcrumbs, vinegar, pepper, salt, paprika, and celery seeds and mix well. Coat the fish fillets with the beaten egg; then, coat them with the breadcrumbs mixture. Pour into the cooking tray. Select the "Air Fry" mode on your air fryer. Press Temp button and then turn the dial to adjust the cooking temperature to 350 degrees F. Press Time button and then turn the dial to adjust the cooking time to 15 minutes. Press the Start button to initiate preheating. When the screen displays "Add Food", transfer the cooking tray to the air fryer basket of your Air Fryer. Close its door, and let the machine do the cooking. Serve.
Per serving: Calories 344; Fat 14.9g; Sodium 227mg; Carbs 14g; Fiber 1g; Sugars 1.4g; Protein 25.7g

Dijon Maple Salmon

Prep time: 15 minutes| Cook time: 12 minutes| Serves: 4

4 salmon fillets
2 tablespoons olive oil
¼ cups Dijon mustard

¼ cups maple syrup
2 garlic cloves, minced
Salt and black pepper, to taste

Line the cooking tray with foil and set aside. Place salmon fillets into the baking pan. Stir Dijon mustard, maple syrup, garlic, olive oil, pepper, salt, and pour over salmon. Coat well and let the food sit for 10 minutes. Select the "Air Fry" mode on your air fryer. Press Temp button and then turn the dial to adjust the cooking temperature to 400 degrees F. Press Time button and then turn the dial to adjust the cooking time to 12 minutes. Press the Start button to initiate preheating. When the screen displays "Add Food", transfer the cooking tray to the air fryer basket of your Air Fryer. Close its door, and let the machine do the cooking. Serve.
Per serving: Calories 236; Fat 13.9g; Sodium 451mg; Carbs 13.2g; Fiber 1.2g; Sugars 1.4g; Protein 14.3g

Air Fried Tilapia

Prep time: 15 minutes| Cook time: 15 minutes| Serves: 2

1-pound tilapia fillets
1 tablespoon garlic, minced
2 tablespoon dried parsley

1 tablespoon olive oil
Salt and black pepper, to taste

Line the cooking tray with foil and set aside. Place the tilapia fillets on the tray. Drizzle with oil and season with salt and black pepper. Sprinkle parsley and garlic over fish fillets. Select the "Air Fry" mode on your air fryer. Press Temp button and then turn the dial to adjust the cooking temperature to 400 degrees F. Press Time button and then turn the dial to adjust the cooking time to 15 minutes. Press the Start button to initiate preheating. When the screen displays "Add Food", transfer the cooking tray to the air fryer basket of your Air Fryer. Close its door, and let the machine do the cooking. Serve warm.
Per serving: Calories 285; Fat 9.8g; Sodium 639mg; Carbs 11.1g; Fiber 1.2g, Sugars 5.1g; Protein 27.8g

Garlic Lime Shrimp

Prep time: 15 minutes| Cook time: 15 minutes| Serves: 4

1-pound shrimp, peel and deveined
3 garlic cloves, pressed

2 tablespoons lime juice
2 tablespoons butter, melted
¼ cups fresh cilantro, chopped

Line the cooking tray with foil and set aside. Add shrimp into

the cooking tray. Stir together lime juice, garlic, and butter and pour over shrimp. Select the "Air Fry" mode on your air fryer. Press Temp button and then turn the dial to adjust the cooking temperature to 375 degrees F. Press Time button and then turn the dial to adjust the cooking time to 15 minutes. Press the Start button to initiate preheating. When the screen displays "Add Food", transfer the cooking tray to the air fryer basket of your Air Fryer. Close its door, and let the machine do the cooking. Garnish with cilantro. Serve warm.
Per serving: Calories 249; Fat 13g; Sodium 556mg; Carbs 10g; Sugar 1.1g; Fiber 0.7g; Protein 31g

Garlic Tilapia

Prep time: 15 minutes| Cook time: 20 minutes| Serves: 4

4 tilapia fillets; boneless
1 bunch kale; chopped.
3 garlic cloves; minced
1 teaspoon Fennel seeds

½ teaspoon red pepper flakes, crushed
3 tablespoons olive oil
Salt and black pepper, to taste

In the cooking tray, stir all the ingredients. Select the "Air Fry" mode on your air fryer. Press Temp button and then turn the dial to adjust the cooking temperature to 360 degrees F. Press Time button and then turn the dial to adjust the cooking time to 20 minutes. Press the Start button to initiate preheating. When the screen displays "Add Food", transfer the cooking tray to the air fryer basket of your Air Fryer. Close its door, and let the machine do the cooking.
Per serving: Calories 285; Fat 9.8g; Sodium 639mg; Carbs 11.1g; Fiber 1.2g, Sugars 5.1g; Protein 27.8g

Golden Beer-Battered Cod

Prep time: 15 minutes| Cook time: 15 minutes| Serves: 4

2 eggs
1 cup malty beer
½ cup cornstarch
1 teaspoon garlic powder

1 cup all-purpose flour
Salt and black pepper, to taste
4 (4-ounce / 113-g) cod fillets
Cooking spray

In a bowl, beat together the 2 eggs with the beer. In another bowl, thoroughly combine the flour and cornstarch. Sprinkle with the garlic powder, pepper and salt. Dredge cod fillet in the flour mixture, then in the 1 egg mixture. Dip piece of fish in the flour mixture a second time. Spritz the cooking tray with cooking spray. Arrange the cod fillets in the cooking tray in a single layer. Select the "Air Fry" mode on your air fryer. Press Temp button and then turn the dial to adjust the cooking temperature to 400 degrees F. Press Time button and then turn the dial to adjust the cooking time to 15 minutes. Press the Start button to initiate preheating. When the screen displays "Add Food", transfer the cooking tray to the air fryer basket of your Air Fryer. Close its door, and let the machine do the cooking. Serve.
Per serving: Calories 361; Fat 10g; Sodium 218mg; Carbs 16g; Sugar 1.2g; Fiber 0.7g; Protein 24g

Greek Pesto Salmon

Prep time: 15 minutes| Cook time: 25 minutes| Serves: 4

4 salmon fillets
½ cup pesto
1 onion, chopped

2 cups grape tomatoes, halved
½ cup feta cheese, crumbled

Line the cooking tray with foil and set aside. Place salmon fillet in cooking tray and top with tomatoes, pesto, onion, and cheese. Select the "Air Fry" mode on your air fryer. Press Temp button

and then turn the dial to adjust the cooking temperature to 350 degrees F. Press Time button and then turn the dial to adjust the cooking time to 25 minutes. Press the Start button to initiate preheating. When the screen displays "Add Food", transfer the cooking tray to the air fryer basket of your Air Fryer. Close its door, and let the machine do the cooking. Serve.
Per serving: Calories 236; Fat 13.9g; Sodium 451mg; Carbs 13.2g; Fiber 1.2g; Sugars 1.4g; Protein 14.3g

Fish and Chips

Prep time: 15 minutes| Cook time: 15 minutes| Serves: 4

1 egg
Old Bay seasoning
½ cup panko breadcrumbs

2 tablespoons almond flour
4-6-ounce tilapia fillets
Frozen crinkle cut fries

Add almond flour to a bowl, beat 1 egg in another bowl, and add panko breadcrumbs to the third bowl, mixed with Old Bay seasoning. Dredge tilapia fillets in flour, then egg, and then breadcrumbs. Place the coated tilapia fillets in the cooking tray along with fries. Select the "Air Fry" mode on your air fryer. Press Temp button and then turn the dial to adjust the cooking temperature to 350 degrees F. Press Time button and then turn the dial to adjust the cooking time to 15 minutes. Press the Start button to initiate preheating. When the screen displays "Add Food", transfer the cooking tray to the air fryer basket of your Air Fryer. Close its door, and let the machine do the cooking. Serve.
Per serving: Calories 285; Fat 9.8g; Sodium 639mg; Carbs 11.1g; Fiber 1.2g, Sugars 5.1g; Protein 27.8g

Mustard-Crusted Sole Fillets

Prep time: 15 minutes| Cook time: 10 minutes| Serves: 4

5 teaspoon low-sodium yellow mustard
1 tablespoon lemon juice
4 (3.5-ounce / 99-g) sole fillets
⅛ teaspoon freshly ground pepper

1 slice low-sodium whole-wheat bread, crumbled
1 teaspoon olive oil
½ teaspoon dried marjoram
½ teaspoon dried thyme

Whisk together the mustard and lemon juice in a bowl until thoroughly mixed and smooth. Spread the mixture evenly over the sole fillets, and then transfer the fillets to the cooking tray. In a separate bowl, combine the olive oil, thyme, marjoram, pepper, and bread crumbs and stir to mix well. Gently but firmly press the mixture over fillets, coating them completely. Select the "Air Fry" mode on your air fryer. Press Temp button and then turn the dial to adjust the cooking temperature to 320 degrees F. Press Time button and then turn the dial to adjust the cooking time to 10 minutes. Press the Start button to initiate preheating. When the screen displays "Add Food", transfer the cooking tray to the air fryer basket of your Air Fryer. Close its door, and let the machine do the cooking. Serve warm.
Per serving: Calories 327; Fat 15g; Sodium 548mg; Carbs 12g; Sugar 1.2g; Fiber 0.7g; Protein 29g

Parmesan Cod

Prep time: 15 minutes| Cook time: 20 minutes| Serves: 4

4 cod fillets; boneless
A drizzle of olive oil
3 spring onions; chopped.
1 cup parmesan

4 tablespoons balsamic vinegar
Salt and black pepper, to taste

Season the cod fillets with pepper, salt, grease with the oil, and coat it in parmesan. Put the fillets in the cooking tray. Select the "Air Fry" mode on your air fryer. Press Temp button and then turn the dial to adjust the cooking temperature to 370 degrees F. Press Time button and then turn the dial to adjust the cooking time to 20 minutes. Press the Start button to initiate preheating. When the screen displays "Add Food", transfer the cooking tray to the air fryer basket of your Air Fryer. Close its door, and let the machine do the cooking. Meanwhile, in a bowl, toss the spring onions with salt, pepper, the vinegar and whisk well. Divide the cod between plates, drizzle the spring onions mix all over and serve with a side salad Serve.

Per serving: Calories 344; Fat 14.9g; Sodium 227mg; Carbs 14g; Fiber 1g; Sugars 1.4g; Protein 25.7g

Parmesan Walnut Salmon

Prep time: 15 minutes| Cook time: 15 minutes| Serves: 4

4 salmon fillets	grated
¼ cups walnuts	1 tablespoon lemon rind
¼ cups parmesan cheese,	1 teaspoon olive oil

Line the cooking tray with foil and set aside. Place salmon fillets in the cooking tray. Add walnuts into the blender and blend until ground. Mix together walnuts, cheese, oil, and lemon rind and spread on top of salmon fillets. Select the "Air Fry" mode on your air fryer. Press Temp button and then turn the dial to adjust the cooking temperature to 400 degrees F. Press Time button and then turn the dial to adjust the cooking time to 15 minutes. Press the Start button to initiate preheating. When the screen displays "Add Food", transfer the cooking tray to the air fryer basket of your Air Fryer. Close its door, and let the machine do the cooking. Serve.

Per serving: Calories 351; Fat 22g; Sodium 502mg; Carbs 15.2g; Sugar 1.1g; Fiber 0.7g; Protein 26.4g

Parmesan-Crusted Halibut Fillets

Prep time: 15 minutes| Cook time: 10 minutes| Serves: 2

2 medium-sized halibut fillets	Kosher salt and freshly
Dash of Tabasco sauce	cracked mixed peppercorns
½ teaspoon hot paprika	2 eggs
1 teaspoon curry powder	1 ½ tablespoon olive oil
½ teaspoon ground coriander	½ cup grated Parmesan cheese

On a clean work surface, drizzle the halibut fillets with the Tabasco sauce. Sprinkle with the curry powder, hot paprika, coriander, salt, and cracked mixed peppercorns. Set aside. In a bowl, beat the 2 eggs until frothy. In another bowl, combine the oil and Parmesan cheese. 1 at a time, dredge the fillets in the beaten 2 eggs, shaking off any excess, then roll them over the Parmesan cheese until evenly coated. Arrange the halibut fillets in the cooking tray in a single layer. Select the "Air Fry" mode on your air fryer. Press Temp button and then turn the dial to adjust the cooking temperature to 365 degrees F. Press Time button and then turn the dial to adjust the cooking time to 10 minutes. Press the Start button to initiate preheating. When the screen displays "Add Food", transfer the cooking tray to the air fryer basket of your Air Fryer. Close its door, and let the machine do the cooking.

Per serving: Calories 254; Fat 28g; Sodium 346mg; Carbs 12.3g; Sugar 1g; Fiber 0.7g; Protein 24.3 g

Parmesan-Crusted Salmon Patties

Prep time: 15 minutes| Cook time: 13 minutes| Serves: 2

1 pound (454 g) salmon,	chopped into ½-inch pieces

2 tablespoon coconut flour	½ teaspoon chipotle powder
2 tablespoon grated Parmesan cheese	½ teaspoon dried parsley flakes
½ tablespoon milk	1 teaspoon acceptable salt
½ white onion, peeled and finely chopped	⅓ teaspoon ground black pepper
½ teaspoon butter, at room temperature	⅓ teaspoon smoked cayenne pepper

Put all the ingredients for the salmon patties in a bowl and stir to combine well. Scoop out 2 tablespoons of the salmon mixture and shape into a patty with your palm, about ½ inches thick. Repeat until all the combination is used. Transfer to the refrigerator for about 120 minutes until firm. When ready, arrange the salmon patties in the cooking tray. Select the "Air Fry" mode on your air fryer. Press Temp button and then turn the dial to adjust the cooking temperature to 395 degrees F. Press Time button and then turn the dial to adjust the cooking time to 13 minutes. Press the Start button to initiate preheating. When the screen displays "Add Food", transfer the cooking tray to the air fryer basket of your Air Fryer. Close its door, and let the machine do the cooking. Serve.

Per serving: Calories 361; Fat 10g; Sodium 218mg; Carbs 16g; Sugar 1.2g; Fiber 0.7g; Protein 24g

Paella

Prep time: 15 minutes| Cook time: 9 minutes| Serves: 4

1 (10-ounce) package frozen cooked rice, thawed	¼ cup vegetable broth
6-ounce jar artichoke hearts, drained and chopped	1 cup frozen cooked small shrimp
½ teaspoon turmeric	½ cup frozen baby peas
½ teaspoon dried thyme	1 tomato, diced

In a suitable pan, combine the rice, artichoke hearts, vegetable broth, turmeric, and thyme, and stir gently. Select the "Air Fry" mode on your air fryer. Press Temp button and then turn the dial to adjust the cooking temperature to 350 degrees F. Press Time button and then turn the dial to adjust the cooking time to 9 minutes. Press the Start button to initiate preheating. When the screen displays "Add Food", transfer the pan to the air fryer basket of your Air Fryer. Close its door, and let the machine do the cooking. Remove from the air fryer and gently stir in the shrimp, peas, and tomato. Serve.

Per serving: Calories 236; Fat 13.9g; Sodium 451mg; Carbs 13.2g; Fiber 1.2g; Sugars 1.4g; Protein 14.3g

Salmon and Cauliflower Rice

Prep time: 15 minutes| Cook time: 15 minutes| Serves: 4

4 salmon fillets; boneless	1 teaspoon turmeric powder
½ cup chicken stock	Salt and black pepper, to taste
1 cup cauliflower, riced	1 tablespoon butter; melted

In the cooking tray, mixes the cauliflower rice with the other ingredients except the salmon, and toss Arrange the salmon fillets over the cauliflower rice. Select the "Air Fry" mode on your air fryer. Press Temp button and then turn the dial to adjust the cooking temperature to 360 degrees F. Press Time button and then turn the dial to adjust the cooking time to 15 minutes. Press the Start button to initiate preheating. When the screen displays "Add Food", transfer the cooking tray to the air fryer basket of your Air Fryer. Close its door, and let the machine do the cooking. Serve.

Per serving: Calories 285; Fat 9.8g; Sodium 639mg; Carbs 11.1g; Fiber 1.2g, Sugars 5.1g; Protein 27.8g

Salmon and Coconut Sauce

Prep time: 15 minutes| Cook time: 25 minutes| Serves: 4

4 salmon fillets; boneless
½ cup coconut; shredded
¼ cup coconut cream
⅓ cup heavy cream

¼ cup lime juice
1 teaspoon lime zest; grated
A pinch of Salt and black pepper, to taste

Take a bowl and mix all the ingredients except the salmon and whisk. Arrange the fish in the cooking tray, drizzle the coconut sauce all over. Select the "Air Fry" mode on your air fryer. Press Temp button and then turn the dial to adjust the cooking temperature to 360 degrees F. Press Time button and then turn the dial to adjust the cooking time to 25 minutes. Press the Start button to initiate preheating. When the screen displays "Add Food", transfer the cooking tray to the air fryer basket of your Air Fryer. Close its door, and let the machine do the cooking. Serve.
Per serving: Calories 305; Fat 15g; Sodium 548mg; Carbs 12g; Sugar 1.2g; Fiber 0.7g; Protein 29g

Salmon and Sauce

Prep time: 15 minutes| Cook time: 25 minutes| Serves: 2

4 salmon fillets; boneless
2 garlic cloves; minced
1 tablespoon Chives; chopped.
1 teaspoon lemon juice
¼ cup ghee; melted

½ cup heavy cream
1 teaspoon Dill; chopped.
A pinch of salt and black pepper

Take a bowl and mix all the ingredients except the salmon, and whisk well. Arrange the salmon in the cooking tray, drizzle the sauce all over. Select the "Air Fry" mode on your air fryer. Press Temp button and then turn the dial to adjust the cooking temperature to 360 degrees F. Press Time button and then turn the dial to adjust the cooking time to 25 minutes. Press the Start button to initiate preheating. When the screen displays "Add Food", transfer the cooking tray to the air fryer basket of your Air Fryer. Close its door, and let the machine do the cooking. Serve.
Per serving: Calories 344; Fat 14.9g; Sodium 227mg; Carbs 14g; Fiber 1g; Sugars 1.4g; Protein 25.7g

Salmon Dill Patties

Prep time: 15 minutes| Cook time: 10 minutes| Serves: 2

1 egg
1 teaspoon dill weeds
½ cup almond flour

14 oz. salmon
¼ cups onion, diced

Add all ingredients into the bowl and stir well. Make patties from bowl mixture and place into the cooking tray. Select the "Air Fry" mode on your air fryer. Press Temp button and then turn the dial to adjust the cooking temperature to 375 degrees F. Press Time button and then turn the dial to adjust the cooking time to 10 minutes. Press the Start button to initiate preheating. When the screen displays "Add Food", transfer the cooking tray to the air fryer basket of your Air Fryer. Close its door, and let the machine do the cooking. Serve.
Per serving: Calories 285; Fat 9.8g; Sodium 639mg; Carbs 11.1g; Fiber 1.2g, Sugars 5.1g; Protein 27.8g

Homemade Salmon Patties

Prep time: 15 minutes| Cook time: 7 minutes| Serves: 2

1 egg, lightly beaten

8 oz. salmon fillet, minced

Salt and black pepper, to taste
¼ teaspoon garlic powder

¼ teaspoon onion powder

Add all ingredients into the bowl and stir until just combined. Make small patties from salmon mixture and place into the cooking tray. Select the "Air Fry" mode on your air fryer. Press Temp button and then turn the dial to adjust the cooking temperature to 400 degrees F. Press Time button and then turn the dial to adjust the cooking time to 7 minutes. Press the Start button to initiate preheating. When the screen displays "Add Food", transfer the cooking tray to the air fryer basket of your Air Fryer. Close its door, and let the machine do the cooking. Serve warm.
Per serving: Calories 249; Fat 13g; Sodium 556mg; Carbs 10g; Sugar 1.1g; Fiber 0.7g; Protein 31g

Sesame Shrimp

Prep time: 15 minutes| Cook time: 12 minutes| Serves: 4

1-pound shrimp; peeled and deveined
1 tablespoon olive oil
1 tablespoon Sesame seeds,

toasted
½ teaspoon Italian seasoning
A pinch of Salt and black pepper, to taste

Take a bowl and mix the shrimp with the rest of the ingredients and stir well Put the shrimp in the cooking tray. Select the "Air Fry" mode on your air fryer. Press Temp button and then turn the dial to adjust the cooking temperature to 370 degrees F. Press Time button and then turn the dial to adjust the cooking time to 12 minutes. Press the Start button to initiate preheating. When the screen displays "Add Food", transfer the cooking tray to the air fryer basket of your Air Fryer. Close its door, and let the machine do the cooking. Serve.
Per serving: Calories 344; Fat 14.9g; Sodium 227mg; Carbs 14g; Fiber 1g; Sugars 1.4g; Protein 25.7g

Salmon

Prep time: 15 minutes| Cook time: 12 minutes| Serves: 2

2 (4-oz. salmon fillets, skin removed
2 tablespoons unsalted butter; melted

⅓ teaspoon Dried dill
1 medium lemon
½ teaspoon Garlic powder

Place fillet on the cooking tray lined with foil. Drizzle with butter and sprinkle with garlic powder. Zest half of the lemon and sprinkle zest over salmon. Slice the other half of the lemon and lay 2 slices on piece of salmon. Sprinkle dill over salmon Gather and fold foil at the top and sides to fully close packets. Place foil packets into the baking pan. Select the "Air Fry" mode on your air fryer. Press Temp button and then turn the dial to adjust the cooking temperature to 400 degrees F. Press Time button and then turn the dial to adjust the cooking time to 12 minutes. Press the Start button to initiate preheating. When the screen displays "Add Food", transfer the cooking tray to the air fryer basket of your Air Fryer. Close its door, and let the machine do the cooking. Serve.
Per serving: Calories 236; Fat 13.9g; Sodium 451mg; Carbs 13.2g; Fiber 1.2g; Sugars 1.4g; Protein 14.3g

Sole and Cauliflower Fritters

Prep time: 15 minutes| Cook time: 28 minutes| Serves: 2

½ pound (227 g) sole fillets
½ pound (227 g) mashed cauliflower

½ cup red onion, chopped
1 egg, beaten
3 garlic cloves, minced

Cooking spray
2 tablespoons fresh parsley, chopped
1 tablespoon olive oil
1 tablespoon coconut amino

½ teaspoon scotch bonnet pepper, minced
½ teaspoon paprika
1 bell pepper, finely chopped
Salt and white pepper

Place the sole fillets in the cooking tray. Select the "Air Fry" mode on your air fryer. Press Temp button and then turn the dial to adjust the cooking temperature to 380 degrees F. Press Time button and then turn the dial to adjust the cooking time to 14 minutes. Press the Start button to initiate preheating. When the screen displays "Add Food", transfer the cooking tray to the air fryer basket of your Air Fryer. Close its door, and let the machine do the cooking. When cooking is complete, transfer the fish fillets to a bowl. Mash the fillets into flakes. Add the remaining ingredients and toss to combine. Scoop out 2 tablespoons of the fish mixture and shape into a patty about ½ inches thick with your hands. Repeat with the remaining fish mixture. Place the cakes in the cooking tray and return to the air fryer. Select Bake, set temperature to 380 degrees F and set time to 14 minutes. When done, serve warm.
Per serving: Calories 361; Fat 10g; Sodium 218mg; Carbs 16g; Sugar 1.2g; Fiber 0.7g; Protein 24g

Spicy Shrimp

Prep time: 15 minutes| Cook time: 6 minutes| Serves: 2

½ pound shrimp, peeled and deveined
½ teaspoon old bay seasoning
½ teaspoon cayenne pepper

¼ teaspoon paprika
1 tablespoon extra-virgin olive oil
Pinch of salt

Add shrimp and remaining ingredients into the bowl and mix well to coat. Add shrimp into the cooking tray.
Select the "Air Fry" mode on your air fryer. Press Temp button and then turn the dial to adjust the cooking temperature to 400 degrees F. Press Time button and then turn the dial to adjust the cooking time to 6 minutes. Press the Start button to initiate preheating. When the screen displays "Add Food", transfer the cooking tray to the air fryer basket of your Air Fryer. Close its door, and let the machine do the cooking. Serve.
Per serving: Calories 285; Fat 9.8g; Sodium 639mg; Carbs 11.1g; Fiber 1.2g, Sugars 5.1g; Protein 27.8g

Spicy Tilapia

Prep time: 15 minutes| Cook time: 15 minutes| Serves: 4

4 tilapia fillets
½ teaspoon red chili powder
1 tablespoon fresh lemon juice
3 teaspoons fresh parsley, chopped

1 teaspoon garlic, minced
3 tablespoon butter, melted
1 lemon, sliced
Salt and black pepper, to taste

Line the cooking tray with foil and set aside. Place fish fillets in the baking pan and season with pepper and salt. Mix together butter, garlic, red chili powder, and lemon juice and pour over fish fillets. Arrange lemon slices on top of fish fillets. Select the "Air Fry" mode on your air fryer. Use the timer (+ / − Time) arrow keys to adjust cooking time to 15 minutes. Adjust its cooking temperature to 350 degrees F, using the temp (+/- Temp) arrow keys. Press the Start button to initiate preheating. When the screen displays "Add Food", transfer the cooking tray to the air fryer basket of your Air Fryer. Close its door, and let the machine do the cooking.
Garnish with parsley. Serve.
Per serving: Calories 305; Fat 15g; Sodium 548mg; Carbs 12g; Sugar 1.2g; Fiber 0.7g; Protein 29g

Sticky Hoisin Tuna

Prep time: 15 minutes| Cook time: 5 minutes| Serves: 4

½ cup hoisin sauce
2 tablespoons rice wine vinegar
1 teaspoon garlic powder
1 cup cooked jasmine rice
¼ teaspoon red pepper flakes
½ small onion, quartered and

thinly sliced
8 ounces (227 g) fresh tuna, cut into 1-inch cubes
Cooking spray
2 teaspoon sesame oil
2 teaspoon dried lemongrass

In a bowl, mix together the hoisin sauce, sesame oil, vinegar, lemongrass, garlic powder, and red pepper flakes. Add the sliced onion and tuna cubes and gently toss until the fish is evenly coated. Arrange the coated tuna cubes in the sprayed cooking tray. Select the "Air Fry" mode on your air fryer. Press Temp button and then turn the dial to adjust the cooking temperature to 350 degrees F. Press Time button and then turn the dial to adjust the cooking time to 5 minutes. Press the Start button to initiate preheating. When the screen displays "Add Food", transfer the cooking tray to the air fryer basket of your Air Fryer. Close its door, and let the machine do the cooking. Serve with the cooked jasmine rice.
Per serving: Calories 344; Fat 14.9g; Sodium 227mg; Carbs 14g; Fiber 1g; Sugars 1.4g; Protein 25.7g

Shrimp Fajitas

Prep time: 15 minutes| Cook time: 15 minutes| Serves: 4

1-pound shrimp, peeled and deveined
1 medium onion, sliced
½ lime juice

½ tablespoon taco seasoning
1 bell pepper, sliced
½ tablespoon extra-virgin olive oil

Layer the cooking tray with foil and set aside. In a bowl, mix shrimp with remaining ingredients.
Spread shrimp mixture on the cooking tray. Select the "Air Fry" mode on your air fryer. Press Temp button and then turn the dial to adjust the cooking temperature to 400 degrees F. Press Time button and then turn the dial to adjust the cooking time to 15 minutes. Press the Start button to initiate preheating. When the screen displays "Add Food", transfer the cooking tray to the air fryer basket of your Air Fryer. Close its door, and let the machine do the cooking. Serve.
Per serving: Calories 285; Fat 9.8g; Sodium 639mg; Carbs 11.1g; Fiber 1.2g, Sugars 5.1g; Protein 27.8g

Tilapia and Salsa

Prep time: 15 minutes| Cook time: 15 minutes| Serves: 4

4 tilapia fillets; boneless
2 tablespoons Sweet red pepper; chopped.
1 tablespoon balsamic vinegar
12 oz. Canned tomatoes; chopped.

2 tablespoons Green onions; chopped.
1 tablespoon olive oil
A pinch of salt and black pepper

Arrange the tilapia in the cooking tray and season with salt and pepper. In a bowl, combine all the other ingredients, stir and spread over the fish Select the "Air Fry" mode on your air fryer. Press Temp button and then turn the dial to adjust the cooking temperature to 350 degrees F. Press Time button and then turn the dial to adjust the cooking time to 15 minutes. Press the Start button to initiate preheating. When the screen displays "Add Food", transfer the cooking tray to the air fryer basket of your Air Fryer. Close its door, and let the machine do the cooking. Serve.

Tilapia Meniere with Vegetables

Prep time: 15 minutes| Cook time: 20 minutes| Serves: 4

10 ounces Yukon Gold potatoes, sliced ¼-inch thick
1 tablespoon unsalted butter, melted, divided
1 teaspoon kosher salt, divided

4 (8-ounce) tilapia fillets
½ pound green beans, trimmed
2 tablespoons chopped fresh parsley, for garnish
Juice of 1 lemon

Drizzle the potatoes with 2 tablespoon of melted butter and ¼ teaspoon of kosher salt in a bowl. Transfer the potatoes to the cooking tray. Select the "Air Fry" mode on your air fryer. Press Temp button and then turn the dial to adjust the cooking temperature to 375 degrees F. Press Time button and then turn the dial to adjust the cooking time to 20 minutes. Press the Start button to initiate preheating. When the screen displays "Add Food", transfer the cooking tray to the air fryer basket of the air fryer. Close its door, and let the machine do the cooking. Meanwhile, season both sides of the fillets with ½ teaspoon of kosher salt. Put the green beans in a bowl and sprinkle with the remaining ¼ teaspoon of kosher salt and 1 tablespoon of butter, tossing to coat. After 10 minutes, remove the tray and push the potatoes to 1 side. Put the fillets in the middle of the tray and add the green beans on the other side. Drizzle the rest of the 2 tablespoon of butter over the fillets. Return it and cook until the fish flakes easily with a fork, and the green beans are crisp-tender. Once cooked, remove and drizzle the lemon juice over the fillets and sprinkle the parsley on top for garnish. Serve.
Per serving: Calories 361; Fat 10g; Sodium 218mg; Carbs 16g; Sugar 1.2g; Fiber 0.7g; Protein 24g

Trout with Mint

Prep time: 15 minutes| Cook time: 16 minutes| Serves: 4

1 avocado, peeled, pitted, and roughly chopped.
4 rainbow trout
⅓ pine nuts
3 garlic cloves; minced
½ cup mint; chopped.

1 cup + 3 tablespoons olive oil
1 cup parsley; chopped
Zest of 1 lemon
Juice of 1 lemon
A pinch of Salt and black pepper, to taste

Pat dry the trout, season with salt and pepper, and rub with 3 tablespoons of oil Put the fish in the cooking tray. Select the "Air Fry" mode on your air fryer. Press Temp button and then turn the dial to adjust the cooking temperature to 350 degrees F. Press Time button and then turn the dial to adjust the cooking time to 16 minutes.
Press the Start button to initiate preheating. When the screen displays "Add Food", transfer the cooking tray to the air fryer basket of your Air Fryer. Close its door, and let the machine do the cooking. Divide the fish between plates and drizzle half of the lemon juice all over In a blender, combine the rest of the oil with the remaining lemon juice, parsley, garlic, mint, pine nuts, lemon zest, and the avocado and pulse well. Spread this over the trout. Serve.
Per serving: Calories 236; Fat 13.9g; Sodium 451mg; Carbs 13.2g; Fiber 1.2g; Sugars 1.4g; Protein 14.3g

Bacon Shrimps

Prep time: 15 minutes| Cook time: 10 minutes| Serves: 6

1 package bacon
1-pound shrimp

½ teaspoon cayenne pepper
½ teaspoon ground cumin

½ teaspoon onion powder
1 teaspoon garlic powder
½ teaspoon lemon zest

1 tablespoon lemon juice
1 tablespoon Worcestershire sauce

In a mixing bowl, whisk the Worcestershire sauce, cumin, lemon zest, lemon juice, cayenne pepper, onion powder, and garlic powder. Add and combine the shrimp. Refrigerate for 1-2 hours to marinate. Take the bacon, slice into 2 parts, and wrap shrimp with them. In the cooking tray, add the wrapped shrimps. Select the "Air Fry" mode on your air fryer. Press Temp button and then turn the dial to adjust the cooking temperature to 380 degrees F. Press Time button and then turn the dial to adjust the cooking time to 10 minutes. Press the Start button to initiate preheating. When the screen displays "Add Food", transfer the cooking tray to the air fryer basket of your Air Fryer. Close its door, and let the machine do the cooking. Serve
Per serving: Calories 351; Fat 22g; Sodium 502mg; Carbs 15.2g; Sugar 1.1g; Fiber 0.7g; Protein 26.4g

Cajuned Salmon

Prep time: 15 minutes| Cook time: 8 minutes| Serves: 2

2 salmon fillets (6 ounces and with skin)
1 tablespoon Cajun seasoning

1 teaspoon brown Sugar
Cooking oil spray

In a mixing bowl, combine the Cajun seasoning and brown sugar. Add the fillets and coat well. Spray the cooking tray with some cooking oil, and add the fillets. Select the "Air Fry" mode on your air fryer. Press Temp button and then turn the dial to adjust the cooking temperature to 350 degrees F. Press Time button and then turn the dial to adjust the cooking time to 8 minutes. Press the Start button to initiate preheating. When the screen displays "Add Food", transfer the cooking tray to the air fryer basket of your Air Fryer. Close its door, and let the machine do the cooking. When the display indicates "turn Food", flip the fillets, and continue cooking for the remaining time. Serve.
Per serving: Calories 344; Fat 14.9g; Sodium 227mg; Carbs 12g; Fiber 1.2g; Sugars 1g; Protein 27g

Coconut Chili Shrimp

Prep time: 15 minutes| Cook time: 12 minutes| Serves: 6

3 cups panko breadcrumbs
½ cup all-purpose flour
2 eggs
¼ cup honey
2 teaspoons fresh cilantro, chopped
3 cups flaked coconut, unsweetened

12-ounce medium-size raw shrimps, peeled, and deveined
1 Serrano chili, thinly sliced
¼ cup lime juice
½ teaspoon kosher salt
½ teaspoon ground black pepper
Cooking spray

In a mixing bowl, combine the honey, Serrano chili with lime juice. In the second bowl, combine the salt, pepper and flour. In the third bowl, beat the 2 eggs. In the fourth bowl, combine the coconut and breadcrumbs. Coat the shrimps with the eggs first, then with the flour, and then with the crumbs. Coat the shrimps with some cooking spray. Line the cooking tray with a parchment paper, add the shrimps.
Select the "Air Fry" mode on your air fryer. Press Temp button and then turn the dial to adjust the cooking temperature to 400 degrees F. Press Time button and then turn the dial to adjust the cooking time to 12 minutes. Press the Start button to initiate preheating. When the screen displays "Add Food", transfer the cooking tray to the air fryer basket of your Air Fryer. Close its door, and let the machine do the cooking. When the display indicates " turn Food", shake the cooking tray and continue cooking for the remaining time. Serve the shrimps warm with

the chili sauce.

Per serving: Calories 305; Fat 15g; Sodium 548mg; Carbs 12g; Sugar 1.2g; Fiber 0.7g; Protein 29g

Creamed Cod

Prep time: 15 minutes| Cook time: 14 minutes| Serves: 2

1 tablespoon lemon juice	Sauce:
1-pound cod fillets	3 tablespoon ground mustard
2 tablespoons olive oil	½ cup heavy cream
½ teaspoon ground black pepper	1 tablespoon butter
½ teaspoon salt	½ teaspoon salt

Spread some olive oil on the fillets. Season the fillets with the pepper, salt, and lemon juice. Grease the cooking tray with some cooking spray. Place the fillets over it. Select the "Air Fry" mode on your air fryer Press Temp button and then turn the dial to adjust the cooking temperature to 400 degrees F. Press Time button and then turn the dial to adjust the cooking time to 10 minutes. Press the Start button to initiate preheating. When the screen displays "Add Food", transfer the cooking tray to the air fryer basket of your Air Fryer. Close its door, and let the machine do the cooking. In a bowl, add the heavy cream, mustard sauce, heavy cream, and salt. Cook the sauce for 3-4 minutes in a saucepan over medium heat. Pour it over the fish and serve warm.

Per serving: Calories 285; Fat 9.8g; Sodium 639mg; Carbs 11.1g; Fiber 1.2g, Sugars 5.1g; Protein 27.8g

Garlic Lemon Shrimp

Prep time: 15 minutes| Cook time: 6 minutes| Serves: 4

¼ teaspoon, crushed red pepper flakes	and deveined
4 cloves garlic, finely grated	lemon juice, zested
1 tablespoon olive oil	¼ cup, parsley, chopped
1 pound small shrimps, peeled	¼ teaspoon salt

Remove the tails of the shrimps. In a mixing bowl, add shrimps, the garlic, lemon zest, red pepper flakes, salt, and oil. Combine the ingredients to stir well with other. In the cooking tray, add the shrimps. Select the "Air Fry" mode on your air fryer. Press Temp button and then turn the dial to adjust the cooking temperature to 400 degrees F. Press Time button and then turn the dial to adjust the cooking time to 6 minutes. Press the Start button to initiate preheating. When the screen displays "Add Food", transfer the cooking tray to the air fryer basket of your Air Fryer. Close its door, and let the machine do the cooking. Serve warm with the lemon juice and parsley on top.

Per serving: Calories 344; Fat 14.9g; Sodium 227mg; Carbs 14g; Fiber 1g; Sugars 1.4g; Protein 25.7g

Mustard Salmon

Prep time: 15 minutes| Cook time: 10 minutes| Serves: 2

2 salmon fillets	½ teaspoon ground black pepper
1 garlic clove, grated	
2 tablespoon mustard, whole grain	1 tablespoon brown sugar
2 teaspoons olive oil	½ teaspoon thyme leaves

Rub the salmon with salt and pepper. In a mixing bowl, combine the mustard grain, thyme, brown sugar, garlic, and oil. Coat the salmon with the mixture. In the cooking tray, add the salmon. Select the "Air Fry" mode on your air fryer. Press Temp button

and then turn the dial to adjust the cooking temperature to 400 degrees F. Press Time button and then turn the dial to adjust the cooking time to 10 minutes. Press the Start button to initiate preheating. When the screen displays "Add Food", transfer the cooking tray to the air fryer basket of your Air Fryer. Close its door, and let the machine do the cooking. When the display indicates "turn Food", flip the salmon, and continue cooking for the remaining time. Serve.

Per serving: Calories 285; Fat 9.8g; Sodium 639mg; Carbs 11.1g; Fiber 1.2g, Sugars 5.1g; Protein 27.8g

Wholesome Fennel Cod Meal

Prep time: 15 minutes| Cook time: 15 minutes| Serves: 2

½ cup red pepper, thinly sliced	2 sprigs tarragon
½ cup carrots, julienned	1 tablespoon vegetable oil
2 ½ ounces cod fillets, frozen and thawed	1 tablespoon lemon juice
½ cup fennel bulbs, julienned	½ teaspoon black pepper powder
2 tablespoons butter, melted	1 tablespoon salt

In a mixing bowl, combine the tarragon, lemon juice, melted butter, and ½ teaspoon of salt. Mix the fennel bulbs, carrots and toss well. Coat the codfish fillets with the oil. Rub pepper and the remaining salt evenly.

Place the fillets over the cooking tray. Add the veggies on top. In the cooking tray, add the fish. Select the "Air Fry" mode on your air fryer. Press Temp button and then turn the dial to adjust the cooking temperature to 400 degrees F. Press Time button and then turn the dial to adjust the cooking time to 15 minutes. Press the Start button to initiate preheating. When the screen displays "Add Food", transfer the cooking tray to the air fryer basket of your Air Fryer. Close its door, and let the machine do the cooking. When the display indicates "turn Food", flip the fillets, and continue cooking for the remaining time. Serve.

Per serving: Calories 236; Fat 13.9g; Sodium 451mg; Carbs 13.2g; Fiber 1.2g; Sugars 1.4g; Protein 14.3g

Air Fryer Salmon Patties

Prep time: 15 minutes| Cook time: 15 minutes| Serves: 4

1 cup almond flour	1 egg
1 tablespoon ghee	1 tablespoon olive oil
¼ teaspoon salt	1 can wild Alaskan pink salmon
⅛ teaspoon pepper	

Drain the salmon into a bowl and keep liquid. Discard skin and bones. Add the ghee, pepper, salt, and 1 egg to salmon, stirring well with hands to incorporate. Make patties. Dredge the patties in flour and remaining egg. If it seems dry, spoon reserved salmon liquid from the can onto patties. Transfer the patties to the cooking tray. Select the "Air Fry" mode on your air fryer. Press Temp button and then turn the dial to adjust the cooking temperature to 380 degrees F. Press Time button and then turn the dial to adjust the cooking time to 7 minutes. Press the Start button to initiate preheating. When the screen displays "Add Food", transfer the cooking tray to the air fryer basket of your Air Fryer. Close its door, and let the machine do the cooking. Serve.

Per serving: Calories 305; Fat 15g; Sodium 548mg; Carbs 12g; Sugar 1.2g; Fiber 0.7g; Protein 29g

Bang Panko Breaded Fried Cod

Prep time: 15 minutes| Cook time: 8 minutes| Serves: 4

Montreal chicken seasoning	1-pound cod fish, boneless,

diced
1 teaspoon paprika
¾ cup panko bread crumbs
½ cup almond flour
1 egg white

Bang Bang Sauce:
⅓ cup plain Greek yogurt
¼ cup sweet chili sauce
2 tablespoon sriracha sauce

Season all cod pieces with seasonings. Add flour to a bowl, 1 egg white in another bowl, and breadcrumbs to a third bowl. Dip seasoned cod in flour, then 1 egg whites, and then breadcrumbs. Spray coated cod with oil and add to the cooking tray. Select the "Air Fry" mode on your air fryer. Press Temp button and then turn the dial to adjust the cooking temperature to 400 degrees F. Press Time button and then turn the dial to adjust the cooking time to 8 minutes. Press the Start button to initiate preheating. When the screen displays "Add Food", transfer the cooking tray to the air fryer basket of your Air Fryer. Close its door, and let the machine do the cooking. To make the sauce, stir together all sauce ingredients until smooth. Pour the sauce over the cod pieces and serve.
Per serving: Calories 249; Fat 13g; Sodium 556mg; Carbs 10g; Sugar 1.1g; Fiber 0.7g; Protein 31g

Crusted White Fish

Prep time: 15 minutes| Cook time: 12 minutes| Serves: 4

4 white fish fillets
1 lemon juiced
4 tablespoon oil

4 oz. cornflakes, crushed
whisked whole 1 egg

Mix the crumbs and oil until it looks nice and loose. Dip the fish in the 1 egg and coat lightly, then move on to the cornflakes Make sure the fillet is covered evenly. Select the "Air Fry" mode on your air fryer. Press Temp button and then turn the dial to adjust the cooking temperature to 350 degrees F. Press Time button and then turn the dial to adjust the cooking time to 12 minutes. Press the Start button to initiate preheating. When the screen displays "Add Food", transfer the fish to the air fryer basket of the air fryer. Close its door, and let the machine do the cooking. Serve with lemon.
Per serving: Calories 361; Fat 10g; Sodium 218mg; Carbs 16g; Sugar 1.2g; Fiber 0.7g; Protein 24g

Lemony Tuna

Prep time: 15 minutes| Cook time: 12 minutes| Serves: 4

2 (6-ounce) cans water packed plain tuna
1 egg
2 teaspoon Dijon mustard
Hot sauce
½ cup bread crumbs

1 tablespoon fresh lime juice
2 tablespoons fresh parsley, chopped
3 tablespoon canola oil
Salt and freshly ground black pepper

Drain most of the liquid from the canned tuna. In a bowl, add the fish, crumbs, mustard, citrus juice, parsley and hot sauce and stir till well combined. Add a little canola oil if it seems too dry. Add egg, salt and toss to combine. Make the patties from tuna mixture. Refrigerate the tuna patties for about 120 minutes. Transfer to the cooking tray. Select the "Air Fry" mode on your air fryer. Press Temp button and then turn the dial to adjust cooking temperature to 355 degrees F. Press Time button and then turn the dial to adjust the cooking time to 12 minutes. Press the Start button to initiate preheating. When the screen displays "Add Food", transfer the cooking tray to the air fryer basket of your Air Fryer. Close its door, and let the machine do the cooking. Serve.
Per serving: Calories 285; Fat 9.8g; Sodium 639mg; Carbs 11.1g; Fiber 1.2g, Sugars 5.1g; Protein 27.8g

Louisiana Shrimp Po Boy

Prep time: 15 minutes| Cook time: 10 minutes| Serves: 6

1-pound deveined shrimp
Lettuce leaves
1 teaspoon creole seasoning
Eight slices of tomato
¼ cup buttermilk
½ cup Louisiana Fish Fry
Remoulade Sauce:
½ teaspoon creole seasoning

1 chopped green onion
1 teaspoon hot sauce
1 teaspoon Worcestershire sauce
1 teaspoon Dijon mustard
Juice of ½ a lemon
½ cup mayo

Combine all sauce ingredients until well incorporated. Chill while you cook shrimp. Stir seasonings together and liberally season shrimp. Add buttermilk to a bowl. Dip shrimp into milk and place in a Ziploc bag. Chill half an hour to marinate. Add Louisiana fish fry to a bowl. Take shrimp from marinating bag and dip into fish fry, and then add to the cooking tray. Select the "Air Fry" mode on your air fryer. Press Temp button and then turn the dial to adjust the cooking temperature to 400 degrees F. Press Time button and then turn the dial to adjust the cooking time to 10 minutes. Press the Start button to initiate preheating. When the screen displays "Add Food", transfer the cooking tray to the air fryer basket of your Air Fryer. Close its door, and let the machine do the cooking. Assemble Po Boy by adding sauce to lettuce leaves, along with shrimp and tomato. Enjoy.
Per serving: Calories 254; Fat 28g; Sodium 346mg; Carbs 12.3g; Sugar 1g; Fiber 0.7g; Protein 24.3 g

Old Bay Crab Cakes

Prep time: 15 minutes| Cook time: 12 minutes| Serves: 4

1-pound lump crabmeat
Slices dried bread, crusts removed
Small amount of milk
1 egg
1 tablespoon mayo
1 tablespoon Worcestershire

sauce
1 tablespoon baking powder
1 tablespoon parsley flakes
1 teaspoon Old Bay®
Seasoning
¼ teaspoon salt

Crush your bread into a bowl until it is broken down into small pieces. Add milk and mix until bread crumbs are moistened. Mix mayo and Worcestershire sauce. Add remaining ingredients and stir well. Shape into 4 patties. Select the "Air Fry" mode on your air fryer. Press Temp button and then turn the dial to adjust the cooking temperature to 360 degrees F. Press Time button and then turn the dial to adjust the cooking time to 12 minutes. Press the Start button to initiate preheating. When the screen displays "Add Food", transfer the patties to the tray of the air fryer. Close its door, and let the machine do the cooking. Assemble 4 sandwiches with bread slices and well-chilled salad. Enjoy!
Per serving: Calories 285; Fat 9.8g; Sodium 639mg; Carbs 11.1g; Fiber 1.2g, Sugars 5.1g; Protein 27.8g

Pistachio-Crusted Lemon-Garlic Salmon

Prep time: 15 minutes| Cook time: 10 minutes| Serves: 6

4 medium-sized salmon filets
3 ounces of melted butter
1 clove of garlic, peeled and finely minced
1 large-sized lemon
2 raw eggs
1 tablespoon of parsley, rinsed,

patted dry and chopped
1 teaspoon of dill, rinsed, patted dry and chopped
½ cup of pistachio nuts, shelled and coarsely crushed
1 teaspoon of salt

Layer the cooking tray with a lining of tin foil, leaving the edges uncovered to allow air to circulate through the tray. In a mixing bowl, beat the 2 eggs until fluffy and until the yolks and whites are fully combined. Add the melted butter, the juice of the lemon, the minced garlic, the parsley and the dill to the beaten 2 eggs, and stir thoroughly. One by one, dunk the salmon filets into the wet mixture, then roll them in the crushed pistachios, coating completely. Place the coated salmon fillets in the cooking tray. Select the "Air Fry" mode on your air fryer. Press Temp button and then turn the dial to adjust the cooking temperature to 350 degrees F. Press Time button and then turn the dial to adjust the cooking time to 10 minutes. Press the Start button to initiate preheating. When the screen displays "Add Food", transfer the cooking tray to the air fryer basket of your Air Fryer. Close its door, and let the machine do the cooking. Serve.

Per serving: Calories 327; Fat 15g; Sodium 548mg; Carbs 12g; Sugar 1.2g; Fiber 0.7g; Protein 29g

Salmon Noodles

Prep time: 15 minutes| Cook time: 15 minutes| Serves: 4

1 Salmon Fillet	3 ½ Oz. Soba Noodles, cooked
1 cup Broccoli	and drained
1 tablespoon Teriyaki	10 oz. Firm Tofu
Marinade	Olive Oil
7 oz. Mixed Salad	Salt and black pepper, to taste

Season the salmon with salt and pepper, then coat with the teriyaki marinate. Set aside for 15 minutes. Transfer salmon, broccoli and tofu to the cooking tray. Select the "Air Fry" mode on your air fryer. Press Temp button and then turn the dial to adjust the cooking temperature to 350 degrees F. Press Time button and then turn the dial to adjust the cooking time to 15 minutes. Press the Start button to initiate preheating. When the screen displays "Add Food", transfer the cooking tray to the air fryer basket of your Air Fryer. Close its door, and let the machine do the cooking. Plate the salmon and broccoli tofu mixture over the soba noodles. Add the mixed salad to the side. Serve.

Per serving: Calories 236; Fat 13.9g; Sodium 451mg; Carbs 13.2g; Fiber 1.2g; Sugars 1.4g; Protein 14.3g

Mustard Salmon Quiche

Prep time: 15 minutes| Cook time: 25 minutes| Serves: 4

5 Oz. Salmon Fillet	1 egg Yolk
Quiche Pan	3 tablespoons Whipped Cream
½ cup Flour	2 teaspoons Mustard
½ tablespoon Lemon Juice	Black pepper, to taste
¼ cups Butter, melted	Salt, to taste
2 eggs	

Clean and cut the salmon into small cubes. Pour the lemon juice over the salmon cubes and allow to marinate for 60 minutes. Combine a 1 tablespoon of water with the flour, butter, and yolk in a bowl. Using your hands, knead the mixture until smooth On a clean surface, use a rolling pin to form a circle of dough. Place this into the quiche pan, using your fingers to adhere the pastry to the edges Whisk the cream, mustard and 2 eggs together. Season the mixture with salt and pepper. Add the marinated salmon into the bowl and combine. Pour the content of the bowl into the dough lined quiche pan Select the "Air Fry" mode on your air fryer Press Temp button and then turn the dial to adjust the cooking temperature to 350 degrees F. Press Time button and then turn the dial to adjust the cooking time to 25 minutes. Press the Start button to initiate preheating. When the screen displays "Add Food", transfer the pan to the air fryer basket of the Air Fryer. Close its door, and let the machine do the cooking. Serve.

Per serving: Calories 344; Fat 14.9g; Sodium 227mg; Carbs 14g; Fiber 1g; Sugars 1.4g; Protein 25.7g

Scallops and Spring Vegetables

Prep time: 15 minutes| Cook time: 2 minutes| Serves: 4

1-pound sea scallops	1 tablespoon lemon juice
½ pound asparagus, ends	½ teaspoon dried thyme
trimmed, cut into 2-inch	2 teaspoons olive oil
pieces	Black pepper, to taste
1 cup snap peas	Salt, to taste

Place the asparagus and snap peas in the cooking tray. Select the "Air Fry" mode on your air fryer. Press Temp button and then turn the dial to adjust the cooking temperature to 350 degrees F. Press Time button and then turn the dial to adjust the cooking time to 2 minutes. Press the Start button to initiate preheating. When the screen displays "Add Food", transfer the cooking tray to the air fryer basket of your Air Fryer. Close its door, and let the machine do the cooking. Meanwhile, check the scallops for a small muscle attached to the side, and pull it off and discard. In a bowl, mix the scallops with the lemon juice, thyme, olive oil, salt, and pepper. Place into the cooking tray over the vegetables. Serve warm.

Per serving: Calories 361; Fat 10g; Sodium 218mg; Carbs 16g; Sugar 1.2g; Fiber 0.7g; Protein 24g

Tuna Stuffed Potatoes

Prep time: 15 minutes| Cook time: 30 minutes| Serves: 4

1 scallion, chopped and	2 tablespoon plain Greek
divided	yogurt
4 starchy potatoes	1 tablespoon caper
½ tablespoon olive oil	1 teaspoon red chili powder
(6-ounce) can tuna, drained	Salt and ground black pepper

In a bowl with water, soak the potatoes for about 30 minutes. Drain well and pat dry with paper towel. Place the potatoes in the cooking tray. Select the "Air Fry" mode on your Air Fryer. Press Temp button and then turn the dial to adjust the cooking temperature to 355 degrees F. Press Time button and then turn the dial to adjust the cooking time to 30 minutes. Press the Start button to initiate preheating. When the screen displays "Add Food", transfer the cooking tray to the air fryer basket of your Air Fryer. Close its door, and let the machine do the cooking. Meanwhile in a bowl, add tuna, red chili powder, yogurt, salt, pepper and half of scallion and with a potato masher, mash the mixture completely. Remove the potatoes from the air fryer and place onto a smooth surface. Carefully, cut potato from top side lengthwise. With your fingers, press the open side of potato halves slightly. Stuff the potato open portion with tuna mixture evenly. Sprinkle with the capers and remaining scallion. Serve.

Per serving: Calories 351; Fat 22g; Sodium 502mg; Carbs 15.2g; Sugar 1.1g; Fiber 0.7g; Protein 26.4g

Coconut Shrimp

Prep time: 15 minutes| Cook time: 5 minutes| Serves: 4

1-pound jumbo shrimp peeled	1 teaspoon baking powder
½ cup all-purpose flour	1 egg
Salt and black pepper, to taste	½ teaspoon garlic powder
For batter	1 cup breadcrumbs
½ a 1 cup all-purpose flour	1 cup shredded coconut

Line your cooking tray with a sheet or parchment paper. On a shallow bout, add ½ a 1 cup of flour for dredging and in another bowl; whish all ingredients together and it should resemble a pan cake consistency. Add a little mineral water or beer if it is too thick. Dredge in the flour and shake off any excess 4 before coating with the breadcrumb and coconut mixture. Lightly press the coconut into the shrimp. Place in a prepared baking sheet and repeat the process for all the remaining shrimp. Select the "Air Fry" mode on your air fryer. Press Temp button and then turn the dial to adjust the cooking temperature to 350 degrees F. Press Time button and then turn the dial to adjust the cooking time to 5 minutes. Press the Start button to initiate preheating. When the screen displays "Add Food", transfer the baking sheet to the air fryer basket of the Air Fryer. Close its door, and let the machine do the cooking. Serve.

Per serving: Calories 344; Fat 14.9g; Sodium 227mg; Carbs 14g; Fiber 1g; Sugars 1.4g; Protein 25.7g

Baked Salmon with Butter Cream Sauce

Prep time: 15 minutes| Cook time: 5 minutes| Serves: 2

4 skinless salmon fillets	For lemon butter cream sauce:
1 teaspoon olive oil	2 teaspoons minced garlic
1 teaspoon minced garlic	¼ cup unsalted butter
2 teaspoons dry white whine	2 teaspoons dry white wine
Salt to season	½ cup heavy cream
Pepper	1 cup freshly squeezed lemon

Pat the salmon to ensure that it is dry. Combine olive oil, lemon juice, garlic and wine together in a small bowl. Rub the salmon with the mixture and arrange them in the cooking tray. Season it with a good pinch of salt and pepper. Select the "Air Fry" mode on your air fryer. Press Temp button and then turn the dial to adjust the cooking temperature to 380 degrees F. Press Time button and then turn the dial to adjust the cooking time to 5 minutes. Press the Start button to initiate preheating. When the screen displays "Add Food", transfer the cooking tray to the air fryer basket of your Air Fryer. Close its door, and let the machine do the cooking. While cooking, mix up all of the sauce ingredients in a suitable bowl. When done, pour sauce over the cooked salmon and mix them. Serve while hot.

Per serving: Calories 344; Fat 14.9g; Sodium 227mg; Carbs 14g; Fiber 1g; Sugars 1.4g; Protein 25.7g

Butter Seared Lobster Tails

Prep time: 15 minutes| Cook time: 5 minutes| Serves: 2

170 grams' lobster tails	4 cloves garlic, crushed
1 teaspoon pepper, to taste	Lemon slice
1 teaspoon cooking oil	2 teaspoons fresh lemon juice
1 teaspoon salt to taste	1 teaspoon parsley to garnish

Thaw your lobster tails if they are frozen in a pot of cold water for an hour. Ensure that the lobster tails are fully thawed. Rinse them and pat dry with paper towels. Using a sharp knife or kitchen shears cut the top shell down through the center of the back of the end of the tail but leaving the tail intact. Remove the shell shards and run your finger between the shell and the meat. Make sure that you are careful not to pull the tail out. Season your lobsters generously with pepper and salt. Oil the cooking tray and then arrange the lobsters to the tray. Select the "Air Fry" mode. Press Temp button and then turn the dial to adjust the cooking temperature to 350 degrees F. Press Time button and then turn the dial to adjust the cooking time to 5 minutes. Press the Start button to initiate preheating. When the screen displays "Add Food", transfer the cooking tray to the air fryer basket of your Air Fryer. Close its door, and let the machine do the cooking. Serve your lobsters with the remaining lemon slices and pan sauce.

Per serving: Calories 305; Fat 15g; Sodium 548mg; Carbs 12g; Sugar 1.2g; Fiber 0.7g; Protein 29g

Creamy Salmon Piccata

Prep time: 15 minutes| Cook time: 12 minutes| Serves: 2

6 oz. skinless salmon fillets	1 cup low sodium chicken
¼ cup flour	broth
2 teaspoons unsalted butter	1 teaspoon cornstarch
⅓ cup dry white wine	1 teaspoon fresh lemon juice
1 teaspoon olive oil	1 teaspoon parsley chopped
4 medium garlic cloves	½ cup cream
minced	2 Lemon slices

Season both sides of your salmon fillets evenly with pepper and salt. Add ¼ cup of flour to the dish and dredge the salmon in the flour to evenly coat it. Shake off the excess flour. Melt 1 teaspoon of butter in a large skillet over medium heat. Add a 1 tablespoon of oil and swill to mix through butter. Transfer this butter, salmon and rest of the ingredients to the cooking tray. Select the "Air Fry" mode on your air fryer. Press Temp button and then turn the dial to adjust the cooking temperature to 350 degrees F. Press Time button and then turn the dial to adjust the cooking time to 12 minutes. Press the Start button to initiate preheating. When the screen displays "Add Food", transfer the cooking tray to the air fryer basket of your Air Fryer. Close its door, and let the machine do the cooking. Serve warm.

Per serving: Calories 285; Fat 9.8g; Sodium 639mg; Carbs 11.1g; Fiber 1.2g, Sugars 5.1g; Protein 27.8g

Garlic Butter Baked Salmon

Prep time: 15 minutes| Cook time: 15 minutes| Serves: 3

2 teaspoons olive oil	⅓ cup lemon juice
½ teaspoon salt	2 ½ teaspoon minced garlic
1-pound baby potatoes	6 oz. skinless salmon fillets
3 bunches of asparagus	1 lemon for garnishing
½ cup melted unsalted butter	1 teaspoon dry white wine

On a large baking sheet toss together your potatoes with oil, ½ of teaspoon salt, ½ teaspoon of garlic, and ¼ teaspoon of pepper. Spread them out evenly in the cooking tray. Select the "Air Fry" mode on your air fryer. Press Temp button and then turn the dial to adjust the cooking temperature to 380 degrees F. Press Time button and then turn the dial to adjust the cooking time to 15 minutes. Press the Start button to initiate preheating. When the screen displays "Add Food", transfer the cooking tray to the air fryer basket of your Air Fryer when the screen displays "Add Food" Close its door, and let the machine do the cooking. Push your potatoes to 1 side of the sheet pan and arrange your salmons at the center. Add 1 ½ teaspoon of minced garlic and 2 teaspoon of parsley and rub every salmon with the mixture. Add asparagus to the other end of the pan. Return them to the oven and continue baking until your potatoes are fork tender and the salmons are opaque throughout. In a bowl, combine the lemon juice, garlic, and the remaining butter with wine or chicken stock. Serve your salmon with vegetables and lemon slices.

Per serving: Calories 236; Fat 13.9g; Sodium 451mg; Carbs 13.2g; Fiber 1.2g; Sugars 1.4g; Protein 14.3g

Shrimp Cakes

Prep time: 15 minutes| Cook time: 10 minutes| Serves: 3

½ teaspoon salt	¼ teaspoon pepper
2 eggs	¼ cup finely diced red bell
1 teaspoon lemon zest	pepper

1-pound raw shrimp deveined and peeled
3 teaspoon chives

2 Lemon wedges
4 teaspoons olive oil

Place the shrimp in a bowl or food processor. Pulse them until they are chopped. When the screen displays "Add Food", transfer your shrimp into a large bowl and add red bell pepper, chives, panko bread crumbs, salt, 2 eggs, pepper, and lemon zest. Stir them until there are well combined. Form your shrimp mixture into 6 patties; heat the olive oil in a pan over medium heat. Select the "Air Fry" mode on your air fryer. Press Temp button and then turn the dial to adjust the cooking temperature to 350 degrees F. Press Time button and then turn the dial to adjust the cooking time to 10 minutes. Press the Start button to initiate preheating. When the screen displays "Add Food", transfer the patties to the air fryer basket of the Air Fryer. Close its door, and let the machine do the cooking. Serve immediately with sour cream and additional chives. Garnish with lemon wedges.
Per serving: Calories 361; Fat 10g; Sodium 218mg; Carbs 16g; Sugar 1.2g; Fiber 0.7g; Protein 24g

Easy Honey Garlic Salmon

Prep time: 15 minutes | Cook time: 8 minutes | Serves: 4

½ test paprika
Salt and black pepper, to taste
4 wild caught salmon
4 cloves garlic
2 teaspoon butter
4 cloves garlic minced

4 teaspoon honey
1 teaspoon water
1 teaspoon soy sauce
Lemon wedges
1 teaspoon freshly squeezed lemon

Season your salmon with paprika, salt and black pepper, to taste and set it aside. Heat the butter in a pan over medium heat; add your garlic and sauté for a minute. Pour honey, soy sauce and water allow for the flavors to fuse. Add lemon juice and mix them thoroughly. Add your salmon steaks to the sauce and cook side for 4 minutes. Season it with pepper and salt to taste. Transfer the salmon steak and sauce to the cooking tray.
Select the "Air Fry" mode on your air fryer. Press Temp button and then turn the dial to adjust the cooking temperature to 350 degrees F. Press Time button and then turn the dial to adjust the cooking time to 8 minutes. Press the Start button to initiate preheating. When the screen displays "Add Food", transfer the cooking tray to the air fryer basket of your Air Fryer when the screen displays "Add Food" Close its door, and let the machine do the cooking. Serve warm.
Per serving: Calories 254; Fat 28g; Sodium 346mg; Carbs 12.3g; Sugar 1g; Fiber 0.7g; Protein 24.3 g

Honey Mustard Salmon in a Foil

Prep time: 15 minutes | Cook time: 13 minutes | Serves: 6

¼ cup whole grain mustard
¼ cup honey
¼ cup butter
2 teaspoons fresh lemon juice
5 cloves garlic minced
2 teaspoon mild Dijon mustard

¼ teaspoon chili powder
2 pounds' salmon
Black pepper
2 teaspoons freshly chopped parsley
Lemon wedges

Line your cooking tray with a piece of foul that is able to fold over and create a packet. You can use 2 foils depending on the size of the foils on use and size of the salmon. In a small pan, combine the butter, honey, mustard, lemon and garlic. Whisk them properly until you achieve an even mix and ensure that honey has melted into the butter. Place your salmon into the cooking tray and pour the mixture over the salmon and use a spoon to spread them over the salmon. Sprinkle 2 teaspoon of salt and pepper. Fold the side of the foils to cover the salmon. Select the "Bake" mode on your air fryer. Press Temp button

and then turn the dial to adjust the cooking temperature to 350 degrees F. Press Time button and then turn the dial to adjust the cooking time to 10 minutes. Press the Start button to initiate preheating. When the screen displays "Add Food", transfer the cooking tray to the air fryer basket of your Air Fryer. Close its door, and let the machine do the cooking. Open the foil and be careful of to avoid escaping steam from injuring you. Bake for 3 minutes more to caramelize it on the top and garnish it with parsley before serving it immediately with lemon wedges.
Per serving: Calories 285; Fat 9.8g; Sodium 639mg; Carbs 11.1g; Fiber 1.2g, Sugars 5.1g; Protein 27.8g

Teriyaki Glazed Salmon

Prep time: 15 minutes | Cook time: 8 minutes | Serves: 5

¼ cup cooking sake
¼ cup soy sauce
3 teaspoon brown sugar
2 teaspoon mirin
1 teaspoon Japanese rice wine vinegar

1 teaspoon sesame
½ teaspoon garlic powder
6 oz. skinless salmon fillets
2 cups of broccoli
1 shallot onion stem
1 large courgetti or zucchini

Combine sake, brown sugar, soy sauce, mirin, garlic powder and vinegar and mix together in a bowl. Mix them properly until the sugar is dissolved. Pour half of the marinade in a small pan and set aside. Rinse and pat dry your salmon with paper towel. Place your salmon fillets in the cooking tray with teriyaki glaze and allow it to coat properly. Select the "Air Fry" mode on your air fryer. Press Temp button and then turn the dial to adjust the cooking temperature to 350 degrees F. Press Time button and then turn the dial to adjust the cooking time to 8 minutes. Press the Start button to initiate preheating. When the screen displays "Add Food", transfer the cooking tray to the air fryer basket of your Air Fryer. Close its door, and let the machine do the cooking. Serve the salmon over steamed vegetables and pour your teriyaki glaze over the top.
Per serving: Calories 249; Fat 13g; Sodium 556mg; Carbs 10g; Sugar 1.1g; Fiber 0.7g; Protein 31g

Delicious Baked Tilapia

Prep time: 15 minutes | Cook time: 15 minutes | Serves: 6

6 tilapia fillets, pat dry with a paper towel
½ cup Asiago cheese, grated
¼ teaspoon dried basil
¼ teaspoon dried thyme

¼ teaspoon onion powder
¼ teaspoon garlic powder
½ cup mayonnaise
⅛ teaspoon black pepper
¼ teaspoon salt

Arrange the tilapia fillets onto the parchment-lined cooking tray. In a small bowl, mix together mayonnaise, garlic powder, onion powder, thyme, basil, Asiago cheese, pepper, and salt. Spread mayonnaise mixture on top of tilapia fillet. Select the "Air Fry" mode on your air fryer. Press Temp button and then turn the dial to adjust the cooking temperature to 350 degrees F. Press Time button and then turn the dial to adjust the cooking time to 15 minutes. Press the Start button to initiate preheating. When the screen displays "Add Food", transfer the tray to the rack of the Air Fryer. Close its door, and let the machine do the cooking. Serve and enjoy.
Per serving: Calories 305; Fat 15g; Sodium 548mg; Carbs 12g; Sugar 1.2g; Fiber 0.7g; Protein 29g

Lemon Butter Tilapia

Prep time: 15 minutes | Cook time: 15 minutes | Serves: 4

4 tilapia fillets

1 lemon, sliced

1 teaspoon pepper
1 teaspoon parsley, chopped

1 teaspoon old bay seasoning
2 tablespoons butter, melted

Arrange fish fillets onto the cooking tray. In a small bowl, mix together butter, old bay seasoning, parsley, and pepper. Brush fish fillets with butter mixture. Arrange lemon slices on top of fish fillets. Select the "Air Fry" mode on your air fryer. Press Temp button and then turn the dial to adjust the cooking temperature to 400 degrees F. Press Time button and then turn the dial to adjust the cooking time to 15 minutes. Press the Start button to initiate preheating. When the screen displays "Add Food", transfer the tray to the air fryer basket of the Air Fryer. Close its door, and let the machine do the cooking. Serve and enjoy.

Per serving: Calories 285; Fat 9.8g; Sodium 639mg; Carbs 11.1g; Fiber 1.2g, Sugars 5.1g; Protein 27.8g

Baked Catfish

Prep time: 15 minutes| Cook time: 20 minutes| Serves: 4

4 catfish fillets
¼ teaspoon garlic powder
2 tablespoon butter, melted
lemon juice
½ teaspoon pepper
½ teaspoon dried basil

½ teaspoon dried oregano
½ teaspoon dried thyme
¾ teaspoon paprika
2 tablespoon parsley, chopped
1 teaspoon salt

Place fish fillets into the cooking tray. Mix together the remaining ingredients and pour over fish fillets. Select the "Air Fry" mode on your air fryer. Press Temp button and then turn the dial to adjust the cooking temperature to 350 degrees F. Press Time button and then turn the dial to adjust the cooking time to 20 minutes. Press the Start button to initiate preheating. When the screen displays "Add Food", transfer the cooking tray to the air fryer basket of your Air Fryer. Close its door, and let the machine do the cooking. Serve and enjoy.

Per serving: Calories 361; Fat 10g; Sodium 218mg; Carbs 16g; Sugar 1.2g; Fiber 0.7g; Protein 24g

Easy Parmesan Tilapia

Prep time: 15 minutes| Cook time: 12 minutes| Serves: 4

1-pound tilapia fillets
½ teaspoon pepper
1 tablespoon olive oil
1 tablespoon dried parsley

1 tablespoon paprika
1 cup parmesan cheese, grated
½ teaspoon salt

In a shallow dish, mix together parmesan cheese, paprika, dried parsley, pepper, and salt. Brush fish fillets with oil and coat with parmesan mixture. Place coated fish fillets onto the cooking tray. Select the "Air Fry" mode on your air fryer. Press Temp button and then turn the dial to adjust the cooking temperature to 400 degrees F. Press Time button and then turn the dial to adjust the cooking time to 12 minutes. Press the Start button to initiate preheating. When the screen displays "Add Food", transfer the tray to the air fryer basket of the Air Fryer. Close its door, and let the machine do the cooking. Serve and enjoy.

Per serving: Calories 344; Fat 14.9g; Sodium 227mg; Carbs 12g; Fiber 1.2g; Sugars 1g; Protein 27g

Garlic Butter Cod

Prep time: 15 minutes| Cook time: 20 minutes| Serves: 2

8 oz. cod fillets
1 tablespoon parsley, chopped
⅛ teaspoon paprika

2 garlic cloves, minced
1 tablespoon olive oil
1 tablespoon butter

⅛ teaspoon salt

Arrange fish fillets onto the cooking tray. In a small bowl, mix together butter, oil, garlic, paprika, parsley, and salt. Brush fish fillets with butter mixture. Select the "Air Fry" mode on your air fryer. Press Temp button and then turn the dial to adjust the cooking temperature to 400 degrees F. Press Time button and then turn the dial to adjust the cooking time to 20 minutes. Press the Start button to initiate preheating. When the screen displays "Add Food", transfer the tray to the air fryer basket of the Air Fryer. Close its door, and let the machine do the cooking. Serve and enjoy.

Per serving: Calories 236; Fat 13.9g; Sodium 451mg; Carbs 13.2g; Fiber 1.2g; Sugars 1.4g; Protein 14.3g

Easy Baked Tilapia

Prep time: 15 minutes| Cook time: 20 minutes| Serves: 4

4 tilapia fillets
2 tablespoon butter, melted

2 teaspoons paprika
½ teaspoon salt

Arrange fish fillets onto the cooking tray. In a small bowl, mix together butter, paprika, and salt. Brush fish fillets with butter mixture. Select the "Air Fry" mode on your air fryer. Press Temp button and then turn the dial to adjust the cooking temperature to 400 degrees F. Press Time button and then turn the dial to adjust the cooking time to 20 minutes. Press the Start button to initiate preheating. When the screen displays "Add Food", transfer the tray to the air fryer basket of the Air Fryer. Close its door, and let the machine do the cooking. Serve and enjoy.

Per serving: Calories 285; Fat 9.8g; Sodium 639mg; Carbs 11.1g; Fiber 1.2g, Sugars 5.1g; Protein 27.8g

Baked Parmesan Cod

Prep time: 15 minutes| Cook time: 15 minutes| Serves: 2

2 cod fillets
¼ tablespoon olive oil
½ teaspoon parsley
½ teaspoon paprika

¼ cups parmesan cheese, grated
Pepper
Salt

In a shallow dish, mix together parmesan cheese, paprika, and parsley. Brush fish fillets with oil and season with pepper and salt. Coat the fish fillets with parmesan cheese mixture and then place onto the cooking tray.
Select the "Air Fry" mode on your air fryer. Press Temp button and then turn the dial to adjust the cooking temperature to 400 degrees F. Press Time button and then turn the dial to adjust the cooking time to 15 minutes. Press the Start button to initiate preheating. When the screen displays "Add Food", transfer the tray to the air fryer basket of the Air Fryer. Close its door, and let the machine do the cooking. Serve and enjoy.

Per serving: Calories 344; Fat 14.9g; Sodium 227mg; Carbs 14g; Fiber 1g; Sugars 1.4g; Protein 25.7g

Delicious Baked Cod

Prep time: 15 minutes| Cook time: 25 minutes| Serves: 4

1-pound cod fillets
1 ½ teaspoon lemon juice
1 teaspoon olive oil
1 garlic clove, chopped

½ teaspoon pepper
½ teaspoon ground cumin
⅛ teaspoon ground turmeric
½ teaspoon salt

Add fish fillets and remaining ingredients into the zip-lock bag, seal bag, and place in the refrigerator overnight. Place marinated fish fillets onto the cooking tray. Select the "Air Fry" mode on your air fryer. Press Temp button and then turn the dial to adjust the cooking temperature to 400 degrees F. Press Time button and then turn the dial to adjust the cooking time to 25 minutes. Press the Start button to initiate preheating. When the screen displays "Add Food", transfer the tray to the air fryer basket of the Air Fryer. Close its door, and let the machine do the cooking. Serve and enjoy.

Per serving: Calories 305; Fat 15g; Sodium 548mg; Carbs 12g; Sugar 1.2g; Fiber 0.7g; Protein 29g

Lemon Parmesan Cod

Prep time: 15 minutes| Cook time: 15 minutes| Serves: 4

½ lbs. cod fillets, boneless	grated
1 teaspoon paprika	2 garlic cloves, minced
¾ cups parmesan cheese,	¼ cups butter, melted

In a small dish, mix together butter and garlic. In a shallow dish, mix together parmesan cheese and paprika. Dip fish fillet in butter mixture then coats with parmesan mixture and place onto the cooking tray. Select the "Air Fry" mode on your air fryer. Press Temp button and then turn the dial to adjust the cooking temperature to 400 degrees F. Press Time button and then turn the dial to adjust the cooking time to 15 minutes. Press the Start button to initiate preheating. When the screen displays "Add Food", transfer the tray to the air fryer basket of the Air Fryer. Close its door, and let the machine do the cooking. Serve and enjoy.

Per serving: Calories 351; Fat 22g; Sodium 502mg; Carbs 15.2g; Sugar 1.1g; Fiber 0.7g; Protein 26.4g

Garlic Herb Cod

Prep time: 15 minutes| Cook time: 12 minutes| Serves: 4

2 lbs. cod fillets	⅓ cup parmesan cheese, grated
1 garlic clove, grated	⅓ cup mayonnaise
1 tablespoon parsley, chopped	Black pepper, to taste
1 tablespoon basil, chopped	Salt, to taste

Arrange fish fillets onto the cooking tray. In a small bowl, mix together mayonnaise, parmesan cheese, basil, parsley, garlic, pepper, and salt. Spread mayonnaise mixture on top of fish fillets. Select the "Air Fry" mode on your air fryer. Press Temp button and then turn the dial to adjust the cooking temperature to 400 degrees F. Press Time button and then turn the dial to adjust the cooking time to 12 minutes. Press the Start button to initiate preheating. When the screen displays "Add Food", transfer the cooking tray to the air fryer basket of your Air Fryer. Close its door, and let the machine do the cooking. Serve and enjoy.

Per serving: Calories 361; Fat 10g; Sodium 218mg; Carbs 16g; Sugar 1.2g; Fiber 0.7g; Protein 24g

Lemon Pepper Sea Bass

Prep time: 15 minutes| Cook time: 20 minutes| Serves: 1

1 oz. sea bass fillet	½ lemon juice
½ teaspoon paprika	2 garlic cloves, minced
½ teaspoon lemon pepper	½ teaspoon pink salt

Place the fish fillet in the cooking tray. Mix together lemon juice, garlic, lemon pepper, paprika, and salt and pour over the fish fillet. Select the "Air Fry" mode on your air fryer. Press Temp button and then turn the dial to adjust the cooking temperature to 400 degrees F. Press Time button and then turn the dial to adjust the cooking time to 20 minutes. Press the Start button to initiate preheating. When the screen displays "Add Food", transfer the

cooking tray to the air fryer basket of your Air Fryer. Close its door, and let the machine do the cooking. Serve and enjoy.

Per serving: Calories 254; Fat 28g; Sodium 346mg; Carbs 12.3g; Sugar 1g; Fiber 0.7g; Protein 24.3 g

Lemon Butter Shrimp

Prep time: 15 minutes| Cook time: 12 minutes| Serves: 4

½ lbs. shrimp, peeled and deveined	1 tablespoon garlic, minced
1 tablespoon parsley, chopped	¼ cups butter, melted
⅛ teaspoon chili flakes	Pepper
2 tablespoon lemon juice	Salt

Add shrimp and remaining ingredients into the baking pan and mix well. Select the "Air Fry" mode on your air fryer. Press Temp button and then turn the dial to adjust the cooking temperature to 350 degrees F. Press Time button and then turn the dial to adjust the cooking time to 12 minutes. Press the Start button to initiate preheating. When the screen displays "Add Food", transfer the cooking tray to the air fryer basket of your Air Fryer. Close its door, and let the machine do the cooking. Serve and enjoy.

Per serving: Calories 236; Fat 13.9g; Sodium 451mg; Carbs 13.2g; Fiber 1.2g; Sugars 1.4g; Protein 14.3g

Shrimp with Grape Tomatoes

Prep time: 15 minutes| Cook time: 25 minutes| Serves: 4

1-pound shrimp, peeled and deveined	4 garlic cloves, sliced
1 tablespoon olive oil	2 cups grape tomatoes
	½ teaspoon salt

Add shrimp and remaining ingredients into the baking pan and mix well. Select the "Air Fry" mode on your air fryer. Press Temp button and then turn the dial to adjust the cooking temperature to 400 degrees F. Press Time button and then turn the dial to adjust the cooking time to 25 minutes. Press the Start button to initiate preheating. When the screen displays "Add Food", transfer the cooking tray to the air fryer basket of your Air Fryer when the screen displays "Add Food" Close its door, and let the machine do the cooking. Serve and enjoy.

Per serving: Calories 285; Fat 9.8g; Sodium 639mg; Carbs 11.1g; Fiber 1.2g, Sugars 5.1g; Protein 27.8g

Greek Shrimp

Prep time: 15 minutes| Cook time: 20 minutes| Serves: 4

1-pound shrimp, peeled and deveined	2 garlic cloves, minced
¾ cups feta cheese, crumbled	1 tablespoon olive oil
⅛ teaspoon red chili flakes	14.5 oz. can tomato, diced
½ teaspoon oregano	¼ teaspoon salt

Add shrimp into the baking pan. Mix together remaining ingredients and pour over shrimp. Select the "Air Fry" mode on your air fryer. Press Temp button and then turn the dial to adjust the cooking temperature to 375 degrees F. Press Time button and then turn the dial to adjust the cooking time to 20 minutes. Press the Start button to initiate preheating. When the screen displays "Add Food", transfer the cooking tray to the air fryer basket of your Air Fryer. Close its door, and let the machine do the cooking. Serve and enjoy.

Per serving: Calories 305; Fat 15g; Sodium 548mg; Carbs 12g; Sugar 1.2g; Fiber 0.7g; Protein 29g

Flavorful Baked Shrimp

Prep time: 15 minutes| Cook time: 10 minutes| Serves: 4

1-pound shrimp, peeled and deveined
⅛ teaspoon ground pepper
¼ teaspoon onion powder
¼ teaspoon cumin

½ teaspoon garlic powder
½ teaspoon chili powder
2 tablespoons olive oil
¼ teaspoon sea salt

In a large bowl, toss shrimp with the remaining ingredients. Transfer shrimp into the cooking tray. Select the "Air Fry" mode on your air fryer. Press Temp button and then turn the dial to adjust the cooking temperature to 400 degrees F. Press Time button and then turn the dial to adjust the cooking time to 10 minutes. Press the Start button to initiate preheating. When the screen displays "Add Food", transfer the cooking tray to the air fryer basket of your Air Fryer. Close its door, and let the machine do the cooking. Serve and enjoy.
Per serving: Calories 285; Fat 9.8g; Sodium 639mg; Carbs 11.1g; Fiber 1.2g, Sugars 5.1g; Protein 27.8g

Italian Shrimp

Prep time: 15 minutes| Cook time: 10 minutes| Serves: 4

1-pound shrimp, peeled and deveined
¾ cups fresh Italian parsley
½ cup olive oil

3 tablespoon lemon juice
¼ teaspoon pepper
¼ teaspoon salt

Add shrimp into the cooking tray. Add parsley, oil, lemon juice, pepper and salt into the blender and blend until smooth. Pour blended mixture over shrimp and mix well. Select the "Air Fry" mode on your air fryer. Press Temp button and then turn the dial to adjust the cooking temperature to 400 degrees F. Press Time button and then turn the dial to adjust the cooking time to 10 minutes. Press the Start button to initiate preheating. When the screen displays "Add Food", transfer the cooking tray to the air fryer basket of your Air Fryer when the screen displays "Add Food" Close its door, and let the machine do the cooking. Serve and enjoy.
Per serving: Calories 344; Fat 14.9g; Sodium 227mg; Carbs 14g; Fiber 1g; Sugars 1.4g; Protein 25.7g

Lemon Dill White Fish Fillets

Prep time: 15 minutes| Cook time: 25 minutes| Serves: 2

2 white fish fillets
2 tablespoon butter, melted

1 teaspoon dried dill

Place fish fillets in the cooking tray. Mix together melted butter and dill and pour over fish fillets. Select the "Air Fry" mode on your air fryer. Press Temp button and then turn the dial to adjust the cooking temperature to 400 degrees F. Press Time button and then turn the dial to adjust the cooking time to 25 minutes. Press the Start button to initiate preheating. When the screen displays "Add Food", transfer the cooking tray to the air fryer basket of your Air Fryer when the screen displays "Add Food" Close its door, and let the machine do the cooking. Serve and enjoy.
Per serving: Calories 361; Fat 10g; Sodium 218mg; Carbs 16g; Sugar 1.2g; Fiber 0.7g; Protein 24g

Herb Salmon

Prep time: 15 minutes| Cook time: 8 minutes| Serves: 2

8 oz. salmon fillets

1 tablespoon butter, melted

1 tablespoon olive oil
¼ teaspoon pepper

1 teaspoon herb de province
¼ teaspoon sea salt

In a small bowl, mix together oil, pepper, herb de Provence, and salt. Brush salmon fillets with oil and place them onto the cooking tray. Select the "Air Fry" mode on your air fryer. Press Temp button and then turn the dial to adjust the cooking temperature to 390 degrees F. Press Time button and then turn the dial to adjust the cooking time to 8 minutes. Press the Start button to initiate preheating. When the screen displays "Add Food", transfer the tray to the air fryer basket of the Air Fryer. Close its door, and let the machine do the cooking. Pour melted butter over salmon and serve.
Per serving: Calories 285; Fat 9.8g; Sodium 639mg; Carbs 11.1g; Fiber 1.2g, Sugars 5.1g; Protein 27.8g

Flavored Crab Cakes

Prep time: 15 minutes| Cook time: 10 minutes| Serves: 4

8 oz. lump crab meat
1 teaspoon old bay seasoning
1 tablespoon Dijon mustard
2 tablespoons almond flour

2 tablespoon mayonnaise
2 green onions, chopped
¼ cups bell pepper, chopped

Add all ingredients into the mixing bowl and mix until well combined. Make small patties from mixture and place onto the parchment-lined cooking tray. Select the "Air Fry" mode on your air fryer. Press Temp button and then turn the dial to adjust the cooking temperature to 370 degrees F. Press Time button and then turn the dial to adjust the cooking time to 10 minutes. Press the Start button to initiate preheating. When the screen displays "Add Food", transfer the tray to the air fryer basket of the Air Fryer. Close its door, and let the machine do the cooking. Serve and enjoy.
Per serving: Calories 236; Fat 13.9g; Sodium 451mg; Carbs 13.2g; Fiber 1.2g; Sugars 1.4g; Protein 14.3g

Lemon Garlic Scallops

Prep time: 15 minutes| Cook time: 12 minutes| Serves: 2

8 scallops, cleaned and pat dry
½ teaspoon garlic, chopped
1 teaspoon lemon zest, grated
1 teaspoon capers, chopped

1 tablespoon parsley, chopped
¼ cups olive oil
¼ teaspoon pepper
⅛ teaspoon salt

Add scallops and remaining ingredients into the baking pan and mix well. Select the "Air Fry" mode on your air fryer. Press Temp button and then turn the dial to adjust the cooking temperature to 400 degrees F. Press Time button and then turn the dial to adjust the cooking time to 12 minutes. Press the Start button to initiate preheating. When the screen displays "Add Food", transfer the cooking tray to the air fryer basket of your Air Fryer. Close its door, and let the machine do the cooking. Flip scallops halfway through. Serve and enjoy.
Per serving: Calories 327; Fat 15g; Sodium 548mg; Carbs 12g; Sugar 1.2g; Fiber 0.7g; Protein 29g

Salmon with Tomato Salsa

Prep time: 15 minutes| Cook time: 15 minutes| Serves: 4

4 salmon fillets
2 tablespoons olive oil
¼ teaspoon pepper
½ teaspoon salt
For salsa:
2 teaspoons olive oil

2 teaspoons fresh lemon juice
1 tablespoon fresh parsley, chopped
1 tablespoon fresh basil, chopped
2 tablespoon onion, chopped

1 cup zucchini, chopped	½ bell pepper, chopped
1 ½ cups tomato, chopped	⅛ teaspoon pepper
1 garlic clove, minced	¼ teaspoon salt
1 ½ teaspoon capers	

Place salmon in the greased cooking tray and drizzle with oil and season with pepper and salt. Select the "Air Fry" mode on your air fryer. Press Temp button and then turn the dial to adjust the cooking temperature to 400 degrees F. Press Time button and then turn the dial to adjust the cooking time to 15 minutes. Press the Start button to initiate preheating. When the screen displays "Add Food", transfer the cooking tray to the air fryer basket of your Air Fryer when the screen displays "Add Food" Close its door, and let the machine do the cooking. In a bowl, mix together all salsa ingredients. Top fish fillets with salsa and serve.
Per serving: Calories 344; Fat 14.9g; Sodium 227mg; Carbs 14g; Fiber 1g; Sugars 1.4g; Protein 25.7g

Delicious Tuna Patties

Prep time: 15 minutes| Cook time: 20 minutes| Serves: 4

14.5 oz. can tuna, drained	½ cup parsley, chopped
1 tablespoon garlic, minced	1 tablespoon Dijon mustard
2 eggs, lightly beaten	Pepper
¼ cups almond flour	Salt

In a mixing bowl, mix together tuna, parsley, mustard, garlic, 2 eggs, almond flour, pepper, and salt. Make small patties from mixture and place onto the parchment-lined cooking tray. Select the "Air Fry" mode on your air fryer. Press Temp button and then turn the dial to adjust the cooking temperature to 400 degrees F. Press Time button and then turn the dial to adjust the cooking time to 20 minutes. Press the Start button to initiate preheating. When the screen displays "Add Food", transfer the tray to the air fryer basket of the Air Fryer. Close its door, and let the machine do the cooking. Serve and enjoy.
Per serving: Calories 285; Fat 9.8g; Sodium 639mg; Carbs 11.1g; Fiber 1.2g, Sugars 5.1g; Protein 27.8g

Feta Tuna Patties

Prep time: 15 minutes| Cook time: 15 minutes| Serves: 6

10 oz. can tuna, drained	egg, lightly beaten
1 tablespoon lemon juice	1 garlic clove, minced
1 tablespoon green onion, minced	½ teaspoon lemon zest
1 tablespoon flax meal	1 teaspoon dried oregano
½ cup feta cheese, crumbled	1 tablespoon fresh mint, chopped

Add all ingredients into the bowl and mix until well combined. Make small patties from tuna mixture and place onto the parchment-lined cooking tray. Select the "Air Fry" mode on your air fryer. Press Temp button and then turn the dial to adjust the cooking temperature to 400 degrees F. Press Time button and then turn the dial to adjust the cooking time to 15 minutes. Press the Start button to initiate preheating. When the screen displays "Add Food", transfer the tray to the air fryer basket of the Air Fryer. Close its door, and let the machine do the cooking. Serve and enjoy.
Per serving: Calories 249; Fat 13g; Sodium 556mg; Carbs 10g; Sugar 1.1g; Fiber 0.7g; Protein 31g

Salmon with Spread

Prep time: 15 minutes| Cook time: 30 minutes| Serves: 6

6 salmon fillets	½ lemon juice
2 garlic cloves, minced	For spread:

½ cup olives, chopped	½ cup feta cheese, crumbled
4 tomatoes, diced	Pepper
3 tablespoons fresh basil, chopped	Salt

Place salmon fillets into the cooking tray. Pour lemon juice over fish fillets and sprinkle with garlic. Select the "Air Fry" mode on your air fryer. Press Temp button and then turn the dial to adjust the cooking temperature to 375 degrees F. Press Time button and then turn the dial to adjust the cooking time to 30 minutes. Press the Start button to initiate preheating. When the screen displays "Add Food", transfer the cooking tray to the air fryer basket of your Air Fryer when the screen displays "Add Food" Close its door, and let the machine do the cooking. In a bowl, mix together all spread ingredients. Top cooked salmon with spread and serve.
Per serving: Calories 361; Fat 10g; Sodium 218mg; Carbs 16g; Sugar 1.2g; Fiber 0.7g; Protein 24g

Rosemary Salmon

Prep time: 15 minutes| Cook time: 15 minutes| Serves: 2

2 salmon fillets	1 tablespoon olive oil
4 fresh rosemary sprigs	Salt
1 lemon, sliced	

Place half lemon slices and 2 rosemary sprigs into the cooking tray and top with salmon fillets. Arrange remaining lemon slices and rosemary sprigs on top of salmon fillets. Drizzle fish fillet with oil and season with salt. Select the "Air Fry" mode on your air fryer. Press Temp button and then turn the dial to adjust the cooking temperature to 400 degrees F. Press Time button and then turn the dial to adjust the cooking time to 20 minutes. Press the Start button to initiate preheating. When the screen displays "Add Food", transfer the cooking tray to the air fryer basket of your Air Fryer. Close its door, and let the machine do the cooking. Serve and enjoy.
Per serving: Calories 236; Fat 13.9g; Sodium 451mg; Carbs 13.2g; Fiber 1.2g; Sugars 1.4g; Protein 14.3g

Basil Tomato Salmon

Prep time: 15 minutes| Cook time: 20 minutes| Serves: 2

2 salmon fillets	grated
1 tomato, sliced	1 tablespoon olive oil
1 tablespoon dried basil	Pepper
2 tablespoon parmesan cheese,	Salt

Place fish fillets into the cooking tray. Season the fillets with basil, salt and pepper. Arrange tomato slices on top of salmon fillets. Drizzle with oil and sprinkle cheese on top. Select the "Air Fry" mode on your air fryer. Press Temp button and then turn the dial to adjust the cooking temperature to 375 degrees F. Press Time button and then turn the dial to adjust the cooking time to 20 minutes. Press the Start button to initiate preheating. When the screen displays "Add Food", transfer the cooking tray to the air fryer basket of your Air Fryer. Close its door, and let the machine do the cooking. Serve and enjoy.
Per serving: Calories 305; Fat 15g; Sodium 548mg; Carbs 12g; Sugar 1.2g; Fiber 0.7g; Protein 29g

Lemon Herb Tilapia

Prep time: 15 minutes| Cook time: 18 minutes| Serves: 4

1-pound tilapia fillets	2 teaspoons olive oil
1 teaspoon fresh lemon juice	½ teaspoon garlic powder

½ teaspoon dried thyme
½ teaspoon dried oregano
¼ teaspoon pepper
1 teaspoon salt

Brush fish fillets with oil and lemon juice and place into a parchment-lined cooking tray. In a small bowl, mix oregano, garlic powder, thyme, pepper, and salt and sprinkle over fish fillets. Select the "Air Fry" mode on your air fryer. Press Temp button and then turn the dial to adjust the cooking temperature to 400 degrees F. Press Time button and then turn the dial to adjust the cooking time to 18 minutes. Press the Start button to initiate preheating. When the screen displays "Add Food", transfer the cooking tray to the air fryer basket of your Air Fryer. Close its door, and let the machine do the cooking. Serve and enjoy.
Per serving: Calories 285; Fat 9.8g; Sodium 639mg; Carbs 11.1g; Fiber 1.2g, Sugars 5.1g; Protein 27.8g

Italian Baked Cod

Prep time: 15 minutes| Cook time: 20 minutes| Serves: 4

½ lbs. cod fillet
1 tablespoon olive oil
1-pound cherry tomatoes, halved
3 garlic cloves, crushed
1 small onion, chopped
¼ cups of water
1 teaspoon Italian seasoning
¼ cups olives, sliced
Pepper
Salt

Place fish fillets, olives, tomatoes, garlic, and onion in the greased cooking tray. Drizzle with oil and sprinkle with Italian seasoning, pepper, and salt. Pour water into the dish. Select the "Air Fry" mode on your air fryer. Press Temp button and then turn the dial to adjust the cooking temperature to 400 degrees F. Press Time button and then turn the dial to adjust the cooking time to 20 minutes. Press the Start button to initiate preheating. When the screen displays "Add Food", transfer the cooking tray to the air fryer basket of your Air Fryer. Close its door, and let the machine do the cooking. Serve and enjoy.
Per serving: Calories 254; Fat 28g; Sodium 346mg; Carbs 12.3g; Sugar 1g; Fiber 0.7g; Protein 24.3 g

Air Fryer Catfish

Prep time: 15 minutes| Cook time: 20 minutes| Serves: 4

4 catfish fillets
1 tablespoon olive oil
1 tablespoon parsley, chopped
Pepper
Salt

Brush fish fillets with oil and season with pepper and salt. Place fish fillets onto the parchment-lined cooking tray. Sprinkle parsley on top of fish fillets. Select the "Air Fry" mode on your air fryer. Press Temp button and then turn the dial to adjust the cooking temperature to 400 degrees F. Press Time button and then turn the dial to adjust the cooking time to 20 minutes. Press the Start button to initiate preheating. When the screen displays "Add Food", transfer the tray to the air fryer basket of the Air Fryer. Close its door, and let the machine do the cooking. Serve and enjoy.
Per serving: Calories 351; Fat 22g; Sodium 502mg; Carbs 15.2g; Sugar 1.1g; Fiber 0.7g; Protein 26.4g

Shrimp and Vegetables

Prep time: 15 minutes| Cook time: 20 minutes| Serves: 4

2 lbs. shrimp, peeled and deveined
1 bag of frozen mixed vegetables
1 tablespoon Cajun seasoning
Pepper
Salt

Arrange shrimp and vegetables onto the cooking tray and season with Cajun seasoning, pepper, and salt. Select the "Air Fry" mode on your air fryer. Press Temp button and then turn the dial to adjust the cooking temperature to 350 degrees F. Press Time button and then turn the dial to adjust the cooking time to 20 minutes. Press the Start button to initiate preheating. When the screen displays "Add Food", transfer the tray to the rack of the air fryer when the screen displays "Add Food" Close its door, and let the machine do the cooking. Serve and enjoy.
Per serving: Calories 361; Fat 10g; Sodium 218mg; Carbs 16g; Sugar 1.2g; Fiber 0.7g; Protein 24g

Air Fryer Shrimp Scampi

Prep time: 15 minutes| Cook time: 6 minutes| Serves: 4

1-pound shrimp
1 teaspoon red pepper flakes
1 tablespoon garlic, minced
1 tablespoon fresh lemon juice
4 tablespoons butter
2 tablespoons white wine
1 teaspoon dried basil
1 teaspoon dried chives

Add all ingredients into the cooking tray and mix well. Select the "Air Fry" mode on your air fryer. Press Temp button and then turn the dial to adjust the cooking temperature to 350 degrees F. Press Time button and then turn the dial to adjust the cooking time to 6 minutes. Press the Start button to initiate preheating. When the screen displays "Add Food", transfer the cooking tray to the air fryer basket of your Air Fryer. Close its door, and let the machine do the cooking. Serve and enjoy.
Per serving: Calories 344; Fat 14.9g; Sodium 227mg; Carbs 14g; Fiber 1g; Sugars 1.4g; Protein 25.7g

Air Fryer Mackerel

Prep time: 15 minutes| Cook time: 20 minutes| Serves: 2

½ lbs. mackerel fish fillets
½ teaspoon olive oil
Pepper
Salt

Place the fish fillet in the cooking tray and drizzle with oil and season with pepper and salt. Select the "Air Fry" mode on your air fryer. Press Temp button and then turn the dial to adjust the cooking temperature to 390 degrees F. Press Time button and then turn the dial to adjust the cooking time to 20 minutes. Press the Start button to initiate preheating. When the screen displays "Add Food", transfer the cooking tray to the air fryer basket of your Air Fryer. Close its door, and let the machine do the cooking. Serve and enjoy.
Per serving: Calories 305; Fat 15g; Sodium 548mg; Carbs 12g; Sugar 1.2g; Fiber 0.7g; Protein 29g

Air Fryer Hot Shrimp

Prep time: 15 minutes| Cook time: 8 minutes| Serves: 4

12 shrimp
½ teaspoon chili flakes
½ teaspoon pepper
½ teaspoon chili powder
½ teaspoon salt

Add all ingredients to the bowl and toss well. Add marinated shrimp onto the parchment-lined cooking tray. Select the "Air Fry" mode on your air fryer. Press Temp button and then turn the dial to adjust the cooking temperature to 350 degrees F. Press Time button and then turn the dial to adjust the cooking time to 8 minutes. Press the Start button to initiate preheating. When the screen displays "Add Food", transfer the tray to the air fryer basket of the Air Fryer. Close its door, and let the machine do the cooking. Serve and enjoy.
Per serving: Calories 285; Fat 9.8g; Sodium 639mg; Carbs 11.1g; Fiber 1.2g, Sugars 5.1g; Protein 27.8g

Creole Seasoned Shrimp

Prep time: 15 minutes| Cook time: 7 minutes| Serves: 2

1-pound shrimp, deveined and shelled	⅛ teaspoon cayenne pepper
1 teaspoon Creole seasoning	¼ teaspoon paprika
1 teaspoon vinegar	1 tablespoon olive oil

Add all ingredients into the bowl and mix well. Add marinated shrimp into the cooking tray. Select the "Air Fry" mode on your air fryer. Press Temp button and then turn the dial to adjust the cooking temperature to 400 degrees F. Press Time button and then turn the dial to adjust the cooking time to 7 minutes. Press the Start button to initiate preheating. When the screen displays "Add Food", transfer the cooking tray to the air fryer basket of your Air Fryer. Close its door, and let the machine do the cooking. Serve and enjoy.

Per serving: Calories 344; Fat 14.9g; Sodium 227mg; Carbs 14g; Fiber 1g; Sugars 1.4g; Protein 25.7g

Shrimp with Cherry Tomatoes

Prep time: 15 minutes| Cook time: 25 minutes| Serves: 4

2 cups cherry tomatoes	1 tablespoon garlic, sliced
1 tablespoon olive oil	Pepper
1-pound shrimp, peeled	Salt

Add shrimp, oil, garlic, tomatoes, pepper, and salt into the bowl and toss well. Transfer shrimp mixture into the cooking tray. Select the "Air Fry" mode on your air fryer. Press Temp button and then turn the dial to adjust the cooking temperature to 400 degrees F. Press Time button and then turn the dial to adjust the cooking time to 25 minutes. Press the Start button to initiate preheating. When the screen displays "Add Food", transfer the cooking tray to the air fryer basket of your Air Fryer. Close its door, and let the machine do the cooking. Serve and enjoy.

Per serving: Calories 285; Fat 9.8g; Sodium 639mg; Carbs 11.1g; Fiber 1.2g, Sugars 5.1g; Protein 27.8g

Spicy Lemon Garlic Shrimp

Prep time: 15 minutes| Cook time: 6 minutes| Serves: 4

1-pound shrimp	1 teaspoon fresh lemon juice
1 teaspoon steak seasoning	1 teaspoon lemon zest, grated
¼ teaspoon red pepper flakes	2 teaspoons olive oil
2 garlic cloves, minced	Pepper
½ tablespoon parsley, chopped	Salt

Add shrimp and remaining ingredients into the bowl and toss well. Transfer shrimp onto the cooking tray. Select the "Air Fry" mode on your air fryer. Press Temp button and then turn the dial to adjust the cooking temperature to 400 degrees F. Press Time button and then turn the dial to adjust the cooking time to 6 minutes. Press the Start button to initiate preheating. When the screen displays "Add Food", transfer the cooking tray to the air fryer basket of the Air Fryer. Close its door, and let the machine do the cooking. Serve and enjoy.

Per serving: Calories 361; Fat 10g; Sodium 218mg; Carbs 16g; Sugar 1.2g; Fiber 0.7g; Protein 24g

Flavorful Crab Cakes

Prep time: 15 minutes| Cook time: 10 minutes| Serves: 5

18 oz. can crab meat, drained	1 teaspoon Old bay seasoning
1-½ tablespoons Dijon mustard	½ teaspoon dried parsley
2 ½ tablespoons mayonnaise	1 tablespoon dried celery
2 eggs, lightly beaten	Pepper
¼ cups almond flour	Salt

Add all ingredients into the bowl and mix until well combined. Make small patties from mixture and place onto the parchment-lined cooking tray. Select the "Air Fry" mode on your air fryer. Press Temp button and then turn the dial to adjust the cooking temperature to 320 degrees F. Press Time button and then turn the dial to adjust the cooking time to 10 minutes. Press the Start button to initiate preheating. When the screen displays "Add Food", transfer the tray to the air fryer basket of the Air Fryer. Close its door, and let the machine do the cooking. Serve and enjoy.

Per serving: Calories 305; Fat 15g; Sodium 548mg; Carbs 12g; Sugar 1.2g; Fiber 0.7g; Protein 29g

Lemon Pepper Tilapia

Prep time: 15 minutes| Cook time: 10 minutes| Serves: 2

2 tilapia fillets	½ teaspoon garlic powder
½ teaspoon lemon pepper seasoning	½ teaspoon onion powder
	Salt

Spray tilapia with cooking spray and season with lemon pepper seasoning, garlic powder, onion powder, and salt. Place tilapia onto the parchment-lined cooking tray. Select the "Air Fry" mode on your air fryer. Press Temp button and then turn the dial to adjust the cooking temperature to 360 degrees F. Press Time button and then turn the dial to adjust the cooking time to 10 minutes. Press the Start button to initiate preheating. When the screen displays "Add Food", transfer the tray to the air fryer basket of the Air Fryer. Close its door, and let the machine do the cooking. Serve and enjoy.

Per serving: Calories 236; Fat 13.9g; Sodium 451mg; Carbs 13.2g; Fiber 1.2g; Sugars 1.4g; Protein 14.3g

Easy Salmon Patties

Prep time: 15 minutes| Cook time: 7 minutes| Serves: 2

1 egg, lightly beaten	Pepper
8 oz. salmon fillet, minced	Salt
¼ teaspoon garlic powder	

Add all ingredients into the bowl and mix until well combined. Make small patties from salmon mixture and place onto the parchment-lined cooking tray. Select the "Air Fry" mode on your air fryer. Press Temp button and then turn the dial to adjust the cooking temperature to 390 degrees F. Press Time button and then turn the dial to adjust the cooking time to 7 minutes. Press the Start button to initiate preheating. When the screen displays "Add Food", transfer the tray to the air fryer basket of the Air Fryer. Close its door, and let the machine do the cooking. Serve and enjoy.

Per serving: Calories 344; Fat 14.9g; Sodium 227mg; Carbs 12g; Fiber 1.2g; Sugars 1g; Protein 27g

Herb Butter Salmon

Prep time: 15 minutes| Cook time: 5 minutes| Serves: 2

2 salmon fillets	2 tablespoons olive oil
¼ teaspoon paprika	Pepper
1 teaspoon herb de Provence	Salt
1 tablespoon butter, melted	

Brush salmon fillets with oil and sprinkle with paprika, herb de Provence, pepper, and salt. Place salmon fillets onto the parchment-lined cooking tray. Select the "Air Fry" mode on your air fryer. Press Temp button and then turn the dial to adjust the cooking temperature to 390 degrees F. Press Time button and then turn the dial to adjust the cooking time to 5 minutes. Press the Start button to initiate preheating. When the screen displays "Add Food", transfer the tray to the air fryer basket of the Air Fryer. Close its door, and let the machine do the cooking. Drizzle melted butter over salmon and serve.

Per serving: Calories 249; Fat 13g; Sodium 556mg; Carbs 10g; Sugar 1.1g; Fiber 0.7g; Protein 31g

Lemon Tilapia with Herbs

Prep time: 15 minutes| Cook time: 18 minutes| Serves: 4

1-pound tilapia	½ teaspoon dried thyme
1 lemon, sliced	½ teaspoon dried oregano
1 teaspoon fresh lemon juice	½ teaspoon pepper
1 teaspoon olive oil	½ teaspoon salt
1 teaspoon garlic powder	

Place a fish fillets in the cooking tray and brush with lemon juice and olive oil. Mix together garlic powder, thyme, oregano, pepper, and salt and sprinkle over fish fillets. Arrange lemon slices on top of fish fillet. Select the "Air Fry" mode on your air fryer. Press Temp button and then turn the dial to adjust the cooking temperature to 400 degrees F. Press Time button and then turn the dial to adjust the cooking time to 18 minutes. Press the Start button to initiate preheating. When the screen displays "Add Food", transfer the cooking tray to the air fryer basket of your Air Fryer. Close its door, and let the machine do the cooking. Serve and enjoy.

Per serving: Calories 305; Fat 15g; Sodium 548mg; Carbs 12g; Sugar 1.2g; Fiber 0.7g; Protein 29g

Greek Salmon

Prep time: 15 minutes| Cook time: 15 minutes| Serves: 2

2 salmon filets	⅓ cup feta cheese, crumbled
½ cup olives, chopped	½ cup tomato, diced
½ tablespoon balsamic vinegar	Pepper
1 tablespoon olive oil	Salt
½ tablespoon parsley, chopped	

Season the salmon with pepper and salt. Place salmon on the cooking tray. Select the "Air Fry" mode on your air fryer. Press Temp button and then turn the dial to adjust the cooking temperature to 350 degrees F. Press Time button and then turn the dial to adjust the cooking time to 15 minutes. Press the Start button to initiate preheating. When the screen displays "Add Food", transfer the tray to the air fryer basket of the Air Fryer. Close its door, and let the machine do the cooking. Meanwhile, mix together tomato, olive oil, vinegar, olives, feta cheese, and parsley. Remove salmon from oven and top with tomato mixture. Serve and enjoy.

Per serving: Calories 285; Fat 9.8g; Sodium 639mg; Carbs 11.1g; Fiber 1.2g, Sugars 5.1g; Protein 27.8g

Orange Chili Salmon

Prep time: 15 minutes| Cook time: 20 minutes| Serves: 4

2 lbs. salmon fillet, skinless and boneless	1 tablespoon olive oil
	1 bunch fresh dill
2 lemon juice	1 chili, sliced
1 orange juice	Pepper

Salt

Place salmon fillets in the cooking tray and drizzle with olive oil, lemon juice, and orange juice. Sprinkle chili slices over the salmon and season with pepper and salt. Select the "Air Fry" mode on your air fryer. Press Temp button and then turn the dial to adjust the cooking temperature to 350 degrees F. Press Time button and then turn the dial to adjust the cooking time to 20 minutes. Press the Start button to initiate preheating. When the screen displays "Add Food", transfer the cooking tray to the air fryer basket of your Air Fryer. Close its door, and let the machine do the cooking. Garnish with dill and serve.

Per serving: Calories 361; Fat 10g; Sodium 218mg; Carbs 16g; Sugar 1.2g; Fiber 0.7g; Protein 24g

Taco Shrimp Fajitas

Prep time: 15 minutes| Cook time: 22 minutes| Serves: 6

1-pound shrimp, tail-off	½ cup onion, diced
1 green bell pepper, diced	Pepper
1 red bell pepper, diced	Salt
½ tablespoon taco seasoning	

Add shrimp, taco seasoning, onion, and bell peppers into the bowl and toss well. Place shrimp mixture onto the cooking tray. Select the "Air Fry" mode on your air fryer. Press Temp button and then turn the dial to adjust the cooking temperature to 390 degrees F. Press Time button and then turn the dial to adjust the cooking time to 22 minutes. Press the Start button to initiate preheating. When the screen displays "Add Food", transfer the tray to the air fryer basket of the Air Fryer. Close its door, and let the machine do the cooking. Serve and enjoy.

Per serving: Calories 236; Fat 13.9g; Sodium 451mg; Carbs 13.2g; Fiber 1.2g; Sugars 1.4g; Protein 14.3g

Chipotle Shrimp

Prep time: 15 minutes| Cook time: 8 minutes| Serves: 4

½ lbs. shrimp, peeled and deveined	½ tablespoon olive oil
	½ tablespoon lime juice
1 teaspoon chipotle in adobo	¼ teaspoon ground cumin

Add shrimp, oil, lime juice, cumin, and chipotle in a zip-lock bag, seal bag, and place in the fridge for 30 minutes. Thread marinated shrimp onto skewers and place skewers onto the cooking tray. Select the "Air Fry" mode on your air fryer. Press Temp button and then turn the dial to adjust the cooking temperature to 350 degrees F. Press Time button and then turn the dial to adjust the cooking time to 8 minutes. Press the Start button to initiate preheating. When the screen displays "Add Food", transfer the cooking tray to the air fryer basket of the Air Fryer. Close its door, and let the machine do the cooking. Serve and enjoy.

Per serving: Calories 285; Fat 9.8g; Sodium 639mg; Carbs 11.1g; Fiber 1.2g, Sugars 5.1g; Protein 27.8g

Lime Shrimp Kababs

Prep time: 15 minutes| Cook time: 8 minutes| Serves: 2

1 cup raw shrimp	Pepper, to taste
1 garlic clove, minced	Salt, to taste
lime juice	

In a bowl, mix shrimp, lime juice, garlic, pepper, and salt. Thread shrimp onto the skewers and place them onto the cooking tray. Select the "Air Fry" mode on your air fryer. Press Temp

button and then turn the dial to adjust the cooking temperature to 350 degrees F. Press Time button and then turn the dial to adjust the cooking time to 8 minutes. Press the Start button to initiate preheating. When the screen displays "Add Food", transfer the cooking tray to the air fryer basket of the air fryer. Close its door, and let the machine do the cooking. Serve and enjoy.
Per serving: Calories 305; Fat 15g; Sodium 548mg; Carbs 12g; Sugar 1.2g; Fiber 0.7g; Protein 29g

Curried Cod Fillets

Prep time: 15 minutes| Cook time: 10 minutes| Serves: 2

2 cod fillets	⅛ teaspoon garlic powder
¼ teaspoon curry powder	⅛ teaspoon paprika
1 tablespoon butter, melted	⅛ teaspoon sea salt
1 tablespoon basil, sliced	

In a small bowl, mix together curry powder, garlic powder, paprika, and salt and set aside. Place cod fillets onto the cooking tray and brush with butter and sprinkle with dry spice mixture. Select the "Air Fry" mode on your air fryer. Press Temp button and then turn the dial to adjust the cooking temperature to 360 degrees F. Press Time button and then turn the dial to adjust the cooking time to 10 minutes. Press the Start button to initiate preheating. When the screen displays "Add Food", transfer the cooking tray to the air fryer basket of the air fryer. Close its door, and let the machine do the cooking. Garnish with basil and serve.
Per serving: Calories 344; Fat 14.9g; Sodium 227mg; Carbs 14g; Fiber 1g; Sugars 1.4g; Protein 25.7g

Air Fryer Cajun Scallops

Prep time: 15 minutes| Cook time: 6 minutes| Serves: 2

12 scallops, clean and pat dry	Salt, to taste
1 teaspoon Cajun seasoning	

Season scallops with Cajun seasoning and salt and place onto the cooking tray. Select the "Air Fry" mode on your air fryer. Press Temp button and then turn the dial to adjust the cooking temperature to 400 degrees F. Press Time button and then turn the dial to adjust the cooking time to 6 minutes. Press the Start button to initiate preheating. When the screen displays "Add Food", transfer the cooking tray to the air fryer basket of the air fryer. Close its door, and let the machine do the cooking. Serve and enjoy.
Per serving: Calories 272; Fat 19g; Sodium 389mg; Carbs 10.4g; Fiber 0.7g, Sugars 1.1g; Protein 15.6g

Tender Cod Fillets

Prep time: 15 minutes| Cook time: 12 minutes| Serves: 2

1-pound cod fillets	¼ cups butter, melted
1 lemon, sliced	½ teaspoon salt

Brush cod fillets with melted butter and season with salt. Place cod fillets into the cooking tray and top with sliced lemon. Select the "Air Fry" mode on your air fryer. Press Temp button and then turn the dial to adjust the cooking temperature to 400 degrees F. Press Time button and then turn the dial to adjust the cooking time to 12 minutes. Press the Start button to initiate preheating. When the screen displays "Add Food", transfer the cooking tray to the air fryer basket of your Air Fryer. Close its door, and let the machine do the cooking. Serve and enjoy.
Per serving: Calories 285; Fat 9.8g; Sodium 639mg; Carbs

11.1g; Fiber 1.2g, Sugars 5.1g; Protein 27.8g

Dill Salmon Patties

Prep time: 15 minutes| Cook time: 10 minutes| Serves: 2

1 egg	½ teaspoon dill weed
14 oz. salmon	½ cup almond flour
¼ cups onion, diced	

Add all ingredients into the bowl and mix well. Make patties from mixture and place onto the parchment-lined cooking tray. Select the "Air Fry" mode on your air fryer. Press Temp button and then turn the dial to adjust the cooking temperature to 375 degrees F. Press Time button and then turn the dial to adjust the cooking time to 10 minutes. Press the Start button to initiate preheating. When the screen displays "Add Food", transfer the tray to the air fryer basket of the air fryer. Close its door, and let the machine do the cooking. Serve and enjoy.
Per serving: Calories 361; Fat 10g; Sodium 218mg; Carbs 16g; Sugar 1.2g; Fiber 0.7g; Protein 24g

Lemon Garlic Cod

Prep time: 15 minutes| Cook time: 20 minutes| Serves: 4

½-1-pound cod fillet	2 lemon juice
1 lemon, sliced	2 tablespoons olive oil
¼ cups butter, diced	Pepper
4 garlic cloves, minced	Salt

Place fish fillets in the cooking tray and season with pepper and salt. Whisk together garlic, lemon juice, and oil and pour over fish fillets. Arrange butter pieces and lemon slices on top of fish fillets. Select the "Air Fry" mode on your air fryer. Press Temp button and then turn the dial to adjust the cooking temperature to 400 degrees F. Press Time button and then turn the dial to adjust the cooking time to 20 minutes. Press the Start button to initiate preheating. When the screen displays "Add Food", transfer the cooking tray to the air fryer basket of your Air Fryer. Close its door, and let the machine do the cooking. Serve and enjoy.
Per serving: Calories 272; Fat 19g; Sodium 389mg; Carbs 10.4g; Fiber 0.7g, Sugars 1.1g; Protein 15.6g

Salmon with Creamy Sauce

Prep time: 15 minutes| Cook time: 30 minutes| Serves: 4

1-pound salmon	1 tablespoon garlic, minced
1 tablespoon dill, chopped	1 tablespoon Dijon mustard
1 tablespoon mayonnaise	Pepper
⅓ cup sour cream	Salt
½ lemon juice	

In a bowl, mix together sour cream, lemon juice, dill, Dijon, and mayonnaise. Place salmon in the cooking tray and top with garlic, pepper, and salt. Pour half sour cream mixture over salmon. Cover the cooking tray with foil. Select the "Air Fry" mode on your air fryer. Press Temp button and then turn the dial to adjust the cooking temperature to 400 degrees F. Press Time button and then turn the dial to adjust the cooking time to 30 minutes. Press the Start button to initiate preheating. When the screen displays "Add Food", transfer the cooking tray to the air fryer basket of your Air Fryer. Close its door, and let the machine do the cooking. Serve with sauce.
Per serving: Calories 344; Fat 14.9g; Sodium 227mg; Carbs 14g; Fiber 1g; Sugars 1.4g; Protein 25.7g

BBQ Parmesan Salmon

Prep time: 15 minutes| Cook time: 15 minutes| Serves: 5

½ lbs. salmon fillets
4 tablespoon parsley, chopped
3 garlic cloves, minced
½ cup parmesan cheese, shredded

1 teaspoon BBQ seasoning
1 teaspoon paprika
1 tablespoon olive oil
Pepper
Salt

Place salmon in the cooking tray. Brush salmon with oil and sprinkle with seasoning. In a small bowl, mix together parsley, cheese, and garlic and sprinkle on top of salmon. Select the "Air Fry" mode on your air fryer. Press Temp button and then turn the dial to adjust the cooking temperature to 400 degrees F. Press Time button and then turn the dial to adjust the cooking time to 15 minutes. Press the Start button to initiate preheating. When the screen displays "Add Food", transfer the cooking tray to the air fryer basket of your Air Fryer. Close its door, and let the machine do the cooking. Serve and enjoy.
Per serving: Calories 236; Fat 13.9g; Sodium 451mg; Carbs 13.2g; Fiber 1.2g; Sugars 1.4g; Protein 14.3g

Delicious Parmesan Halibut

Prep time: 15 minutes| Cook time: 12 minutes| Serves: 6

1-pound halibut fillets
1 tablespoon almond flour
3 tablespoon parmesan cheese, grated
1 tablespoon dried parsley

1 teaspoon garlic powder
1 stick butter
Pepper
Salt

In a bowl, mix together all ingredients except fish fillets. Place fish fillets in the cooking tray and spread bowl mixture on top of fish fillets. Select the "Bake" mode on your air fryer. Press Temp button and then turn the dial to adjust the cooking temperature to 400 degrees F. Press Time button and then turn the dial to adjust the cooking time to 12 minutes. Press the Start button to initiate preheating. When the screen displays "Add Food", transfer the cooking tray to the air fryer basket of your Air Fryer. Close its door, and let the machine do the cooking. Serve and enjoy.
Per serving: Calories 327; Fat 15g; Sodium 548mg; Carbs 12g; Sugar 1.2g; Fiber 0.7g; Protein 29g

Ginger Garlic Fish Fillet

Prep time: 15 minutes| Cook time: 20 minutes| Serves: 2

12 oz. white fish fillets
2 garlic cloves, minced
2 teaspoon ginger, grated
lime zest
1 tablespoon butter, cut into

pieces
¼ teaspoon onion powder
Pepper
Salt

Place fish fillets in the cooking tray. Top with ginger, garlic, and lime zest. Season the fillets with onion powder, pepper, and salt. Spread butter pieces on top of fish fillets. Select the "Air Fry" mode on your air fryer. Press Temp button and then turn the dial to adjust the cooking temperature to 350 degrees F. Press Time button and then turn the dial to adjust the cooking time to 20 minutes. Press the Start button to initiate preheating. When the screen displays "Add Food", transfer the cooking tray to the air fryer basket of your Air Fryer. Close its door, and let the machine do the cooking. Serve and enjoy.
Per serving: Calories 285; Fat 9.8g; Sodium 639mg; Carbs 11.1g; Fiber 1.2g; Sugars 5.1g; Protein 27.8g

Chili Prawns

Prep time: 15 minutes| Cook time: 8 minutes| Serves: 2

6 prawns
1 teaspoon chili flakes
¼ teaspoon pepper

1 teaspoon chili powder
¼ teaspoon salt

In a bowl, add all ingredients and toss well. Select the "Air Fry" mode on your air fryer. Press Temp button and then turn the dial to adjust the cooking temperature to 350 degrees F. Press Time button and then turn the dial to adjust the cooking time to 8 minutes. Press the Start button to initiate preheating. When the screen displays "Add Food", transfer the cooking tray to the air fryer basket of your Air Fryer. Close its door, and let the machine do the cooking. Serve and enjoy.
Per serving: Calories 344; Fat 14.9g; Sodium 227mg; Carbs 14g; Fiber 1g; Sugars 1.4g; Protein 25.7g

Salmon Beans and Mushrooms

Prep time: 15 minutes| Cook time: 5 minutes| Serves: 6

4 salmon fillets
2 tablespoons fresh parsley, minced
¼ cups fresh lemon juice
1 teaspoon garlic, minced
1 tablespoon olive oil

1 pound mushrooms, sliced
1 pound green beans, trimmed
½ cup parmesan cheese, grated
Pepper
Salt

Heat the oil in a small saucepan over medium-high heat. Add garlic and sauté for 30 seconds. Remove from heat and stir in lemon juice, parsley, pepper, and salt. Arrange fish fillets, mushrooms, and green beans in baking pan and drizzle with oil mixture. Sprinkle with grated parmesan cheese. Select the "Air Fry" mode on your air fryer. Press Temp button and then turn the dial to adjust the cooking temperature to 400 degrees F. Press Time button and then turn the dial to adjust the cooking time to 5 minutes. Press the Start button to initiate preheating. When the screen displays "Add Food", transfer the cooking tray to the air fryer basket of your Air Fryer. Close its door, and let the machine do the cooking. Serve and enjoy.
Per serving: Calories 351; Fat 22g; Sodium 502mg; Carbs 15.2g; Sugar 1.1g; Fiber 0.7g; Protein 26.4g

Glazed Tuna and Fruit Kebabs

Prep time: 15 minutes| Cook time: 10 minutes| Serves: 4

Kebabs:
1 pound (454 g) tuna steaks, cut into 1-inch cubes
½ cup canned pineapple chunks, drained, juice reserved
½ cup large red grapes
Marinade:

1 tablespoon honey
1 teaspoon olive oil
2 teaspoon grated fresh ginger
Pinch cayenne pepper
Special Equipment:
4 metal skewers

Thread the alternating tuna cubes, pineapple chunks, and red grapes, onto the metal skewers. Whisk together the honey, olive oil, ginger, and cayenne pepper in a small bowl. Brush generously the marinade over the kebabs and allow the food to sit for 10 minutes. When ready, transfer the kebabs to the cooking tray. Select the "Air Fry" mode on your air fryer. Press Temp button and then turn the dial to adjust the cooking temperature to 370 degrees F. Press Time button and then turn the dial to adjust the cooking time to 10 minutes. Press the Start button to initiate preheating. When the screen displays "Add Food", transfer the cooking tray to the air fryer basket of your Air Fryer. Close its door, and let the machine do the cooking.

Serve hot.

Per serving: Calories 272; Fat 19g; Sodium 389mg; Carbs 10.4g; Fiber 0.7g, Sugars 1.1g; Protein 15.6g

Roasted Scallops with Snow Peas

Prep time: 15 minutes| Cook time: 8 minutes| Serves: 4

1 pound (454 g) sea scallops	3 teaspoons vegetable oil,
1 tablespoon hoisin sauce	divided
½ cup toasted sesame seeds	1 teaspoon soy sauce
6 ounces (170 g) snow peas,	1 teaspoon sesame oil
trimmed	1 cup roasted mushrooms

Brush the scallops with the hoisin sauce. Put the sesame seeds in a shallow dish. Roll the scallops in the sesame seeds until evenly coated. Combine the snow peas with 1 teaspoon of vegetable oil, the sesame oil, and soy sauce in a medium bowl. Grease the cooking tray with the remaining 2 teaspoons of vegetable oil. Put the scallops in the middle of the pan and arrange the snow peas around the scallops in a single layer. Select the "Air Fry" mode on your air fryer. Press Temp button and then turn the dial to adjust the cooking temperature to 375 degrees F. Press Time button and then turn the dial to adjust the cooking time to 8 minutes. Press the Start button to initiate preheating. When the screen displays "Add Food", transfer the pan to the air fryer basket of your Air Fryer. Close its door, and let the machine do the cooking. Serve warm.

Per serving: Calories 361; Fat 10g; Sodium 218mg; Carbs 16g; Sugar 1.2g; Fiber 0.7g; Protein 24g

Spicy Halibut

Prep time: 15 minutes| Cook time: 17 minutes| Serves: 4

1-pound halibut fillets	¼ teaspoon garlic powder
½ teaspoon chili powder	Pepper
½ teaspoon smoked paprika	Salt
¼ cups olive oil	

Place halibut fillets in the cooking tray. In a small bowl, mix oil, garlic powder, paprika, pepper, chili powder, and salt. Brush fish fillets with oil mixture. Select the "Air Fry" mode on your air fryer. Press Temp button and then turn the dial to adjust the cooking temperature to 400 degrees F. Press Time button and then turn the dial to adjust the cooking time to 17 minutes. Press the Start button to initiate preheating. When the screen displays "Add Food", transfer the cooking tray to the air fryer basket of your Air Fryer. Close its door, and let the machine do the cooking. Serve and enjoy.

Per serving: Calories 305; Fat 15g; Sodium 548mg; Carbs 12g; Sugar 1.2g; Fiber 0.7g; Protein 29g

Seafood Spring Rolls

Prep time: 15 minutes| Cook time: 10 minutes| Serves: 4

1 tablespoon olive oil	4 teaspoon soy sauce
1 teaspoon minced garlic	Salt and freshly ground black
1 cup matchstick cut carrots	pepper, to taste
2 cups finely sliced cabbage	16 square spring roll wrappers
2 (4-ounce / 113-g) cans tiny	Cooking spray
shrimp, drained	

Spray the baking pan with cooking spray. Set aside. Heat the olive oil in a medium skillet over medium heat until it shimmers. Add the garlic to the skillet and cook for 30 seconds. Stir in the cabbage and carrots and sauté for about 5 minutes. Fold in the shrimp and soy sauce and sprinkle with salt and pepper, then

stir to combine. Sauté for another 2 minutes or until the moisture is evaporated. Remove from the heat and set aside to cool. Put a spring roll wrapper on a work surface and spoon 1 tablespoon of the shrimp mixture onto the lower end of the wrapper. Roll the wrapper away from you halfway, and then fold in the right and left sides, like an envelope. Continue to roll to the very end, using a little water to seal the edge. Repeat with the remaining wrappers and filling. Place the spring rolls in the cooking tray in a single layer, leaving space between spring roll. Mist them lightly with cooking spray. Select the "Air Fry" mode on your air fryer. Press Temp button and then turn the dial to adjust the cooking temperature to 375 degrees F. Press Time button and then turn the dial to adjust the cooking time to 10 minutes. Press the Start button to initiate preheating. When the screen displays "Add Food", transfer the cooking tray to the air fryer basket of your Air Fryer. Close its door, and let the machine do the cooking. When cooking is complete, the spring rolls will be heated through and start to brown. If necessary, continue cooking for 5 minutes more. Remove from the oven and cool for a few minutes before serving. When the display indicates "turn Food", flip the rolls halfway through the cooking time. Serve warm.

Per serving: Calories 249; Fat 13g; Sodium 556mg; Carbs 10g; Sugar 1.1g; Fiber 0.7g; Protein 31g

Parmesan-Crusted Hake with Garlic Sauce

Prep time: 15 minutes| Cook time: 10 minutes| Serves: 3

Fish:	3 hake fillets, patted dry
6 tablespoons mayonnaise	Nonstick cooking spray
1 tablespoon fresh lime juice	Garlic Sauce:
1 teaspoon Dijon mustard	¼ cup plain Greek yogurt
1 cup grated Parmesan cheese	2 tablespoons olive oil
Salt, to taste	2 cloves garlic, minced
¼ teaspoon ground black	½ teaspoon minced tarragon
pepper, or more to taste	leaves

Mix the mayo, lime juice, and mustard in a shallow bowl and whisk to combine. In another shallow bowl, stir together the grated Parmesan cheese, salt, and pepper. Dredge fillet in the mayo mixture, and then roll them in the cheese mixture until they are evenly coated on both sides. Spray the baking pan with nonstick cooking spray. Place the fillets in the pan. Select the "Air Fry" mode on your air fryer. Press Temp button and then turn the dial to adjust the cooking temperature to 395 degrees F. Press Time button and then turn the dial to adjust the cooking time to 10 minutes. Press the Start button to initiate preheating. When the screen displays "Add Food", transfer the pan to the air fryer basket of your Air Fryer. Close its door, and let the machine do the cooking. When cooking is complete, the fish should flake apart with a fork. Remove the fillets from the oven and serve warm alongside the sauce. When the display indicates "turn Food", flip the fillets halfway through the cooking time. Meanwhile, in a small bowl, whisk all the ingredients for the sauce until well incorporated.

Per serving: Calories 236; Fat 13.9g; Sodium 451mg; Carbs 13.2g; Fiber 1.2g; Sugars 1.4g; Protein 14.3g

Crispy Cheesy Fish Fingers

Prep time: 15 minutes| Cook time: 20 minutes| Serves: 4

2 Large codfish filets,	home will do)
approximately 6-8 ounces,	2 tablespoons of shredded or
fresh or frozen and thawed,	powdered parmesan cheese
cut into 1 ½-inch strips	1 tablespoon of shredded
2 raw 2 eggs	cheddar cheese
½ cup of breadcrumbs (we	Pinch of Salt and black pepper,
like Panko, but any brand or	to taste

In a large mixing bowl, beat the 2 eggs until fluffy and until the yolks and whites are fully combined. Dunk all the fish strips in the beaten 2 eggs, fully submerging. In a separate mixing bowl, combine the bread crumbs with the parmesan, cheddar, and salt and pepper, until evenly mixed. 1 by one, coat the egg-covered fish strips in the mixed dry ingredients so that they're fully covered, and place on the foil-lined cooking tray. Select the "Air Fry" mode on your air fryer. Press Temp button and then turn the dial to adjust the cooking temperature to 350 degrees F. Press Time button and then turn the dial to adjust the cooking time to 20 minutes. Press the Start button to initiate preheating. When the screen displays "Add Food", transfer the cooking tray to the air fryer basket of your Air Fryer. Close its door, and let the machine do the cooking. Serve warm.

Per serving: Calories 285; Fat 9.8g; Sodium 639mg; Carbs 11.1g; Fiber 1.2g, Sugars 5.1g; Protein 27.8g

Perfect Baked Cod

Prep time: 15 minutes| Cook time: 20 minutes| Serves: 4

4 cod fillets
1 tablespoon olive oil
1 teaspoon dried parsley
2 teaspoons paprika
¾ cups parmesan cheese, grated
¼ teaspoon salt

In a shallow dish, mix parmesan cheese, paprika, parsley, and salt. Brush fish fillets with oil and coat with parmesan cheese mixture. Place coated fish fillets into the baking pan. Select the "Air Fry" mode on your air fryer. Press Temp button and then turn the dial to adjust the cooking temperature to 400 degrees F. Press Time button and then turn the dial to adjust the cooking time to 20 minutes. Press the Start button to initiate preheating. When the screen displays "Add Food", transfer the cooking tray to the air fryer basket of your Air Fryer when the screen displays "Add Food" Close its door, and let the machine do the cooking. Serve and enjoy.

Per serving: Calories 305; Fat 15g; Sodium 548mg; Carbs 12g; Sugar 1.2g; Fiber 0.7g; Protein 29g

Rosemary Garlic Shrimp

Prep time: 15 minutes| Cook time: 15 minutes| Serves: 2

1-pound shrimp, peeled and deveined
2 garlic cloves, minced
½ tablespoon fresh rosemary,
chopped
1 tablespoon olive oil
Pepper
Salt

Add shrimp and remaining ingredients in a large bowl and toss well. Pour shrimp mixture into the cooking tray. Select the "Air Fry" mode on your air fryer. Press Temp button and then turn the dial to adjust the cooking temperature to 400 degrees F. Press Time button and then turn the dial to adjust the cooking time to 15 minutes. Press the Start button to initiate preheating. When the screen displays "Add Food", transfer the cooking tray to the air fryer basket of your Air Fryer. Close its door, and let the machine do the cooking. Serve and enjoy.

Per serving: Calories 344; Fat 14.9g; Sodium 227mg; Carbs 14g; Fiber 1g; Sugars 1.4g; Protein 25.7g

Roasted Halibut Steaks with Parsley

Prep time: 15 minutes| Cook time: 10 minutes| Serves: 4

1 pound (454 g) halibut steaks
¼ cup vegetable oil
2½ tablespoon Worcester sauce

2 tablespoon honey
2 tablespoon vermouth
1 tablespoon lemon juice
1 tablespoon fresh parsley
leaves, chopped
Salt and pepper, to taste
1 teaspoon dried basil

Put all the ingredients in a large mixing dish and gently stir until the fish is coated evenly. Transfer the fish to the cooking tray. Select the "Air Fry" mode on your air fryer. Press Temp button and then turn the dial to adjust the cooking temperature to 390 degrees F. Press Time button and then turn the dial to adjust the cooking time to 10 minutes. Press the Start button to initiate preheating. When the screen displays "Add Food", transfer the cooking tray to the air fryer basket of your Air Fryer. Close its door, and let the machine do the cooking. Serve warm.

Per serving: Calories 361; Fat 10g; Sodium 218mg; Carbs 16g; Sugar 1.2g; Fiber 0.7g; Protein 24g

Greek Cod with Asparagus

Prep time: 15 minutes| Cook time: 25 minutes| Serves: 2

1-pound cod, cut into 4 pieces
8 asparagus spears
leek, sliced
1 onion, quartered
2 tomatoes, halved
½ teaspoon oregano
½ teaspoon red chili flakes
½ cup olives, chopped
2 tablespoons olive oil
¼ teaspoon pepper
¼ teaspoon salt

Arrange fish pieces, olives, asparagus, leek, onion, and tomatoes in the cooking tray. Season the food with oregano, chili flakes, pepper, and salt and drizzle with olive oil. Select the "Air Fry" mode on your air fryer. Press Temp button and then turn the dial to adjust the cooking temperature to 400 degrees F. Press Time button and then turn the dial to adjust the cooking time to 25 minutes. Press the Start button to initiate preheating. When the screen displays "Add Food", transfer the cooking tray to the air fryer basket of your Air Fryer. Close its door, and let the machine do the cooking. Serve and enjoy.

Per serving: Calories 254; Fat 28g; Sodium 346mg; Carbs 12.3g; Sugar 1g; Fiber 0.7g; Protein 24.3 g

Speedy Fried Scallops

Prep time: 15 minutes| Cook time: 6 minutes| Serves: 4

12 fresh scallops
3 tablespoon flour
Salt and black pepper to taste
1 egg, lightly beaten
1 cup breadcrumbs

Coat the scallops with flour. Dip into the egg, then into the breadcrumbs. Spray with olive oil and arrange them in the cooking tray. Select the "Air Fry" mode on your air fryer. Press Temp button and then turn the dial to adjust the cooking temperature to 360 degrees F. Press Time button and then turn the dial to adjust the cooking time to 6 minutes. Press the Start button to initiate preheating. When the screen displays "Add Food", transfer the cooking tray to the air fryer basket of your Air Fryer. Close its door, and let the machine do the cooking. Serve.

Per serving: Calories 344; Fat 14.9g; Sodium 227mg; Carbs 12g; Fiber 1.2g; Sugars 1g; Protein 27g

Crispy Coated Scallops

Prep time: 15 minutes| Cook time: 12 minutes| Serves: 4

Nonstick cooking spray
1-pound sea scallops, patted dry
1 teaspoon onion powder
½ teaspoon pepper
1 egg
1 tablespoon water
¼ cup Italian bread crumbs

Paprika   1 tablespoon fresh lemon juice

Sprinkle scallops with onion powder and pepper. In a shallow dish, whisk together 1 egg and water. Place bread crumbs in a separate shallow dish. Dip scallops in 1 egg then bread crumbs coating them lightly. Place in the cooking tray. Select the "Air Fry" mode on your air fryer. Press Temp button and then turn the dial to adjust the cooking temperature to 400 degrees F. Press Time button and then turn the dial to adjust the cooking time to 12 minutes. Press the Start button to initiate preheating. When the screen displays "Add Food", transfer the cooking tray to the air fryer basket of your Air Fryer. Close its door, and let the machine do the cooking. Drizzle with lemon juice and serve.
Per serving: Calories 272; Fat 19g; Sodium 389mg; Carbs 10.4g; Fiber 0.7g, Sugars 1.1g; Protein 15.6g

Easy Salmon Cakes

Prep time: 15 minutes| Cook time: 10 minutes| Serves: 2

8 oz. salmon, cooked   A handful of parsley, chopped
½ oz. potatoes, mashed   Zest of 1 lemon
A handful of capers   ¾ oz. plain flour

Carefully flake the salmon in a bowl. Stir in zest, capers, dill, and mashed potatoes. Shape the mixture into cakes and dust them with flour. Place in the fridge for 60 minutes. Select the "Air Fry" mode on your air fryer. Press Temp button and then turn the dial to adjust the cooking temperature to 350 degrees F. Press Time button and then turn the dial to adjust the cooking time to 10 minutes. Press the Start button to initiate preheating. When the screen displays "Add Food", transfer the salmon cakes to the air fryer basket of the air fryer. Close its door, and let the machine do the cooking. Serve chilled.
Per serving: Calories 285; Fat 9.8g; Sodium 639mg; Carbs 11.1g; Fiber 1.2g, Sugars 5.1g; Protein 27.8g

Maryland Crab Cakes

Prep time: 15 minutes| Cook time: 10 minutes| Serves: 6

Nonstick cooking spray   grated
2 eggs   1 teaspoon Italian seasoning
1 cup Panko bread crumbs   1 tablespoon fresh parsley,
1 stalk celery, chopped   chopped
3 tablespoon mayonnaise   1 teaspoon pepper
1 teaspoon Worcestershire   ¾ pound lump crabmeat,
sauce   drained
¼ cup mozzarella cheese,

Lightly spray the cooking tray with cooking spray. In a large bowl, combine all ingredients except crab meat, mix well. Fold in crab carefully so it retains some chunks. Form mixture into 12 patties. Place patties in a single layer in the cooking tray. Select the "Air Fry" mode on your air fryer. Press Temp button and then turn the dial to adjust the cooking temperature to 350 degrees F. Press Time button and then turn the dial to adjust the cooking time to 10 minutes. Press the Start button to initiate preheating. When the screen displays "Add Food", transfer the cooking tray to the air fryer basket of your Air Fryer. Close its door, and let the machine do the cooking. Serve immediately.
Per serving: Calories 236; Fat 13.9g; Sodium 451mg; Carbs 13.2g; Fiber 1.2g, Sugars 1.4g; Protein 14.3g

Fish Spicy Lemon Kebab

Prep time: 15 minutes| Cook time: 25 minutes| Serves: 4

1-pound boneless fish roughly   chopped

2 onions chopped   3 tablespoon cream
5 green chilies-roughly   2 tablespoon coriander powder
chopped   4 tablespoons fresh mint
½ tablespoon ginger paste   chopped
1 ½ teaspoon garlic paste   3 tablespoon chopped
½ teaspoon salt   capsicum
1 teaspoon lemon juice   3 2 eggs
1 teaspoon garam masala   2 ½ tablespoon white sesame
1 tablespoon chopped   seeds
coriander

Take all the ingredients mentioned under the first heading and mix them in a bowl. Grind them thoroughly to make a smooth paste. Take the 2 eggs in a different bowl and beat them. Add a pinch of salt and leave them aside. Take a flat plate and in it mix the sesame seeds and breadcrumbs. Mold the fish mixture into small balls and flatten them into round and flat kebabs. Dip these kebabs in the 1 egg and salt mixture and then in the mixture of breadcrumbs and sesame seeds. Leave these kebabs in the fridge for an hour or so to set. Select the "Air Fry" mode on your air fryer. Press Temp button and then turn the dial to adjust the cooking temperature to 350 degrees F. Press Time button and then turn the dial to adjust the cooking time to 25 minutes. Press the Start button to initiate preheating. When the screen displays "Add Food", transfer the kebabs to the air fryer basket of the air fryer. Close its door, and let the machine do the cooking. Serve the kebabs with mint sauce.
Per serving: Calories 344; Fat 14.9g; Sodium 227mg; Carbs 14g; Fiber 1g; Sugars 1.4g; Protein 25.7g

Spicy Grilled Halibut

Prep time: 15 minutes| Cook time: 15 minutes| Serves: 4

½ cup fresh lemon juice   4 6 oz. halibut fillets
2 jalapeno peppers, seeded   Nonstick cooking spray
and chopped fine   ¼ cup cilantro, chopped

In a small bowl, combine lemon juice and chilies, mix well. Place fish in a large Ziploc bag and add marinade. Toss to coat. Refrigerate 30 minutes. Lightly spray the cooking tray with cooking spray. Select the "Air Fry" mode on your air fryer. Press Temp button and then turn the dial to adjust the cooking temperature to 350 degrees F. Press Time button and then turn the dial to adjust the cooking time to 15 minutes. Press the Start button to initiate preheating. When the screen displays "Add Food", transfer the cooking tray to the air fryer basket of your Air Fryer. Close its door, and let the machine do the cooking. Sprinkle with cilantro before serving. Serve warm.
Per serving: Calories 361; Fat 10g; Sodium 218mg; Carbs 16g; Sugar 1.2g; Fiber 0.7g; Protein 24g

Baked Lemon Swordfish

Prep time: 15 minutes| Cook time: 15 minutes| Serves: 2

12 oz. swordfish fillets   chopped
⅛ teaspoon crushed red pepper   1 tablespoon olive oil
1 garlic clove, minced   ½ teaspoon lemon zest, grated
1 teaspoon fresh parsley,   ½ teaspoon ginger, grated

In a small bowl, mix oil, lemon zest, red pepper, ginger, garlic, and parsley. Season fish fillets with salt. Transfer fish fillets in the cooking tray and pour the seasoning on top. Select the "Air Fry" mode on your air fryer. Press Temp button and then turn the dial to adjust the cooking temperature to 350 degrees F. Press Time button and then turn the dial to adjust the cooking time to 15 minutes. Press the Start button to initiate preheating. When the screen displays "Add Food", transfer the cooking tray to the air fryer basket of your Air Fryer. Close its door, and let the machine do the cooking. Serve warm.

Per serving: Calories 285; Fat 9.8g; Sodium 639mg; Carbs 11.1g; Fiber 1.2g, Sugars 5.1g; Protein 27.8g

Cheese Carp Fries

Prep time: 15 minutes| Cook time: 25 minutes| Serves: 4

1-pound carp Oregano Fingers
Ingredients for the marinade:
1 tablespoon olive oil
1 teaspoon mixed herbs
½ teaspoon red chili flakes

A pinch of salt to taste
1 tablespoon lemon juice
For the garnish:
1 cup melted cheddar cheese

Mix the marinade ingredients in the cooking tray and place the oregano fingers in it. Select the "Air Fry" mode on your air fryer. Press Temp button and then turn the dial to adjust the cooking temperature to 350 degrees F. Press Time button and then turn the dial to adjust the cooking time to 25 minutes. Press the Start button to initiate preheating. When the screen displays "Add Food", transfer the cooking tray to the air fryer basket of your Air Fryer. Close its door, and let the machine do the cooking. Towards the end of the cooking process (the last 2 minutes or so), sprinkle the melted cheddar cheese over the fries and serve hot.

Per serving: Calories 249; Fat 13g; Sodium 556mg; Carbs 10g; Sugar 1.1g; Fiber 0.7g; Protein 31g

Oyster Club Sandwich

Prep time: 15 minutes| Cook time: 15 minutes| Serves: 2

2 slices of white bread
1 tablespoon softened butter
½ pound shelled oyster
small capsicum
For Barbeque Sauce:
¼ tablespoon Worcestershire sauce
½ teaspoon olive oil
½ flake garlic crushed

¼ cup chopped onion
¼ teaspoon mustard powder
1 tablespoon tomato ketchup
½ tablespoon sugar
¼ tablespoon red chili sauce
½ cup water.
A pinch of salt and black pepper to taste

Take the slices of bread and remove the edges. Now cut the slices horizontally. Cook the ingredients for the sauce and wait till it thickens. Now, add the oyster to the sauce and stir till it obtains the flavors. Roast the capsicum and peel the skin off. Cut the capsicum into slices. Mix the ingredients together and apply it to the bread slices. Place the prepared Classic Sandwiches in the cooking tray. Select the "Air Fry" mode on your air fryer. Press Temp button and then turn the dial to adjust the cooking temperature to 350 degrees F. Press Time button and then turn the dial to adjust the cooking time to 15 minutes. Press the Start button to initiate preheating. When the screen displays "Add Food", transfer the cooking tray to the air fryer basket of your Air Fryer. Close its door, and let the machine do the cooking. Turn the Classic Sandwiches in between the cooking process to cook both slices. Serve the Classic Sandwiches with tomato ketchup or mint sauce.

Per serving: Calories 272; Fat 19g; Sodium 389mg; Carbs 10.4g; Fiber 0.7g, Sugars 1.1g; Protein 15.6g

Grilled Soy Salmon Fillets

Prep time: 15 minutes| Cook time: 9 minutes| Serves: 4

4 salmon fillets
¼ teaspoon ground black pepper
½ teaspoon cayenne pepper
½ teaspoon salt

1 teaspoon onion powder
1 tablespoon fresh lemon juice
½ cup soy sauce
½ cup water
1 tablespoon honey

1 tablespoon extra-virgin olive oil

Firstly, pat the salmon fillets dry using kitchen towels. Season the salmon with black pepper, cayenne pepper, salt, and onion powder. To make the marinade, combine together the lemon juice, soy sauce, water, honey, and olive oil. Marinate the salmon for at least 2 hours in your refrigerator. Arrange the fish fillets on in the cooking tray. Select the "Air Fry" mode on your air fryer. Press Temp button and then turn the dial to adjust the cooking temperature to 330 degrees F. Press Time button and then turn the dial to adjust the cooking time to 9 minutes. Press the Start button to initiate preheating. When the screen displays "Add Food", transfer the cooking tray to the air fryer basket of your Air Fryer. Close its door, and let the machine do the cooking. Work with batches and serve warm.

Per serving: Calories 272; Fat 19g; Sodium 389mg; Carbs 10.4g; Fiber 0.7g, Sugars 1.1g; Protein 15.6g

Italian Salmon

Prep time: 15 minutes| Cook time: 25 minutes| Serves: 4

¾ lbs. salmon fillet
¼ cups sun-dried tomatoes, drained
1 tablespoon fresh dill, chopped
¼ cups capers

¼ cups olives, pitted and chopped
⅓ cup basil pesto
⅓ cup artichoke hearts
¼ teaspoon paprika
¼ teaspoon salt

Arrange salmon fillet in the cooking tray and season with paprika and salt. Pour the remaining ingredients on top of salmon. Select the "Air Fry" mode on your air fryer. Press Temp button and then turn the dial to adjust the cooking temperature to 400 degrees F. Press Time button and then turn the dial to adjust the cooking time to 25 minutes. Press the Start button to initiate preheating. When the screen displays "Add Food", transfer the cooking tray to the air fryer basket of your Air Fryer. Close its door, and let the machine do the cooking. Serve and enjoy.

Per serving: Calories 285; Fat 9.8g; Sodium 639mg; Carbs 11.1g; Fiber 1.2g, Sugars 5.1g; Protein 27.8g

Honey Glazed Salmon

Prep time: 15 minutes| Cook time: 8 minutes| Serves: 4

4 salmon fillets
2 teaspoon soy sauce
1 tablespoon honey

Pepper
Salt

Brush salmon with soy sauce and season with pepper and salt. Place salmon in the cooking tray. Select the "Air Fry" mode on your air fryer. Press Temp button and then turn the dial to adjust the cooking temperature to 375 degrees F. Press Time button and then turn the dial to adjust the cooking time to 8 minutes. Press the Start button to initiate preheating. When the screen displays "Add Food", transfer the cooking tray to the air fryer basket of your Air Fryer. Close its door, and let the machine do the cooking. Brush salmon with honey and serve.

Per serving: Calories 305; Fat 15g; Sodium 548mg; Carbs 12g; Sugar 1.2g; Fiber 0.7g; Protein 29g

Parsley Catfish Fillets

Prep time: 15 minutes| Cook time: 16 minutes| Serves: 4

4 catfish fillets, rinsed and dried
¼ cup seasoned fish fry

1 tablespoon olive oil
1 tablespoon fresh parsley, chopped

Add seasoned fish fry and fillets in a large Ziploc bag; massage well to coat. Spread the fish in the cooking tray. Select the "Air Fry" mode on your air fryer. Press Temp button and then turn the dial to adjust the cooking temperature to 360 degrees F. Press Time button and then turn the dial to adjust the cooking time to 16 minutes. Press the Start button to initiate preheating. When the screen displays "Add Food", transfer the cooking tray to the air fryer basket of your Air Fryer. Close its door, and let the machine do the cooking. Top with parsley. Serve warm.
Per serving: Calories 236; Fat 13.9g; Sodium 451mg; Carbs 13.2g; Fiber 1.2g; Sugars 1.4g; Protein 14.3g

Snapper with Vegetables

Prep time: 15 minutes| Cook time: 20 minutes| Serves: 4

10 ounces (283 g) Yukon Gold potatoes, sliced ¼-inch thick
5 tablespoons unsalted butter, melted, divided
1 teaspoon kosher salt, divided
4 (8-ounce / 227-g) snapper

fillets
½ pound (227 g) green beans, trimmed
Juice of 1 lemon
2 tablespoon chopped fresh parsley, for garnish

In a large bowl, drizzle the potatoes with 2 tablespoons of melted butter and ¼ teaspoon of kosher salt. Transfer the potatoes to the cooking tray. Select the "Air Fry" mode on your air fryer. Press Temp button and then turn the dial to adjust the cooking temperature to 375 degrees F. Press Time button and then turn the dial to adjust the cooking time to 20 minutes. Press the Start button to initiate preheating. When the screen displays "Add Food", transfer the cooking tray to the air fryer basket of your Air Fryer. Close its door, and let the machine do the cooking. Meanwhile, season both sides of the fillets with ½ teaspoon of kosher salt. Put the green beans in the medium bowl and sprinkle with the remaining ¼ teaspoon of kosher salt and 1 tablespoon of butter, tossing to coat. After 10 minutes, remove from the oven and push the potatoes to 1 side. Put the fillets in the middle of the pan and add the green beans on the other side. Drizzle the remaining 2 tablespoons of butter over the fillets then return the pan to the air fryer and resume cooking. Drizzle the lemon juice over the fillets and sprinkle the parsley on top for garnish. Serve hot.
Per serving: Calories 254; Fat 28g; Sodium 346mg; Carbs 12.3g; Sugar 1g; Fiber 0.7g; Protein 24.3 g

Carp Flat Cakes

Prep time: 15 minutes| Cook time: 25 minutes| Serves: 2

2 tablespoon garam masala
1-pound fileted carp
1 teaspoon ginger finely chopped
1-2 tablespoon fresh coriander

leaves
2 or 3 green chilies finely chopped
½ tablespoon lemon juice
Salt and black pepper to taste

Mix the ingredients in a clean bowl and add water to it. Make sure that the paste is not too watery but is enough to apply on the sides of the carp filets. Place the carp filets in the cooking tray. Select the "Air Fry" mode on your air fryer. Press Temp button and then turn the dial to adjust the cooking temperature to 350 degrees F. Press Time button and then turn the dial to adjust the cooking time to 25 minutes. Press the Start button to initiate preheating. When the screen displays "Add Food", transfer the cooking tray to the air fryer basket of your Air Fryer. Close its door, and let the machine do the cooking. Serve either with mint sauce or ketchup.
Per serving: Calories 361; Fat 10g; Sodium 218mg; Carbs 16g; Sugar 1.2g; Fiber 0.7g; Protein 24g

Delicious Coconut Shrimp

Prep time: 15 minutes| Cook time: 7 minutes| Serves: 4

(8-ounce) can crushed pineapple
½ cup sour cream
¼ cup pineapple preserves
2 egg whites
⅔ 1 cup cornstarch

⅔ 1 cup sweetened coconut
1 cup panko bread crumbs
1-pound uncooked large shrimp, thawed if frozen, deveined and shelled
Olive oil for misting

Drain the crushed pineapple well, reserving the juice. In a small bowl, combine the pineapple, sour cream, and preserves, and mix well. Set aside. In a shallow bowl, beat the 1 egg whites and mix with 2 tablespoons of the reserved pineapple liquid. Place the cornstarch on a plate. Combine the coconut and bread crumbs on another plate. Dip the shrimp into the cornstarch, shake it off, then dip into the 1 egg white mixture and finally into the coconut mixture. Place the shrimp in the cooking tray and mist with oil. Select the "Air Fry" mode on your air fryer. Press Temp button and then turn the dial to adjust the cooking temperature to 350 degrees F. Press Time button and then turn the dial to adjust the cooking time to 7 minutes. Press the Start button to initiate preheating. When the screen displays "Add Food", transfer the cooking tray to the air fryer basket of your Air Fryer. Close its door, and let the machine do the cooking. Serve warm.
Per serving: Calories 272; Fat 19g; Sodium 389mg; Carbs 10.4g; Fiber 0.7g, Sugars 1.1g; Protein 15.6g

Easy Shrimp Fajitas

Prep time: 15 minutes| Cook time: 20 minutes| Serves: 10

1-pound shrimp
1 tablespoon olive oil
2 bell peppers, diced

2 tablespoon taco seasoning
½ cup onion, diced

Add shrimp and remaining ingredients into the bowl and toss well. Add shrimp mixture to the cooking tray. Select the "Air Fry" mode on your air fryer. Press Temp button and then turn the dial to adjust the cooking temperature to 390 degrees F. Press Time button and then turn the dial to adjust the cooking time to 20 minutes. Press the Start button to initiate preheating. When the screen displays "Add Food", transfer the cooking tray to the air fryer basket of your Air Fryer. Close its door, and let the machine do the cooking. Serve and enjoy.
Per serving: Calories 351; Fat 22g; Sodium 502mg; Carbs 15.2g; Sugar 1.1g; Fiber 0.7g; Protein 26.4g

Squab Oregano Fingers

Prep time: 15 minutes| Cook time: 25 minutes| Serves: 2

½ pound squab Oregano Fingers
2 cups of dry breadcrumbs
1 ½ tablespoon ginger-garlic paste
3 tablespoons lemon juice

2 teaspoons salt
½ teaspoon pepper powder
1 teaspoon red chili flakes or to taste
3 eggs
5 tablespoons corn flour

To make the marinade, in a suitable bowl, combine the ingredients except for the Oregano Fingers and breadcrumbs. Transfer the Oregano Fingers into the marinade. Leave them on a plate to dry for 15 minutes. Now cover the Oregano Fingers with the breadcrumbs and transfer to the cooking tray. Select the "Air Fry" mode on your air fryer. Press Temp button and then turn the dial to adjust the cooking temperature to 350 degrees F. Press Time button and then turn the dial to adjust the cooking time to 25 minutes. Press the Start button to initiate preheating.

When the screen displays "Add Food", transfer the cooking tray to the air fryer basket of your Air Fryer. Close its door, and let the machine do the cooking. Serve warm.
Per serving: Calories 344; Fat 14.9g; Sodium 227mg; Carbs 14g; Fiber 1g; Sugars 1.4g; Protein 25.7g

Fired Shrimp with Mayonnaise Sauce

Prep time: 15 minutes| Cook time: 7 minutes| Serves: 4

Shrimp
12 jumbo shrimp
½ teaspoon garlic salt
¼ teaspoon freshly cracked mixed peppercorns
Sauce:
4 tablespoon mayonnaise
1 teaspoon grated lemon rind
1 teaspoon Dijon mustard
1 teaspoon chipotle powder
½ teaspoon cumin powder

In a medium bowl, season the shrimp with garlic salt and cracked mixed peppercorns. Place the shrimp in the cooking tray. Select the "Air Fry" mode on your air fryer. Press Temp button and then turn the dial to adjust the cooking temperature to 400 degrees F. Press Time button and then turn the dial to adjust the cooking time to 7 minutes. Press the Start button to initiate preheating. When the screen displays "Add Food", transfer the cooking tray to the air fryer basket of your Air Fryer. Close its door, and let the machine do the cooking. Meanwhile, stir together all the ingredients for the sauce in a small bowl until well mixed. When cooking is complete, remove the shrimp from the oven and serve alongside the sauce.
Per serving: Calories 285; Fat 9.8g; Sodium 639mg; Carbs 11.1g; Fiber 1.2g, Sugars 5.1g; Protein 27.8g

Air-fried Scallops

Prep time: 15 minutes| Cook time: 10 minutes| Serves: 2

⅓ 1 cup shallots, chopped
1 ½ tablespoon olive oil
1 ½ tablespoon coconut aminos
1 tablespoon Mediterranean seasoning mix
½ tablespoon balsamic vinegar
½ teaspoon ginger, grated
1 clove garlic, chopped
1 pound (454 g) scallops, cleaned
Cooking spray
Belgian endive, for garnish

Place all the ingredients except the scallops and Belgian endive in a small skillet over medium heat and stir to combine. Let this mixture simmer for about 2 minutes. Remove the mixture from the skillet to a large bowl and set aside to cool. Add the scallops, coating them all over, then transfer to the refrigerator to marinate for at least 2 hours. When ready, place the scallops in the cooking tray and spray with cooking spray. Select the "Air Fry" mode on your air fryer. Press Temp button and then turn the dial to adjust the cooking temperature to 345 degrees F. Press Time button and then turn the dial to adjust the cooking time to 10 minutes. Press the Start button to initiate preheating. When the screen displays "Add Food", transfer the cooking tray to the air fryer basket of your Air Fryer. Close its door, and let the machine do the cooking. Flip the scallops halfway through the cooking time. Serve warm.
Per serving: Calories 236; Fat 13.9g; Sodium 451mg; Carbs 13.2g; Fiber 1.2g; Sugars 1.4g; Protein 14.3g

Italian Cod

Prep time: 15 minutes| Cook time: 25 minutes| Serves: 4

½ lbs. cod fillet
¼ cups olives, sliced
1-pound cherry tomatoes, halved

3 garlic cloves, crushed
1 small onion, chopped
1 tablespoon olive oil
¼ cups of water
1 teaspoon Italian seasoning
Pepper
Salt

Place fish fillets, olives, tomatoes, garlic, and onion in the cooking tray. Drizzle with oil. Sprinkle with Italian seasoning, pepper, and salt. Pour water into the dish. Select the "Air Fry" mode on your air fryer. Press Temp button and then turn the dial to adjust the cooking temperature to 400 degrees F. Press Time button and then turn the dial to adjust the cooking time to 25 minutes. Press the Start button to initiate preheating. When the screen displays "Add Food", transfer the cooking tray to the air fryer basket of your Air Fryer. Close its door, and let the machine do the cooking. Serve and enjoy.
Per serving: Calories 344; Fat 14.9g; Sodium 227mg; Carbs 14g; Fiber 1g; Sugars 1.4g; Protein 25.7g

Easy Blackened Shrimp

Prep time: 15 minutes| Cook time: 15 minutes| Serves: 6

1-pound shrimp, deveined
1 tablespoon olive oil
¼ teaspoon pepper
2 teaspoon blackened seasoning
¼ teaspoon salt

Toss shrimp with oil, pepper, blackened seasoning, and salt. Transfer shrimp into the cooking tray. Select the "Air Fry" mode on your air fryer. Press Temp button and then turn the dial to adjust the cooking temperature to 400 degrees F. Press Time button and then turn the dial to adjust the cooking time to 15 minutes. Press the Start button to initiate preheating. When the screen displays "Add Food", transfer the cooking tray to the air fryer basket of your Air Fryer. Close its door, and let the machine do the cooking. Serve and enjoy.
Per serving: Calories 305; Fat 15g; Sodium 548mg; Carbs 12g; Sugar 1.2g; Fiber 0.7g; Protein 29g

Old Bay Crab Cakes

Prep time: 15 minutes| Cook time: 20 minutes| Serves: 4

2 slices dried bread, crusts removed
Small amount of milk
1 tablespoon mayonnaise
1 tablespoon Worcestershire sauce
1 tablespoon baking powder
1 tablespoon parsley flakes
1 teaspoon Old Bay® Seasoning
¼ teaspoon salt
1 egg
1-pound lump crabmeat

Crush your bread over a large bowl until it is broken down into small pieces. Add milk and stir until bread crumbs are moistened. Mix in mayo and Worcestershire sauce. Add remaining ingredients and mix well. Shape into 4 patties then place in a baking pan. Select the "Air Fry" mode on your air fryer. Press Temp button and then turn the dial to adjust the cooking temperature to 360 degrees F. Press Time button and then turn the dial to adjust the cooking time to 20 minutes. Press the Start button to initiate preheating. When the screen displays "Add Food", transfer the cooking tray into the air fryer. Close its door, and let the machine do the cooking. Serve warm.
Per serving: Calories 285; Fat 9.8g; Sodium 639mg; Carbs 11.1g; Fiber 1.2g, Sugars 5.1g; Protein 27.8g

Lemon Salmon

Prep time: 15 minutes| Cook time: 14 minutes| Serves: 2

2 salmon fillets
Salt to taste
Zest of 1 lemon

Rub the fillets with salt and lemon zest. Place them in a baking pan and spray with cooking spray. Select the "Air Fry" mode on your air fryer. Press Temp button and then turn the dial to adjust the cooking temperature to 360 degrees F. Press Time button and then turn the dial to adjust the cooking time to 14 minutes. Press the Start button to initiate preheating. When the screen displays "Add Food", transfer the cooking tray into the air fryer. Close its door, and let the machine do the cooking. Serve with steamed asparagus and a drizzle of lemon juice.
Per serving: Calories 344; Fat 14.9g; Sodium 227mg; Carbs 14g; Fiber 1g; Sugars 1.4g; Protein 25.7g

Cajun and Lemon Pepper Cod

Prep time: 15 minutes| Cook time: 12 minutes| Serves: 2

1 tablespoon Cajun seasoning	½ teaspoon lemon pepper
1 teaspoon salt	½ teaspoon freshly ground

black pepper
2 (8-ounce / 227-g) cod fillets, cut to fit into the baking pan
Cooking spray

2 tablespoons unsalted butter, melted
lemon, cut into 4 wedges

Spritz the baking pan with cooking spray. Thoroughly combine the Cajun seasoning, salt, lemon pepper, and black pepper in a small bowl. Rub this mixture all over the cod fillets until completely coated. Put the fillets in the prepared pan and brush the melted butter over both sides of fillet. Select the "Air Fry" mode on your air fryer. Press Temp button and then turn the dial to adjust the cooking temperature to 360 degrees F. Press Time button and then turn the dial to adjust the cooking time to 12 minutes. Press the Start button to initiate preheating. When the screen displays "Add Food", transfer the cooking tray into the air fryer. Close its door, and let the machine do the cooking. Flip the fillets halfway through the cooking time. Serve warm.
Per serving: Calories 254; Fat 28g; Sodium 346mg; Carbs 12.3g; Sugar 1g; Fiber 0.7g; Protein 24.3 g

Vegetable and Sides

Air Fried Leeks

Prep time: 5 minutes| Cook time: 10 minutes| Serves: 4

4 leeks; ends cut off and halved	1 tablespoon lemon juice
1 tablespoon butter; melted	Salt and black pepper to the taste

Coat the leeks in melted butter, season with salt & pepper. Cook for 7 minutes at 400 degrees F on Air Fry mode in an air fryer. Arrange on a plate and sprinkle with lemon juice before serving.
Per Serving: Calories 100; Fat 4g; Sodium 338mg; Carbs 6g; Fiber 2g; Sugar 2g; Protein 2g

Air Fryer Radish

Prep time: 5 minutes| Cook time: 15 minutes| Serves: 4

½ teaspoon onion powder	1 pound radishes; sliced
⅓ cup parmesan; grated	Salt and black pepper to the taste
4 eggs	

Combine radishes, salt, pepper, onion, eggs, and parmesan in a mixing bowl and toss well. Cook the radishes for 7 minutes at 400 degrees F on Air Fry mode in a pan that fits your air fryer. Serve the hash on individual plates.
Per Serving: Calories 80; Fat 5g; Sodium 449mg; Carbs 5g; Fiber 2g; Sugar 2g; Protein 7g

Broccoli Air Fryer Salad

Prep time: 5 minutes| Cook time: 20 minutes| Serves: 4

1 broccoli head; florets separated	1 tablespoon peanut oil
1 tablespoon Chinese rice wine vinegar	6 garlic cloves; minced
	Salt and black pepper to the taste

Toss broccoli with salt, pepper, and half of the oil in a bowl, then put to your air fryer. Cook for 8 minutes at 400 degrees F on Air Fry mode, shaking the air fryer basket halfway through. Transfer broccoli to a salad dish, mix with the remaining peanut oil, garlic, and rice vinegar, and serve.
Per Serving: Calories 121; Fat 3 g; Sodium 383mg; Carbs 4 g; Fiber 4 g; Sugar 2g; Protein 4 g

Spicy Broccoli

Prep time: 5 minutes| Cook time: 15 minutes| Serves: 4

1 pound broccoli florets	Juice of 1 lime
1 tablespoons olive oil	A pinch of salt and black pepper
1 tablespoons chili sauce	

In a large mixing basin, combine all of the ingredients and toss thoroughly. Place the broccoli in the air fryer basket. cook for 15 minutes at 400 degrees F on Air Fry mode. Serve by dividing the mixture amongst plates.
Per Serving: Calories 173 g; Fat 6 g; Sodium 299mg; Carbs 6 g; Fiber 2 g; Sugar 1g; Protein 8 g

Cheesy Asparagus and Broccoli

Prep time: 5 minutes| Cook time: 15 minutes| Serves: 4

1 broccoli head, florets separated	taste
½ pound asparagus, trimmed	2 tablespoons olive oil
Juice of 1 lime	3 tablespoons parmesan, grated
Salt and black pepper to the	

Stir the asparagus with the broccoli and all of the other ingredients, except the parmesan, in a small bowl, toss, put to your air fryer basket. Cook for 15 minutes at 400 degrees F on Air Fry mode. Serve by dividing the pasta amongst plates and sprinkling the parmesan on top.
Per Serving: Calories 172; Fat 5 g; Sodium 399mg; Carbs 4 g; Fiber 2 g; Sugar 1g; Protein 9g

Buttery Mix with Broccoli

Prep time: 5 minutes| Cook time: 15 minutes| Serves: 4

1 pound broccoli florets
A pinch of salt and black pepper

1 teaspoon sweet paprika
½ tablespoon butter, melted

Toss the broccoli with the other ingredients in a small mixing dish. Place the broccoli in the air fryer basket. Cook for 15 minutes at 350 degrees F on Air Fry mode, then divide into plates and serve.
Per Serving: Calories 130; Fat 3 g; Sodium 267mg; Carbs 4 g; Fiber 3 g; Sugar 1g; Protein 8 g

Kale with Balsamic

Prep time: 2 minutes| Cook time: 12 minutes| Serves: 6

2 tablespoons olive oil
3 garlic cloves, minced
2 and ½ pounds kale leaves

Salt and black pepper to the taste
2 tablespoons balsamic vinegar

Toss all of the ingredients together in the cooking tray. Place the tray in your air fryer. Cook for 12 minutes at 400 degrees F on Air Fry mode. Serve by dividing the mixture amongst plates.
Per Serving: Calories 122; Fat 4 g; Sodium 336mg; Carbs 4 g; Fiber 3 g; Sugar 2g; Protein 5 g

Olives with Kale

Prep time: 5 minutes| Cook time: 15 minutes| Serves: 4

½ pounds kale, torn
1 tablespoon olive oil
Salt and black pepper to the taste

1 tablespoon hot paprika
1 tablespoon black olive, pitted and sliced

Toss all of the ingredients together in an air fryer-safe pan. Place the pan in your air fryer and cook for 15 minutes at 400 degrees F on Air Fry mode. Divide into plates and serve.
Per Serving: Calories 154 g; Fat 3 g; Sodium 298mg; Carbs 4 g; Fiber 2 g; Sugar 2g; Protein 6 g

Mushrooms with Kale

Prep time: 5 minutes| Cook time: 15 minutes| Serves: 4

1 pound brown mushrooms, sliced
1 pound kale, torn
Salt and black pepper to the

taste
2 tablespoons olive oil
14 ounces coconut milk

Toss the kale with the rest of the ingredients in a saucepan that fits your air fryer. Place the pan in the air fryer and cook for 15 minutes at 400 degrees F on Air Fry mode. Divide into plates and serve.
Per Serving: Calories 162; Fat 4 g; Sodium 331mg; Carbs 3 g; Fiber 1 g; Sugar 0g; Protein 5 g

Kale with Oregano

Prep time: 5 minutes| Cook time: 10 minutes| Serves: 4

1 pound kale, torn

1 tablespoon olive oil

A pinch of salt and black pepper

2 tablespoons oregano, chopped

Toss all of the ingredients together in an air fryer-safe pan. Place the pan in the air fryer and cook for 10 minutes at 380 degrees F on Roast mode. Serve by dividing the mixture amongst plates.
Per Serving: Calories 140; Fat 3 g; Sodium 220mg; Carbs 3 g; Fiber 2 g; Sugar 0g; Protein 5 g

Brussels Sprout with Kale

Prep time: 5 minutes| Cook time: 15 minutes| Serves: 8

1 pound Brussels sprouts, trimmed
1 cups kale, torn
1 tablespoon olive oil

Salt and black pepper to the taste
3 ounces mozzarella, shredded

Toss all of the ingredients, except the mozzarella, in a pan that fits the air fryer. Place the pan in the air fryer and cook for 15 minutes at 380 degrees F on Roast mode. Serve by dividing the mixture across plates and sprinkling the cheese on top.
Per Serving: Calories 170; Fat 5 g; Sodium 449mg; Carbs 4 g; Fiber 3 g; Sugar 0g; Protein 7 g

Avocado and Olives Mix

Prep time: 5 minutes| Cook time: 15 minutes| Serves: 4

2 cups kalamata olives, pitted
2 small avocados, pitted, peeled, and sliced
¼ cup cherry tomatoes, halved

Juice of 1 lime
1 tablespoon coconut oil, melted

Combine the olives with the other ingredients in a pan that fits in your air fryer, stir, place the pan in your air fryer. Cook at 400 degrees F for 15 minutes on Air Fry mode. Serve the mixture by dividing it amongst plates.
Per Serving: Calories 153; Fat 3 g; Sodium 331mg; Carbs 4 g; Fiber 3 g; Sugar 1g; Protein 6 g

Bacon with Green Beans and Olives

Prep time: 5 minutes| Cook time: 15 minutes| Serves: 4

½ pound green beans, trimmed and halved
1 cup black olives, pitted and halved

¼ cup bacon, cooked and crumbled
1 tablespoon olive oil
¼ cup tomato sauce

Combine all of the ingredients in a pan that fits in the air fryer, stir, place the pan in the air fryer. Cook for 15 minutes at 380 degrees F on Roast mode. Serve by dividing the mixture amongst plates.
Per Serving: Calories 160; Fat 4 g; Sodium 270mg; Carbs 5 g; Fiber 3 g; Sugar 1g; Protein 4 g

Peppers with Cajun Olives

Prep time: 4 minutes| Cook time: 12 minutes| Serves: 4

1 tablespoon olive oil
½ pound mixed bell peppers, sliced

1 cup black olives, pitted and halved
½ tablespoon Cajun seasoning

Combine all of the ingredients in an air fryer-safe pan. Place the pan in your air fryer and cook for 12 minutes at 400 degrees F on Roast mode. Serve the mixture by dividing it amongst plates.
Per Serving: Calories 151; Fat 3 g; Sodium 226mg; Carbs 4 g; Fiber 2 g; Sugar 2g; Protein 5 g

Air Fryer Tomatoes

Prep time: 5 minutes| Cook time: 8 minutes| Serves: 4

1 tablespoon of herbed butter
4 large tomatoes

1 cup of mozzarella cheese, shredded

Set the air fryer to Roast for 10 minutes at 380 degrees F. Scoop out the tomato's interior contents and stuff it with cheese. Toss the filled tomatoes with the herbed butter and place on the baking pan. When it says "Add Food," place the cooking tray in the air fryer. When the cooking time is up, remove the tray from the air fryer. Warm the dish before serving.
Per Serving: Calories 75; Fat 3.2g; Sodium 310mg; Carbs 7.5g; Fiber 2g; Sugar 2g; Protein 5g

Yummy Beans Chips

Prep time: 10 minutes| Cook time: 8 hours| Serves: 4

2 ½ pounds green beans, frozen & thawed
2 ½ tablespoons coconut oil, melted

½ teaspoon garlic powder
½ teaspoon onion powder
2 teaspoons salt

Green beans should be added to the big mixing basin. Toss green beans with melted oil, garlic powder, onion powder, and salt, and toss well. Place the cooking plate in the air fryer and arrange the green beans on it. Select Dehydrate mode, then set the temperature to 280 degrees F and the timer to 8 hours, and then hit the start button. Green beans should be stored in an airtight container.
Per Serving: Calories 105; Fat 8.5 g; Sodium 335mg; Carbs 6.3 g; Fiber 2g; Sugar 2g; Protein 1.5 g

Chips of Zucchinis

Prep time: 10 minutes| Cook time: 10 minutes| Serves: 4

4 cups zucchini slices
½ teaspoon crushed red pepper flakes
½ tablespoon onion powder
½ tablespoon garlic powder
1 tablespoon dried parsley

1 tablespoon dried basil
1 tablespoon dried oregano
1 tablespoon olive oil
1 tablespoon balsamic vinegar
½ teaspoon black pepper
½ teaspoon salt

Toss the sliced zucchini with the remaining ingredients in a mixing dish until well covered. Place the cooking tray in the air fryer and arrange zucchini slices on it. Select Dehydrate mode, then set the temperature to 280 degrees F and the timer to 10 hours, and then hit the Start button. Zucchini chips should be kept in an airtight container.
Per Serving: Calories 91; Fat 7.4 g; Sodium 190mg; Carbs 6.4 g; Fiber 2g; Sugar 1g; Protein 1.9 g

Almonds Crackers with Cashew

Prep time: 10 minutes| Cook time: 9 hours| Serves: 12

1 cup ground almonds
1 cup ground cashews

½ cup water
⅓ cup ground flax

¾ teaspoon dried garlic
2 teaspoons rosemary

Salt

In a large mixing bowl, combine all of the ingredients and stir thoroughly. Spread the mixture onto the parchment-lined baking pan to a thickness of approximately 13 inches. In the air fryer, place the cooking tray. Select Dehydrate mode, then set the temperature to 260 degrees F and the timer to 1 hour, and then hit the start button. Change the temperature to 280 degrees F and the timer to 8 hours after 1 hour. Serve by slicing into pieces.
Per Serving: Calories 113; Fat 9 g; Sodium 221mg; Carbs 5.5 g; Fiber 2g; Sugar 1g; Protein 4 g

Crackers of Walnuts

Prep time: 10 minutes| Cook time: 9 hours| Serves: 12

2 cups walnuts, soak in water for overnight
1 teaspoon oregano
¼ cup olives, sliced
⅓ cup sun-dried tomatoes,

chopped
¼ cup water
½ cup ground flax
Salt

Process the walnuts in a food processor until they are finely ground. Blend the olives and sun-dried tomatoes separately. To make the dough, combine ground walnuts, blended olives and sun-dried tomatoes, ground flax, water, and salt. Spread a ¼-inch thick layer of dough onto the parchment-lined baking sheet. In the air fryer, place the cooking tray. Set the temperature to 280 degrees F and the timer to 8 hours on Dehydrate mode. Serve by slicing into pieces.
Per Serving: Calories 153; Fat 14.1 g; Sodium 190mg; Carbs 3.8 g; Fiber 2g; Sugar 0g; Protein 6.1 g

Spicy and Herby Eggplants

Prep time: 15 minutes| Cook time: 15 minutes| Serves: 2

½ teaspoon dried marjoram, crushed
½ teaspoon dried oregano, crushed
½ teaspoon dried thyme, crushed

½ teaspoon garlic powder
Salt and ground black pepper, as required
1 large eggplant, cubed
Olive oil cooking spray

Preheat the air fryer to 400 degrees F. Grease air fryer basket. Combine herbs, garlic powder, salt, and black pepper in a small bowl. After uniformly spraying the eggplant cubes with cooking spray, combine them with the herb mixture. Arrange eggplant cubes in a single layer in the air fryer basket. Select Air Fry mode. Set temperature to 400 degrees F. Cook for around 6 minutes. Cook for another6 minutes in the air fryer Spray the eggplant cubes with cooking spray again after flipping. Cook for another 2-3 minutes in the air fryer. Remove the eggplant cubes from the air fryer and place them on serving plates.
Per Serving: Calories 62; Fat 0.5g; Sodium 310mg; Carbs 14.5g; Fiber 7g; Sugar 3g; Protein 2.4g

Veggies with Basil

Prep time: 15 minutes| Cook time: 20 minutes| Serves: 2

1 small eggplant, halved and sliced
1 yellow bell pepper, sliced into 1 inch strips
1 red bell pepper, sliced into 1 inch strips
1 garlic clove, quartered
1 red onion, sliced

1 tablespoon extra-virgin olive oil
Salt and freshly ground black pepper, to taste
½ cup chopped fresh basil, for garnish
Cooking spray

Grease a nonstick baking dish with cooking spray. In a greased baking dish, combine the eggplant, bell peppers, garlic, and red onion. Drizzle the olive oil over the top and toss to evenly coat. Using cooking spray, saturate all exposed surfaces. Select Bake, set the temperature to 365 degrees F, and the cooking time to 20 minutes. To begin preheating, choose Start. Place the baking dish in the air fryer after it has been warmed. Halfway through the cooking time, flip the veggies. Remove the dish from the air fryer and season with salt and pepper. Serve with a sprinkling of basil on top as a finishing touch.
Per Serving: Calories 164; Fat 4.1 g; Sodium 222mg; Carbs 6 g; Fiber 2g; Sugar 4g; Protein 7 g

Celery Roots with Cinnamon

Prep time: 10 minutes| Cook time: 20 minutes| Serves: 4

2 celery roots, peeled and diced
1 teaspoon extra-virgin olive oil
1 teaspoon butter, melted

½ teaspoon ground cinnamon
Sea salt and freshly ground black pepper, to taste

Aluminum foil should be used to line a baking pan. In a large mixing basin, toss the celery roots with the olive oil until completely coated. Place them on the baking sheet that has been prepared. Select Roast and set the temperature to 365 degrees F for 20 minutes. To begin preheating, choose Start. Place the baking sheet in the air fryer after it has been warmed. Celery roots should be quite sensitive when done. Remove the dish from the air fryer and place it in a serving bowl. Add the butter and cinnamon and mash until frothy with a potato masher. Season with salt and pepper. Serve right away.
Per Serving: Calories 134; Fat 3 g; Sodium 170mg; Carbs 7 g; Fiber 1g; Sugar 3g; Protein 9 g

Parmesan Broccoli

Prep time: 20 minutes| Cook time: 15 minutes| Serves: 4

12 ounces frozen broccoli, thawed, drained, and patted dry
1 large egg, lightly beaten
½ cup seasoned whole-wheat bread crumbs
¼ cup shredded reduced-fat

sharp Cheddar cheese
¼ cup grated Parmesan cheese
1½ teaspoons minced garlic
Salt and freshly ground black pepper, to taste
Cooking spray

Using cooking spray, gently coat a perforated pan. In a food processor, combine the other ingredients and pulse until the mixture resembles coarse meal. Place the ingredients in a mixing basin. Scoop out the broccoli mixture with a tablespoon and shape into 24 oval "tater tot" shapes with your hands. Place the tots in a single layer in the prepared perforated pan, spacing them 1 inch apart. Using a thin mist of cooking spray, gently coat the tots. Choose Air Fry, set the temperature to 400 degrees F, and the timer to 15 minutes. To begin preheating, choose Start. Place the pan in the air fryer after it has been warmed. Halfway through the cooking time, flip the tots. When done, the tots will be lightly browned and crispy. Remove from the air fryer and serve on a plate.
Per Serving: Calories 211; Fat 12 g; Sodium 443mg; Carbs 14 g; Fiber 2g; Sugar 4g; Protein 8 g

Crunchy Broccoli

Prep time: 10 minutes| Cook time: 8 minutes| Serves: 2

¼ teaspoon Masala
½ teaspoon Red chili powder
½ teaspoon Salt

¼ teaspoon Turmeric powder
1 tablespoon Chickpea flour
1 tablespoon Yogurt

1 pound broccoli

Broccoli should be cut into florets. To eliminate impurities, soak for at least half an hour in a bowl of water with 2 tablespoons of salt. Remove the broccoli florets from the water and set them aside to drain. Wipe off the surface completely. To make a marinade, combine all of the other ingredients. In a large mixing bowl, toss the broccoli florets with the marinade. Chill for 15-30 minutes, covered. Preheat the air fryer to 400 degrees F. Place the marinated broccoli florets in the fryer basket, heat to 400 degrees F, and cook for 10 minutes at 400 degrees F on Air Fry mode. When the Florets are done, they will be crispy.
Per Serving: Calories 96; Fat 1.3g; Sodium 241mg; Carbs 3g; Fiber 2g; Sugar 1g; Protein 7g

Carrot, Zucchini and Squash

Prep time: 5 minutes| Cook time: 35 minutes| Serves: 4

1 tablespoon chopped tarragon leaves
½ teaspoon white pepper
1 teaspoon salt

1 pound yellow squash
1 pound zucchini
6 teaspoons olive oil
½ pound carrots

Squash and zucchini should be stemmed and rooted before being cut into 3/4-inch half-moons. Carrots should be peeled and sliced into 1-inch pieces. Toss carrot chunks with 2 tablespoons olive oil until well coated. Select Air Fry mode. Set the temperature to 400 degrees F and the timer to 5 minutes. While the carrots are cooking, pour the remaining olive oil over the squash and zucchini, seasoning with pepper and salt. Toss well to coat. When the timer for the carrots goes off, add the squash and zucchini. Cook for 30 minutes, tossing 2-3 times during the cooking time. Remove the vegetables and mix with tarragon after they're done. Warm it up before serving.
Per Serving: Calories 122; Fat 9g; Sodium 441mg; Carbs 7g; Fiber 2g; Sugar 1g; Protein 6g

Tomatoes with Basil

Prep time: 10 minutes| Cook time: 10 minutes| Serves: 2

3 tomatoes, halved
olive oil cooking spray
salt and ground black pepper

1 tablespoon fresh basil, chopped

Spritz cooking spray on the cut sides of the tomato halves equally. Add salt, black pepper, and basil to taste. Select Air Fry mode. Set temperature to 400 degrees F and time to 10 minutes. To begin, press the Start button. Open the lid when the device beeps to indicate that it has warmed. Place the tomatoes in an air fryer basket and cook them. Serve warm.
Per Serving: Calories 34; Fat 0.4 g; Sodium 225mg; Carbs 7.2 g; Fiber 2g; Sugar 2g; Protein 1.7 g

Delicious Tomatoes

Prep time: 15 minutes| Cook time: 15 minutes| Serves: 2

2 large tomatoes
½ cup broccoli, chopped finely
½ cup Cheddar cheese, shredded
Salt and ground black pepper

1 tablespoon unsalted butter, melted
½ teaspoon dried thyme, crushed

Cut the tops off each tomato carefully and scoop out the pulp and seeds. Chop the broccoli and combine it with the cheese, salt, and black pepper in a mixing bowl. Fill each tomato equally with the broccoli mixture. Select Air Fry mode. Set temp to

400 degrees F and time to 15 minutes. To begin, press the Start button. Open the lid, when the device shows Add Food. Place the tomatoes in an Air fryer basket that has been oiled and placed in the air fryer. Serve warm with the garnishing of thyme.
Per Serving: Calories 206; Fat 15.6 g; Sodium 229mg; Carbs 9 g; Fiber 2g; Sugar 2g; Protein 9.4 g

Brussels Sprout with Honey

Prep time: 10 minutes| Cook time: 15 minutes| Serves: 4

½ pound Brussels sprouts, cut stems then cut each in half	1 tablespoon vinegar
1 tablespoon olive oil	1 tablespoon lemon juice
½ tsp salt	1 teaspoon sugar
For sauce:	1 tablespoon honey
1 tablespoon sriracha sauce	1 teaspoon garlic, minced
	½ teaspoon olive oil

In a small saucepan, combine all sauce ingredients and cook over low heat for 2-3 minutes, or until thickened. Take the saucepan from the heat and set it aside. In a zip-lock bag, combine the Brussels sprouts, oil, and salt and shake thoroughly. Place Brussels sprouts on the cooking tray and set "air fry"mode for 15 minutes at 400 degrees F. Shake the bottle halfway through. Fill a mixing dish halfway with Brussels sprouts. Toss with the prepared sauce until fully coated. Serve and have fun.
Per Serving: Calories 86; Fat 4.3 g; Sodium 223mg; Carbs 11.8 g; Fiber 2g; Sugar 7.6 g; Protein 2 g

Air Fried Carrots

Prep time: 10 minutes| Cook time: 20 minutes| Serves: 6

2 pounds' carrots, peeled, slice in half again slice half	1 teaspoon dried thyme
2 ½ tablespoons dried parsley	3 tablespoons olive oil
1 teaspoon dried oregano	Pepper
	Salt

In a mixing basin, combine the carrots. Toss in the remaining ingredients on top of the carrots. Arrange carrots on the cooking tray and cook for 10 minutes at 400 degrees F on Air Fry mode. After 10 minutes, flip the carrot slices over and roast for another 10 minutes. Serve and have fun.
Per Serving: Calories 124; Fat 7.1 g; Sodium 410mg; Carbs 15.3 g; Fiber 5.5g; Sugar 7.5 g; Protein 1.3 g

Cheesy Broccoli

Prep time: 10 minutes| Cook time: 5 minutes| Serves: 4

1 pound broccoli florets	1 tablespoon olive oil
¼ cup parmesan cheese, grated	Pepper
1 tablespoon garlic, minced	Salt

Broccoli florets should be added to the mixing basin. Toss the broccoli florets with the cheese, garlic, oil, pepper, and salt. Arrange broccoli florets on the cooking tray and bake for 4 minutes at 365 degrees F. Cook for another 2 minutes on the opposite side of the broccoli florets. Serve and have fun.
Per Serving: Calories 252; Fat 16.4 g; Sodium 331mg; Carbs 8.2 g; Fiber 2g; Sugar 2 g; Protein 15.3 g

Cheesy Green Beans

Prep time: 10 minutes| Cook time: 5 minutes| Serves: 6

2 pounds fresh green beans	½ cup flour

2 eggs, lightly beaten	½ cup parmesan cheese, grated
¾ tablespoon garlic powder	1 cup breadcrumbs

Add flour to a small dish. Add the eggs to a second shallow dish. Combine breadcrumbs, garlic powder, and cheese in a third shallow dish. Coat the beans in flour, then in eggs, and finally in breadcrumbs. Place coated beans on the cooking tray and air fry for 5 minutes at 400 degrees F on Air Fry mode. Serve and have fun.
Per Serving: Calories 257; Fat 8.6 g; Sodium 429mg; Carbs 27.2 g; Fiber 4g; Sugar 2.6 g; Protein 14.9 g

Delicious Asparagus

Prep time: 10 minutes| Cook time: 9 minutes| Serves: 4

1-pound asparagus, cut the ends	Pepper
1 teaspoon olive oil	Salt

Arrange asparagus on the pan of the air fryer. Season it with pepper and salt and drizzle with olive oil. Bake asparagus at 365 degrees F for 7-9 minutes on Bake mode in your air fryer. While cooking, turn the asparagus. Serve and have fun.
Per Serving: Calories 33; Fat 1.3 g; Sodium 312mg; Carbs 4.4 g; Fiber 1g; Sugar 2.1 g; Protein 2.5 g

Yummy Veggies

Prep time: 10 minutes| Cook time: 18 minutes| Serves: 4

1 cup carrots, sliced	1 tablespoon olive oil
1 cup cauliflower, cut into florets	Pepper
1 cup broccoli florets	Salt

In a mixing dish, combine all of the veggies. Season with pepper and salt and then drizzle with olive oil. Toss thoroughly. Select Roast mode. Place the veggies in the air fryer basket and Roast for 18 minutes at 380 degrees F. Serve and have fun.
Per Serving: Calories 55; Fat 3.6 g; Sodium 331mg; Carbs 5.6 g; Fiber 1g; Sugar 2.3 g; Protein 1.4 g

Air Fryer Sweet Potatoes

Prep time: 10 minutes| Cook time: 40 minutes| Serves: 4

4 sweet potatoes, scrubbed and washed	½ tablespoon butter, melted
	½ teaspoon sea salt

By using a fork, prick the sweet potatoes. Sweet potatoes should be rubbed with melted butter and seasoned with salt. Select Bake option. Cook sweet potatoes for 40 minutes at 365 degrees F on an air fryer basket. Serve and have fun.
Per Serving: Calories 125; Fat 1.5 g; Sodium 410mg; Carbs 26.2 g; Fiber 7g; Sugar 5.4 g; Protein 2.1 g

Pudding of Cauliflower

Prep time: 10 minutes| Cook time: 30 minutes| Serves: 4

2 ½ cups water	2 cinnamon sticks
1 cup coconut; Sugar	½ cup coconut, shredded
2 cups cauliflower rice	

Mix water with coconut in a saucepan that fits your air fryer; sugar, cauliflower rice, cinnamon, and coconut, whisk, then place in the air fryer and cook for 30 minutes at 365 degrees F on Bake mode. Serve the pudding cold, divided into cups. Enjoy!
Per Serving: Calories 203; Fat 4 g; Sodium 331mg; Carbs 9 g; Fiber 1g; Sugar 2g; Protein 4 g

Curry of Zucchini

Prep time: 5 minutes| Cook time: 8-10 minutes| Serves: 2

2 zucchinis, washed & sliced
1 tablespoon olive oil

1 pinch sea salt
Curry mix, pre-made

Preheat your air fryer to 400 degrees F. Combine the zucchini slices, salt, oil, and spices in a mixing bowl. Select Air Fry mode. Set temp to 400 degrees F and time to 10 minutes. Cook the zucchini for 8-10 minutes in the air fryer. Serve alone or with sour cream.
Per Serving: Calories 100; Fat 1g; Sodium 170mg; Carbs 4g; Fiber 2g; Sugar 1g; Protein 2g

Air Fryer Fries of Carrot

Prep time: 5 minutes| Cook time: 12-15 minutes| Serves: 2

5 large carrots
1 tablespoon olive oil

½ teaspoon sea salt

Preheat the air fryer to 400 degrees F, then wash and peel the carrots. Cut them into fries-like shapes. Combine the carrot sticks, olive oil, and salt in a mixing bowl and coat evenly. Select Air Fry mode. Set temp to 400 degrees F and timer to 14 minutes. Place them in an air fryer and cook for 12 minutes. Cook for an additional 2 to 3 minutes if they aren't crispy enough. Serve with sour cream, ketchup, or your favorite main dish alone.
Per Serving: Calories 140; Fat 3g; Sodium 221mg; Carbs 6g; Fiber 1g; Sugar 1g; Protein 7g

Tasty Stuffed Potatoes

Prep time: 15 minutes| Cook time: 35 minutes| Serves: 2

4 large potatoes, peeled
2 bacon, rashers

½ brown onion, diced
¼ cup cheese, grated

Preheat your air fryer to 400 degrees F. After cutting your potatoes in half, brush them with oil. Place it in your air fryer for 10 minutes to cook. Brush the potatoes with oil once more and bake for 10 minutes more. To prepare the cooked potatoes for stuffing, make a hole in them. In a frying pan, cook the bacon and onion. Over medium heat, add the cheese and whisk to combine. Remove the pan from the heat. Select Air Fry mode. Set temp to 400 degrees F and timer to 5 minutes. Cook for 4 to 5 minutes after stuffing your potatoes.
Per Serving: Calories 180; Fat 8g; Sodium 221mg; Carbs 10g; Fiber 2g; Sugar 3g; Protein 11g

Carrots in Air Fryer

Prep time: 5 minutes| Cook time: 35 minutes| Serves: 2

4 cups carrots, chopped
1 teaspoon herbs de Provence

2 teaspoons olive oil
4 tablespoons orange juice

Preheat your air fryer to 400 degrees F. Combine the carrots, herbs, and oil in a mixing bowl. Select Air Fry mode. Set temp to 400 degrees F and timer to 28 minutes. Cook for around 25 to 28 minutes. Remove it from the pan and dip the pieces in orange juice before continuing to cook for another 7 minutes.
Per Serving: Calories 125; Fat 2g; Sodium 229mg; Carbs 5g; Fiber 1g; Sugar 1g; Protein 6g

Cheddar Broccoli

Prep time: 5 minutes| Cook time: 9 minutes| Serves: 2

1 head broccoli, washed & chopped
salt & pepper to taste

1 tablespoon olive oil
Sharp cheddar cheese, shredded

Preheat your air fryer to 400 degrees F. Combine the broccoli, olive oil, and salt in a mixing bowl. Select Air Fry mode. Set temp to 400 degrees F and timer to 6 minutes. Place it in the air fryer for 6 minutes to cook. Remove it from the air fryer and top it with cheese before cooking for another 3 minutes. Serve with a side dish of your choice.
Per Serving: Calories 170; Fat 5g; Sodium 221mg; Carbs 9g; Fiber 2g; Sugar 1g; Protein 7g

Yummy Plantains

Prep time: 5 minutes| Cook time: 10 minutes| Serves: 2

2 ripe plantains, peeled and cut at a diagonal into ½-inch-thick pieces

3 tablespoons ghee, melted
¼ teaspoon kosher salt

Combine the plantains, ghee, and salt in a mixing dish. In the air fryer basket, arrange the plantain pieces. Select Air Fry mode. Set the air fryer to 400 degrees F for 8 minutes. When the plantains are soft and delicate on the inside and have a lot of crisp, delicious brown spots on the exterior, they're ready.
Per Serving: Calories 180; Fat 5g; Sodium 321mg; Carbs 10g; Fiber 1g; Sugar 2g; Protein 7g

Asparagus Wrap with Bacon

Prep time: 5 minutes| Cook time: 10 minutes| Serves: 4

1 pound asparagus, trimmed (about 24 spears)
4 slices bacon or beef bacon
½ cup Ranch Dressing for

serving
3 tablespoons chopped fresh chives, for garnish

Avocado oil should be used to grease the air fryer basket. Preheat the air fryer to 400 degrees F. Long, thin strips of bacon may be made by slicing the bacon along the middle. Wrap one piece of bacon around 3 asparagus spears and fasten with a toothpick at each end. Using the leftover bacon and asparagus, repeat the process. Select Air Fry mode. Set temp to 400 degrees F and timer to 10 minutes. Arrange the asparagus bundles in a single layer in the air fryer. (If required, cook in batches if using a smaller air fryer.) Cook until the asparagus is slightly browned on the ends and the bacon is crispy, about 8 minutes for thin stalks and 10 minutes for medium to thick stalks. Serve with ranch dressing and chives on top. It's best to eat it right away.
Per Serving: Calories 241; Fat 22g; Sodium 231mg; Carbs 6g; Fiber 3g; Sugar 2g; Protein 7g

Roasted Cob and Corn

Prep time: 5 minutes| Cook time: 10 minutes| Serves: 4

1 tablespoon vegetable oil
4 ears of corn
Unsalted butter, for topping

Salt, for topping
Freshly ground black pepper, for topping

Rub the vegetable oil all over the corn, making sure it's well covered. Select Air Fry mode. Set the temperature of your Air

fryer to 400 degrees F. Set the timer for 5 minutes. Press Start to begin. Flip the corn. Cook for another 5 minutes. With a pat of butter and a hefty pinch of salt and pepper, serve.
Per Serving: Calories 265; Fat 17g; Sodium 441mg; Carbs 29g; Fiber 4g; Sugar 5g; Protein 5g

Bacon with Green Beans

Prep time: 15 minutes| Cook time: 20 minutes| Serves: 4

3 cups frozen cut green beans	¼ cup water
1 medium onion, chopped	Kosher salt and black pepper
3 slices bacon, chopped	

Combine the frozen green beans, onion, bacon, and water in a 6 x 3-inch circular heatproof pan. Toss everything together. In the basket, place the saucepan. Set the air fryer to 365 degrees F for 15 minutes on Bake mode. Season the beans to taste with salt and pepper, mix well, and cook. Cover the pan with foil after removing it from the air fryer basket. Allow for 5 minutes of rest before serving.
Per Serving: Calories 230; Fat 10g; Sodium 342mg; Carbs 14g; Fiber 4g; Sugar 2g; Protein 17g

Roasted Carrots with Honey

Prep time: 5 minutes| Cook time: 15 minutes| Serves: 4

3 cups baby carrots	Salt
1 tablespoon extra-virgin olive oil	Freshly ground black pepper
1 tablespoon honey	Fresh dill (optional)

Combine honey, olive oil, carrots, salt, and pepper in a mixing bowl. Make sure the carrots are well covered with oil. In the air fryer basket, place the carrots. Set your air fryer to 380 degrees F on Roast mode. Set the timer for 12 minutes, or until the potatoes are fork-tender. Remove the air fryer basket from the air fryer. Serve the carrots in a dish with a sprinkling of dill, if preferred.
Per Serving: Calories 140; Fat 3g; Sodium 331mg; Carbs 7g; Fiber 2g; Sugar 1g; Protein 9g

Delicious Cabbage

Prep time: 5 minutes| Cook time: 10 minutes| Serves: 4

1 head cabbage, sliced in 1-inch-thick ribbons	pepper
1 tablespoon olive oil	1 teaspoon garlic powder
Salt and freshly ground black	1 teaspoon red pepper flakes

Mix together the olive oil, cabbage, salt, pepper, garlic powder, and red pepper flakes in a mixing bowl. Make sure the cabbage is well covered with oil. In the air fryer basket, place the cabbage. Set your Air Fryer to 380 degrees F on Roast mode. Set the timer for 4 minutes and roast. Flip the cabbage with tongs. Restart the timer to 3 minutes and cook for another 3 minutes.
Per Serving: Calories 100; Fat 1g; Sodium 221mg; Carbs 3g; Fiber 1g; Sugar 1g; Protein 3g

Yummy Delicious Tomatoes

Prep time: 5 minutes| Cook time: 5 minutes| Serves: 4

4 medium tomatoes	4 (2-ounce) Burrata balls
½ teaspoon fine sea salt	Fresh basil leaves, for garnish

Extra-virgin olive oil, for drizzling

Using a melon baller or a spoon, remove the tomato seeds and membranes. Sprinkle the salt on the insides of the tomatoes. Fill each tomato with a Burrata ball. Select Air Fry mode. Set temp to 400 degrees F and timer to 5 minutes. Cook it for 5 minutes in the air fryer, or until the cheese has melted. Garnish with basil leaves and olive oil. Warm the dish before serving.
Per Serving: Calories 108; Fat 7g; Sodium 290mg; Carbs 5g; Fiber 2g; Sugar 1g; Protein 6g

Broccoli with Parmesan

Prep time: 5 minutes| Cook time: 5 minutes| Serves: 4

1 pound broccoli florets	¼ cup grated or shaved
2 teaspoons minced garlic	Parmesan cheese
2 tablespoons olive oil	

Combine the broccoli florets, garlic, olive oil, and Parmesan cheese in a mixing bowl. Select Bake mode. Set temp to 365 degrees F and timer to 5 minutes. Set the timer for 4 minutes and steam the broccoli in the air fryer basket in a single layer.
Per Serving: Calories 130; Fat 3g; Sodium 190mg; Carbs 5g; Fiber 2g; Sugar 1g; Protein 4g

Mayo Broccoli

Prep time: 5 minutes| Cook time: 10 minutes| Serves: 4

4 cups broccoli florets	smoked salt
3 tablespoons melted ghee or butter-flavored coconut oil	Mayonnaise, for serving (optional; omit for egg-free)
1½ teaspoons fine sea salt or	

Avocado oil should be used to grease the basket. In a large mixing basin, place the broccoli. Drizzle the ghee over it, stir to coat, and season with salt. Select Air fry mode. Set temp to 400 degrees F and timer to 8 minutes. Cook it for 8 minutes, or until the broccoli is soft and crisp around the edges, in the air fryer basket.
Per Serving: Calories 120; Fat 2g; Sodium 221mg; Carbs 4g; Fiber 1g; Sugar 1g; Protein 3g

Brussels Sprouts with Balsamic

Prep time: 5 minutes| Cook time: 15 minutes| Serves: 4

¼ teaspoon salt	halved
1 tablespoon balsamic vinegar	3 tablespoons olive oil
2 cups Brussels sprouts,	

In a mixing bowl, combine all of the ingredients until the zucchini fries are well covered. Place in the air fryer basket. Bake at 365 degrees F for 15 minutes.
Per Serving: Calories 82; Fat 6.8g; Sodium 221mg; Carbs 7g; Fiber 1g; Sugar 1g; Protein 1.5g

Mushrooms with Thyme and Garlic

Prep time: 5 minutes| Cook time: 10 minutes| Serves: 4

3 tablespoons unsalted butter, melted	2 cloves garlic, minced
1 (8 ounce) package button mushrooms, sliced	3 sprigs fresh thyme leaves
	½ teaspoon fine sea salt

Avocado oil should be used to grease the air fryer basket. Preheat the air fryer to 400 degrees F. In a medium-sized mixing bowl, combine all of the ingredients. Coat the mushroom slices with a spoon or your hands. Select Air Fry mode. Set temp to 400 degrees F and time to 15 minutes. Place the mushrooms in a single layer in the basket; if necessary, work in batches. Cook for 10 minutes, or until golden brown and crispy. Before serving, garnish with thyme sprigs. Cook it for 5 minutes in a preheated at 400 degrees F air fryer, or until thoroughly heated.
Per Serving: Calories 82; Fat 9g; Sodium 190mg; Carbs 1g; Fiber 0.2g; Sugar 0g; Protein 1g

Cheesy Zucchini Chips

Prep time: 10 minutes| Cook time: 10 minutes| Serves: 10

½ teaspoon paprika
½ cup grated parmesan cheese
½ cup Italian breadcrumbs
1 lightly beaten egg
2 thinly sliced zucchinis

Slice zucchini as finely as possible using a very sharp knife or a mandolin slicer. Remove any excess moisture with a paper towel. Mix the egg with a sprinkle of salt and pepper, as well as a little water. In a mixing dish, combine paprika, cheese, and breadcrumbs. Slices of zucchini should be dipped in the egg mixture before being dipped in the breadcrumb mixture. To coat, lightly press. Mist zucchini slices with olive oil cooking spray. Place in a single layer in your air fryer. Select Bake mode. Set temperature to 365 degrees F, and set time to 8 minutes. Select Start to begin cooking. Serve with salsa and a pinch of salt.
Per Serving: Calories 130; Fat 2g; Sodium 90mg; Carbs 5g; Fiber 2g; Sugar 1g; Protein 3g

Fries of Jicama

Prep time: 10 minutes| Cook time: 5 minutes| Serves: 4

1 tablespoon dried thyme
¾ cup arrowroot flour
½ large Jicama
Eggs

Jicama fries made with sliced jicama. Combine the eggs and pour over the fries. Toss to evenly coat. Mix together a bit of salt, thyme, and arrowroot flour. Toss the egg-coated jicama into the dry mixture and toss well to coat. Add the fries to the air fryer basket after spraying it with olive oil. Select air fry mode. Set temperature to 400 degrees F, and set time to 5 minutes. Select Start to begin. Toss halfway through the cooking time.
Per Serving: Calories 211; Fat 19g; Sodium 229mg; Carbs 16g; Fiber 4g; Sugar 3g; Protein 9g

Yummy Cauliflower Pizza

Prep time: 5 minutes| Cook time: 20 minutes| Serves: 6

1 (12 ounces) Steamer bag cauliflower
1 large egg
½ cup shredded sharp cheddar cheese.
2 tablespoons Blanched finely ground almond flour
1 teaspoon Italian blend seasoning

Cook the cauliflower according to the package directions. Remove from bag and place on a paper towel to absorb any excess moisture. In a large mixing basin, place the cauliflower. Toss together the almond flour, cheese, egg, and Italian spice in a mixing bowl. To fit your air fryer, cut a sheet of parchment to fit. Cauliflower should be pressed into a 6-inch circular round. Place the ingredients in the air fryer basket. Select Air Fry mode. Adjust the temperature to 400 degrees F and set the timer for 11 minutes. Flip the pizza crust after 7

minutes. Toppings can be added to the pizza as desired. Return to the air fryer basket and cook for an additional 4 minutes, or until golden. Serve right away.
Per Serving: Calories 230; Fat 14.2g; Sodium 331mg; Carbs 10.0g; Fiber 4.7g; Sugar 5g; Protein 14.9g

Delicious Tomatoes and Cabbage

Prep time: 5 minutes| Cook time: 20 minutes| Serves: 4

2 spring onions; chopped.
1 savoy cabbage, shredded
1 tablespoon parsley; chopped.
2 tablespoons tomato sauce
Salt and black pepper to taste

Stir the cabbage with the remaining ingredients (save the parsley) in a pan that fits your air fryer, toss, place the pan in the air fryer, and cook at 400 degrees F for 15 minutes on Air Fry mode. Serve with a sprinkling of parsley on top of each serving.
Per Serving: Calories 163; Fat 4g; Sodium 223mg; Carbs 6g; Fiber 3g; Sugar 1g; Protein 7g

Steak of Cauliflower

Prep time: 5 minutes| Cook time: 10 minutes| Serves: 4

1 medium head cauliflower
¼ cup blue cheese crumbles
¼ cup hot sauce
¼ cup full-fat ranch dressing
2 tablespoons Salted butter; melted.

Remove the leaves from the cauliflower. By using a 1/2-inch thick slicer, cut the skull into ½ inch thick slices. Combine the spicy sauce and butter in a small bowl. Brush the cauliflower with the mixture. Working in batches if required, place each cauliflower steak in the air fryer. Select Air Fry mode. Adjust the temperature to 400 degrees F and set the timer for 7 minutes When cooked, the edges begin to darken and caramelize. To serve, top steaks with blue cheese crumble. Drizzle ranch dressing over the top.
Per Serving: Calories 122; Fat 8.4g; Sodium 221mg; Carbs 7.7g; Fiber 3.0g; Sugar 2g; Protein 4.9g

Green Beans with Avocado and Tomatoes

Prep time: 5 minutes| Cook time: 20 minutes| Serves: 4

¼ pound green beans, trimmed and halved
1 avocado, peeled, pitted and cubed
1 pint mixed cherry tomatoes; halved
2 tablespoons olive oil

Toss the tomatoes with the rest of the ingredients in a pan that fits your air fryer. Place the pan in the air fryer and cook for 15 minutes at 365 degrees F on Bake mode. Serve immediately in bowls.
Per Serving: Calories 151; Fat 3g; Sodium 221mg; Carbs 4g; Fiber 2g; Sugar 1g; Protein 4g

Green Beans with Dill and Garlic

Prep time: 5 minutes| Cook time: 20 minutes| Serves: 4

1 pound green beans, trimmed
½ cup bacon cooked and chopped.
2 garlic cloves; minced
2 tablespoons dill; chopped.
Salt and black pepper to taste

Toss the green beans with the rest of the ingredients in a pan

that fits the air fryer. Place the pan in the air fryer and cook for 15 minutes at 380 degrees F on Bake mode. Serve by dividing everything across plates.
Per Serving: Calories 180; Fat 3g; Sodium 90mg; Carbs 4g; Fiber 2g; Sugar 1g; Protein 6g

Stacks of Eggplant

Prep time: 5 minutes| Cook time: 15 minutes| Serves: 4

2 large tomatoes; cut into ¼-inch slices	into ½-oz. slices
¼ cup fresh basil, sliced	1 medium eggplant; cut into ¼-inch slices
4 ounces fresh mozzarella; cut	2 tablespoons olive oil

Place 4 slices of eggplant on the bottom of a 6-inch round baking dish. Place a piece of tomato, mozzarella, and eggplant on each eggplant round. As needed, repeat the process. Drizzle with extra virgin olive oil. Place the dish in the air fryer basket after covering it with foil. Select Air Fry mode. Set temp to 400 degrees F and time to 15 minutes. The eggplant will be soft when done. To serve, garnish with fresh basil.
Per Serving: Calories 195; Fat 12.7g; Sodium 221mg; Carbs 12.7g; Fiber 5.2g; Sugar 1g; Protein 8.5g

Garlic Squash Spaghetti

Prep time: 5 minutes| Cook time: 40 minutes| Serves: 4

½ large spaghetti squash	1 tablespoon coconut oil
2 tablespoons salted butter; melted.	1 teaspoon dried parsley
	½ teaspoon garlic powder

Apply coconut oil to the shell of the spaghetti squash. Brush the interior with butter and place the skin side down. Garlic powder and parsley are sprinkled on top. Place the squash in the air fryer basket with the skin side down. Adjust the temperature to 400 degrees F and set the timer for 30 minutes on Air Fry mode. When the timer goes off, turn the squash over and cook for another 15 minutes, or until fork soft. Warm the dish before serving.
Per Serving: Calories 182; Fat 11.7g; Sodium 112mg; Carbs 18.2g; Fiber 3.9g; Sugar 2g; Protein 1.9g

Simple Beet Salad with Blue Cheese

Prep time: 10 minutes| Cook time: 15 minutes| Serves: 6

6 beets, peeled and quartered	¼ cup blue cheese, crumbled
Salt and black pepper to the taste	1 tablespoon olive oil

Cook the beets in your air fryer for 14 minutes at 400 degrees F on Air Fry mode before transferring them to a bowl. Toss in the blue cheese, salt, pepper, and oil before serving. Enjoy!
Per Serving: Calories 100; Fat 4g; Sodium 331mg; Carbs 10g; Fiber 4g; Sugar 2g; Protein 5g

Tomatoes and Brussels Sprouts

Prep time: 5 minutes| Cook time: 10 minutes| Serves: 4

1 pound Brussels sprouts, trimmed	taste
Salt and black pepper to the	6 cherry tomatoes, halved
	¼ cup green onions, chopped

1 tablespoon olive oil

Season Brussels sprouts with salt and pepper before placing them in your air fryer and cooking for 10 minutes at 400 degrees F on Air Fry mode. Add salt, pepper, cherry tomatoes, green onions, and olive oil to a mixing bowl, toss well, and serve. Enjoy!
Per Serving: Calories 121; Fat 4g; Sodium 221mg; Carbs 11g; Fiber 4g; Sugar 2g; Protein 4g

Parmesan Brussels Sprout

Prep time: 10 minutes| Cook time: 10 minutes| Serves: 4

1 pound Brussels sprouts, washed	taste
Juice of 1 lemon	2 tablespoons butter
Salt and black pepper to the	3 tablespoons parmesan, grated

Place Brussels sprouts in an air fryer and cook for 8 minutes at 400 degrees F on Air Fry mode before transferring to a bowl. Warm the butter in a skillet over medium heat, and then add the lemon juice, salt, and pepper, mix well, and pour over the Brussels sprouts. Toss in the parmesan until it melts, then serve. Enjoy!
Per Serving: Calories 152; Fat 6g; Sodium 225mg; Carbs 8g; Fiber 6g; Sugar 2g; Protein 12g

Sweet and Spicy Baby Carrots

Prep time: 10 minutes| Cook time: 10 minutes| Serves: 4

2 cups baby carrots	1 tablespoon brown; Sugar
A pinch of salt and black pepper	½ tablespoon butter, melted

Stir baby carrots with butter, salt, pepper, and sugar in a dish that fits your air fryer, toss, place in the air fryer. Cook at 400 degrees F for 10 minutes on Air Fry mode. Serve by dividing the mixture among plates. Enjoy!
Per Serving: Calories 100; Fat 2g; Sodium 331mg; Carbs 7g; Fiber 3g; Sugar 1g; Protein 4g

Spicy Leeks

Prep time: 10 minutes| Cook time: 10 minutes| Serves: 4

4 leeks, washed, halved	1 tablespoon butter, melted
Salt and black pepper to taste	1 tablespoon lemon juice

Rub the leeks with melted butter, season with salt & pepper, and cook for 7 minutes at 400 degrees F in an air fryer on Air Fry mode. Arrange on a plate and sprinkle with lemon juice before serving. Enjoy!
Per Serving: Calories 100; Fat 4g; Sodium 90mg; Carbs 6g; Fiber 2g; Sugar 1g; Protein 2g

Potatoes with Parsley

Prep time: 10 minutes| Cook time: 10 minutes| Serves: 4

1 pound gold potato, cut into wedges	taste
Salt and black pepper to the	2 tablespoons olive oil
	Juice from ½ lemon

Season potatoes with salt, pepper, lemon juice, and olive oil. Place them in your air fryer and cook for 10 minutes at 400

degrees F on Air Fry mode. Serve by dividing among dishes and garnishing with parsley. Enjoy!
Per Serving: Calories 152; Fat 3g; Sodium 221mg; Carbs 17g; Fiber 7g; Sugar 2g; Protein 4g

Tomatoes with Garlic

Prep time: 10 minutes| Cook time: 15 minutes| Serves: 4

4 garlic cloves, crushed
1 pound mixed cherry tomatoes
3 thyme springs, chopped

Salt and black pepper to the taste
¼ cup olive oil

Toss tomatoes with salt, black pepper, garlic, olive oil, and thyme in a dish to coat. Place in your air fryer and cook for 15 minutes at 400 degrees F on Air Fry mode. Serve the tomato mixture on plates. Enjoy!
Per Serving: Calories 100; Fat 0g; Sodium 223mg; Carbs 1g; Fiber 1g; Sugar 0g; Protein 6g

Potatoes with Green Beans

Prep time: 10 minutes| Cook time: 15 minutes| Serves: 5

2 pounds green beans
6 new potatoes, halved
Salt and black pepper to the taste

A drizzle of olive oil
6 bacon slices, cooked and chopped

Toss green beans with potatoes, salt, pepper, and oil in a bowl, then add to your air fryer and cook for 15 minutes at 400 degrees F on Air Fry mode. Serve with bacon sprinkled on top, divided among plates. Enjoy!
Per Serving: Calories 374; Fat 15g; Sodium 331mg; Carbs 28g; Fiber 12g; Sugar 7g; Protein 12g

Yummy Tomatoes and Green Beans

Prep time: 10 minutes| Cook time: 15 minutes| Serves: 4

1 pint cherry tomatoes
1 pound green beans
2 tablespoons olive oil

Salt and black pepper to the taste

Toss cherry tomatoes with green beans, olive oil, salt, and pepper in a bowl, then put to your air fryer and cook for 15 minutes at 400 degrees F on Air Fry mode. Serve immediately after dividing among plates. Enjoy!
Per Serving: Calories 162; Fat 6g; Sodium 224mg; Carbs 8g; Fiber 5g; Sugar 2g; Protein 9g

Tasty Asparagus

Prep time: 5 minutes| Cook time: 10 minutes| Serves: 2

Nutritional yeast
Olive oil non-stick spray

1 bunch of asparagus

After washing the asparagus, take off the bushy, woody ends. Drizzle olive oil spray over asparagus and top with yeast. Arrange asparagus in a single layer in your air fryer. Select Air Fry mode. Cook for 8 minutes at 400 degrees F.
Per Serving: Calories 17; Fat 4 g; Sodium 210mg; Carbs 32 g; Fiber 7g; Sugar 2g; Protein 24 g

Fries of Avocado

Prep time: 5 minutes| Cook time: 5 minutes| Serves: 6

1 avocado
½ teaspoon salt
½ cup panko breadcrumbs

Bean liquid (aquafaba) from a 15-ounce can of white or garbanzo beans

Avocado should be peeled, pitted, and sliced. In a mixing dish, combine the salt and breadcrumbs. Place the aquafaba in a separate basin. Dredge avocado slices in aquafaba first, then panko, ensuring sure they are evenly coated. In the air fryer, arrange the avocado slices in a single layer. Select Air Fry mode. Cook 5 minutes at 400 degrees F, shaking at 5 minutes. Serve with a keto dipping sauce of your choice!
Per Serving: Calories 102; Fat 22g; Sodium 229mg; Carbs 9g; Fiber 4g; Sugar: 1g; Protein 9g

Squash Spaghetti

Prep time: 5 minutes| Cook time: 15 minutes| Serves: 10

¼ teaspoon pepper
½ teaspoon salt

1 thinly sliced scallion
1 spaghetti squash

Wash the squash and chop it lengthwise. Remove the seeds using a scraper. Remove strands of spaghetti flesh with a fork and discard skins. Toss the squash in a clean towel and squeeze out as much liquid as possible. Place the meat in a bowl and chop it up with a knife a few times to make it smaller. Mix in the pepper, salt, and scallions with the squash. Toss "tot" shapes in the air fryer using your hands. Olive oil is sprayed over the surface. Select Air Fry mode. Cook for 15 minutes at 400 degrees F, or until golden and crispy!
Per Serving: Calories 231; Fat 18g; Sodium 210mg; Carbs 6g; Fiber 1g; Sugar: 0g; Protein 5g

Buttery Fries of Cinnamon

Prep time: 10 minutes| Cook time: 10 minutes| Serves: 2

1 pinch of salt
1 tablespoon powdered unprocessed; Sugar
2 tablespoons cinnamon

1 tablespoon coconut oil
10 ounces pre-cut butternut squash fries

Pour all items into a plastic bag. Coat the fries in the other ingredients until they are completely covered and the sugar has dissolved. In the air fryer, arrange the coated fries in a single layer. Select Air Fry mode. Cook it at 400 degrees for 10 minutes, or until crispy.
Per Serving: Calories 175; Fat 8g; Sodium 221mg; Carbs 5g; Fiber 0g; Sugar: 5g; Protein 1g

Garlic Potatoes

Prep time: 5 minutes| Cook time: 40 minutes| Serves: 2

2 russet potatoes, scrubbed
½ tablespoon butter, melted
½ teaspoon garlic & herb

blend seasoning
½ teaspoon garlic powder
Salt, as required

Combine all of the spices and salt in a mixing dish. Prick the potatoes with a fork. Butter the potatoes and then sprinkle with the spice mixture. Arrange the potatoes on the wire rack to boil. Select "Air Fry" and set the temperature to 400 degrees F. Press "Start" after setting the timer for 40 minutes. Place the frying rack in the

center position when the display says "Add Food". Do nothing when the display says "Turn Food." Remove the tray from the air fryer after the cooking is completed. Serve immediately.
Per Serving: Calories 176; Fat 2.1g; Sodium 331mg; Carbs 34.2g; Fiber 12g; Sugar 7g; Protein 3.8g

Salty and Spicy Zucchini

Prep time: 10 minutes| Cook time: 15 minutes| Serves: 4

1 pound zucchini, cut into ½-inch thick slices lengthwise	½ teaspoon cayenne pepper salt and ground black pepper, as required
1 tablespoon olive oil ½ teaspoon garlic powder	

Toss all of the ingredients in a bowl to evenly coat them. Place the zucchini slices on a baking sheet. Select "Air Fry" and set the temperature to 400 degrees F. Press "Start" after setting the timer for 12 minutes. Place the mixture in the cooking tray in the air fryer when the display says "Add Food". Do nothing when the display says "Turn Food." Remove the tray from the air fryer after the cooking is completed. Serve immediately.
Per Serving: Calories 67; Fat 5g; Sodium 331mg; Carbs 5.6g; Fiber 1g; Sugar 2g; Protein 2g

Spicy Yellow Squash

Prep time: 5 minutes| Cook time: 10 minutes| Serves: 4

4 large yellow squash, cut into slices	¾ tablespoon Italian seasoning ½ tablespoon garlic salt
¼ cup olive oil ½ onion, sliced	¼ tablespoon seasoned salt

Combine all of the ingredients in a mixing bowl. Fill the prepared baking tray halfway with the vegetable mixture. Select "Air Fry" and set the temperature to 400 degrees F. Press "Start" after setting the timer for 10 minutes. Place the mixture in the cooking tray, when the display says "Add Food". Turn the veggies when the display says "Turn Food". Remove the tray from the air fryer after the cooking is completed. Serve immediately.
Per Serving: Calories 113; Fat 9g; Sodium 221mg; Carbs 8.1g; Fiber 2g; Sugar 2g; Protein 4.2g

Asparagus with Butter

Prep time: 5 minutes| Cook time: 10 minutes| Serves: 4

1 pound fresh thick asparagus spears trimmed	Salt and ground black pepper, as required
1 pound butter melted	

Toss all of the ingredients in a bowl to evenly coat them. Place the asparagus on a baking sheet. Select "Air Fry" and set the temperature to 350 degrees F. Press "Start" after setting the timer for 10 minutes. Place the mixture in the cooking tray in the air fryer when the display says "Add Food". Turn the asparagus when the display says "Turn Food." Remove the tray from the air fryer after the cooking is completed. Serve immediately.
Per Serving: Calories 64; Fat 4g; Sodium 228mg; Carbs 5.9g; Fiber 2g; Sugar 2g; Protein 3.4g

Buttery Broccoli

Prep time: 5 minutes| Cook time: 15 minutes| Serves: 4

1 pound broccoli florets	1 tablespoon butter, melted

½ teaspoon red pepper flakes, crushed	salt and ground black pepper, as required

In a large mixing basin, combine all of the ingredients and toss thoroughly to coat. Attach the cover to the air fryer basket and add the broccoli florets. Select "Air Fry" and set the temperature to 400 degrees F. Set the timer for 15 minutes and hit the "Start" button. Arrange the air fryer basket in the air fryer when the display says "Add Food". When the cooking time is over, remove from the air fryer. Serve right away.
Per Serving: Calories 55; Fat 3g; Sodium 228mg; Carbs 6.1g; Fiber 1g; Sugar 1g; Protein 2.3g

Broccoli and Sweet Potatoes

Prep time: 5 minutes| Cook time: 20 minutes| Serves: 4

2 medium sweet potatoes, peeled and cut in 1-inch cubes	2 tablspoons vegetable oil salt and ground black pepper, as required
1 broccoli head, cut in 1-inch florets	

Prepare a baking dish that will fit in the Air Fryer by lightly greasing it. Toss all of the ingredients together in a bowl to evenly coat them. Place the vegetable mixture in a single layer in the prepared baking dish. Select "Roast" and set the temperature to 400 degrees F. Set the timer for 20 minutes in the centre and hit the "Start" button. Insert the baking dish in the centre position when the display says "Add Food". Turn the veggies when the display says "Turn Food." Remove the baking dish from the air fryer when the cooking time is finished. Serve immediately.
Per Serving: Calories 170; Fat 7.1g; Sodium 281mg; Carbs 25.2g; Fiber 2g; Sugar 2g; Protein 2.9g

Edamame with Garlic

Prep time: 5 minutes| Cook time: 10 minutes| Serves: 4

Olive oil	pepper
1 (16-ounce) bag frozen edamame in pods	½ teaspoon garlic salt ½ teaspoon red pepper flakes (optional)
salt and freshly ground black	

Using olive oil, gently coat the air fryer basket. Add the frozen edamame to a medium mixing bowl and gently spray with olive oil. Toss to evenly coat. Combine the garlic salt, salt, black pepper, and red pepper flakes in a mixing bowl (if using). Toss the edamame with the mixture until they are uniformly covered. Half of the edamame should be placed in the air fryer basket. Make sure the basket isn't overflowing. Select Air Fry mode. Set temp to 400 degrees F and timer to 10 minutes. Air fry it for 5 minutes. Shake the basket and heat for another 3 to 5 minutes, or until the edamame begins to brown and crisp. Repeat with the rest of the edamame and serve right away.
Per Serving: Calories 100; Fat 3g; Sodium 496mg; Carbs 9g; Fiber 4g; Sugar 2g; Protein 8g

Yummy Chickpeas

Prep time: 5 minutes| Cook time: 20 minutes| Serves: 4

Olive oil	¼ teaspoon salt
½ teaspoon ground cumin	1 (19-ounce) can chickpeas, drained and rinsed
½ teaspoon chili powder	
¼ teaspoon cayenne pepper	

Using olive oil, gently coat the air fryer basket. Combine the chili powder, cumin, cayenne pepper, and salt in a mixing bowl. Add the chickpeas to a medium mixing bowl and gently spray with olive oil. Toss in the spice mixture until it is uniformly covered. Select Air Fry mode. Set temp to 400 degrees F and timer to 20 minutes. Fill the air fryer basket halfway with chickpeas. Air fry for 15 to 20 minutes, shaking the basket every 5 minutes, until the chickpeas reach your preferred level of crunchiness.

Per Serving: Calories 122; Fat 1g; Sodium 152mg; Carbs 22g; Fiber 6g; Sugar 2g; Protein 6g

Yummy Broccoli and Cauliflower

Prep time: 15 minutes| Cook time: 20 minutes| Serves: 4

1½ cups broccoli, cut into 1-inch pieces	1-inch pieces
1½ cups cauliflower, cut into	1 tablespoon olive oil
	Salt, as required

Toss the veggies, oil, and salt in a mixing bowl to coat well. Select Air Fry mode. Set temp to 400 degrees F and time to 20 minutes. Place the veggie mixture in an air fryer basket that has been oiled and place it in the air fryer. Serve immediately.

Per Serving: Calories 51; Fat 3.7 g; Sodium 61 mg; Carbs 4.3 g; Fiber 1.8 g; Sugar 1.5 g; Protein 1.7 g

Buffalo Sauce and Cauliflower

Prep time: 13 minutes| Cook time: 12 minutes| Serves: 4

1 large head cauliflower, cut into bite-size florets	Salt and ground black pepper, as required
1 tablespoon olive oil	4 tablespoons butter, melted
2 teaspoons garlic powder	⅔ cup warm buffalo sauce

Toss cauliflower florets with olive oil, garlic powder, salt, and pepper in a large mixing basin to coat. Select Air Fry mode. Set temp to 400 degrees F and time to 12 minutes. Arrange the cauliflower florets in the air fryer basket and cook. Coat the cauliflower florets with buffalo sauce after 7 minutes of cooking and cook again. Serve immediately.

Per Serving: Calories 183; Fat 17.1 g; Sodium 826 mg; Carbs 5.9 g; Fiber 1.8 g; Sugar 1.9 g; Protein 1.6 g

Cauliflower Yummy Curry

Prep time: 15 minutes| Cook time: 10 minutes| Serves: 4

2 tablespoons golden raisins	½ tablespoon curry powder
½ head cauliflower, cored and cut into 1-inch pieces	Salt, to taste
½ cup olive oil, divided	2 tablespoons pine nuts, toasted

Set aside the raisins after soaking them in hot water. Combine the cauliflower, oil, curry powder, and salt in a mixing bowl. Select Air Fry mode. Set temp to 400 degrees F and time to 10 minutes. Arrange the cauliflower florets in the air fryer basket and cook. Using a sieve, drain the golden raisins. Toss the cauliflower, raisins, and pine nuts together in a bowl to coat. Serve right away.

Per Serving: Calories 269; Fat 28.3 g; Sodium 50mg; Carbs 6.4 g; Fiber 1.4 g; Sugar 3.7 g; Protein 1.5 g

Green Beans with Lime

Prep time: 15 minutes| Cook time: 12 minutes| Serves: 4

1 lb. green beans, trimmed	1 tablespoon fresh lemon juice
1 tablespoon butter, melted	¼ teaspoon garlic powder

Salt and ground black pepper, as required   ½ teaspoon lemon zest, grated

Toss all of the ingredients in a large mixing basin, except the lemon zest, to coat well. Select Air Fry mode. Set temp to 400 degrees F and time to 12 minutes. Arrange the green beans in the air fryer basket and cook. Serve hot with a sprinkling of lemon zest on top.

Per Serving: Calories 62; Fat 3.1 g; Sodium 67 mg; Carbs 8.4 g; Fiber 3.9 g; Sugar 1.7 g; Protein 2.2 g

Spicy Green Beans with Soy Sauce

Prep time: 10 minutes| Cook time: 10 minutes| Serves: 2

8 ounces fresh green beans, trimmed and cut in half	1 teaspoon sesame oil
1 tablespoon soy sauce	¼ teaspoon sesame seeds

Combine the green beans, soy sauce, and sesame oil in a mixing bowl. Select Air Fry mode. Set temp to 400 degrees F and time to 10 minutes. Arrange the green beans in the air fryer basket and cook. Serve immediately with sesame seeds as a garnish.

Per Serving: Calories 62; Fat 2.6 g; Sodium 458 mg; Carbs 8.8 g; Fiber 4 g; Sugar 1.7 g; Protein 2.6 g

Okra and Green Beans

Prep time: 15 minutes| Cook time: 20 minutes| Serves: 2

½ (10-oz.) bag frozen cut okra	3 tablespoons balsamic vinegar
½ (10-oz.) bag frozen cut green beans	Salt and ground black pepper, as required
¼ cup nutritional yeast	

Toss the okra, green beans, nutritional yeast, vinegar, salt, and black pepper in a mixing bowl to evenly coat. Select Air Fry mode. Set temp to 400 degrees F and time to 20 minutes. Place the okra mixture in an air fryer basket that has been oiled and place it in the air fryer then cook. Serve immediately.

Per Serving: Calories 126; Fat 1.3 g; Sodium 100 mg; Carbs 19.7 g; Fiber 9.7 g; Sugar 2.1 g; Protein 11.9 g

Casserole of Green Beans and Mushrooms

Prep time: 15 minutes| Cook time: 12 minutes| Serves: 6

24 oz. fresh green beans, trimmed	1 teaspoon ground sage
2 cups fresh button mushrooms, sliced	1 teaspoon garlic powder
3 tablespoons olive oil	1 teaspoon onion powder
2 tablespoons fresh lemon juice	Salt and ground black pepper, as required
	⅓ cup French fried onions

Toss the green beans, mushrooms, oil, lemon juice, sage, and spices together in a mixing bowl to coat well. Select Air Fry mode. Set temp to 400 degrees F and time to 12 minutes. Place the mushroom mixture in an air fryer basket that has been oiled and place it in the air fryer then cook. Shake the mushroom mixture while cooking. Fill a serving dish halfway with the mushroom mixture. Serve with fried onions on top.

Per Serving: Calories 125; Fat 8.6 g; Sodium 52 mg; Carbs 11 g; Fiber 4.2 g; Sugar 2.4 g; Protein 3 g

Mushrooms with Wine

Prep time: 15 minutes| Cook time: 32 minutes| Serves: 6

4 tablespoons butter	2 pounds fresh mushrooms,
2 teaspoons Herbs de Provence	quartered
½ teaspoon garlic powder	2 tablespoons white wine

Stir together the butter, Herbs de Provence, and garlic powder in a frying pan over medium-low heat for about 2 minutes. Remove the pan from the heat and stir in the mushrooms. Fill a baking pan halfway with the mushroom mixture. Select Air Fry mode. Set temp to 400 degrees F and time to 30 minutes. Place the pan in your air fryer. After 25 minutes of cooking, stir the wine into mushroom mixture. Serve hot.
Per Serving: Calories 54; Fat 2.4 g; Sodium 23 mg; Carbs 5.3 g; Fiber 1.5 g; Sugar 2.7 g; Protein 4.8 g

Mushrooms with Honey

Prep time: 10 minutes| Cook time: 15 minutes| Serves: 5

½ cup low-sodium soy sauce	2 teaspoons Chinese 5-spice
2 teaspoons honey	powder
4 tablespoons balsamic	½ teaspoon ground ginger
vinegar	20 oz. fresh cremini
4 garlic cloves, finely chopped	mushrooms, halved

Combine the soy sauce, honey, vinegar, garlic, 5-spice powder, and powdered ginger in a mixing bowl and combine well. Remove from the equation. Place the mushrooms in a single layer in a greased baking pan. Select Air Fry mode. Set temp to 400 degrees F and time to 15 minutes. Place pan in the air fryer and cook. Add the vinegar mixture to the pan after 10 minutes of cooking and swirl to incorporate.
Per Serving: Calories 54; Fat 0.1 g; Sodium 1400 mg; Carbs 9.6 g; Fiber 0.8 g; Sugar 5.9 g; Protein 4.6 g

Herby Peppers

Prep time: 10 minutes| Cook time: 8 minutes| Serves: 4

1½ lbs. bell peppers, seeded	crushed
and cubed	Salt and ground black pepper,
½ teaspoon dried thyme,	as required
crushed	2 teaspoons butter, melted
½ teaspoon dried savory,	

Toss the bell peppers, herbs, salt, and black pepper in a bowl to evenly coat. Select Air Fry mode. Set temp to 400 degrees F and time to 8 minutes. Place the bell peppers in the air fryer basket and cook them. Drizzle the bell peppers with butter in a mixing basin. Serve right away.
Per Serving: Calories 32; Fat 2 g; Sodium 54 mg; Carbs 3.6 g; Fiber 0.7 g; Sugar 2.3 g; Protein 0.5 g

Spinach with Feta

Prep time: 10 minutes| Cook time: 15 minutes| Serves: 6

2 pounds fresh spinach,	Salt and ground black pepper,
chopped	as required
3 garlic cloves, minced	1 cup feta cheese, crumbled
1 jalapeño pepper, minced	1 teaspoon fresh lemon zest,
4 tablespoons butter, melted	grated

In a mixing bowl, combine the spinach, garlic, jalapeno, butter,

salt, and black pepper. Select Air Fry mode. Set temp to 400 degrees F and time to 15 minutes. Place the spinach in the air fryer basket and cook it. Place the spinach in a mixing basin. Stir in the cheese and lemon zest right away, and serve immediately.
Per Serving: Calories 170; Fat 13.6 g; Sodium 480 mg; Carbs 6.9 g; Fiber 3.4g; Sugar 1.8 g; Protein 8 g

Delicious Yellow Squash with Tarragon

Prep time: 15 minutes| Cook time: 15 minutes| Serves: 6

4 teaspoons olive oil	½ teaspoon ground white pepper
2 lbs. yellow squash, sliced	1 tablespoon tarragon leaves,
1 teaspoon salt	chopped

Combine the oil, yellow squash, salt, and white pepper in a large mixing basin. Select Air Fry mode. Set temp to 400 degrees F and time to 15 minutes. Place the yellow squash slices in air fryer basket in the air fryer and cook. Toss the yellow squash slices twice or three times while cooking. Combine the yellow squash and tarragon leaves in a mixing dish and toss thoroughly. Serve right away.
Per Serving: Calories 53; Fat 3.4 g; Sodium 403 mg; Carbs 5.3 g; Fiber 1.7 g; Sugar 2.9 g; Protein 1.9 g

Spicy Zucchini and Squash

Prep time: 15 minutes| Cook time: 10 minutes| Serves: 6

2 large yellow squash, cut into	½ onion, sliced
slices	¾ teaspoon Italian seasoning
2 large zucchinis cut into slices	½ teaspoon garlic salt
¼ cup olive oil	¼ teaspoon seasoned salt

Combine all of the ingredients in a large mixing basin. Select Air Fry mode. Set temp to 400 degrees F and time to 10 minutes. Place the squash mixture in an air fryer basket and cook it. Serve immediately.
Per Serving: Calories 113; Fat 9 g; Sodium 85 mg; Carbs 8.3 g; Fiber 2.6 g; Sugar 0.9 g; Protein 4.2 g; Protein 2.8 g

Yummy Brussels Sprout

Prep time: 15 minutes| Cook time: 12 minutes| Serves: 4

1 lb. Brussels sprouts, cut in	¼ teaspoon red pepper flakes,
half	crushed
1 tablespoons oil	Salt and ground black pepper,
3 garlic cloves, minced	as required

Combine all of the ingredients in a mixing bowl and toss well to combine. Select Air Fry mode. Set temp to 400 degrees F and time to 12 minutes. Place the Brussels sprouts in the air fryer basket and cook them. Serve immediately.
Per Serving: Calories 113; Fat 9 g; Sodium 185 mg; Carbs 8.3 g; Fiber 2.6 g; Sugar 4.2 g; Protein 2.8 g

Spicy and Sweet Brussels Sprout

Prep time: 10 minutes| Cook time: 10 minutes| Serves: 2

2 cups Brussels sprouts,	1 tablespoon maple syrup
trimmed and halved	¼ teaspoon red pepper flakes,
lengthwise	crushed
1 tablespoon balsamic vinegar	Salt, as required

Combine all of the ingredients in a mixing bowl and toss well to combine. Select Air Fry mode. Set temp to 400 degrees F and time to 10 minutes. Place the Brussels sprouts in the air fryer basket and cook them. Serve immediately.
Per Serving: Calories 66; Fat 0.4 g; Sodium 101 mg; Carbs 14.9 g; Fiber 3.4 g; Sugar 7.9 g; Protein 3 g

Delicious Spicy Eggplant

Prep time: 15 minutes| Cook time: 25 minutes| Serves: 3

2 medium eggplants, cubed	1 teaspoon onion powder
2 tablespoons butter, melted	Salt and ground black pepper,
1 tablespoon Maggi seasoning	as required
sauce	1 tablespoon fresh lemon juice
1 teaspoon sumac	1 tablespoons Parmesan
1 teaspoon garlic powder	cheese, shredded

Combine the eggplant cubes, butter, seasoning sauce, and spices in a mixing dish. Select Air Fry mode. Set temp to 400 degrees F and time to 15 minutes. Place the eggplant cubes in the air fryer basket and cook them. Toss the eggplant cubes after 15 minutes of cooking. Set the air fryer again to 400 degrees F for 10 minutes and cook. Transfer the eggplant cubes into a bowl with the lemon juice, and Parmesan and toss to coat well. Serve immediately.
Per Serving: Calories 180; Fat 9.3 g; Sodium 304 mg; Carbs 23 g; Fiber 13.1 g; Sugar 11.6g; Protein 5.2 g

Curry with Eggplants

Prep time: 15 minutes| Cook time: 15 minutes| Serves: 2

1 large eggplant, cut into	1 tablespoon vegetable oil
½-inch thick slices	¼ teaspoon curry powder
1 garlic clove, minced	Salt, as required
½ fresh red chili, chopped	

Combine all of the ingredients in a mixing bowl and toss well to combine. Select Air Fry mode. Set temp to 400 degrees F and time to 15 minutes. Place the eggplant cubes in the air fryer basket and cook them. Serve immediately.
Per Serving: Calories 121; Fat 7.3 g; Sodium 83 mg; Carbs 14.2 g; Fiber 8.3 g; Sugar 7 g; Protein 2.4 g

Spicy Potatoes

Prep time: 10 minutes| Cook time: 16 minutes| Serves: 4

6 small potatoes, chopped	as required
3 tablespoons olive oil	2 tablespoons fresh parsley,
2 teaspoons mixed dried herbs	chopped
Salt and ground black pepper,	

Toss the potatoes, oil, herbs, salt, and black pepper in a large mixing basin to coat well. Select Air Fry mode. Set temp to 400 degrees F and time to 16 minutes. Arrange the potato pieces in the air fryer basket and cook. Serve garnished with parsley.
Per Serving: Calories 268; Fat 10.8 g; Sodium 55 mg; Carbs 40.4 g; Fiber 6.3 g; Sugar 3 g; Protein 4.4 g

Creamy Potatoes

Prep time: 15 minutes| Cook time: 15 minutes| Serves: 2

2 potatoes	2 tablespoons mozzarella
cheese, shredded	1 teaspoon chives, minced
1 tablespoon sour cream	Salt and ground black pepper,
1 tablespoon butter, softened	as required

Prick the potatoes with a fork. Select Air Fry mode. Set temp to 400 degrees F and time to 15 minutes. Place the potatoes in air fryer basket that has been oiled and placed in the air fryer. Meanwhile, place the other ingredients in a mixing dish and stir until thoroughly mixed. Place the potatoes on a serving dish. Make a hole in the center of the potatoes and fill them with the cheese mixture.
Per Serving: Calories 277; Fat 12.2 g; Sodium 225 mg; Carbs 34.8 g; Fiber 25.1 g; Sugar 2.6 g; Protein 8.2 g

Yummy Stuffed Potatoes

Prep time: 15 minutes| Cook time: 31 minutes| Serves: 4

4 potatoes, peeled	2 tablespoons chives, chopped
2-3 tablespoons canola oil	½ cup Parmesan cheese,
2 tablespoons butter	grated
½ of brown onion, chopped	

Brush some oil on the potatoes. Select Air Fry mode. Set temp to 400 degrees F and time to 26 minutes. Place the potatoes in air fryer basket that has been oiled and place it in the air fryer then cook. By using the remaining oil, coat the potatoes twice. Meanwhile, melt the butter in a frying pan over medium heat and cook the onion for 4-5 minutes. Remove the onion from the flame and place it in a basin. Stir together the potato flesh, chives, and half of the cheese in the onion dish. After 20 minutes of cooking, pause the device and move the potatoes to a dish. Cut each potato in half with care. Scoop out the meat from each side using a tiny scooper. Fill the potato halves halfway with the potato mixture and the remaining cheese. Place the potato halves in a air fryer basket that has been oiled and placed in the air fryer. Serve right away.
Per Serving: Calories 276; Fat 12.5 g; Sodium 120 mg; Carbs 34.8 g; Fiber 5.4 g; Sugar 3.1 g; Protein 7.8 g

Parmesan Potatoes

Prep time: 20 minutes| Cook time: 30 minutes| Serves: 4

4 potatoes	cheese, shredded
2 tablespoons olive oil	1 tablespoon fresh chives,
2 tablespoons Parmesan	chopped

Cut slits down the short side of each potato, approximately 14 inches apart, with a sharp knife, making sure the slices stay together at the bottom. Using a gentle brush, evenly coat each potato in oil. Select Air Fry mode. Set temp to 400 degrees F and time to 30 minutes. Place the potatoes in air fryer basket that has been oiled and place it in the Air Fryer then cook. While cooking brush the potatoes with the oil.
Per Serving: Calories 218; Fat 7.9 g; Sodium 55 mg; Carbs 33.6 g; Fiber 5.1 g; Sugar 2.5 g; Protein 4.6 g

Gratin of Potatoes

Prep time: 15 minutes| Cook time: 20 minutes| Serves: 4

2 large potatoes, sliced thinly	2 tablespoons plain flour
5 ½ tablespoons cream	½ cup cheddar cheese, grated
2 eggs	

Arrange the potato slices in the air fryer basket. Select Air Fry mode. Set temp to 400 degrees F and time to 10 minutes. Meanwhile, combine cream, eggs, and flour in a mixing dish

and whisk until a thick sauce develops. Take the potato slices out of the basket and set them aside. In 4 ramekins, equally distribute the potato pieces, and then evenly distribute the egg mixture, followed by the cheese. Place the ramekins in the air fryer basket and cook them. Set the air fryer on "Air Fry" mode and adjust cooking temperature to 400 degrees F and time to 10 minutes. Warm the dish before serving.
Per Serving: Calories 233; Fat 8 g; Sodium 135 mg; Carbs 31.3 g; Fiber 4.5 g; Sugar 2.7 g; Protein 9.7 g

Yummy Okra

Prep time: 15 minutes| Cook time: 12 minutes| Serves: 2

8 oz. large okra	powder
¼ cup chickpea flour	½ teaspoon ground turmeric
¼ of onion, chopped	½ teaspoon red chili powder
2 tablespoons coconut, grated freshly	½ teaspoon ground cumin
1 teaspoon garam masala	Salt, to taste

Make a vertical incision in each okra with a knife without splitting it in half. Combine the flour, onion, shredded coconut, and spices in a mixing bowl. Stuff the mixture inside each okra. Place the filled okra in an air fryer basket and cook it. Select Air Fry mode. Set temp to 400 degrees F and time to 12 minutes. Serve immediately.
Per Serving: Calories 166; Fat 3.7 g; Sodium 103 mg; Carbs 26.6 g; Fiber 9.1 g; Sugar 5.3 g; Protein 7.6 g

Stuffed Bells

Prep time: 15 minutes| Cook time: 15 minutes| Serves: 5

½ small bell pepper, seeded and chopped	1½ teaspoons Italian seasoning
1 (15-oz.) can diced tomatoes with juice	5 large bell peppers, tops removed and seeded
1 (15-oz.) can red kidney beans, rinsed and drained	½ cup mozzarella cheese, shredded
1 cup cooked rice	1 tablespoon Parmesan cheese, grated

Combine the diced bell pepper, tomatoes with juice, beans, rice, and Italian spice in a mixing dish. Stuff the rice mixture inside each bell pepper. Place the bell peppers in the air fryer basket and cook them. Select Air Fry mode. Set temp to 400 degrees F and time to 15 minutes. Meanwhile, combine the mozzarella and Parmesan cheese in a mixing dish. After 12 minutes of cooking, top each bell pepper with cheese mixture. Serve warm.
Per Serving: Calories 287; Fat 2.5 g; Sodium 113 mg; Carbs 55.8 g; Fiber 10.2 g; Sugar 9 g; Protein 12.3 g

Yummy Pumpkin

Prep time: 20 minutes| Cook time: 30 minutes| Serves: 5

1 sweet potato, peeled and chopped	1 egg, beaten
1 parsnip, peeled and chopped	2 teaspoons mixed dried herbs
1 carrot, peeled and chopped	Salt and ground black pepper, as required
½ cup fresh peas, shelled	½ of butternut pumpkin, seeded
1 onion, chopped	
1 garlic cloves, minced	

Combine the veggies, garlic, egg, herbs, salt, and black pepper in a large mixing basin. Fill half of the pumpkin with the veggie mixture. Select Air Fry mode. Set temp to 400 degrees F and time to 30 minutes. Place the pumpkin half in the air fryer basket and cook it. Before serving, place the pumpkin on a serving dish

and let aside to cool somewhat.
Per Serving: Calories 223; Fat 1.3 g; Sodium 70 mg; Carbs 53 g; Fiber 9.9 g; Sugar 12 g; Protein 6 g

Ratatouille of Vegetables

Prep time: 15 minutes| Cook time: 15 minutes| Serves: 4

1 green bell pepper, seeded and chopped	2 garlic cloves, minced
1 yellow bell pepper, seeded and chopped	2 tablespoons Herbs de Provence
1 eggplant, chopped	1 tablespoon olive oil
1 zucchini, chopped	1 tablespoon balsamic vinegar
3 tomatoes, chopped	Salt and ground black pepper, as required
2 small onions, chopped	

Toss the veggies, garlic, Herbs de Provence, oil, vinegar, salt, and black pepper in a large mixing basin to coat well. Fill a greased baking pan halfway with the vegetable mixture. Select Air Fry mode. Set temp to 400 degrees F and time to 15 minutes. Place the pan in the air fryer and cook. Serve immediately.
Per Serving: Calories 119; Fat 4.2 g; Sodium 54 mg; Carbs 20.3 g; Fiber 7.3 g; Sugar 11.2 g; Protein 3.6 g

Veggies with Mustard

Prep time: 15 minutes| Cook time: 20 minutes| Serves: 4

2 ounces cherry tomatoes	2 tablespoons honey
2 large zucchinis, chopped	2 teaspoons Dijon mustard
2 green bell peppers, seeded and chopped	1 teaspoon dried herbs
6 tablespoons olive oil, divided	1 teaspoon garlic paste
	Salt, as required

Place the veggies in a baking sheet lined with parchment paper and sprinkle with 3 tablespoons of oil. Select Air Fry mode. Set temp to 400 degrees F and time to 15 minutes. Place the pan in the air fryer and cook. Meanwhile, combine the remaining oil, honey, mustard, herbs, garlic, salt, and black pepper in a mixing bowl and well combine. Add the honey mixture to the vegetable mixture after 15 minutes of simmering and stir thoroughly. Now, set the temperature to 400 degrees F for 5 minutes. Serve immediately.
Per Serving: Calories 262; Fat 21.5 g; Sodium 72 mg; Carbs 19.5 g; Fiber 2.9 g; Sugar 14.8 g; Protein 2.8 g

Cheesy Veggies

Prep time: 15 minutes| Cook time: 18 minutes| Serves: 5

1 tablespoon olive oil	1 small onion, sliced
1 tablespoon garlic, minced	¼ cup balsamic vinegar
1 cup cauliflower florets	1 teaspoon red pepper flakes
1 cup broccoli florets	Salt and ground black pepper, as required
1 cup zucchini, sliced	
½ cup yellow squash, sliced	¼ cup Parmesan cheese, grated
½ cup fresh mushrooms, sliced	

Toss all of the ingredients, except the cheese, in a large mixing bowl to coat well. Select Air Fry mode. Set temp to 400 degrees F and time to 18 minutes. Place the veggies in an air fryer basket that has been oiled and placed in the air fryer. Flip the veggies after 8 minutes of cooking. After 16 minutes of cooking, evenly sprinkle the cheese over the veggies. Serve hot.
Per Serving: Calories 102; Fat 6.2 g; Sodium 352 mg; Carbs 6.6 g; Fiber 1.9 g; Sugar 2.2 g; Protein 6.6 g

Kabobs of Vegetables

¼ cup carrots, peeled and chopped	½ cup cottage cheese
¼ cup French beans	2 medium boiled potatoes, mashed
½ cup green peas	
1 teaspoon ginger	½ teaspoon 5 spice powder
1 garlic cloves, peeled	Salt, to taste
1 green chilies	2 tablespoons corn flour
¼ cup fresh mint leaves	Olive oil cooking spray

Pulse the carrot, beans, peas, ginger, garlic, mint, and cheese in a food processor until smooth. Place the ingredients in a mixing basin. Mix in the potato, 5 spice powder, salt, and corn flour until smooth. Make equal-sized tiny balls out of the mixture. In a sausage form, wrap each ball around a skewer. Using frying spray, coat the skewers. Select "Air Fry" as the cooking mode. Set the timer for 10 minutes of cooking. Adjust the temperature to 400 degrees F. To begin, press the "Start" button. When the device shows "Add Food", place the skewers in an air fryer basket that has been oiled and placed in the air fryer. Serve warm.

Per Serving: Calories 120; Fat 0.8 g; Sodium 115 mg; Carbs 21.9 g; Fiber 4.9 g; Sugar 1.8 g; Protein 6.3 g

Burgers with Vegetables and Beans

1 cup cooked black beans	1 cup fresh mushrooms, chopped
1 cup boiled potatoes, peeled and mashed	
1 cup fresh spinach, chopped	1 teaspoon Chile lime seasoning
	Olive oil cooking spray

Mix the beans, potatoes, spinach, mushrooms, and spice in a large mixing basin with your hands until thoroughly mixed. Form the ingredients into 4 equal-sized patties. Evenly coat the patties with cooking spray. Select Air Fry mode. Set temp to 400 degrees F and time to 22 minutes. Place the skewers in air fryer basket that has been oiled and placate in the air fryer then cook.

Per Serving: Calories 113; Fat 0.4 g; Sodium 166 mg; Carbs 23.1 g; Fiber 6.2 g; Sugar 1.7 g; Protein 6 g

Spicy Tofu

2 tablespoons low-sodium soy sauce	12 oz. extra-firm tofu, drained and cubed into 1-inch size
2 tablespoons fish sauce	1 teaspoon butter, melted
1 teaspoon olive oil	

Incorporate the soy sauce, fish sauce, and oil in a large mixing basin and stir to combine. Toss in the tofu cubes to evenly cover them. Set aside for 30 minutes to marinate, stirring occasionally. Select Air Fry mode. Set temp to 400 degrees F and time to 25 minutes. Place the tofu cubes in an air fryer basket that has been oiled and place it in the air fryer then cook. Serve hot.

Per Serving: Calories 102; Fat 7.1 g; Sodium 1100 mg; Carbs 2.5 g; Fiber 0.3 g; Sugar 1.3 g; Protein 9.4 g

Crispy Tofu

1 (14-oz.) block firm tofu,	pressed and cubed into ½-inch

size

1 tablespoons cornstarch	Salt and ground black pepper, as required
¼ cup rice flour	2 tablespoons olive oil

Combine the cornstarch, rice flour, salt, and black pepper in a mixing bowl. Evenly coat the tofu in the flour mixture. Then pour some oil over the tofu. Select Air Fry mode. Set temp to 400 degrees F and time to 28 minutes. Place the tofu cubes in an air fryer basket that has been oiled and place it in the air fryer then cook. While cooking flip the tofu chunks. Serve hot.

Per Serving: Calories 241; Fat 15 g; Sodium 67 mg; Carbs 17.7 g; Fiber 1.6 g; Sugar 0.8 g; Protein 11.6 g

Orange Sauce and Tofu

For Tofu	1 tablespoon honey
2 lb. extra-firm tofu, pressed and cubed	1 teaspoon orange zest, grated
1 tablespoon cornstarch	1 teaspoon garlic, minced
1 tablespoon tamari	1 teaspoon fresh ginger, minced
For Sauce	2 teaspoons cornstarch
½ cup water	¼ teaspoon red pepper flakes, crushed
⅓ cup fresh orange juice	

Toss the tofu, cornstarch, and tamari together in a bowl to coat thoroughly. Allow at least 15 minutes for the tofu to marinade. Select Air Fry mode. Set temp to 400 degrees F and time to 10 minutes. Place the tofu cubes in an air fryer basket that has been oiled and place it in the air fryer then cook. While cooking flip the tofu chunks. Meanwhile, for the sauce, combine all of the ingredients in a small saucepan over medium-high heat and bring to a boil, stirring constantly. Toss the tofu with the sauce in a serving dish and gently toss to incorporate. Serve immediately.

Per Serving: Calories 147; Fat 6.7 g; Sodium 262 mg; Carbs 12.7 g; Fiber 0.7 g; Sugar 6.7 g; Protein 12.1 g

Capers and Tofu

For Marinade	1 cup panko breadcrumbs
¼ cup fresh lemon juice	For Sauce
2 tablespoons fresh parsley	1 cup vegetable broth
2 garlic cloves, peeled	¼ cup lemon juice
Salt and ground black pepper, as required	3 garlic cloves, peeled
For Tofu	1 tablespoon fresh parsley
1 (14-oz.) block extra-firm tofu, pressed and cut into 8 rectangular cutlets	1 teaspoon cornstarch
	Salt and ground black pepper, as required
½ cup mayonnaise	2 tablespoons capers

To make the marinade, combine all of the ingredients in a food processor and pulse until smooth. Combine the marinade and tofu in a mixing basin. Allow for 15-30 minutes of rest time. Place the mayonnaise and panko breadcrumbs in separate shallow basins. Coat the tofu slices with mayonnaise before rolling them in panko. Select Air Fry mode. Set temp to 400 degrees F and time to 20 minutes. Place the tofu cubes in an air fryer basket that has been oiled and place it in the air fryer then cook. While cooking flip the tofu chunks. Meanwhile, make the sauce by pulsing broth, lemon juice, garlic, parsley, cornstarch, salt, and black pepper until smooth in a food processor. Place the sauce in a small saucepan and add the capers. Bring the water to a boil in the pan over medium heat. Reduce the heat to low and cook, stirring constantly, for about 5-7 minutes. Place the cubes of tofu on serving plates. Serve with the sauce on top.

Per Serving: Calories 327; Fat 18 g; Sodium 540 mg; Carbs 15.7 g; Fiber 0.8 g; Sugar 3 g; Protein 12.4 g

Tofu with Spicy Sauce

Prep time: 20 minutes| Cook time: 20 minutes| Serves: 4

For Tofu
1 (14-oz.) block firm tofu, pressed and cubed
½ cup arrowroot flour
½ teaspoon sesame oil
For Sauce
4 tablespoons low-sodium soy sauce

1½ tablespoons rice vinegar
1½ tablespoons chili sauce
1 tablespoon agave nectar
1 large garlic cloves, minced
1 teaspoon fresh ginger, peeled and grated
2 scallions (green part), chopped

Combine the tofu, arrowroot flour, and sesame oil in a mixing bowl. Select Air Fry mode. Set temp to 400 degrees F and time to 20 minutes. Place the tofu cubes in an air fryer basket that has been oiled and place it in the air fryer then cook. Halfway through, flip the tofu chunks. Meanwhile, make the sauce by combining all of the ingredients (excluding the scallions) in a mixing bowl and mixing thoroughly. Transfer the tofu into a skillet with sauce over medium heat and cook for about 3 minutes, stirring occasionally. Garnish with scallions and serve hot.
Per Serving: Calories 115; Fat4.8 g; Sodium 1000 mg; Carbs 10.2 g; Fiber 1.7 g; Sugar 5.6 g; Protein 10.1 g

Cauliflower with Tofu

Prep time: 15 minutes| Cook time: 15 minutes| Serves: 2

½ (14-oz.) block firm tofu, pressed and cubed
½ small head cauliflower, cut into florets
1 tablespoon canola oil
1 tablespoon nutritional yeast

¼ teaspoon dried parsley
1 teaspoon ground turmeric
¼ teaspoon paprika
Salt and ground black pepper, as required

Combine the tofu, cauliflower, and the remaining ingredients in a mixing bowl. Select Air Fry mode. Set temp to 400 degrees F and time to 15 minutes. Place the tofu mixture in an air fryer basket that has been oiled and place it in the air fryer then cook. While cooking, flip the tofu mixture. Serve immediately.
Per Serving: Calories 170; Fat 11.6 g; Sodium 113 mg; Carbs 8.3 g; Fiber 4.2 g; Sugar 2.3 g; Protein 11.9 g

Cauliflower with Blue Cheese

Prep time: 5 minutes| Cook time: 10 minutes| Serves: 4

1 pound cauliflower florets
1 tablespoon olive oil
½ teaspoon ground turmeric
½ teaspoon smoked paprika
1 teaspoon fennel seeds

Sea salt and ground black pepper, to taste
4 tablespoons blue cheese, crumbled

In a mixing dish, combine all of the ingredients. Set the air fryer on "Air Fry" mode and adjust temperature to 400 degrees F. Adjust time to 9 minutes. To begin, press the "Start" key. Arrange the cauliflower florets on the cooking tray, being careful not to crowd them. Air fry the cauliflower florets for 9 minutes, or until golden brown, shaking the tray once or twice throughout the frying process. Bon appétit!
Per Serving: Calories105; Fat 5.2g; Sodium 221mg; Carbs 8g; Fiber 2.9g; Sugars 2.7g; Protein 3.9g

Peppers in Air Fryer

Prep time: 5 minutes| Cook time: 20 minutes| Serves: 4

4 bell peppers, seeded and   sliced

1 onion, sliced
1 tablespoon olive oil
Kosher salt and ground black pepper, to taste

1 teaspoon cayenne pepper
1 teaspoon dried oregano
1 teaspoon dried basil

In a mixing dish, combine all of the ingredients. Set the air fryer on Air Fry mode and adjust temperature to 400 degrees F and time to 15 minutes. To begin, press the "Start" key. Arrange the peppers and onions on the cooking tray, being careful not to crowd them. Cook for 15 minutes or until the peppers and onions are caramelized, shaking the pan once or twice throughout cooking. Bon appétit!
Per Serving: Calories 119; Fat 7.2g; Sodium 443mg; Carbs 13.5g; Fiber 2.2g; Sugars 0.7g; Protein 2.3g

Asparagus in Air Fryer

Prep time: 5 minutes| Cook time: 10 minutes| Serves: 4

½ pounds asparagus, trimmed
1 tablespoon olive oil
1 teaspoon cayenne pepper
1 teaspoon granulated garlic

(or garlic powder)
1 teaspoon grated lemon zest
Kosher salt and freshly cracked black pepper, to taste

In a mixing dish, combine all of the ingredients. Set the air fryer on Air Fry mode and adjust temperature to 400 degrees F and time to 8 minutes To begin, press the "Start" key. Arrange the asparagus stalks on the perforated pan in the air fryer, being careful not to crowd them. Air fried the asparagus for 8 minutes, turning midway during the cooking time, or until tender and bright green. Bon appétit!
Per Serving: Calories 96; Fat 7g; Sodium 442mg; Carbs 7.2g; Fiber 3.7g; Sugars 3.2g; Protein 3.8g

Salad of Green Beans

Prep time: 5 minutes| Cook time: 15 minutes| Serves: 4

1 pound fresh green beans, trimmed
1 tablespoon sesame oil
Kosher salt and ground black pepper, to taste
2 garlic cloves, minced
1 teaspoon cayenne pepper

1 cup grape tomatoes, halved
1 bell pepper, sliced
1 jalapeno pepper, sliced
2 tablespoons apple cider vinegar
1 tablespoon Dijon mustard
4 tablespoons olive oil

In a mixing dish, toss green beans with sesame oil, salt, and black pepper. Set the air fryer on Air Fry mode and adjust temperature to 400 degrees F and time to 10 minutes. To begin, press the "Start" key. Arrange green beans on the air fryer basket that has been coated with parchment paper. Green beans should be air fried for 10 minutes or until they get a light brown hue. Toss green beans with the other ingredients in a large mixing bowl. Bon appétit!
Per Serving: Calories 211; Fat 17g; Sodium 441mg; Carbs 12.7g; Fiber 4.3g; Sugars 6.1g; Protein 3.2g

Breaded Portobellas in Air Fryer

Prep time: 5 minutes| Cook time: 15 minutes| Serves: 4

3 medium eggs
1 teaspoon stone-ground mustard
1 tablespoon soy sauce
½ cup all-purpose flour
1 cup seasoned breadcrumbs

1 teaspoon smoked paprika
Sea salt and ground black pepper, to taste
1 tablespoon olive oil
1 pound Portobello mushrooms

Combine the egg, mustard, soy sauce, and flour in a small basin.

Place the breadcrumbs, spices, and olive oil in a small basin. In a separate bowl, dredge the mushrooms in the egg mixture. After that, thoroughly cover the mushrooms in the breadcrumb mixture. Set the air fryer on Air Fry mode and adjust temperature to 400 degrees F and time to 10 minutes. To begin, press the "Start" key. Arrange the mushrooms on the air fryer basket of the air fryer, being careful not to crowd them. Cook the mushrooms in an air fryer for 10 minutes, or until golden brown. Bon appétit!
Per Serving: Calories 289; Fat 8g; Sodium 441mg; Carbs 38.7g; Fiber 7g; Sugars 8.1g; Protein 10.4g

Garlic and Fennel

Prep time: 5 minutes| Cook time: 20 minutes| Serves: 4

1 pound fennel, cut into wedges
1 tablespoon olive oil
1 teaspoon garlic, minced
1 teaspoon lemon zest, grated

1 teaspoon dried basil
1 teaspoon dried oregano
½ teaspoon dried dill weed
Kosher salt and ground black pepper, to taste

In a mixing dish, combine all of the ingredients. Set the air fryer on Air Fry mode and adjust temperature to 400 degrees F and time to 15 minutes. To begin, press the "Start" key. Arrange the fennel wedges on the air fryer basket coated with parchment paper. Fennel wedges should be air fried for 15 minutes or until tender and cooked through. Bon appétit!
Per Serving: Calories 99; Fat 7.1g; Sodium 321mg; Carbs 8.9g; Fiber 3.7g; Sugars 4.5g; Protein 1.5g

Eggplant with Butter

Prep time: 5 minutes| Cook time: 20 minutes| Serves: 4

1 pound eggplant, cut into 1 ½ -inch pieces
1 tablespoon butter, melted
1 tablespoon olive oil

½ teaspoon onion powder
¼ teaspoon cumin, ground
1 teaspoon garlic powder
½ teaspoon ancho chile powder

In a mixing dish, combine all of the ingredients. Set the air fryer on Air Fry mode and adjust temperature to 400 degrees F and time to 20 minutes. To begin, press the "Start" key. Arrange the eggplant slices on the air fryer basket that has been coated with parchment paper. Cook the eggplant slices in the air fryer for 20 minutes, or until they are soft and cooked through. Bon appétit!
Per Serving: Calories 115; Fat 9.3g; Sodium 331mg; Carbs 7.6g; Fiber 3.7g; Sugars 4g; Protein 1.4g

Cheesy Beet Salad

Prep time: 5 minutes| Cook time: 20 minutes| Serves: 4

1 pound fresh beets, peeled and cut into 1-inch pieces cubes
1 tablespoon extra-virgin olive oil
1 tablespoon red wine vinegar

½ teaspoon cumin
½ teaspoon mustard seeds
Kosher salt and ground black pepper, to taste
4 ounces Gruyere cheese, crumbled

Except for the cheese, combine all of the ingredients in a mixing dish. Set the air fryer on Air Fry mode and adjust temperature to 400 degrees F and time to 20 minutes. To begin, press the "Start" key. Arrange the beets on the air fryer basket of the air fryer, being careful not to crowd them. Cook the beets in the air fryer for 20 minutes or until browned, shaking the pan once or twice throughout cooking. Enjoy the cheese-topped roasted beets!
Per Serving: Calories 235; Fat 16.4g; Sodium 341mg; Carbs 12.2g; Fiber 3.4g; Sugars 8.3g; Protein 10.6g

Carrots with Butter

Prep time: 5 minutes| Cook time: 20 minutes| Serves: 4

1 pound carrots, sliced lengthwise
1 teaspoon butter, melted
1 teaspoon cayenne pepper

1 teaspoon dried oregano
Kosher salt and ground black pepper, to taste

In a mixing dish, combine all of the ingredients. Set the air fryer on Roast mode and adjust temperature to 380 degrees F and time to 20 minutes. To begin, press the "Start" key. Arrange the carrots on the air fryer basket that has been coated with parchment paper. Cook your carrots in the air for 20 minutes, or until they are soft and cooked through. Bon appétit!
Per Serving: Calories 66; Fat 2.4g; Sodium 444mg; Carbs 11.2g; Fiber 3.4g; Sugars 5.4g; Protein 1.6g

Cheesy Bites of Broccoli

Prep time: 5 minutes| Cook time: 10 minutes| Serves: 4

1 pound broccoli florets
1 tablespoon olive oil
1 teaspoon fresh garlic, minced
½ teaspoon onion powder

Kosher salt and freshly ground black pepper, to taste
2 ounces parmesan cheese, grated

In a mixing dish, combine all of the ingredients. Set the air fryer on Air Fry mode and adjust temperature to 400 degrees F and time to 6 minutes. To begin, press the "Start" key. Arrange the broccoli florets on the air fryer basket in the air fryer, being careful not to crowd them. Broccoli florets should be air fried for 6 minutes or until cooked through, turning once or twice during that period. Bon appétit!
Per Serving: Calories 165; Fat 11.2g; Sodium 443mg; Carbs 9.8g; Fiber 3g; Sugars 1.9g; Protein 7.3g

Cauliflower in Air Fryer

Prep time: 5 minutes| Cook time: 10 minutes| Serves: 4

1 pound cauliflower florets
1 large egg
1 cup seasoned breadcrumbs
1 teaspoon hot paprika
½ teaspoon garlic powder

1 teaspoon onion powder
1 teaspoon dried dill weed
Sea salt and ground black pepper, to taste
2 teaspoons olive oil

Dry the cauliflower florets with a paper towel. In a small dish, whisk the egg. Combine the remaining ingredients in a separate bowl. The cauliflower florets should be dipped in the whisked egg. The cauliflower florets should then be rolled in the breadcrumb mixture. Set the air fryer on Air Fry mode and adjust temperature to 400 degrees F and time to 9 minutes. To begin, press the "Start" key. Arrange the cauliflower florets on the air fryer basket of the air fryer, being careful not to crowd them. Air fried the cauliflower florets for 9 minutes, or until golden brown, shaking the pan once or twice throughout the frying process. Bon appétit!
Per Serving: Calories 188; Fat 3.8g; Sodium 431mg; Carbs 27.8g; Fiber 7g; Sugars 6.6g; Protein 5.7g

Parsnip in French Style

Prep time: 5 minutes| Cook time: 20 minutes| Serves: 4

½ pounds parsnip, cut into

½-inch chunks

1 tablespoon extra-virgin olive oil
1 tablespoon Herbs de Province

Kosher salt and cayenne pepper, to taste
2 tablespoons fresh parsley, chopped

In a mixing dish, combine all of the ingredients. Set the air fryer on Air Fry mode and adjust temperature to 400 degrees F and time to 20 minutes. To begin, press the "Start" key. Arrange the parsnips on the parchment-lined air fryer basket. Cook your parsnips in the air fryer for 20 minutes, or until they are soft and cooked through. Bon appétit!
Per Serving: Calories 186; Fat 7.3g; Sodium 541mg; Carbs 30.1g; Fiber 7g; Sugars 6.7g; Protein 2.5g

Squash in Grand Maa Style

Prep time: 5 minutes| Cook time: 15 minutes| Serves: 4

1 pound butternut squash, cut into ½-inch chunks
1 tablespoon coconut oil
1 tablespoon pure maple syrup

A pinch of kosher salt
A pinch of grated nutmeg
½ teaspoon ground cinnamon
½ teaspoon ground cloves

In a mixing dish, combine all of the ingredients. Set the air fryer on Roast mode and adjust temperature to 380 degrees F and time to 12 minutes. To begin, press the "Start" key. Arrange the squash on the air fryer basket that has been lined with parchment paper. Cook the squash in the air fryer for 12 minutes, or until it is soft and cooked through. Bon appétit!
Per Serving: Calories 133; Fat 6.9g; Sodium 483mg; Carbs 18.7g; Fiber 1.7g; Sugars 6g; Protein 0.9g

Delicious Sweet Potatoes

Prep time: 5 minutes| Cook time: 40 minutes| Serves: 4

1 pound sweet potatoes, peeled and diced
1 teaspoon olive oil
1 teaspoon cayenne pepper

½ teaspoon dried dill weed
Sea salt and freshly ground black pepper, to taste

In a mixing dish, combine all of the ingredients. Set the air fryer on Roast mode and adjust temperature to 380 degrees F and time to 35 minutes. To begin, press the "Start" key. Arrange the sweet potatoes on the air fryer basket that has been coated with parchment paper. Roast it for 35 minutes, or until sweet potatoes are soft and cooked through. Bon appétit!
Per Serving: Calories 119; Fat 2.3g; Sodium 441mg; Carbs 23.1g; Fiber 3.5g; Sugars 4.6g; Protein 1.9g

Eggplants in Greek Style

Prep time: 5 minutes| Cook time: 20 minutes| Serves: 4

½ pounds eggplants, diced
1 teaspoon garlic, minced
1 teaspoon dried oregano
1 teaspoon dried basil
2 tablespoons extra-virgin

olive oil
1 teaspoon paprika
Coarse sea salt and ground black pepper, to taste

In a mixing dish, combine all of the ingredients. Set the air fryer on Air Fry mode and adjust temperature to 380 degrees F and time to 15 minutes. To begin, press the "Start" key. Arrange the eggplant on the air fryer basket that has been coated with parchment paper. Roast it for 15 minutes, or until the eggplant is soft and cooked through. Bon appétit!
Per Serving: Calories 111; Fat 7.2g; Sodium 421mg; Carbs 11.8g; Fiber 5.7g; Sugars 6.6g; Protein 2.1g

Herby Zucchini

Prep time: 5 minutes| Cook time: 20 minutes| Serves: 4

1 pound zucchini, quartered lengthwise
1 tablespoon Italian seasoning
Coarse sea salt and ground black pepper, to taste
4 tablespoons extra-virgin olive oil

2 tablespoons freshly squeezed lemon juice
1 teaspoon Dijon mustard
1 tablespoon fresh parsley, chopped
1 tablespoon fresh basil, chopped
1 tablespoon fresh mint, chopped

In a mixing dish, combine all of the ingredients. Set the air fryer on Air Fry mode and adjust temperature to 400 degrees F and time to 15 minutes. To begin, press the "Start" key. Arrange the zucchini on the air fryer basket that has been coated with parchment paper. Cook for 15 minutes, or until zucchini is soft and cooked through. Bon appétit!
Per Serving: Calories 158; Fat 14.6g; Sodium 332mg; Carbs 6.6g; Fiber 1.9g; Sugars 1g; Protein 2.1g

Mushrooms with Ritzy

Prep time: 5 minutes| Cook time: 20 minutes| Serves: 4

1 pound button mushrooms, stalks removed
½ cup crackers, crushed
2 cloves garlic, minced
2 tablespoons butter, softened
Kosher salt and freshly ground

black pepper, to taste
¼ cup Pecorino cheese, grated
2 tablespoons fresh parsley, chopped
2 tablespoons fresh cilantro, chopped

Dry the mushrooms with a paper towel. In a mixing basin, combine the remaining ingredients. Fill the mushrooms halfway with the filling. Set the air fryer on Air Fry mode and adjust temperature to 400 degrees F and time to 12 minutes. To begin, press the "Start" key. Arrange the mushrooms on the air fryer basket that has been coated with parchment paper. Bake it for 12 minutes, or until the mushrooms are soft and cooked through. Bon appétit!
Per Serving: Calories 148; Fat 10.6g; Sodium 321mg; Carbs 8.3g; Fiber 1.4g; Sugars 2.8g; Protein 6.1g

Air Fryer Brussels Sprout

Prep time: 5 minutes| Cook time: 15 minutes| Serves: 4

½ pounds Brussels sprouts, trimmed and halved
1 tablespoon butter, melted
1 teaspoon cayenne pepper

½ teaspoon dried thyme
1 teaspoon dried parsley flakes
Sea salt and ground black pepper, to taste

In a mixing basin, toss the Brussels sprouts with the remaining ingredients. Set the air fryer on Air Fry mode and adjust temperature to 375 degrees F and time to 5 minutes. select the "Air Fry" mode. To begin, press the "Start" key. Arrange the Brussels sprouts on the air fryer basket coated with parchment paper. Cook the Brussels sprouts for 5 minutes in the air fryer. Raise the temperature to 400 degrees F. Continue to simmer for another 8 minutes, or until the vegetables are soft. Bon appétit!
Per Serving: Calories 128; Fat 6.3g; Sodium 332mg; Carbs 15.5g; Fiber 6.4g; Sugars 3.8g; Protein 6g

Yummy Baby Potatoes

Prep time: 5 minutes| Cook time: 35 minutes| Serves: 4

½ pounds baby potatoes,

scrubbed and halved

1 tablespoon fresh lemon juice
2 tablespoons olive oil
1 teaspoon garlic powder
1 teaspoon onion powder

1 teaspoon Italian seasoning mix
Kosher salt and ground black pepper, to taste

In a mixing dish, combine the young potatoes and the remaining ingredients. Set the air fryer on Air Fry mode and adjust temperature to 400 degrees F and time to 30 minutes. To begin, press the "Start" key. Arrange the tiny potatoes on the air fryer basket coated with parchment paper. Cook the baby potatoes for 30 minutes, turning them over halfway through. Bon appétit!
Per Serving: Calories 188; Fat 7.1g; Sodium 542mg; Carbs 28.7g; Fiber 3.4g; Sugars 2.4g; Protein 3.6g

Green Beans with Butter

Prep time: 5 minutes| Cook time: 15 minutes| Serves: 4

1 pound fresh green beans, trimmed
1 teaspoon butter, melted
Sea salt and ground black

pepper, to taste
1 teaspoon hot paprika
½ teaspoon onion powder
½ teaspoon garlic powder

In a mixing dish, combine the green beans and the remaining ingredients. Set the air fryer on air fryer on Air Fry mode and adjust temperature to 400 degrees F and time to 10 minutes. To begin, press the "Start" key. Arrange the green beans on the cooking tray that has been coated with parchment paper. Green beans should be air fried for 10 minutes or until they get a light brown hue. Bon appétit!
Per Serving: Calories 68; Fat 2.2g; Sodium 435mg; Carbs 9.8g; Fiber 3.5g; Sugars 4.3g; Protein 2.7g

Broccoli with Feta

Prep time: 5 minutes| Cook time: 10 minutes| Serves: 4

1 pound broccoli florets
1 teaspoon lemon zest, grated
2 tablespoons butter, melted
2 garlic cloves, minced

1 teaspoon Dijon mustard
1 ounces feta cheese crumbled
Sea salt and ground black pepper, to taste

In a mixing dish, combine all of the ingredients. Set the air fryer on Air Fry mode and adjust temperature to 400 degrees F and time to 6 minutes. To begin, press the "Start" key. Arrange the broccoli florets on the cooking tray in the air fryer, being careful not to crowd them. Broccoli florets should be air fried for 6 minutes or until cooked through, turning once or twice during that period. Bon appétit!
Per Serving: Calories 118; Fat 9.3g; Sodium 443mg; Carbs 4.5g; Fiber 3.3g; Sugars 1.6g; Protein 5.8g

Salad of Peppers

Prep time: 5 minutes| Cook time: 20 minutes| Serves: 4

4 large bell peppers
2 tablespoons olive oil
2 tablespoons apple cider vinegar
Sea salt and ground black pepper, to taste

2 garlic cloves, crushed
2 tablespoons fresh parsley, chopped
2 tablespoons fresh scallions, chopped

In a mixing dish, combine all of the ingredients. Set the air fryer on Air Fry mode and adjust temperature to 400 degrees F and time to 15 minutes. To begin, press the "Start" key. Arrange the peppers on the air fryer basket of the air fryer, being careful not to crowd them. Cook the peppers in the air fryer for 15 minutes or until browned, shaking the pan once or twice throughout

the process. If preferred, peel away the browned outer shell of the peppers, then cut them into strips and combine with the remaining ingredients. Toss thoroughly to mix, then serve cold. Enjoy!
Per Serving: Calories 119; Fat 7.3g; Sodium 463mg; Carbs 11.7g; Fiber 3.8g; Sugars 7.5g; Protein 2g

Mushrooms with Sauce

Prep time: 5 minutes| Cook time: 10 minutes| Serves: 3

1 pound brown mushrooms
1 tablespoon olive oil
½ teaspoon cumin powder
½ teaspoon onion powder
½ teaspoon garlic powder
½ teaspoon turmeric powder

2 teaspoons Worcestershire sauce
1 teaspoon rice vinegar
Kosher salt and ground black pepper, to taste

In a mixing dish, combine all of the ingredients. Set the air fryer on Air Fry mode and adjust temperature to 400 degrees F and time to 9 minutes. To begin, press the "Start" key. Arrange the mushrooms on the cooking tray of the air fryer, being careful not to crowd them. Cook the mushrooms in an air fryer for 9 minutes, shaking the pan once or twice during the process. Bon appétit!
Per Serving: Calories 129; Fat 9.3g; Sodium 543mg; Carbs 9.9g; Fiber 1.4g; Sugars 3.8g; Protein 4.2g

Roasted Carrot Mash

Prep time: 5 minutes| Cook time: 20 minutes| Serves: 4

½ pound carrots, trimmed and sliced
1 tablespoon olive oil
1 tablespoon butter
1 teaspoon ground cumin

¼ teaspoon dried dill weed
Sea salt and ground black pepper, to season
1 teaspoon cayenne pepper
½ cup whole milk

In a mixing basin, toss the carrots with the olive oil. Set the air fryer on Air Fry mode and adjust temperature to 400 degrees F and time to 20 minutes. To begin, press the "Start" key. Arrange the carrots on the cooking tray that has been coated with parchment paper. Cook your carrots in the air fryer for 20 minutes, or until they are soft and cooked through. By using a fork, mash the carrots with the remaining ingredients until smooth and creamy. Bon appétit!
Per Serving: Calories 219; Fat 14.1g; Carbs 21.8g; Fiber 5g; Sugars 12.6g; Protein 2.9g

Spicy Sweet Potatoes

Prep time: 5 minutes| Cook time: 40 minutes| Serves: 4

4 medium sweet potatoes, scrubbed
6 ounces smoked sausage, chopped
4 ounces tofu cheese, chopped
1 medium onion, chopped
1 clove garlic, minced
1 tablespoon fresh parsley,

chopped
1 bell pepper, seeded and chopped
1 cup canned kidney beans, drained
½ cup tomato sauce
1 cup Colby cheese, shredded

Set the air fryer on Air Fry mode and adjust temperature to 400 degrees F and time to 15 minutes. To begin, press the "Start" key. Sweet potatoes should be pierced and air-fried for 15 minutes or until tender. In a mixing basin, thoroughly combine the remaining ingredients, except the cheese. Bake for another 15 minutes after stuffing the sweet potatoes with the prepared mixture. Choose the "Bake" option. Top each potato with cheese and bake for an

additional 5 minutes at 365 degrees F. Bon appétit!
Per Serving: Calories 502; Fat 23.1g; Sodium 441mg; Carbs 49.2g; Fiber 7.1g; Sugars 8.2g; Protein 25.9g

Cheesy Zucchini Tots

Prep time: 5 minutes| Cook time: 15 minutes| Serves: 4

1 pound zucchini, grated
4 tablespoons almond flour
1 teaspoon Italian seasoning mix

1 large egg, whisked
½ cup parmesan cheese, shredded
1 cup breadcrumbs

Set the air fryer on Air Fry mode and adjust temperature to 400 degrees F and time to 10 minutes. To begin, press the "Start" key. In the cooking tray, place a layer of parchment paper. Combine all the ingredients well. Form the mixture into equal-sized balls and arrange them in a single layer in the cooking tray. Toss the zucchini tots in the air fryer for 10 minutes, rotating halfway through. Bon appétit!
Per Serving: Calories 192; Fat 11.1g; Sodium 337mg; Carbs 13.6g; Fiber 3.1g; Sugars 1.2g; Protein 25.9g

Salad of Lebanese Eggplant

Prep time: 5 minutes| Cook time: 20 minutes| Serves: 4

1 pound eggplant, diced
1 teaspoon olive oil
1 cup cherry tomatoes, halved
1 small onion, chopped
2 cloves garlic, pressed
¼ cup extra-virgin olive oil
Coarse sea salt and ground

black pepper, to taste
½ teaspoon cumin
1 teaspoon oregano
1 teaspoon sumac
4 ounces canned chickpeas, drained
¼ cup almonds, slivered

Toss the eggplant with 1 teaspoon of olive oil in a mixing basin. Set the air fryer on Air Fry mode and adjust temperature to 400 degrees F and time to 15 minutes. To begin, press the "Start" key. Arrange the eggplant on the cooking tray that has been coated with parchment paper. Cook it for 15 minutes, or until the eggplant is soft and cooked through. Bon appétit!
Per Serving: Calories 258; Fat 19.1g; Sodium 445mg; Carbs 49.2g; Fiber 7.1g; Sugars 7.6g; Protein 19.5g

Cheesy Zucchini Bites

Prep time: 5 minutes| Cook time: 20 minutes| Serves: 4

1 pound zucchini, sliced
1 tablespoon olive oil
½ cup parmesan cheese, grated
1 teaspoon garlic powder

1 teaspoon paprika
Sea salt and ground black pepper, to taste

In a mixing dish, combine all of the ingredients. Set the air fryer on Air Fry mode and adjust temperature to 400 degrees F and time to 15 minutes. To begin, press the "Start" key. Arrange the zucchini on the cooking tray that has been coated with parchment paper. Cook for 15 minutes, or until zucchini is soft and cooked through. Bon appétit!
Per Serving: Calories 155; Fat 10.7g; Sodium 337mg; Carbs 7.2g; Fiber 1.2g; Sugars 0.6g; Protein 7g

Yummy Bowl of Brussels Sprout

Prep time: 5 minutes| Cook time: 20 minutes| Serves: 5

½ pounds Brussels sprouts,   trimmed

1 bell pepper, sliced
1 tablespoon olive oil
1 cloves garlic, peeled
½ teaspoon dried dill weed
1 teaspoon dried parsley flakes

Sea salt and ground black pepper to taste
1 tablespoon Dijon mustard
1 tablespoon balsamic vinegar

In a mixing basin, toss the Brussels sprouts with the remaining ingredients. Set the air fryer on Air Fry mode and adjust temperature to 400 degrees F and time to 8 minutes. To begin, press the "Start" key. Arrange the Brussels sprouts and peppers on the cooking tray coated with parchment paper. Cook 7 minutes in the with Brussels sprouts and peppers Set temp to 400 degrees F. Continue to cook for another 8 minutes, or until the vegetables are soft. Bon appétit!
Per Serving: Calories 165; Fat 8.7g; Sodium 227mg; Carbs 19.2g; Fiber 6.2g; Sugars 3.9g; Protein 5.8g

Potatoes Fingerlings

Prep time: 5 minutes| Cook time: 20 minutes| Serves: 4

½ pound fingerling potatoes, scrubbed
1 tablespoon olive oil
Kosher salt and freshly cracked black pepper, to taste

1 tablespoon fresh rosemary, chopped
1 tablespoon fresh parsley, chopped

In a mixing dish, combine the fingerling potatoes and the remaining ingredients. Set the air fryer on Air Fry mode and adjust temperature to 400 degrees F and time to 30 minutes. To begin, press the "Start" key. Arrange fingerling potatoes on the cooking tray coated with parchment paper. Cook fingerling potatoes for 30 minutes, turning them over halfway through. Bon appétit!
Per Serving: Calories 236; Fat 10.3g; Sodium 332mg; Carbs 30.9g; Fiber 4.2g; Sugars 1.9g; Protein 3.7g

Smoky Bites of Cauliflower

Prep time: 5 minutes| Cook time: 10 minutes| Serves: 4

1 pound cauliflower florets
1 tablespoon butter, at room temperature
1 cloves garlic, crushed

1 tablespoon olive oil
1 teaspoon smoked paprika
Sea salt and ground black pepper, to taste

In a mixing dish, combine all of the ingredients. Set the air fryer on Air Fry mode and adjust temperature to 400 degrees F and time to 9 minutes. To begin, press the "Start" key. Arrange the cauliflower florets on the cooking tray of the air fryer, being careful not to crowd them. Air fry the cauliflower florets for 9 minutes, or until golden brown, shaking the pan once or twice throughout the frying process. Bon appétit!
Per Serving: Calories 118; Fat 9.5g; Sodium 229mg; Carbs 6.4g; Fiber 2.5g; Sugars 2.2g; Protein 2.7g

Mushrooms with Beans

Prep time: 5 minutes| Cook time: 15 minutes| Serves: 4

1 pound fresh green beans, trimmed
½ pound button mushrooms, sliced
1 tablespoon sesame oil

1 tablespoon soy sauce
1 teaspoon rice wine vinegar
2 cloves garlic, pressed
A few dashes of hot sauce

In a mixing dish, combine the green beans and mushrooms with the remaining ingredients. Set the air fryer on Air Fry mode and adjust temperature to 400 degrees F and time to 10 minutes.

To begin, press the "Start" key. Arrange the green beans and mushrooms on the cooking tray coated with parchment paper. For 10 minutes, air fried the green beans and mushrooms. Serve right away!

Per Serving: Calories98; Fat 4.5g; Sodium 285mg; Carbs 11.2g; Fiber 3.5g; Sugars 5.6g; Protein 4.2g

Yummy Fennel Salad

Prep time: 5 minutes| Cook time: 20 minutes| Serves: 4

1 pound fennel bulbs, quartered	1 teaspoon Dijon mustard
1 shallot, sliced	1 tablespoon apple cider vinegar
4 cups lightly packed mixed greens	1 clove garlic, chopped
1 bell pepper, sliced	¼ cup extra-virgin olive oil
1 tablespoon pure maple syrup	Kosher salt and freshly ground black pepper
1 tablespoon fresh lime juice	¼ cup pine nuts, toasted

Set the air fryer on Air Fry mode and adjust temperature to 400 degrees F and time to 15 minutes. To begin, press the "Start" key. Arrange the fennel wedges on the cooking tray coated with parchment paper. Fennel wedges should be air fried for 15 minutes or until tender. Add the remaining veggies after cutting the fennel into tiny pieces. Whisk together the maple syrup, lime juice, mustard, vinegar, garlic, olive oil, salt, and black pepper in a small mixing basin. Serve the salad immediately after dressing it and garnishing it with toasted nuts. Bon appétit!

Per Serving: Calories318; Fat 21.3g; Carbs 30.5g; Fiber 5g; Sugars 19.6g; Protein 4.8g

Salad of Apple, Beet and Cranberry

Prep time: 5 minutes| Cook time: 25 minutes| Serves: 4

1 pound beets, peeled and cut into bite-sized pieces	⅓ cup extra-virgin olive oil
1 teaspoon olive oil	3 tablespoons apple cider vinegar
1 cup baby spinach	1 teaspoon yellow mustard
1 apple, cored and diced	1 garlic clove, minced
½ cup dried cranberries	Kosher salt and ground black pepper, to taste
Vinaigrette.	

Toss the beets in the olive oil until they are well covered. Set the air fryer on Air Fry mode and adjust temperature to 400 degrees F and time to 20 minutes. To begin, press the "Start" key. Arrange the beets on the cooking tray. Cook the beets in an air fryer for 20 minutes, shaking the tray once or twice during the process. Toss the roasted beets with the rest of the ingredients and serve.

Per Serving: Calories 281; Fat 20.6g; Sodium 442mg; Carbs 23.1g; Fiber 5g; Sugars 16g; Protein 2.8g

Yummy Salad of Asparagus

Prep time: 5 minutes| Cook time: 10 minutes| Serves: 4

½ pounds asparagus	2 tablespoons apple cider vinegar
1 tablespoon butter, melted	1 tablespoon Dijon mustard
1 teaspoon hot paprika	1 tablespoon fresh lemon juice
1 teaspoon dried oregano	¼ cup extra-virgin olive oil
Sea salt and ground black pepper, to taste	2 pickles, crushed

In a mixing dish, combine the asparagus and butter. Set the air fryer on Air Fry mode and adjust temperature to 400 degrees F and time to 8 minutes. To begin, press the "Start" key. Arrange the asparagus stalks on the cooking tray in the air fryer, being careful not to crowd them. Air fry the asparagus for 8 minutes, turning halfway during cooking time, or until tender and brilliant green. Toss the asparagus with the remaining ingredients, tossing well to incorporate. Serve at room temperature. Bon appétit!

Per Serving: Calories 223; Fat 19.9g; Sodium 442mg; Carbs 10.4g; Fiber 4.9g; Sugars 4.8g; Protein 4.6g

Sweet Potatoes with Lime

Prep time: 5 minutes| Cook time: 40 minutes| Serves: 4

1 small onion, finely chopped	1 jalapeno pepper, seeded and chopped
1 tablespoon grated lemon zest	1 tablespoon fresh mint, chopped
1 tablespoon fresh lemon juice	2 tablespoon fresh chives, chopped
1 ½ pounds sweet potatoes, peeled and diced	2 tablespoons fresh parsley, chopped
2 tablespoons butter, melted	
Kosher salt and ground black pepper, to taste	

In a mixing dish, combine all of the ingredients. Set the air fryer on Roast mode and adjust temperature to 380 degrees F and time to 35 minutes. To begin, press the "Start" key. Arrange the sweet potatoes on the cooking tray that has been coated with parchment paper. Roast it for 35 minutes, or until sweet potatoes are soft and cooked through. Bon appétit!

Per Serving: Calories 214; Fat 5.9g; Sodium 412mg; Carbs 37.8g; Fiber 5.8g; Sugars 8.7g; Protein 3.3g

Delicious Eggplants

Prep time: 5 minutes| Cook time: 20 minutes| Serves: 4

1 pound eggplant	½ teaspoon mustard seeds
1 teaspoon butter, melted	1 garlic clove, minced
1 medium tomato, diced	1 tablespoon freshly squeezed lemon juice
1 sweet onion, diced	6 tablespoons extra-virgin olive oil
1 red chili pepper, chopped	Kosher salt and ground black pepper, to taste
1 tablespoon fresh mint leaf chopped	
½ teaspoon ground cumin	

Toss the eggplant with 1 teaspoon of melted butter in a mixing bowl. Set the air fryer on Air Fry mode and adjust temperature to 400 degrees F and time to 15 minutes. To begin, press the "Start" key. Place the eggplant on the cooking tray that has been lined with parchment paper. For 10 minutes, cook the eggplant. Cook for a further 5 minutes after adding the tomato and onion. Toss the roasted vegetables with the other ingredients in a large mixing bowl. Bon appétit!

Per Serving: Calories 258; Fat 21.7g; Sodium 445mg; Carbs 16.2g; Fiber 4.8g; Sugars 9.7g; Protein 2.5g

Broccoli with Sesame

Prep time: 5 minutes| Cook time: 15 minutes| Serves: 4

1 pound broccoli, grated	½ cup Cheddar cheese, shredded
1 cup seasoned breadcrumbs	Kosher salt and ground black pepper, to taste
2 large eggs, beaten	
1 small onion, finely chopped	2 tablespoons sesame seeds
1 teaspoon garlic, minced	

Set the air fryer on Air Fry mode and adjust temperature to 400 degrees F and time to 10 minutes. To begin, press the "Start" key. In the air fryer pan, place a layer of parchment paper. Combine all the ingredients well. Form the mixture into equal-sized balls and arrange them in a single layer in the cooking tray of the air fryer. Cook the croquettes in the air for 10 minutes,

rotating halfway through. Bon appétit!
Per Serving: Calories201; Fat 10.5g; Sodium 621mg; Carbs 16.4g; Fiber 4.2g; Sugars 4g; Protein 12.2g

minutes, rotating halfway through. Bon appétit!
Per Serving: Calories 266; Fat 11.4g; Sodium 442mg; Carbs 34.4g; Fiber 5g; Sugars 5.7g; Protein 7.7g

Cheesy Brussels Sprout

Prep time: 5 minutes| Cook time: 15 minutes| Serves: 4

½ pounds Brussels sprouts, trimmed and halved
1 tablespoon olive oil
Sea salt and freshly ground black pepper, to taste

1 teaspoon lemon zest
½ cup Parmesan cheese, grated
2 tablespoons fresh parsley leaves, roughly chopped

In a mixing basin, toss the Brussels sprouts with the olive oil, salt, black pepper, and lemon zest. Set the air fryer on Air Fry mode and adjust temperature to 400 degrees F and time to 13 minutes. To begin, press the "Start" key. Arrange the Brussels sprouts on the cooking tray coated with parchment paper. Cook the Brussels sprouts for 5 minutes. Select the "Air Fry" mode and top your Brussels sprouts with cheese and parsley. Bake for an additional 8 minutes, or until the cheese melts. Bon appétit!
Per Serving: Calories 201; Fat 10.5g; Sodium 441mg; Carbs 16.4g; Fiber 4.2g; Sugars 4g; Protein 12.2g

Spicy Potatoes with Garlic

Prep time: 5 minutes| Cook time: 40 minutes| Serves: 4

½ pound potatoes, peeled and diced
1 tablespoon olive oil
1 tablespoon butter, softened
Coarse sea salt and ground

black pepper, to taste
1 teaspoon smoked paprika
1 teaspoon garlic, minced
1 teaspoon rosemary, chopped
1 teaspoon thyme, chopped

In a mixing dish, combine all of the ingredients. Set the air fryer on Roast mode and adjust temperature to 380 degrees F and time to 35 minutes. To begin, press the "Start" key. Arrange the potatoes on the air fryer basket that has been coated with parchment paper. Roast it for 35 minutes, or until potatoes are soft and cooked through. Warm it up and enjoy it!
Per Serving: Calories 254; Fat 13.5g; Sodium 337mg; Carbs 31.4g; Fiber 4.2g; Sugars 1.9g; Protein 3.8g

Greek-Style Marathokeftedes

Prep time: 5minutes| Cook time: 15 minutes| Serves: 4

1 pound fennel bulbs, trimmed and chopped
4 spring onions, finely chopped
1 teaspoon dried Greek oregano
1 tablespoon fresh mint leaf,

chopped
1 tablespoon fresh parsley leaf, chopped
1 cup all-purpose flour
½ cup feta cheese, crumbled
2 tablespoons olive oil

Set the air fryer on Air Fry mode and adjust temperature to 400 degrees F and time to 13 minutes. To begin, press the "Start" key. In the air fryer basket, place a layer of parchment paper. Combine all the ingredients well. Form the mixture into equal-sized balls and arrange them in a single layer in the basket of the air fryer. The Greek marathokeftedes should be air fried for 13

Sticky and Spicy Carrots

Prep time: 5 minutes| Cook time: 25 minutes| Serves: 4

1 pound carrots, trimmed and cut into 1 inch pieces
1 tablespoon butter, melted
1 tablespoon agave nectar

A pinch of kosher salt
A pinch of grated nutmeg
½ teaspoon garlic powder

In a mixing dish, combine all of the ingredients. Set the air fryer on Air Fry mode and adjust temperature to 400 degrees F and time to 20 minutes. To begin, press the "Start" key. Arrange the carrots on the cooking tray that has been coated with parchment paper. Cook your carrots in the air fryer for 20 minutes, or until they are soft and cooked through. Bon appétit!
Per Serving: Calories 108; Fat 6g; Sodium 543mg; Carbs 13.4g; Fiber 4.4g; Sugars 5.7g; Protein 1.2g

Eastern Style Salad

Prep time: 5 minutes| Cook time: 20 minutes| Serves: 4

1 pound eggplant, sliced
1 cup cherry tomato
½ cup fresh scallion, chopped
1 garlic clove, minced
1 tablespoon fresh cilantro, roughly chopped

1 tablespoon fresh parsley, roughly chopped
½ lemon, freshly squeezed
¼ cup extra-virgin olive oil
Sea salt and ground black pepper, to taste

Toss the eggplant with 1 teaspoon of olive oil in a mixing basin. Set the air fryer on Air Fry mode and adjust temperature to 400 degrees F and time to 15 minutes. To begin, press the "Start" key. Arrange the eggplant on the cooking tray that has been coated with parchment paper. Cook the eggplant for 10 minutes before adding the cherry tomatoes and roasting for another 5 minutes. Toss the remaining ingredients with the roasted vegetables and serve at room temperature. Bon appétit!
Per Serving: Calories 166; Fat 13.6g; Sodium 387mg; Carbs 10.7g; Fiber 4.5g; Sugars 5.7g; Protein 2.1g

Mushrooms with Garlic and Butter

Prep time: 5 minutes| Cook time: 15 minutes| Serves: 4

1 pound button mushrooms
4 cloves garlic minced
4 tablespoons unsalted butter
2 tablespoons scallions, chopped
2 tablespoons dry white wine

2 teaspoons fresh thyme leaves, chopped
2 tablespoons chopped fresh parsley
Sea salt and ground black pepper, to taste

Toss the mushrooms with the other ingredients after patting them dry. Set the air fryer on Air Fry mode and adjust temperature to 400 degrees F and time to 12 minutes. To begin, press the "Start" key. Arrange the mushrooms on the cooking tray that has been coated with parchment paper. Cook it for 12 minutes, or until the mushrooms are soft and cooked through. Bon appétit!
Per Serving: Calories 116; Fat 8.1g; Sodium 498mg; Carbs 6.4g; Fiber 1.5g; Sugars 3g; Protein 4.5g

Poultry Recipes

Chimichurri Chicken Breasts

Prep time: 5 minutes| Cook time: 35 minutes| Serves: 1

1 chicken breast, bone-in, skin-on
Chimichurri
½ bunch fresh cilantro
¼ bunch fresh parsley
½ shallot, peeled, cut in quarters
½ tablespoon paprika ground
½ tablespoon chili powder
½ tablespoon fennel ground
½ teaspoon black pepper,
ground
½ teaspoon onion powder
1 teaspoon salt
½ teaspoon garlic powder
½ teaspoon cumin ground
½ tablespoon canola oil
2 tablespoons olive oil
4 garlic cloves, peeled
1 zest and juice of lemon
1 teaspoon kosher salt

Oil the cooking tray. To preheat the air fryer, select the Air Fry function. Set the time to 35 minutes and temperature to 400 degrees F. Touch Start to begin. In a good bowl, combine all of the spices and season the chicken with them. Drizzle the chicken with canola oil and place it in the cooking tray. Cook for 35 minutes, and then serve on a plate. In a blender, combine all of the other ingredients and mix until smooth. Toss the chicken with the Chimichurri sauce and serve.
Per serving: Calories 140; Fat 7.9g; Sodium 581mg; Carbs 1.8g; Fiber 0.1g; Sugar 7.1g; Protein 7.2g

Chicken Wings from Korea

Prep time: 5 minutes| Cook time: 10 minutes| Serves: 8

For Wings
1 teaspoon pepper
1 teaspoon salt
2 pounds chicken wings
For Sauce
2 packets Splenda
1 tablespoon minced garlic
1 tablespoon minced ginger
1 tablespoon sesame oil
1 teaspoon agave nectar
1 tablespoon mayo
2 tablespoons gochujang
For Finishing
¼ cup chopped green onions
2 teaspoons sesame seeds

Select Air Fry function. Select time to 20 minutes and temperature to 400 degrees F. Touch Start to begin. Ensure your air fryer is preheated. Season the wings with salt and pepper. Place the wings on a cooking tray lined with foil in the air fryer. Cook it for 20 minutes, flipping after 10 minutes. As the chicken air fries, combine all of the sauce ingredients in a mixing bowl. Remove the wings and set them in a basin once the chicken has reached 160 degrees F on a thermometer. Pour half of the sauce mixture over the wings and toss to coat thoroughly. Return the coated wings to the air fryer for another 5 minutes or until they reach 165 degrees F. Remove the green onions and sesame seeds from the tray. Extra sauce can be dipped in.
Per serving: Calories 356; Fat 26g; Sodium 440mg; Carbs 9g; Fiber 0.5g; Sugar 2g; Protein 23g

Cornish Game Hens with Harissa Rub

Prep time: 10 minutes plus 30 minutes to marinate| Cook time: 20 minutes| Serves: 4

For the Harissa
½ cup olive oil
6 cloves garlic, minced
2 tablespoons smoked paprika
1 tablespoon ground coriander
1 tablespoon ground cumin
1 teaspoon ground caraway
1 teaspoon kosher salt
½ to 1 teaspoon cayenne pepper
For the Hens
½ cup yogurt

Cornish game hens, any giblets removed, split in half lengthwise
To make the harissa, mix the oil, garlic, paprika, coriander, cumin, caraway, salt, and cayenne in a medium microwave-safe bowl. Microwave for 1 minute on high, stirring halfway during cooking time. (Alternatively, heat the oil on the burner until it is hot and boiling.) Select Air Fry function. Cook it in the air fryer by setting temperature to 400 degrees F and time to 5 minutes. Combine 1 to 2 tablespoon harissa and the yogurt in a small bowl for the chickens. Whisk all of these together until it's get a smooth texture. Pour this mixture and the hen halves in a re-sealable plastic bag. Seal the bag and massage all of the pieces until they are completely covered with mixture of harissa and yogurt. Then let it marinate at room temperature for 30 minutes or in the refrigerator for up to 24 hours In the cooking tray, arrange the hen halves in a single layer. Set the air fryer temperature to 400 degrees F and time to 20 minutes. Touch Start to begin. Cook in it and make sure the game hens have attained an internal temperature with a meat thermometer.
Per serving: Calories 590; Fat 38g; Sodium 490mg; Carbs 3.2g; Fiber 0.1g; Sugar 0.1g; Protein 32.5g

Easy Chicken Thighs with Lemon

Prep time: 5 minutes| Cook time: 10 minutes| Serves: 4

1 teaspoon salt
1 teaspoon freshly ground black pepper
2 tablespoons olive oil
2 tablespoons Italian seasoning
2 tablespoons freshly squeezed lemon juice
1 lemon, sliced

Season the chicken thighs with salt and pepper and place them in a medium mixing basin. Toss the chicken thighs with the olive oil, Italian seasoning, and lemon juice until they are well coated in oil. Add the lemon slices. Place the chicken thighs in a single layer in the cooking tray. Preheat your air fryer. Select Air Fry function. Select time to 10 minutes and temperature to 400 degrees F. Cook for 10 minutes after setting the timer. Flip the chicken using tongs. Cook for another 10 minutes after resetting the timer. Check that the chicken has achieved a temperature of 165 degrees F on the inside. If necessary, increase the cooking time. Plate, serve, and enjoy the chicken after it's thoroughly cooked.
Per serving: Calories 325; Fat 26g; Sodium 670mg; Carbs 1g; Fiber 0.1g; Sugar 1g; Protein 20g

Southern Style Fried Chicken

Prep time: 15 minutes plus 1 hour for marinating| Cook time: 26 minutes| Serves: 4

½ cup buttermilk
2 teaspoons salt, plus 1 tablespoon
1 teaspoon freshly ground black pepper
1 pound chicken thighs and
drumsticks
1 cup all-purpose flour
2 teaspoons onion powder
2 teaspoons garlic powder
½ teaspoon sweet paprika

Whisk together the buttermilk, 2 teaspoons of salt, and pepper in a large mixing basin. Place the chicken pieces in the basin and marinate for at least an hour in the refrigerator, covered. Prepare the dredging mixture about 5 minutes before the chicken is done marinating. Combine the flour, 1 tablespoon of salt, onion powder, garlic powder, and paprika in a large mixing basin. Olive oil should be sprayed on the cooking tray. Dredge the chicken in the flour mixture after removing it from the buttermilk mixture. Remove any extra flour by shaking it. Place the chicken pieces in a single layer in the oiled cooking tray, allowing space between each piece. Using a spray bottle, liberally coat the chicken with olive oil. Preheat your air fryer to 390 degrees F. Select Air Fry function. Select time to 13 minutes and temperature to 400 degrees F. Touch Start to begin cooking. Cook it for 13 minutes after setting the timer. Flip the chicken using tongs. Olive oil should be sprayed liberally. Restart the timer and cook for another 13 minutes. Check that the chicken has achieved a temperature of 165 degrees F on the inside. If necessary, increase the cooking time. Plate, serve, and enjoy the chicken after it's thoroughly cooked!

Per serving: Calories 377; Fat 18g; Sodium 1182mg; Carbs 28g; Fiber 1g; Sugar 2g; Protein 25g

Grilled Breast Chicken

Prep time: 5 minutes| Cook time: 14 minutes| Serves: 4

½ teaspoon garlic powder	1 teaspoon dried parsley
1 teaspoon salt	2 tablespoons olive oil, divided
½ teaspoon freshly ground black pepper	3 boneless, skinless chicken breasts

Combine the garlic powder, salt, pepper, and parsley in a small mixing bowl. Rub each chicken breast with 1 tablespoon of olive oil and half of the spice mix. In the cooking tray, place the chicken breasts. Select Air Fry function. Set the timer for 7 minutes on the air fryer. Adjust temperature to 370 degrees F. Touch Start to begin cooking. Flip the chicken with tongs and brush the remaining olive oil and seasonings on top. Restart the air fryer and cook for another 7 minutes. Check that the chicken has achieved a temperature of 165 degrees F on the inside. If necessary, increase the cooking time. Transfer the chicken to a dish and serve after it is thoroughly done.

Per serving: Calories 182; Fat 9g; Sodium 657mg; Carbs 3.2g; Fiber 0.1g; Sugar 0.1g; Protein 26g

Chicken Breast Stuffed with Cheese and Garlic

Prep time: 5 minutes| Cook time: 30 minutes| Serves: 2

½ cup Cottage cheese	salt
2 eggs, beaten	Seasoned breadcrumbs
2 medium-sized chicken breasts, halved	⅓ teaspoon freshly ground black pepper, to savor 3 cloves
2 tablespoons fresh coriander, chopped 1 teaspoon fine sea	garlic, finely minced

To begin, use a meat tenderizer to flatten the chicken breast. Combine the cottage cheese, garlic, coriander, salt, and black pepper in a medium mixing bowl. ⅓ of the mixture should be spread over the first chicken breast. Repeat with the rest of the ingredients. Roll the chicken around the filling, securing it with toothpicks as needed. In a small dish, whisk the egg. Combine the salt, ground black pepper, and seasoned breadcrumbs in a small dish. Roll the chicken breasts in the breadcrumbs after coating them with the whisked egg. Select Air Fry function. Select time to 22 minutes and temperature to 400 degrees F. Cook for 22 minutes in a cooking tray. Serve right away.

Per serving: Calories 424; Fat 24.5g; Sodium 580mg; Carbs 7.5g; Fiber 1g; Sugar 1.4g; Protein 43.4g

Aioli Sauce Chicken Strips

Prep time: 5 minutes| Cook time: 15 minutes| Serves: 4

3 chicken breasts cut into strips	½ tablespoon garlic powder
2 tablespoons olive oil	½ cup mayonnaise
1 cup breadcrumbs	1 tablespoon lemon juice
Salt and black pepper to taste	½ tablespoon ground chili

Combine the breadcrumbs, salt, pepper, and garlic in a mixing bowl and lay out on a platter. Roll the chicken in the breadcrumb mixture after brushing it with olive oil. Select time to 10-12 minutes and temperature to 400 degrees F on Air Fry function, cook while flipping once halfway through, on the greased cooking tray. To make the aioli, whisk together mayonnaise, lemon juice, and ground chili. Serve the chicken with aioli that is still hot.

Per serving: Calories 311; Fat 11g; Sodium 780mg; Carbs 22g; Fiber 0.1g; Sugar 0.1g; Protein 31g

Crisped Chicken Thigh

Prep time: 10 minutes| Cook time: 35 minutes| Serves: 6

6 chicken thighs	½ teaspoon pepper
1 tablespoon olive oil	1 teaspoon garlic powder
For Rub:	1 teaspoon onion powder
½ teaspoon basil	½ teaspoon salt
½ teaspoon oregano	

Preheat your air fryer to 365 degrees F. Olive oil should be brushed over the chicken thighs. Combine the rub ingredients in a small dish and rub all over the chicken. Select Bake function. Set time to 30 minutes and temperature to 365 degrees F. Bake for 30 minutes, depending on the size of the chicken. Serve and have fun.

Per serving: Calories 250; Fat 19g; Sodium 680mg; Carbs 0.9g; Fiber 0.1g; Sugar 0.1g; Protein 18g

Classic Chicken

Prep time: 10 minutes| Cook time: 30 minutes| Serves: 4

1 pound chicken breasts, skinless and boneless	¼ teaspoon oregano
	3 garlic cloves, minced
For marinade:	1 tablespoon lemon juice
½ teaspoon dill	3 tablespoons olive oil
1 teaspoon onion powder	¼ teaspoon pepper
¼ teaspoon basil	½ teaspoon salt

In a mixing dish, combine all of the marinade ingredients and stir thoroughly. Coat the chicken with the marinade well. Refrigerate the bowl overnight after covering it. Place the dish into the air fryer. Set the air fryer to bake, the temperature to 390 degrees F, and the timer to 30 minutes. To preheat the air fryer, press Start. Select Bake function. Select time 30 minutes and temperature 365 degrees F. Bake the marinated chicken for 30 minutes in a cooking tray. Serve and have fun.

Per serving: Calories 313; Fat 19g; Sodium 770mg; Carbs 20g; Fiber 1g; Sugar 0.1g; Protein 33g

Chicken Breast

Prep time: 10 minutes| Cook time: 15 minutes| Serves: 8

4 chicken breasts, skinless and   boneless

1 tablespoon olive oil
For Rub:
1 teaspoon garlic powder
1 teaspoon onion powder

4 teaspoons brown sugar
4 teaspoons paprika
1 teaspoon black pepper
1 teaspoon salt

Set the air fryer to bake, the temperature to 390 degrees F, and the timer to 30 minutes. To preheat the air fryer, press Start. Olive oil should be brushed on the chicken breasts. Combine the rub ingredients in a small dish and massage all over the chicken breasts. Select Bake function. Set time to 15 minutes and the temperature to 365 degrees F. Place chicken breasts on a cooking tray and bake for 15 minutes, or until an internal temperature of 165 degrees F is reached. Serve and have fun.
Per serving: Calories 165; Fat 7.3g; Sodium 600mg; Carbs 2.7g; Fiber 0.1g; Sugar 1.8g; Protein 21.4g

Chicken Broccoli Bacon Ranch

Prep time: 10 minutes| Cook time: 30 minutes| Serves: 4

4 chicken breasts, skinless and boneless
⅓ cup mozzarella cheese, shredded
1 cup cheddar cheese, shredded

½ cup ranch dressing
5 bacon slices, cooked and chopped
2 cups broccoli florets, blanched and chopped

Set the air fryer to bake, the temperature to 365 degrees F, and the timer to 30 minutes. To preheat the air fryer, press Start. Place the chicken in a casserole dish. Bacon and broccoli go on top. Top the chicken with ranch dressing and shredded mozzarella and cheddar cheese. Preheat air fryer to 365 degrees F and select Bake function and bake chicken for 30 minutes. Serve and have fun.
Per serving: Calories 551; Fat 30.8g; Sodium 650mg; Carbs 5.4g; Fiber 0.1g; Sugar 1.7g; Protein 60.4g

Perfect Chicken Leg

Prep time: 10 minutes| Cook time: 50 minutes| Serves: 10

10 chicken legs
½ teaspoon ground nutmeg
½ teaspoon ground cinnamon
1 teaspoon ground allspice
1 teaspoon black pepper
1 tablespoon fresh thyme
1 ½ tablespoons brown sugar
¼ cup soy sauce

⅓ cup fresh lime juice
1 tablespoon ginger, sliced
2 habanera peppers, remove the stem
4 garlic cloves, peeled and smashed
6 green onions, chopped

Place the chicken in a big zip-lock bag. In a food processor, combine the remaining ingredients and pulse until combined. Pour the sauce over the chicken. Refrigerate the chicken overnight after sealing the bag and shaking it thoroughly to coat it. Set the air fryer to bake, the temperature to 365 degrees F, and the timer to 50 minutes. To preheat the air fryer, press Start. Using foil, line a cooking tray. Select Bake function. Bake the marinated chicken legs for 45-50 minutes on the cooking tray. Serve and have fun.
Per serving: Calories 232; Fat 14.2g; Sodium 586mg; Carbs 4.8g; Fiber 1g; Sugar 2.2g; Protein 21.9g

Full Protein Baked Chicken

Prep time: 10 minutes| Cook time: 25 minutes| Serves: 6

6 chicken breasts, skinless and boneless
¼ teaspoon paprika

½ teaspoon garlic salt
1 teaspoon Italian seasoning
2 tablespoons olive oil

¼ teaspoon pepper

Set the air fryer to bake, the temperature to 365 degrees F, and the timer to 25 minutes. To preheat the air fryer, press Start. Brush the chicken with olive oil. Rub the chicken with a mixture of Italian spice, garlic salt, paprika, and pepper. Select Bake function. Place the chicken breasts on a cooking tray and bake for 25 minutes, or until the internal temperature reaches 165 degrees F. Cut into slices and serve.
Per serving: Calories 321; Fat 15.7g; Sodium 677mg; Carbs 0.4g; Fiber 0.1g; Sugar 0.1g; Protein 42.3g

Balsamic Flavored Chicken

Prep time: 10 minutes| Cook time: 25 minutes| Serves: 4

4 chicken breasts, skinless and boneless
2 teaspoons dried oregano
2 garlic cloves, minced

½ cup balsamic vinegar
2 tablespoons soy sauce
¼ cup olive oil
Pepper and salt

Insert the cooking tray into the air fryer. Set the air fryer to bake, the temperature to 390 degrees F, and the timer to 25 minutes. To preheat the air fryer, press Start. Combine soy sauce, oil, black pepper, oregano, garlic, and vinegar in a mixing bowl. Pour the soy sauce mixture over the chicken in a baking dish. Allow for a 10-minute rest period. Preheat air fryer and select Bake function, set time 25 minutes and temperature 365 degrees F and bake chicken for 25 minutes. Serve and have fun.
Per serving: Calories 401; Fat 23.5g; Sodium 667mg; Carbs 1.9g; Fiber 0.1g; Sugar 0.3g; Protein 42.9g

Easy Thigh Chicken

Prep time: 10 minutes| Cook time: 35 minutes| Serves: 6

6 chicken thighs
2 teaspoons poultry seasoning

2 tablespoons olive oil
Pepper and salt

Place the cooking tray into the air fryer. Set the air fryer to bake, the temperature to 390 degrees F, and the timer to 40 minutes. To preheat the air fryer, press Start. Brush the chicken with oil and season with salt, pepper, and poultry spice. Select Bake function. Set time to 35 minutes and temperature to 365 degrees F. Place the chicken on a cooking tray and bake for 35 minutes, or until the internal temperature reaches 165 degrees F. Serve and have fun.
Per serving: Calories 319; Fat 15.5g; Sodium 558mg; Carbs 0.3g; Fiber 0.1g; Sugar 0.1g; Protein 42.3g

Tender Buffalo Chicken

Prep time: 60 minutes| Cook time: 25 minutes| Serves: 5

Nonstick cooking spray
⅔ cup panko bread crumbs
½ teaspoon cayenne pepper
½ teaspoon paprika
½ teaspoon garlic powder

½ teaspoon salt
3 chicken breasts, boneless, skinless and cut in 10 strips
½ cup butter, melted
½ cup hot sauce

Combine bread crumbs and spices in a shallow dish. Coat the chicken in the crumb mixture on all sides. Refrigerate for 1 hour after placing on prepared pan. Whisk together butter and spicy sauce in a small bowl. Select Bake function. Spray the cooking tray lightly with cooking spray and line it with foil. Place each piece of chicken in the foil basket after dipping it in the butter mixture. Place the cooking tray in air fryer. Preheat the air fryer, select Air Fry function and set time 25 minutes and temperature to 400 degrees F. Cook until the chicken is no longer pink and

the exterior is crispy and golden brown. Halfway through the cooking time, flip the chicken. Serve right away.
Per serving: Calories 371; Fat 23g; Sodium 777mg; Carbs 10g; Fiber 1g; Sugar 1g; Protein 31g

Parmesan Chicken

Prep time: 10 minutes| Cook time: 35 minutes| Serves: 4

Nonstick cooking spray	2 tablespoons fresh parsley,
½ cup flour	chopped
2 eggs	½ teaspoon salt
⅔ cup panko bread crumbs	¼ teaspoon pepper
⅔ cup Italian seasoned bread	4 chicken breast halves,
crumbs	skinless and boneless
⅓ + ¼ cup parmesan cheese,	24 ounces marinara sauce
divided	1 cup mozzarella cheese, grated

Spray the cooking tray lightly with cooking spray. Fill a small dish halfway with flour. Beat the eggs in a separate shallow bowl. Combine both bread crumbs, ⅓ cup parmesan cheese, 2 tablespoons parsley, salt, and pepper in a third shallow dish. Pound the chicken between two pieces of plastic wrap to a thickness of 1-2 inches. To coat the chicken, first coat it in flour, then in eggs, and finally in the bread crumb mixture. Place the items in the tray and place the tray in air fryer. Preheat the air fryer and select Bake function. Set time to 10 minutes and temperature to 365 F. Bake for 10 minutes. Halfway through the cooking time, flip the chicken. Remove the chicken from the air fryer. In the bottom of a drip pan, pour ½ cup marinara. Place the chicken on top of the sauce and top with another 2 tablespoons marinara. Add mozzarella and parmesan cheese on the top of the chicken. Bake for 20-25 minutes on Bake mode at 365 degrees F, until bubbling and cheese is golden brown. Serve.
Per serving: Calories 529; Fat 13g; Sodium 1437mg; Carbs 52g; Fiber 5g; Sugar 9g; Protein 51g

Crispy Nutty Chicken Wings

Prep time: 5 minutes| Cook time: 18 minutes| Serves: 4

1 tablespoon fish sauce	2 fresh lemongrass stalks,
1 tablespoon fresh lemon juice	chopped finely
1 teaspoon sugar	¼ cup unsalted cashews,
12 chicken middle wings cut	crushed
into half	

Combine the fish sauce, lime juice, and sugar in a mixing bowl. Add the wings and thoroughly cover them in the mixture. Refrigerate for 1-2 hours to marinate. Preheat the air fryer and select Air Fry function. Set time to 2 minutes and temperature at 400 degrees F. Place lemongrass stems in the cooking tray. Cook for approximately a minute and a half. Transfer the cashew mixture to a bowl from the air fryer. In a cooking tray, place the chicken wings. Select Air Fry function. Set time to 15 minutes and temperature 400 degrees F. Cook for a further 13 to 15 minutes. Place the wings on plates to serve. Serve with a cashew mixture on top.
Per serving: Calories 233; Fat 20g; Sodium 233mg; Carbs 15g; Fiber 2g; Sugar 11g; Protein 2g

Chicken with Honey and Wine

Prep time: 5 minutes| Cook time: 15 minutes| Serves: 4

2 chicken breasts, rinsed and	¾ teaspoon sea salt, or to taste
halved	1 teaspoon paprika
1 tablespoon melted butter	1 teaspoon dried rosemary
½ teaspoon freshly ground	2 tablespoons dry white wine
pepper, or to taste	1 tablespoon honey

To begin, blot the chicken breasts dry using a paper towel. Using the melted butter, lightly coat them. After that, combine the remaining ingredients. Place them in the cooking tray and select Bake function. Set time to 15 minutes and temperature to 365 degrees F. Bake for 15 minutes at 365 degrees F. Warm it up and enjoy it!
Per serving: Calories 189; Fat 14g; Sodium 568mg; Carbs 3.2g; Fiber 0.1g; Sugar 1g; Protein 11g

Brie, Ham and Chicken Fillet

Prep time: 5 minutes| Cook time: 15 minutes| Serves: 4

2 large chicken fillets	1 tablespoon freshly chopped
freshly ground black pepper	chives
4 small slices of brie (or your	4 slices cured ham
cheese of choice)	

Cut the fillets into four pieces and make incisions like a hamburger bun. At the rear, leave a little "hinge" uncut. Season the interior and stuff it with brie and chives. Put a piece of ham around each one. Brush them with oil before placing them in the cooking tray. Preheat the air fryer to 400 degrees F and select Air Fry function and set the timer for 15 minutes. Roast the little packages until they appear to be delicious (15 minutes)
Per serving: Calories 375; Fat 18.3g; Sodium 553mg; Carbs 0.8g; Fiber 0.1g; Sugar 0.1g; Protein 49.2g

Chicken Buttermilk

Prep time: 5 minutes| Cook time: 55 minutes| Serves: 2

½ teaspoon cayenne pepper	8 ounces panko breadcrumbs
200 ml buttermilk	2 sweet potatoes, sliced into
1 teaspoon garlic, minced	chips
2 pieces chicken breast fillet	1 tablespoon sweet smoked
4 tablespoons flour	paprika
Salt and pepper to taste	1 tablespoon olive oil
1 egg, beaten	

Combine the cayenne pepper, buttermilk, and garlic in a mixing bowl. Marinate chicken breasts for 2 hours or overnight in this mixture. Preheat your air fryer for about 3 minutes. Using salt and pepper, season the flour. Using seasoned flour, dredge the chicken. Coat with breadcrumbs after dipping in the beaten egg. Select Air Fry function. Set time to 20 minutes and temperature to 400 degrees F. Cook the chicken in the air fryer. Paprika and oil should be used to coat the sweet potato chips. Cook again for 20 minutes in the air fryer at Air Fry function at 400 degrees F. To ensure uniform cooking, give it a good shake. Serve the chicken with sweet potatoes on the side.
Per serving: Calories 934; Fat 16g; Sodium 980mg; Carbs 79.5g; Fiber 6.5g; Sugar 5.4g; Protein 58.4g

Avocado Mix Chicken

Prep time: 5 minutes| Cook time: 20 minutes| Serves: 2

2 cups chicken	2 radish (sliced)
½ avocado (sliced)	parsley (chopped) for dressing
salt and pepper to taste	

Slice the chicken and toss it into the bowl. Place the radish slices and avocado slices on top of the chicken. When it's done, add the parsley and stir it in. Place it in the air fryer with the cooking tray. Select Air Fry function. Set time to 14 minutes and temperature to 400 degrees F. Cook for 14 minutes. When the salad is done, season it with salt and pepper before serving.

Per serving: Calories 227; Fat 8g; Sodium 200mg; Carbs 19g; Fiber 7g; Sugar 11g; Protein 20g

Coconut, Turmeric Chicken

Prep time: 5 minutes| Cook time: 27 minutes| Serves: 3

1 ½ ounces coconut milk
3 teaspoons ginger, grated
4 teaspoons ground turmeric

½ teaspoon sea salt
3 chicken legs (skin removed)

Combine the coconut milk, ginger, turmeric, and salt in a large mixing bowl. Make a few slits in the flesh of the bird. Marinate the chicken for 4 hours in the mixture. Store in the refrigerator. Preheat the air fryer. Select Air Fry function. Set time to 10 minutes and temperature to 400 degrees F. Cook for 10 minutes on one side. Cook for another 10 to 12 minutes on the other side.
Per serving: Calories 112; Fat 6.5g; Sodium 390mg; Carbs 4g; Fiber 0.1g; Sugar 0.1g; Protein 9.6g

Chicken Strip Crunchy Curry

Prep time: 5 minutes| Cook time: 25 minutes| Serves: 4

12 ounces chicken breast, cut into strips
salt and pepper to taste
1 egg, beaten

¼ cup whole wheat flour
½ cup panko breadcrumbs
¼ cup curry powder

Sprinkle the salt and pepper over the chicken pieces. Each chicken strip should be floured first, then dipped in the egg. Combine the curry powder and breadcrumbs in a mixing dish. Using the curry powder mixture, coat each of the chicken strips. Select Air Fry function. Set time to 10 minutes and temperature to 400 degrees F. Cook for 10 minutes on one side. Cook for another 5 minutes on the other side.
Per serving: Calories 170; Fat 4.1g; Sodium 477mg; Carbs 11.4g; Fiber 1g; Sugar 1.4g; Protein 21.2g

Stir Fried Orange Chicken

Prep time: 5 minutes| Cook time: 30 minutes| Serves: 4

olive oil to mist
1 sliced red onion
1 bell pepper, yellow
¾ pound chicken thighs
3 teaspoons curry powder

1 tablespoon cornstarch
¼ cup orange juice
2 tablespoons honey
¼ cup chicken stock

In the cooking tray, place the red onion, pepper, and chicken thighs, and drizzle with olive oil. Select Air Fry. Set time to 12 minutes and temperature 400 degrees F. Cook chicken 12 minutes. While cooking, shake the tray around a little. Remove the veggies and chicken from the tray and place them on a plate to the side. Combine the curry powder, cornstarch, orange juice, honey, and stock in a metal bowl and stir well. Toss in the veggies and chicken, then place everything in the tray. Select Air Fry function. Set time 10 minutes and temp 400 degrees F. After 10 minutes of cooking when the sauce is thick and bubbling, serve.
Per serving: Calories 230; Fat 7g; Sodium 478mg; Carbs 16g; Fiber 1g; Sugar 2g; Protein 26g

Spicy Chicken Curry

Prep time: 5 minutes| Cook time: 25 minutes| Serves: 4

1 teaspoon olive oil

1 pound chicken breast;

skinless, boneless
½ cup chicken stock
2 tablespoons curry paste
1 onion diced
2 tablespoons minced garlic

1 tablespoon apple cider vinegar
1 tablespoon lemongrass
½ cup coconut milk

Chicken breasts should be cut into cubes. Peel and dice the onion. Then, in the cooking tray, mix the chicken cubes and chopped onion. Preheat the air fryer. Select Air Fry function. Set time to 5 minutes and temperature to 400 degrees F Cook the chicken mixture in the air fryer for 5 minutes. In a separate bowl, combine the minced garlic, apple cider vinegar, lemongrass, coconut milk, chicken stock, and curry paste. Using a wooden spatula, combine the ingredients. Continue to cook the chicken curry for another 10 minutes at the same temperature of Air Fry function. Remove the chicken curry from the air fryer when the timer goes off and it is done cooking. Place the dish on the serving plates now.
Per serving: Calories 275; Fat 15g; Sodium 569mg; Carbs 7.2g; Fiber 1g; Sugar 0.1g; Protein 25.6g

Pandan Chicken

Prep time: 5 minutes| Cook time: 30 minutes| Serves: 4

15 ounces chicken
1 Pandan leaf
½ onion diced
1 teaspoon turmeric
1 tablespoon butter
¼ cup coconut milk

1 tablespoon chives
1 teaspoon minced garlic
1 teaspoon chili flakes
1 teaspoon Stevie
1 teaspoon ground black pepper

The chicken should be cut into four large pieces. In a large mixing basin, place the chicken chunks. Mix the minced garlic, chopped onion, chili flakes, Stevie, ground black pepper, chives, and turmeric into the chicken. Using your hands, combine the meat. After that, chop the Pandan leaf into four pieces. Pandan leaf is used to wrap the chicken cubes. Place the wrapped chicken in a dish with the coconut milk and let aside for 10 minutes. To preheat the air fryer, select Air Fry function. Set time to 10 minutes and temperature to 400 degrees F. Press Start to begin. In the cooking tray, place the Pandan chicken and cook for 10 minutes. When the chicken is done, move it to serving dishes and refrigerate for at least 2-3 minutes before serving.
Per serving: Calories 250; Fat 12.6g; Sodium 750mg; Carbs 3.1g; Fiber 0.1g; Sugar 0.1g; Protein 29.9g

Rosemary Chicken with Lemon and Garlic

Prep time: 5 minutes| Cook time: 27 minutes| Serves: 2

2 chicken thighs (skin removed)
Sea salt and pepper to taste
1 tablespoon lemon juice

3 teaspoons dried rosemary
3 cloves garlic, crushed and minced
1 teaspoon olive oil

Using the sea salt, pepper, lemon juice, and dried rosemary, season the chicken thighs. Marinate for 1 hour. Meanwhile, heat the olive oil and sauté the smashed garlic. Select Air Fry function. Cook the chicken thighs in the air fryer by setting time to 12 minutes and temperature to 400 degrees F. Cook for 6 minutes on each side by flipping the chicken. Before serving, drizzle the garlic oil over the chicken.
Per serving: Calories 188; Fat 12.3g; Sodium 450mg; Carbs 3.2g; Fiber 0.1g; Sugar 0.1g; Protein 16g

Easy Chicken Pie

Prep time: 5 minutes| Cook time: 31 minutes| Serves: 8-10

2 chicken thighs (boneless, sliced into cubes)
1 teaspoon reduced-sodium soy sauce
1 onion, diced
1 carrot, diced
2 potatoes, diced

1 cup mushrooms
1 teaspoon garlic powder
1 teaspoon flour
½ cup milk
2 hard-boiled eggs, sliced in half
2 sheets puff pastry

Season the chicken cubes with the low sodium soy sauce. Sauté the onions, carrots, and potatoes in a pan over low heat. Combine the chicken cubes and mushrooms in a large mixing bowl. Add the garlic powder, flour, and milk and season with salt and pepper. Mix thoroughly. Place the pastry sheet on the cooking tray. Use a fork to poke holes in it. On top of the pastry sheet, arrange the eggs. On top of the eggs, pour the chicken mixture. Place the second pastry layer on top. Press a little harder. Select Air Fry function. Set time to 6 minutes and temperature to 400 degrees F. Cook in air fryer. Serve by slicing into numerous pieces.

Per serving: Calories 114; Fat 3.4g; Sodium 500mg; Carbs 9.7g; Fiber 2g; Sugar 1.9g; Protein 11.2g

Turkey Breast in Air Fryer

Prep time: 10 minutes| Cook time: 40 minutes| Serves: 6

2 ¾ pounds turkey breast
2 tablespoons unsalted butter
1 tablespoon chopped fresh rosemary
1 teaspoon chopped fresh

chives
1 teaspoon minced fresh garlic
¼ teaspoon black pepper
½ teaspoon salt

Preheat the air fryer to 400 degrees F. Combine chives, rosemary, garlic, salt, and pepper in a mixing bowl. Using a pastry cutter, cut in the butter and mash until thoroughly combined. Select Air Fry function. Set timer to 40 minutes and temperature 400 degrees F. Rub the herbed butter all over the turkey breast and place it in the cooking tray; cook for 20 minutes. Cook for another 20 minutes after turning the turkey breast. Wrap the cooked turkey in aluminum foil and let it to rest for at least 10 minutes before slicing. Warm the dish before serving.

Per serving: Calories 263; Fat 10.1g; Sodium 290mg; Carbs 0.3g; Fiber 0.1g; Sugar 0.1g; Protein 40.2g

Lemon Olive Chicken in Air Fryer

Prep time: 10 minutes| Cook time: 15 minutes| Serves: 4

4 boneless skinless chicken breasts
½ teaspoon organic cumin
1 teaspoon sea salt (real salt)
¼ teaspoon black pepper
½ cup butter, melted

1 lemon, ½ juiced, ½ thinly sliced
1 cup chicken bone-broth
1 can pitted green olives
½ cup red onions, sliced

Season the chicken breasts liberally with salt, cumin, and black pepper. Preheat your air fryer and brush the chicken breasts with melted butter. Select Air Fry function. Set time to 15 minutes and temperature to 400 degrees F Cook for around 5 minutes in the pan of your air fryer, until uniformly toasted. Cook for 10 minutes at 400 degrees F with the remaining ingredients. Serve immediately!

Per serving: Calories 310; Fat 9.4g; Sodium 660mg; Carbs 10.2g; Fiber 3g; Sugar 1.5g; Protein 21.8g

Mustard Vinaigrette Chicken

Prep time: 15 minutes| Cook time: 10 minutes| Serves: 1

Salad:
250g chicken breast
1 cup shaved Brussels sprouts
2 cups baby spinach
2 cups mixed greens
½ avocado sliced
1 segments of orange
1 teaspoon raw pumpkin seeds
1 teaspoon toasted almonds
1 teaspoon hemp seeds

Dressing:
½ shallot, chopped
1 garlic clove, chopped
2 teaspoons balsamic vinegar
1 teaspoon extra virgin olive oil
½ cup fresh orange juice
1 teaspoon Dijon mustard
1 teaspoon raw honey
fresh ground pepper

Blend all dressing ingredients until smooth in a blender; put aside. Oil the cooking tray. To preheat your air fryer, select Air Fry function. Set time to 10 minute and temperature to 400 degrees F. Press Start to begin. Cook for 10 minutes, 5 minutes per side, with the chicken breasts in the tray. Remove the tray from the air fryer and place it on a platter. Allow for 5 minutes of resting time before cutting into bite-sized bits. In a large mixing basin, combine all salad ingredients; sprinkle with dressing and toss to coat well before serving.

Per serving: Calories 457; Fat 37g; Sodium 760mg; Carbs 13.6g; Fiber 3g; Sugar 2.5g; Protein 31.8g

Chicken Wings with Lemon Pepper

Prep time: 10 minutes| Cook time: 20 minutes| Serves: 4

8 whole chicken wings
½ lemon Juice
½ teaspoon garlic powder
1 teaspoon onion powder

salt and pepper
¼ cup low-fat buttermilk
½ cup all-purpose flour
Cooking oil

Place the wings in a plastic bag that can be sealed. Drizzle lemon juice over the wings. Garlic powder, onion powder, and salt and pepper to taste should be used to season the wings. Close the bag. To mix the ingredients and coat the wings, give it a good shake. Fill separate basins with buttermilk and flour large enough to dip the wings in. Cooking oil should be sprayed on the cooking tray. Dip the wings in buttermilk and then flour one at a time. Place the wings in the cooking tray of the air fryer. Select Air Fry function. Set time to 20 minutes and temperature to 400 degrees F. It's ok to stack them on top of one another. Cooking oil should be sprayed on the bottom layer of the wings. Halfway flip the wings every 5 minutes in the air fryer. Remove the tray from the air fryer and shake it to verify that all of the pieces are completely cooked. Continue to cook the chicken in the tray of the air fryer. Shake the container every 5 minutes for a total of 20 minutes. Allow to cool before serving.

Per serving: Calories 347; Fat 12g; Sodium 440mg; Carbs 1g; Fiber 1g; Sugar 0.1g; Protein 46g

Cheese and Leek Tomato Sauce Chicken

Prep time: 10 minutes| Cook time: 20 minutes| Serves: 4

2 large-sized chicken breasts, cut in half lengthwise
Salt and ground black pepper, to taste
4 ounces Cheddar cheese, cut into sticks
1 tablespoon sesame oil

1 cup leeks, chopped
2 cloves garlic, minced
⅔ cup roasted vegetable stock
⅔ cup tomato puree
1 teaspoon dried rosemary
1 teaspoon dried thyme

Season the chicken breasts with salt & pepper, then lay a slice of Cheddar cheese in the centre. Then, with a kitchen string drizzled with sesame oil, knot it and set it aside. In an air fryer-safe bowl, combine the leeks and garlic. Select Air Fry function. Set time to 5 minutes and temperature to 400 degrees F. Cook for 5 minutes in an air fryer until tender. Return the chicken to the air fryer. Add the other ingredients and simmer for another 12 to 13 minutes, or until the chicken is done. Enjoy.
Per serving: Calories 257.7; Fat 1.5g; Sodium 90mg; Carbs 40.8g; Fiber 6.2g; Sugar 7.5g; Protein 22.1g

Fried Chicken Wings in Air Fryer

Prep time: 10 minutes| Cook time: 25 minutes| Serves: 3

1 ½ pounds chicken wings
⅓ cup grated Parmesan cheese
⅓ cup breadcrumbs
⅛ teaspoon garlic powder
⅛ teaspoon onion powder
¼ cup melted butter
Salt and black pepper to taste
Cooking spray

Spray a cooking tray with nonstick cooking spray. Combine Parmesan cheese, garlic powder, onion powder, black pepper, breadcrumbs, and salt in a large mixing bowl. Stir everything together thoroughly. One at a time, dip chicken wings into melted butter and then into the bread mixture until completely covered. Arrange the wings on the cooking tray in a single layer. Select Air Fry function. Set time to 20 minutes and temperature to 400 degrees F. Cook for 10 minutes on one side. Cook for another 10 minutes on the other side, until the wings are no longer pink in the middle and the juices flow clear. Remove from the air fryer as soon as possible and serve.
Per serving: Calories 371; Fat 22.6g; Sodium 443mg; Carbs 11.8g; Fiber 1g; Sugar 2g; Protein 27.8g

Beer Chicken

Prep time: 10 minutes| Cook time: 40 minutes| Serves: 4

Brine
2 cups water
2 cans beer
¼ cup kosher salt
½ cup brown sugar
8 thyme sprigs
3 pounds whole chicken, cleaned
Rub
2 teaspoons paprika
1 tablespoon thyme, dried
½ teaspoon salt
¼ teaspoon onion powder
¼ teaspoon garlic powder
¼ teaspoon freshly ground black pepper
2 tablespoons extra-virgin olive oil

In a saucepan, bring 1 cup of water to a low heat. In a saucepan of hot water, dissolve the kosher salt, sugar, and thyme. To make the brine, add 1 cup of water and the beer. Overnight in the brine, marinate the chicken. In a mixing dish, combine the rub ingredients. After removing the chicken from the brine, pat it dry. Apply the rub to the chicken after brushing it with olive oil. Place chicken in cooking tray. Select Air Fry mode. Set temperature to 400 degrees F and time to 30 minutes then cook.
Per serving: Calories 311; Fat 11g; Sodium 390mg; Carbs 22g; Fiber 4g; Sugar 3.7g; Protein 31g

Glazed Balsamic Chicken

Prep time: 10 minutes| Cook time: 19 minutes| Serves: 6

Balsamic Glaze
⅔ cup balsamic vinegar
2 cloves garlic, grated
¼ cup Dijon mustard
¼ cup honey
1 teaspoon. salt
½ teaspoon. freshly ground black pepper
1 cup extra virgin olive oil
small boneless and skinless chicken breasts

In a mixing bowl, combine the balsamic vinegar, garlic, Dijon mustard, honey, salt, and pepper. To emulsify the glaze, drizzle the olive oil into it while whisking. Refrigerate the chicken breasts for 45 minutes after marinating them in the marinade. Select Air Fry function. Set the time to 30 minutes and temperature to 400 degrees F. Press Start to begin cooking. While the chicken is cooking, brush it with the glaze every 10 minutes. Carefully remove the chicken using the fetch tool.
Per serving: Calories 127; Fat 0.5g; Sodium 450mg; Carbs 2.7g; Fiber 0.1g; Sugar 0.1g; Protein 26g

Rosemary Paprika Style Chicken

Prep time: 5 minutes| Cook time: 80 minutes and marinating time| Serves: 4

1 (3 ½- 4 pound) whole chicken
2 tablespoons salt
2 cups buttermilk
1 teaspoon lime juice
3 tablespoons butter, melted
1 tablespoon paprika
black pepper and sea salt to taste

In a large mixing basin, combine the salt, lemon juice, and buttermilk and stir until the salt is completely dissolved. Submerge the chicken in the water. Refrigerate the bowl for 2 hours or overnight after covering it. Remove the chicken from the refrigerator, toss off the marinade, and wipe dry with kitchen towels. Brush the legs with butter after tying them with butcher's twine. Paprika, sea salt, and black pepper should be applied to the top and sides of the chicken. Place the chicken in the air fryer. Select the Roast mode on your air fryer and set the temperature to 380 degrees F and time to 50 minutes. Start testing for doneness with a meat thermometer around 10-15 minutes before the end of the recommended cooking time. The internal temperature of the chicken should be 165 degrees F. Remove the chicken from the air fryer with the removal tool when it is fully cooked. Place the chicken on a chopping board and carefully remove it off the pole using gloves. Before carving, cover with foil and set aside for 10-15 minutes. Warm the dish before serving.
Per serving: Calories 160; Fat 11g; Sodium 360mg; Carbs 0.1g; Fiber 0g; Sugar 0g; Protein 14g

Yogurt Sauce and Harrisa Chicken

Prep time: 5 minutes| Cook time: 80 minutes and marinating time| Serves: 4

2 cups sour cream
salt and black pepper to taste
3 tablespoons olive oil
3 cloves garlic, minced
2 teaspoons harissa seasoning
1 teaspoon dried dill
1 teaspoon dried tarragon
1 (4-pound) whole chicken
Yogurt Sauce:
2 tablespoons olive oil
Salt to taste
¼ teaspoon red pepper flakes, crushed
1 cup full-fat yogurt
1 teaspoon dried dill weed

Combine all of the sauce's components and chill until ready to use. Pour the sour cream over the chicken in a large mixing basin. Refrigerate for 2-3 hours after covering with a lid. Remove the chicken from the refrigerator and set it aside to come to room temperature for 30 minutes. Remove the chicken from the marinade and set it aside. Butcher's twine is used to tie the legs together. Whisk together the olive oil, garlic, paprika, sage, thyme, tarragon, salt, and pepper to taste in a small bowl. Apply the mixture to the top and sides of the chicken. Select the Roast mode on your air fryer and set the temperature to 380 degrees F with a 60-minute cooking duration. In the air fryer, place the chicken. To begin cooking, press Start. Remove the pan from the air fryer after the cooking is finished. Before carving, cover with foil and set aside for 10-15 minutes. Serve the chicken with a yoghurt sauce that has been cooled.

Roasted Spicy Chicken

Prep time: 5 minutes| Cook time: 75 minutes and marinating time| Serves: 4

1 (4 pound) whole chicken
4 tablespoons olive oil
1 tablespoon ground coriander
2 teaspoons garlic powder

1 teaspoon onion powder
1 teaspoon chili pepper
1 tablespoon allspice

In a large zip-lock bag, add the olive oil, coriander, garlic powder, onion powder, chili pepper, and allspice; shake well to blend. Massage the chicken in the bag to coat it. Refrigerate for 30 minutes to enable the flavors to meld. On the air fryer, choose the Roast function and set the temperature to 380 degrees F and time to 40 minutes. To begin cooking, press Start.
Remove the chicken from the bag and place it in the air fryer. Roast for 40 minutes, or until the skin of the chicken is golden and burnt, rotating the bird halfway through. Using a meat thermometer, check for doneness. Remove the chicken from the spit and set aside for 10 minutes before serving.
Per serving: Calories 127; Fat 0.5g; Sodium 390mg; Carbs 3.2g; Fiber 0.1g; Sugar 0.1g; Protein 26g

Spiced Whole Chicken

Prep time: 10 minutes| Cook time: 45 minutes| Serves: 4

3 pounds (1.4 kg) tied whole chicken
3 cloves garlic, halved
1 whole lemon, quartered
2 sprigs fresh rosemary whole
2 tablespoons olive oil
Chicken Rub:
½ teaspoon fresh ground

pepper
½ teaspoon salt
1 teaspoon garlic powder
1 teaspoon dried oregano
1 teaspoon paprika
1 spring rosemary (leaves only)

In a small dish, combine the rub ingredients. Remove from the equation. Place the chicken on a chopping board that has been cleaned. Make sure the chicken's cavity is clean. Garlic, lemon, and rosemary should be stuffed into the cavity of the bird. If necessary, tie your bird with thread. Dry the chicken with a paper towel. Drizzle the olive oil all over the chicken and use a brush to coat it completely. Rub the rub into the chicken until it is completely coated. To preheat the air fryer to 400 degrees F, select Air Fry mode, and set the temperature to 400 degrees F. Set the timer for 40 minutes. To begin preheating, choose Start. Place the prepared chicken into the air fryer when the display shows "Add Food". Check the temperature every 5 minutes while cooking, or until the chicken reaches 165 degrees F (74 degrees Celsius) in the breast and 165 degrees F (85 degrees Celsius) in the thigh. After the chicken has finished roasting, carefully remove it from the spit. Allow the chicken to rest for 5 to 10 minutes, covered. Slice and serve.
Per serving: Calories 160; Fat 11g; Sodium 360mg; Carbs 0.1g; Fiber 0g; Sugar 0g; Protein 14g

Montreal Chicken and Cornish Hen

Prep time: 5 minutes| Cook time: 30 minutes| Serves: 2

2 tablespoons Montreal chicken seasoning

1 (1½- to 2-pound / 680- to 907-g) Cornish hen

Preheat the air fryer to 380 degrees F and select Roast function. Rub the spice all over the chicken, making sure it's well covered. Place the chicken in the air fryer. Set the timer for 30 minutes

and roast on one side. Roast for another 15 minutes after flipping the chicken. Check that the chicken has achieved a temperature of 165 degrees F on the inside (74 degrees Celsius). If necessary, increase the cooking time.
Per serving: Calories 220; Fat 16g; Sodium 70mg; Carbs 0.1g; Fiber 0g; Sugar 0g; Protein 19g

Air Fryer Roasted Cornish Hen

Prep time: 6 minutes| Cook time: 20 minutes| Serves: 2

½ cup olive oil
1 teaspoon chopped fresh rosemary
1 teaspoon chopped fresh thyme
1 teaspoon grated fresh lemon zest

¼ teaspoon sugar
¼ teaspoon crushed red pepper flakes
salt and ground black pepper, as required
2 pounds Cornish game hen, backbone removed and halved

Combine the oil, herbs, lemon zest, sugar, and spices in a mixing bowl. Add the hen pieces and liberally cover them in the marinade. Refrigerate for at least 24 hours after covering. Place the hen pieces in a colander and put aside to drain any liquid. Place the hen pieces on the oiled cooking tray. Select "Air Fry" and set the temperature to 400 degrees F. Set the timer for 20 minutes and hit the "Start" button. Place the cooking tray in the air fryer when the display says "Add Food." Do not flip the food when the display says "Turn Food." Remove the hen pieces when the cooking time is up. Serve immediately.
Per serving: Calories 665; Fat 57.7g; Sodium 780mg; Carbs 0.8g; Fiber 0.1g; Sugar 0.1g; Protein 38.5g

Roasted Chicken Cajun

Prep time: 10 minutes| Cook time: 1 hour and 30 minutes| Serves: 6

¼ cup butter, softened
2 teaspoons dried rosemary
2 teaspoons dried thyme
1 tablespoon Cajun seasoning
1 tablespoon onion powder
1 tablespoon garlic powder

1 tablespoon paprika
1 teaspoon cayenne pepper
salt, as required
1 (3-pound) whole chicken, neck and giblets removed

Combine the butter, herbs, spices, and salt in a mixing dish. Rub the spice mixture all over the chicken. Tie the wings and legs together using kitchen thread. Place the chicken on a prepared baking sheet. Place it in cooking tray. Select "Roast" and set the temperature to 380 degrees F. Set the timer for 70 minutes and hit the "Start" button. Place the cooking tray in air fryer when the display says "Add Food." Do not flip the food when the display says "Turn Food." Remove the cooking tray after the cooking time is over. Before slicing, place the chicken on a plate for 10 minutes. Cut the chicken into desired-sized pieces with a sharp knife and serve.
Per serving: Calories 421; Fat 14.8g; Sodium 540mg; Carbs 2.3g; Fiber 0.1g; Sugar 0.1g; Protein 66.3g

Spicy Chicken Roasted in Air Fryer

Prep time: 10 minutes| Cook time: 40 minutes| Serves: 6

1 teaspoon dried oregano
1 teaspoon dried rosemary
1 teaspoon paprika
1 teaspoon garlic powder
salt and ground black pepper, as required

1 (3-pound) whole chicken, neck and giblets removed
1 lemon, quartered
3 garlic cloves, halved
2 fresh rosemary sprigs
2 tablespoons olive oil

Combine the dried herbs, spices, salt, and black pepper in a small bowl. Fill the cavity of the bird with lemon, garlic, and rosemary sprigs. Tie the bird with kitchen twine. Apply a thin layer of oil to the chicken and then massage in the herb mixture. Select "Roast" and set the temperature to 380 degrees F. Set the timer for 40 minutes and hit the "Start" button. Place the peprared chicken into the air fryer when the display says "Add Food." Carefully remove the chicken from the air fryer after the cooking time is up. Remove the chicken onto a pan and set it aside for 5-10 minutes before cutting. Cut the chicken into desired-sized pieces with a sharp knife and serve.

Per serving: Calories 389; Fat 11.7g; Sodium 390mg; Carbs 1.6g; Fiber 0.1g; Sugar 0.1g; Protein 66g

Chicken Roasted with Buttermilk

Prep time: 10 minutes| Cook time: 50 minutes| Serves: 6

2 cups buttermilk	3 pounds whole chicken neck
¼ cup olive oil	and giblets removed
1 teaspoon garlic powder	Ground black pepper, as
salt, as required	required

Combine the buttermilk, oil, garlic powder, and 1 tablespoon. salt in a large re-sealable bag. Seal the bag securely after adding the whole chicken. Refrigerate for up to two days to marinate. Using paper towels, blot the chicken dry after removing it from the bag. Season the chicken with black pepper and salt. Tie the wings and legs together using kitchen thread. Place the chicken inside the air fryer basket. Select "Air Fry" and set the temperature to 400 degrees F. Set the timer for 50 minutes and hit the "Start" button. Arrange the air fryer basket in the air fryer when the display says "Add Food." Carefully remove the chicken from the air fryer after the cooking time is up. Before carving, remove the chicken onto a pan and lay it on a dish for roughly 10 minutes. Cut the chicken into desired-sized pieces with a sharp knife and serve.

Per serving: Calories 449; Fat 16g; Sodium 450mg; Carbs 4.3g; Fiber 0.1g; Sugar 0.1g; Protein 68.5g

Chicken Leg in Air Fryer

Prep time: 7 minutes| Cook time: 25 minutes| Serves: 6

2½ pounds chicken legs	½ teaspoon ground cumin
2 tablespoons olive oil	salt and ground black pepper,
1 teaspoon smoked paprika	as required
1 teaspoon garlic powder	

In a mixing dish, combine all of the ingredients and stir thoroughly. Arrange the chicken legs evenly on two oiled cooking trays. Place the drip pan in the cooking chamber of the air fryer. Select "Air Fry" and set the temperature to 400 degrees F. Set the timer for 25 minutes and hit the "Start" button. Insert one tray in the top position and the other in the bottom position when the display says "Add Food." When the display says "turn Food," don't turn the food; instead, swap the cooking trays. Remove from the air fryer when the cooking time is up. Serve immediately.

Per serving: Calories 402; Fat 18.8g; Sodium 390mg; Carbs 0.6g; Fiber 0.1g; Sugar 0.1g; Protein 54.8g

Chicken Drumsticks Spicy Herbed

Prep time: 5 minutes| Cook time: 20 minutes| Serves: 4

2 tablespoons olive oil	rosemary
½ teaspoon crushed dried thyme	½ teaspoon crushed dried oregano
½ teaspoon crushed dried	salt and ground black pepper,

as required
4 (6-ounce) chicken

drumsticks

Combine the oil, herbs, salt, and black pepper in a large mixing basin. Add the chicken drumsticks and liberally cover them in the mixture. In the air fryer basket, arrange the chicken drumsticks and secure the cover. Select "Air Fry" and set the temperature to 400 degrees F. Set the timer for 20 minutes and hit the "Start" button. Place the air fryer basket in the air fryer when the display says "Add Food." Carefully remove the chicken drumsticks from the basket after the cooking time is up. Serve immediately.

Per serving: Calories 349; Fat 16.8g; Sodium 560mg; Carbs 0.3g; Fiber 0.1g; Sugar 0.1g; Protein 46.8g

Chicken Drumsticks with Ginger Flavoring

Prep time: 5 minutes| Cook time: 25 minutes| Serves: 3

¼ cup full-fat coconut milk	2 teaspoons ground turmeric
2 teaspoons fresh ginger minced	Salt, as required
2 teaspoons fresh galangal minced	3 (6-ounce) chicken drumsticks

Combine the coconut milk, galangal, ginger, and spices in a large mixing basin and stir well. Add the chicken drumsticks and liberally cover them in the marinade. Refrigerate for at least 6-8 hours to marinate. Place the chicken drumsticks on a prepared cooking tray. Select "Air Fry" and set the temperature to 400 degrees F. Set the timer for 25 minutes and hit the "Start" button. Place the cooking tray in the centre position when the display says "Add Food." Turn the chicken drumsticks when the display says "Turn Food." Transfer the chicken drumsticks to a plate after the cooking time is over. Serve immediately.

Per serving: Calories 347; Fat 14.8g; Sodium 333mg; Carbs 3.8g; Fiber 0.1g; Sugar 0.2g; Protein 47.6g

Chicken Drumstick Fully Glazed

Prep time: 5 minutes| Cook time: 20 minutes| Serves: 4

¼ cups Dijon mustard	minced
1 tablespoon honey	salt and ground black pepper,
2 tablespoons olive oil	as required
1 tablespoon fresh thyme minced	4 (6 ounce) boneless chicken drumsticks
½ tablespoon fresh rosemary	

All of the ingredients, except the drumsticks, should be mixed thoroughly in a mixing basin. Add the drumsticks and liberally cover them in the mixture. Refrigerate the bowl overnight to let the flavors to meld. Place the chicken drumsticks on a prepared cooking tray. Place the drip pan in the cooking chamber of the air fryer. Select "Air Fry" and set the temperature to 400 degrees F. Set the timer for 20 minutes and hit the "Start" button. Place the cooking tray in the centre position when the display says "Add Food". Transfer the chicken drumsticks to a plate after the cooking time is over.

Per serving: Calories 377; Fat 17.5g; Sodium 445mg; Carbs 5.9g; Fiber 0.1g; Sugar 0.1g; Protein 47.6g

Simple Thigh Chicken

Prep time: 5 minutes| Cook time: 20 minutes| Serves: 2

4 (4 ounce) skinless, boneless   chicken thighs

salt and ground black pepper, as required   2 tablespoons butter melted

Season the chicken thighs evenly with salt and black pepper, then brush them with melted butter. Place the chicken thighs on a greased cooking tray. Place the drip pan in the cooking chamber of the air fryer. Select "Roast" and set the temperature to 380 degrees F. Press "Start" to start the timer for 20 minutes. Place the cooking tray in the centre position when the display says "Add Food". Remove the chicken from air fryer after the cooking time is over. Serve immediately.
Per serving: Calories 183; Fat 9.8g; Sodium 230mg; Carbs 0g; Fiber 0g; Sugar 0g; Protein 25.4g

Thigh Chicken Fully Spiced

Prep time: 5 minutes| Cook time: 20 minutes| Serves: 2

1 teaspoon garlic powder
1 teaspoon ground cumin
½ teaspoon ground coriander
½ teaspoon smoked paprika

Salt and ground black pepper, as required
4 (5 ounce) chicken thighs
2 tablespoons olive oil

Combine the spices, salt, and black pepper in a large mixing basin and stir well. Rub the chicken thighs with the spice mixture after coating them in oil. Place the chicken thighs on a greased cooking tray. Place the drip pan in the cooking chamber of the air fryer. Select "Air Fry" and set the temperature to 400 degrees F. Press "Start" to start the timer for 20 minutes. Place the cooking tray in the centre position when the display says "Add Food." Turn the chicken thighs when the display says "Turn Food." Transfer the chicken thighs to a plate after the cooking time is over. Serve immediately.
Per serving: Calories 334; Fat 17.7g; Sodium 507mg; Carbs 0.9g; Fiber 0.1g; Sugar 0.1g; Protein 41.3g

Chicken Breast Crisped

Prep time: 8 minutes| Cook time: 40 minutes| Serves: 3

¼ cup flour
Salt and ground black pepper, as required
1 large egg, beaten

¼ cup fresh cilantro, chopped
1 cup Croutons, crushed
3 (5-ounce) boneless, skinless chicken breasts

Combine flour, salt, and black pepper in a small bowl and stir thoroughly. Combine the egg and cilantro in a second shallow dish. Place croutons in a third shallow dish. Coat the chicken breasts in flour, then dip them in eggs, and then coat them in croutons. Place the chicken breasts on a greased cooking tray. Place the drip pan in the cooking chamber of the air fryer. Select "Roast" and set the temperature to 380 degrees F. Set the timer for 40 minutes and hit the "Start" button. Place the cooking tray in the centre position when the display says "Add Food". Remove the cooking tray after the cooking time is over. Serve immediately.
Per serving: Calories 372; Fat 12.9g; Sodium 605mg; Carbs 15.5g; Fiber 1g; Sugar 0.9g; Protein 45.4g

Cheese Loaded Chicken Wings

Prep time: 5 minutes| Cook time: 25 minutes| Serves: 4

4 tablespoons Parmesan cheese grated
2 tablespoons cornstarch
1 tablespoon garlic powder

salt and ground black pepper, as required
1½ pounds chicken wings
Nonstick cooking spray

Combine the Parmesan cheese, cornstarch, garlic powder, salt, and black pepper in a mixing dish and stir well. Add the chicken

wings and thoroughly cover them in the mixture. Place the chicken wings on a prepared cooking tray. Place the drip pan in the cooking chamber of the air fryer. Select "Air Fry" and set the temperature to 400 degrees F. Set the timer for 25 minutes and hit the "Start" button. Place the cooking tray in the centre position when the display says "Add Food." Using cooking spray, coat the tops of the chicken wings. Turn the chicken wings when the display says "Turn Food." Remove from the air fryer when the cooking time is up. Serve right away.
Per serving: Calories 363; Fat 13.8g; Sodium 657mg; Carbs 5.2g; Fiber 1g; Sugar 0.1g; Protein 51.6g

Wings of Chicken with Full Spices

Prep time: 5 minutes| Cook time: 30 minutes| Serves: 3

1 tablespoon granulated garlic
1 low-sodium chicken bouillon cube
1 tablespoon garlic and herb seasoning blend
ground black pepper, as required

1 teaspoon smoked paprika
1 teaspoon cayenne pepper
1 teaspoon old bay seasoning
1 teaspoon onion powder
½ teaspoon dried oregano
1 pound chicken wings
Nonstick cooking spray

Combine all ingredients in a mixing basin, except the chicken wings and cooking spray, and stir well. Half of the spice mixture should be rubbed into the chicken wings, and cooking spray should be used liberally. Place the chicken wings on a cooking tray. Place the drip pan in the cooking chamber of the air fryer. Select "Air Fry" and set the temperature to 400 degrees F. Press "Start" after setting the timer for 19 minutes. Place the cooking tray in the centre position when the display says "Add Food." Turn the chicken wings when the display says "Turn Food." Remove the trays after the cooking time is over. Transfer the wings into the bowl and cover with the remaining spice mixture and toss to coat well. Serve immediately.
Per serving: Calories 315; Fat 11.6g; Sodium 400mg; Carbs 4.9g; Fiber 0.1g; Sugar 0.1g; Protein 44.7g

Sweet and Sour Flavor Wings

Prep time: 5 minutes| Cook time: 25 minutes| Serves: 4

2 pounds chicken wings and drumettes
½ cup ketchup
3 tablespoons white vinegar
2 tablespoons honey

2 tablespoons molasses
½ teaspoon liquid smoke
¼ teaspoon paprika
¼ teaspoon garlic powder
Pinch of cayenne pepper

Arrange the wingettes and drumettes in a single layer on two oiled cooking trays. In the bottom of the air fryer's cooking chamber, place the drip pan. Select "Air Fry" and set the temperature to 400 degrees F. Set the timer for 25 minutes and hit the "Start" button. Insert one tray in the top position and the other in the bottom position when the display says "Add Food." When the display says "turn Food," don't turn the food; instead, swap the two cooking trays. Meanwhile, boil the other ingredients in a small saucepan over medium heat for about 10 minutes, stirring periodically. Remove the trays after the cooking time is over. Toss the chicken wings with the honey mixture in a large mixing basin until well coated. Serve right away.
Per serving: Calories 524; Fat 16.9g; Sodium 657mg; Carbs 24g; Fiber 5.4g; Sugar 3.9g; Protein 66.2g

BBQ Wings of Chicken

Prep time: 4 minutes| Cook time: 19 minutes| Serves: 4

2 pounds chicken wings   1 teaspoon olive oil

1 teaspoon smoked paprika
1 teaspoon garlic powder
salt and ground black pepper,

as required
¼ cup BBQ sauce

Combine the chicken wings, smoked paprika, garlic powder, oil, salt, and pepper in a large mixing basin. Place the chicken wings on a prepared cooking tray. In the bottom of the air fryer's cooking chamber, place the drip pan. Select "Air Fry" and set each temperature to 400 degrees F. Press "Start" after setting the timer for 19 minutes. Place the cooking tray in the centre position when the display says "Add Food." Turn the chicken wings over and cover with BBQ sauce when the display says "Turn Food." Remove the trays after the cooking time is over. Serve right away.

Per serving: Calories 468; Fat 18.1g; Sodium 609mg; Carbs 6.5g; Fiber 1g; Sugar 0.1g; Protein 65.8g

Tender Chicken Parmesan

Prep time: 5 minutes| Cook time: 15 minutes| Serves: 4

½ cup flour
Salt and ground black pepper, as required
2 eggs, beaten
¾ cup Panko breadcrumbs

¾ cup Parmesan cheese, grated finely
1 teaspoon Italian seasoning
8 chicken tenders

Combine flour, salt, and black pepper in a small bowl and stir thoroughly. Place the beaten eggs in a second shallow dish. Combine the breadcrumbs, parmesan cheese, and Italian seasoning in a third shallow dish. Coat the chicken tenders in the flour mixture, then dunk them in the beaten eggs before finishing with the breadcrumb mixture. Arrange the tenders in a single layer on two oiled cooking trays. Place the drip pan in the cooking chamber of the air fryer. Select "Air Fry" and set the temperature to 400 degrees F. Set the timer for 15 minutes and hit the "Start" button. Insert one tray in the top position and the other in the bottom position when the display says "Add Food." Remove the trays after the cooking time is over. Serve immediately.

Per serving: Calories 435; Fat 16.1g; Sodium 609mg; Carbs 15.3g; Fiber 3g; Sugar 2.7g; Protein 43.7g

Chicken Tenders

Prep time: 4 minutes| Cook time: 10 minutes| Serves: 2

8 ounces chicken tenders
1 teaspoon BBQ seasoning

Salt and ground black pepper, as required

BBQ spice, salt, and black pepper are used to season the chicken tenders. Arrange the chicken tenders in a single layer on the oiled cooking tray. Place the drip pan in the cooking chamber of the air fryer. Select "Bake" and set the temperature to 365 degrees F. Set the timer for 10 minutes and hit the "Start" button. Place the rack in the centre position when the display says "Add Food." Turn the chicken tenders when the display says "Turn Food." Remove when the cooking time is up. Serve immediately.

Per serving: Calories 220; Fat 8.4g; Sodium 530mg; Carbs 0.5g; Fiber 0.1g; Sugar 0.1g; Protein 32.8g

Cordon Blue Chicken

Prep time: 7 minutes| Cook time: 30 minutes| Serves: 2

2 (6 ounces) boneless, skinless chicken breast halves
2 (¾ ounces) Deli ham slices
2 Swiss cheese slices

½ cup all-purpose flour
⅛ teaspoon paprika
salt and ground black pepper, as required

1 large egg
2 tablespoons 2% milk
½ cup seasoned breadcrumbs

1 tablespoon olive oil
1 tablespoon butter melted

Prepare a baking dish that will fit in the air fryer by lightly greasing it. Using a meat mallet, pound each chicken breast half to a thickness of 14 inches. Place the chicken breast halves on a flat surface and arrange them. Place 1 ham slice on top of each chicken breast half, then the cheese. Roll up each chicken breast piece and tuck in ends. Secure the rolls with toothpicks. Combine the flour, paprika, salt, and black pepper in a shallow dish. In a second shallow dish, whisk together the egg and milk. Place the breadcrumbs in a third shallow dish. Coat each chicken roll in the flour mixture, then in the egg mixture, and then in breadcrumbs. Heat the oil in a small pan over medium heat and cook the chicken rolls for about 3-5 minutes, or until golden brown on both sides. Place the chicken rolls in the baking dish that has been prepared. Place the drip pan in the cooking chamber of the air fryer. Select "Bake" and set the temperature to 365 degrees F. Set the timer for 25 minutes and hit the "Start" button. Insert the baking dish in the centre position when the display says "Add Food." Remove the baking dish from the air fryer when the cooking time is over. Serve the chicken rolls on serving dishes with melted butter drizzled on top. Serve right away.

Per serving: Calories 672; Fat 28g; Sodium 507mg; Carbs 45.9g; Fiber 7g; Sugar 5.5g; Protein 56.2g

Turkey Breast Full Spicy

Prep time: 10 minutes| Cook time: 45 minutes| Serves: 8

2 tablespoons fresh rosemary chopped
1 teaspoon ground cumin
1 teaspoon ground cinnamon
1 teaspoon smoked paprika

1 teaspoon Cayenne pepper
Salt and ground black pepper, as required
1 (3 pound) Turkey breast

Combine the rosemary, spices, salt, and black pepper in a mixing bowl. Rub the rosemary mixture evenly over the turkey breast. Tie the turkey breast with kitchen twines to keep it compact. Attach the cover to the air fryer basket and place the turkey breast inside. Select "Air Fry" and set the temperature to 400 degrees F. Set the timer for 45 minutes and hit the "Start" button. Place the air fryer basket in the air fryer when the display says "Add Food". Carefully remove the chicken from the air fryer basket after the cooking time is up. Remove the turkey breast from the air fryer and let it aside for 5-10 minutes before slicing. Cut the turkey breast into desired-sized pieces with a sharp knife and serve.

Per serving: Calories 190; Fat 0.9g; Sodium 430mg; Carbs 1g; Fiber 0.1g; Sugar 0.1g; Protein 42.4g

Spicy Duck Breast

Prep time: 5 minutes| Cook time: 20 minutes| Serves: 2

1 cup beer
1 tablespoon olive oil
1 teaspoon mustard
1 tablespoon fresh thyme

chopped
salt and ground black pepper, as required
1 (10½ oz) duck breast

Combine the beer, oil, mustard, thyme, salt, and black pepper in a mixing bowl and stir well. Add the duck breast and liberally cover it with the marinade. Refrigerate for 4 hours after covering the bowl. Place the duck breasts on a greased cooking tray. Place the drip pan in the cooking chamber of the air fryer. Select "Air Fry" and set the temperature to 400 degrees F. Set the timer for 20 minutes and hit the "Start" button. Place the cooking tray in the centre position when the display says "Add Food". Turn the duck breast when the display says "Turn Food." Remove the tray from the air fryer when the cooking time is finished. Before slicing the duck breast, place it on a cutting board for about 5 minutes. Cut the duck breast into desired-sized pieces with a sharp knife and serve.

Per serving: Calories 315; Fat 13.5g; Sodium 776mg; Carbs 5.7g; Fiber 1.2g; Sugar 1g; Protein 33.8g

Garlic Flavor Duck Legs

Prep time: 5 minutes| Cook time: 30 minutes| Serves: 2

2 garlic cloves, minced
1 tablespoon fresh parsley chopped
1 teaspoon five spice powder

Salt and ground black pepper, as required
2 duck legs

Combine the garlic, parsley, five-spice powder, salt, and black pepper in a mixing bowl. Brush the duck legs liberally with the garlic mixture. Place the duck legs on a greased cooking tray. Place the drip pan in the cooking chamber of the air fryer. Select "Air Fry" and set the temperature to 400 degrees F. Set the timer for 30 minutes and hit the "Start" button. Place the cooking tray in the centre position when the display says "Add Food." Turn the duck legs when the display says "Turn Food." Remove the tray from the air fryer when the cooking time is finished. Serve immediately.

Per serving: Calories 234; Fat 14.4g; Sodium 510mg; Carbs 1.1g; Fiber 0.1g; Sugar 0.1g; Protein 70.4g

Spiced Breast Turkey

Prep time: 5 minutes| Cook time: 1 hour| Serves: 4

3 pounds boneless turkey breast
¼ cup Mayonnaise

2 teaspoons poultry seasoning
Salt and pepper to taste
½ teaspoon garlic powder

To preheat your air fryer, select Air Fry function and set time to 1 hour and temperature to 400 degrees F. Mayonnaise, seasoning, salt, garlic powder, and black pepper are used to season the turkey. Then place the turkey into the air fryer and cook the turkey for 1 hour. Every 15 minutes, rotate the dish. When the temperature of the turkey hits 165 degrees F, it is ready.

Per serving: Calories 558; Fat 18g; Sodium 330mg; Carbs 1g; Fiber 0.1g; Sugar 0.1g; Protein 98g

Turkey Breast with Thyme

Prep time: 10 minutes| Cook time: 40 minutes| Serves: 4

2 pounds turkey breast
Salt to taste
Black pepper to taste
4 tablespoons butter, melted

3 cloves garlic, minced
1 teaspoon thyme, chopped
1 teaspoon rosemary, chopped

In a bowl, combine butter, salt, black pepper, garlic, thyme, and rosemary. Season the turkey breast well with this seasoning and set it in the cooking tray. Select the "Air Fry" mode. Set the time to 40 minutes and temperature to 400 degrees F. Place the cooking tray into the air fryer after it has been warmed. Slice and serve fresh.

Per serving: Calories 334; Fat 4.7g; Sodium 607mg; Carbs 54.1g; Fiber 8g; Sugar 6.1g; Protein 26.2g

Spicy Easy Chicken Drumsticks

Prep time: 10 minutes| Cook time: 20 minutes| Serves: 8

8 chicken drumsticks

2 tablespoons olive oil

1 teaspoon salt
1 teaspoon pepper
1 teaspoon garlic powder

1 teaspoon paprika
½ teaspoon cumin

In a bowl, combine olive oil, salt, black pepper, garlic powder, paprika, and cumin. This mixture should be applied liberally to all of the drumsticks. In the cooking tray, place these drumsticks. Select the "Air Fry" mode. Set the time to 20 minutes and temperature to 400 degrees F. Place the cooking tray into the air fryer after it has been preheated. When the drumsticks are halfway done, flip them. Continue air frying for the remaining 10 minutes. Warm the dish before serving.

Per serving: Calories 212; Fat 11.8g; Sodium 448mg; Carbs 14.6g; Fiber 4g; Sugar 3.9g; Protein 17.3g

Baked Blackened Chicken

Prep time: 10 minutes| Cook time: 18 minutes| Serves: 4

4 chicken breasts
2 teaspoons olive oil
For Seasoning:
1 ½ tablespoons brown sugar
1 teaspoon paprika

1 teaspoon dried oregano
¼ teaspoon garlic powder
½ teaspoon salt and pepper
Chopped parsley, for garnish

In a mixing bowl, combine olive oil, brown sugar, paprika, oregano, garlic powder, salt, and black pepper. Place the chicken breasts in the cooking tray. This mixture should be poured and rubbed thoroughly over all of the chicken breasts. Select the "Bake" mode. Set the time to 18 minutes and temperature to 365 degrees F. Place the cooking tray inside the air fryer after it has been warmed. Warm the dish before serving.

Per serving: Calories 412; Fat 24.8g; Sodium 657mg; Carbs 43.8g; Fiber 7.1g; Sugar 5g; Protein 18.9g

Crispy Drumsticks

Prep time: 10 minutes| Cook time: 10 minutes| Serves: 4

1 pound chicken drumsticks
½ cup buttermilk
½ cup panko breadcrumbs
½ cup flour
¼ teaspoon baking powder
Spice Mixture:
½ teaspoon salt
½ teaspoon celery salt
¼ teaspoon oregano

¼ teaspoon cayenne
1 teaspoon paprika
¼ teaspoon garlic powder
¼ teaspoon dried thyme
½ teaspoon ground ginger
½ teaspoon white pepper
½ teaspoon black pepper
3 tablespoons butter melted

Soak the chicken in buttermilk and refrigerate it overnight to marinate. In a shallow tray, combine spices, flour, breadcrumbs, and baking powder. Remove the chicken from the milk and cover it in the flour spice mixture well. Place the chicken drumsticks in the cooking tray. Melt the butter and brush it over the drumsticks. Select the "Air Fry" mode. Set the cooking time to 10 minutes and adjust the temperature to 400 degrees F. Place the cooking tray inside the air fryer after it has been preheated. Cook for another 10 minutes after flipping the drumsticks. Serve warm.

Per serving: Calories 331; Fat 2.5g; Sodium 402mg; Carbs 69g; Fiber 5g; Sugar 2g; Protein 28.7g

Turkey in Brine

Prep time: 10 minutes| Cook time: 45 minutes| Serves: 8

7 pound. bone-in, skin-on turkey breast
Brine:

½ cup salt
1 lemon
½ onion

3 cloves garlic, smashed
5 sprigs fresh thyme
3 bay leaves
black pepper
Turkey Breast:

4 tablespoons butter, softened
½ teaspoon black pepper
½ teaspoon garlic powder
¼ teaspoon dried thyme
¼ teaspoon dried oregano

In a saucepan, combine the turkey brine ingredients and soak the turkey overnight. Remove the saturated turkey from the brine the next day. Combine the butter, black pepper, garlic powder, oregano, and thyme in a large mixing bowl. Place the turkey in a cooking tray after brushing it with the butter mixture. To choose the "Roast" mode, press the "Start" on the air fryer. Adjust the cooking time to 45 minutes. Set the temperature to 380 degrees F. Place the turkey in the air fryer and seal the cover after it has been preheated. Slice and serve while still warm.
Per serving: Calories 397; Fat 15.4g; Sodium 690mg; Carbs 58.5g; Fiber 4.5g; Sugar 3.1g; Protein 7.9g

Chicken Tenderloin in Air Fryer

Prep time: 5 minutes| Cook time: 15 minutes| Serves: 8

½ cup almond flour
1 egg, beaten
2 tablespoons coconut oil

8 chicken tenderloins
Salt and pepper to taste

Preheat your air fryer by select Air Fry function. Set time to 15 minutes and temperature to 400 degrees F. Season the chicken tenderloin with salt and pepper. Dredge the chicken tenderloins in almond flour after soaking in beaten eggs. Brush with coconut oil and place in the air fryer. Cook for 15 minutes. Shake the cooking tray halfway during the cooking period to ensure equal frying.
Per serving: Calories 130.3; Fat 10.3g; Sodium 307mg; Carbs 0.7g; Fiber 0.1g; Sugar 0.1g; Protein 8.7g

Chicken Breast with Oregano

Prep time: 10 minutes| Cook time: 25 minutes| Serves: 6

2 pounds chicken breasts, minced
1 tablespoon avocado oil
1 teaspoon smoked paprika

1 teaspoon garlic powder
1 teaspoon oregano
½ teaspoon salt
Black pepper to taste

In a mixing basin, combine all of the meatball ingredients and stir thoroughly. Make tiny meatballs with the ingredients and cook them in a cooking tray. Select Air Fry function. Adjust the cooking time to 25 minutes and set the temperature to 400 degrees F. Press Start to begin. Place the cooking tray into the preheated air fryer. Cook and serve warm.
Per serving: Calories 352; Fat 14g; Sodium 447mg; Carbs 15.8g; Fiber 4.5g; Sugar 3.1g; Protein 26g

Chicken with Lemon

Prep time: 10 minutes| Cook time: 30 minutes| Serves: 4

¼ cup olive oil
3 tablespoons garlic, minced
⅓ cup dry white wine
1 tablespoon lemon zest, grated
2 tablespoons lemon juice
1 ½ teaspoons dried oregano,

crushed
1 teaspoon thyme leaves, minced
Salt and black pepper
4 skin-on boneless chicken breasts
1 lemon, sliced

In a cooking tray, whisk together all of the ingredients to thoroughly coat the chicken breasts. Serve the chicken breasts with lemon wedges on top. Over the toasted bread slices,

spread the mustard mixture. To preheat the air fryer, select Bake function. Set timer to 30 minutes and temperature to 365 degrees F. Press Start to begin. Place the cooking tray inside when the display shows "Add Food". Warm the dish before serving.
Per serving: Calories 388; Fat 8g; Sodium 200mg; Carbs 8g; Fiber 2.1g; Sugar 0.1g; Protein 13g

Chicken Cordon Blue with Almonds Flour Battering

Prep time: 5 minutes| Cook time: 30 minutes| Serves: 2

¼ cup almond flour
1 slice cheddar cheese
1 slice ham
1 small egg, beaten

1 teaspoon parsley
2 chicken breasts, butter-flied
Salt and pepper to taste

Season the chicken to taste with parsley, salt, and pepper. Roll in cheese and ham in center of chicken and secure it with tooth pick. Then soak it in egg then dredge chicken in almond flour to cover it completely. Select Bake function. Set time to 30 minutes and temperature to 365 degrees F. Place the chicken in the air fryer. Bake for 30 minutes. When cooking time is over, remove it from air fryer and serve hot.
Per serving: Calories 1142; Fat 89.1g; Sodium 980mg; Carbs 5.5g; Fiber 2.1g; Sugar 1.1g; Protein 79.4g

Chicken with Almonds Flour and Coco Milk Battering

Prep time: 5 minutes| Cook time: 30 minutes| Serves: 4

¼ cup coconut milk
½ cup almond flour
1 ½ tablespoons old bay Cajun seasoning

1 egg, beaten
4 small chicken thighs
Salt and pepper to taste

To preheat your air fryer, select Bake function. Set time to 30 minutes and temperature to 365 degrees F. Press Start to begin. In a bowl, whisk together the egg and coconut milk. Using the beaten egg mixture, soak the chicken thighs. Combine the almond flour, Cajun spice, salt, and pepper in a mixing bowl. Using the almond flour mixture, coat the chicken thighs. Place in the cooking tray when the display shows "Add Food". Let it cook. Halfway through cooking, turn the food around. When cooked, remove from the air fryer and serve warm.
Per serving: Calories 590; Fat 38.6g; Sodium 657mg; Carbs 3.2g; Fiber 0.1g; Sugar 0.1g; Protein 32.5g

Baked Chicken with Basil and Garlic

Prep time: 5 minutes| Cook time: 30 minutes| Serves: 2

2 boneless skinless chicken breast halves (4 ounces each)
1 tablespoon butter, melted
1 large tomato, seeded and chopped
2 garlic cloves, minced
1 ½ tablespoons minced fresh basil

½ tablespoon olive oil
½ teaspoon salt
¼ cup all-purpose flour
¼ cup egg substitute
¼ cup grated Parmesan cheese
¼ cup dry bread crumbs
¼ teaspoon pepper

Egg replacement should be whisked well in a shallow dish, and flour should be placed in a separate bowl. Chicken should be floured first, then dipped in whisked egg substitute, and then floured again. Whisk together the butter, bread crumbs, and cheese in a small bowl. Sprinkle on top of the chicken. Spray the air fryer's cooking tray lightly with cooking spray. In the bottom of the tray, place the breaded chicken. Wrap foil around the dish. Select Bake function. Set time to 20 minutes and temperature to 365 degrees F. Cook for 20 minutes in air fryer. Meanwhile cooking, whisk together the remaining ingredients in a mixing dish. Remove the foil from the pan and pour the remaining ingredients over the chicken. Cook for an additional 8 minutes on same temperature and function. Serve and have fun.

Per serving: Calories 311; Fat 11g; Sodium 670mg; Carbs 22g; Fiber 4.1g; Sugar 1.9g; Protein 31g

Greece BBQ Chicken

Prep time: 5 minutes| Cook time: 24 minutes| Serves: 2

1 (8 ounces) container fat-free plain yogurt
2 tablespoons fresh lemon juice
2 teaspoons dried oregano
1-pound skinless, boneless chicken breast halves - cut into 1-inch pieces
1 large red onion, cut into wedges
½ teaspoon lemon zest

½ teaspoon salt
1 large green bell pepper, cut into 1 ½-inch pieces
⅓ cup crumbled feta cheese with basil and sun-dried tomatoes
¼ teaspoon ground black pepper
¼ teaspoon crushed dried rosemary

Combine rosemary, pepper, salt, oregano, lemon juice, lemon zest, feta cheese, and yoghurt in a shallow dish. Toss in the chicken and coat well. Marinate for 3 hours in the refrigerator. Using skewers, thread bell pepper, onion, and chicken pieces. Place skewer rack on top. Select Air Fry function. Set time to 12 minutes and temperature to 400 degrees F. Cook it at 400 degrees F for 12 minutes. Halfway through the cooking period, flip the skewers. Cook in batches as necessary. Serve and have fun.

Per serving: Calories 242; Fat 7.5g; Sodium 474mg; Carbs 12.3g; Fiber 4.3g; Sugar 2.1g; Protein 31g

Pineapple and Teriyaki Glazed Chicken

Prep time: 5 minutes | Cook time: 20 minutes| Serves: 2

¼ cup pineapple juice
¼ teaspoon pepper
½ cup brown sugar
½ cup soy sauce
½ teaspoon salt
1 green bell pepper, cut into 1-inch cubes
1 red bell pepper, cut into 1-inch cubes
1 red onion, cut into 1-inch cubes

1 tablespoon cornstarch
1 tablespoon water
1 yellow red bell pepper, cut into 1-inch cubes
2 boneless skinless chicken breasts cut into 1-inch cubes
2 cups fresh pineapple cut into 1-inch cubes
2 garlic cloves, minced
Green onions for garnish

Bring the salt, pepper, garlic, pineapple juice, soy sauce, and brown sugar to a boil in a saucepan. Whisk together cornstarch and water in a small bowl. Slowly add into the pan's mixture, whisking frequently. Cook for about 3 minutes, or until the sauce has thickened. Set aside a quarter cup of the sauce for basting. Combine the chicken with the leftover thickened sauce in a shallow dish. Toss well to coat. Refrigerate for 30 minutes after marinating. Using skewers, thread bell pepper, onion, pineapple, and chicken pieces. In the air fryer, place on skewer rack. Select Air Fry function. Set time to 10 minutes and temperature to 400 degrees F. Cook for 10 minutes. Halfway through the cooking period, flip the skewers. In addition, baste with sauce. Cook in batches as necessary. Serve and enjoy with a sprinkle of green onions.

Per serving: Calories 391; Fat 3.4g; Sodium 607mg; Carbs

58.7g; Fiber 5.1g; Sugar 1.7g; Protein 31.2g

Turkey Meatballs and Cranberry Sauce

Prep time: 5 minutes| Cook time: 20 minutes| Serves: 4

1 ½ tablespoons water
2 teaspoons cider vinegar
1 teaspoon. salt and more to taste

1-pound ground turkey
1 ½ tablespoons barbecue sauce
⅓ cup cranberry sauce
¼-pound ground bacon

Combine the turkey, ground bacon, and a teaspoon of salt in a mixing basin. Form 16 equal-sized balls evenly. Boil cranberry sauce, barbecue sauce, water, cider vinegar, and a pinch of salt in a small pot. Simmer for 3 minutes after well mixing. Using skewers, thread meatballs and baste with cranberry sauce. In the air fryer, place on skewer rack. Select Air Fry function. Set the time to 15 minutes and temperature to 400 degrees F. Cook it for 15 minutes. Turn skewers after 5 minutes of cooking time and baste with sauce. Cook in batches as necessary. Serve and enjoy.

Per serving: Calories 217; Fat 10.9g; Sodium 517mg; Carbs 11.5g; Fiber 3.1g; Sugar 2.1g; Protein 28g

Chicken Dip in Buffalo Style

Prep time: 5 minutes| Cook time: 10 minutes| Serves: 4

1 (8 ounce) package cream cheese, softened
1 tablespoon shredded pepper Jack cheese
½ pinch cayenne pepper for garnish
½ pinch cayenne pepper, or to taste
¼ cup and 2 tablespoons hot pepper sauce (such as Frank's

Reshoot)
¼ cup blue cheese dressing
¼ cup crumbled blue cheese
¼ cup shredded pepper Jack cheese
¼ teaspoon seafood seasoning (such as Old Bay)
1-½ cups diced cooked rotisserie chicken

Spray the air fryer's cooking tray lightly with cooking spray. Cayenne pepper, seafood seasoning, blue cheese crumbles, blue cheese dressing, pepper Jack, spicy pepper sauce, cream cheese, and chicken are all mixed together. Select Air Fry function. Set the time to 15 minutes and temperature to 400 degrees F. Cook it for 15 minutes. After 10 minutes, garnish with cayenne pepper and continue to cook. Serve and have fun.

Per serving: Calories 405; Fat 35.9g; Sodium 780mg; Carbs 3.2g; Fiber 1.1g; Sugar 0.1g; Protein 17.1g

Chicken Stuffed with Cheese

Prep time: 5 minutes| Cook time: 25 minutes| Serves: 4

1 tablespoon Creole seasoning
1 tablespoon olive oil
1 teaspoon garlic powder
1 teaspoon onion powder

4 chicken breasts, butter-flied and pounded
4 slices Colby cheese
4 slices pepper jack cheese

To preheat, set the air fryer to Roast function. Set the temperature to 390 degrees F. Press Start to begin. In the air fryer, place the pan attachment. To make the dry rub, combine the Creole spice, garlic powder, and onion powder in a dish. If desired, season with salt and pepper. Season the chicken with the seasoning. Place a piece of pepper jack and a slice of Colby cheese on top of the chicken on a work surface. Fold the chicken in half and use toothpicks to seal the sides. Olive oil should be brushed on the chicken. Select Roast function. Set time to 30 minutes and temperature to 380 degrees F. Roast the beef for 30 minutes, flipping it after 10 minutes.

Per serving: Calories 727; Fat 45.9g; Sodium 787mg; Carbs 5.4g; Fiber 2.1g; Sugar 0.1g; Protein 73.1g

Meatballs Made with Turkey

Prep time: 10 minutes| Cook time: 20 minutes| Serves: 6

1 pound turkey mince	4 tablespoons parsley, minced
1 red bell pepper, deseeded and chopped	1 tablespoon cilantro, minced
1 large egg, beaten	Salt and black pepper, to taste

In a mixing basin, combine all of the meatball ingredients and stir thoroughly. Make tiny meatballs with the ingredients and cook them in an cooking tray. To choose the "Air Fry" mode, press the "Start" on the air fryer. Set time to 20 minutes and temperature to 400 degrees F. Place the cooking tray into the preheated air fryer. Warm the dish before serving.

Per serving: Calories 338; Fat 9.7g; Sodium 660mg; Carbs 32.5g; Fiber 6.1g; Sugar 3.2g; Protein 10.3g

Grounded Meatballs of Chicken

Prep time: 10 minutes| Cook time: 10 minutes| Serves: 4

1 pound. ground chicken	½ teaspoon garlic powder
⅓ cup panko	1 teaspoon thyme
1 teaspoon salt	1 egg
2 teaspoons chives	

In a mixing basin, combine all of the meatball ingredients and stir thoroughly. Make tiny meatballs with the ingredients and cook them in a cooking tray. Choose the "Air Fry" mode. Set time to 10 minutes and temperature to 400 degrees F. Press Start to begin. Place the cooking tray into the preheated air fryer. Warm the dish before serving.

Per serving: Calories 453; Fat 2.4g; Sodium 390mg; Carbs 18g; Fiber 4.1g; Sugar 0.9g; Protein 23.3g

Parmesan Meatballs of Chicken

Prep time: 10 minutes| Cook time: 12 minutes| Serves: 4

1 pound ground chicken	1 teaspoon paprika
1 large egg, beaten	1 teaspoon kosher salt
½ cup Parmesan cheese, grated	½ teaspoon pepper
½ cup pork rinds, ground	½ cup ground pork rinds, for crust
1 teaspoon garlic powder	

In a mixing basin, combine all of the meatball ingredients and stir thoroughly. Form tiny meatballs from the ingredients and coat them with pig rinds. In the cooking tray, place the coated meatballs. Select the Bake function. Set time to 12 minutes and temperature to 365 degrees F. Press Start to begin. Place the cooking tray into the preheated air fryer. Warm the dish before serving.

Per serving: Calories 529; Fat 17g; Sodium 657mg; Carbs 55g; Fiber 4.7g; Sugar 3.4g; Protein 41g

Chicken BBQ Breast

Prep time: 5 minutes| Cook time: 15 minutes| Serves: 4

4 (about 6 ounces) boneless, skinless chicken breast	2 tablespoons BBQ seasoning Cooking spray

Rub the chicken with BBQ spice and marinate for 45 minutes in the refrigerator. To preheat the air fryer, select Air Fry function.

Set time to 14 minutes and temperature to 400 degrees F. Place the chicken in the cooking tray that has been greased with oil. Then squirt some oil on top. Cook for 14 minutes at 400 degrees F. At the midway point, keep flipping. Serve.

Per serving: Calories 131; Fat 3g; Sodium 240mg; Carbs 2g; Fiber 0.1g; Sugar 0.1g; Protein 24g

Skewer of Chicken Sweet and Sour Flavor

Prep time: 5 minutes| Cook time: 18 minutes| Serves: 4

1 pound. of chicken tenders	2 tablespoons pineapple juice
¼ teaspoon of pepper	1 tablespoon sesame oil
4 garlic cloves, minced	½ teaspoon ginger, minced
1 ½ tablespoons soy sauce	

Except for the chicken, combine all of the ingredients in a mixing dish. Skewer the chicken tenders, then marinate for 2 hours in a bowl. Select Air Fry function. Set time to 18 minutes and temperature to 400 degrees F. Cook for 18 minutes in the air fryer with the tenders. Serve immediately!

Per serving: Calories 217; Fat 3g; Sodium 290mg; Carbs 15.3g; Fiber 1g; Sugar 1.1g; Protein 21.3g

Duck Legs with Full Spices

Prep time: 5 minutes| Cook time: 30 minutes| Serves: 2

2 duck legs, bone-in, and skin on	1 tablespoon herbs that you like, such as thyme, parsley, etc., chopped
Salt and pepper to taste	
1 teaspoon five-spice powder	

Spices should be rubbed all over the duck legs. Select Bake function. Set time to 25 minutes and temperature to 365 degrees F. Cook the duck legs in the air fryer for 25 minutes at 325 degrees F. After that, cook again on Air Fry function by setting time to 5 minutes and temperature to 400 degrees F.

Per serving: Calories 207; Fat 10.6g; Sodium 340mg; Carbs 1.9g; Fiber 0.1g; Sugar 0.1g; Protein 24.5g

Turkey with Stuffing

Prep time: 5 minutes| Cook time: 1 hour and 5 minutes| Serves: 4

1 whole turkey, bone-in, with skin	2 cups turkey broth
2 celery stalks, chopped	4 cloves garlics, minced
1 lemon, sliced	1 onion, chopped
Fresh oregano leaves, chopped	2 eggs
1 cup fresh parsley, minced	1 ½ pounds. sage sausage
1 teaspoon sage leaves, dry	4 tablespoons butter

Melt 2 ½ tablespoons butter in a pan over medium heat and mash in the sausage (separate the flesh from the skin). Select Air Fry function. Set time to 18 minutes and temperature to 400 degrees F. Cook the sausage flesh in the pan for 8 minutes, stirring occasionally. Cook for a further 10 minutes, stirring to incorporate celery, onions, garlic, and sage. Remove the sausage from the heat and stir in the broth. Whisk together the eggs and two tablespoons of parsley in a mixing dish. Stir the egg mixture into the sausage mixture. This will be your turkey's stuffing. Stuff the bird with stuffing mixture. Combine the remaining butter, parsley, oregano, salt, and pepper in a separate dish and massage it into the turkey skin. Cook for 45 minutes in the air fryer with the turkey. Serve with lemon slices as a garnish.

Per serving: Calories 1046; Fat 69.7g; Sodium 440mg; Carbs 12.7g; Fiber 1g; Sugar 2.1g; Protein 91.5g

Baked Chicken

Prep time: 5 minutes| Cook time: 1 hour| Serves: 4

1 whole chicken, cleaned and patted dry

2 tablespoons olive oil
1 tablespoon Seasoned salt

The giblet package should be removed from the cavity. Season the chicken with salt and oil. Place breast-side down in the cooking tray. Select Bake function. Set time to 30 minutes and temperature to 365 degrees F. Bake for 30 minutes. Cook for another 30 minutes after flipping. When the temperature of the chicken hits 165 degrees F, it is ready to serve.
Per serving: Calories 534; Fat 36g; Sodium 140mg; Carbs 0g; Fiber 0g; Sugar 0g; Protein 35g

Chicken in Greek Style

Prep time: 10 minutes| Cook time: 15 minutes| Serves: 4

2 tablespoons olive oil
Juice from 1 lemon
1 teaspoon oregano, dried
3 garlic cloves, minced
1 pound chicken thighs

Salt and black pepper to the taste
½ pound asparagus, trimmed
1 zucchini, roughly chopped
1 lemon sliced

Stir chicken pieces with oil, lemon juice, oregano, garlic, salt, pepper, asparagus, zucchini, and lemon slices in a heat-proof dish that fits your air fryer, toss, then place in the prepared air fryer. Select Air Fry function and set time to 15 minutes and temperature to 400 degrees F. Cook for 15 minutes. Serve by dividing everything across plates. Enjoy.
Per serving: Calories 300; Fat 8g; Sodium 4000mg; Carbs 20g; Fiber 2.1g; Sugar 1.7g; Protein 18g

Orange Sauce and Red Wine Duck Breast

Prep time: 10 minutes| Cook time: 35 minutes| Serves: 4

½ cup honey
2 cups orange juice
4 cups red wine
2 tablespoons sherry vinegar
2 cups chicken stock
2 teaspoons pumpkin pie spice

2 tablespoons butter
2 duck breasts, skin on and halved
2 tablespoons olive oil
Salt and black pepper to the taste

Heat the orange juice in a skillet over medium heat, then add the honey and simmer for 10 minutes, stirring constantly. Stir in the wine, vinegar, stock, pie spice, and butter, then simmer for another 10 minutes before turning off the heat. Select Air Fry function. Set time to 14 minutes and temperature to 400 degrees F. Season duck breasts with salt and pepper, massage with olive oil, and cook for 7 minutes on each side in air fryer set at 400 degrees F. Serve immediately after dividing the duck breasts among plates and drizzling them with wine and orange juice. Enjoy!
Per serving: Calories 300; Fat 8g; Sodium 280mg; Carbs 24g; Fiber 3.1g; Sugar 2.2g; Protein 11g

Simple Duck Breast

Prep time: 10 minutes| Cook time: 15 minutes| Serves: 4

4 duck breasts, skinless and boneless
4 garlic heads, peeled, tops cut

off and quartered
2 tablespoons lemon juice
Salt and black pepper to the

taste
½ teaspoon lemon pepper

1 and ½ tablespoons olive oil

Toss the duck breasts in a bowl with the garlic, lemon juice, salt, pepper, lemon pepper, and olive oil. Select Air Fry Function. Set time to 15 minutes and temperature to 400 degrees F. Cook for 15 minutes in your air fryer with the duck and garlic. Serve the duck breasts with the garlic on plates. Enjoy!
Per serving: Calories 200; Fat 7g; Sodium 340mg; Carbs 11g; Fiber 1.1g; Sugar 0.9g; Protein 17g

Fig Sauce and Duck Breast

Prep time: 10 minutes| Cook time: 20 minutes| Serves: 4

2 duck breasts, skin on, halved
1 tablespoon olive oil
½ teaspoon thyme, chopped
½ teaspoon garlic powder
¼ teaspoon sweet paprika
Salt and black pepper to the taste

1 cup beef stock
3 tablespoons butter, melted
1 shallot, chopped
½ cup port wine
4 tablespoons fig preserves
1 tablespoon white flour

Season the duck breasts with salt and pepper, then sprinkle with half of the melted butter, massage well, and place in the cooking tray. Select Air Fry function. Set time to 10 minutes and temperature to 400 degrees F. Cook for 5 minutes on each side at 400 degrees F. Meanwhile, heat the olive oil and remaining butter in a pan over medium-high heat, then add the shallot, swirl, and cook for 2 minutes. Cook for 7-8 minutes after adding the thyme, garlic powder, paprika, stock, salt, pepper, wine, and figs. Add the flour, mix thoroughly, and simmer until the sauce thickens slightly before removing it from the heat. Serve the duck breasts on plates with fig sauce drizzled all over. Enjoy!
Per serving: Calories 246; Fat 12g; Sodium 440mg; Carbs 22g; Fiber 3.1g; Sugar 1.5g; Protein 3g

Raspberry Sauce and Duck Breast

Prep time: 10 minutes| Cook time: 15 minutes| Serves: 4

2 duck breasts, skin on and scored
Salt and black pepper to the taste
Cooking spray

½ teaspoon cinnamon powder
½ cup raspberries
1 tablespoon sugar
1 teaspoon red wine vinegar
½ cup water

Season duck breasts with salt and pepper and coat with cooking spray then place skin side down in a preheated air fryer. Select Air Fry function. Set time to 10 minutes and temperature to 400 degrees F. Cook for 10 minutes. Warm the water in a pan over medium heat, then add the raspberries, cinnamon, sugar, and wine, stirring constantly. Bring to a simmer, then move to a blender, purée, and return to the pan. Add the duck breasts from the air fryer to the pan as well, toss to coat, distribute among plates, and serve immediately. Enjoy!
Per serving: Calories 456; Fat 22g; Sodium 440mg; Carbs 14g; Fiber 2.6g; Sugar 1.8g; Protein 45g

Yummy Fruit Sauce with Chicken Breast

Prep time: 10 minutes| Cook time: 10 minutes| Serves: 4

4 chicken breasts
Salt and black pepper to the taste
4 passion fruits, halved, deseeded and pulp reserved

1 tablespoon whiskey
2 star anise
2 ounces maple syrup
1 bunch chives, chopped

Heat the passion fruit pulp in a skillet over medium heat, then add the whiskey, star anise, maple syrup, and chives, stirring constantly. Simmer for 5–6 minutes, then remove from the heat. Season the chicken with salt and pepper, then place it in the preheated air fryer and select Air Fry function. Set time to 10 minutes and temperature to 400 degrees F. Cook for 10 minutes, flipping halfway through. Divide the chicken amongst dishes, warm the sauce slightly, and drizzle it over the chicken before serving. Enjoy!

Per serving: Calories 374; Fat 8g; Sodium 350mg; Carbs 34g; Fiber 4g; Sugar 2.1g; Protein 37g

Cherries with Duck Breast

Prep time: 10 minutes| Cook time: 20 minutes| Serves: 4

½ cup sugar
¼ cup honey
⅓ cup balsamic vinegar
1 teaspoon garlic, minced
1 tablespoon ginger, grated
1 teaspoon cumin, ground
½ teaspoon clove, ground
½ teaspoon cinnamon powder
4 sage leaves, chopped

1 jalapeno, chopped
2 cups rhubarb, sliced
½ cup yellow onion, chopped
2 cups cherries, pitted
4 duck breasts, boneless, skin on and scored
Salt and black pepper to the taste

Season the duck breast with salt and pepper, then place it in the air fryer. Select Bake function. Set the timer to 10 minutes and temperature to 365 degrees F. Cook for 5 minutes on each side. In a separate pan, boil the sugar, honey, vinegar, garlic, ginger, cumin, clove, cinnamon, sage, jalapeño, rhubarb, onion, and cherries over medium heat, stirring constantly. Bring to a simmer and then select Air Fry function in air fryer. Set time to 10 minutes and temperature to 400 degrees F. Cook for 10 minutes. Toss in the duck breasts, divide everything among plates, and serve. Enjoy!

Per serving: Calories 456; Fat 13g; Sodium 440mg; Carbs 64g; Fiber 4.1g; Sugar 2.7g; Protein 31g

Tea Sauce with Duck Breast

Prep time: 10 minutes| Cook time: 20 minutes| Serves: 4

2 duck breast halves, boneless
2 ¼ cups chicken stock
¾ cup shallot, chopped
1 and ½ cups orange juice
Salt and black pepper to the

taste
3 teaspoons earl gray tea leaves
3 tablespoons butter, melted
1 tablespoon honey

To preheat, select the Air Fry function. Set time to 10 minutes and temperature to 400 degrees F. Press Start to begin. Season duck breast halves with salt and pepper, then place them in a preheated air fryer and select Air Fry function. Cook for 10 minutes. Meanwhile, melt the butter in a skillet over medium heat, add the shallot, and cook for 2-3 minutes, stirring occasionally. Cook for another minute after adding the stock and stirring it in. Stir in the orange juice, tea leaves, and honey, then simmer for another 2-3 minutes before straining into a bowl. Serve the duck on plates with tea sauce drizzled all over it. Enjoy!

Per serving: Calories 228; Fat 11g; Sodium 270mg; Carbs 20g; Fiber 5g; Sugar 2g; Protein 12g

Chicken Breast with Honey and Mustard

Prep time: 5 minutes| Cook time: 25 minutes| Serves: 6

6 (6 ounces) boneless, skinless   chicken breasts

2 tablespoons fresh rosemary minced
3 tablespoons honey

1 tablespoon Dijon mustard
Salt and pepper to taste

In a mixing dish, combine the mustard, honey, pepper, rosemary, and salt. This mixture should be rubbed all over the bird. Grease the cooking tray. Select Air Fry function. Set time to 24 minutes and temperature to 400 degrees F. Air fry the chicken for 24 minutes or until it reaches 165 degrees F internally. Serve hot.

Per serving: Calories 236; Fat 9.8g; Sodium 330mg; Carbs 5g; Fiber 0.1g; Sugar 0.1g; Protein 38g

Parmesan Chicken Wings

Prep time: 5 minutes| Cook time: 15 minutes| Serves: 4

2 pounds chicken wings cut into drumettes, pat dried
½ cup Parmesan, plus 6 tablespoon grated

1 teaspoon Herbs de Provence
1 teaspoon paprika
Salt to taste

In a bowl, combine the parmesan, herbs, paprika, and salt, and spread the mixture all over the chicken. Preheat the air fryer to 400 degrees F. Select Air Fry function. Set the time to 15 minutes and temperature to 400 degrees F. Spray the cooking tray with nonstick frying spray. Cook for 15 minutes in the air fryer. At the halfway point, flip once more. Serve with a parmesan garnish.

Per serving: Calories 490; Fat 22g; Sodium 540mg; Carbs 1g; Fiber 0.1g; Sugar 0.1g; Protein 72g

Chicken in Air Fryer

Prep time: 5 minutes| Cook time: 30 minutes| Serves: 4

2 pounds chicken wings
salt and pepper to taste

cooking spray

Season the chicken wings with salt and pepper before serving. Using cooking spray, coat the cooking tray. Select Air Fry function. Set the time to 35 minutes and temperature to 400 degrees F. Cook the chicken wings in air fryer. To ensure uniform cooking, flip the pan three times during the cooking process. Serve.

Per serving: Calories 277; Fat 8g; Sodium 240mg; Carbs 1g; Fiber 0.1g; Sugar 0.1g; Protein 50g

Easy Chicken Whole

Prep time: 5 minutes| Cook time: 40 minutes| Serves: 6

1 (2 ½ pounds) whole chicken washed and pat dried
2 tablespoons dry rub

1 teaspoon salt
Cooking spray

To preheat, set the air fryer on Bake function. Set the time to 40 minutes and temperature to 365 degrees F. Press Start to begin. The chicken should be rubbed with the dry rub. After that, massage with salt. Place the chicken into the air fryer when the display shows "Add Food". Bake for 20 minutes on one side. Cook for another 20 minutes after flipping the chicken. When the temperature of the chicken hits 165 degrees F, it is ready.

Per serving: Calories 412; Fat 28g; Sodium 430mg; Carbs 1g; Fiber 0.1g; Sugar 0.1g; Protein 35g

Coconut Creamy Chicken

Prep time: 5 minutes| Cook time: 20 minutes| Serves: 4

4 big chicken legs
5 teaspoons turmeric powder
2 tablespoons ginger grated

salt and black pepper to taste
4 tablespoons coconut cream

Combine salt, pepper, ginger, turmeric, and cream in a mixing basin. Whisk. Add the chicken pieces, coat them, and set aside for 2 hours to marinate. Select Air Fry function. Set time to 25 minutes and temperature to 400 degrees F. Cook the chicken for 25 minutes in air fryer. Serve.
Per serving: Calories 300; Fat 4g; Sodium 440mg; Carbs 22g; Fiber 4g; Sugar 2.1g; Protein 20g

Chicken Tenders with Buffalo Sauce

Prep time: 5 minutes| Cook time: 20 minutes| Serves: 4

1 pound boneless, skinless chicken tenders
¼ cup hot sauce
1 ½ ounces pork rinds, finely

ground
1 teaspoon chili powder
1 teaspoon garlic powder

Pour the spicy sauce over the chicken breasts in a bowl. Toss to evenly coat. In a separate dish, combine the ground pork rinds, chili powder, and garlic powder. Coat each tender with a thick layer of ground pork rinds. Press the pork rinds into the chicken with moist hands. Select Air Fry function. Set time to 20 minutes and temperature to 400 degrees F. Place the tenders in the cooking tray in a single layer. Cook for 20 minutes. Flip the coin once while cooking in air fryer. Serve.
Per serving: Calories 160; Fat 4.4g; Sodium 140mg; Carbs 0.6g; Fiber 0g; Sugar 0g; Protein 27.3g

Teriyaki Wings

Prep time: 5 minutes| Cook time: 20 minutes| Serves: 4

2 pounds chicken wings
½ cup teriyaki sauce
2 teaspoons minced garlic

¼ teaspoon ground ginger
2 teaspoons baking powder

Place all ingredients in a bowl, except the baking powder, and marinate for 1 hour in the refrigerator. Sprinkle baking powder on the wings before placing them in the cooking tray. Rub gently into the wings. Preheat air fryer to 365 degrees F by selecting Bake function and setting time to 25 minutes and temperature to 365 degrees F. Press Start to begin. When the display shows "Add Food", place the wings into the air fryer. Bake for 25 minutes. During the cooking process, shake the tray two or three times. Serve.
Per serving: Calories 446; Fat 29.8g; Sodium 440mg; Carbs 3.1g; Fiber 0.1g; Sugar 0.1g; Protein 41.8g

Drumsticks with Lemon

Prep time: 5 minutes| Cook time: 20 minutes| Serves: 2

2 teaspoons baking powder
½ teaspoon garlic powder
8 chicken drumsticks
4 tablespoons salted butter

melted
1 tablespoon lemon pepper seasoning

Garlic powder and baking powder should be sprinkled over the drumsticks and rubbed into the skin. In the cooking tray, place the drumsticks. Select Air Fry function. Set the time to 25 minutes and temperature to 400 degrees F. Cook for 25 minutes. Halfway through the cooking time, flip the drumsticks. When the food is done, remove it. In a mixing dish, combine the seasonings and butter. Toss the drumsticks in the dish to coat them. Serve.
Per serving: Calories 532; Fat 32.3g; Sodium 240mg; Carbs 1.2g; Fiber 0.1g; Sugar 0.1g; Protein 48.3g

Chicken Tenders with Parmesan

Prep time: 5 minutes| Cook time: 10 minutes| Serves: 4

1 pound chicken tenderloins
3 large egg whites
½ cup Italian-style bread

crumbs
¼ cup grated Parmesan cheese

Getting the ingredients ready and olive oil should be sprayed on the cooking tray. Any white fat on the chicken tenders should be removed. Whisk the egg whites until foamy in a mixing dish. Combine the bread crumbs and parmesan cheese in a separate small mixing dish. Mix thoroughly. The chicken tenders should be dipped in the egg mixture, then in the parmesan and bread crumbs. Remove any extra breading by shaking it off. Place the chicken tenders in a single layer in the cooking tray. To avoid powdery, undercooked breading, generously spray the chicken with olive oil. To preheat your air fryer to 370 degrees F, select Air Fry function. Set the timer for 4 minutes and temperature to 365 degrees F then bake. Flip the chicken tenders with tongs and bake for another 4 minutes. Check that the chicken has achieved a temperature of 165 degrees F on the inside. If necessary, increase the cooking time. Plate, serve, and enjoy the chicken after it is thoroughly done.
Per serving: Calories 210; Fat 4g; Sodium 440mg; Carbs 10g; Fiber 1g; Sugar 1g; Protein 33g

Simple Thigh Chicken with Lemon

Prep time: 5 minutes | Cook time: 10 minutes| Serves: 4

Salt and black pepper to taste
2 tablespoons olive oil
2 tablespoons Italian seasoning

2 tablespoons freshly squeezed lemon juice
1 lemon, sliced

Season the chicken thighs with salt and pepper and place them in a medium mixing basin. Toss the chicken thighs with the olive oil, Italian seasoning, and lemon juice until they are well coated in oil. Add the lemon slices. Place the chicken thighs in a single layer in the cooking tray. To preheat your air fryer to 350 degrees F, select Air Fry function. Set time to 10 minutes and temperature to 400 degrees F. Cook for 10 minutes after setting the timer. Flip the chicken using tongs. Cook for another 10 minutes after resetting the timer. Check that the chicken has achieved a temperature of 165 degrees F on the inside. If necessary, increase the cooking time. Plate, serve, and enjoy the chicken after it is thoroughly done.
Per serving: Calories 325; Fat 26g; Sodium 310mg; Carbs 1g; Fiber 0.1g; Sugar 0.1g; Protein 20g

Bake Chicken Breast in Air Fryer

Prep time: 5 minutes| Cook time: 14 minutes| Serves: 4

½ teaspoon garlic powder
Salt and black pepper to taste
1 teaspoon dried parsley
2 tablespoons olive oil,

divided
3 boneless, skinless chicken breasts

Combine the garlic powder, salt, pepper, and parsley in a small bowl. Rub each chicken breast with 1 tablespoon olive oil and half of the spice mix. In the cooking tray, place the chicken breasts. To preheat your air fryer to 400 degrees F, select Air Fry function. Set the timer for 7 minutes and temperature to 400 degrees F. Flip the chicken with tongs and brush the remaining olive oil and seasonings on top. Reset timer to 7 minutes and cook for another 7 minutes. Check that the chicken has achieved a temperature of 165 degrees F on the inside. If necessary, increase the cooking time. When the chicken is done, place it on a serving dish and serve.

Per serving: Calories 182; Fat 9g; Sodium 140mg; Carbs 9g; Fiber 1g; Sugar 0.9g; Protein 26g

Butter Chicken in Air Fryer

Prep time: 5 minutes| Cook time: 15 minutes| Serves: 4

2 (8-ounce) boneless, skinless chicken breasts
1 sleeve Ritz crackers

4 tablespoons (½ stick) cold unsalted butter, cut into 1 tablespoon slices

Spray an air fryer baking sheet with olive oil or cooking spray, or spray the cooking tray with olive oil. In a bowl of water, dunk the chicken breasts. Fill a re-sealable plastic bag halfway with crackers. Crush the crackers with a mallet or your hands. One by one, place the chicken breasts in the bag and cover them with the cracker crumbs. Place the chicken in the greased baking sheet that has been placed in the cooking tray. Apply 1 to 2 coats of butter to each chicken piece. Select Bake function. Set the timer for 7 minutes and temperature to 365 degrees F then bake. Flip the chicken using tongs. To avoid undercooked breading, liberally coat the chicken with olive oil. Restart the timer to 7 minutes and bake for another 7 minutes. Check that the chicken has achieved a temperature of 165 degrees F on the inside. If necessary, increase the cooking time. Remove the chicken from the air fryer with tongs and serve.

Per serving: Calories 750; Fat 40g; Sodium 940mg; Carbs 38g; Fiber 5.1g; Sugar 4.3g; Protein 57g

Breaded Chicken Breast in Air Fryer

Prep time: 5 minutes| Cook time: 15 minutes| Serves: 2

2 large eggs
1 cup bread crumbs or panko bread crumbs
1 teaspoon Italian seasoning

4 to 5 tablespoons vegetable oil
2 boneless, skinless, chicken breasts

Using olive oil or cooking spray, coat the cooking tray. Whisk the eggs in a small bowl until foamy. Combine the bread crumbs, Italian seasoning, and oil in a separate small mixing dish. The chicken should be dipped in the egg mixture first, then in the bread crumb mixture. Place the chicken into the oiled air fryer basket or on the greased baking sheet that has been placed in the basket. Select Air Fry function. To avoid powdery, undercooked breading, generously spray the chicken with olive oil. Set the timer for 7 minutes and temperature to 400 degrees F then air fry. Flip the chicken with tongs and liberally sprinkle it with olive oil. Restart the timer and cook for another 7 minutes. Check that the chicken has achieved a temperature of 165 degrees F on the inside. If necessary, increase the cooking time. Remove the chicken from the air fryer with tongs after it is thoroughly cooked and serve.

Per serving: Calories 833; Fat 46g; Sodium 640mg; Carbs 40g; Fiber 6.1g; Sugar 7g; Protein 65g

Brie and Ham Chicken Fillets

Prep time: 5 minutes| Cook time: 15 minutes| Serves: 4

2 large chicken fillets
freshly ground black pepper
4 small slices brie (or your cheese of choice)

1 tablespoon freshly chopped chives
4 slices cured ham

Cut the fillets into four pieces and make incisions like a hamburger bun. At the rear, leave a little "hinge" uncut. Season the interior and stuff it with brie and chives. Close them and put a piece of ham around each one. Brush them with oil before placing them in the cooking tray. To preheat your air fryer to 380 degrees F. Select Roast function. Set time to 15 minutes and temperature to 380 degrees F. Press Start to begin. Roast the little packages until they appear to be delicious (15 minutes).

Per serving: Calories 850; Fat 50g; Sodium 370mg; Carbs 43g; Fiber 7g; Sugar 5.5g; Protein 76g

Cornish Hen in Air Fryer

Prep time: 5 minutes| Cook time: 30 minutes| Serves: 2

2 tablespoons Montreal chicken seasoning

1 (1½ to 2 pound) Cornish hen

To preheat the air fryer to 380 degrees F, select Roast function and set time to 30 minutes and temperature to 380 degrees F. Rub the spice all over the chicken, making sure it's well covered. Place the chicken in the air fryer basket and then roast on one side. Cook for another 15 minutes after flipping the chicken. Check that the chicken has achieved a temperature of 165 degrees F on the inside. If necessary, increase the cooking time.

Per serving: Calories 520; Fat 36g; Sodium 390mg; Carbs 0g; Fiber 0g; Sugar 0g; Protein 45g

Turkey Wings in Air Fryer

Prep time: 5 minutes| Cook time: 26 minutes| Serves: 4

2 pounds turkey wings
3 tablespoons olive oil or

sesame oil
3 to 4 tablespoons chicken rub

In a large mixing dish, place the turkey wings. Add the rub to the bowl with the olive oil. Rub the oil mixture over the turkey wings with your hands. In the air fryer basket, place the turkey wings. To preheat your air fryer to 380 degrees F, select Roast function. Set the timer for 13 minutes and temperature to 380 degrees F then roast.. Reset the timer for another 13 minutes of roasting. Take the turkey wings out of the air fryer and place them on a platter to serve.

Per serving: Calories 521; Fat 34g; Sodium 440mg; Carbs 4g; Fiber 1g; Sugar 0.5g; Protein 52g

Streak Supreme Chicken in Air Fryer

Prep time: 10 minutes| Cook time: 30 minutes| Serves: 8

½ pound beef bottom round, sliced into strips
1 cup breadcrumbs

2 medium-sized eggs
Pinch of salt and pepper
½ tablespoon ground thyme

Cover the cooking tray with a sheet of tin foil, leaving the sides free to enable air to flow through. To preheat your air fryer to

400 degrees F, select Air Fry function and set time to 15 minutes and temperature to 400 degrees F. Press Start to begin. Set aside the eggs, which should be whisked until frothy and the yolks and whites are thoroughly mixed in a dish. Set aside the breadcrumbs, thyme, salt, and pepper in a separate dish. Dip each piece of raw steak into the dry ingredients bowl one at a time, covering all sides; then immerse into the wet ingredients bowl, then dip back into the dry ingredients. This second coating ensures a crispier taste. Place the coated steak pieces in a single flat layer on the foil that covers the cooking tray. Select Air Fry function. Set the timer on the air fryer for 15 minutes and temperature to 400 degrees F. The air fryer will switch off after 15 minutes, and the steak should be halfway done with the breaded coating beginning to brown. Turn each piece of steak over with tongs to get a complete all-over fry. Remove the fried steak strips with tongs and place them on a serving dish after 15 minutes, when the air fryer goes off. Eat as soon as it's cool enough to handle.

Per serving: Calories 421; Fat 26g; Sodium 390mg; Carbs 8g; Fiber 1g; Sugar 1g; Protein 46g

Baked Chicken with Caser Marinating

Prep time: 10 minutes| Cook time: 25 minutes| Serves: 4

¼ cup crouton	1 pound ground chicken
1 teaspoon lemon zest. Form into ovals, skewer and grill.	2 tablespoons Caesar dressing and more for drizzling
½ cup Parmesan	2-4 romaine leaves
¼ cup breadcrumbs	

Combine the chicken, 2 tablespoons of Caesar dressing, parmesan, and breadcrumbs in a shallow dish. Hands-on mixing is recommended. Make 1-inch oval patties out of the mixture. Using skewers, thread chicken pieces together. In the air fryer, place on the cooking tray. Select Bake function. Set time to 12 minutes and temperature to 365 degrees F. Cook for 12 minutes. Turn the skewers halfway through the cooking time. Cook in batches as necessary. Serve on a bed of lettuce with croutons and additional dressing on the side.

Per serving: Calories 342; Fat 12g; Sodium 270mg; Carbs 8g; Fiber 1g; Sugar 1g; Protein 36g

Chicken Tenders Full of Cheese

Prep time: 10 minutes| Cook time: 30 minutes| Serves: 4

1 large white meat chicken breast	Pinch of salt and pepper
1 cup breadcrumbs	1 tablespoon grated or powdered parmesan cheese
2 medium sized eggs	

Cover the cooking tray with a sheet of tin foil, leaving the sides free to enable air to flow through. To preheat your air fryer to 350 degrees F, select Air Fry function. Set time to 15 minutes and temperature to 400 degrees F. Press Start to begin. Set aside the eggs, which should be whisked until frothy and the yolks and whites are thoroughly mixed in a dish.
Set aside the breadcrumbs, parmesan, salt, and pepper in a separate bowl. Dip each piece of raw chicken into the dry ingredients bowl one at a time, covering both sides; then immerse into the wet ingredients bowl, then dip back into the dry ingredients. Place the breaded chicken pieces in a single flat layer on the foil that covers the cooking tray. The air fryer will switch off after 15 minutes, and the chicken should be halfway done with the breaded coating beginning to brown. To guarantee a complete fry, turn each piece of chicken over. For another 15 minutes, reset timer to 15 minutes at temp 400 degrees F. When the air fryer goes off after 15 minutes, remove the fried chicken strips with tongs and place them on a serving platter. Enjoy after it's cold enough to handle.

Per serving: Calories 278; Fat 15g; Sodium 270mg; Carbs 10g; Fiber 2g; Sugar 7g; Protein 29g

Mint Flavor Fried Pork Chops

Prep time: 10 minutes| Cook time: 30 minutes| Serves: 4

4 medium-sized pork chops	½ tablespoon mint, either dried and ground; or fresh, rinsed, and finely chopped
1 cup breadcrumbs	
2 medium sized eggs	
Pinch of salt and pepper	

Cover the cooking tray with a sheet of tin foil, leaving the sides free to enable air to flow through. To preheat the air fryer, select Air Fry function. Set time to 15 minutes and temperature to 400 degrees F. Press Start to begin. Whisk the eggs in a mixing dish until frothy and the yolks and whites are thoroughly mixed, then put aside. Set aside the breadcrumbs, mint, salt, and pepper in a separate dish. Dip each raw pork chop into the dry ingredients bowl one at a time, covering all sides; then immerse into the wet ingredients bowl, then dip again into the dry ingredients. Place the coated pork chops in a single flat layer on the foil that covers the cooking tray into the air fryer, when the display shows "Add Food". The air fryer will switch off after 15 minutes, at which point the pork should be halfway done and the breaded coating should be beginning to brown. Turn each piece of steak over with tongs to get a complete all-over fry. Cook it for another 15 minutes, for that reset timer again to 15 minutes. Remove the fried pork chops with tongs after 15 minutes and place them on a serving dish.

Per serving: Calories 262; Fat 17g; Sodium 370mg; Carbs 7g; Fiber 1g; Sugar 1g; Protein 32g

Stuffed Chicken for Bacon Lovers

Prep time: 10 minutes| Cook time: 20 minutes| Serves: 4

4 (5 ounce) boneless, skinless chicken breasts, sliced into ¼-inch-thick	8 slices thin cut bacon or beef bacon
2 packages Boursin cheese	sprig of fresh cilantro for garnish
	avocado oil for cooking spray

Getting the ingredients ready. Avocado oil should be sprayed on the cooking tray. To preheat your air fryer to 400 degrees F, select Air Fry function. Press Start to begin. On a chopping board, place one of the chicken breasts. Make a 1-inch-wide incision at the top of the breast with a sharp knife held parallel to the cutting board. Carefully cut a big pocket into the breast, leaving a 1- to 2- inch border on the sides and bottom. Repeat with the remaining three chicken breasts. To make a 3- to 4-inch hole, snip the corner of a big re-sealable plastic bag. Place the Boursin cheese in the bag and pipe it into the pockets in the chicken breasts, evenly distributing the cheese. Each chicken breast should be wrapped in two slices of bacon and tooth-picked at the ends. Select Air Fry function. Cook the bacon-wrapped chicken in the cooking tray for 18 to 20 minutes, turning after 10 minutes, until the bacon is crisp and the internal temperature of the chicken reaches 165 degrees F. If preferred, garnish with a sprig of cilantro before serving.

Per serving: Calories 446; Fat 17g; Sodium 350mg; Carbs 13g; Fiber 1.9g; Sugar 1.2g; Protein 36g

Easy Turkey Breast

Prep time: 5 minutes| Cook time: 60 minutes| Serves: 6

pepper and salt	turkey seasonings of choice
1 oven-ready turkey breast	

To preheat your air fryer, select Air Fry function. Set time to 60

minutes and temperature to 400 degrees F. Season the turkey with pepper, salt, and any other seasonings you like. When the display shows "Add Food", place the turkey on the cooking tray in the air fryer. When the meat is done, it should be 165 degrees. Allow 10-15 minutes for resting before slicing. Enjoy.
Per serving: Calories 212; Fat 12g; Sodium 340mg; Carbs 3g; Fiber 1g; Sugar 0g; Protein 24g

Chicken Tenders with Mustard

Prep time: 5 minutes| Cook time: 20 minutes| Serves: 4

½ cup coconut flour
1 tablespoon spicy brown mustard

2 beaten eggs
1 pound chicken tenders

Season the tenders with salt and pepper. Apply a perfect coating of mustard to the tenders. Dip coated tenders in egg and then cover tenders with flour completely. Select Air Fry function. Set the temperature to 400 degrees F and the timer to 20 minutes in the air fryer. Cook for 20 minutes and remove from air fryer when cooking time is over. Serve hot.
Per serving: Calories 346; Fat 10g; Sodium 170mg; Carbs 12g; Fiber 1.9g; Sugar 1g; Protein 31g

Air Fryer Chicken Meatballs

Prep time: 5 minutes| Cook time: 15 minutes| Serves: 2

½ pound chicken breast
1 tablespoon garlic
1 tablespoon onion

½ chicken broth
1 tablespoon oatmeal, whole wheat flour, or of your choice

In a food processor, combine all of the ingredients and pulse until well combined and ground. If you don't have a food processor, have the butcher ground it for you, then mix in the rest of the ingredients thoroughly. Form the balls into balls and set them in the cooking tray. Select Air Fry function. Set temperature to 400 degrees F and time to 15 minutes. Shake the tray halfway through to loosen the meatballs and ensure consistent cooking.
Per serving: Calories 45; Fat 1.57g; Sodium 70mg; Carbs 1.94g; Fiber 0.1g; Sugar 0.1g; Protein 5.34g

Air Fryer Chicken Breast

Prep time: 30 minutes| Cook time: 20 minutes| Serves: 6

1 pound diced clean chicken breast
½ lemon
smoked paprika to taste

black pepper or chili powder to taste
salt to taste

Season the chicken with salt, paprika, and pepper and set it aside to marinade. Select Air Fry function. Place in the air fryer and set time to 20 minutes and temperature to 400 degrees F. Place the chicken into the air fryer. Cook for 20 minutes. Turn the chicken over after 10 minutes. Cook for another 10 minutes, or until golden. Serve right away.
Per serving: Calories 124; Fat 1.4g; Sodium 170mg; Carbs 0g; Fiber 0g; Sugar 0g; Protein 26.1g

Crispy Breaded Chicken Without Flour

Prep time: 10 minutes| Cook time: 15 minutes| Serves: 6

1 ⅛ ounce grated parmesan   cheese

1 unit egg
1 pound chicken (breast)

Salt and black pepper to taste

Season the chicken breast with salt & pepper and cut it into 6 fillets. In a mixing dish, beat the egg. Pass the chicken breast through the egg, then sprinkle the fillets with shredded cheese. Select Air Fry function. Set timer to 30 minutes and temperature to 400 degrees F. Air fry for about 30 minutes or until golden brown at 400 degrees F. When cooked, serve.
Per serving: Calories 114; Fat 5.9g; Sodium 270mg; Carbs 13g; Fiber 2g; Sugar 3.2g; Protein 2.3g

Easy Spicy Chicken Wings

Prep time: 15 minutes| Cook time: 15 minutes| Serves: 6

4 pounds chicken wings
½ tablespoon ginger
2 tablespoons vinegar
1 fresh lime juice
1 tablespoon olive oil

2 tablespoons soy sauce
6 garlic cloves, minced
1 habanero, chopped
¼ teaspoon cinnamon
½ teaspoon sea salt

To preheat your air fryer to 400 degrees F, select Air Fry function and set time to 15 minutes and temperature to 400 degrees F. Press Start to begin. In a large mixing basin, combine all of the ingredients. Refrigerate the chicken wings for 2 hours after dipping them in the marinade. When the display shows "Add Food", place the marinated chicken wings onto the cooking tray. Cook for 15 minutes in the air fryer. Serve immediately!
Per serving: Calories 673; Fat 29g; Sodium 370mg; Carbs 9g; Fiber 1g; Sugar 1g; Protein 39g

Chorizo and Chicken Barbecue

Prep time: 5 minutes | Cook time: 35 minutes| Serves: 4

4 chicken thighs
2 Tuscan sausages

4 small onions

To preheat your air fryer to 400 degrees F, select Air Fry function. Set time to 30 minutes and temperature to 400 degrees F. Press Start to begin. Season the meat as you would if you were going to cook it on the air fryer. Check after 20 minutes to see whether any of the meat has reached your desired temperature. If that's the case, remove whichever one is done and put it back in the air fryer with the others for another 10 minutes at 400 degrees F. If not, finish them in the air fryer at 400 degrees F for the last 10 minutes.
Per serving: Calories 135; Fat 5g; Sodium 170mg; Carbs 0g; Fiber 0g; Sugar 0g; Protein 6g

Chicken Thigh Roasted in Air Fryer

Prep time: 5 minutes| Cook time: 30 minutes| Serves: 1

3 chicken thighs and thighs
2 red seasonal bags
1 clove garlic

½ teaspoon salt
1 pinch black pepper

Red seasoning, minced garlic, salt, and pepper should be to season the chicken. Allow 5-10 minutes for the taste to develop. Select Roast function. Place the chicken in the cooking tray and set time to 20 minutes and temperature to 365 degrees F then bake. Remove the cooking tray and inspect the chicken spot after that time has passed. Turn it over and bake for another 10 minutes at 365 degrees F if it's still raw or not brown enough. Your chicken will be ready to cook in the air fryer after the previous stage! Serve with a leaf salad and doer potatoes.
Per serving: Calories 278; Fat 18g; Sodium 370mg; Carbs 0.1g;

Fiber 0g; Sugar 0g; Protein 31g

Fit Coxinha

Prep time: 10 minutes| Cook time: 10-15 minutes| Serves: 4

½ pound seasoned and minced chicken
1 cup light cottage cheese

1 egg
Condiments to taste
Flaxseed or oatmeal

Combine all of the ingredients, except the flour, in a mixing bowl. Knead well with your hands and form into a Coxinha shape. You may fill it with chicken or cheese if you like. Repeat the procedure until all of the dough has been used up. Dredge the drumsticks in flour before placing them in the air fryer. Preheat the air fryer to 365 degrees F and select Bake function then set timer to 15 minutes and temperature to 365 degrees F after that bake it.
Per Serving: Calories 220; Fat 18g; Sodium 170mg; Carbs 40g; Fiber 7g; Sugar 5.1g; Protein 100g

Turkey Breast with Cherry Tomatoes

Prep time: 5 minutes| Cook time: 10 minutes| Serves: 4

1 box of cherry tomatoes
¼ pound turkey blanket

Tomatoes are wrapped around the turkey and covered with toothpicks. Select Air Fry function. Set timer to 10 minutes and temperature to 400 degrees F. Cook for 10 minutes in air fryer. Ricotta and other light ingredients can be added to the filling to make it more substantial.
Per serving: Calories 172; Fat 2g; Sodium 140mg; Carbs 3g; Fiber 1g; Sugar 1g; Protein 34g

Beer Air Fryer Chicken

Prep time: 5 minutes| Cook time: 10 minutes| Serves: 4

2 ¼ pounds chicken thigh and thigh
½ can of beer

4 cloves of garlic
1 large onion
Pepper and salt to taste

To make the chicken pieces healthier, wash them and remove the skin if required. Arrange on an air fryer-safe platter. In a blender, combine the remaining ingredients: beer, onion, garlic, and salt & pepper. Cover the chicken in this mixture and leave it to float in the beer. Select Air Fry function. Set timer to 45 minutes and temperature to 400 degrees F. Cook for 45 minutes. When it has a brown cone on top and the beer has dried a little, it is ready to roast.
Per serving: Calories 674; Fat 41.94g; Sodium 170mg; Carbs 5.47g; Fiber 1g; Sugar 1.62g; Protein 61.94g

Fillets of Chicken in Air Fryer

Prep time: 5 minutes| Cook time: 20 minutes| Serves: 4

4 chicken fillets
Salt to taste
1 garlic clove, crushed

Thyme to taste
Black pepper to taste

Season the fillets and wrap them tightly for taste. Select Bake function. Place the fillets in the basket and set timer to 20 minutes and temperature to 365 degrees F then bake. Turn the fillets after 5 minutes. Serve!
Per serving: Calories 90; Fat 1g; Sodium 270mg; Carbs 1g; Fiber 0g; Sugar 0g; Protein 17g

Lemon and Bahian Seasoning Chicken

Prep time: 2 hours| Cook time: 20 minutes| Serves: 4

5 pieces chicken to bird
2 garlic cloves, crushed
4 tablespoons lemon juice

1 coffee spoon Bahian spices
Salt and black pepper to taste

Combine the chicken pieces and seasonings in a covered bowl. Lemon juice should be added now. Allow the chicken to marinade for 2 hours in the covered container. Place each piece of chicken in the air fryer basket without them overlapping. Select Air Fry function. Set timer to 20 minutes and temperature to 400 degrees F then cook for 20 minutes. Serve!
Per serving: Calories 316.2; Fat 15.3g; Sodium 170mg; Carbs 15.3g; Fiber 2g; Sugar 2.5g; Protein 32.8g

BBQ Chicken in Air Fryer

Prep time: 5 minutes| Cook time: 20 minutes| Serves: 4

2 tablespoons Worcestershire Sauce
1 tablespoon honey
¾ cup ketchup

2 teaspoons chipotle chili powder
6 chicken drumsticks

Combine the Worcestershire sauce, honey, ketchup, and chili powder in a large mixing basin. Mix everything up thoroughly. Place the drumsticks in the mixture and flip them to coat them completely. Place 3 chicken drumsticks in the cooking tray and coat them with nonstick spray. Select Air Fry function. Set timer to 17 minutes and 15 minutes for tiny drumsticks and temperature to 400 degrees F. Cook by flipping halfway through. Continue with the last three drumsticks.
Per serving: Calories 145; Fat 2.6g; Sodium 240mg; Carbs 4.5g; Fiber 1g; Sugar 1g; Protein 13g

Easy No Frills Turkey Breast

Prep time: 5 minutes| Cook time: 50 minutes| Serves: 4

1 bone in turkey breast (about 8 pounds)
2 tablespoons olive oil

2 tablespoons sea salt
1 tablespoon black pepper

Preheat the air fryer to 400 degrees F for around 8 minutes. Both the skin and the interior of the cavity of the cleaned turkey breast should be rubbed with olive oil. Season it with black pepper and sea salt. Remove the basket from the air fryer and spray it with nonstick spray that has a butter or olive oil taste. Place the turkey breast side down in the pan. Select Air Fry function. Set Timer to 40 minutes and temperature to 400 degrees F. Cook for 20 minutes before carefully flipping the breast. Cook for another 20 minutes after spraying with cooking oil. When you're finished, check the temperature with a thermometer; it should register 165 degrees F. If not, reinsert it for a few moments. Allow at least 15 minutes for the breast to rest before carving and serving.
Per serving: Calories 375; Fat 6.8g; Sodium 220mg; Carbs 8.2g; Fiber 1g; Sugar 1g; Protein 15g

Yummy Turkey Legs

Prep time: 5 minutes| Cook time: 10 minutes| Serves: 4

1 turkey leg
1 teaspoon olive oil
1 teaspoon poultry seasoning
1 teaspoon garlic powder
Salt and black pepper to taste

Preheat the air fryer to 400 degrees F for about 4 minutes. Olive oil should be applied to the leg. Simply massage it in with your hands. Combine the chicken seasoning, garlic powder, salt, and pepper in a small bowl. It should be rubbed on the turkey leg. Select Air Fry function. Set timer to 27 minutes and temperature to 400 degrees F. Place the turkey leg in the cooking tray after spraying the interior with nonstick spray. Cook for 27 minutes, with a 14-minute turn. Insert a meat thermometer into the meaty portion of the leg to check for doneness; it should register 165 degrees F.
Per serving: Calories 325; Fat 10g; Sodium 270mg; Carbs 8.3g; Fiber 1g; Sugar 1g; Protein 18g

Herby Fried Chicken

Prep time: 5 minutes| Cook time: 50 minutes| Serves: 4

2 pounds deboned chicken thighs
1 teaspoon rosemary
1 teaspoon thyme
1 teaspoon garlic powder
1 large lemon

Trim the fat off the thighs and season them on all sides with salt and pepper. Combine the rosemary, thyme, and garlic powder in a bowl. Sprinkle the chicken thighs with the mixture and press it in, then place them on a baking sheet. Squeeze the lemon juice over all of the chicken thighs. Refrigerate for 30 minutes after wrapping in plastic wrap. Select Air Fry function. Set timer to 15 minutes and temperature to 400 degrees F. Place as many thighs as will fit in one layer in the cooking tray. Cook for 15 minutes, with a 7-minute turn. Serve hot.
Per serving: Calories 534; Fat 27.8g; Sodium 370mg; Carbs 2.5g; Fiber 0.1g; Sugar 0.5g; Protein 66.2g

Spicy Wings

Prep time: 5 minutes| Cook time: 10 minutes| Serves: 4

2 teaspoons salt
2 teaspoons fresh ground
pepper
2 pounds chicken wings

Combine the salt and pepper in a bowl. Toss the wings into the dish and coat each one with your hands. In a cooking tray coated with nonstick cooking spray, place 8 to 10 wings. Select Bake function (no need to preheat) and set timer to 15 minutes and temperature to 365 degrees F then bake for 15 minutes, rotating once after 7 minutes. Repeat with the remaining wings and serve immediately.
Per serving: Calories 342; Fat 14.8g; Sodium 440mg; Carbs 1g; Fiber 0g; Sugar 0g; Protein 49.2g

Chicken Wings with Parmesan

Prep time: 10 minutes| Cook time: 25 minutes| Serves: 4

1 ½ pounds. chicken wings
¾ tablespoon garlic powder
¼ cup parmesan cheese, grated
2 tablespoons arrowroot powder
Salt and pepper

Preheat the air fryer to 400 degrees F. Combine garlic powder, parmesan cheese, arrowroot powder, pepper, and salt in a mixing bowl. Toss in the chicken wings until fully coated. In the cooking tray, place the chicken wings. Cooking spray the tops of the chicken wings. Start by selecting air fryer and time for 20 minutes and temperature at 400 degrees F and pressing the start button. Halfway through, shake the cooking tray.

Air Fried Western Wings

Prep time: 10 minutes| Cook time: 15 minutes Serves: 4

2 pounds chicken wings
1 teaspoon Herb de Provence
1 teaspoon paprika
½ cup parmesan cheese, grated
Salt and pepper

In a large mixing bowl, combine the cheese, paprika, herb de Provence, pepper, and salt. Toss the chicken wings in the basin to evenly coat them. Preheat the air fryer to 350 degrees F. Select Air Fry function. In the cooking tray, place the chicken wings. Cooking spray the tops of the chicken wings. Set the cooking time to 15 minutes and temperature at 400 degrees F for chicken wings. Cook by flipping wings halfway. Serve and have fun.
Per serving: Calories 473; Fat 19.6g; Sodium 370mg; Carbs 0.8g; Fiber 0g; Sugar 0.1g; Protein 69.7g

Simple Air Fried Thighs

Prep time: 10 minutes| Cook time: 15 minutes| Serves: 4

4 chicken thighs, bone-in & skinless
¼ teaspoon ground ginger
2 teaspoons paprika
2 teaspoons garlic powder
Salt and pepper

Preheat the air fryer to 400 degrees F. Rub ginger, paprika, garlic powder, pepper, and salt all over the chicken thighs in a bowl. Using frying spray, coat the chicken thighs. Select Air Fry function. Set timer to 15 minutes and temperature to 400 degrees F. Cook for 10 minutes in the cooking tray with chicken thighs. Cook for another 5 minutes after turning the chicken thighs. Serve and enjoy.
Per serving: Calories 286; Fat 11g; Sodium 190mg; Carbs 1.8g; Fiber 0.1g; Sugar 0.5g; Protein 42.7g

Spicy Chicken Tenders

Prep time: 10 minutes| Cook time: 13 minutes| Serves: 4

6 chicken tenders
1 teaspoon onion powder
1 teaspoon garlic powder
1 teaspoon paprika
1 teaspoon kosher salt

Preheat the air fryer to 400 degrees F. Combine onion powder, garlic powder, paprika, and salt in a dish and coat chicken tenders evenly. Using cooking spray, coat the chicken tenders. Select Air Fry function. Set timer to 13 minutes and temperature to 400 degrees F. Cook for 13 minutes in the cooking tray with chicken tenders. Serve and have fun.
Per serving: Calories 423; Fat 16.4g; Sodium 270mg; Carbs 1.5g; Fiber 0.1g; Sugar 0.5g; Protein 63.7g

Chicken with Spicy Mustard Sauce

Prep time: 15 minutes| Cook time: 20 minutes| Serves: 6

2 eggs
1 ½ pounds chicken breasts,
boneless, skinless, cut into bite-sized chunks

½ cup crushed pretzels
1 teaspoon shallot powder
1 teaspoon paprika
Sea salt and ground black pepper to taste
½ cup vegetable broth
1 tablespoon cornstarch
3 tablespoons Worcestershire

sauce
3 tablespoons tomato paste
1 tablespoon apple cider vinegar
2 tablespoons olive oil
2 garlic cloves, chopped
1 jalapeno pepper, minced
1 teaspoon yellow mustard

Preheat your air fryer to 400 degrees F. Whisk the eggs until foamy in a mixing bowl; throw the chicken bits into the whisked eggs and coat thoroughly. Combine the crushed pretzels, shallot powder, paprika, salt, and pepper in a separate dish. Then, place the chicken chunks in the pretzel mixture and toss them around until they're evenly covered. In the cooking tray, place the chicken pieces. Select Air Fry function. Set timer to 12 minutes and temperature to 400 degrees F. Cook the chicken in the air fryer for 12 minutes, shaking halfway through. Meanwhile, combine the vegetable broth, cornstarch, Worcestershire sauce, tomato paste, and apple cider vinegar in a large mixing bowl. Over medium heat, preheat a cast-iron skillet. Sauté the garlic with the jalapeño pepper in the olive oil for 30 to 40 seconds, stirring regularly. Allow the sauce to thicken slightly before adding the cornstarch mixture. Add the air-fried chicken and mustard and continue to cook for another 2 minutes, or until cooked through. Serve right away and enjoy.

Per Serving: Calories 357; Fat 17.6g; Sodium 470mg; Carbs 20.3g; Fiber 4g; Sugar 2.8g; Protein 28.1g

Turkey Chicken Thigh in Chinese Style

Prep time: 20 minutes| Cook time: 35 minutes| Serves: 6

1 tablespoon sesame oil
2 pounds turkey thighs
1 teaspoon Chinese Five spice powder
1 teaspoon pink Himalayan salt
¼ teaspoon Sichuan pepper

6 tablespoons honey
1 tablespoon Chinese rice vinegar
2 tablespoons soy sauce
1 tablespoon sweet chili sauce
1 tablespoon mustard

Preheat the air fryer to 400 degrees F. Brush the turkey thighs with the sesame oil. Spices are used to season them. Select Air Fry function. Set time to 23 minutes and temperature to 400 degrees F. Cook for 23 minutes, flipping once or twice throughout cooking. To achieve uniform cooking, make sure to operate in batches. Meanwhile, mix the other ingredients in a prepared wok (or similar style pan) over medium-high heat. Cook, stirring constantly, until the sauce has been reduced by approximately a third. In the same wok, add the fried turkey thighs and gently swirl to coat them in the sauce. Allow 10 minutes for the turkey to rest before slicing and serving. Enjoy!

Per serving: Calories 279; Fat 10.1g; Sodium 430mg; Carbs 19g; Fiber 4g; Sugar 17.9g; Protein 27.7g

Simple Hot Drumsticks

Prep time: 40 minutes| Cook time: 30 minutes| Serves: 6

6 chicken drumsticks
For Sauce:
6 ounces hot sauce
3 tablespoons olive oil

3 tablespoons tamari sauce
1 teaspoon dried thyme
½ teaspoon dried oregano

Using a nonstick cooking spray, coat the sides and bottom of the cooking tray. Select Air Fry function. Set time to 35 minutes and temperature to 400 degrees F. Cook the chicken drumsticks for 35 minutes, turning halfway through. Meanwhile, in a skillet over medium-low heat, combine the spicy sauce, olive oil,

tamari sauce, thyme, and oregano; set aside. Drizzle the sauce over the cooked chicken drumsticks and toss well to coat. Bon appétit!

Per serving: Calories 280; Fat 18.7g; Sodium 470mg; Carbs 2.6g; Fiber 1g; Sugar 1.4g; Protein 24.1g

Crunchy Chicken Tenders with Peanuts

Prep time: 25 minutes| Cook time: 20 minutes| Serves: 4

1 ½ pounds chicken tenderloins
2 tablespoons peanut oil
½ cup tortilla chips, crushed
Sea salt and ground black

pepper to taste
½ teaspoon garlic powder
1 teaspoon red pepper flakes
2 tablespoons peanuts, roasted and roughly chopped

Preheat your air fryer to 400 degrees F. Brush the chicken tenderloins on all sides with peanut oil. Combine the crumbled chips, salt, black pepper, garlic powder, and red pepper flakes in a mixing bowl. Dredge the chicken in the breading and shake off any excess. Select Air Fry function. Set timer to 13 minutes and temperature to 400 degrees F. In the cooking tray, place the chicken tenderloins. Cook for 13 minutes, or until the Centre is no longer pink. Cook in batches until an instant-read thermometer registers 165 degrees F. Serve with toasted peanuts on top. Bon appétit!

Per serving: Calories 343; Fat 16.4g; Sodium 370mg; Carbs 10.6g; Fiber 3g; Sugar 1g; Protein 36.8g

Baby Potatoes and Turkey Tenderloins

Prep time: 50 minutes| Cook time: 50 minutes| Serves: 6

2 pounds turkey tenderloins
2 teaspoons olive oil
Salt and ground black pepper to taste
1 teaspoon smoked paprika

2 tablespoons dry white wine
1 tablespoon fresh tarragon leaves, chopped
1-pound baby potatoes, rubbed

Olive oil should be brushed on the turkey tenderloins. Season with paprika, salt, and black pepper. Add the white wine and tarragon after that. Select Air Fry function. Set timer to 30 minutes and temperature to 400 degrees F. Cook the turkey tenderloins for 30 minutes, turning halfway through. Allow for 5 to 9 minutes of resting time before slicing and serving. Using the remaining 1 teaspoon of olive oil, spray the sides and bottom of the cooking tray. Preheat the air fryer to 400 degrees F and fry the tiny potatoes for 15 minutes. Serve with the turkey and have a good time!

Per serving: Calories 317; Fat 7.4g; Sodium 430mg; Carbs 14.2g; Fiber 2g; Sugar 1.1g; Protein 45.7g

Mediterranean Chicken in Air Fryer

Prep time: 1 hour| Cook time: 30 minutes| Serves: 8

2 teaspoons olive oil, melted
3 pounds chicken breasts, bone-in
½ teaspoon black pepper, freshly ground
½ teaspoon salt
1 teaspoon cayenne pepper

2 tablespoons fresh parsley, minced
1 teaspoon fresh basil, minced
1 teaspoon fresh rosemary, minced
4 medium-sized Roma tomatoes, halved

Preheat your air fryer to 400 degrees F. Using 1 teaspoon olive oil, brush over the cooking tray. All of the ingredients mentioned above should be sprinkled over the chicken breasts. Select Air Fry function. Set timer to 25 minutes and temperature to 400 degrees F. Cook for 25 minutes, or until the chicken breasts have little bit browned. Organize your work in chunks. Brush the tomatoes with the remaining teaspoon of olive oil and arrange them in the cooking tray. Season with a pinch of salt. Cook the tomatoes for 10 minutes at 400 degrees F at Air Fry function, shaking halfway through the process. Serve with chicken breasts on the side. Bon appétit!

Per serving: Calories 315; Fat 17.1g; Sodium 370mg; Carbs 2.7g; Fiber 1g; Sugar 1.7g; Protein 36g

Red Duck with Onions

Prep time: 25 minutes| Cook time: 25 minutes| Serves: 4

1 ½ pounds duck breasts, skin removed	1 tablespoon Thai red curry paste
1 teaspoon kosher salt	1 cup candy onions, halved
½ teaspoon cayenne pepper	¼ small pack coriander, chopped
⅓ teaspoon black pepper	
½ teaspoon smoked paprika	

Place the duck breasts between two pieces of foil and pound them with a rolling pin until they are 1-inch-thick. Preheat the air fryer to 400 degrees F. Salt, cayenne pepper, black pepper, paprika, and red curry paste are rubbed into the duck breasts. In the cooking tray, place the duck breast. Select Air Fry function. Set timer to 12 minutes and temperature to 400 degrees F. Cook for 12 minutes. Cook for another 10 to 11 minutes after adding the candied onions. Serve with coriander as a garnish and enjoy!

Per serving: Calories 362; Fat 18.7g; Sodium 450mg; Carbs 4g; Fiber 1g; Sugar 1.3g; Protein 42.3g

Chicken Leg with Turnip

Prep time: 30 minutes| Cook time: 25 minutes| Serves: 3

1-pound chicken legs	pepper
1 teaspoon Himalayan salt	1 teaspoon butter, melted
1 teaspoon paprika	1 turnip, trimmed, and sliced
½ teaspoon ground black	

Using a nonstick cooking spray, coat the sides and bottom of the cooking tray. Using salt, paprika, and ground black pepper, season the chicken legs. Select Air Fry function. Set timer to 10 minutes and temperature to 400 degrees F. Cook for 10 minutes. Drizzle melted butter over turnip slices and place them in the cooking tray with the chicken. Cook the turnips and chicken for a further 15 minutes, turning halfway through. An instant-read thermometer should read at least 165 degrees F for the chicken. Serve and have fun!

Per serving: Calories 207; Fat 7.8g; Sodium 190mg; Carbs 3.4g; Fiber 1g; Sugar 1.6g; Protein 29.5g

Chicken Drumettes

Prep time: 30 minutes| Cook time: 22 minutes| Serves: 3

⅓ cup all-purpose flour	1 teaspoon rosemary
½ teaspoon ground white pepper	1 whole egg + 1 egg white
1 teaspoon seasoning salt	6 chicken drumettes
1 teaspoon garlic paste	1 heaping tablespoon fresh chives, chopped

Preheat your air fryer to 400 degrees F. In a small mixing bowl, combine the flour, white pepper, salt, garlic paste, and rosemary.

In a separate dish, whisk the eggs until they are foamy. Dip the chicken in the flour mixture, then the beaten eggs, then back into the flour mixture. Select Air Fry function. Set timer to 22 minutes and temperature to 400 degrees F. Cook for 22 minutes the chicken drumettes. Garnish with chives and serve warm.

Per serving: Calories 347; Fat 9.1g; Sodium 430mg; Carbs 11.3g; Fiber 1g; Sugar 0.1g; Protein 41g

Chicken Nuggets in Air Fryer

Prep time: 20 minutes | Cook time: 8 minutes | Serves: 4

1 ½ pounds chicken tenderloins, cut into small pieces	freshly cracked
	4 tablespoons olive oil
½ teaspoon garlic salt	⅓ cup saltines (e.g., Ritz crackers), crushed
½ teaspoon cayenne pepper	4 tablespoons Parmesan cheese, freshly grated
¼ teaspoon black pepper,	

Preheat your air fryer to 400 degrees F. Garlic salt, cayenne pepper, and black pepper are sprinkled over each piece of chicken. Combine the olive oil and crushed saltines in a mixing dish and stir well. Each piece of chicken should be dipped in the cracker mixture. Roll the chicken pieces in the Parmesan cheese at the end. Select Air Fry function. Set timer to 8 minutes and temperature to 400 degrees F each time. Working in batches, cook. If you wish to reheat the chicken nuggets later, place them in the basket and cook for another minute. If preferred, serve with French fries.

Per serving: Calories 355; Fat 20.1g; Sodium 470mg; Carbs 5.3g; Fiber 1g; Sugar 0.2g; Protein 36.6g

Asian Style Cheese Chicken Fillets

Prep time: 50 minutes| Cook time: 20 minutes| Serves: 2

4 rashers smoked bacon	1 teaspoon black mustard seeds
2 chicken fillets	
½ teaspoon coarse sea salt	1 teaspoon mild curry powder
¼ teaspoon black pepper, preferably freshly ground	½ cup coconut milk
1 teaspoon garlic, minced	⅓ cup tortilla chips, crushed
1 (2-inch) piece ginger, peeled and minced	½ cup Pecorino Romano cheese, freshly grated

Preheat your air fryer to 400 degrees F. Cook for 5 to 7 minutes in the preheated air fryer with the smoked bacon. Set aside. Put the chicken fillets, salt, black pepper, garlic, ginger, mustard seeds, curry powder, and milk in a mixing bowl. Allow it to marinade for 30 minutes in the refrigerator. Combine the crumbled chips and shredded Pecorino Romano cheese in a separate bowl. Select Air Fry function. Set timer to 12 minutes and temperature to 400 degrees F. Transfer the chicken fillets to the cooking tray after dredging them in the chips mixture. Cook the chicken for 6 minutes on one side. Cook for another 6 minutes on the other side. Repeat until you've used up all of your components. Serve with reserved bacon. Enjoy!

Per serving: Calories 376; Fat 19.6g; Sodium 445mg; Carbs 12.1g; Fiber 2g; Sugar 3.4g; Protein 36.2g

Brussels Sprouts Paprika Chicken Legs

Prep time: 30 minutes| Cook time: 20 minutes| Serves: 2

2 chicken legs	½ teaspoon black pepper
½ teaspoon paprika	1-pound Brussels sprouts
½ teaspoon kosher salt	1 teaspoon dill, fresh or dried

Preheat your air fryer to 400 degrees F. Season the chicken with paprika, salt, and pepper at this point. Place the chicken legs in the cooking tray and set aside. Select Air Fry function. Set timer to 10 minutes and temperature to 400 degrees F. Cook for 10 minutes before serving. Cook for another 10 minutes after flipping the chicken legs. Set aside. Sprinkle the dill over the Brussels sprouts in the cooking basket. Cook for 15 minutes at 400 degrees F again on Air Fry function, shaking the basket halfway through. Serve with the chicken legs that were set aside. Bon appétit!

Per serving: Calories 355; Fat 20.1g; Sodium 290mg; Carbs 5.3g; Fiber 1.2g; Sugar 0.2g; Protein 36.6g

Chinese Style Duck

Prep time: 30 minutes| Cook time: 20 minutes| Serves: 6

2 pounds duck breast, boneless
2 green onions, chopped
1 tablespoon light soy sauce
1 teaspoon Chinese 5 spice powder
1 teaspoon Szechuan peppercorns
3 tablespoons Shaoxing rice

wine
1 teaspoon coarse salt
½ teaspoon ground black pepper
Glaze:
¼ cup molasses
3 tablespoons orange juice
1 tablespoon soy sauce

Place the duck breasts, green onions, light soy sauce, Chinese 5 spice powder, Szechuan peppercorns, and Shaoxing rice wine in a ceramic bowl and mix well. Allow it to marinade in the refrigerator for 1 hour. Preheat your air fryer for 5 minutes at 400 degrees F. Select Air Fry function. Set timer to 15 minutes and temperature to 400 degrees F. Remove the duck breasts

from the marinade and season them with salt and pepper. Cook for 15 minutes, or until the duck breasts are golden brown. Repeat with the remaining ingredients. Meanwhile, transfer the remaining marinade to a prepared saucepan over medium-high heat. Combine the molasses, orange juice, and 1 tablespoon soy sauce in a mixing bowl.

Per serving: Calories 403; Fat 25.3g; Sodium 670mg; Carbs 16.4g; Fiber 5g; Sugar 13.2g; Protein 27.5g

Scrambled Egg and Turkey Bacon

Prep time: 25 minutes| Cook time: 20 minutes| Serves: 4

½-pound turkey bacon
4 eggs
⅓ cup milk
2 tablespoons yogurt

½ teaspoon sea salt
1 bell pepper, finely chopped
2 green onions, finely chopped
½ cup Colby cheese, shredded

In the cooking tray, place the turkey bacon. Select Air Fry function. Set timer to 11 minutes and temperature to 400 degrees F. Cook for 11 minutes. Organize your work in chunks. Keep the fried bacon aside. Whisk the eggs, milk, and yoghurt together thoroughly in a mixing dish. Season with salt, pepper, and green onions. Use the remaining 1 teaspoon of bacon oil to brush the sides and bottom of the baking pan. Fill the baking pan halfway with the egg mixture. Select Air Fry again and set temperature to 400 degrees F and timer to 10 minutes. Cook for about 5 minutes. Cook for a further 5 to 6 minutes after adding the shredded Colby cheese. Enjoy the scrambled eggs with the bacon that was set aside!

Per serving: Calories 456; Fat 38.3g; Sodium 470mg; Carbs 6.3g; Fiber 1g; Sugar 4.5g; Protein 1.4g

Beef, Lamb, and Pork

Garlicky Herbed Lamb Cutlets

Prep time: 30 minutes| Cook time: 25 minutes| Serves: 2

2 lamb racks (with 3 cutlets per rack)
2 cloves garlic, peeled and thinly sliced
2 long sprigs of fresh

rosemary, leaves removed
2 tablespoons wholegrain mustard
1 tablespoon honey
2 tablespoon mint sauce

Trim fat and cut slits in the top of the lamb. Insert the garlic and rosemary leaves in the slits and set the lamb aside. Whisk the mustard, honey, and mint sauce together for marinade and brush over the lamb racks. Let the lamb marinade in a fridge for 20 minutes. Preheat the air fryer to 360 degrees F for about 5 minutes at the "Air Fry" setting. Spray the air fryer cooking tray with cooking spray and place the marinated lamb rack into the cooking tray. Air fry the lamb for 10 minutes, flipping halfway, and air fry for 10 more minutes. Once done, place on a platter and cover with foil to rest for 10 minutes before slicing and serving. Serve warm with your favorite sauce and salad on the side and enjoy.

Per Serving: Calories 248; Fat 10g; Sodium 546mg; Carbs 5g; Fiber 2.1g; Sugar 1g; Protein 45g

Aromatic Lamb Chops with Garlic Sauce

Prep time: 15 minutes| Cook time: 25 minutes| Serves: 4

1 garlic bulb
1 teaspoon + 3 tablespoons olive oil
1 tablespoon fresh oregano,

chopped fine
¼ teaspoon ground pepper
½ teaspoon sea salt
8 lamb chops

Preheat the air fryer to 400 ° F for 5 minutes at the "roast" setting. While the air fryer is preheating, take the excess paper for the garlic bulb. Spray the air fryer cooking tray with cooking oil. Coat the garlic bulb with 1 teaspoon of olive oil and wrap it in the foil, drop it in the greased cooking tray. Roast the garlic for 12 minutes. In a bowl, combine the 3 tablespoons of olive oil, oregano, salt, and pepper and mix well. Lightly coat the lamb chops on both with the resulting oil. Let the chops sit at room temperature for 5 minutes. Remove the garlic bulb from the air fryer and if it is cool, preheat again to 400 degrees F for 3 minutes. Spray the air fryer cooking tray with cooking oil and place chops in roasting at 400 degrees F for 5 minutes. Place them on a platter and cover to keep them warm while you do the other chops. In a small bowl, squeeze garlic clove between the thumb and index finger. Taste and add salt and pepper and mix well into a fine sauce. Serve garlic sauce along with the chops like serving ketchup.

Per Serving: Calories 425; Fat 12g; Sodium 652mg; Carbs 9g; Fiber 2g; Sugar 3g; Protein 36g

Herb Coated Lamb Chops

Prep time: 5 minutes| Cook time: 15 minutes| Serves: 2

1 teaspoon oregano
1 teaspoon coriander
1 teaspoon thyme
1 teaspoon rosemary
½ teaspoon salt

¼ teaspoon pepper
2 tablespoons lemon juice
1 tablespoon olive oil
1 pound lamb chops

In a resealable bag, add the oregano, coriander, thyme, rosemary, salt, pepper, lemon juice, and olive oil and shake well to mix. Place the chops in the spiced mix bag and squish to toss the chop with the mixture. Refrigerate 1 hour for well marinated. Preheat the air fryer to 390 degrees F for 5 minutes at the "Air Fry" setting. Place the chops in the air fryer cooking tray that has been sprayed with cooking spray. Air fry the meat for 3 minutes, flip the chops, and cook for another 4 minutes for medium-rare. Serve hot with ranch sauce.

Per Serving: Calories 624; Fat 25g; Sodium 1070mg; Carbs 7g; Fiber 3g; Sugar 0.3g; Protein 58g

Spiced Rack of Lamb

Prep time: 15 minutes| Cook time: 35 minutes| Serves: 2

1 tablespoon olive oil
1 clove garlic, peeled and minced
1 ½ teaspoon fresh ground pepper
1 tablespoon fresh rosemary, chopped

chopped
1 tablespoon fresh thyme, chopped
¾ cup breadcrumbs
1 egg
2 pounds rack of lamb

In a small bowl, add the olive oil and then the garlic. Mix well. Brush the garlic oil on the rack of lamb and season well with pepper. In a large bowl, combine the rosemary, thyme, and breadcrumbs. In another bowl, break the egg and whisk well. Preheat the air fryer at 350 degrees F for 5 minutes on the "Air Fry" setting. Spray the cooking tray with cooking spray. Dip the marinated lamb rack in the egg and then place in the breadcrumb mixture and coat the rack. Place rack in the air fryer cooking tray and air fry for 20 minutes. Increase the temperature to 400 degrees F and set for 5 more minutes. Take a foil and wrap the fried lamb carefully in it and wrap it well and sit for about 10 minutes. Foil wraps the meat carefully and rests it for about 10 minutes. Unwrap the meat and serve with the fresh salad as an aside.

Per Serving: Calories 321; Fat 23g; Sodium 845mg; Carbs 7g; Fiber 2g; Sugar 7g; Protein 48g

Roasted Lamb and Root Vegetables

Prep time: 35 minutes| Cook time: 1 hour 55 minutes| Serves: 6

4 cloves garlic,
2 springs fresh rosemary,
4 pounds leg of lamb
Salt and pepper to taste, divided
Medium-sized sweet potatoes,

peeled and cut into wedges
1 tablespoon oil, divided
1 cup baby carrots
1 teaspoon butter
2 large red potatoes, cubed

Preheat the air fryer at 400 degrees F for 10 minutes at the "Air Fry" setting. Chop the rosemary and the garlic. Cut slits in the top of the lamb and insert slices of garlic and some rosemary in each. Seasoned with salt and pepper as per your taste and set aside to cook after the vegetables are done. Coat the sweet potatoes in olive oil and season with salt and pepper lightly.

Spray the cooking tray of the air fryer with cooking spray and put it in the wedges. Air fry the sweet potato wedges for 8 minutes, shake and cook another 8 minutes or so. Dump into a bowl and cover with foil. Place the carrots in foil and put the butter on top of them. Enclose them in the foil and place the packet in the air fryer. Set for 400 degrees F for 20 minutes. Remove from the air fryer. Coat the cooking tray again with cooking spray. Mix the red potatoes with the oil and salt and pepper to taste. Place in the air fryer cooking tray and cook at 400 degrees F for 20 minutes, shaking after 10 minutes. Use a baking dish that fits into the air fryer and coat with cooking spray. Place the leftover garlic and rosemary in the bottom and place the lamb on top. Set the air fryer for 380 degrees F and air fry for 1 hour, checking after 30 minutes and 45 minutes to make sure it isn't getting too dark. Increase the air fryer heat to 400 degrees F and cook for 10 to 15 minutes. Once done, remove the roast from the air fryer and set it on a platter. Foil wrap it and rest 10 minutes while you place all the vegetables back in the cooking tray and air fry at 350 degrees F for 8 to 10 minutes or until heated through. Serve lamb with roasted veggies all together with the sauce and enjoy.

Per Serving: Calories 425; Fat 32g; Sodium 648mg; Carbs 10g; Fiber 4.6g; Sugar 2.3g; Protein 28g

Lemony Rack of Lamb

Prep time: 15 minutes| Cook time: 3 hours 20 minutes| Serves: 4

1 ½ to 1 ¾ pound Frenched rack of lamb
Salt and pepper to taste
½ cup breadcrumbs
1 teaspoon cumin seed
1 teaspoon ground cumin
½ teaspoon salt

1 teaspoon garlic, peeled and grated
Lemon zest (¼ of a lemon)
1 teaspoon vegetable or olive oil
1 egg, beaten

Season the lamb rack well with pepper and salt to taste and set it aside. Combine the breadcrumbs, cumin seed, ground cumin, salt, garlic, lemon zest, and oil in a bowl and set aside. In another bowl, beat the egg well. Preheat to air fryer to 250 degrees F for 5 minutes at "Air Fry" setting. Dip the lamb rack in the egg and then into the breadcrumb mixture. Make sure it is well coated. Spray the air fryer cooking tray and put the crusted lamb rack in. Set the air fryer for 250 degrees F and cook for 25 minutes. Increase temperature to 400 degrees F and cook another 5 minutes. Check internal temperature to make sure it is 145 degrees F for medium-rare or more. Remove rack when done and cover with foil for 10 minutes before servings. Serve and enjoy.

Per Serving: Calories 325; Fat 19g; Sodium 874mg; Carbs 6g; Fiber 2.5g; Sugar 3g; Protein 41g

Nutty Macadamia Lamb

Prep time: 20 minutes| Cook time: 32 minutes| Serves: 4

1 tablespoon olive oil
1 clove garlic, peeled and minced
1 ½ to 1 ¾ pound rack of lamb
Salt and pepper to taste
¾ cups unsalted macadamia

nuts
1 tablespoon fresh rosemary, chopped
1 tablespoon breadcrumbs
1 egg, beaten

In a small bowl, mix the olive oil and garlic Brush the garlic oil all over the rack of lamb. Season the lamb with salt and pepper to taste. Preheat the air fryer at 250 degrees F for 8 minutes at the "Air Fry" setting. Chop the macadamia nuts as fine as possible and put them in a bowl. Mix the rosemary and breadcrumbs with finely chopped macadamia nuts and set them aside. In another bowl, beat the egg well. Dredge the lamb rack in the egg mixture and then into a nutty breadcrumb mixture.

Coat the rack well with the mixture. Spray the air fryer cooking tray with cooking spray and place the rack inside. Air fry the lamb at 250 degrees F for 25 minutes and then increase to 400 degrees F and cook another 5 to 10 minutes or until done. Cover with foil paper for 10 minutes, uncover and separate into chops and serve with hot sauce or ranch sauce.
Per Serving: Calories 258; Fat 19g; Sodium 745mg; Carbs 12g; Fiber 3.6g; Sugar 0g; Protein 28g

Lamb Burgers with Moroccan Spices

Prep time: 10 minutes| Cook time: 20 minutes| Serves: 4

For the Moroccan spice mix:	1 ½ pound ground lamb
1 teaspoon ground ginger	1 teaspoon Harissa paste
1 teaspoon ground cumin	1 tablespoon Moroccan spice
1 teaspoon sea salt	mix, divided
¾ teaspoon ground black	1 teaspoon garlic, peeled and
pepper	minced
½ teaspoon ground coriander	¼ teaspoon fresh chopped
½ teaspoon ground allspice	oregano
½ teaspoon ground cloves	1 tablespoon plain Greek
½ teaspoon ground cinnamon	yogurt
½ teaspoon cayenne	1 small lemon, juiced
For burgers and dip:	

Moroccan Spice Mix: In a small bowl, whisk the ginger, cumin, salt, pepper, coriander, allspice, cloves, cinnamon, and cayenne well and set aside.
Burgers and dip: In a large bowl, place the lamb and add the Harissa sauce, 1 tablespoon of the Moroccan spice mix, and the garlic. Mix everything with the hands well until incorporated and form 4 patties. Preheat the air fryer to 360 degrees F for 5 minutes on the "Air Fry" setting. Spray the cooking tray of the air fryer with cooking spray and place 2 of the burgers in. Air fry the burger patties for 12 minutes, flipping after 6 minutes for even cooking. Repeat with the other 2 burgers. While burgers are cooking, make the dip; in a bowl, add freshly chopped oregano with the yogurt, 1 teaspoon of the Moroccan spice mix, and the juice of the lemon. Whisk the sauce well with a fork and divide it into small containers to serve with the burgers when they are done.
Per Serving: Calories 304; Fat 19g; Sodium 754mg; Carbs 12g; Fiber 4g; Sugar 2g; Protein 38g

Simple Lamb Chops

Prep time: 15 minutes| Cook time: 30 minutes| Serves: 4

1 clove of garlic	½ tablespoon fresh oregano,
1 ½ tablespoons olive oil	chopped
1 pound lamb chops	Salt and pepper to taste

Preheat the air fryer to 400 degrees F for 6 minutes at the "air fry" setting. In a foil, place the garlic with little oil and a pinch of salt and wrap it. Place the foil packet in the cooking tray of the air fryer and air fry for 12 minutes. In a small bowl, mix the oregano, salt, and pepper. Add all the remaining olive oil and mix well. Spread a thin coating of the oregano mixture on both sides of the lamb chops and reserve the rest. Remove the garlic from the cooking tray of the air fryer. Spray the cooking tray of the air fryer using cooking spray and place the lamb chops in, 2 at a time in 2 batches. Air fry the lamb chops for 5 minutes, turn and cook another 4 minutes for even cooking. When chops are done, squeeze the garlic out of the papery shell into the oregano mixture and mix it well in form of paste. Serve the chops with the oregano garlic on the side like ketchup and enjoy.
Per Serving: Calories 435; Fat 25g; Sodium 1258mg; Carbs 11g; Fiber 0g; Sugar 0.2g; Protein 28g

Hot Tandoori Lamb

Prep time: 10 minutes| Cook time: 20 minutes| Serves: 4

½ onion, peeled and quartered	½ teaspoon ground cardamom
5 cloves garlic, peeled	½ teaspoon cayenne
1 slices fresh ginger, peeled	1 teaspoon salt
1 teaspoon ground fennel	1 pound b1less lamb sirloin
1 teaspoon Garam Masala	steaks
1 teaspoon ground cinnamon	

Ground the onion, garlic, ginger, fennel, Garam Masala, cinnamon, cardamom, cayenne, and salt in a blender. In a large bowl, place the lamb steaks and slash the meat so the spices will be absorbed well into it. Pour the spice mix over the top of the lamb in a bowl and rub it on both sides of the lamb. Let the meat sit at room temperature for 30 minutes or cover and refrigerate overnight to marinate. Preheat the air fryer to 350 degrees F for 10 minutes at the "Air Fry" setting. Spray the cooking tray with cooking spray and place lamb steaks in without letting them overlap. Cook 7 minutes, turn and cook another 8 minutes. Test with the meat thermometer to make sure they are done. The medium-well will be 150 degrees F. Serve with sauce and roasted veggies if desire.
Per Serving: Calories 542; Fat 23g; Sodium 1052mg; Carbs 12g; Fiber 2g; Sugar 1g; Protein 30g

Greek Air Fried Lamb Leg with Herbs

Prep time: 25 minutes| Cook time: 1 hour 30 minutes| Serves: 6

3 pounds leg of lamb, bone-in	1 teaspoon ground black
For the Marinade:	pepper
1 tablespoon lemon zest	For the Herb Dressing:
3 tablespoons lemon juice	1 tablespoon lemon juice
3 cloves garlic, minced	¼ cup chopped fresh oregano
1 teaspoon onion powder	1 teaspoon fresh thyme
1 teaspoon fresh thyme	1 tablespoon olive oil
¼ cup fresh oregano	1 teaspoon sea salt
¼ cup olive oil	Ground black pepper, to taste

In a large resealable bag, place lamb leg. In a small bowl, combine the ingredients for the marinade. Stir to mix well. Pour the marinade mix over the lamb, making sure the meat is completely coated. Seal the bag and place it in the refrigerator for marinating. Marinate the meat for 4 to 6 hours before roasting. Remove the lamb leg from the marinade. Place the lamb leg inside the air fryer basket.
Set the air fryer to the "Roast" setting, set the temperature to 350 degrees F and set the time to 1 hour 30 minutes. Baste the lamb leg with marinade for every 30 minutes. While the lamb is roasting, combine the ingredients for the herb dressing in a bowl. Stir to mix well. When cooking is complete, remove the lamb leg carefully from the air fryer basket using hot pads or gloves. Cover lightly with aluminum foil for 8 to 10 minutes. Carve the leg in serving sizes and arrange on a platter. Drizzle with herb dressing. Serve immediately and enjoy.
Per Serving: Calories 324; Fat 19g; Sodium 1704mg; Carbs 16g; Fiber 0.3g; Sugar 0.3g; Protein 58g

Lemony Lamb Chops with Mustard

Prep time: 10 minutes| Cook time: 15 minutes| Serves: 2

1 tablespoon Dijon mustard	½ teaspoon olive oil
½ tablespoon fresh lemon	½ teaspoon dried tarragon
juice	Salt and ground black pepper,

as required | 4 (4-oz) lamb loin chops

Mix the mustard, lemon juice, oil, tarragon, salt, and black pepper in a small bowl. In a bowl, add the chops with the spice mix and coat with the mixture generously. Arrange the chops onto the greased air fryer cooking tray. Arrange the drip pan in the bottom of the Air Fryer cooking chamber. Select "Bake" setting to 390 degrees F. Set the time for 15 minutes and press "Start". Bake the chops until tender for 5 minutes. When cooking time is complete, remove the tray from the air fryer. Serve hot with sauce.

Per Serving: Calories 543; Fat 23g; Sodium 804mg; Carbs 14g; Fiber 2g; Sugar 3g; Protein 38g

Herbed Lamb Chops

Prep time: 5 minutes| Cook time: 10 minutes| Serves: 2

4(4-oz, ½ inch thick) lamb loin chops
2 tablespoons fresh rosemary, minced

4 garlic cloves, crushed
¼ teaspoon red chili powder
Salt and ground black pepper, as required

Place all ingredients in a bowl and mix well. Marinade the lamb in the refrigerator overnight. Arrange the marinated chops onto the greased cooking tray. Select "Bake" setting to 400 degrees F for 11 minutes and press "Start". Bake the chops until tender. When cooking time is complete, remove the tray from the air fryer. Serve hot with sauce.

Per Serving: Calories 258; Fat 14g; Sodium 1597mg; Carbs 14g; Fiber 1.2g; Sugar 1.3g; Protein 38g

Minty Lamb Meatballs

Prep time: 5 minutes| Cook time: 15 minutes| Serves: 4

1 pound ground lamb
1 egg white
½ teaspoon sea salt
2 tablespoons parsley, fresh, chopped

1 tablespoon coriander, chopped
2 garlic cloves, minced
1 tablespoon olive oil
1 tablespoon mint, chopped

Preheat the air fryer to 320 degrees F for 10 minutes at the "Air Fry" setting. In a bowl, add all the ingredients and combine well. Shape small meatballs from the mixture and place them in the air fryer cooking tray. Air fry the meatballs for 15 minutes until done. Serve hot with fresh salad and sauce.

Per Serving: Calories 304; Fat 29g; Sodium 904mg; Carbs 14g; Fiber 3.6g; Sugar 0.6g; Protein 27g

Baked Lamb Chops with Delicious Rosemary Sauce

Prep time: 10 minutes| Cook time: 52 minutes| Serves: 8

8 lamb loin chops
1 small onion, peeled and chopped
Salt and black pepper, to taste
For the sauce:
1 onion, peeled and chopped
1 tablespoon rosemary leaves

1 oz butter
1 oz plain flour
6 fl oz milk
6 fl oz vegetable stock
2 tablespoons cream, whipping
Salt and black pepper, to taste

Place the lamb loin chops along with onion in a baking tray. Season the lamb with salt and black pepper on top as per taste. Select the "Bake" setting of the air fryer and preheat at 350 degrees F for 5 minutes. Once preheated, place the lamb baking tray in the air fryer. Bake the lamb for 45 minutes. While meat is

baking, prepare the white sauce by melting butter in a saucepan then stir in onions. Sauté onions for 5 minutes, then stir flour and cook for 2 minutes. Put all ingredients in the onion flour mix and stir well until well incorporated in a silky smooth sauce. Pour the sauce over baked chops and serve. Enjoy yummy chops with white creamy sauce.

Per Serving: Calories 254; Fat 12g; Sodium 638mg; Carbs 16g; Fiber 3.6g; Sugar 5g; Protein 24g

Roast Spiced Lamb Shoulder

Prep time: 10 minutes| Cook time: 60 minutes| Serves: 2

1 pound boneless lamb shoulder roast
4 cloves garlic, minced
1 tablespoon rosemary, chopped
2 teaspoons thyme leaves

3 tablespoons olive oil, divided
Salt
Black pepper
2 pounds baby potatoes halved

In a baking tray, toss potatoes with all the herbs, seasonings, and oil. Select the "Roast" setting at 370 degrees F for 5 minutes and preheat. Once the preheating is done, set the cooking time to 60 minutes. Place the lamb baking tray in the air fryer. Roast for 60 minutes until tender and done. Remove from the air fryer and slice and serve warm with veggies and sauce.

Per Serving: Calories 454; Fat 19g; Sodium 844mg; Carbs 4g; Fiber 1.2g; Sugar 0.3g; Protein 20g

Garlicky Fried Lamb Chops

Prep time: 10 minutes| Cook time: 45 minutes| Serves: 8

8 medium lamb chops
¼ cup olive oil
3 thin lemon slices
2 garlic cloves, crushed

1 teaspoon dried oregano
1 teaspoon salt
½ teaspoon black pepper

Rub the chops with olive oil in the baking tray. Add lemon slices, garlic, oregano, salt, and black pepper on top of the oiled lamb chops. Select the "Roast" setting at 400 degrees F for 5 minutes. Once preheated, select the temperature for 45 minutes and place the lamb baking tray in the cooking tray. Roast until tender and done. Remove from the air fryer once done. Slice and serve warm.

Per Serving: Calories 404; Fat 12g; Sodium 1504mg; Carbs 2g; Fiber 0.3g; Sugar 0.6g; Protein 25g

New England Lamb with Veggies

Prep time: 10 minutes| Cook time: 60 minutes| Serves: 6

2 tablespoons canola oil
2 pounds boneless leg of lamb, diced
1 onion, chopped
2 leeks white portion only, sliced
2 carrots, sliced
2 tablespoons minced fresh parsley, divided

½ teaspoon dried rosemary, crushed
½ teaspoon salt
¼ teaspoon black pepper
¼ teaspoon dried thyme, crushed
3 potatoes, peeled and sliced
3 tablespoons butter, melted

In a baking tray, toss the lamb cubes with all the veggies, oil, and seasonings. Select the "Roast" setting of the air fryer at 350 degrees F for 5 minutes. Once preheated, turn on the timer dial to 60 minutes, place the lamb baking tray in the air fryer. Roast the lamb until done and tender. Slice and serve warm with ranch sauce and veggies.

Per Serving: Calories 354; Fat 10g; Sodium 844mg; Carbs 6g;

Fiber 3.6g; Sugar 6g; Protein 26g

Tasty Onion Lamb Kebabs

Prep time: 10 minutes| Cook time: 20 minutes| Serves: 4

18 ounces lamb kebab
1 teaspoon chili powder
1 teaspoon cumin powder
1 egg

2 ounces onion, bite-sized chunks
2 teaspoons sesame oil

In a bowl, whisk the egg with chili powder, oil, cumin powder, and salt. Add lamb kebabs and onion chunks to coat well then thread it on the skewers. Place these lamb skewers in the air fryer cooking tray. Select the "Air Fry" setting of the air fryer at 395 degrees F for 20 minutes. Once preheated, place the cooking tray in the air fryer. Air fry the lamb kebabs for 20 minutes until fully tender. Serve warm with sauce and enjoy.
Per Serving: Calories 254; Fat 9g; Sodium 502mg; Carbs 3g; Fiber 1g; Sugar 0.2g; Protein 28g

Pesto Lamb

Prep time: 10 minutes| Cook time: 45 minutes| Serves: 4

1 cup parsley
1 cup mint
1 small yellow onion, roughly chopped
⅓ cup pistachios, chopped.
1 teaspoon lemon zest, grated
5 tablespoons olive oil

2 pounds lamb riblets
½ onions, chopped.
5 garlic cloves, minced
Juice from 1 orange
Salt and black pepper to the taste

Mix parsley with mint, onion, pistachios, lemon zest, salt, pepper, and oil and blend very well into mint pesto puree. Rub lamb with this pesto sauce, place in a bowl; cover and leave in the fridge for 1 hour to marinate. Transfer lamb to a baking dish and adds garlic, drizzle orange juice. Preheat the air fryer at 300 degrees F for 45 minutes on the "Air Fry" setting. Air fry the lamb for 45 minutes flipping halfway until tender. Serve on a plate with salad and sauce and enjoy.
Per Serving: Calories 652; Fat 20g; Sodium 1986mg; Carbs 15g; Fiber 6g; Sugar 2g; Protein 50g

Classical Roast Lamb

Prep time: 5 minutes| Cook time: 15 minutes| Serves: 2

10 ounces lamb leg roast, patted dry
1 tablespoon olive oil
1 teaspoon rosemary, fresh or

dried
1 teaspoon thyme, fresh or dried
½ teaspoon black pepper

Preheat the air fryer to 360 degrees F for 15 minutes at the air fry setting. In a large bowl, mix the olive oil, rosemary, and thyme. Coat the lamb well into the oil mixture. Put the lamb into the air fryer cooking tray. Air fryer the lamb for 15 minutes on the "Air Fry" setting. Check if the lamb is cooked with a meat thermometer – the temperature in the center should be 145 degrees F (medium). Air fry for 3 more minutes until desired tenderness. Remove from the air fryer, cover with foil and let it rest for 5 minutes before serving. Serve warm with sauce and fresh salad as a side and enjoy.
Per Serving: Calories 521; Fat 15g; Sodium 985mg; Carbs 13g; Fiber 6g; Sugar 2g; Protein 45g

Spiced Lamb Kebabs

Prep time: 10 minutes| Cook time: 60 minutes| Serves: 3

1 ½ pounds lamb shoulder, bones removed and cut into pieces
2 tablespoons cumin seeds, toasted
2 teaspoons caraway seeds, toasted

1 tablespoon Sichuan peppercorns
1 teaspoon sugar
2 teaspoons crushed red pepper flakes
Salt and pepper

In a large bowl, place all ingredients and allow the meat to marinate in the refrigerator for at least 2 hours. Preheat the air fryer to 390 degrees F for 15 minutes at the "Roast" setting. Roast the meat for 15 minutes per batch. Flip the meat every 8 minutes for even roasting. Serve hot with sauce and enjoy.
Per Serving: Calories 522; Fat 12g; Sodium 1184mg; Carbs 6g; Fiber 2.6g; Sugar 3.2g; Protein 24g

Crispy Taquitos

Prep time: 10 minutes| Cook time: 16 minutes| Serves: 5

1 cup shredded cheese of your choice
½ cup diced onions
2 cups shredded meat

Spray cooking oil
1 package corn tortillas
Sour cream, salsa, cheese, and guacamole for garnish

Place tortilla bread on a tray or plate. Place a small amount of onion, meat, and cheese on the tortilla and roll around. Make all the rolls with the same procedure. Place the rolled tortillas on the air fryer cooking tray. Do not crowd taquitos. Preheat your cooking to 350 degrees F for 8 minutes at the "Air Fry" setting. Air fry your taquitos for 8 minutes per side flipping them to ensure that they cook evenly. Garnish with guacamole, sour cream, cheese, and onion. Serve warm and enjoy.
Per Serving: Calories 444; Fat 20g; Sodium 1784mg; Carbs 9g; Fiber 2.6g; Sugar 2.3g; Protein 28g

Savory Lamb Chops With Fresh Herbs

Prep time: 10 minutes| Cook time: 10 minutes| Serves: 1

⅓ lb lamb chop
1 tablespoon fresh thyme, chopped
1 tablespoon fresh rosemary, chopped

½ tablespoon Dijon mustard
½ tablespoon olive oil
Pepper
Salt

Mix oil, Dijon mustard, rosemary, thyme, pepper, and salt well in a small bowl. Brush lamb chop with oil mixture and place onto the cooking tray. Select "Air Fry" setting to 375 degrees F to 10 minutes, then press Start. Air fry the lamb for 10 minutes flipping halfway until fully cooked. Serve hot with sauce and enjoy.
Per Serving: Calories 252; Fat 9g; Sodium 524mg; Carbs 3g; Fiber 0.23g; Sugar 0.1g; Protein 21g

Minty Lamb Patties

Prep time: 10 minutes| Cook time: 8 minutes| Serves: 4

1 pound ground lamb
6 basil leaves, minced

8 mint leaves, minced
¼ cup fresh parsley, chopped

1 teaspoon dried oregano
1 cup feta cheese, crumbled
1 tablespoon garlic, minced

1 jalapeno pepper, minced
¼ teaspoon pepper
½ teaspoon kosher salt

In a large bowl, add all ingredients and mix until well combined. Make the equal shape of patties from seasoned meat mixture and place them onto the parchment-lined cooking tray. Select "Bake" setting to 400 degrees F to 8 minutes, then press Start. Bake the patties for 8 minutes flipping halfway until done. Serve with salad and sauce and enjoy.
Per Serving: Calories 374; Fat 11g; Sodium 325mg; Carbs 15g; Fiber 3.6g; Sugar 0.6g; Protein 38g

Fresh Herbed Lamb Chops

Prep time: 10 minutes| Cook time: 12 minutes| Serves: 4

4 lamb loin chops
1 tablespoon garlic, chopped
2 tablespoons olive oil
¼ cup lemon juice

¼ teaspoon cayenne pepper
½ teaspoon thyme
1 teaspoon rosemary
1 teaspoon sea salt

In a zip lock bag, add lamb chops and remaining ingredients, seal bag, and place in the refrigerator for 1 hour for marinating. Place marinated lamb chops onto the cooking tray. Select "Air Fry" setting to 390 degrees F to 12 minutes, then press Start. Air fry lamb chops for 12 minutes flipping halfway until tender. Serve hot with sauce and enjoy.
Per Serving: Calories 351; Fat 9g; Sodium 904mg; Carbs 12g; Fiber 3.6g; Sugar 0g; Protein 32g

Flavorful Lamb Steak with Cardamom

Prep time: 10 minutes| Cook time: 15 minutes| Serves: 4

1 pound lamb sirloin steaks, blless
1 teaspoon ground fennel
1 teaspoon garam masala
5 garlic cloves
1 tablespoon ginger

1 teaspoon cayenne
½ teaspoon ground cardamom
1 teaspoon ground cinnamon
½ onion
1 teaspoon salt

In a blender, add all ingredients except steak and blend until smooth. Add puree mixture and steak into the bowl and coat well. Cover and place the seasoned meat in the refrigerator for 1 hour to marinate. Place marinated meat onto the cooking tray. Select "Air Fry" setting to 330 degrees F to 15 minutes, then press Start. Air fry the meat until tender for 15 minutes. Flip the meat halfway for even cooking. Serve hot with sauce and enjoy.
Per Serving: Calories 642; Fat 24g; Sodium 1855mg; Carbs 14g; Fiber 1.6g; Sugar 2.3g; Protein 24g

Seasoned Lamb Chunks

Prep time: 10 minutes| Cook time: 10 minutes| Serves: 4

1 pound lamb, cut into 1-inch pieces
2 tablespoons olive oil
½ teaspoon cayenne

2 tablespoons ground cumin
2 chili peppers, chopped
1 tablespoon garlic, minced
1 teaspoon salt

In a zip lock bag, add lamb chops and remaining ingredients, seal bag, and place in the refrigerator for 1 hour for marinating. Place marinated meat onto the cooking tray. Select "Air Fry" setting to 360 degrees F to 10 minutes, then press Start. Air fry the lamb meat for 10 minutes until tender. Serve hot and enjoy.
Per Serving: Calories 554; Fat 17g; Sodium 1325mg; Carbs

12g; Fiber 6g; Sugar 0g; Protein 24g

Fried Thyme Lamb Chops

Prep time: 10 minutes| Cook time: 12 minutes| Serves: 4

4 lamb chops
1 tablespoon dried thyme
3 tablespoons olive oil

Pepper
Salt

In a small bowl, mix oil, thyme, pepper, and salt. Brush lamb chops with oil mixture and place onto the cooking tray. Select "Air Fry" setting to 390 degrees F and the time to 12 minutes, and then press Start. Air fry the lamb chops for 12 minutes until tender. Flip the chop halfway for even cooking. Serve hot and enjoy.
Per Serving: Calories 435; Fat 9.7g; Sodium 870mg; Carbs 5g; Fiber 2g; Sugar 2g; Protein 35g

Herbed Marinated Lamb Chops

Prep time: 10 minutes| Cook time: 8 minutes| Serves: 4

1 pound lamb chops
1 teaspoon oregano
1 teaspoon thyme
1 teaspoon rosemary

2 tablespoons lemon juice
2 tablespoons olive oil
1 teaspoon coriander
1 teaspoon salt

In a zip lock bag, add lamb chops and remaining ingredients, seal bag, and place in the refrigerator for 1 hour for marinating. Place marinated lamb chops onto the cooking tray. Select "Air Fry" setting to 390 degrees F to 8 minutes, then press Start. Air fry the chop for 8 minutes until tender and done flipping halfway. Serve with sauce and fresh salad and enjoy.
Per Serving: Calories 534; Fat 19g; Sodium 1704mg; Carbs 13g; Fiber 5g; Sugar 0.13g; Protein 21g

Lamb Spicy Lemony Kebab

Prep time: 10 minutes| Cook time: 25 minutes| Serves: 2

3 teaspoons lemon juice
2 teaspoons garam masala
4 tablespoons chopped coriander
3 tablespoons cream
1 pound of lamb
3 onions chopped
5 green chilies-roughly chopped
1 ½ tablespoon ginger paste

1 ½ teaspoon garlic paste
1 ½ teaspoon salt
4 tablespoons fresh mint chopped
3 tablespoons chopped capsicum
3 eggs
2 ½ tablespoons white sesame seeds

Cube the lamb into medium-sized chunks. Marinate lamb chunks overnight in any marinade of your choice. Take the lemon juice, garam masala, coriander, and cream in a bowl and mix them well. Grind them thoroughly to make a smooth paste. In another bowl, crack the eggs. Add a pinch of salt and beat them and leave them aside. Take a flat plate and in it mix the sesame seeds and breadcrumbs. Mold the lamb mixture into small balls and flatten them into a round and flat patties like kebabs. Dip these kebabs in the egg and salt mixture and then in the mixture of breadcrumbs and sesame seeds. Leave these kebabs in the fridge for an hour or so to set. Pre heats the Air fryer at 160 degrees F for 5 minutes at the "Air Fry" setting. Place the kebabs in the cooking tray and let them air fry for another 25 minutes at 160 degrees F. Turn the kebabs over in between the cooking process for even cooking. Serve the kebabs with mint sauce and salad.
Per Serving: Calories 321; Fat 7g; Sodium 670mg; Carbs 5g; Fiber 1.6g; Sugar 1g; Protein 21g

Mutton French Galette

Prep time: 10 minutes| Cook time: 25 minutes| Serves: 2

2 tablespoons garam masala
1 pound minced mutton
3 teaspoons ginger finely chopped
1-2 tablespoon fresh coriander
leaves
2 or 3 green chilies finely chopped
1 ½ tablespoon lemon juice
Salt and pepper to taste

In a bowl, mix the ingredients until well incorporated. Mold this mixture into a round and flat French Cuisine Galettes. Wet the French Cuisine Galettes slightly with water to prevent from sticking. Preheat the air fryer at 160 degrees F for 5 minutes at the "Air Fry" setting. Place the French Cuisine Galettes in the air fry cooking tray and let them cook for another 25 minutes at 160 degrees F. Keep rolling them over to get a uniform cook. Serve either with mint sauce or ketchup and enjoy.
Per Serving: Calories 421; Fat 7.9g; Sodium 604mg; Carbs 7g; Fiber 2g; Sugar 0.3g; Protein 25g

Spicy Corn Flour Lamb Fries

Prep time: 10 minutes| Cook time: 15 minutes| Serves: 2

2 teaspoons salt
1 teaspoon pepper powder
1 pound b1less lamb cut into
Oregano Fingers
2 cups dry breadcrumbs
2 teaspoons oregano
2 teaspoons red chili flakes
1 ½ tablespoon ginger-garlic
paste
4 tablespoons lemon juice
1 teaspoon red chili powder
6 tablespoons cornflour
4 eggs

In a bowl, mix all the ingredients for the marinade. Put the lamb Oregano Fingers inside marinate and let it rest overnight. Mix the breadcrumbs, oregano, and red chili flakes well. Place the marinated Oregano Fingers on this mixture. Cover it with plastic wrap and leave it till right before you serve to cook. Preheat the Air fryer at 160 degrees F for 5 minutes on the "Air Fry" setting. Place the Oregano Fingers in the cooking tray. Let them air fry at 160 degrees F for another 15 minutes or so. Toss the Oregano Fingers well so that they are cooked uniformly. Serve hot with sauce and enjoy.
Per Serving: Calories 554; Fat 10g; Sodium 1706mg; Carbs 14g; Fiber 3.6g; Sugar 0.6g; Protein 32g

Crispy Veggies and Pork Patties

Prep time: 10 minutes| Cook time: 20 minutes| Serves: 5

1 pound ground pork
2 teaspoons butter, melted
1 medium carrot, grated
1 small zucchini, grated
1 bell pepper, chopped
1 small leek, finely chopped
1 teaspoon garlic, minced
1 teaspoon Italian seasoning
mix

Combine all the ingredients in a large mixing bowl. Shape the meat and veggies mixture into equal patties. Select the "Air Fry" setting of the air fryer to 370 degrees F for 8 minutes. Place the patties into the greased cooking tray and air fry for 8 minutes, flipping halfway until done. Once done, remove from the air fryer and serve hot with toasted buns and salad. Bon appétit!
Per Serving: Calories 288; Fat 20.2g; Sodium 478mg; Carbs 5.7g; Fiber 1.3g; Sugar 2.3g; Protein 16g

Herbed Blade Steaks

Prep time: 10 minutes| Cook time: 32 minutes| Serves: 4

1 ½ pound blade pork steaks
2 tablespoons olive oil
1 teaspoon cayenne pepper
1 teaspoon dried oregano
1 teaspoon dried basil
1 teaspoon dried rosemary
Sea salt and ground black
pepper, to taste

In a mixing bowl, add all ingredients along with steak and mix well. Marinate the steak for 30 minutes in refrigerator. Select the "Air Fry" setting of air fryer to 360 degrees F for 16 minutes. Place the steak in the air fryer cooking tray and air fry it for 8 minutes. Flip the steaks over halfway and continue to cook them for a further 8 minutes. Serve hot with roasted veggies as the side. Bon appétit!
Per Serving: Calories 379; Fat 27.8g; Sodium 623mg; Carbs 0.5g; Fiber 0.3g; Sugar 0g; Protein 29.6g

Hawaiian Pork Skewers

Prep time: 10 minutes| Cook time: 30 minutes| Serves: 4

1 pound pork loin, cut into
bite-sized cubes
¼ cup soy sauce
¼ cup honey
¼ cup olive oil
1 tablespoon chili sauce
4 tablespoons apple cider
vinegar
2 garlic cloves, minced
1 teaspoon crushed red pepper
flakes
1 teaspoon ginger, peeled and
grated
Sea salt and ground black
pepper, to taste
1 cup pineapple cubes
1 large onion, cut into wedges
2 bell peppers, sliced

In a mixing bowl, toss all the ingredients and marinate the spiced meat for 1 hour in a refrigerator. Select the "Roast" setting of the air fryer to 360 degrees F for 30 minutes. Lightly grease the air fryer cooking tray with olive oil. Thread bamboo skewers, alternating with pork and veggies. Place the skewers in the air fryer cooking tray. Roast the skewers for about 25 minutes, rotating them once or twice. Serve hot with any sauce you like. Bon appétit!
Per Serving: Calories 458; Fat 21.1g; Sodium 841mg; Carbs 39.5g; Fiber 2.3g; Sugar 33g; Protein 28.8g

Sticky Pork

Prep time: 10 minutes| Cook time: 40 minutes| Serves: 4

1 ½ pound boneless pork butt
2 tablespoons cilantro,
chopped
½ cup orange juice
¼ cup sweet chili sauce
4 garlic cloves (finely
chopped)
2 tablespoons sesame oil (or
melted ghee)
1 teaspoon Chinese five-spice
Kosher salt and ground black
pepper, to taste

In a mixing bowl, add all the ingredients and mix well. Marinate the pork for at least 3 hours in the refrigerator. Select the "Roast" setting of the air fryer to 390 degrees F for 40 minutes. Place the pork in the air fryer cooking tray and air fry for 40 minutes. Reserve the marinade. Baste the roasting pork with the marinade and continue to roast for about 20 minutes or until cooked through. Serve immediately with sauce and enjoy!
Per Serving: Calories 418; Fat 27.9g; Sodium 1320mg; Carbs 8.1g; Fiber 1.2g; Sugar 4.2g; Protein 30.4g

Crusted Cauliflower Pork Chops

Prep time: 10 minutes| Cook time: 20 minutes| Serves: 4

1 ½ pounds boneless pork
chops
1 teaspoon brown mustard
1 tablespoon butter
½ cup seasoned breadcrumbs
Coarse sea salt and ground
black pepper, to taste
1 pound cauliflower florets

Select the "Air Fry" setting of the air fryer to 400 degrees F for 20 minutes. Grease the air fryer cooking tray with olive oil. In a large mixing bowl, toss the pork chops with mustard, butter, breadcrumbs, sea salt, and black pepper. Place the pork chops and cauliflower florets in the air fryer cooking tray. Air fry the chops with cauliflower for 15 minutes or until cooked through. Serve hot. Bon appétit!

Per Serving: Calories 379; Fat 15.1g; Sodium 621mg; Carbs 16.6g; Fiber 4.8g; Sugar 4.6g; Protein 40g

Hot Ribs

Prep time: 10 minutes| Cook time: 40 minutes| Serves: 5

2 pounds Country-style pork ribs	¼ cup apple cider
1 teaspoon paprika	2 tablespoons olive oil
2 teaspoons garlic powder	1 cup tomato sauce
1 teaspoon dried thyme	2 tablespoons molasses
Sea salt and ground black pepper	1 tablespoon mustard powder
	1 teaspoon Tabasco

In a mixing bowl, add all the ingredients and mix well. Let the spiced ribs marinate for at least 1 hour in the refrigerator. Select the "Air Fry" setting of the air fryer to 350 degrees F for 5 minutes. Add the pork ribs to the air fryer basket. Air fry the pork ribs for about 35 minutes or until they are thoroughly cooked. Serve hot. Bon appétit!

Per Serving: Calories 396; Fat 16.1g; Sodium 745mg; Carbs 19.6g; Fiber 3.8g; Sugar 12.6g; Protein 36.9g

Sweet and Sour Crispy Pork

Prep time: 10 minutes| Cook time: 12 minutes| Serves: 6

2 tablespoons olive oil	Sweet and Sour sauce:
1/16 teaspoon Chinese five spice	¼ teaspoon sea salt
¼ teaspoon pepper	½ teaspoon garlic powder
½ teaspoon sea salt	1 tablespoon low sodium soy sauce
1 teaspoon pure sesame oil	½ cup rice vinegar
2 eggs	1 tablespoon tomato paste
1 cup almond flour	1/8 teaspoon water
2 pounds pork, sliced into chunks	½ cup sweetener of choice

For the dipping sauce, whisk all sauce ingredients over medium heat in a saucepan, stirring for 5 minutes. Simmer the sauce uncovered 5 minutes till thickened. Meanwhile, in a mixing bowl, combine almond flour, five-spice, pepper, and salt. Mix eggs with a sesame oil well in another bowl. Dredge pork in flour mixture, then in the egg mixture. Shake well any excess off before adding to the cooking tray. Set the air fryer on the "Air fryer" setting to 340 degrees Ffor for 12 minutes. Air fry the chops for 12 minutes. Serve hot with sweet and sour dipping sauce and enjoy!

Per Serving: Calories 371; Fat 17g; Sodium 875mg; Carbs 14g; Fiber 2g; Sugar 3g; Protein 27g

Pork Ribs Ole

Prep time: 10 minutes| Cook time: 25 minutes| Serves: 4

1 rack of pork ribs	½ teaspoon ground black pepper
½ cup low-fat milk	
1 tablespoon envelope taco seasoning mix	1 teaspoon seasoned salt
1 can tomato sauce	1 tablespoon cornstarch
	1 teaspoon canola oil

In a mixing bowl, mix all ingredients and let them marinate for 1 hour in the refrigerator. Set the air fryer to the "Air Fry" setting and air fry the marinated ribs for 25 minutes at 390 ° F. Serve hot with your favorite sauce and Enjoy.

Per Serving: Calories 218; Fat 8g; Sodium 657mg; Carbs 14g; Fiber 2g; Sugar 1g; Protein 11g

Sirloin Sandwich

Prep time: 10 minutes| Cook time: 50 minutes| Serves: 4

1 pound pork sirloin	Sea salt and cayenne pepper, to taste
2 tablespoons olive oil	
2 tablespoons soy sauce	4 Kaiser rolls, split
2 garlic cloves, pressed	4 lettuce leaves
2 teaspoons brown sugar	1 medium tomato, sliced
2 teaspoons brown mustard	

Select the "Roast" setting of the air fryer to 360 degrees F for 50 minutes. In a mixing bowl, toss the pork with olive oil, soy sauce, garlic, sugar, mustard, salt, and cayenne pepper. Place the loin in the air fryer cooking tray. Roast the pork for about 25 minutes. Turn the pork over and continue roasting for about 20 minutes or until it reaches an internal temperature of 145 degrees F and is tender. Assemble your sandwiches with Kaiser Rolls, lettuce, and tomato, and roast shavings. Serve the sandwich hot. Bon appétit!

Per Serving: Calories 456; Fat 22g; Sodium 568mg; Carbs 35.2g; Fiber 1.8g; Sugar 4.4g; Protein 29g

Granny Mini Meat-Loaves

Prep time: 10 minutes| Cook time: 30 minutes| Serves: 4

1 pound ground pork	1 small shallot, chopped
1 small carrot, grated	1 teaspoon garlic, minced
1 small bell pepper, chopped	1 egg, whisked
1 cup tortilla chips, crushed	

Select the "Air Fry" setting of the air fryer to 390 degrees F for 25 minutes. Meanwhile, brush silicon muffin cups with cooking oil. In a mixing bowl, mix all the ingredients until well combined. Divide the mixture between the muffin cups. Place the muffin cups on the cooking tray. Air fry the mini meatloaves in the preheated air fryer until cooked through. Serve hot. Bon appétit!

Per Serving: Calories 425; Fat 25.9g; Sodium 532mg; Carbs 23.7g; Fiber 2g; Sugar 1.7g; Protein 24.2g

Mexican-Style Carnitas

Prep time: 10 minutes| Cook time: 40 minutes| Serves: 4

1 ½ pound pork shoulder	½ cup dry red wine
4 burger buns	¼ cup dark brown sugar
Marinade:	1 tablespoon chili powder
2 tablespoons Worcestershire sauce	1 tablespoon mustard seeds
2 tablespoons fresh lime juice	Sea salt and ground black pepper, to taste

In a mixing bowl, add the pork along with all ingredients and mix well. Marinate the pork for at least 3 hours. On the air fryer, select the "Air Fry" setting to 390 degrees F for 40 minutes. Place the pork in the cooking tray. Reserve the marinade. Air fry the pork for about 20 minutes. Baste the pork with the marinade and roast for about 20 minutes or until cooked through. Shred the pork well and serve the roast in toasted buns and salad and enjoy.

Per Serving: Calories 486; Fat 22.9g; Sodium 230mg; Carbs 33.2g; Fiber 1.8g; Sugar 16.8g; Protein 33.3g

Smoked Meatballs

Prep time: 10 minutes| Cook time: 20 minutes| Serves: 4

1 ½ pounds ground pork	2 garlic cloves, minced
2 tablespoons butter	1 teaspoon mustard seeds
Sea salt and ground black pepper, to taste	1 teaspoon smoked paprika
1 small onion, chopped	½ teaspoon ground cumin

Select the "Air Fry" setting of the air fryer to 380 degrees F for 20 minutes. Place a sheet of parchment paper in the air fryer cooking tray. In a mixing bowl, combine all the ingredients well. Make meatballs from it or you can directly scoop a small amount on the cooking tray. Air fry the meatballs for 10 minutes. Select the "Broil" setting and broil meatballs for a further 5 minutes or until cooked through. Serve hot topped on fresh salad and Bon appétit!
Per Serving: Calories 511; Fat 42.1g; Sodium 245mg; Carbs 3.8g; Fiber 0.8g; Sugar 1.4g; Protein 29g

Pork Belly with Toasted Brussels Sprouts

Prep time: 10 minutes| Cook time: 20 minutes| Serves: 5

1 pound pork belly cubes	½ teaspoon ground cumin
1 pound Brussels sprouts	1 teaspoon red pepper flakes, crushed
1 tablespoon brown sugar	
1 teaspoon onion powder	Kosher salt and ground black pepper, to season
1 teaspoon garlic powder	

Select the "Air Fry" setting of the air fryer to 390 ° F for 20 minutes. In a mixing bowl, toss all the ingredients. Place the pork and Brussels sprouts in the air fryer cooking tray. Cook the pork and Brussels sprouts for about 10 minutes. Flip over and continue to cook for a further 8 minutes. Serve hot immediately with sauce and enjoy!
Per Serving: Calories 521; Fat 48.1g; Sodium 953mg; Carbs 10.7g; Fiber 3.6g; Sugar 3.4g; Protein 11.7g

Tropical Pineapple Picnic Shoulder

Prep time: 10 minutes| Cook time: 3 hours| Serves: 6

2 pounds cooked pork picnic shoulder	¼ cup brown sugar
	1 teaspoon garlic powder
½ can pineapple, chopped	1 teaspoon onion powder
2 tablespoons Dijon mustard	

Pat the ham dry with a paper towel. On the air fryer, select the "Roast" setting to 250 degrees F for 3 hours. Press the "Start" key. Place the prepared ham onto the air fryer basket. Meanwhile, make the glaze by mixing all the remaining ingredients. When the ham has reached 145 degrees F, brush the glaze over all surfaces of the ham. Allow the glazed ham to rest for 10 minutes before slicing and serving. Serve hot Bon appétit!
Per Serving: Calories 375; Fat 19.3g; Sodium 530mg; Carbs 6.4g; Fiber 0.4g; Sugar 5.4g; Protein 40.7g

Spicy Pork Chops with Peppers

Prep time: 10 minutes| Cook time: 20 minutes| Serves: 5

2 pounds pork blade chops	2 bell peppers, sliced
1 tablespoon butter, melted	2 tablespoons sugar
1 teaspoon mixed peppercorns	1 teaspoon garlic, minced
1 teaspoon chili powder	

Select the "Air Fry" setting of the air fryer to 400 degrees F for 20 minutes. Grease the air fryer cooking pan with olive oil. In a mixing bowl, toss the pork chops and peppers with the remaining ingredients. Place the pork chops and peppers in the air fryer cooking tray. Air fry the chops for 15 minutes or until cooked through. Serve hot and Bon appétit!
Per Serving: Calories 299; Fat 11.4g; Sodium 569mg; Carbs 5.6g; Fiber 0.5g; Sugar 4.1g; Protein 40g

Smoked Mustardy Ribs

Prep time: 10 minutes| Cook time: 40 minutes| Serves: 5

2 pounds St. Louis-style ribs	2 garlic cloves, pressed
2 tablespoons lime juice	1 tablespoon smoked paprika
2 tablespoons brown sugar	1 tablespoon Dijon mustard
Kosher salt and ground black pepper, to taste	1 cup tomato ketchup
	2 tablespoons soy sauce

In a mixing bowl, place all the ingredients and mix well. Let the meat marinate for at least 1 hour in the refrigerator. Select the "Air Fry" setting of air fryer to 350 degrees F for 40 minutes. Add the pork ribs to the air fryer basket. Air fry the pork ribs for about 35 minutes or until they are thoroughly cooked. Serve hot with a chilled drink and Bon appétit!
Per Serving: Calories 395; Fat 22.7g; Sodium 841mg; Carbs 8.6g; Fiber 1.3g; Sugar 5.8g; Protein 36.5g

Spicy Savory Pork Cakes

Prep time: 10 minutes| Cook time: 20 minutes| Serves: 4

1 pound ground pork	2 tablespoons olive oil
1 large shallot, finely chopped	1 red chili pepper, minced
2 garlic cloves, minced	Sea salt and ground black pepper, to season
1 tablespoon of lemongrass	
1 tablespoon fish sauce	

In a mixing bowl, combine all the ingredients. Shape the mixture into four patties. Select the "Air Fry" setting of the air fryer to 370 degrees F for 16 to 20 minutes. Place the pork burgers in the air fryer cooking tray. Cook your burgers for about 8 minutes. Flip the burgers halfway and continue to cook them for a further 8 minutes. Serve hot with toasted buns and Bon appétit!
Per Serving: Calories 393; Fat 30.7g; Sodium 230mg; Carbs 8g; Fiber 1.4g; Sugar 3.7g; Protein 20.6g

Summer-Style Spareribs

Prep time: 10 minutes| Cook time: 45 minutes| Serves: 4

1 ½ pounds pork spareribs	1 teaspoon liquid smoke
2 tablespoons brown mustard	¼ cup apple cider vinegar
1 teaspoon cayenne pepper	¼ cup seedless blackberry preserves
½ teaspoon dried thyme	
2 tablespoons Worcestershire sauce	½ cup cream of celery soup

In a mixing bowl, place all the ingredients. Cover the meat and let it marinate for at least 1 hour in the refrigerator. Select the "Air Fry" setting of the air fryer to 350 degrees F for 45 minutes. Press the "Start" key. Add the pork ribs to the air fryer basket. Cook the pork ribs for about 40-45 minutes or until they are thoroughly cooked. Serve hot and Bon appétit!
Per Serving: Calories 365; Fat 22.2g; Sodium 402mg; Carbs 33.5g; Fiber 1.1g; Sugar 4.1g; Protein 33.5g

Teriyaki Pork Rolls with Mushrooms

Prep time: 10 minutes| Cook time: 8 minutes| Serves: 6

1 teaspoon almond flour
1 tablespoon low sodium soy sauce
1 tablespoon mirin
1 tablespoon brown sugar
Thumb sized amount of ginger, chopped
Pork belly slices
Enoki mushrooms

In a large mixing bowl, mix brown sugar, mirin, soy sauce, almond flour, and ginger until brown sugar dissolves. Take pork belly slices and wrap gently around a bundle of enoki mushrooms. Brush the mushroom pork rolls with teriyaki sauce. Chill half an hour for marinates. Preheat your Air fryer to 350 degrees F for 5 minutes at the "Air Fry" setting and add marinated pork rolls. Air fry the rolls to 350 degrees F for8 minutes. Serve hot with fresh salad on the side.
Per Serving: Calories 412; Fat 9g; Sodium 852mg; Carbs 14g; Fiber 2g; Sugar 4g; Protein 19g

Buttery Pork Loin

Prep time: 5 minutes| Cook time: 30 minutes| Serves: 6

2 pounds pork loin
3 tablespoons butter, melted and divided
Salt and ground black pepper, as required

Arrange a wire rack in a cooking tray of the Air Fryer. Grease the pork loin with melted butter and rub with salt and black pepper generously. Arrange the pork loin into the prepared cooking tray. Select the "Air Fry" setting of the air fryer to 350 degrees F for 30 minutes and press "Start". Place the cooking rack in the center position and air fry the pork for 30 minutes flipping halfway for even cooking. Once cooked, place the pork loin onto a cutting board. With a piece of foil, cover the pork loin for about 10 minutes before slicing. Cut the slice of pork loin into the desired size and serve hot.
Per Serving: Calories 417; Fat 26.8g; Sodium 452mg; Carbs 0g; Fiber 0g; Sugar 0g; Protein 41g

Pork Milanese with Fresh Parsley

Prep time: 10 minutes| Cook time: 12 minutes| Serves: 4

1 pound boneless pork chops
Fine sea salt and ground black pepper
2 large eggs
¾ cup powdered Parmesan
cheese about 2¼ ounces
Chopped fresh parsley, for garnish
Lemon slices, for serving

Spray the air fryer cooking tray with avocado oil and set it aside. Preheat the Air Fryer to 400 degrees F for 5 minutes at the "Air Fry" setting. Pound the pork chops with the flat side of a meat tenderizer between 2 sheets of plastic wrap, until they're ¼ inch thick. Lightly season the chops with salt and pepper. Beat the eggs in a shallow bowl. In 2 medium bowls, divide the Parmesan cheese evenly and set the bowls in this order: Parmesan, eggs, Parmesan. Dredge the pork chop in the Parmesan cheese bowl, then dip it in the eggs, and then dredge it again in the Parmesan cheese bowl. Make sure both sides are well coated. Repeat with the chops. Place the chops in the cooking tray and air fry for 12 minutes, flipping halfway through. Garnish with freshly chopped parsley and serve immediately with lemon slices and enjoy.
Per Serving: Calories 351; Fat 18g; Sodium 841mg; Carbs 3g; Fiber 1g; Sugar 0.6g; Protein 42g

Southern Crispy Pork Chops

Prep time: 10 minutes| Cook time: 25 minutes| Serves: 4

½ cup all-purpose flour
½ cup low-fat buttermilk
½ teaspoon black pepper
½ teaspoon Tabasco sauce
½ teaspoon paprika
1 pound bone-in pork chops

In a Ziploc bag, add the buttermilk and hot sauce and add the pork chops and mix well. Allow marinating for at least 1 hour in the refrigerator. In a mixing bowl, combine the flour, paprika, and black pepper. Remove marinated pork from the Ziploc bag and dredge in the flour mixture. Preheat the air fryer to 390 degrees F for 5 minutes at the "Air Fry" setting. Spray the crusted pork chops with cooking oil. Place in the air fryer cooking tray and air fry for 25 minutes, flipping halfway for even cooking. Serve hot with sauce and done.
Per Serving: Calories 427; Fat 21.2g; Sodium 912mg; Carbs 12g; Fiber 2g; Sugar 2g; Protein 46g

Veggies with Italian Sausages

Prep time: 5 minutes| Cook time: 28 minutes| Serves: 3

1 medium onion, thinly sliced
1 yellow or orange bell pepper, thinly sliced
1 red bell pepper, thinly sliced
¼ cup avocado oil or melted
coconut oil
1 teaspoon fine sea salt
Italian sausages
Dijon mustard, for serving (optional)

Preheat the Air fryer to 400 degrees F for 5 minutes at "Air Fry" setting. In a large mixing bowl, place the onion and peppers and drizzle with the oil, and toss well to coat oil in the veggies. Season the veggies with salt. Place the onion and peppers in a 6-inch pie pan and air fry for 8 minutes, stirring halfway at 400 degrees F. Remove the veggies from the air fryer and set them aside. Spray the air fryer cooking tray with avocado oil. Place the sausages in the cooking tray and air fry for 20 minutes at 400 degrees F, until crispy and golden brown. In the last 2 minutes, add veggies with sausages to warm through. Place the onion and peppers on a serving platter and arrange the sausages on top. Serve Dijon mustard on the side, if desired.
Per Serving: Calories 576; Fat 49g; Sodium 654mg; Carbs 8g; Fiber 2g; Sugar 1g; Protein 25g

Thai Style Minty BBQ Pork

Prep time: 5 minutes| Cook time: 15 minutes| Serves: 3

1 minced hot Chile
1 minced shallot
1 pound ground pork
2 tablespoons fish sauce
2 tablespoons lime juice
2 tablespoons basil
2 tablespoons chopped mint
2 tablespoons cilantro

Mix all ingredients with hands in a shallow dish. Form ground pork into 1-inch oval rolls. Thread oval rolls in skewers. Place the skewers on the air fryer cooking tray. Set the air fryer at the "Air Fry" setting for 15 minutes on 360 degrees F and air fry the rolls. Turnover the skewers halfway through cooking time. Serve hot with sauce and enjoy.
Per Serving: Calories 455; Fat 31g; Sodium 895mg; Carbs 6g; Fiber 2g; Sugar 1g; Protein 40g

Asian Pork Roast in Coconut Sauce

Prep time: 10 minutes| Cook time: 20 minutes| Serves: 6

½ teaspoon curry powder
½ teaspoon ground turmeric

powder
1 can unsweetened coconut milk
1 tablespoon sugar

1 tablespoon fish sauce
1 tablespoon soy sauce
1 pound pork shoulder
Salt and pepper to taste

In the bowl, place all ingredients and mix well and allow the meat to marinate in the refrigerator for at least 2 hours. Preheat the air fryer to 390 degrees F for 5 minutes at the "Roast" setting. Place the air fryer cooking tray in the air fryer. Roast the meat for 20 minutes, flipping the pork every 10 minutes for even roasting, and cook in batches. Meanwhile, meat is cooking, pour the marinade reserve in a saucepan and allow simmering for 10 minutes until the sauce thickens. Baste the meat with the sauce before serving and serve hot and enjoy.

Per Serving: Calories 688; Fat 52g; Sodium 947mg; Carbs 12g; Fiber 2g; Sugar 3g; Protein 17g

Crispy Garlic Pork Roast

Prep time: 5 minutes| Cook time: 45 minutes| Serves: 4

1 teaspoon Chinese five-spice powder
1 teaspoon white pepper

2 pounds pork belly
2 teaspoons garlic salt

Preheat the air fryer to the "Air Fry" setting for 5 minutes to 390 degrees F. In a mixing bowl, mix all the spices to create the dry rub. With a sharp knife, score the skin of the pork belly and season the entire pork with the spice rub. Marinate the pork for about 2 hours in the refrigerator for the best taste. Place the meat in the air fryer cooking tray and air fry for 40 to 45 minutes until the skin is crispy. Select the "Broil" setting for 5 minutes for extra crispy skin. Chop before serving and serve with your favorite sauce.

Per Serving: Calories 785; Fat 79g; Sodium 1745mg; Carbs 54g; Fiber 12g; Sugar 6g; Protein 14g

Chinese Style Pork Chop Stir Fry

Prep time: 10 minutes| Cook time: 35 minutes| Serves: 4

Pork Chops:
Olive oil
¾ cup almond flour
¼ teaspoon pepper
½ teaspoon salt
1 egg white
1 pound pork chops

Stir fry:
¼ teaspoon pepper
1 teaspoon sea salt
1 tablespoon olive oil
4 sliced scallions
2 sliced jalapeno peppers

Coat the air fryer cooking tray with olive oil. In a clear bowl, whisk pepper, salt, and egg white together till foamy and airy. Cut pork chops into pieces with little bone on. Add pork to egg white mixture, coating well. Marinade the pork for 20 minutes. Dredge the chops in the almond flour and shake off excess and place into the air fryer. Set the air fryer to 360 degrees F, and 12 minutes at the "Air Fry" setting. Air fry the chops for 12 minutes at 360 degrees F. Turn up the heat to 400 degrees F and cook another 6 minutes till pork chops are nice and crispy. Remove the jalapeno seeds and chop them up finely. Chop scallions and mix with jalapeno pieces. Over a high heat, heat oil in a wok. Stir fry pepper, salt, scallions, and jalapenos for 60 seconds. Then add fried pork pieces to the wok and toss with scallion mixture firmly. Stir fry pork with veggies for 12 minutes till well coated and hot. Serve hot with boiled rice and enjoy.

Per Serving: Calories 294; Fat 17g; Sodium 874mg; Carbs 15g; Fiber 3g; Sugar 4g; Protein 36g

Buttery Pork Chops

Prep time: 10 minutes| Cook time: 15 minutes| Serves: 4

2 teaspoons parsley
2 teaspoons grated garlic cloves

1 tablespoon coconut oil
1 tablespoon coconut butter
4 pork chops

Ensure your air fryer is preheated to 350 degrees F for 5 minutes at the "Air Fry" setting. In a mixing bowl, mix coconut butter, coconut oil, and spice seasoning. Rub the seasoning mixture over the pork chops completely. Place in foil, seal, and chill for 1 hour to marinating. Remove pork chops from foil and place them into an air fryer cooking tray. Place the rack on the middle shelf of the air fryer to 350 degrees F, and time to 7 minutes. Air fry the chops for 7 minutes on 1 side and 8 minutes on the other. Once done, drizzle with olive oil and serve alongside a green salad and enjoy.

Per Serving: Calories 526; Fat 23g; Sodium 871mg; Carbs 16g; Fiber 3g; Sugar 4g; Protein 41g

Fried Pork with Sweet And Sour Glazed

Prep time: 5 minutes| Cook time: 30 minutes| Serves: 4

¼ cup rice wine vinegar
¼ teaspoon Chinese five-spice powder
1 cup potato starch
1 green onion, chopped
2 large eggs, beaten

2 pounds pork chops cut into chunks
1 tablespoon cornstarch + 3 tablespoon water
1 tablespoon brown sugar
Salt and pepper to taste

Preheat the air fryer to 390° F for 5 minutes at the "Air Fry" setting. Season pork chops with spices as per taste. Dip the pork chops in egg. Set aside. Combine the potato starch and Chinese five-spice powder in a bowl well. Dredge the egg-dipped pork chops in the flour mixture. Place in the air fryer cooking tray and air fry for 30 minutes. Meanwhile, in a saucepan, place the vinegar and brown sugar. Season the mix with salt and pepper to taste. Stir in the cornstarch slurry and allow simmering until thick over medium heat and keep stirring to avoid burning. Serve the pork chops with the sweet and sour sauce and garnish with green onions you can serve the sauce in a bowl or brush evenly on chop as a glaze as desire.

Per Serving: Calories 420; Fat 7.9g; Sodium 704mg; Carbs 6g; Fiber 3.6g; Sugar 6g; Protein 18g

Hot Herby Breaded Pork

Prep time: 10 minutes| Cook time: 30 minutes| Serves: 4

¼ cup water
¼ teaspoon dry mustard
½ teaspoon black pepper
½ teaspoon cayenne pepper
½ teaspoon garlic powder
½ teaspoon salt

1 cup panko breadcrumbs
1 egg, beaten
2 teaspoons oregano
1 pound lean pork chops
2 teaspoons paprika

Preheat the air fryer to 390 degrees F for 5 minutes at the "Air Fry" setting. Pat dry the pork chops with a paper towel. In a mixing bowl, combine the egg and water and mix well. Then set the egg mixture aside. Combine the rest of the ingredients in a bowl. Dredge the pork chops in the egg mixture and then in the flour mixture evenly. Do with all chops. Place in the air fryer cooking tray and air fry chops for 25 to 30 minutes until golden and crispy. Serve hot with ranch sauce and enjoy.

Per Serving: Calories 364; Fat 20g; Sodium 982mg; Carbs 9g;

Fiber 2g; Sugar 0.4g; Protein 42g

Cajun Spiced Steaks

Prep time: 5 minutes| Cook time: 20 minutes| Serves: 6

4 -6 pork steaks
BBQ sauce:
Cajun seasoning
1 tablespoon vinegar

1 teaspoon low sodium soy sauce
½ cup brown sugar
½ cup vegan ketchup

Ensure air fryer is preheated to 290 degrees F for 10 minutes at the "Air Fry" setting. Sprinkle steaks with Cajun seasoning evenly. Combine remaining ingredients and brush onto steaks and marinate for 2 hours for best taste. Place coated steaks in an air fryer cooking tray. Transfer the air fryer basket inside the air fryer. Air Fry the steaks to 290 degrees F for 20 minutes. Cook 15- 20 minutes till just browned. Serve hot with mashed potatoes as the side.
Per Serving: Calories 209; Fat 11g; Sodium 958mg; Carbs 15g; Fiber 4g; Sugar 2g; Protein 28g

Stuffed Cutlet Rolls

Prep time: 10 minutes| Cook time: 15 minutes| Serves: 4

4 pork cutlets
4 sundried tomatoes in oil
2 tablespoons parsley, finely chopped
1 green onion, finely chopped

Black pepper to taste
2 teaspoons paprika
½ tablespoon olive oil
String for rolled meat

Preheat the air fryer to 390 degrees F for 5 minutes at the "Air Fry" setting. Finely chop the tomatoes with the parsley and green onion and mix them well. Add salt and pepper to taste in the tomatoes mix. Spread out the cutlets over a cutting board and coat them with the tomato mixture. Roll up the cutlets and secure them intact with a string or toothpicks. Rub the rolls with salt, pepper, and paprika powder and grease them with olive oil. Put the cutlet rolls in the cooking tray and air fry for 15 minutes. Air fry until nicely brown and done. Serve with tomato sauce and enjoy.
Per Serving: Calories 422; Fat 27g; Sodium 674mg; Carbs 14g; Fiber 3g; Sugar 2g; Protein 34g

Crispy Pork Scotch Egg

Prep time: 10 minutes| Cook time: 25 minutes| Serves: 2

3 soft boiled eggs, peeled
8 ounces of raw minced pork, or sausage outside the casings
2 teaspoons of ground rosemary

2 teaspoons of garlic powder
Pinch of salt and pepper
2 raw eggs
1 cup of breadcrumbs

Cover the cooking tray of the air fryer with a lining of tin foil, leaving the edges uncovered to allow air to circulate through the cooking tray. Preheat the air fryer to 350 degrees F for 5 minutes at the "Air fry" setting. Mix the raw pork with the rosemary, garlic powder, salt, and pepper in the bowl. Divide the meat mixture into 3 equal portions and form it into balls. Lay a plastic wrap on the countertop, and flatten 1 of the balls of meat on top of it, to form a wide, flat meat circle. Place 1 peeled soft boiled eggs in the center of the meat circle and then, pull the meat circle so that it fully covers the soft boiled egg. Make 3 meat eggs balls and set them aside. Beat the eggs until fluffy and until the yolks and whites are fully combined in a bowl. Dunk the pork-covered balls into the egg, and then roll them in the bread crumbs, covering fully and generously. Place each of the bread

crumb covered meatballs onto the foil-lined cooking tray of the air fryer. Set the air fryer to 25 minutes and air fry. Shake the egg balls halfway for even cooking. Once cooked plate the egg balls. The egg yolks will be still runny on the inside, and crispy and golden brown at the outsides. Place them on serving plates, slice in half, and enjoy.
Per Serving: Calories 785; Fat 80g; Sodium 1569mg; Carbs 25g; Fiber 11g; Sugar 7g; Protein 14.2g

Braised Pork Loin

Prep time: 40 minutes| Cook time: 40 minutes| Serves: 2

1 pound pork loin roast, boneless and cubed
3 tablespoons butter, melted and divided
Salt and black pepper, to taste
1 cup chicken stock
¼ cup dry white wine

1 clove garlic, minced
½ teaspoon thyme, chopped
½ thyme sprig
1 bay leaf
¼ yellow onion, chopped
1 tablespoon white flour
¼ pound red grapes

Season the pork cubes well with salt and pepper. With the melted butter, grease the spiced pork and put it in the air fryer. Set the air fryer to the "Air Fry" setting for 8 minutes at 370 degrees F and air fry the meat. Meanwhile, in the cooking pan, heat butter over medium-high heat and sauté onion and garlic in it. Add bay leaf, flour, thyme, salt, pepper, stock, and wine to the cooking pan. Mix well. Bring the sauce to simmer and take off the heat. Add grapes and pork cubes to the sauce. Place the sauce with pork in a heat-proof pan and place in the air fryer. Air fry the meat with sauce at 360 degrees F for 30 minutes. Once done, serve hot and enjoy.
Per Serving: Calories 320; Fat 4g; Sodium 624mg; Carbs 14g; Fiber 1.2g; Sugar 3g; Protein 38g

Country-Style Tenderloin

Prep time: 15 minutes| Cook time: 25 minutes| Serves: 3

1 pound pork tenderloin
1 tablespoon garlic, minced
2 tablespoons soy sauce
2 tablespoons honey

1 tablespoon Dijon mustard
1 tablespoon grain mustard
1 teaspoon Sriracha sauce

Add ingredients except for pork in a bowl and mix well. Add the pork tenderloin in the spice mix and coat with the mixture generously until all meat is covered. Marinade the meat for 2 -3 hours in the refrigerator. Remove the marinated pork tenderloin from the bowl, reserving the marinade. Place the pork tenderloin onto the greased cooking tray. Select the "Air Fry" setting of the air fryer to 380 degrees F for 25 minutes and press the "Start". Air fry the chops for 25 minutes, flipping halfway for even cooking. Place the pork tenderloin onto a platter for about 10 minutes before slicing. Serve the tenderloin into desire slices and enjoy.
Per Serving: Calories 277; Fat 5.7g; Sodium 741mg; Carbs 12g; Fiber 2.3g; Sugar 0.2g; Protein 40.7g

Smoked Raspberry Pork Chops

Prep time: 15 minutes| Cook time: 15 minutes| Serves: 4

Cooking spray
2 large eggs
¼ cup Coconut milk
1 cup Panko bread crumbs
1 cup finely chopped walnuts
4 smoked bone-in pork chops

(7 ½ ounces each)
¼ cup coconut flour
2 tablespoons stevia
2 tablespoons raspberry
1 tablespoon fresh orange juice

Preheat the air fryer to 400 degrees F for 5 minutes at the "Air Fry" setting. Spray some oil in the cooking tray. In a shallow bowl, mix the eggs and coconut milk. In another bowl, mix the panko breadcrumbs with walnuts and cover the pork chops with the flour. Shake off excess. Dip the chops into the egg mixture and then into the crumb mixture and tap on it to help it stick. Place the chops in a single layer in the cooking tray of the air fryer. Spray with oil and air fry for 12 to 15 minutes until golden brown, turn after half the cooking time and sprinkle with additional cooking spray. In the meantime, put the remaining ingredients in a small saucepan. Bring to a boil and stir until it gets a little thick, 6- 8 minutes. Serve the sauce with chops.
Per Serving: Calories 542; Fat 31g; Sodium 1845mg; Carbs 24g; Fiber 5g; Sugar 2g; Protein 41g

Italian Cheesy Breaded Pork Chops

Prep time: 5 minutes| Cook time: 25 minutes| Serves: 5

5(3½ to 5 ounce) pork chops (bone-in or boneless)
1 teaspoon Italian seasoning
Seasoning salt
Pepper
¼ cup all-purpose flour
1 tablespoon Italian bread crumbs
1 tablespoon finely grated Parmesan cheese
Cooking oil

Spice the pork chops with the Italian seasoning, salt and pepper to taste. Sprinkle the flour on each side of the pork chops well. Coat both sides with bread crumbs and Parmesan cheese. Place the pork chops in the air fryer. Spray the pork chops with cooking oil. Set the air fryer to 360 degrees F for 6 minutes at the "Air Fry" setting. Air fry the chops and flip the pork chops. Cook for an additional 6 minutes. Serve hot with sauce and enjoy.
Per Serving: Calories 334; Fat 7g; Sodium 1256mg; Carbs 4g; Fiber 0g; Sugar 2g; Protein 34g

Sweet Caramelized Pork Shoulder

Prep time: 10 minutes| Cook time: 20 minutes| Serves: 8

⅓ cup soy sauce
1 tablespoon sugar
1 tablespoon honey
2 pounds pork shoulder, cut into 1½ inch thick slices

In a bowl, mix all the ingredients with pork and marinate for about 24 hours in the refrigerator. Preheat the air fryer to 335 degrees F for 5 minutes at the "Air Fry" setting. Place the pork in an air fryer cooking tray. Air fry the pork for about 10 minutes. Now, adjust the Air fryer to 390 ° F and air fry further for about 10 minutes. Serve hot with salad on the side and enjoy.
Per Serving: Calories 268; Fat 10g; Sodium 742mg; Carbs 8g; Fiber 2g; Sugar 5g; Protein 23g

Herbed Roasted Pork Tenderloin

Prep time: 5 minutes| Cook time: 1 hour| Serves: 4

1 (3 pounds) pork tenderloin
1 tablespoon extra virgin olive oil
2 garlic cloves, minced
1 teaspoon dried basil
1 teaspoon dried oregano
1 teaspoon dried thyme
Salt
Pepper

Grease the pork fillet with olive oil. Rub the garlic, basil, oregano, thyme, and salt and pepper to taste throughout the fillet. Place the fillet in the air fryer cooking tray. Set the air fryer to

the "Roast" setting at 350 degrees F for 45 minutes. Roast the pork fillets for 45 minutes flipping halfway for even cooking. Once the fillets are roasted, let it rest for 10 minutes in a foil warp. Slice and serve fillets with mashed potatoes on the side and enjoy.
Per Serving: Calories 283; Fat 10g; Sodium 952mg; Carbs 14g; Fiber 4g; Sugar 4g; Protein 48g

Wrapped Pork Tenderloin with Apple Gravy

Prep time: 5 minutes| Cook time: 15 minutes| Serves: 4

Pork:
1- 2 tablespoon Dijon mustard
3 -4 strips of bacon
1 pork tenderloin
Apple Gravy:
½ -1 teaspoon Dijon mustard
1 tablespoon almond flour
1 tablespoon ghee
1 chopped onion
2 - 3 Granny Smith apples
1 cup vegetable broth

Grease the tenderloin with Dijon mustard all over and wrap the meat with strips of bacon. Set the air fryer to 360 degrees F for 15 minutes at the "Air Fry" setting, and cook for 10-15 minutes. While meat is cooking, heat a pan over medium heat, and add ghee with shallots. Cook 1-2 minutes to make the sauce. Add apples and cook for 3- 5 minutes until softened. Add flour and ghee to make a roux in a pan. Add broth and mustard, stirring well to combine until starting to thicken. Add sautéed apples to the sauce and cook till sauce thickens. Once the pork tenderloin is cooked, let it sit 5 -10 minutes to rest before slicing. Serve tenderloin slices topped with apple gravy and enjoy.
Per Serving: Calories 552; Fat 25g; Sodium 847mg; Carbs 15g; Fiber 6g; Sugar 6g; Protein 29g

Pork Neck with Tomato Salad

Prep time: 10 minutes| Cook time: 10 minutes| Serves: 2

For Pork:
1 tablespoon soy sauce
1 tablespoon fish sauce
½ tablespoon oyster sauce
½ pound pork neck
For Salad:
1 ripe tomato, sliced tickly
8 10 Thai shallots, sliced
1 scallion, chopped
1 bunch fresh basil leaves
1 bunch fresh cilantro leaves
For Dressing:
1tablespoon fish sauce
2 tablespoon olive oil
1 teaspoon apple cider vinegar
1 tablespoon palm sugar
1bird's eye chili
1 tablespoon garlic, minced

In a mixing bowl, mix all the ingredients along with the pork neck and marinated for about 4 hours in the refrigerator. Preheat the air fryer to 340 ° F for 5 minutes at the "Air Fry" setting. Place the pork neck in a cooking tray and air fry for 12 minutes. Meanwhile, in a large mixing bowl, combine all of the salad ingredients. In another bowl, add all the dressing ingredients and beat until well combined and creamy, you can also blend them in a blender. Remove the pork neck from the air fryer and slice it into the desired size. Place the pork slices on top of the salad and drizzle dressing on top and serve.
Per Serving: Calories 296; Fat 20g; Sodium 578mg; Carbs 15g; Fiber 4g; Sugar 8g; Protein 24g

Chinese-Style Braised Pork Belly

Prep time: 5 minutes| Cook time: 20 minutes| Serves: 8

1 pound pork belly, sliced
1 tablespoon oyster sauce
1 tablespoon sugar
1 tablespoon red fermented bean curd paste
1 tablespoon cooking wine

½ tablespoon soy sauce
1 teaspoon sesame oil

1 cup all-purpose flour

Preheat the air fryer to 390 degrees F for 5 minutes at the "Air Fry" setting. In a shallow bowl, mix all the ingredients. Rub the pork thoroughly with a spice mixture Marinate the pork for at least 30 minutes or overnight for the flavors to marinate the meat well. Coat each marinated meat slice in flour and place in the air fryer cooking tray. Air fry the meat for 20 minutes until crispy and tender. Serve hot with sauce and enjoy.
Per Serving: Calories 409; Fat 14g; Sodium 589mg; Carbs 14g; Fiber 3g; Sugar 9g; Protein 19g

Mustardy Pork Chops

Prep time: 10 minutes| Cook time: 20 minutes| Serves: 4

1 ½ pound pork blade chops
4 tablespoons mayonnaise
1 tablespoon Dijon mustard
½ cup seasoned breadcrumbs

1 teaspoon garlic powder
½ onion powder
Sea salt and ground black pepper, to taste

Select the "Air Fry" setting of the air fryer to 400 degrees F for 5 minutes and preheat. Grease the air fryer cooking tray with olive oil. Toss the pork chops with the other ingredients in a bowl. Place the pork chops in the air fryer cooking tray. Air fry the chops for 15 minutes or until the internal temperature reaches 145 degrees F. Serve warm with sauce and enjoy!
Per Serving: Calories 425; Fat 23.9g; Sodium 124mg; Carbs 13.1g; Fiber 2.5g; Sugar 2.6g; Protein 40g

Hot Sticky Pork Tenderloin

Prep time: 20 minutes| Cook time: 25 minutes| Serves: 3

11½ lbs pork tenderloin
2 tablespoons honey
2 tablespoons sriracha hot

sauce
1½ teaspoon kosher salt

Insert the spit through the center of the tenderloin. In a bowl, mix the honey, sriracha, and salt in a small bowl. Brush the prepared mixture evenly over the screwed pork. Transfer the air fryer basket inside the air fryer. Set the air fryer for 20 minutes at 350 degrees F on the "Air Fry" setting. Air fry the tenderloin to the internal temperature of the meat is 145 degrees F in the center of the tenderloin. If not, increase the cooking time. Once cook release from the forks and rest for 5 minutes before slicing. Serve warm with fresh salad on the side and enjoy.
Per Serving: Calories 120; Fat 3g; Sodium 430mg; Carbs 5g; Fiber 0.6g; Sugar 1g; Protein 20g

Crispy Pork Belly Bites

Prep time: 20 minutes| Cook time: 20 minutes| Serves: 15

1½ pounds pork belly patted dry, cut into 1inch pieces
3 tablespoons canola oil
1 tablespoon brown sugar

1 teaspoon garlic powder
1 teaspoon salt
1 teaspoon pepper

Preheat the air fryer to 400 degrees F for 5 minutes at the "Air Fry" setting. In a large mixing bowl, mix the oil, garlic powder, brown sugar, salt, and pepper. Add the belly pieces and toss in the spices, covering each piece. Arrange the pieces in a single layer in the air fryer cooking tray. Air fry the chops for 18-20 minutes, shaking and flipping after 9-10 minutes for even cooking. Serve warm with your favorite sauce and enjoy.
Per Serving: Calories 144; Fat 11g; Sodium 251mg; Carbs 2g; Fiber 0.1g; Sugar 0.2g; Protein 10g

Sticky Pork Chops

Prep time: 10 minutes| Cook time: 15 minutes| Serves: 4

4 pork chops
Salt and pepper to taste
¼ cup honey
2 garlic cloves, minced

2 tablespoons lemon juice
1 tablespoon sweet chili sauce
1 tablespoon extra virgin olive oil

Preheat the air fryer to 400 degrees F for 5 minutes at the "Air Fry" setting. Season the pork with salt and pepper on each side as per your desire taste. Arrange the chops in a single layer in the air fryer cooking tray. Air fry the chops for 10-15 minutes, flipping halfway until they reach 145 degrees F. In a pan heat oil over medium heat and cook the garlic for 30 seconds until fragrant. Add the lemon juice, honey, and chili sauce, and mix to combine well with the garlic in form of sauce. Then, simmer the sauce and cook for 3 to 4 minutes until thickened and silky in texture. Transfer the crispy pork chops to a plate and glaze with sauce on top and enjoy.
Per Serving: Calories 435; Fat 21g; Sodium 250mg; Carbs 21g; Fiber 3g; Sugar 6g; Protein 40g

Memphis-Style Pork Ribs

Prep time: 10 minutes| Cook time: 40 minutes| Serves: 2

2 ¼ pounds individually cut pork spareribs
1 tablespoon kosher salt
1 tablespoon dark brown sugar
1 tablespoon sweet paprika
1 teaspoon garlic powder

1 teaspoon onion powder
1 teaspoon poultry seasoning
½ teaspoon mustard powder
½ teaspoon freshly ground black pepper

In a mixing bowl, mix salt, paprika, brown sugar, garlic and onion powders, poultry seasoning, mustard powder, and pepper well. Add the ribs to the mixing bowl and rub the spice mix until completely coated. Arrange the ribs standing up on their ends in the air fryer cooking tray. Set the air fryer on the "Air Fry" setting for 35 minutes at 350 degrees F and air fry the ribs until tender and crispy golden brown. Transfer the cooked ribs to plates and serve with your favorite sauce and fresh salad on the side.
Per Serving: Calories 165; Fat 12g; Sodium 210mg; Carbs 5g; Fiber 0.2g; Sugar 0.6g; Protein 9g

Roast Pork in Cajun Sweet and Sour Sauce

Prep time: 10 minutes| Cook time: 12 minutes| Serves: 3

1 pound pork loin, sliced into 1inch cubes
2 tablespoons Cajun seasoning

3 tablespoons brown sugar + ¼ cup
¼ cup cider vinegar

In a shallow dish, mix pork loin, Cajun seasoning, and 3 tablespoons brown sugar. Coat the meat with the spice mix. Marinate in the refrigerator for 3 hours. Mix the brown sugar and vinegar to baste the meat in a small bowl. Thread pork pieces onto skewers. Baste with sauce and place on skewer rack in the air fryer. Set the air fryer to the "Roast" setting at 360 degrees F for 12 minutes. Flip halfway through cooking time, turn skewers over and baste with sauce, and then roast in batches. Serve hot and enjoy.
Per Serving: Calories 428; Fat 16.7g; Sodium 853mg; Carbs 30.3g; Fiber 9g; Sugar 12g; Protein 39g

Ribs with Coriander

2 slabs spare-ribs
2 teaspoons Cajun seasoning
¼ cup brown sugar
½ teaspoon lemon
1 tablespoon paprika

1 teaspoon coriander seed powder
2 tablespoons onion powder
1 tablespoon salt

Preheat the air fryer to 390 degrees F for 5 minutes at the "Roast" setting. Place the cooking tray in the air fryer. In a bowl, mix paprika, lemon, coriander, onion, and salt. Rub the spice mixture onto the spare ribs. Place the ribs on the cooking pan and roast for 20 minutes per batch flipping halfway. Serve with your favorite barbecue sauce and enjoy.
Per Serving: Calories 354; Fat 35.5g; Sodium 1247mg; Carbs 18.2g; Fiber 3g; Sugar 3g; Protein 24.4g

Buttermilk Pork Chops

1 cup buttermilk
2 boneless pork chops
½ cup of flour

1 teaspoon garlic
Cooking oil spray
Salt and pepper to taste

In a Ziploc bag, add pork chops with buttermilk. Marinate the chops for at least 30 minutes. Add salt, garlic, and pepper to the flour and mix it well. Dredge the marinated pork chops well with flour. Allow pork chops to sit for 5 minutes for the flour to adhere. Preheat the air fryer to 380 degrees F for 5 minutes at the "Air Fry" setting. Place the pork chops on the cooking tray and spray them with oil. Air fry pork chops for 30 minutes until golden-brown color. Flip the pork chops and re-spray the trays to ensure that the chops do not burn. Once they are golden brown, serve them with sauce. Enjoy!
Per Serving: Calories 304; Fat 4g; Sodium 210mg; Carbs 1g; Fiber 0g; Sugar 0g; Protein 23g

Tasty Beef Jerky

1½ pounds beef round, trimmed
½ cup Worcestershire sauce
½ cup low-sodium soy sauce
2 teaspoons honey

1 teaspoon liquid smoke
2 teaspoons onion powder
½ teaspoon red pepper flakes
Ground black pepper, as required

In a Ziploc bag, place the beef and freeze for 1-2 hours to firm up. Place the meat onto a cutting board and cut against the grain into 1/8- to ¼-inch strips. Add the remaining ingredients in a large bowl, and mix until well combined. Add in the steak slices and coat with the mixture generously. Refrigerate the meat to marinate for about 4-6 hours. Remove the beef slices from the bowl and with paper towels, pat dry them. Divide the steak strips onto the cooking trays and arrange them in an even layer. Set the Air Fryer to 160 degreees F at the "Air Fry" setting for 3 hours. After 1½ hours, switch the position of the steak for even cooking. Add the remaining marinade sauce in a small pan over medium heat and cook for about 10 minutes until thicken. When cooking time is complete, remove the trays from Air Fryer. Serve hot topped with the sauce and enjoy.
Per Serving: Calories 372 g; Fat 10.7 g; Sodium 2000 mg; Carbs 12 g; Fiber 0.2 g; Sugar 11.3 g; Protein 53.8g

Beef Roast

2 ½ pounds beef roast

2 tablespoons Italian seasoning

Arrange the roast on the air fryer basket. Rub roast with Italian seasoning, then put it into the air fryer. Set the air fryer to 350 degrees F for 45 minutes at the "Roast" setting. Roast the meat for 45 minutes while cooking. When it is done, slice the roast and serve with salad and sauce and enjoy.
Per Serving: Calories 365 g; Fat 13.2 g; Sodium 567 mg; Carbs 0.5 g; Fiber 0 g; Sugar 0 g; Protein 57.4g

Garlic Beef Patties

1 pound ground beef
½ teaspoon garlic powder
¼ teaspoon onion powder

Pepper
Salt

Preheat the air fryer to 400 degrees F at the "Air Fry" setting for 5 minutes. In a mixing bowl, mix the ground meat, garlic powder, onion powder, pepper, and salt. Make even shape patties from the meat mixture and arrange on the air fryer cooking tray. Place the cooking tray in air fryer. Air fry the patties for 10 minutes. Turn patties after 5 minutes for even cooking. Serve hot with toasted buns and enjoy with sauce.
Per Serving: Calories 212 g; Fat 7.1 g; Sodium 742 mg; Carbs 0.4 g; Fiber 0g; Sugar 0 g; Protein 34.5g

Juicy Beef Roast

1½ pounds beef round, trimmed
½ cup Worcestershire sauce
½ cup low-sodium soy sauce
2 teaspoons honey

1 teaspoon liquid smoke
2 teaspoons onion powder
½ teaspoon red pepper flakes
Ground black pepper, as required

Put the beef in a zip-lock bag and freeze for 1-2 hours. Place the freeze meat onto a cutting board and cut against the grain into 1/8- to ¼-inch strips. Combine the remaining ingredients in a large bowl. Add in the steak slices and coat with the spice mixture. Refrigerate the spiced meat to marinate for about 4-6 hours or for 24 hours. Remove the beef slices from the bowl and dry them with paper towel. Divide the steak strips onto the cooking trays and arrange them in an even layer. Set the Air Fryer to the 160 degrees F at the "Roast" setting for 3 hours. Roast the steak for 3 hours, flipping every 30 minutes for even cooking. In a small pan, add the reserved marinade mix and cook over medium heat for about 10 minutes. When cooking time is complete, remove the tray from Air Fryer. Slice the roast and serve hot and enjoy
Per Serving: Calories 372 g; Fat 10.7 g; Sodium 255 mg; Carbs 12 g; Fiber 2 g; Sugar 3 g; Protein 53.8g

Tasty Madeira Beef

1 cup Madeira
1 and ½ pounds beef meat, cubed
Salt and black pepper to the

taste
1 yellow onion, thinly sliced
1 chili pepper, sliced

Mix all the ingredients along with meat in the air fryer cooking tray then place it in the air fryer. Set the air fryer at 380 degrees F for 25 minutes at the "air fry" setting. Air fry the beef for 25 minutes, stirring once for even cooking. When the meat is ready, divide the mix into bowls with fresh salad and sauce of your choice and serve.

Per Serving: Calories 295 g; Fat 16 g; Sodium 931 mg; Carbs 20 g; Fiber 9 g; Sugar 2 g; Protein 15g

Braised Corned Beef

Prep time: 10 minutes| Cook time: 40 minutes| Serves: 2

1 medium onion, chopped	2 tablespoons Dijon mustard
2 cups of water	2 pounds corned beef brisket

Preheat the air fryer to 400 degrees F at the "Air Fry" setting for 5 minutes. Slice the brisket to chunks and add in the bowl along with the onion, mustard and water. Marinade the meat in the mix for about 12 hours in the refrigerator. In the air fryer cooking tray, pour all the marinated meat with marinade and air fry for 40 minutes, stirring once for even cooking. Serve hot with boiled rice and enjoy

Per Serving: Calories 320 g; Fat 22 g; Sodium 193 mg; Carbs 10 g; Fiber 2 g; Sugar 3 g; Protein 21g

Easy Beef Schnitzel

Prep time: 5 minutes| Cook time: 20 minutes| Serves: 2

2 tablespoons vegetable oil	1 thin beef schnitzel, cut into
12 ounces' breadcrumbs	strips
1 whole egg, whisked	1 whole lemon

Preheat the air fryer to 356 degrees F at the "Air Fry" setting for 5 minutes. Add breadcrumbs and oil in a bowl, and stir well to get a loose mixture. Dip schnitzel in egg, and then dip in breadcrumbs to coat well. Put the prepared schnitzel in air fryer's cooking tray and air fry for 12 minutes, flipping halfway for even cooking. Serve with a drizzle of lemon juice and enjoy.

Per Serving: Calories 205 g; Fat 11 g; Sodium 522 mg; Carbs 12 g; Fiber 2 g; Sugar 1 g; Protein 25g

Beef Liver Soufflé

Prep time: 15 minutes| Cook time: 30 minutes| Serves: 2

½ pound of beef liver	1 cup warm milk
2 eggs	Salt and black pepper to taste
5 ounces buns	

Set the air fryer to the "Bake" setting for 20 minutes at 350 degrees F. Slice the liver and put it in the fridge for 15 minutes. Divide the buns into pieces and soak them in milk for 10 minutes. Put the liver in a blender, along with the yolks, the bun mixture, and the spices. Blend the mixture into a fine puree and stuff in the ramekins. Line the ramekins in the cooking tray and bake for 20 minutes until cook and set. Insert a toothpick in one of the ramekin, if it comes out clean the soufflé is ready. Serve hot topped with the sour cream and chopped dill and enjoy.

Per Serving: Calories 230 g; Fat 11 g; Sodium 421 mg; Carbs 15 g; Fiber 4 g; Sugar 2 g; Protein 26g

Tasty Wiener Beef Schnitzel

Prep time: 5 minutes| Cook time: 30 minutes| Serves: 4

1 pound beef schnitzel cutlets	½ cup flour

2 eggs, beaten	1 cup breadcrumbs
Salt and black pepper	

Set the air fryer to the "Air Fry" setting for 10 minutes at 360 degrees F. Dip the beef cutlets in flour then dip the coated cutlets into the egg mixture. Season the beef cutlets with salt and black pepper as per taste. Then dip it into the breadcrumbs and coat well. Drizzle the cutlets with oil and air fry for 10 minutes, turning once halfway through. Serve hot with ranch sauce and enjoy.

Per Serving: Calories 195 g; Fat 11 g; Sodium 630 mg; Carbs 8 g; Fiber 2 g; Sugar 1 g; Protein 18g

Oregano Beef Roast

Prep time: 5 minutes| Cook time: 40 minutes| Serves: 2

2 teaspoons olive oil	½ teaspoon dried oregano
1 pound beef roast	Salt and black pepper to taste
½ teaspoon dried rosemary	

Preheat the Air Fryer to 400 degrees F at the "Air Fry" setting time for 5 minutes. In a cooking tray, drizzle oil over the beef, and sprinkle with salt, pepper, and herbs. Rub spices onto the meat with hands. Air fry the meat for 40 minutes. Flip to ensure they cook evenly. Once done, wrap the beef in foil for 10 minutes. Slice the beef and serve with a side of steamed asparagus and enjoy.

Per Serving: Calories 235 g; Fat 13 g; Sodium 532 mg; Carbs 11 g; Fiber 6 g; Sugar 2 g; Protein 28g

Delicious Carrot Beef Cake

Prep time: 10 minutes| Cook time: 60 minutes| Serves: 6

2 eggs, beaten	2 cups shredded carrots
½ cup almond milk	2 pounds lean ground beef
1-ounce onion soup mix	½-pound ground pork
1 cup dry bread crumbs	

In a bowl, mix ground beef with carrots and all other ingredients until well incorporated. Grease a meatloaf pan with oil or butter and spread the minced beef in the pan. Set the Air Fryer to 350 degrees F at the "Air Fry" setting for 60 minutes. Place the air fryer cooking tray in the preheated air fryer. Air fry the meatloaf for 60 minutes until cooked through. Slice the meatloaf and serve hot with sauce and fresh salad and enjoy.

Per Serving: Calories 212 g; Fat 11.8 g; Sodium 321 mg; Carbs 14.6 g; Fiber 4.4 g; Sugar 8 g; Protein 17.3g

Tasty Creole Beef Meatloaf

Prep time: 10 minutes| Cook time: 15 minutes| Serves: 6

1 pound ground beef	1 tablespoon creole seasoning
½ tablespoon butter	½ teaspoon turmeric
1 red bell pepper diced	½ teaspoon cumin
⅓ cup red onion diced	½ teaspoon coriander
⅓ cup cilantro diced	2 garlic cloves minced
⅓ cup zucchini diced	Salt and black pepper to taste

In a bowl, mix the beef minced with all the meatloaf ingredients. Make meatloaf from the mixture and place them in the air fryer cooking tray. Set the Air Fryer to 370 degrees F at the "Air Fry" setting for 15 minutes. Place the air fryer cooking tray in the air fryer. Air fry the meatloaf for 15 minutes, shaking once for even cooking. Slice the loaf and serve warm with sauce and fresh salad and enjoy.

Per Serving: Calories 331 g; Fat 2.5 g; Sodium 595 mg; Carbs 69 g; Fiber 12.2 g; Sugar 12.5 g; Protein 26.7g

Egg Beef Short Ribs

Prep time: 10 minutes| Cook time: 35 minutes| Serves: 4

1 ⅔ pounds short ribs	¼ cup panko crumbs
Salt and black pepper, to taste	1 teaspoon ground cumin
1 teaspoon grated garlic	1 teaspoon avocado oil
½ teaspoon salt	½ teaspoon orange zest
1 teaspoon cumin seeds	1 egg, beaten

In a cooking tray, place the beef ribs and pour the whisked egg on top. In another bowl, whisk rest of the crusting ingredients and spread over the meaty side of beef ribs. Set the Air Fryer to 350 degrees F at the "Air Fry" setting for 35 minutes. Place the air fryer cooking tray in the air fryer. Air fry the ribs for 35 minutes until cooked through and crust is golden brown and crispy. Serve warm with sauce and enjoy.
Per Serving: Calories 267 g; Fat 15.4 g; Sodium 203 mg; Carbs 58.5 g; Fiber 4 g; Sugar 1.1 g; Protein 22.9g

Tasty Tarragon Beef Shanks

Prep time: 10 minutes| Cook time: 1 hour 30 minutes| Serves: 6

2 tablespoons olive oil	2 stalks celery, diced
2 pounds beef shank	1 cup Marsala wine
Salt and black pepper to taste	2 tablespoons dried tarragon
1 onion, diced	

In a cooking tray, place the beef shanks. In a another bowl, whisk rest of the ingredients and pour over the shanks. Put the shanks in the Air fryer cooking tray. Set the Air Fryer to 400 degrees F at the "Air Fry" setting for 1 hr 30 minutes. Place the air fryer cooking tray in the air fryer. Air fry the lamb for 1 hour 30 minutes until tender, flipping every 30 minutes for even cooking. Serve hot with ranch sauce and enjoy.
Per Serving: Calories 438 g; Fat 9.7 g; Sodium 245 mg; Carbs 32.5 g; Fiber 0.3 g; Sugar 1.8 g; Protein 30.3g

Saucy BBQ Beef Roast

Prep time: 10 minutes| Cook time: 15 minutes| Serves: 4

1 pound beef roast	½ cup BBQ sauce

Rub the beef roast with BBQ sauce in a bowl. Put the saucy roast in the air fryer cooking tray . Set the air fryer to 390 degrees F at the "Roast" setting for 15 minutes. Place the air fryer cooking tray in the air fryer. Roast the meat for 15 minutes and turn over the roast when cooked halfway through then resume cooking. Serve hot with sauce and enjoy.
Per Serving: Calories 529 g; Fat 17 g; Sodium 391 mg; Carbs 55 g; Fiber 6 g; Sugar 8 g; Protein 41g

Effortless Beef Roast

Prep time: 10 minutes| Cook time: 15 minutes| Serves: 4

2 pounds beef roast	1 teaspoon salt
1 tablespoon olive oil	2 teaspoons rosemary and
1 medium onion	thyme

In the air fryer cooking tray, put in the beef roast. Rub the beef roast with olive oil, salt, rosemary, thyme, and onion. Set the Air Fryer to 390 degrees F at the "Roast" setting for 15 minutes. Place the air fryer cooking tray in the air fryer. Roast the meat for 15 minutes until tender and turn over the roast when cooked halfway

through then resume cooking. Serve hot with sauce and enjoy.
Per Serving: Calories 297 g; Fat 14 g; Sodium 364 mg; Carbs 8 g; Fiber 1 g; Sugar 3 g; Protein 32 g

Bake Beef Pesto

Prep time: 10 minutes| Cook time: 35 minutes| Serves: 6

25 ounces potatoes, boiled	8 ounces pesto
20 ounces beef mince	1 tablespoon olive oil
23 ounces jar tomato pasta	

In a bowl, mash the potatoes and stir in pesto. In a frying pan, sauté the beef mince with olive oil. Layer a casserole dish with tomato pasta sauce. Top with the cooked beef mince. Spread the green pesto potato mash over the beef in an even layer. Set the Air Fryer to 350 degrees F at the "Air Fry" setting for 35 minutes. Air fry the casserole for 35 minutes until top is golden brown and cooked. Serve slices with the salad and enjoy.
Per Serving: Calories 352 g; Fat 14 g; Sodium 220 mg; Carbs 15.8 g; Fiber 0.2 g; Sugar 1g; Protein 26 g

Crispy Beef Potato Meatballs

Prep time: 10 minutes| Cook time: 20 minutes| Serves: 4

½ pound minced beef	1 pound potato cooked, mashed
1 tablespoon parsley, chopped	1 ounce cheese, grated
2 teaspoons curry powder	1 ½ ounce potato chips,
1 pinch salt and black pepper	crushed

In a bowl, mix the beef with potato and all other ingredients. Make small meatballs from the mixture then place them in the air fryer cooking tray. Set the Air Fryer to 350 degrees F at the "Air Fry" setting for 20 minutes. Place the air fryer cooking tray in the air fryer. Air fry the meatballs for 20 minutes and turn over the meatballs halfway through cooking. Serve warm with fresh garden salad and enjoy.
Per Serving: Calories 301 g; Fat 15.8 g; Sodium 189 mg; Carbs 31.7 g; Fiber 0.3g; Sugar 0.1g; Protein 28.2g

Beef Pork Meatballs

Prep time: 10 minutes| Cook time: 20 minutes| Serves: 6

1 pound ground beef	1 teaspoon Italian seasoning
1 pound ground pork	1 egg
½ cup Italian breadcrumbs	¼ cup parsley chopped
⅓ cup milk	¼ cup shredded parmesan
¼ cup onion, diced	salt and pepper to taste
½ teaspoon garlic powder	

In a bowl, mix the beef with all other ingredients for meatballs. Make the small meatballs from the mixture then place them in the air fryer cooking tray. Set the Air Fryer to 400 degrees F at the "Air Fry" setting for 20 minutes. Place the air fryer cooking tray in the air fryer. Air fry the meatballs for 20 minutes and turn over the meatballs halfway through cooking then resume cooking. Serve hot with sauce and enjoy.
Per Serving: Calories 380 g; Fat 20 g; Sodium 686mg; Carbs 33 g; Fiber 1g; Sugar 1.2g; Protein 21g

Meaty Noodle Casserole

Prep time: 10 minutes| Cook time: 35 minutes| Serves: 6

2 tablespoons olive oil	½ pound ground beef
1 medium onion, chopped	fresh mushrooms, sliced

1 cup pasta noodles, cooked
2 cups marinara sauce
1 teaspoon butter
2 teaspoons flour

1 cup milk
1 egg, beaten
1 cup cheddar cheese, grated

Place the pan on moderate heat and add oil to heat. Add in the onion and sauté until soft. Add in mushrooms and beef, and then cook until meat is brown. Add in the marinara sauce and cook it to a simmer. Stir in pasta then spread this mixture in a casserole dish. Prepare the sauce by melting butter in a saucepan over moderate heat. Stir in flour and whisk well, pour in the milk. Mix well and whisk ¼ cup sauce with egg then return it to the saucepan. Stir and cook for 1 minute then pour this sauce over the beef. Drizzle cheese over the beef casserole. Set the Air Fryer to 350 degrees F at the "Air Fry" setting for 30 minutes. Place the air fryer cooking tray with beef casserole in the air fryer. Air fry the casserole for 30 minutes until cooked and top is golden brown. Serve slices and enjoy.
Per Serving: Calories 361 g; Fat 16.3 g; Sodium 515 mg; Carbs 19.3 g; Fiber 0.1g; Sugar 18.2g; Protein 33.3g

Saucy Oregano Beef Bake

Prep time: 10 minutes| Cook time: 66 minutes| Serves: 6

2 tablespoons olive oil
1 large onion, diced
2 pounds ground beef
2 teaspoons salt
½ cup red wine
2 cloves garlic, chopped
1 teaspoon ground cinnamon

2 teaspoons ground cumin
2 teaspoons dried oregano
1 teaspoon black pepper
1 can (28-ounce) crushed tomatoes
1 tablespoon tomato paste

Over the moderate heat, put a pan and add in the oil. Add in the onion, salt, and beef meat then and cook for 12 minutes, stiring frequently. Stir in red wine and cook for 2 minutes. Put in the cinnamon, garlic, oregano, cumin, and pepper, then stir cook for 2 minutes. Add in the tomato paste and tomatoes and cook for 20 minutes on a simmer. Spread this mixture in a casserole dish. Set the Air Fryer to 350 degrees F at the "Bake" setting for 30 minutes. Place the air fryer cooking tray in the air fryer. Bake the beef for 30 minutes until cooked through. Serve hot and enjoy.
Per Serving: Calories 405 g; Fat 22.7 g; Sodium 227mg; Carbs 26.1 g; Fiber 1.4g; Sugar 0.9g; Protein 45.2g

Cheesy Tricolor Beef Skewers

Prep time: 10 minutes| Cook time: 25 minutes| Serves: 4

2 garlic cloves, minced
2 tablespoons rapeseed oil
1 cup cottage cheese, cubed
Cherry tomatoes

2 tablespoons cider vinegar
Large bunch thyme
1 ¼ pound boneless beef, diced

In a bowl, mix the beef with all its thyme, oil, vinegar, and garlic. Marinate the thyme beef for 2 hours in the refrigerator. Thread the marinated beef, cheese, and tomatoes on the skewers. Put the skewers in an air fryer cooking tray. Set the Air Fryer to 350 degrees F at the "Air Fry" setting for 25 minutes. Place the air fryer cooking tray in the air fryer. Air fry the meat for 25 minutes. Flip the skewers halfway through cooking then resume cooking. Serve warm with sauce and enjoy.
Per Serving: Calories 695 g; Fat 17.5 g; Sodium 355mg; Carbs 26.4 g; Fiber 1.8g; Sugar 0.8g; Protein 117.4g

Tasty Yogurt Beef Kebabs

Prep time: 10 minutes| Cook time: 25 minutes| Serves: 4

½ cup yogurt

1½ tablespoon mint

1 teaspoon ground cumin
1 cup eggplant, diced

10.5ounces lean beef, diced
½ small onion, cubed

In a bowl, whisk yogurt with mint and cumin. Mix in the beef cubes and mix well to coat. Marinate for 30 minutes in refrigerator. Thread the beef, onion, and eggplant on the skewers. Put the beef skewers in the air fry cooking tray. Set the air fryer to 360 degrees F at the "Air Fry" setting for 25 minutes. Place the air fryer cooking tray in the preheated air fryer. Turn over the skewers halfway through cooking then resume cooking. Serve warm and enjoy.
Per Serving: Calories 301 g; Fat 8.9 g; Sodium 3450mg; Carbs 24.7 g; Fiber 1.2g; Sugar 1.3g; Protein 15.3g

Delicious Agave Beef Kebabs

Prep time: 10 minutes| Cook time: 20 minutes| Serves: 6

2 pounds beef steaks, cubed
2 tablespoons jerk seasoning
zest and juice of 1 lime

1 tablespoon agave syrup
½ teaspoon thyme leaves, chopped

In a bowl, mix the beef with jerk seasoning, lime juice, zest, agave syrup, and thyme. Mix the meat well then marinate for 30 minutes in the refrigerator. Thread the beef on the skewers. Put the beef skewers in the air fry cooking tray. Set the Air Fryer to 360 degrees F at the "Air Fry" setting for 20 minutes. Place the air fryer cooking tray in the air fryer. Air fry the skewers for 20 minutes until cooked. Turn over the skewers when cooked halfway through then resume cooking. Serve warmed and enjoy with fresh salad.
Per Serving: Calories 548 g; Fat 22.9 g; Sodium 350 mg; Carbs 17.5 g; Fiber 6.3g; Sugar 10.9g; Protein 40.1g

Tasty Beef Skewers with Potato Salad

Prep time: 10 minutes| Cook time: 25 minutes| Serves: 4

juice ½ lemon
2 tablespoons olive oil
1 garlic clove, crushed
1 ¼ pound diced beef
For the salad
2 potatoes, boiled, peeled and diced

2 large tomatoes, chopped
1 cucumber, chopped
1 handful black olives, chopped
12 ounces pack feta cheese, crumbled
1 bunch of mint, chopped

In a bowl, whisk lemon juice with garlic and olive oil. Mix in beef cubes and mix well to coat. Marinate for 30 minutes. Thread the beef on the skewers. Place these beef skewers in the air fry cooking tray. Set the air fryer to 360 degrees F at the "Air Fry" setting for 25 minutes. Place the air fryer cooking tray in the air fryer. Air fry the meat for 25 minutes until done. Turn over the skewers when cooked halfway through, and then resume cooking. Whisk all the salad ingredients in a salad bowl. Serve the skewers hot with tasty fresh salad and enjoy.
Per Serving: Calories609 g; Fat 50.5 g; Sodium 463 mg; Carbs 9.9 g; Fiber 1.5g; Sugar 0.3g; Protein 29.3g

Harissa Dipped Beef Skewers

Prep time: 10 minutes| Cook time: 16 minutes| Serves: 6

1 pound beef mince
2 tablespoons harissa
2 ounces feta cheese
1 large red onion, shredded

1 handful parsley, chopped
1 handful mint, chopped
1 tablespoon olive oil
juice 1 lemon

Whisk beef mince with harissa, onion, feta, and seasoning in a bowl. Make 12 sausages out of meat mixture then thread them on the skewers. Place these beef skewers in the air fry cooking tray. Set the air fryer to 360 degrees F at the "Air Fry" setting for 16 minutes. Place the air fryer cooking tray in the air fryer. Air fry the meat sausages for 16 minutes. Turn over the skewers when cooked halfway through then resume cooking. Mix the remaining ingredients in a salad bowl. Serve hot with fresh salad and enjoy.
Per Serving: Calories 452 g; Fat 4 g; Sodium 220mg; Carbs 23.1 g; Fiber 0.3g; Sugar 1g; Protein 26g

Tasty Onion Pepper Beef Kebobs

Prep time: 10 minutes| Cook time: 20 minutes| Serves: 4

2 tablespoons pesto paste
⅔ pound beefsteak, diced
2 red peppers, cut into chunks
2 red onions, cut into wedges
1 tablespoon olive oil

In a bowl, mix the beef cubes with harissa and oil. Marinate the meat for 30 minutes. Thread the beef, onion, and peppers on the skewers. Put the beef skewers in the air fry cooking tray. Set the air fryer to 360 degrees F at the "Air Fry" setting for 20 minutes. Place the air fryer cooking tray in the air fryer. Air fry the skewers for 20 minutes. Turn over the skewers when cooked halfway through then resume cooking. Serve warm with sauce and enjoy.
Per Serving: Calories 301 g; Fat 15.8 g; Sodium 389mg; Carbs 11.7 g; Fiber 0.3g; Sugar 0.1g; Protein 28.2g

Tasty Beef with Orzo Salad

Prep time: 10 minutes| Cook time: 27 minutes| Serves: 4

⅔ pounds beef shoulder, cubed
1 teaspoon ground cumin
½ teaspoon cayenne pepper
1 teaspoon sweet smoked paprika
1 tablespoon olive oil
24 cherry tomatoes
Salad:
½ cup orzo, boiled
½ cup frozen pea
1 large carrot, grated
1 small pack coriander, chopped
1 small pack mint, chopped
juice 1 lemon
2 tablespoons olive oil

In a bowl, mix the tomatoes and beef with oil, paprika, pepper, and cumin. Thread the beef and tomatoes on the skewers. Put the beef skewers in the air fry cooking tray. Set the Air Fryer to 370 degrees F at the "Air Fry" setting for 25 minutes. Place the air fryer cooking tray in the preheated Air Fryer. Air fry the meat for 25 minutes. Turn over the skewers when cooked halfway through then resume cooking. Sauté the carrots and peas with olive oil in a pan for 2 minutes. Add mint, lemon juice, coriander in the carrots and cooked couscous. Serve hot skewers with the warm couscous salad.
Per Serving: Calories 231 g; Fat 20.1 g; Sodium 941 mg; Carbs 20.1 g; Fiber 0.9g; Sugar 1.4g; Protein 14.6g

Rosemary Beef Zucchini Shashliks

Prep time: 10 minutes| Cook time: 25 minutes| Serves: 4

1pound beef, b1d and diced
1 lime, juiced and chopped
1 tablespoon olive oil
20 garlic cloves, chopped
1 handful rosemary, chopped
2 green peppers, cubed
2 zucchinis, cubed
2 red onions, cut into wedges

In a bowl, add the beef with the rest of the skewer's ingredients. Thread the beef, peppers, zucchini, and onion on the skewers. Put the beef skewers in the air fry cooking tray. Set the Air

Fryer to 370 degrees F at the "Air Fry" setting for 25 minutes. Place the air fryer cooking tray in the in the air fryer. Air fry the skewers for 25 minutes until done. Turn over the skewers when cooked halfway through then resume cooking. Serve warm with sauce and enjoy.
Per Serving: Calories 472 g; Fat 11.1 g; Sodium 749 mg; Carbs 19.9 g; Fiber 0.2g; Sugar 0.2 g; Protein 13.5g

Spicy Lemon Beef Skewers

Prep time: 10 minutes| Cook time: 18 minutes| Serves: 4

2 teaspoons ground cumin
2 teaspoons ground coriander
¼ teaspoon ground cinnamon
1/8 teaspoon ground smoked paprika
2 teaspoons lime zest
½ teaspoon salt
½ teaspoon black pepper
1 tablespoon lemon juice
2 teaspoons olive oil
1 ½ pounds lean beef, cubed

In a bowl, mix the beef with the rest of the skewer's ingredients. Thread the beef and veggies on the skewers alternately. Put the beef skewers in the air fry cooking tray. Set the air fryer to 370 degrees F at the "Air Fry" setting for 18 minutes. Place the air fryer cooking tray in the air fryer. Air fry the skewers for 18 minutes. Turn over the skewers when cooked halfway through then resume cooking. Serve warm with sauce and enjoy.
Per Serving: Calories 327 g; Fat 3.5 g; Sodium 142 mg; Carbs 33.6 g; Fiber 0.4g; Sugar 0.5g; Protein 24.5g

Delicious Beef Sausage with Cucumber Sauce

Prep time: 10 minutes| Cook time: 15 minutes| Serves: 6

Beef Kabobs
1 pound ground beef
½ an onion, finely diced
2 garlic cloves, finely minced
2 teaspoons cumin
2 teaspoons coriander
1 ½ teaspoon salt
2 tablespoons chopped mint
Yogurt Sauce:
1 cup Greek yogurt
2 tablespoons cucumber, chopped
2 garlic cloves, minced
¼ teaspoon salt

In a bowl, mix the beef with the rest of the kebob ingredients. Make 6 sausages out of the mince and thread them on the skewers. Put the beef skewers in the air fry cooking tray. Set the air fryer to 370 degrees F at the "Air Fry" setting for 15 minutes. Place the air fryer cooking tray in the air fryer. Air fry the kebobs for 15 minutes. Turn over the skewers when cooked halfway through then resume cooking. Prepare the cucumber sauce by whisking all its ingredients in a bowl. Serve the skewers with chilled cucumber sauce and enjoy.
Per Serving: Calories 353 g; Fat 7.5 g; Sodium 297 mg; Carbs 10.4 g; Fiber 0.2g; Sugar 0.1g; Protein 13.1g

Crispy Beef Eggplant Medley

Prep time: 10 minutes| Cook time: 20 minutes| Serves: 4

2 cloves of garlic
1 teaspoon dried oregano
2 tablespoons olive oil
1 pound beef steaks, diced
2 eggplant, cubed
fresh bay leaves
2 lemons, juiced
a few sprigs parsley, chopped

In a bowl, mix the beef with the rest of the skewer's ingredients. Thread the beef and veggies on the skewers alternately. Put the beef skewers in the air fry cooking tray. Set the air fryer to 370 degrees F at the "Air Fry" setting for 20 minutes. Air fry the skewers for 20 minutes. Turn over the skewers when cooked

halfway through then resume cooking. Serve warm and enjoy.
Per Serving: Calories 248 g; Fat 13 g; Sodium 353mg; Carbs 1 g; Fiber 0.4g; Sugar 1g; Protein 29g

Oregano Beef Kebobs

Prep time: 10 minutes| Cook time: 20 minutes| Serves: 6

2 pounds beef, cubed	¼ teaspoon dried thyme,
½ cup olive oil	1 teaspoon salt
1 lemon, juice only	¼ teaspoon black pepper
3 cloves garlic, minced	1 tablespoon parsley, chopped
1 onion, sliced	1 cup Worcestershire sauce
1 teaspoon oregano, dried	

In a bowl, mix the beef with the rest of the kebab ingredients. Marinate the beef for 30 minutes. Thread the beef and veggies on the skewers alternately. Put the beef skewers in the air fry cooking tray. Brush the skewers with the Worcestershire sauce. Set the air fryer to 370 degrees F at the "Air Fry" setting for 20 minutes. Put the air fryer cooking tray in the air fryer. Air fry the meat for 20 minutes until tender. Turn the skewers when cooked halfway through then resume cooking. Serve warm and enjoy.
Per Serving: Calories 457 g; Fat 19.1 g; Sodium 635 mg; Carbs 18.9 g; Fiber 1.7g; Sugar 1.2g; Protein 32.5g

Lemon Beef Kebobs with Cream Dip

Prep time: 10 minutes| Cook time: 20 minutes| Serves: 6

Beef Kebabs	1 tablespoon olive oil
2 pounds beef, diced	2 tablespoons lemon juice
1 large onion, squares	1 teaspoon yellow mustard
Salt	¼ teaspoon salt
For the Dressing	1/8 teaspoon black pepper
1 tablespoon mayonnaise	

In a bowl, mix the beef and onion with salt. Thread the beef and onion on the skewers. Put the beef skewers in the air fry cooking tray Set the air fryer to 370 degrees F at the "Air Fry" setting for 20 minutes. Place the air fryer cooking tray in the air fryer. Air fry the meat for 20 minutes. Turn over the skewers when cooked halfway through then resume cooking. In a bowl, mix the cream dip and its ingredients. Serve skewers with cream dip and enjoy.
Per Serving: Calories392 g; Fat 16.1 g; Sodium 466mg; Carbs 3.9 g; Fiber 0.9g; Sugar 0.6g; Protein 48g

BBQ Sauce Beef Skewers

Prep time: 10 minutes| Cook time: 15 minutes| Serves: 4

2 tablespoons hoisin sauce	2 cloves garlic, minced
2 tablespoons sherry	1 tablespoon minced fresh
¼ cup soy sauce	ginger root
1 teaspoon barbeque sauce	1 ½ pounds flank steak, cubed
2 green onions, chopped	

In a bowl, toss steak cubes with sherry, all the sauces and other ingredients marinate the saucy spiced skewers for 30 minutes. Put the beef skewers in the air fry cooking tray. Set the Air Fryer to 350 degrees F at the "Air Fry" setting for 15 minutes. Place the air fryer cooking tray in the air fryer and cook for 15 minutes. Turn the skewers when cooked halfway through then resume cooking. Serve warm and enjoy.
Per Serving: Calories 321 g; Fat 7.4 g; Sodium 353mg; Carbs 19.4 g; Fiber 2.7g; Sugar 6.5g; Protein 37.2g

Buttery Roasted Beef Brisket

Prep time: 10 minutes| Cook time: 1 hour 30 minutes| Serves: 12

2 pounds beef brisket,	Salt to taste
boneless	Black pepper to taste
Spice Rub:	1 stick butter, melted
1 cup olive oil	½ cup olive oil
juice of 1 lemon	1 ounce soy sauce
1 teaspoon thyme	1 ounce brown sugar
1teaspoon minced garlic	1 tablespoon black pepper

In an air fryer cooking tray, place the beef brisket. In a bowl, mix the spices rub ingredients. Brush the brisket with the spice mixture. In a bowl, whisk the baste ingredients and keep it aside. Set the air fryer to 370 degrees F at the "Air Fry" setting for 1 hour 30 minutes. Air fry the beef brisket for 1 hour 30 minutes. Baste the meat with sauce every 30 minute of cooking. Serve warm and enjoy.
Per Serving: Calories 378 g; Fat 21 g; Sodium 146mg; Carbs 7.1 g; Fiber 0.4g; Sugar 0.1g; Protein 23g

Rosemary Roast Beef

Prep time: 10 minutes| Cook time: 45 minutes| Serves: 6

2 pounds roast beef	1 teaspoon fresh basil, chopped
2 tablespoons olive oil	1 teaspoon fresh thyme, chopped
2 cloves garlic, minced	1 teaspoon cayenne pepper
1 teaspoon fresh rosemary,	Kosher salt and ground black
chopped	pepper, to taste

Set the air fryer to 360 degrees F at the "Air Fry" setting for 45 minutes. Tap the roast dry with paper towel. Grease the air fryer cooking tray with olive oil. Place the beef in the air fryer cooking tray. Roast the beef for 25 minutes in the air fryer. Flip the roast over and continue roasting for 20 minutes. Serve hot with sauce and enjoy.
Per Serving: Calories 325 g; Fat 17.3 g; Sodium 602mg; Carbs 0.6 g; Fiber 0.2g; Sugar 0g; Protein 40g

Fresh Beef Chuck Salad

Prep time: 10 minutes| Cook time: 50 minutes| Serves: 6

2 pounds beef chuck roast	2 tablespoons lemon juice
3 cups Romaine lettuce, torn	¼ cup extra-virgin olive oil
into pieces	1 teaspoon garlic
1 large tomato, diced	1 teaspoon ginger, peeled and
2 tablespoons fresh cilantro	minced
2 tablespoons fresh parsley	1 tablespoon fish sauce
2 tablespoons fresh basil	2 tablespoons soy sauce

Set the air fryer to 360 degrees F at the "Air Fry" setting for 50 minutes. Grease the air fryer cooking tray with olive oil. Place the beef in the air fryer cooking tray. Roast the beef for 25 minutes in the air fryer. Flip the roast over and continue roasting for 25 minutes. Cut the beef into strips; add in the remaining salad ingredients and toss to combine. Serve the salad well-chilled. Bon appétit!
Per Serving: Calories 325 g; Fat 21.3 g; Sodium 347mg; Carbs 4.6 g; Fiber 1.2g; Sugar 2.3g; Protein 30.3g

Tasty BBQ Beef Ribs

Prep time: 10 minutes| Cook time: 20 minutes| Serves: 4

1 ½ pounds chuck short ribs	1 teaspoon smoked paprika

1 teaspoon onion powder
1 teaspoon garlic powder
2 tablespoons brown sugar
1 tablespoon apple cider vinegar

1 tablespoon Dijon mustard
2 tablespoons BBQ sauce
2 tablespoons oil
Sea salt and ground black pepper

In a ceramic bowl, add all the ingredients. Marinate the beef for at least 3 hours. Set the air fryer to 360 degrees F at the "Air Fry" setting for 15 minutes. Place aluminum foil onto the cooking tray. Place the beef ribs in the air fryer cooking tray. Reserve the marinade. Cook the beef for about 15 minutes flipping halfway cooking and baste the reserved marinade evenly and resume cooking. Serve hot immediately and enjoy!
Per Serving: Calories 365 g; Fat 22.3 g; Sodium 986mg; Carbs 6.3 g; Fiber 0.7g; Sugar 4.5g; Protein 34.8g

Buttery BBQ Beef Brisket

Prep time: 10 minutes| Cook time: 40 minutes| Serves: 5

2 pounds beef brisket, sliced
½ cup BBQ sauce

2 tablespoons butter
2 garlic cloves, pressed

Set the air fryer to 365 degrees F at the "Air Fry" setting for 20 minutes. Combine the beef with the other ingredients. Place aluminum foil onto the cooking tray. Place the beef in the air fryer cooking tray. Cook the beef for about 20 minutes. Flip the beef and continue to cook for 15 minutes more. Serve warm and enjoy!
Per Serving: Calories 410 g; Fat 31.6 g; Sodium 945mg; Carbs 2.4 g; Fiber 0.5g; Sugar 1g; Protein 27.1g

Beef Meatloaf with Veggies

Prep time: 10 minutes| Cook time: 30 minutes| Serves: 5

1 ½ pounds ground beef
1 egg
2 garlic cloves, minced
1 small leek, chopped
½ cup cream of celery soup
1 cup tortilla chips, crushed
1 tablespoon olive oil

Kosher salt and ground black pepper, to taste
Glaze:
½ cup tomato paste
1 tablespoon brown mustard
2 tablespoons brown sugar

Combine all the ingredients for the meatloaf; press the meatloaf into a lightly greased cooking tray. Set the air fryer to 400 degrees F at the "Air Fry" setting for 20 minutes. Add the cooking tray to the air fryer. Air Fry the meatloaf for 20 minutes. Toss the glaze ingredients and spread the mixture over the top of the meatloaf. Select the "Broil" function and cook the meatloaf for 5 minutes more. Serve hot and enjoy.
Per Serving: Calories 301 g; Fat 16.6 g; Sodium 428mg; Carbs 17.9 g; Fiber 2.5g; Sugar 7.8g; Protein 21.1g

Classic Minty Beef Patties

Prep time: 10 minutes| Cook time: 30 minutes| Serves: 4

1 pound ground beef
1 carrot, grated
1 medium onion, chopped
1 teaspoon garlic, minced
2 tablespoons fresh cilantro, chopped
1 tablespoon fresh mint, chopped

1 tablespoon fresh parsley, chopped
1 tablespoon Worcestershire sauce
A few drops of liquid smoke
Sea salt and ground black pepper, to taste

Set the air fryer to 360 degrees F at the "Air Fry" setting for 25 minutes. In the air fryer cooking tray, place a sheet of parchment paper. Combine all the ingredients in a bowl. Make 4 patties

from the mixture and place it in the air fryer cooking tray. Air Fry the beef patties for 25 minutes. Serve warm with toasted buns and fresh salad and enjoy.
Per Serving: Calories 326 g; Fat 19.8 g; Sodium 856mg; Carbs 8.3 g; Fiber 1.5g; Sugar 3.8g; Protein 30.3g

Hot Beef Back Ribs

Prep time: 10 minutes| Cook time: 20 minutes| Serves: 4

1 ½ pounds beef back ribs
1 cup barbecue sauce
1 tablespoon mustard
1 tablespoon hot paprika

2 tablespoons scallions, chopped
2 tablespoons garlic, chopped

In a ceramic bowl, mix all the ingredients and marinate the beef for at least 3 hours. Set the air fryer to 360 degrees F at the "Air Fry" setting for 15 minutes. Place aluminum foil onto the cooking tray. Place the beef in the air fryer cooking tray. Cook the beef for about 15 minutes. Serve immediately with sauce and enjoy!
Per Serving: Calories 513 g; Fat 27.7 g; Sodium 733mg; Carbs 8 g; Fiber 2.2g; Sugar 2.8g; Protein 34.8g

Delicious Teriyaki Beef Brisket

Prep time: 10 minutes| Cook time: 55 minutes| Serves: 4

1 ½ pounds beef brisket, b1less
2 tablespoons agave nectar
2 garlic cloves, minced
1 teaspoon chili powder

1 teaspoon mustard powder
Sea salt and ground black pepper, to taste
¼ cup teriyaki sauce

Set the air fryer to 350 degrees F at the "Air Fry" setting for 25 minutes. Mix the beef with the other ingredients. Place aluminum foil onto the cooking tray. Place the beef in the air fryer cooking tray. Cook the beef for about 25 minutes. Increase the temperature to 390 degrees F. Turn it over and continue to cook for 25 minutes more. Serve warm with sauce and enjoy!
Per Serving: Calories 377 g; Fat 25.4 g; Sodium 744mg; Carbs 6.2 g; Fiber 0.6g; Sugar 4.2g; Protein 26.3g

Tasty Beef Chuck with Carrots

Prep time: 10 minutes| Cook time: 35 minutes| Serves: 5

1 ½ pounds beef chuck shoulder steak
1 clove garlic, minced
2 tablespoons fresh chives, chopped
2 tablespoons soy sauce
¼ cup dry red wine
1 tablespoon st1-ground

mustard
1 teaspoon red pepper flakes, crushed
1-pound carrots, sliced
2 tablespoons butter, at room temperature
Kosher salt and freshly ground black pepper, to taste

In a ceramic bowl, place the beef, garlic, chives, soy sauce, red wine, mustard, and red pepper flakes and marinate the beef for at least 3 hours. Set the air fryer to 390 degrees F at the "Air Fry" setting for 35 minutes. Place aluminum foil onto the cooking tray. Place the beef in the air fryer cooking tray. Cook the beef for about 15 minutes. Turn the temperature of the air fryer to 380 degrees F. Add in the carrots, butter, salt, and black pepper, baste the beef with the reserved marinade and continue to cook for 15 minutes more. Serve warm with veggies and enjoy!
Per Serving: Calories 302 g; Fat 14.4 g; Sodium 533mg; Carbs 10.9 g; Fiber 2.9g; Sugar 5.6g; Protein 29.8g

Cheese Stuffed Beef Rolls

Prep time: 10 minutes| Cook time: 25 minutes| Serves: 4

1 pound beef tenderloin, thinly sliced
2 tablespoons Worcestershire sauce
2 tablespoons yellow mustard
1 teaspoon dried oregano

1 teaspoon garlic powder
1 teaspoon onion powder
2 teaspoons olive oil
2 tablespoons mayonnaise
8 ounces Gruyere cheese, crumbled

In a ceramic bowl, place the beef, Worcestershire sauce, mustard, spices, and olive oil. Marinate the beef to marinate for at least 3 hours. Divide the mayonnaise and Gruyere cheese between the beef tenderloin slices. Roll the meat up and secure with toothpicks. Set the air fryer to 400 degrees F at the "Air Fry" setting for 20 minutes. Place the aluminum foil on the air fryer cooking tray. Place the beef in the air fryer cooking tray. Reserve the marinade. Cook the beef rolls for about 20 minutes, basting them with the marinade occasionally. Serve hot and enjoy.
Per Serving: Calories 482 g; Fat 37.1 g; Sodium 235mg; Carbs 3.9 g; Fiber 0.7g; Sugar 1.2g; Protein 32g

Tender Beef Roast

Prep time: 10 minutes| Cook time: 50 minutes| Serves: 6

2 ½ pounds beef roast
2 tablespoons olive oil
¼ cup wine vinegar
1 tablespoon mustard
1 teaspoon dried thyme
1 teaspoon garlic powder

1 teaspoon onion powder
1 teaspoon turmeric powder
1 teaspoon cayenne pepper
Sea salt and ground black pepper, to taste

In a ceramic bowl, mix all the ingredients and marinate it for 1 hour. Set the air fryer to 360 degrees F at the "Roast" setting for 50 minutes. Spray the air fryer cooking tray with nonstick spray. Place the beef in the air fryer cooking tray. Roast for 20 minutes in the air fryer. Flip the roast over, baste with the reserved marinade, and roast for a further 30 minutes for medium-rare. When the roast is done, slice and serve hot with sauce and enjoy.
Per Serving: Calories 303 g; Fat 15.5 g; Sodium 731mg; Carbs 1.4 g; Fiber 0.4g; Sugar 0.1g; Protein 39.2g

Hot Beef Brisket

Prep time: 10 minutes| Cook time: 50 minutes| Serves: 4

1 ½ pounds beef brisket
2 tablespoons brown sugar
Kosher salt and ground black pepper, to taste
1 teaspoon chili powder
1 teaspoon garlic powder
1 teaspoon hot paprika
2 tablespoons butter, melted

2 tablespoons scallions, sliced thinly
2 garlic cloves, smashed
½ cup ketchup
2 tablespoons white vinegar
1 tablespoon st1-ground mustard
2 tablespoons molasses

Set the air fryer to 390 degrees F at the "Bake" setting for 50 minutes. Mix the beef brisket with the other ingredients. Place aluminum foil onto the cooking tray. Place the beef in the air fryer cooking tray. Bake the beef brisket for about 25 minutes. Increase the temperature to 400 degrees F. Turn it over and continue to cook for 25 minutes more. Serve warm with sauce and enjoy!
Per Serving: Calories 484 g; Fat 31.9 g; Sodium 777mg; Carbs 23.2 g; Fiber 1.1g; Sugar 18.3 g; Protein 26.2g

Beef Croquettes

Prep time: 10 minutes| Cook time: 25 minutes| Serves: 4

1 pound ground beef
1 small leek, chopped
2 garlic cloves, minced
1 bell pepper, seeded and chopped
2 tablespoons fresh mint, chopped
2 tablespoons fresh parsley,

chopped
2 tablespoons olive oil
2 large eggs
¼ cup cream cheese
1 teaspoon red pepper flakes, crushed
Sea salt and freshly ground black pepper, to taste

Set the air fryer to 390 degrees F at the "Air Fry" setting for 25 minutes. Place a sheet of parchment paper in the air fryer cooking tray. Combine all the ingredients in a mixing bowl. Make 8 balls from the mixture and place it on the cooking tray. Cook for 20 minutes. After 20 minutes serve with sauce and enjoy.
Per Serving: Calories 380 g; Fat 27.9 g; Sodium 455mg; Carbs 5.8 g; Fiber 0.7g; Sugar 2.1g; Protein 26.9g

Memphis Back Ribs

Prep time: 10 minutes| Cook time: 20 minutes| Serves: 4

1 ½ pounds beef back ribs
1 cup BBQ sauce
Kosher salt and freshly ground black pepper, to taste
1 tablespoon brown sugar

1 tablespoon brown mustard
1 teaspoon hot paprika
1 teaspoon garlic powder
1 teaspoon onion powder

In a ceramic bowl, add all the ingredients and marinate the beef for at least 3 hours. Set the air fryer to 360 degrees F at the "Air Fry" setting for 20 minutes. Place aluminum foil onto the cooking tray. Place the beef ribs in the air fryer cooking tray. Cook the beef for about 15 minutes. Serve hot immediately and enjoy!
Per Serving: Calories 412 g; Fat 28 g; Sodium 732mg; Carbs 8.2 g; Fiber 1.7g; Sugar 4.6g; Protein 34.4g

Flanken Beef Ribs

Prep time: 10 minutes| Cook time: 20 minutes| Serves: 4

1 ½ pounds Flanken-style beef ribs
¼ cup brown sugar
1 tablespoon kosher salt
1 teaspoon freshly ground black pepper
1 tablespoon chili powder

1 teaspoon garlic powder
1 teaspoon cayenne pepper
1 tablespoon brown mustard
2 tablespoons butter
¼ cup bourbon
½ cup tomato sauce

In a ceramic bowl, add all the ingredients, and then marinate the beef for at least 3 hours. Set the air fryer to 360 degrees F at the "Air Fry" setting for 20 minutes. Place aluminum foil onto the cooking tray. Place the beef ribs in the air fryer cooking tray. Cook the beef for about 20 minutes. Serve hot immediately and enjoy!
Per Serving: Calories 570 g; Fat 40.5 g; Sodium 423mg; Carbs 15.1 g; Fiber 2g; Sugar 9.3g; Protein 33.9g

Cold Beef Brisket Salad

Prep time: 10 minutes| Cook time: 50 minutes| Serves: 4

1 pound beef brisket
2 green onions, chopped
1 garlic clove, minced
¼ cup fresh mint leaves,

chopped
¼ cup fresh lime juice
1 teaspoon sweet chili sauce
1 head Romaine lettuce, torn

into bite-size pieces
1 medium cucumber, diced
1 cup grape tomatoes, halved
1 bell pepper, sliced

Set the air fryer to 350 degrees F at the "Air Fry" setting. Mix the beef brisket with all the ingredients, now place the aluminum foil on the air fryer cooking tray. Place the beef in the air fryer cooking tray and cook the beef brisket for about 25 minutes. Increase the temperature to 390 degrees F. Turn it over and continue to cook for 25 minutes more. Slice the beef into strips and toss it with the remaining ingredients. Serve your salad chilled and enjoy!
Per Serving: Calories 347 g; Fat 22.5 g; Sodium 632mg; Carbs 25 g, Fiber 5.1g, Sugar 5.9g; Protein 42g

Tasty Beef Zucchini Cakes

Prep time: 10 minutes| Cook time: 30 minutes| Serves: 5

1 pound ground beef
½ pound beef sausage
1 zucchini, grated
2 tablespoons olive oil
1 medium onion, chopped
2 garlic cloves, chopped
1 tablespoon garam masala
1 teaspoon ground cumin
1 jalapeno pepper, minced
Kosher salt and ground black pepper, to taste
2 large eggs, beaten
½ cup crackers, crushed

Set the air fryer to 390 F at the "Air Fry" setting for 30 minutes. In the air fryer cooking tray, place the parchment paper. Combine all the ingredients in a mixing bowl. Make 10 balls from the mixture and place them in the air fryer cooking tray and cook for 30 minutes. When it is nicely done, serve hot and enjoy.
Per Serving: Calories 451 g; Fat 34.5 g; Sodium 953mg; Carbs 27.6 g; Fiber 5g; Sugar 8g; Protein 27.6g

Italian Beef Braciole

Prep time: 10 minutes| Cook time: 20 minutes| Serves: 4

1 pound beef steak
1 cup dry Italian wine
2 large tomatoes, chopped
1 bay leaf
1 red chili pepper, minced
2 cloves garlic, minced
¼ cup olive oil
1 teaspoon black peppercorns, whole
2 tablespoons Worcestershire
sauce
1 cup Pecorino Romano cheese, shredded
¼ cup fresh Italian parsley, chopped
¼ cup fresh basil, chopped
Kosher salt and freshly ground black pepper, to taste
1 small onion, chopped

In a ceramic bowl, place the beef, wine, tomatoes, bay leaf, chili pepper, garlic, olive oil, black peppercorns, and Worcestershire sauce. Marinate the beef for at least 3 hours. Pound the meat with the flat side of a mallet. Divide the remaining ingredients between the beef steaks; roll them up and secure with toothpicks. Set the air fryer to 400 degrees F at the "Air Fry" setting for 20 minutes. Place aluminum foil onto the cooking tray. Place the beef in the air fryer cooking tray. Cook the beef rolls for about 20 minutes. When it is done, serve hot and enjoy.
Per Serving: Calories431 g; Fat 27.5 g; Sodium 832mg; Carbs 10 g; Fiber 1.9g; Sugar 5.2g; Protein 33.1g

Gyudon (Delicious Beef Bowl)

Prep time: 10 minutes| Cook time: 20 minutes| Serves: 4

1 pound rib-eye steak, cubed
½ cup dashi (or beef bones stock)
2 tablespoons rice vinegar
2 tablespoons soy sauce (or Shoyu sauce)
1 teaspoon ginger-garlic paste
2 tablespoons agave nectar
1 teaspoon red pepper flakes, crushed
Sea salt and ground black

pepper, to taste
1 pound Chinese cabbage, cut
into wedges
1 medium shallot, sliced

In a ceramic bowl, add the steak, dashi, rice vinegar, soy sauce, ginger-garlic paste, agave nectar, red pepper flakes, salt, and black pepper. Cover and allow the beef to marinate for 3 hours. Set the air fryer to 380 degrees F at the "Air Fry" setting for 20 minutes. Place the aluminum foil on the cooking tray of air fryer. Place the steak, cabbage, and shallot in the parchment-lined air fryer cooking tray. Cook the steak for about 8 minutes, turning it twice during the cooking time. Increase the temperature to 400 degrees F and continue cooking for 8 minutes more. Served hot and enjoy
Per Serving: Calories377 g; Fat 25.5 g; Sodium 245mg; Carbs 10 g; Fiber 2.1g; Sugar 2g; Protein 23.3g

Bbq Flat Beef Ribs

Prep time: 10 minutes| Cook time: 15 minutes| Serves: 4

1 ½ pounds flat 2g Fat; 1
1 cup BBQ sauce
1 teaspoon smoked paprika
½ teaspoon chili powder
2 tablespoons brown sugar
1 teaspoon onion powder
Kosher salt and ground black pepper, to taste

Mix all the ingredients in a ceramic bowl. Marinate the beef for at least 3 hours. Set the air fryer to 360 degrees F at the "Air Fry" setting for 15 minutes. Place the aluminum foil on the cooking tray. Place the beef ribs in the air fryer cooking tray and cook the beef for about 15 minutes. Serve immediately and enjoy!
Per Serving: Calories472 g; Fat 33.2 g; Sodium 236mg; Carbs 11.5 g; Fiber 1.8g; Sugar 7.1g; Protein 33.2g

Herb Loaded Beef Eye Round Roast

Prep time: 10 minutes| Cook time: 45 minutes| Serves: 5

2 pounds beef eye round roast
2 tablespoon olive oil
2 garlic cloves, pressed
1 teaspoon dried basil
1 teaspoon dried oregano
1 teaspoon dried rosemary
1 teaspoon red pepper flakes, crushed
Sea salt and ground black pepper, to taste

Select the "Roast" setting of the air fryer at 360 degrees F for 45 minutes of the air fryer. Pat the beef dry with paper towel. Grease the steak with olive oil and rub garlic, and spices all over the round roast. Place the beef in the air fryer basket. Roast the beef until it reaches an internal temperature of 160 degrees F on a meat thermometer. Serve hot and Bon appétit!
Per Serving: Calories393 g; Fat 20.9 g; Sodium 852mg; Carbs 0.6 g; Fiber 0.2g; Sugar 0.1g; Protein 38.5g

Tasty Beef Steaks

Prep time: 10 minutes| Cook time: 6 minutes| Serves: 2

2 New York strip, filet mignon, ribeye, or similar steaks, at room temperature
2 tablespoons extra virgin olive oil
salt and pepper, to taste

Preheat the air fryer to 400 degrees F at the "Air Fry" setting for 5 minutes. Pat dry the steaks completely with paper towel. Drizzle with oil and season with salt and pepper. Place in the cooking tray and cook for 6 minutes. Check the steak properly, when it is done place it in the plate and leave it for 5 minutes then serve and enjoy.
Per Serving: Calories 449g; Fat 32 g; Sodium 663mg; Carbs 1 g; Fiber 0g; Sugar 0g; Protein 37g

Saucy Beef Satay

1 pound flank steak, cut across the grain in 3x6-inch pieces
1½ cups Tamari
1 teaspoon fish sauce
1 tablespoon black-strap molasses
1 teaspoon ground coriander powder
1 teaspoon ground cumin
1 teaspoon ground turmeric
1 teaspoon ground black pepper
1 teaspoon grated ginger
1 clove garlic grated or minced
1 teaspoon grated onion
For the sauce:
½ cup homemade mayo
1 tablespoon Sriracha hot sauce
1 teaspoon grated ginger
1 teaspoon minced garlic

Tap the beef with a meat tenderizer on a cutting board. In a small bowl, mix the mayo, hot sauce, ginger, and garlic. Mix the sauce and put in the fridge until needed. Mix the fish sauce, tamari, molasses, coriander, cumin, turmeric, black pepper, ginger, garlic, and onion in a bowl. Add the meat and put in the fridge for 1 hour covered. Preheat the air fryer to 360 degrees F at the "Air Fry" setting for 10 minutes. Thread the meat pieces onto skewers. Arrange the skewers in a single layer in the cooking tray and cook for 9 minutes. Work in batches until all of the meat is cooked. Serve with the prepared sauce alongside and enjoy.
Per Serving: Calories 163g; Fat 12 g; Sodium 444mg; Carbs 8 g; Fiber 0.5g; Sugar 1.3g; Protein 9g

Delicious Beefsteak with Olives and Capers

1 anchovy fillet, minced
1 clove of garlic, minced
1 cup pitted olives
1 tablespoon capers, minced
2 tablespoons fresh oregano
2 tablespoons garlic powder
2 tablespoons onion powder
2 tablespoons smoked paprika
⅓ cup extra-virgin olive oil
2 pounds' flank steak, pounded
Salt and pepper

Preheat the air fryer with the grill pan to 390 degrees F at the "Roast" setting for 5 minutes. Season the steak with pepper and salt. Spread the onion powder, oregano, paprika, and garlic powder all over the steak and rub generously. Place on the cooking tray and roast for 45 minutes. Stir the olive oil, capers, garlic, olives, and anchovy fillets in a pan. When meat is ready, serve hot with anchovy sauce on top and enjoy.
Per Serving: Calories553; Fat 33.4 g; Sodium 763mg; Carbs 11.6 g; Fiber 1g; Sugar 1.2g; Protein 51.5g

Memphis Back Ribs

1 ½ pounds beef back ribs
1 cup BBQ sauce
Kosher salt and freshly ground black pepper, to taste
1 tablespoon brown sugar
1 tablespoon brown mustard
1 teaspoon hot paprika
1 teaspoon garlic powder
1 teaspoon onion powder

In a ceramic bowl add all the ingredients and marinate the beef for at least 3 hours. Place aluminum foil onto the cooking tray. Place the beef ribs in the air fryer cooking tray. Select Air Fry mode, adjust the cooking temperature to 360☐F and cooking time to 20 minutes. When the display indicates "Add Food," place the tray in the air fryer basket and cook. Serve hot immediately and enjoy!
Per Serving: Calories 412 g; Fat 28 g; Sodium 732mg; Carbs 8.2 g; Fiber 1.7g; Sugar 4.6g; Protein 34.4g

Desserts

Syrup Coated Banana

2 ripe bananas, peeled and sliced lengthwise
1 teaspoon fresh lime juice
4 teaspoons maple syrup
⅛ teaspoon ground cinnamon

Coat each banana half with lime juice. Arrange the banana pieces onto the greased cooking tray cut sides up. Drizzle the banana pieces with maple syrup and sprinkle with cinnamon. Touch Air Fry then adjust the temp to 350 degrees F, set the time to 10 minutes. Press "Start" to begin cooking. When the unit beeps to show message Add Food, insert the cooking tray in the Air Fryer. When cooking time is complete, remove the cooking tray from Air Fryer and serve immediately.
Per Serving: Calories 70; Fat 0.2g; Sodium 1mg; Carbs 18g; Fiber 1.6g; Sugar 11.2g; Protein 0.6 g

Raspberry Sweet Roll

1 tube full-sheet crescent roll dough
4 ounces cream cheese, softened
¼ cup raspberry jam
½ cup fresh raspberries, chopped
1 cup powdered sugar
2-3 tablespoons heavy whipping cream

Place the sheet of crescent roll dough onto a flat surface and unroll it. In a microwave-safe bowl, add the cream cheese and microwave for about 20-30 seconds. Remove from microwave and stir until creamy and smooth. Spread the cream cheese over the dough sheet, followed by the raspberry jam. Now, place the raspberry pieces evenly across the top. From the short side, roll the dough and pinch the seam to seal. Arrange a greased parchment paper onto the Cooking tray of Air Fryer. Carefully, curve the rolled pastry into a horseshoe shape and arrange onto the prepared Cooking tray. Press Bake then adjust the temp to 350 degrees F, set the time to 25 minutes. Press "Start" to begin cooking. When the unit beeps to show that it is Add Food, insert the tray in the Air Fryer. When cooking time is complete, remove the tray from Air Fryer and place onto a rack for cooling. Meanwhile, in a bowl, mix together the powdered sugar and cream. Drizzle the cream mixture over cooled Danish and serve.
Per Serving: Calories 335; Fat 15.3g; Sodium 342mg; Carbs 45.3g; Fiber 0.7g; Sugar 30.1g; Protein 4.4 g

Blueberry Cupcakes

Prep time: 15 minutes| Cook time: 15 minutes| Serves: 8

¼ cup unsweetened coconut milk	¼ teaspoon ground cinnamon
2 large eggs	Pinch of ground cloves
½ teaspoon vanilla extract	Pinch of ground nutmeg
1½ cups almond flour	⅛ teaspoon salt
¼ cup Swerve	½ cup fresh blueberries
1 teaspoon baking powder	¼ cup pecans, chopped

In a blender, add the coconut milk, eggs and vanilla extract and pulse for about 20-30 seconds. Add the almond flour, Swerve, baking powder, spices and salt and pulse for about 30-45 seconds until well blended. Transfer the mixture into a bowl Gently, fold in half of the blueberries and pecans. Place the mixture into 8 silicone muffin cups and top each with remaining blueberries. Press Bake then adjust the temp to 325 degrees F, set the time to 15 minutes. Press "Start" to begin cooking. When the unit beeps to show Add Food message, place the cups over the cooking tray and insert in the Air Fryer. When cooking time is complete, remove the cups from Air Fryer and place onto a wire rack to cool for about 10 minutes. Carefully, invert the muffins onto the wire rack to completely cool before serving.
Per Serving: Calories 191; Fat 16.5g; Sodium 54mg; Carbs 14.8g; Fiber 3.2g; Sugar 9.7g; Protein 6.8 g

Yummy Cranberry Muffins

Prep time: 15 minutes| Cook time: 15 minutes| Serves: 10

4½ ounces self-rising flour	4¾ ounces butter, softened
½ teaspoon baking powder	4¼ ounces caster sugar
Pinch of salt	2 eggs
½ ounce cream cheese, softened	2 teaspoons fresh lemon juice
	½ cup fresh cranberries

In a bowl, mix together the flour, baking powder, and salt. In another bowl, mix together the cream cheese, and butter. Add the sugar and beat until fluffy and light. Add the eggs, one at a time and whisk until just combined. Add the flour mixture and stir until well combined. Stir in the lemon juice. Place the mixture into silicone cups and top each with cranberries evenly, pressing slightly. Press Bake then adjust the temp to 365 degrees F, set the time to 15 minutes. Press "Start" to begin cooking. When the unit beeps and show message Add Food, place the cups over the cooking tray and insert in the Air Fryer. When cooking time is complete, remove the cups from Air Fryer and place onto a wire rack to cool for about 10 minutes. Carefully, invert the cupcakes onto the wire rack to completely cool before serving.
Per Serving: Calories 209; Fat 12.4g; Sodium 110mg; Carbs 22.6g; Fiber 0.6g; Sugar 12.4g; Protein 2.7 g

Zucchini Cup Cake

Prep time: 15 minutes| Cook time: 20 minutes| Serves: 1

¼ cup whole-wheat pastry flour	milk
1 tablespoon sugar	2 tablespoons zucchini, grated and squeezed
¼ teaspoon baking powder	2 tablespoons almonds, chopped
¼ teaspoon ground cinnamon	1 tablespoon raisins
Pinch of salt	2 teaspoons maple syrup
2 tablespoons plus 2 teaspoons	

In a bowl, mix together the flour, sugar, baking powder, cinnamon and salt. Add the remaining ingredients and mix until well combined. Place the mixture into a lightly greased ramekin.

Press Bake then adjust the temp to 350 degrees F, set the time to 20 minutes. Press "Start" to begin cooking When the unit beeps to show message Add Food, place the ramekin over the cooking tray and insert in the Air Fryer. When cooking time is complete, remove the ramekin from Air Fryer and place onto a wire rack to cool slightly before serving.
Per Serving: Calories 310; Fat 7g; Sodium 175mg; Carbs 57.5g; Fiber 3.2g; Sugar 27.5g; Protein 7.2 g

Apple Oats Crumbly

Prep time: 15 minutes| Cook time: 40 minutes| Serves: 2

1½ cups apple, peeled, cored and sliced	¼ teaspoon ground cinnamon
¼ cup sugar, divided	Pinch of salt
1½ teaspoons cornstarch	1½ tablespoons cold butter, chopped
3 tablespoons all-purpose flour	3 tablespoons rolled oats

In a bowl, place apple slices, 1 teaspoon of sugar and cornstarch and toss to coat well. Divide the plum mixture into lightly greased 2 (8-ounce) ramekins. In a bowl, mix together the flour, remaining sugar, cinnamon and salt. With 2 forks, blend in the butter until a crumbly mixture form. Add the oats and gently, stir to combine. Place the oat mixture over apple slices into each ramekin. Press Bake then adjust the temp to 350 degrees F, set the time to 40 minutes. Press "Start" to begin cooking When the unit beeps to show message Add Food, place the ramekin over the cooking tray and insert in the Air Fryer. When cooking time is complete, remove the ramekins from Air Fryer and place onto a wire rack to cool for about 10 minutes before serving.
Per Serving: Calories 337; Fat 9.6g; Sodium 141mg; Carbs 64.3g; Fiber 5.3g; Sugar 42.5g; Protein 2.8 g

Crunchy Banana and Walnut Cake

Prep time: 10 minutes| Cook time: 25 minutes| Serves: 6

1 pound bananas, mashed	3.5 ounces butter, melted
8 ounces flour	2 eggs, lightly beaten
6 ounces sugar	¼ teaspoon baking soda
3.5 ounces walnuts, chopped	

Select the Bake function and preheat to 355 degrees F (179 degrees Celsius). In a bowl, combine the sugar, butter, egg, flour, and baking soda with a whisk. Stir in the bananas and walnuts. Transfer the mixture to a greased baking pan. Press Bake then adjust the temp to 350 degrees F, set the time to 10 minutes. Press "Start" to begin cooking When the unit beeps to show message Add Food, place the baking pan the cooking tray and insert in the Air Fryer. After 10 minutes, reduce the temperature to 330 degrees F and bake for another 15 minutes. Serve hot.
Per Serving: Calories 70; Fat 0.2g; Sodium 1mg; Carbs 18g; Fiber 1.6g; Sugar 11.2g; Protein 0.6 g

Apple Lemon Pasty

Prep time: 05 minutes| Cook time: 35 minutes| Serves: 4

½ teaspoon vanilla extract	1 tablespoon ground cinnamon
1 beaten egg	1 tablespoon raw sugar
1 large apple, chopped	2 tablespoons sugar
1 Pillsbury Refrigerator pie crust	2 teaspoons lemon juice
1 tablespoon butter	Cooking spray

Lightly grease baking pan of Air Fryer with cooking spray. Spread pie crust on bottom of pan up to the sides. In a bowl, mix vanilla, sugar, cinnamon, lemon juice, and apple. Pour on top of

pie crust. Top apples with butter slices. Cover apples with the other pie crust. Pierce with knife the tops of pie. Spread beaten egg on top of crust and sprinkle sugar. Cover with foil. Press Bake then adjust the temp to 390 degrees F, set the time to 25 minutes. Press "Start" to begin cooking When the unit beeps to show message Add Food, place the baking pan the cooking tray and insert in the Air Fryer. Cook in the Air Fryer for 25 minutes. Remove foil cook for 10 minutes at 330 degrees F until tops are browned. Serve and enjoy.
Per Serving: Calories 372; Fat 19g; Sodium 190mg; Carbs 5.8g; Fiber 3.6g; Sugar 5g; Protein 4.2 g

Delicious Blueberry Lemon Muffins

Prep time: 05 minutes| Cook time: 10 minutes| Serves: 12

1 teaspoon vanilla	½ cup cream
Juice and zest of 1 lemon	¼ cup avocado oil
2 eggs	½ cup monk fruit
1 cup blueberries	2½ cups almond flour

Mix monk fruit and flour together. In another bowl, mix vanilla, egg, lemon juice, and cream together. Add mixtures together and blend well. Spoon batter into cupcake holders.
Place the mixture into 12 silicone muffin cups. Press Bake then adjust the temp to 320 degrees F, set the time to 10 minutes. Press "Start" to begin cooking. When the unit beeps to show Add Food message, place the cups over the cooking tray and insert in the Air Fryer. When cooking time is complete, remove the cups from Air Fryer and place onto a wire rack to cool for about 10 minutes. Carefully, invert the muffins onto the wire rack to completely cool before serving.
Per Serving: Calories 317; Fat 11g; Sodium 190mg; Carbs 5.8g; Fiber 3.6g; Sugar 5g; Protein 3 g

Air Fryer Cinnamon Sweet Rolls

Prep time: 15 minutes| Cook time: 05 minutes| Serves: 8

1½ tablespoon cinnamon	½ teaspoon vanilla
¾ cup brown sugar	1 ¼ cup powdered erythritol
¼ cup melted coconut oil	2 tablespoons softened ghee
1-pound frozen bread dough, thawed	2 ounces softened cream cheese
Glaze:	

Lay out bread dough and roll out into a rectangle. Brush melted ghee over dough and leave a 1-inch border along edges. Mix cinnamon and sweetener together and then sprinkle over dough. Roll dough tightly and slice into 8 pieces. Let sit 1-2 hours to rise. To make the glaze, simply mix ingredients together till smooth. Once rolls rise, press Bake then adjust the temp to 350 degrees F, set the time to 5 minutes. Press "Start" to begin cooking. When the unit beeps to show Add Food message, place the rolls over the cooking tray and insert in the Air Fryer. Serve rolls drizzled in cream cheese glaze. Enjoy!
Per Serving: Calories 390; Fat 8g; Sodium 268mg; Carbs 64.8g; Fiber 1.6g; Sugar 15g; Protein 5.4 g

Raspberry Jelly Roll

Prep time: 10 minutes| Cook time: 25 minutes| Serves: 4

1 cup of fresh raspberries, rinsed and patted dry	milk
	1 egg
½ cup of cream cheese softened to room temperature	1 teaspoon of corn starch
¼ cup of brown sugar	6 spring roll wrappers (any brand will do, we like Blue
¼ cup of sweetened condensed	Dragon or Tasty Joy, both

available through Target or Walmart, or any large grocery chain) ¼ cup of water

Preparing the Ingredients. Cover the cooking tray of the Air Fryer with a lining of tin foil, leaving the edges uncovered to allow air to circulate through the basket. In a mixing bowl, combine the cream cheese, brown sugar, condensed milk, cornstarch, and egg. Beat or whip thoroughly, until all ingredients are completely mixed and fluffy, thick and stiff. Spoon even amounts of the creamy filling into each spring roll wrapper, then top each dollop of filling with several raspberries. Roll up the wraps around the creamy raspberry filling, and seal the seams with a few dabs of water. Place each roll on the foil-lined cooking tray, seams facing down. Place the drip pan in the bottom of the cooking chamber. Using the control panel, select Air Fry, then adjust the temperature to 330 degrees F and the time to 10 minutes, then touch Start. When the display indicates "Add Food", insert one cooking tray in the center position. After 10 minutes, when the Air Fryer times up, the spring rolls should be golden brown and perfect on the outside, while the raspberries and cream filling will have cooked together in a glorious fusion. Repeat the cooking steps for the rest rolls. Remove with tongs and serve hot or cold.
Per Serving: Calories 335; Fat 15.3g; Sodium 342mg; Carbs 45.3g; Fiber 0.7g; Sugar 30.1g; Protein 4.4 g

Yummy Chocolate Banana Muffins

Prep time: 05 minutes| Cook time: 25 minutes| Serves: 12

¾ cup whole wheat flour	mashed
¾ cup plain flour	1 cup sugar
¼ cup cocoa powder	⅓ cup canola oil
¼ teaspoon baking powder	1 egg
1 teaspoon baking soda	½ teaspoon vanilla essence
¼ teaspoon salt	1 cup mini chocolate chips
2 large bananas, peeled and	

Prepare the Ingredients. In a large bowl, mix together flour, cocoa powder, baking powder, baking soda, and salt. In another bowl, add bananas, sugar, oil, egg and vanilla extract and beat till well combined. Slowly, add flour mixture in egg mixture and mix till just combined. Fold in chocolate chips. Grease 12 muffin tins. Press Bake then adjust the temp to 320 degrees F, set the time to 25 minutes. Press "Start" to begin cooking. When the unit beeps to show Add Food message, place the cups over the cooking tray and insert in the Air Fryer. When cooking time is complete, remove the cups from Air Fryer and place onto a wire rack to cool for about 10 minutes.
Per Serving: Calories 75; Fat 6.5g; Sodium 342mg; Carbs 45.3g; Fiber 1.7g; Sugar 2g; Protein 1.7 g

Fried Bananas with Cinnamon

Prep time: 05 minutes| Cook time: 10 minutes| Serves: 2

1 cup panko breadcrumbs	8 ripe bananas
3 tablespoons cinnamon	3 tablespoons vegan coconut
½ cup almond flour	oil
3 egg whites	

Prepare the ingredients. Heat coconut oil and add breadcrumbs. Mix around 2-3 minutes until golden. Pour into bowl. Peel and cut bananas in half. Roll each bananas half into flour, eggs, and crumb mixture. Place the drip pan in the bottom of the cooking chamber. Press Air Fry then adjust the temp to 280 degrees F, set the time to 10 minutes. Press "Start" to begin cooking. When the unit beeps to show Add Food message, place the prepared banana over the cooking tray and insert in the Air Fryer. When cooking time is complete, remove the cooking tray from Air Fryer

Per Serving: Calories 219; Fat 10g; Sodium 56mg; Carbs 45.3g; Fiber 1.7g; Sugar 5g; Protein 3 g

Tasty Chinese Beignet

Prep time: 10 minutes| Cook time: 8 minutes| Serves: 8

1 tablespoon baking powder	6teaspoons sugar
1 tablespoon coconut oil	2 cups all-purpose flour
¾ cup of coconut milk	½ teaspoon sea salt

Mix baking powder, flour, sugar, and salt in a bowl. Add coconut oil and mix well. Add coconut milk and mix until well combined. Knead dough for 3 to 4 minutes. Roll dough half inch thick and using cookie cutter cut doughnuts. Using the control panel, select Air Fry, adjust temperature to 375 degrees F and set time to 8 minutes. Preheat the unit until display indicates Add Food. When preheated, insert the cooking tray inside the Air Fryer. Cook until golden. Let cool 5 minutes, then transfer to a wire rack and cool completely. Repeat with the rest. Serve and enjoy.
Per Serving: Calories 259; Fat 15.9g; Sodium 56mg; Carbs 27g; Fiber 1.7g; Sugar 5g; Protein 3.8 g

Crusty Bananas

Prep time: 10 minutes| Cook time: 10 minutes| Serves: 4

4 sliced ripe bananas	1 tablespoon almond meal
1 egg	1½ tablespoons coconut oil
½ cup breadcrumbs	1 tablespoon crushed cashew
1½ tablespoons cinnamon sugar	¼ cup corn flour

Add coconut oil over medium heat and add breadcrumbs in the pan and stir for 3 to 4 minutes. Remove pan from heat and transfer breadcrumbs in a bowl. Add almond meal and crush cashew in breadcrumbs and mix well. Dip banana half in corn flour then in egg and finally coat with breadcrumbs. Place coated banana in Air Fryer cooking tray. Sprinkle with cinnamon sugar. Press Air Fry then adjust the temperature to 350 degrees F, set the time to 10 minutes. Press "Start" to begin cooking. When the unit beeps to show Add Food message, place the prepared banana over the cooking tray and insert in the Air Fryer.
Per Serving: Calories 282; Fat 9g; Sodium 116mg; Carbs 44.5g; Fiber 4.7g; Sugar 15.6 g; Protein 5.7 g

Banana and Walnuts Quick Bread

Prep time: 10 minutes| Cook time: 10 minutes| Serves: 2

¼ cup flour	1 tablespoon chopped walnuts
½ teaspoon baking powder	¼ cup oats
¼ cup mashed banana	Sugar, as needed
¼ cup butter	

Spray 4 muffin molds with cooking spray and set aside. In a bowl, mix together mashed bananas, walnuts, sugar, and butter. In another bowl, mix oat flour, and baking powder. Combine the flour mixture to the banana mixture. Pour batter into prepared muffin mold. Press Bake then adjust the temp to 325 degrees F, set time to 10 minutes. Press "Start" to begin cooking. When the unit beeps to show Add Food message, place the cups over the cooking tray and insert in the Air Fryer. When cooking time is complete, remove the cups from Air Fryer and place onto a wire rack to cool for about 10 minutes. Carefully, invert the muffins onto the wire rack to completely cool before serving.
Per Serving: Calories 192; Fat 12.3g; Sodium 116mg; Carbs 19.4g; Fiber 4.7g; Sugar 15.6 g; Protein 1.9 g

Appetizing Nut Mix

Prep time: 05 minutes| Cook time: 05 minutes| Serves: 6

2 cups mix nuts	1 tablespoon melted butter
1 teaspoon ground cumin	1 teaspoon salt
1 teaspoon chili powder	1 teaspoon pepper

Set all ingredients in a large bowl and toss until well coated. Press Air Fry then adjust the temperature to 330 degrees F, set the time to 5 minutes. Press "Start" to begin cooking. When the unit beeps to show Add Food message, place the nut mixer over the cooking tray and insert in the Air Fryer. When cooking time is complete, remove the cups from Air Fryer and place onto a wire rack to cool for about 10 minutes. Serve and enjoy.
Per Serving: Calories 438; Fat 38.3g; Sodium 618mg; Carbs 18.4g; Fiber 6.6g; Sugar 0.1 g; Protein 12.9 g

Vanilla Spiced Puffed up

Prep time: 20 minutes| Cook time: 32 minutes| Serves: 6

¼ cup all-purpose flour	4 egg yolks
1 cup whole milk	1-ounce sugar
2 teaspoons vanilla extract	¼ cup softened butter
1 teaspoon cream of tartar	¼ cup sugar
1 vanilla bean	5 egg whites

Combine flour and butter in a bowl until the mixture becomes a smooth paste. Set the pan over medium flame to heat the milk. Add sugar and stir until dissolved. Mix in the vanilla bean and bring to a boil. Beat the mixture using a wire whisk as you add the butter and flour mixture. Lower the heat to simmer until thick. Discard the vanilla bean. Turn off the heat. Place them on an ice bath and allow to cool for 10 minutes. Grease 6 ramekins with butter. Sprinkle each with a bit of sugar. Beat the egg yolks in a bowl. Add the vanilla extract and milk mixture. Mix until combined. Whisk together the tartar cream, egg whites, and sugar until it forms medium stiff peaks. Gradually fold egg whites into the soufflé base. Transfer the mixture to the ramekins. Press Bake then adjust the temperature to 330 degrees F, set the time to 16 minutes. Press "Start" to begin cooking. When the unit beeps to show Add Food message, place the ramekins over the cooking tray and insert in the Air Fryer. When cooking time is complete, remove the cups from Air Fryer and place onto a wire rack to cool for about 10 minutes. Sprinkle powdered sugar on top and drizzle with chocolate sauce before serving.
Per Serving: Calories 201; Fat 12.4g; Sodium 61mg; Carbs 14.4g; Fiber 0.1g; Sugar 7.3 g; Protein 6.7 g

Chocolate Caster Sugar Patty Cakes

Prep time: 05 minutes| Cook time: 12 minutes| Serves: 6

3 eggs	1 cup milk
¼ cup caster sugar	¼ teaspoon vanilla essence
¼ cup cocoa powder	2 cups all-purpose flour
1 teaspoon baking powder	4 tablespoons butter

Beat eggs with sugar in a bowl until creamy. Add butter and beat again for 1-2 minutes. Now add flour, cocoa powder, milk, baking powder, and vanilla essence, mix with a spatula. Fill ¾ of muffin tins with the mixture. Press Bake then adjust the temperature to 400 degrees F, set the time to 12 minutes. Press "Start" to begin cooking. When the unit beeps to show Add Food message, place the patty cakes over the cooking tray and insert in the Air Fryer. When cooking time is complete, remove the cups from Air Fryer and place onto a wire rack to cool for about 10 minutes. Serve!

Per Serving: Calories 268; Fat 6.6g; Sodium 53mg; Carbs 44.7g; Fiber 2.2g; Sugar 10.5 g; Protein 9.1 g

Tempting Cheesecake

Prep time: 20 minutes| Cook time:20 minutes| Serves: 8

Crust	1 cup cashews, soaked in
½ cup dates, chopped, soaked in water for at least 15 min, soaking liquid reserved	water for at least 2 hours
	1 teaspoon vanilla extract
	2 tablespoons lemon juice
½ cup walnuts	1 to 2 teaspoon grated lemon
1 cup quick oats	zest
Filling	½ cup fresh berries or 6 figs,
½ cup vanilla almond milk	sliced
¼ cup coconut palm sugar	1 tablespoon arrowroot
½ cup coconut flour	powder

Make the crust: in a food processor, process together all the crust ingredients until smooth and press the mixture into the bottom of a spring form pan. Make the filling: add cashews along with soaking liquid to a blender and process until very smooth; add milk, palm sugar, coconut flour, lemon juice, lemon zest, and vanilla and blend until well combined; add arrowroot and continue blending until mixed and pour into the crust. Smooth the top and cover the spring form pan with foil. Press Bake then adjust the temp to 375 degrees F, set the time to 20 minutes. Press "Start" to begin cooking. When the unit beeps to show Add Food message, place the pan over the cooking tray and insert in the Air Fryer. When cooking time is complete, remove the cups from Air Fryer and place onto a wire rack to cool for about 10 minutes. Serve! Top with fruit to serve.

Per Serving: Calories 303; Fat 17.2g; Sodium 55mg; Carbs 33.7g; Fiber 3.8g; Sugar 9.2 g; Protein 7.4 g

Roasted Peanuts

Prep time: 10 minutes| Cook time:20 minutes| Serves: 8

1 cup raw peanuts	2 tablespoons olive oil
½ teaspoon cayenne pepper	salt
3 teaspoons seafood seasoning	

In a bowl, whisk together cayenne pepper, olive oil, and seafood seasoning; stir in peanuts until well coated. Transfer to the cooking tray. Press Roast then adjust the temperature to 380 degrees F, set the time to 10 minutes. Press "Start" to begin cooking. When the unit beeps to show Add Food message, place the cooking tray and insert in the Air Fryer. When cooking time is complete, remove the cups from Air Fryer and place onto a wire rack to cool for about 10 minutes. Serve! Top with fruit to serve. Transfer the peanuts to a dish and season with salt. Let cool before serving.

Per Serving: Calories 134; Fat 12.5g; Sodium 23mg; Carbs 3g; Fiber 1.6g; Sugar 0.7 g; Protein 4.7 g

Roasted Salty Corn

Prep time: 10 minutes| Cook time: 40 minutes| Serves: 8

2 cups giant white corn	1-½ teaspoons sea salt
3 tablespoons olive oil	

Soak the corn in a bowl of water for at least 8 hours or overnight; drain and spread in a single layer on a baking tray; pat dry with paper towels. In a bowl, mix corn, olive oil and salt and toss to coat well. Press Roast then adjust the temperature to 400 degrees F, set the time to 20 minutes. Press "Start" to begin cooking. When the unit beeps to show Add Food message, place the cooking tray with corn and insert in the Air Fryer. When cooking time is complete, remove the cups from Air Fryer and place onto a wire rack to cool for about 10 minutes. Serve. Let cool before serving.

Per Serving: Calories 78; Fat 5.6g; Sodium 356mg; Carbs 7.7g; Fiber 0.8g; Sugar 1.3g; Protein 1.1g

Luscious Fruit Cake

Prep time: 05 minutes| Cook time: 45 minutes| Serves: 8

Dry Ingredients	milk
⅛ teaspoon sea salt	2 tablespoons ground flax
½ teaspoon baking powder	seeds
½ teaspoon baking soda	¼ cup agave
½ teaspoon ground cardamom	1-½ cups water
1-¼ cup whole wheat flour	Mix-Ins
Wet Ingredients	½ cup chopped cranberries
2 tablespoons coconut oil	1 cup chopped pear
½ cup unsweetened nondairy	

Grease a Bundt pan; set aside. In a mixing, mix all dry ingredients together. In another bowl, combine together the wet ingredients; whisk the wet ingredients into the dry until smooth. Fold in the add-ins and spread the mixture into the pan; cover with foil. Press Bake then adjust the temperature to 370 degrees F, set the time to 35 minutes. Press "Start" to begin cooking. When the unit beeps to show Add Food message, place the cake pan into cooking tray and insert in the Air Fryer. When cooking time is complete, remove the pan from Air Fryer and place onto a wire rack to cool for about 10 minutes Serve. Let cool before serving. Enjoy!

Per Serving: Calories 309; Fat 27g; Sodium 278mg; Carbs 33.7g; Fiber 2.8g; Sugar 6.3g; Protein 4.1g

Ultimate Dried Apples

Prep time: 05 minutes| Cook time: 2 hr.| Serves: 6

6 apples, cored	1 cup red wine
1 teaspoon cinnamon powder	¼ cup raisins
½ cup sugar	

Add apples to your Air Fryer cooking tray and then add wine, cinnamon powder, sugar and raisins. Insert in the Air Fryer. Using the control panel, select Dehydrate, then adjust the temperature to 160 degrees F and the time to 3 hours, then touch Start. Halfway through cooking, flip the apples. When the Dehydrate program has nearly completed, test a piece of apple by bending it at a 90-degree angle. If any moisture seeps out, return for an additional 20-30 minutes. If it bends, but there is no moisture seepage, it is done. If it cracks and breaks, it is overdone.

Per Serving: Calories 229; Fat 0.4g; Sodium 5mg; Carbs 53.7g; Fiber 5.6g; Sugar 43.3g; Protein 0.8 g

Nutty Slice with Cinnamon

Prep time: 10 minutes| Cook time: 30 minutes| Serves: 4

4 cups fresh or frozen mixed berries	1 cup oven roasted walnuts, sunflower seeds, pistachios.
1 cup almond meal	½ teaspoon ground cinnamon
½ cup almond butter	

Crush the nuts using a mortar and pestle. In a bowl, combine the nut mix, almond meal, and cinnamon and combine well. In a pie dish, spread half the nut mixture over the bottom of the dish, then

top with the berries and finish with the rest of the nut mixture. Press Bake then adjust the temperature to 350 degrees F, set the time to 35 minutes. Press "Start" to begin cooking. When the unit beeps to show Add Food message, place the pie dish over cooking tray and insert in the Air Fryer. When cooking time is complete, remove the pan from Air Fryer and place onto a wire rack to cool for about 10 minutes. Serve. Let cool before serving. Enjoy!
Per Serving: Calories 278; Fat 15.4g; Sodium 1mg; Carbs 23.7g; Fiber 8.8g; Sugar 11.3g; Protein 7.8 g

Hemp Seed Brownies

Prep time: 10 minutes| Cook time: 35 minutes| Serves: 10

1-½ cups unsweetened shredded coconut	½ cup coconut butter
½ cup dried cranberries	1 cup hemp seeds
½ cup golden flax meal	A good pinch of sea salt
	Stevia, as needed

Combine the cranberries, flax, and hemp seeds in the bowl of your food processor and pulse until well-ground. Add the shredded coconut, coconut butter, stevia, and salt and pulse until it forms thick dough. Transfer the dough to a baking dish. Press Bake then adjust the temperature to 370 degrees F, set the time to 10 minutes. Press "Start" to begin cooking. When the unit beeps to show Add Food message, place the baking dish over cooking tray and insert in the Air Fryer. When cooking time is complete, remove the pan from Air Fryer and place onto a wire rack to cool for about 10 minutes. Serve. Let cool before serving. Enjoy!
Per Serving: Calories 245; Fat 21.1g; Sodium 47mg; Carbs 8.5g; Fiber 5.8g; Sugar 1.8g; Protein 6.8 g

Avocado Chocolate Bars

Prep time: 05 minutes| Cook time: 25 minutes| Serves: 4

1 cup chopped chocolate	4 eggs
2 ripe avocados	1 cup ground almonds
1 teaspoon raw honey	½ cup cocoa powder
2 teaspoons vanilla extract	¼ teaspoon salt

Prepare an 8-inch baking pan by lining it with foil and then coating with non-stick cooking spray. Add chocolate to a bowl and place over a large saucepan of boiling water. Stir until chocolate is melted. Remove from heat and let cool. Meanwhile, prepare the batter: in a bowl, mash the avocados; add honey and stir to combine. Whisk in vanilla extract and eggs until well blended. Gradually whisk in the chocolate until well incorporated. Stir in ground almonds, cocoa powder, and salt until well blended. Transfer the batter to the prepared baking pan and cover with a paper towel and then with aluminum foil. Press Bake then adjust the temperature to 375 degrees F, set the time to 30 minutes. Press "Start" to begin cooking. When the unit beeps to show Add Food message, place the baking pan over cooking tray and insert in the Air Fryer. When cooking time is complete, remove the pan from Air Fryer and place onto a wire rack to cool for about 10 minutes. Serve. Let cool before serving. Enjoy!
Per Serving: Calories 665; Fat 49.7g; Sodium 251mg; Carbs 46.5g; Fiber 14.3g; Sugar 25.4g; Protein 17.6 g

Banana Pudding with Cinnamon

Prep time: 05 minutes| Cook time: 60 minutes| Serves: 8

1 cup caster sugar	¼ cup mashed banana
1½ cups self-rising flour, sifted	1 egg, lightly beaten
⅓ cup butter, melted and cooled	¾ cups milk
1 teaspoon vanilla extract	½ cup packed brown sugar

⅛ teaspoon nutmeg	½ cups boiling water
1 teaspoon cinnamon	ice cream, to serve

Grease the Air Fryer pan with butter using wax paper. Combine the first 7 ingredients above in a large mixing bowl; whisk until well-combined. Sift sugar, nutmeg, and cinnamon over the pudding mix. Spoon the boiling water gently and evenly over the mixture. Press Bake then adjust the temp to 375 degrees F, set the time to 60 minutes.
Press "Start" to begin cooking. When the unit beeps to show Add Food message, place the pan over cooking tray and insert in the Air Fryer. When cooking time is complete, remove the pan from Air Fryer and place onto a wire rack to cool for about 10 minutes. Serve. Let cool before serving. Enjoy!
Per Serving: Calories 307; Fat 9g; Sodium 76mg; Carbs 54.3g; Fiber 0.9g; Sugar 25.4g; Protein 4 g

Molten Chocolate Lava Cake

Prep time: 05 minutes| Cook time: 1 hr 10 minutes| Serves: 8

1 box of Devil's Food Chocolate Cake mix, prepared according to box instructions	1 (15 ounce) can of milk chocolate frosting, divided Non-stick cooking spray

Spray the Air Fryer pan with cooking spray. Add cake batter prepared as instructed on the box. Spoon half of the chocolate frosting into the middle of the cake batter. Press Bake then adjust the temperature to 375 degrees F, set the time to 60 minutes. Press "Start" to begin cooking. When the unit beeps to show Add Food message, place the pan over cooking tray and insert in the Air Fryer. When cooking time is complete, remove the pan from Air Fryer and place onto a wire rack to cool for about 10 minutes. Serve. Let cool before serving.
Per Serving: Calories 253; Fat 11.8g; Sodium 137mg; Carbs 37.8g; Fiber 1.1g; Sugar 32.7 g; Protein 0.5 g

Mouth-Watering Banana Loaf

Prep time: 05 minutes| Cook time: 60 minutes| Serves: 8

1½ cup unbleached flour	1 cup ripe bananas, mashed
½ cup sugar or sugar substitute	⅓ cup softened butter
2 teaspoons baking powder	¼ cup milk
½ teaspoon baking soda	1 egg
½ teaspoon vanilla extract	¼ cup walnuts chopped
½ teaspoon sea salt	

Combine the flour, sugar, baking powder, baking soda and salt in a large mixing bowl; whisk until the ingredients are well mixed. Fold in the bananas, butter, milk, egg and vanilla extract. Use an electric mixer to mix until the batter has a uniform thick consistency.
Fold in chopped walnuts. Grease the bottom loaf pan with non-stick cooking spray. Pour batter into loaf pan and press Bake then adjust the temperature to 375 degrees F, set the time to 60 minutes. Press "Start" to begin cooking. When the unit beeps to show Add Food message, place the loaf pan over cooking tray and insert in the Air Fryer. When cooking time is complete, remove the pan from Air Fryer and place onto a wire rack to cool for about 10 minutes. Serve. Let cool before serving.
Per Serving: Calories 255; Fat 11g; Sodium 211mg; Carbs 36.1g; Fiber 1.4g; Sugar 32.7 g; Protein 4.6g

Vanilla Choco Mug Cake

Prep time: 05 minutes| Cook time: 20 minutes| Serves: 1

1 teaspoon Softened butter	1 Egg

1 teaspoon butter
1 teaspoon Vanilla extract
2 tablespoons Erythritol
2 tablespoons unsweetened
cocoa powder
¼ teaspoon baking powder
1 tablespoon heavy cream

Combine all ingredients in a mixing bowl. Pour into a greased mug. Press Bake then adjust the temperature to 400 degrees F, set the time to 20 minutes. Press "Start" to begin cooking. When the unit beeps to show Add Food message, place the mug over cooking tray and insert in the Air Fryer. When cooking time is complete, remove the pan from Air Fryer and place onto a wire rack to cool for about 10 minutes. Serve. Let cool before serving.

Per Serving: Calories 220; Fat 19g; Sodium 125mg; Carbs 37.7g; Fiber 3.6g; Sugar 31.1 g; Protein 8.1 g

Baked Coconut Raspberry

Prep time: 05 minutes| Cook time: 20 minutes| Serves: 12

1 teaspoon Vanilla bean
1 cup Pulsed raspberries
1 cup coconut milk
3 cups desiccated coconut
¼ cup coconut oil
⅓ cup Erythritol powder

Combine all ingredients in a mixing bowl. Pour into a greased baking dish. Press Bake then adjust the temperature to 375 degrees F, set the time to 20 minutes. Press "Start" to begin cooking. When the unit beeps to show Add Food message, place the mug over cooking tray and insert in the Air Fryer. When cooking time is complete, remove the pan from Air Fryer and place onto a wire rack to cool for about 10 minutes. Serve. Let cool before serving.

Per Serving: Calories 152; Fat 14.2g; Sodium 9mg; Carbs 9.3g; Fiber 2.3g; Sugar 2.6 g; Protein 1.3 g

Crunchy Almond Cherry Bars

Prep time: 05 minutes| Cook time: 35 minutes| Serves: 12

1 tablespoon Xanthan gum
1½ cup almond flour
½ teaspoon salt
1 cup pitted fresh cherries
½ cup softened butter
2 eggs
¼ cup water
½ teaspoon Vanilla
1 cup Erythritol

Combine almond flour, softened butter, salt, vanilla, eggs, and erythritol in a large bowl until you form a dough. Press the dough in a baking dish that will fit in the Air Fryer. Press Bake then adjust the temperature to 375 degrees F, set the time to 10 minutes. Press "Start" to begin cooking. When the unit beeps to show Add Food message, place the mug over cooking tray and insert in the Air Fryer. When cooking time is complete, remove the pan from Air Fryer Meanwhile, mix the cherries, water, and xanthan gum in a bowl. Take the dough out and pour over the cherry mixture. Bake again for 25 minutes more at 375 degrees F in the Air Fryer.

Per Serving: Calories 172; Fat 15.3g; Sodium 445mg; Carbs 33.3g; Fiber 9.9g; Sugar 20.6 g; Protein 4.8 g

Coffee Aroma Doughnuts

Prep time: 05 minutes| Cook time: 06 minutes| Serves: 6

1 teaspoon baking powder
½ teaspoon salt
1 tablespoon sunflower oil
¼ cup coffee
¼ cup coconut sugar
1 cup white all-purpose flour
2 tablespoons Aquafaba

Combine sugar, flour, baking powder, and salt in a mixing

bowl. In another bowl, combine the aquafaba, sunflower oil, and coffee. Mix to form a dough. Let the dough rest inside the fridge. Press Bake then adjust the temperature to 400 degrees F, set the time to 10 minutes. Press "Start" to begin cooking. When the unit beeps to show Add Food message, place the donuts over cooking tray and insert in the Air Fryer. When cooking time is complete, remove the pan from Air Fryer. Cooling first then serve

Per Serving: Calories 101; Fat 2.7g; Sodium 197mg; Carbs 16.9g; Fiber 0.6; Sugar 0.1 g; Protein 2.2 g

Simple Strawberry Pie

Prep time: 10 minutes| Cook time: 25 minutes| Serves: 4

¼ cup heavy whipping cream
1½ teaspoons cornstarch
1½ teaspoons white sugar
½ cup water
¼ teaspoon salt
2 teaspoons butter
1½ cups hulled strawberries
1½ teaspoons white sugar
1 tablespoon diced butter
1 tablespoon butter
½ cup all-purpose flour
¾ teaspoon baking powder

Lightly grease baking pan of Air Fryer with cooking spray. Add water, cornstarch, and sugar. Cook for 10 minutes 390 degrees F or until hot and thick. Add strawberries and mix well. Dot tops with 1 tablespoon butter. Press Roast then adjust the temperature to 400 degrees F, set the time to 10 minutes. Press "Start" to begin cooking. When the unit beeps to show Add Food message, place the baking pan over cooking tray and insert in the Air Fryer. When time up, stop the unit by press Start In a bowl, mix well salt, baking powder, sugar, and flour. Cut in 2 teaspoons butter. Mix in cream. Spoon on the top of berries. Press Bake then adjust the temp to 390 degrees F, set the time to 15 minutes. Press "Start" to begin cooking. When the unit beeps to show Add Food message, place the baking pan over cooking tray and insert in the Air Fryer. Cook until top is lightly browned. Serve and enjoy.

Per Serving: Calories 364; Fat 5.4g; Sodium 183mg; Carbs 76.2g; Fiber 2; Sugar 18 g; Protein 2.6 g

Simple Pumpkin Tart

Prep time: 5minutes| Cook time: 35 minutes| Serves: 8

2 egg yolks
1 large egg
½ teaspoon ground ginger
½ teaspoon fine salt
⅛ teaspoon Chinese 5-spice powder
19-inch unbaked pie crust
¼ teaspoon freshly grated nutmeg
14 ounces sweetened condensed milk
15 ounces pumpkin puree
1 teaspoon ground cinnamon

Lightly grease baking pan of Air Fryer with cooking spray. Press pie crust on bottom of pan, stretching all the way up to the sides of the pan. Pierce all over with fork. In blender, blend well egg, egg yolks, and pumpkin puree. Add Chinese 5-spice powder, nutmeg, salt, ginger, cinnamon, and condensed milk. Pour on top of pie crust. Cover pan with foil. Press Bake then adjust the temp to 390 degrees F, set the time to 20 minutes. Press "Start" to begin cooking. When the unit beeps to show Add Food message, place the baking pan over cooking tray and insert in the Air Fryer. Allow to cool completely. Serve and enjoy.

Per Serving: Calories 326; Fat 6.4g; Sodium 224mg; Carbs 31.2g; Fiber 1.7; Sugar 28.8 g; Protein 6 g

Toothsome Cheesecake

Prep time: 10 minutes| Cook time: 19 minutes| Serves: 5

1 cup crumbled graham   crackers

½ teaspoon vanilla extract
4 tablespoons sugar
2 tablespoons butter

1 pound cream cheese
2 eggs

Mix crackers with the butter in a bowl. Press crackers mixture on the bottom of a lined cake pan. Press Bake then adjust the temperature to 350 degrees F, set the time to 4 minutes. Press "Start" to begin cooking. When the unit beeps to show Add Food message, place the cake pan over cooking tray and insert in the Air Fryer. Meanwhile, in a bowl, mix eggs, cream cheese, sugar and vanilla, and whisk well. Spread filling over crackers crust and bake for 310 degrees F for 15 minutes. Cool and keep in the refrigerator for 3 hours. Slice and serve.
Per Serving: Calories 246; Fat 12g; Sodium 224mg; Carbs 20g; Fiber 1.7; Sugar 28.8 g; Protein 3 g

Delicious Strawberry Danish

Prep time: 10 minutes| Cook time: 15 minutes| Serves: 4

4 ounces whole milk
1 egg
1 teaspoon baking powder
1 tablespoon brown sugar
1 tablespoon white sugar
8ounces flour

½ tablespoons butter
For the strawberry icing:
1 tablespoon whipped cream
½ teaspoon pink coloring
2 tablespoons butter
¼ cup chopped strawberries

In a bowl, mix flour, 1 tablespoon white sugar, 1 tablespoon brown sugar and butter, and stir. Stir together the egg with milk, and 1½ tablespoon butter in another bowl. Combine the 2 mixtures, stir, and then shape donuts from this mix. Press Air Fry then adjust the temperature to 350 degrees F, set the time to 15 minutes. Press "Start" to begin cooking. When the unit beeps to show Add Food message, place the donuts over cooking tray and insert in the Air Fryer. Mix strawberry puree, whipped cream, food coloring, icing sugar and 1 tablespoon butter, and whisk well. Arrange donuts on a platter and serve with strawberry icing on top.
Per Serving: Calories 250; Fat 12g; Sodium 224mg; Carbs 32g; Fiber 1.7; Sugar 28.8 g; Protein 4 g

Yummy Apricot Blackberry Crisp

Prep time: 10 minutes| Cook time: 20 minutes| Serves: 8

1 cup flour
2 tablespoons lemon juice
2oz cubed and deseeded fresh apricots

½ cup sugar
2 tablespoons cold butter
5.5 ounces fresh blackberries
salt.

Put the apricots and blackberries in a bowl. Add lemon juice and 2 tablespoons of sugar. Mix until combined. Transfer the mixture to a baking dish. Mix flour, the rest of the sugar, and a pinch of salt in a bowl. Add a tablespoon of cold butter. Combine the mixture until it becomes crumbly. Put this on top of the fruit mixture and press it down lightly. Press Bake then adjust the temperature to 390 degrees F, set the time to 20 minutes. Press "Start" to begin cooking. When the unit beeps to show Add Food message, place the pan over cooking tray and insert in the Air Fryer. Allow to cool before slicing and serving.
Per Serving: Calories 154; Fat 3.6g; Sodium 49mg; Carbs 28.2g; Fiber 1.9; Sugar 14.8 g; Protein 3.5g

Spiced Sugary Squash

Prep time: 05 minutes| Cook time: 15 minutes| Serves: 2

1 medium acorn squash,
halved crosswise and deseeded

1 teaspoon coconut oil
1 teaspoon light brown sugar

Few dashes of ground cinnamon

Few dashes of ground nutmeg

On a clean work surface, rub the cut sides of the acorn squash with coconut oil. Scatter with the brown sugar, cinnamon, and nutmeg. Put the squash halves in the Air Fryer cooking tray, cut-side up. Press Air Fry then adjust the temperature to 340 degrees F, set the time to 15 minutes. Press "Start" to begin cooking. When the unit beeps to show Add Food message, place cooking tray and insert in the Air Fryer. When cooking is complete, the squash halves should be just tender when pierced in the center with a paring knife. Remove from the oven. Rest for 5 to 10 minutes and serve warm.
Per Serving: Calories 40; Fat 1g; Sodium 2mg; Carbs 8.7g; Fiber 1.1; Sugar 0.8 g; Protein 0.5g

Tasty Chocolate Coconut Mug Cake

Prep time: 7 minutes| Cook time: 13 minutes| Serves: 3

½ cup of cocoa powder
½ cup stevia powder
1 cup coconut cream
1 package cream cheese, room

temperature
1 tablespoon vanilla extract
1 tablespoon butter

In a mixing bowl, combine all the listed ingredients using a hand mixer until fluffy. Pour into greased mugs. Press Bake then adjust the temperature to 350 degrees F, set the time to13 minutes. Press "Start" to begin cooking. When the unit beeps to show Add Food message, place mug over cooking tray and insert in the Air Fryer. When cooking is complete cool for 5 minutes and serve.
Per Serving: Calories 361; Fat 34.7g; Sodium 126mg; Carbs 13.7g; Fiber 6; Sugar 3.5g; Protein 6.5g

Chocolate Almond Cake

Prep time: 06 minutes| Cook time: 35 minutes| Serves: 9

½ cups hot water
1 teaspoon vanilla
¼ cups olive oil
½ cups almond milk
1 egg
½ teaspoon Salt

¾ teaspoon Baking soda
¾ teaspoon baking powder
½ cups unsweetened cocoa powder
2 cups almond flour
1 cup brown sugar

Stir all dry ingredients together and then stir in wet ingredients. Add hot water last. The batter should be thin. Pour cake batter into a pan that fits into the Air Fryer. Press Bake then adjust the temperature to 350 degrees F, set the time to 35 minutes. Press "Start" to begin cooking. When the unit beeps to show Add Food message, place pan over cooking tray and insert in the Air Fryer. When cooking is complete cool for 5 minutes and serve.
Per Serving: Calories 301; Fat 22.4g; Sodium 247mg; Carbs 24.8g; Fiber 4.6; Sugar 17.1g; Protein 7.2g

Chocolate Honey Cookies

Prep time: 10 minutes| Cook time: 15 minutes| Serves: 3

75g self-raising flour
100g butter
75g brown sugar

75g milk chocolate
30 millilitres honey
30 millilitres whole milk

Beat the butter until smooth and fluffy. Add the butter to the sugar and beat together in a smooth mixture. Now add and mix in the milk, sugar, chocolate (broken into small chunks/chips),

and flour. Shape the mixture into cookie shapes and put them on a baking sheet Press Bake then adjust the temperature to 350 degrees F, set the time to 15 minutes. Press "Start" to begin cooking. When the unit beeps to show Add Food message, place cookies over cooking tray and insert in the Air Fryer. When cooking is complete cool for 5 minutes and serve.
Per Serving: Calories 608; Fat 35g; Sodium 224mg; Carbs 70.6g; Fiber 1.6; Sugar 49.4g; Protein 5.2g

Doughnuts with Sugary Glaze

Prep time: 35 minutes| Cook time: 60 minutes| Serves: 8

¼ cup warm water, warmed (100 F to 110 F)	¼ cup whole milk, at room temperature
1 tablespoon active yeast	2 tablespoons unsalted butter, melted
¼ cup, plus half teaspoon granulated sugar, divided	1 large egg, beaten
2 cups (about 8½ ounce) all-purpose flour	1 cup (about 4 ounces) powdered sugar
¼ teaspoon kosher salt	4 teaspoons tap water

Mix water, yeast, and ½ teaspoon of the granulated sugar in a small bowl; let stand until foamy, around five minutes. Combine flour, salt, and remaining ¼ cup granulated sugar in a medium bowl. Add yeast mixture, milk, butter, and egg; stir it with a wooden spoon until a soft dough comes together. Turn dough out onto a lightly floured surface and knead until smooth, 1 to 2 minutes. Switch dough to a lightly greased tub. Cover and let rise in a warm place ud's'xntil doubled in volume, around 1 hour. Turn dough out onto a lightly floured surface. Gently roll to ¼-inch thickness. Cut out eight doughnuts using a 3-inch round cutter and a 1-inch round cutter to delete core Place doughnuts and doughnuts holes on a lightly floured surface. Cover loosely with plastic wrap and let stand for about 30 minutes, until doubled in volume. Place 2 doughnuts and 2 doughnuts holes in a single layer in an Air Fryer cooking tray, Press Air Fry then adjust the temperature to 350 degrees F, set the time to 05 minutes. Press "Start" to begin cooking. When the unit beeps to show Add Food message, place doughnut over cooking tray and insert in the Air Fryer. When cooking is complete cool for 5 minutes and serve. Whisk powdered sugar together and tap water until smooth in a medium bowl. In a glaze, dip doughnuts and doughnut holes. Place them on a wire rack set above a rimmed baking sheet to allow excess glaze to drip off. Let stand for about 10 minutes, until the glaze hardens.
Per Serving: Calories 216; Fat 4.2g; Sodium 108mg; Carbs 39.8g; Fiber 1.2; Sugar 15.4g; Protein 5g

Chocolate Chia Almond Bars

Prep time: 07 minutes| Cook time: 15 minutes| Serves: 8

¼ teaspoon salt	½ cup quinoa, cooked
½ cup almonds, sliced	¾ cup almond butter
½ cup chia seeds	⅓ cup honey
½ cup dark chocolate, chopped	2 cups oats
½ cup dried cherries, chopped	2 tablespoons coconut oil
½ cup prunes, pureed	

In a bowl, combine the oats, quinoa, chia seeds, almond, cherries, and chocolate. In a saucepan, heat the almond butter, honey, and coconut oil. Pour the butter mixture over the dry mix, then add salt and prunes and mix until well combined. Pour over a baking dish that can fit inside the Air Fryer. Press Bake then adjust the temperature to 375 degrees F, set the time to 15 minutes. Press "Start" to begin cooking. When the unit beeps to show Add Food message, place pan over cooking tray and insert in the Air Fryer When cooking is complete cool for 5 minutes and serve
Per Serving: Calories 328; Fat 12.9g; Sodium 86mg; Carbs

48.8g; Fiber 5.2; Sugar 21.4g; Protein 7.2g

Pancakes Nutella-Stuffed

Prep time: 15 minutes| Cook time: 20 minutes| Serves: 12

4 teaspoons of chocolate-hazelnut spread, such as Nutella ®, at room temperature	¼ cup of granulated sugar
	1 teaspoon baking soda
	1 teaspoon baking soda
¼ cup vegetable oil, plus	1 egg
¼ cup all-purpose flour	A pinch of salt
1¼ cups buttermilk	Sugar for dusting
	Maple syrup for serving

Line a parchment baking sheet and drop 12 different teaspoonful mounds of chocolate-hazelnut spread over it. Place the baking sheet on a counter to flatten the dollops and freeze for about 15 minutes until firm. In a large bowl, whisk together the flour, buttermilk, oil, granulated sugar, baking powder, baking soda, egg, and a pinch of salt until smooth. Press Air Fry then adjust the temperature to 350 degrees F, set the time to 10 minutes. Press "Start" to begin cooking. When the unit beeps to show Add Food message, place pancake over cooking tray and insert in the Air Fryer. After 2 minutes, stop the unit and open the door then add frozen chocolate-hazelnut dish spread on pancake then cook for 2 more minutes. When cooking is complete cool for 5 minutes and serve. Stub the pancakes with the sugar of the confectioners and serve warmly with syrup.
Per Serving: Calories 91; Fat 5.9g; Sodium 186mg; Carbs 8.8g; Fiber 0.2; Sugar 6.4g; Protein 1.7g

Chocolate Bananas

Prep time: 07 minutes| Cook time: 10 minutes| Serves: 2

1 large egg	2 bananas, halved crosswise
¼ cup corn-starch	Cooking oil
¼ cup plain breadcrumbs	Chocolate sauce

In a small bowl, beat the egg. In another bowl, place the corn-starch. Place the breadcrumbs in a different bowl. Dip the bananas in the corn-starch, then the egg, and then the breadcrumbs. Spray the cooking tray with cooking oil. Place the bananas in the cooking tray and spray them with cooking oil. Press Air Fry then adjust the temperature to 350 degrees F, set the time to 10 minutes. Press "Start" to begin cooking. When the unit beeps to show Add Food message, place cooking tray and insert in the Air Fryer. When time reaming 2 minutes when show message turn food the unit and open the door then turn the banana cook for 2 more minutes. Drizzle the chocolate sauce over the bananas and serve.
Per Serving: Calories 347; Fat 10.9g; Sodium 176mg; Carbs 58.8g; Fiber 4.2; Sugar 15.4g; Protein 7.2g

Easy Graham Cheesecake

Prep time: 10 minutes| Cook time: 19 minutes| Serves: 15

1 pound cream cheese	2 tablespoons butter
½ teaspoon vanilla extract	2 eggs
1 cup graham crackers, crumbled	4 tablespoons sugar

In a bowl, mix crackers with butter. Press crackers mix on the bottom of a lined cake pan, Press Air Fry then adjust the temperature to 350 degrees F, set the time to 4 minutes. Press "Start" to begin cooking. When the unit beeps to show Add Food message, place pan cooking tray and insert in the Air Fryer. Meanwhile in a bowl, mix sugar with cream cheese, eggs

and vanilla and whisk well. When times up open the Air Fryer and Spread filling over crackers crust and cook your cheesecake in your Air Fryer at 310 degrees F for 15 minutes. Leave cake in the fridge for 3 hours, slice and serve.
Per Serving: Calories 164; Fat 13.9g; Sodium 146mg; Carbs 8.8g; Fiber 0.2; Sugar 5.4g; Protein 3.4g

Coconut Macaroons

Prep time: 10 minutes| Cook time: 08 minutes| Serves: 20

2 tablespoons sugar	4 egg whites
2 cups coconut, shredded	1 teaspoon vanilla extract

In a bowl, mix egg whites with stevia and beat using your mixer. Add coconut and vanilla extract, whisk again, shape small balls out of this mix. Press Air Fry then adjust the temperature to 340 degrees F, set the time to 8 minutes. Press "Start" to begin cooking. When the unit beeps to show Add Food message, place macaroons into cooking tray and insert in the Air Fryer. Meanwhile in a bowl, mix sugar with cream cheese, eggs and vanilla and whisk well. Serve macaroons cold.
Per Serving: Calories 37; Fat 2.7g; Sodium 8mg; Carbs 2.5g; Fiber 0.7; Sugar 1.8 g; Protein 1g

Luscious Orange cake

Prep time: 10 minutes| Cook time: 16 minutes| Serves: 12

1 orange, peeled and cut into quarters	4 ounces cream cheese
1 teaspoon vanilla extract	1 teaspoon baking powder
6 eggs	9 ounces flour
2 tablespoons orange zest	2 ounces sugar+ 2 tablespoons
	4 ounces yogurt

In your food processor, pulse orange very well. Add flour, 2 tablespoons of sugar, eggs, baking powder, vanilla extract and pulse well again. Transfer this into 2 spring form pans. Carefully transfer the pastries to a cooking tray. Using the control panel, select bake, then adjust the temperature to 330 degrees F and the time to 16 minutes, and then touch Start. When the display indicates "Add Food", insert one cooking tray in the Air Fryer. Meanwhile in a bowl, mix cream cheese with orange zest, yogurt and the rest of the sugar and stir well. Place one cake layer on a plate, add half of the cream cheese mix, add the other cake layer and top with the rest of the cream cheese mix. Spread it well, slice and serve.
Per Serving: Calories 176; Fat 5.7g; Sodium 66mg; Carbs 24.3g; Fiber 1.1; Sugar 7.1 g; Protein 6.4g

Bread with Amaretto Sauce

Prep time: 07 minutes| Cook time: 8 minutes| Serves: 12

1 pound Bread dough	½ cup butter, melted
1 cup heavy cream	2 tablespoons Amaretto
12 ounces Chocolate chips	liqueur
1 cup sugar	

Roll dough, cut into 20 slices and then cut each slice in halves. Brush dough pieces with butter, sprinkle sugar, place them in your cooking tray. Using the control panel, select Air Fry, then adjust the temperature to 350 degrees F and the time to 8 minutes, and then touch Start. When the display indicates "Add Food", insert one cooking tray in the center position. When the display shows turn food, turn the food and cook 3 minutes more. Heat up a pan with the heavy cream over medium heat, add chocolate chips and stir until they melt. Add liqueur stir again. Transfer to a bowl and serve bread dippers with this sauce.

Per Serving: Calories 419; Fat 20.7g; Sodium 444mg; Carbs 52g; Fiber 1.6; Sugar 34.6 g; Protein 5.4g

Easy Granola with Apple Pie Spice

Prep time: 20 minutes| Cook time:25 minutes| Serves: 4

1 cup coconut, shredded	½ cup sunflower seeds
½ cup almonds	2 tablespoons sunflower oil
½ cup pecans, chopped.	1 teaspoon nutmeg ground
2 tablespoons sugar	1 teaspoon apple pie spice mix
½ cup pumpkin seeds	

In a bowl, mix almonds and pecans with pumpkin seeds, sunflower seeds, coconut, nutmeg and apple pie spice mix and stir well. Heat up a pan with the oil over medium heat, add sugar and stir well. Pour this over nuts and coconut mix and stir well. Spread this on a lined baking sheet that fits your Air Fryer. Using the control panel, select Bake, then adjust the temperature to 300 degrees F and the time to 25 minutes, and then touch Start. When the display indicates "Add Food", insert pan over cooking tray in the Air Fryer. Leave your granola to cool down, cut and serve.
Per Serving: Calories 419; Fat 20.7g; Sodium 444mg; Carbs 52g; Fiber 1.6; Sugar 34.6 g; Protein 5.4g

Mascarpone Pears and Espresso Cream

Prep time: 10 minutes| Cook time:30 minutes| Serves: 4

4 pears, halved and cored	For the Cream:
2 tablespoons water	1 cup whipping cream
2 tablespoons lemon juice	2 tablespoons espresso, cold
1 tablespoon sugar	1 cup mascarpone
2 tablespoons butter	⅓ cup sugar

In a bowl, mix pears halves with lemon juice, 1 tablespoon sugar, butter and water, toss well; transfer them to your cooking tray Place the drip pan in the bottom of the cooking chamber. Using the control panel, select Air Fry, then adjust the temperature to 360 degrees F and the time to 30 minutes, and then touch Start. When the display indicates "Add Food", insert cooking tray with pears in the center position. Meanwhile in a bowl, mix whipping cream with mascarpone, ⅓ cup sugar and espresso, whisk really well and keep in the fridge until pears are done. Divide pears on plates, top with espresso cream and serve them
Per Serving: Calories 380; Fat 23.7g; Sodium 109mg; Carbs 5.2g; Fiber 1.6; Sugar 24.6 g; Protein 8.4g

Vanilla Cranberries Pudding

Prep time: 05 minutes| Cook time: 45 minutes| Serves: 4

1-½ cups milk	¾ cup heavy whipping cream
2-½ eggs	¾ teaspoon lemon zest
½ cup cranberries	¾ teaspoon kosher salt
1 teaspoon butter	¾ French baguettes cut into
¼ cup and 2 tablespoons white sugar	2-inch slices
¼ cup golden raisins	3/8 vanilla bean, split and seeds scraped away
⅛ teaspoon ground cinnamon	

Lightly grease baking pan of Air Fryer with cooking spray. Spread baguette slices, cranberries, and raisins. In blender, blend well vanilla bean, cinnamon, salt, lemon zest, eggs, sugar, and cream. Pour over baguette slices. Let it soak for an hour. Cover pan with foil. Using the control panel, select Bake, then adjust the temperature to 330 degrees F and the time to 10 minutes, and then touch Start. When the display indicates "Add Food", insert baking pan over cooking tray in the Air Fryer. Let it rest for 10 minutes. Serve and enjoy.

Per Serving: Calories 269; Fat 15.7g; Sodium 615mg; Carbs 28.1g; Fiber 1.2; Sugar 14.6 g; Protein 6.4g

White Choco Chips Brownies

Prep time: 10 minutes| Cook time: 20 minutes| Serves: 8

1 egg	¼ cup cocoa powder
¼ cup brown sugar	⅓ cup all-purpose flour
2 tablespoons white sugar	¼ cup white chocolate chips
2 tablespoons safflower oil	Nonstock baking spray with
1 teaspoon vanilla	flour

In a medium bowl, beat the egg with the brown sugar and white sugar. Beat in the oil and vanilla. Add the cocoa powder and flour, and stir just until combined. Fold in the white chocolate chips. Spray a baking pan with non-stick spray. Spoon the brownie batter into the pan. Using the control panel, select Bake, then adjust the temperature to 390 degrees F and the time to 20 minutes, and then touch Start. When the display indicates "Add Food", insert baking pan over cooking tray in the Air Fryer. Let cool for 30 minutes before slicing to serve.

Per Serving: Calories 121; Fat 6.1g; Sodium 15mg; Carbs 16.1g; Fiber 1; Sugar 10.6 g; Protein 2g

Nutmeg Apple with Walnuts

Prep time: 10 minutes| Cook time: 20 minutes| Serves: 1

¼ cup water	2 tablespoons raisins
¼ teaspoon nutmeg	2 tablespoon chopped walnuts
¼ teaspoon cinnamon	1 medium apple
1½ teaspoons melted ghee	

Preheat your Air Fryer to 350 degrees F. Slice apple in half and discard some of the flesh from the center. Place into pan. Mix remaining ingredients together except water. Spoon mixture into the middle of the apple halves. Pour water over filled apples. Using the control panel, select bake, then adjust the temperature to 350 degrees F and the time to 20 minutes, then touch Start. When the display indicates "Add Food", insert baking pan over cooking tray in the Air Fryer.

Per Serving: Calories 455; Fat 30.1g; Sodium 6mg; Carbs 46.1g; Fiber 7.6; Sugar 34.6 g; Protein 5g

Vanilla Blueberry Pecans Cake

Prep time: 05minutes| Cook time: 35 minutes| Serves: 6

1 cup white sugar	½ teaspoon vanilla extract
1 egg	¼ cup brown sugar
½ cup butter, softened	¼ cup chopped pecans
½ cup fresh or frozen	⅛ teaspoon salt
blueberries	1-½ teaspoons confectioners'
½ cup sour cream	sugar for dusting
½ teaspoon baking powder	¾ cup and 1 tablespoon all-
½ teaspoon ground cinnamon	purpose flour

In a small bowl, whisk well pecans, cinnamon, and brown sugar. In a blender, blend well all wet ingredients. Add dry ingredients except for confectioner's sugar and blueberries. Blend well until smooth and creamy. Lightly grease baking pan of Air Fryer with cooking spray. Pour half of batter in pan. Sprinkle half of pecan mixture on top. Pour the remaining batter. And then top with

remaining pecan mixture. Cover pan with foil. Using the control panel, select bake, then adjust the temperature to 330 degrees F and the time to 35 minutes, and then touch Start. When the display indicates "Add Food", insert baking pan over cooking tray in the Air Fryer. When times up, open the door of unit and put pan into wire rack for cooling. Serve and enjoy with a dusting of confectioner's sugar.

Per Serving: Calories 405; Fat 20.6g; Sodium 132mg; Carbs 54.1g; Fiber 1; Sugar 41.6 g; Protein 3.5g

Cashew Lemon Bars

Prep time: 05minutes| Cook time: 25 minutes| Serves: 6

¼ cup cashew	1 cup desiccated coconut
¼ cup fresh lemon juice,	1 teaspoon baking powder
freshly squeezed	2 eggs, beaten
¾ cup coconut milk	2 tablespoons coconut oil
¾ cup erythritol	salt

Combine all ingredients. Use a hand mixer to mix everything. Pour into a baking dish that will fit in the Air Fryer. Using the control panel, select Bake, then adjust the temperature to 350 degrees F and the time to 25 minutes, and then touch Start. When the display indicates "Add Food", insert baking pan over cooking tray in the Air Fryer. When times up, open the door of unit and put pan into wire rack for cooling.

Per Serving: Calories 196; Fat 18.6g; Sodium 32mg; Carbs 34.1g; Fiber 1.7; Sugar 32 g; Protein 3.8g

Almond Coffee Cake

Prep time: 10 minutes| Cook time: 20 minutes| Serves: 2

¼ cup butter	¼ cup of sugar
½ teaspoon instant coffee	¼ cup almond flour
1 tablespoon black coffee,	1 teaspoon of cocoa powder
brewed	A pinch of salt
1 egg	Powdered sugar, for icing

Grease a small ring cake pan. Beat the sugar and egg along in a very bowl. Beat in cocoa, instant coffee and black coffee; stir in salt and flour. Transfer the batter to the prepared pan. Using the control panel, select Bake, then adjust the temperature to 350 degrees F and the time to 15 minutes, and then touch Start. When the display indicates "Add Food", insert baking pan over cooking tray in the Air Fryer. When times up, open the door of unit and put pan into wire rack for cooling

Per Serving: Calories 285; Fat 23.3g; Sodium 242mg; Carbs 17.1g; Fiber 1; Sugar 4 g; Protein 2.8g

Lime Coconut Cheesecake

Prep time: 05 minutes| Cook time: 20 minutes| Serves: 10

2 tablespoons butter, melted	1 pound cream cheese
2 teaspoons sugar	Zest from 1 lime, grated
4 ounces flour	Juice from 1 lime
¼ cup coconut, shredded	2 cups hot water
For the filling:	2 sachets lime jelly

In a bowl, mix coconut with flour, butter, and sugar, stir well and press this on the bottom of a pan that fits your Air Fryer. Meanwhile, put the hot water in a bowl, add jelly sachets and until it dissolves. Put cream cheese in a bowl, add jelly, lime juice, and zest and whisk really well. Spread this over the crust. Using the control panel, select Bake, then adjust the temperature to 300 degrees F and the time to 5 minutes, and then touch Start. When the display indicates "Add Food", insert baking pan over cooking tray in the Air Fryer. Keep in the fridge for 4 hours before serving. Enjoy!

Per Serving: Calories 245; Fat 18.3g; Sodium 173mg; Carbs 15.1g; Fiber 0.5; Sugar 4.7g; Protein 4.8g

Coconut Lemon Cookie

Prep time: 05 minutes| Cook time: 10 minutes| Serves: 4

½ cup softened unsalted butter
5 cups of coconut flour
1 lemon juice and zest
2 cups of coconut milk
2 teaspoons of yeast

¼ cup of granulated sugar
1 teaspoon of salt
1 teaspoon of baking soda
1 teaspoon of baking powder

Using a bowl, add and stir the coconut flour, yeast, baking soda, baking powder, salt, and granulated sugar. Add and stir in the coconut milk, lemon juice, lemon zest, unsalted butter and mix it properly until it has soft dough's texture. Roll out the pastry and cut it into cookies. Place the cookies on a baking sheet and place into cooking tray. Using the control panel, select bake, then adjust the temperature to 360 degrees F and the time to 5 minutes, and then touch Start. When the display indicates "Add Food", insert cooking tray with cookies in the Air Fryer. Remove and allow it to cool off until it is cool enough to eat. Sprinkle it with icing sugar. Serve and enjoy!

Per Serving: Calories 568; Fat 54.3g; Sodium 959mg; Carbs 19.1g; Fiber 9.5; Sugar 6.7g; Protein 6.4g

Corn Banana Fritters

Prep time: 05 minutes| Cook time: 15 minutes| Serves: 8

8 bananas
3 tablespoons vegetable oil
3 tablespoons corn flour

1 egg white
¾ cup breadcrumbs

Combine the oil and breadcrumbs, in a small bowl. Coat the bananas with the corn flour first, brush them with egg white, and dip them in the breadcrumb mixture. Arrange on a lined baking sheet. Using the control panel, select Air Fry, then adjust the temperature to 350 degrees F and the time to 15 minutes, and then touch Start. When the display indicates "Add Food", insert cooking tray with baking sheet in the Air Fryer. When the display indicates "Turn Food", turn food cook for reaming time. Remove and allow it to cool off until it is cool enough to eat.

Per Serving: Calories 202; Fat 6.2g; Sodium 80mg; Carbs 36.4g; Fiber 3.5; Sugar 15.7g; Protein 3.4g

Tasty Chocolate Chips Banana

Prep time: 05 minutes| Cook time: 15 minutes| Serves: 8

16 baking cups crust
1 banana; peeled and sliced
into 16 pieces

¼ cup peanut butter
¾ cup of chocolate chips
1 tablespoon vegetable oil

Put chocolate chips in a small pot, heat up over low heat; stir until it melts and takes off heat. In a bowl; mix peanut butter with coconut oil and whisk well. Spoon 1 teaspoon chocolates mix in a cup, add 1 banana slice and top with 1 teaspoon butter mix. Repeat with the rest of cups; place them all into a cooking tray of air fryer, Using the control panel, select Air Fry, then adjust the temperature to 320 degrees F and the time to 5 minutes, and then touch Start. When the display indicates "Add Food", insert cooking tray with baking sheet in the Air Fryer. Transfer to a freezer and keep there until you serve

Per Serving: Calories 33; Fat 2g; Sodium 1mg; Carbs 3.4g; Fiber 0.5; Sugar 2.7g; Protein 0.4g

Lemon Strawberry Cobbler

Prep time: 05 minutes| Cook time: 35 minutes| Serves: 6

A ¾ cup of sugar
6 cups strawberries, halved
⅛ teaspoon baking powder
1 tablespoon lemon juice
½ cup flour

A pinch of baking soda
½ cup of water
3 and ½ tablespoon olive oil
Cooking spray

In a bowl, mix strawberries with half of the sugar, sprinkle some flour, add lemon juice, whisk and pour into the baking dish that fits your Air Fryer and greased with cooking spray. In another bowl, mix flour with the rest of the sugar, baking powder and soda and stir well. Add the olive oil and mix until the whole thing with your hands. Add ½ cup water and spread over strawberries. Using the control panel, select Bake, then adjust the temperature to 355 degrees F and the time to 25 minutes, and then touch Start. When the display indicates "Add Food", insert pan over cooking tray in the Air Fryer. Leave cobbler aside to cool down, slice and serve. Enjoy!

Per Serving: Calories 180; Fat 0.7g; Sodium 33mg; Carbs 44.1g; Fiber 3.2; Sugar 32.7g; Protein 2.4g

Brownies with Chocolate Chips

Prep time: 05 minutes| Cook time: 25 minutes| Serves: 4

4-ounces of softened unsalted butter
8-ounces of bittersweet chocolate chips

3 eggs
1 cup of granulated sugar
½ teaspoon of salt
1 cup of all-purpose flour

Grease a heat-safe dish that is convenient with your Air Fryer. Using a saucepan, soften the butter and chocolate. Then using a large bowl, add and mix all the ingredients properly. Add the brownie batter to the greased heat-safe dish and smoothen the surface. Press Bake then adjust the temperature to 350 degrees F, set the time to 25 minutes. Press "Start" to begin cooking. When the unit beeps to show Add Food message, place cooking tray and insert in the Air Fryer. Remove the brownies and allow it to chill it is cool enough to eat, thereafter cut it into squares. Serve and enjoy!

Per Serving: Calories 703; Fat 26.7g; Sodium 383mg; Carbs 107.1g; Fiber 2.8; Sugar 79.7g; Protein 11.4g

Sugary Cinnamon Churros

Prep time: 05 minutes| Cook time: 10 minutes| Serves: 4

½ cup water ¼ teaspoon
kosher salt
Unsalted butter split half cup
2 tablespoons All-purpose

flour
2 large eggs
⅓ cup granulated sugar
cinnamon

In a small saucepan over medium-high heat, bring 14 cups water, salt, and butter to a boil. Reduce the heat to low; add the flour and whisk briskly with a wooden spoon for about 30 seconds, or until the dough is smooth. Cook, stirring constantly, until the dough begins to pull away from the pan's sides and forms a movie picture on the back of the pan, about 2 to 3 minutes. Place the dough in a medium mixing basin. Stir constantly for about 1 minute, or until the mixture has somewhat cooled. 1 at a time, add eggs, stirring constantly until smooth after each addition. Fill a piping bag halfway with the ingredients with a medium celebrity tip. Allow 30 minutes to chill. Pipe 6 (3 inches long) pieces into one layer in a cooking tray. Press Air Fry then adjust the temperature to 380 degrees F, set the time to 10 minutes. Press "Start" to begin cooking. When the unit beeps to show Add

Food message, place cooking tray and insert in the Air Fryer. In a medium bowl, collectively stir the sugar and cinnamon. Brush the cooked churros with the remaining 2 tablespoons of melted butter, and roll in a sugar mixture. Serve churros with chocolate sauce.
Per Serving: Calories 121; Fat 3.5g; Sodium 42mg; Carbs 19.1g; Fiber 0.1; Sugar 16.9g; Protein 3.6 g

Stuffed Apples with Vanilla Sauce

Prep time: 10 minutes| Cook time: 10 minutes| Serves: 4

For Stuffed Apples:
½ cup golden raisins
½ cup blanched almonds
2 tablespoons sugar
4 cored small firm apples

For Vanilla Sauce:
½ cup whipped cream
2 tablespoons sugar
½ teaspoon vanilla extract

Pulse the raisins, almonds, and sugar in a food processor until finely chopped. Fill each apple with the raisin mixture carefully. Line a baking dish that will fit in the Air Fryer with parchment paper. Place the apples in the baking dish that has been prepared. Select "Air Fry" and set the temperature to 355 degrees F. Set the timer for 10 minutes and hit the "Start" button. Insert the baking dish in the centre position when the display says "Add Food". Do not flip the food when the display says "Turn Food". Meanwhile, make the vanilla sauce by heating the cream, sugar, and vanilla extract in a saucepan over medium heat until the sugar is dissolved, stirring constantly. Remove the baking dish from the unit when the cooking time is up. Place the apples on plates to cool somewhat before serving. Serve with the vanilla sauce on top.
Per Serving: Calories 212; Fat 9.2g; Sodium 5mg; Carbs 32.4g; Fiber 7; Sugar 19g; Protein 4.2 g

Fried Oreo Cookies

Prep time: 02 minutes| Cook time: 4 minutes| Serves: 9

1 crescent sheet roll

9 Oreo cookies

Unroll the crescent roll dough sheet onto a clean, flat surface. Cut the dough into 9 even squares with a knife. Each cookie should be entirely wrapped in 1 dough square. Place the Oreos on a baking sheet. Place the drip pan in the Air Fryer's cooking chamber's bottom. Select "Air Fry" and set the temperature to 360 degrees F. Set the timer for 4 minutes and hit the "Start" button. Place the cooking tray in the Air Fryer when the display says "Add Food". Turn the Oreos when the display says "Turn Food". Remove the tray from the Air Fryer when the cooking time is up. Warm the dish before serving.
Per Serving: Calories 58; Fat 2.1g; Sodium 75mg; Carbs 9.3g; Fiber 0.4; Sugar 4.1g; Protein 0.9 g

Chocolate Cupcakes with Pistachios

Prep time: 02 minutes| Cook time: 15 minutes| Serves: 6

1 cup all-purpose flour
2 tablespoons unsweetened cocoa powder
¼ teaspoon baking soda
1 teaspoon baking powder
¼ teaspoon salt
½ cup coconut milk

¼ cup granulated sugar
3 tablespoons coconut oil melted
½ teaspoon vanilla extract
½ cup dark chocolate chips
¼ cup pistachios – ¼ cup, chopped

In a mixing dish, combine the flour, cocoa powder, baking powder, baking soda, and salt. In another dish, whisk together the coconut milk, sugar, coconut oil, and vanilla extract until

smooth. Mix in the flour mixture until it is completely mixed. Combine the chocolate chips and pistachios in a mixing bowl. Grease a 6-cup muffin tray with cooking spray. Fill the muffin cups approximately 3/4 full with the mixture. Place a cooking tray on top of the muffin pan. Place the drip pan in the cooking chamber of the Air Fryer. Select "Air Fry" and set the temperature to 300 degrees Fahrenheit. Set the timer for 15 minutes and hit the "Start" button. Do not flip the food when the display says "Turn Food". Remove the ramekins from the Air Fry when the cooking time is up. Allow the muffin tray to cool for 10-15 minutes on a wire rack. Before serving, carefully slide the muffins onto the wire rack to cool completely.
Per Serving: Calories 259; Fat 13.6g; Sodium 209mg; Carbs 34.1g; Fiber 1.9; Sugar 14.1g; Protein 4.1 g

Apple Pie Crumble

Prep time: 02 minutes| Cook time: 25 minutes| Serves: 4

1 (14-ounce) can apple pie filling
¼ cup, butter softened

9 tablespoons self-rising flour
7 tablespoons caster sugar
1 pinch of salt

Prepare a baking dish that will fit in the Air Fryer by lightly greasing it. Fill the prepared baking dish equally with apple pie filling. Combine the remaining ingredients in a medium mixing bowl and stir until a crumbly mixture form. Evenly spread the mixture over the apple pie filling. Place the baking dish on top of a cooking tray in the Air Fryer. Place the drip pan in the cooking chamber of the Air Fryer. Select "Air Fry" and set the temperature to 320 degrees F. Set the timer for 25 minutes and hit the "Start" button. When the display shows Add Food, place the cooking tray in the Air Fryer. When the display shows "Turn Food", do not turn food. When cooking time is complete, remove the baking dish from the Air Fryer. Place the baking dish onto a wire rack to cool for about 10 minutes. Serve warm.
Per Serving: Calories 152; Fat 0.1g; Sodium 85mg; Carbs 36.1g; Fiber 2.9; Sugar 21.1g; Protein 0.1 g

Almond Strawberry Cheesecake

Prep time: 02 minutes| Cook time: 1 hr. 37 minutes| Serves: 8

For Crust:
7 tablespoons almond flour
2 tablespoons natural peanut butter
1 tablespoon honey
For Filling:
2 eggs
10½ ounces plain Greek yogurt
10½ ounces cream cheese
2 scoops vanilla whey protein powder

2 tablespoons strawberry preserve
2 tablespoons splenda
¼ teaspoon vanilla extract
1 cup, hulled and sliced fresh strawberries
For Topping:
2 tablespoons fat-free plain Greek yogurt
1 tablespoon splenda
2 tablespoons vanilla whey protein powder

Line a greased circular baking dish with parchment paper. To make the crust, combine all of the crust ingredients in a mixing dish and stir until a dough ball form. Place the dough ball in the center of the baking dish that has been prepared. Press down with your fingertips until the dough is uniformly distributed in the bottom of the baking dish. Select "Air Fry" and set the temperature to 250 degrees F. Set the timer for 7 minutes and hit the "Start" button. Place the baking dish over the drip pan when the display says "Add Food". Do not flip the food when the display says "Turn Food". Remove the baking dish from the unit when the cooking time is finished. Meanwhile, make the filling by whisking together all of the filling ingredients (except the strawberries) in a large mixing bowl until smooth. Combine the strawberry slices and fold them in. Spread the strawberry mixture evenly over the crust. Smooth the top surface of the strawberry mixture with the back of a spatula. Select "Air Fry" once more, and then set the temperature to 250 degrees F. Set the timer for 30 minutes and hit the "Start" button. Insert the baking dish in the Air Fryer, when the display says "Add Food". Adjust the temperature to 195 degrees F after 30 minutes. Preheat the unit to 350 degrees F and set the timer for 60 minutes. Do not flip the food when the display says "Turn Food". Remove the baking dish from the Air Fryer, when the cooking time is up. Place the baking dish aside for about 1-2 hours to cool. For topping: in a bowl, put all the topping ingredients and mix well. After cooling, top the cheesecake with the topping mixture. Refrigerate for about 4-8 hours before serving.

Per Serving: Calories 301; Fat 8.1g; Sodium 149mg; Carbs 18.1g; Fiber 1.9; Sugar 13.1g; Protein 40.1 g

Cinnamon Whole Wheat Bread

Prep time: 10 minutes| Cook time: 5 minutes| Serves: 6

2 teaspoons pepper	1 cup coconut oil
1½ teaspoon cinnamon	12 slices whole-wheat bread
½ cup sweetener of choice	

Melt the coconut oil and stir in the sweetener until it is completely dissolved. Mix in the remaining ingredients, minus the bread, until well combined. Cover all regions of the bread with the mixture. Using the control panel, select Air Fry, then adjust the temperature to 400 degrees F and the time to 5 minutes, and then touch Start. When the display indicates "Add Food" insert baking pan over cooking tray in the Air Fryer. Remove and cut diagonally. Enjoy!

Per Serving: Calories 541; Fat 38.1g; Sodium 266mg; Carbs 48.1g; Fiber 4.9; Sugar 23.1g; Protein 7.1 g

Strawberry Tartar Cake

Prep time: 05 minutes| Cook time: 30 minutes| Serves: 12

¼ cup butter, melted	12 egg whites
1 cup powdered Erythritol	2 teaspoons cream of tartar
1 teaspoon strawberry extract	

Combine the cream of tartar and egg whites in a mixing bowl. Whip the egg whites with a hand mixer until they are white and fluffy. Whisk in the other ingredients, except the butter, for another minute. Fill a baking dish halfway with the mixture. Using the control panel, select Bake, then adjust the temperature to 400 degrees F and the time to 30 minutes, and then touch Start. When the display indicates "Add Food", insert baking pan over cooking tray in the Air Fryer.

Per Serving: Calories 73; Fat 3.8g; Sodium 61mg; Carbs 12.1g; Fiber 0; Sugar 0.3 g; Protein 3.6g

Apple Won Ton with Raisins

Prep time: 10 minutes| Cook time: 25 minutes| Serves: 4

2 tablespoons melted coconut oil	1 tablespoon brown sugar
2 puff pastry sheets	2 tablespoons raisins
	2 small apples of choice

Apples should be cored and peeled before being combined with raisins and sugar. Brush the sides of puff pastry sheets with melted coconut oil and a dab of the apple mixture. Using the control panel, select Air Fry, then adjust the temperature to 400 degrees F and the time to 25 minutes, and then touch Start. When the display indicates "Add Food", insert baking pan over cooking tray in the Air Fryer.

Per Serving: Calories 231; Fat 13.8g; Sodium 102mg; Carbs

27.1g; Fiber 3g; Sugar 13 g; Protein 1.6g

Chocolate Jamb Biscuits

Prep time: 05 minutes| Cook time: 20 minutes| Serves: 10

(8-ounce) can jumbo biscuits	Chocolate sauce, such as
Cooking oil	Hershey's

Place the biscuit dough on a flat work surface and cut it into 8 biscuits. Cut a hole in the centre of each biscuit with a small circular cookie cutter or a biscuit cutter. You can also use a knife to cut the holes. Cooking oil should be used to grease the basket. Place 4 donuts in the cooking tray. Do not stack. Spray with cooking oil. Using the control panel, select Air Fry, then adjust the temperature to 400 degrees F and the time to 20 minutes, then touch Start. When the display indicates "Add Food", insert baking pan over cooking tray in the Air Fryer. Drizzle chocolate sauce over the donuts and enjoy while warm.

Per Serving: Calories 93; Fat 5.8g; Sodium 276mg; Carbs 11.6g; Fiber 0.8g; Sugar 2g; Protein 1.6g

Yummy Apple Tart

Prep time: 05 minutes| Cook time: 10 minutes| Serves: 6

15-ounces no-sugar-added apple pie filling	1 store-bought crust

Roll out the pie crust and cut it into squares of similar size. Fill each square with 2 tablespoons of filling and seal with a fork. Using the control panel, select Air Fry, then adjust the temperature to 390 degrees F and the time to 10 minutes, and then touch Start. When the display indicates "Add Food", insert cooking tray in the Air Fryer. When cooked, remove from the Air Fryer and serve.

Per Serving: Calories 89; Fat 0.8g; Sodium 42mg; Carbs 18.6g; Fiber 0; Sugar 10.2g; Protein 0.1g

Cream Cheese Dumplings

Prep time: 05 minutes| Cook time: 05 minutes| Serves: 16

1 egg with a little water	8 ounces softened cream
Wonton wrappers	cheese
½ cup powdered Erythritol	olive oil

Combine the sweetener and cream cheese in a mixing bowl. To prevent drying out, roll out 4 wontons at a time and cover with a dish towel. Fill each wrapper with 12 teaspoon cream cheese mixture. Dip your finger into the egg/water mixture and fold the triangle in half diagonally. Make sure the edges are securely sealed. Repeat with the rest of the ingredients. Place filled wontons into the cooking tray. Using the control panel, select Air Fry, then adjust the temperature to 400 degrees F and the time to 5 minutes, and then touch Start. When the display indicates "Add Food", insert the cooking tray in the Air Fryer.

Per Serving: Calories 75; Fat 6.2g; Sodium 58mg; Carbs 6.1g; Fiber 0g; Sugar 0.2g; Protein 1.7g

Cinnamon French Toast Bites

Prep time: 05 minutes| Cook time: 15 minutes| Serves: 8

Almond milk	3 eggs
Cinnamon	4 pieces wheat bread
Sweetener	

Thin with almond milk after whisking the eggs. Add ⅓ cup sweetener plus a generous amount of cinnamon. Tear the bread in half, then roll the pieces into a ball and press them together. Soak bread balls in egg, then roll them in cinnamon sugar, ensuring sure they are completely covered. Using the control panel, select Air Fry, then adjust the temperature to 360 degrees F and the time to 15 minutes, then touch Start. When the display indicates "Add Food", insert the cooking tray in the Air Fryer.
Per Serving: Calories 128; Fat 9.2g; Sodium 94mg; Carbs 8.1g; Fiber 1.9g; Sugar 1.2g; Protein 4.7g

Sugary Cinnamon Chickpeas

Prep time: 05 minutes| Cook time: 10 minutes| Serves: 2

1 tablespoon sweetener   1 cup chickpeas
1 tablespoon cinnamon

Chickpeas should be rinsed and drained. Combine all ingredients and place in the Air Fryer. Using the control panel, select Roast, then adjust the temperature to 390 degrees F and the time to 10 minutes, and then touch Start. When the display indicates "Add Food", insert cooking tray in the center position.
Per Serving: Calories 372; Fat 6.2g; Sodium 24mg; Carbs 64.1g; Fiber 19.7g; Sugar 10.2g; Protein 19.7g

Walnuts Brownie Muffins

Prep time: 10 minutes| Cook time: 10 minutes| Serves: 12

1 package Betty Crocker fudge   1 egg
brownie mix   ⅓ cup vegetable oil
¼ cup walnuts, chopped   2 teaspoons water

Grease 12 muffin molds. Set aside. In a bowl, put all ingredients together. Place the mixture into the prepared muffin molds. Using the control panel, select Bake, then adjust the temperature to 390 degrees F and the time to 10 minutes, then touch Start. When the display indicates "Add Food", insert cooking tray with muffins in the Air Fryer. Place the muffin molds onto a wire rack to cool for about 10 minutes. Carefully invert the muffins onto the wire rack to completely cool before serving.
Per Serving: Calories 84; Fat 8.2g; Sodium 12mg; Carbs 2g; Fiber 0.3g; Sugar 1.2g; Protein 1.7g

Choco Milk Mug Cake

Prep time: 15 minutes| Cook time: 13 minutes| Serves: 1

¼ cup self-rising flour   3 tablespoons coconut oil
5 tablespoons caster sugar   3 tablespoons whole milk
1 tablespoon cocoa powder

In a shallow mug, add all the ingredients and mix until well combined. Using the control panel, select Bake, then adjust the temperature to 390 degrees F and the time to 13 minutes, and then touch Start. When the display indicates "Add Food", insert cooking tray with mug in the Air Fryer. Place the mug onto a wire rack to cool slightly before serving.
Per Serving: Calories 729; Fat 43.3g; Sodium 20mg; Carbs 88.8g; Fiber 2.3g; Sugar 62.6 g; Protein 5.7g

Grilled Graham Cracker Peaches

Prep time: 10 minutes| Cook time: 10 minutes| Serves: 2

2 peaches, cut into wedges,   and remove pits

¼ cup butter, diced into pieces   ¼ cup graham cracker crumbs
¼ cup brown sugar

Using the control panel, select Air Fry, then adjust the temperature to 350 degrees F and the time to 5 minutes, and then touch Start. When the display indicates "Add Food", insert the cooking tray with peaches in the Air Fryer. In a bowl, put the butter, graham cracker crumbs, and brown sugar together. Turn peaches skin side down. Spoon butter mixture over top of peaches and then arrange cooking tray again in the Air Fryer and cook for 5 minutes. Top with whipped cream and serve.
Per Serving: Calories 378; Fat 24.3g; Sodium 262mg; Carbs 40.8g; Fiber 3g; Sugar 33.6 g; Protein 2.3g

Delicious Sweet and Spiced Apples

Prep time: 10 minutes| Cook time: 10 minutes| Serves: 4

4 apples, sliced   2 tablespoons sugar
1 teaspoon apple pie spice   2 tablespoons ghee, melted

Add apple slices into the mixing bowl. Add remaining ingredients on top of apple slices and toss until well coated. Transfer apple slices on cooking tray of air fryer. Using the control panel, select Air Fry, then adjust the temperature to 350 degrees F and the time to 10 minutes, and then touch Start. When the display indicates "Add Food" insert cooking tray with apple in Air Fryer. Top with ice cream and serve.
Per Serving: Calories 196; Fat 6.8g; Sodium 2mg; Carbs 37.8g; Fiber 5.5g; Sugar 29.6 g; Protein 0.3g

Tangy Honey Mango Slices

Prep time: 10 minutes| Cook time: 12 hrs.| Serves: 6

4 mangoes, peel, and cut into   ¼ cup fresh lemon juice
¼-inch slices   1 tablespoon honey

In a big bowl, combine together honey and lemon juice and set aside. Add mango slices in lemon-honey mixture and coat well. Arrange mango slices on the cooking tray of air fryer. Using the control panel, select Dehydrate, then adjust the temperature to 175 degrees F and the time to 12 hours, and then touch Start. When the display indicates "Add Food", insert cooking tray in the Air Fryer.
Per Serving: Calories 221; Fat 1.4g; Sodium 7mg; Carbs 55g; Fiber 5.5g; Sugar 50.6 g; Protein 2.3g

Dried Raspberries with Lemon Juice

Prep time: 10 minutes| Cook time: 15 hr.| Serves: 4

4 cups raspberries wash and dry   ¼ cup fresh lemon juice

Add raspberries and lemon juice to a bowl and toss well. Arrange raspberries on a cooking tray. Using the control panel, select Dehydrate, then adjust the temperature to 175 degrees F and the time to 15 hr, then touch Start. When the display indicates "Add Food", insert the cooking tray in the Air Fryer.
Per Serving: Calories 54; Fat 1.4g; Sodium 7mg; Carbs 55g; Fiber 5.5g; Sugar 50.6 g; Protein 2.3g

Sweet and Savoy Peach Wedges

Prep time: 10 minutes| Cook time: 8 hour| Serves: 4

3 peaches, cut and remove   pits, and sliced

½ cup fresh lemon juice

Add lemon juice and peach slices into the bowl and toss well. Arrange peach slices on the cooking tray. Using the control panel, select Dehydrate, then adjust the temperature to 175 degrees F and the time to 8 hour, and then touch Start. When the display indicates "Add Food", insert cooking tray in the Air Fryer.

Per Serving: Calories 52; Fat 0.4g; Sodium 6mg; Carbs 11.1g; Fiber 1.9g; Sugar 11.6 g; Protein 1.3g

Sandwich Cookies

Prep time: 05 minutes| Cook time: 05 minutes| Serves: 9

½ cup pancake mix
½ cup water
cooking spray
9 chocolate sandwich cookies
(e.g. Oreo)
1 tablespoon confectioners' sugar: or to taste

Blend the pancake mixture with the water until well mixed. Line the parchment paper on the basket of an Air Fryer. Spray non-stick cooking spray on parchment paper. Dip each cookie into the mixture of the pancake and place it in the basket. Make sure they do not touch; if possible, cook in batches. Using the control panel, select Air Fry, then adjust the temperature to 400 degrees F and the time to 5 minutes then touch Start. When the display indicates "Add Food", insert cooking tray in the Air Fryer. When display indicates "turn food", turn the food and cook 3 minutes more. Sprinkle the sugar over the cookies and serve.

Per Serving: Calories 242; Fat 9.2g; Sodium 316mg; Carbs 37.1g; Fiber 2.1g; Sugar 18 g; Protein 3.2g

Buttery Cake

Prep time: 10 minutes| Cook time: 15 minutes| Serves: 4

7 tablespoons of butter, at ambient temperature
¼ cup plus 2 tablespoons white sugar
1 ⅔ cups all-purpose flour
1 pinch salt or to taste
6 tablespoons milk

In a large mixing bowl, combine 1/4 cup butter and 2 teaspoons sugar. To make the sugar and butter smooth and fluffy, use an electric mixer. Combine the flour and salt in a mixing bowl. Mix in the milk until the batter is completely combined. Transfer the batter to the prepared saucepan and smooth the top with a spoon. Using the control panel, select Bake, then adjust the temperature to 350 degrees F and the time to 15 minutes then touch Start. When the display indicates "Add Food", insert cooking tray with baking pan in the Air Fryer. Turn the cake out of the baking pan and allow it to cool for about five minutes.

Per Serving: Calories 426; Fat 21.2g; Sodium 194mg; Carbs 53.1g; Fiber 1.4g; Sugar 13.7 g; Protein 6.3g

Marshmallows S'mores

Prep time: 05 minutes| Cook time: 03 minutes| Serves: 4

4 graham crackers (each half split to make 2 squares, for a total of 8 squares)
8 Squares of Hershey's
chocolate bar, broken into squares
4 Marshmallows

Put 4 squares of graham crackers on a cooking tray of the Air Fryer. Place 2 squares of chocolate bars on each cracker. Using the control panel, select Air Fry, then adjust the temperature to 390 degrees F and the time to 1 minutes then touch Start. When the display indicates "Add Food", insert cooking tray with

baking pan in the Air Fryer. Top with a marshmallow over each cracker. Throw the marshmallow down a little bit into the melted chocolate. This will help to make the marshmallow stay over the chocolate. Put back the cooking tray in the Air Fryer and Air Fry at 390 °F for 2 minutes. (The marshmallows should be puffed up and browned at the tops. Using tongs to carefully remove each cracker from the cooking tray of the Air Fryer and place it on a platter. Top each marshmallow with another square of graham crackers. Enjoy it right away.

Per Serving: Calories 285; Fat 13.5g; Sodium 111mg; Carbs 46.9g; Fiber 3.4g; Sugar 32 g; Protein 3.1 g

Sugar Peanut Buttery Biscuit

Prep time: 02minutes| Cook time: 05 minutes| Serves: 10

1 cup peanut butter
1 cup sugar
1 egg

Using a hand mixer, combine all of the ingredients. Canola oil should be sprayed on the Air Fryer cooking trays. (Alternatively, parchment paper can be used, but the cookies will take longer to bake.) Place rounded dough balls onto the Air Fryer cooking tray. Press down softly with the back of a fork. Using the control panel, select Air Fry, then adjust the temperature to 350 degrees F and the time to 5 minutes then touch Start. When the display indicates "Add Food", insert cooking tray with baking pan in the Air Fryer.

Per Serving: Calories 233; Fat 13.4g; Sodium 125mg; Carbs 25.1g; Fiber 1.4g; Sugar 22.5 g; Protein 7 g

Cinnamon Cream Pudding

Prep time: 05 minutes| Cook time: 12 minutes| Serves: 2

4 eggs; whisked
4 tablespoons erythritol
2 tablespoons heavy cream
½ teaspoon cinnamon powder
¼ teaspoon allspice, ground
Cooking spray

Take a bowl and mix all the ingredients, except the cooking spray, whisk well and pour into a ramekin greased with cooking spray. Add the cooking tray to your Air Fryer, put the ramekin inside. Using the control panel, select Bake, then adjust the temperature to 400 degrees F and the time to 12 minutes then touch Start. When the display indicates "Add Food", insert cooking tray in the Air Fryer. Serve.

Per Serving: Calories 45; Fat 3g; Sodium 36mg; Carbs 15.5g; Fiber 0g; Sugar 15.2 g; Protein 3.1 g

Tasty Carrot Cinnamon Mug Cake

Prep time: 15 minutes| Cook time: 20 minutes| Serves: 1

¼ cup whole-wheat pastry flour
1 tablespoon coconut sugar
¼ teaspoon baking powder
⅛ teaspoon ground cinnamon
⅛ teaspoon ground ginger
Pinch of ground cloves
Pinch of ground allspice
Pinch of salt
2 tablespoons plus 2 teaspoons unsweetened almond milk
2 tablespoons carrot, peeled and grated
2 tablespoons walnuts, chopped
1 tablespoon raisins
2 teaspoons applesauce

Combine the flour, sugar, baking powder, spices, and salt in a mixing basin. Mix in the other ingredients until everything is nicely mixed. Place the mixture in a ramekin that has been lightly buttered. Place ramekins into cooking tray. Using the control panel, select bake, then adjust the temperature to 350 degrees F and the time to 20 minutes then touch Start. When the display indicates "Add Food", insert cooking tray in the Air Fryer. When cooked, remove from the air fryer and serve.

Per Serving: Calories 357; Fat 9.8g; Sodium 209mg; Carbs 58.5g; Fiber 4.3g; Sugar 7.2 g; Protein 8.1 g

Vanilla Rice Pudding with Nutmeg

Prep time: 10 minutes| Cook time: 40 minutes| Serves: 4

For the Rice Pudding:
3½ tablespoons unsalted butter, plus more for the dish
3 tablespoons superfine sugar
Scant½ cup short-grain rice (not risotto rice)
1-quart whole milk
⅔ cup heavy cream
Pinch of salt

Lots of freshly grated nutmeg
Finely grated zest of½ unwaxed lemon
¼ teaspoon vanilla extract
To Serve:
Quince jelly (blackcurrant jelly is a good substitute)
⅓ pound (151 g) blackberries

Using butter, grease a baking dish. In a saucepan, combine the butter, sugar, rice, milk, and cream and bring to a gentle boil, stirring to dissolve the sugar. Return to a simmer with the salt, nutmeg, lemon zest, and vanilla extract. Cook, stirring constantly, for about 4 minutes, or until the rice grains have become slightly (very slightly) swelled. Pour the mixture into the dish that has been prepared. Using the control panel, select bake, then adjust the temperature to 325 degrees F and the time to 2 hr then touch Start. When the display indicates "Add Food", insert cooking tray in the Air Fryer. The rice should be creamy and cooked when done, but not dry or excessively sticky. Take the pudding to the table in the baking dish once it has baked and developed a wonderful golden skin on top, and serve the quince jelly and blackberries separately in separate serving bowls so people may assist themselves.

Per Serving: Calories 682; Fat 60g; Sodium 461mg; Carbs 29.9g; Fiber 0g; Sugar 21.9 g; Protein 9.5 g

Creamy Plums

Prep time: 10 minutes| Cook time: 20 minutes| Serves: 6

For the Cream:
¼ cup plus 2 tablespoons heavy cream
⅔ cup Greek yogurt
3 to 4 heaping tablespoons dark brown sugar
For the Plums:
1¾ pounds (793 g) plums (preferably crimson-fleshed),

halved and pitted
2 slices of crystallized ginger, very finely chopped
½ cup light brown sugar
½ teaspoon ground ginger
3 broad strips of lime zest, plus juice of 1 lime
⅔ cup dark rum, plus 3 tablespoons

Make the whipped cream at least 12 hours ahead of time. Whip the heavy cream until it is light and fluffy, and then fold in the yoghurt. Place in a bowl and evenly sprinkle with sugar. Refrigerate after wrapping in plastic wrap. The sugar will become molasses-like and mushy. Place the plums in a single layer in a baking pan. Arrange the fruits so that the sliced sides are facing out. Arrange the plums in a circle with the crystallised ginger. Sprinkle the sugar over the top, along with the ground ginger. Squeeze the lime juice over the fruits and tuck the lime zest under them before pouring the 2/3 cup rum around them. Using the control panel, select Bake, then adjust the temperature to 375 degrees F and the time to 20 minutes then touch Start. When the display indicates "Add Food", insert cooking tray with baking pan in the Air Fryer. When done, the fruit should be soft but not collapse when penetrated with a sharp knife. Allow cooling entirely; as the juices cool, they should thicken. Drain the juices and boil them in a pot until they become more syrupy if they aren't thick enough. The remaining 3 tablespoons of rum should be added now. Serve the plums with the brown sugar cream at room temperature.

Per Serving: Calories 208; Fat 10.6g; Sodium 9mg; Carbs 9.9g; Fiber 0.5g; Sugar 9.1 g; Protein 2.5 g

Orange Sloe Gin

Prep time: 10 minutes| Cook time: 40 minutes| Serves: 4

1½ pounds (680 g) hothouse or main crop rhubarb stalks, all about the same thickness
½ cup granulated sugar
Finely grated zest of½ orange

7 tablespoons sloe gin
3 tablespoons orange juice
2 rosemary sprigs, bruised
Whipped cream or heavy cream, to serve

Trim the bottoms of the rhubarb and remove any leaves. Place them in a large ovenproof baking dish, cut into 1¼ in lengths. Scatter the sugar and orange zest on top, then pour in the sloe gin, orange juice, and 2 tablespoons of water, and tuck the rosemary sprigs beneath the rhubarb with your hands. Wrap the foil around the dish tightly. Using the control panel, select bake, then adjust the temperature to 350 degrees F and the time to 30 minutes then touch Start. When the display indicates "Add Food" insert cooking tray with foil in the Air Fryer. When done, the rhubarb should be soft yet still keep its shape rather than collapsing. Remove from the oven and allow cooling in the dish for a few minutes. Serve warm with whipped cream or heavy cream, at room temperature, or chilled.

Per Serving: Calories 281; Fat 2.6g; Sodium 27mg; Carbs 69.9g; Fiber 12.5g; Sugar 37.1 g; Protein 6.5 g

Creme Fraîche with Apricot

Prep time: 10 minutes| Cook time: 25 minutes| Serves: 6

6 thick slices of brioche
2 tablespoons superfine sugar, plus 4 teaspoons
¼ cup amaretto or Marsala
5 tablespoons very soft unsalted butter
3¾ ounces (106 g) good-quality marzipan, broken into

small chunks
12 small ripe apricots, or 6 plums, pitted and quartered
Juice of ½ lemon
Generous ¼ cup sliced almonds Confectioners' sugar, to dust (optional)
Crème fraîche, to serve

Place the brioche slices in a single layer on a sheet pan or in a baking pan. Pour 14 cups boiling water over the 2 teaspoons sugar in a small heatproof bowl. Stir until the sugar is completely dissolved, then set aside to cool. Add the amaretto or Marsala and mix well. Cover both sides of the brioche slices with the cooled syrup. Butter each slice of brioche on both sides with care, as the brioche will be quite tender at this point. Arrange marzipan chunks on top, then top with apricot quarters. Sprinkle the 4 teaspoons of superfine sugar on top of the lemon juice. Using the control panel, select Bake, then adjust the temperature to 400 degrees F and the time to 25 minutes then touch Start. When the display indicates "Add Food", insert cooking tray with pan in the Air Fryer. Sprinkle the almonds on top after 15 minutes and bake for another 10 minutes. The apricots should be soft when done, and the bread and marzipan should both be golden.

Per Serving: Calories 1166; Fat 67.6g; Sodium 1174mg; Carbs 119.9g; Fiber 2.5g; Sugar 23.1 g; Protein 16.5 g

Bundt Cake with Glaze

Prep time: 10 minutes| Cook time: 55 minutes| Serves: 8

For the Cake:
1½ cups unsalted butter, at room temperature, plus more for preparing the pan

2 cups light brown sugar
1 cup sugar
5 large eggs
3 cups all-purpose flour, plus

more for preparing the pan
1 teaspoon table salt
1 cup sour cream, at room temperature

1 tablespoon vanilla extract
For the Glaze:
1 cup confectioners' sugar
2 tablespoons milk

A 10-cup Bundt pan should be butter and floured. Cream the butter, brown sugar, and sugar together in a large mixing bowl with a wooden spoon or an electric mixer until pale yellow and fluffy. One at a time, add the eggs, mixing after each addition until fully integrated. Combine the flour, salt, sour cream, and vanilla in a mixing bowl. Place the batter in the pan that has been prepared. Place the drip pan in the bottom of the cooking chamber. Using the control panel, select bake, then adjust the temperature to 350 degrees F and the time to 55 minutes then touch Start. When the display indicates "Add Food", insert cooking tray with baking pan in the Air Fryer. Remove the cake from the oven and cool for 10 minutes on a wire rack before flipping it onto a cake dish to cool fully. Produce the Glaze Whisk the confectioners' sugar and milk together in a small bowl until smooth. Drizzle the glaze over the cake once it has completely cooled.
Per Serving: Calories 880; Fat 44.6g; Sodium 364mg; Carbs 113.9g; Fiber 1.5g; Sugar 61 g; Protein 10.5 g

Cinnamon Chocolate Brownie

Prep time: 10 minutes| Cook time: 25 minutes| Serves: 8

½ cup unsalted butter, plus more for greasing
8 ounces (227 g) dark chocolate (60 to 72 percent cocoa)
1 cup sugar
2 teaspoons vanilla extract

Pinch salt
2 large eggs, at room temperature
1 teaspoon ground cinnamon
¼ teaspoon cayenne
¾ cup all-purpose flour

Aluminium foil should be used to line a square baking pan, with the ends extending over the pan's edges on two sides. Butter the foil as well as the pan. Gently melt the butter and chocolate together in a small saucepan over low heat, stirring constantly, until completely melted. Remove from the heat and set aside to cool. Pour into a big mixing basin. Combine the sugar, vanilla, and salt in a mixing bowl. Stir in the eggs one at a time until well combined. Combine the cinnamon and cayenne pepper with the flour and stir until equally distributed. Add the flour to the chocolate mixture and beat for about a minute, or until completely combined. The batter may appear to be gritty. Pour the batter into the pan that has been prepared. Using the control panel, select bake, then adjust the temperature to 350 degrees F and the time to 25 minutes then touch Start. When the display indicates "Add Food", insert cooking tray with baking pan in the Air Fryer. A toothpick put into the centre of the cake should come out with crumbs but no uncooked batter stuck to it when it's done. Allow for a 10-minute cooling period. Carefully take the brownies out of the pan using the foil's edges. Remove the foil and set aside for another 5 minutes to cool. Squares should be cut off.
Per Serving: Calories 408; Fat 21.6g; Sodium 79mg; Carbs 50.7g; Fiber 2.5g; Sugar 38.9 g; Protein 4.2 g

Vanilla Butter Cookies with Nutmeg

Prep time: 10 minutes| Cook time: 11 minutes| Serves: 4 dozen

½ cup (1 stick) unsalted butter, melted
1 cup sugar
1 teaspoon vanilla extract
¼ teaspoon kosher salt

1 large egg
1 cup all-purpose flour
1½ teaspoons freshly grated nutmeg

Silicone baking mats should be used to line two sheet pans (or use one sheet pan and bake in batches). Combine the butter and sugar in a large mixing basin. Combine the vanilla and salt in a mixing bowl. Add the egg and continue to beat until the mixture is completely smooth. Combine the flour and nutmeg in a small mixing dish. Just until combined, stir the flour mixture into the sugar and butter mixture. Drop the batter into the prepared pans by level teaspoons, leaving about 2 inches around the dough balls. Using the control panel, select bake, then adjust the temperature to 350 degrees F and the time to 11 minutes then touch Start. When the display indicates "Add Food", insert cooking tray in the Air Fryer. The cookies will spread as they bake, the edges will turn golden brown, and the tops will begin to collapse. Allow to cool for a few minutes on the pans before transferring to a cooling rack to cool fully.
Per Serving: Calories 45; Fat 2.1g; Sodium 27mg; Carbs 5.7g; Fiber 0.1g; Sugar 4.3 g; Protein 0.4 g

Cinnamon Blueberry and Peach Crisp with Lemon

Prep time: 15minutes| Cook time: 30 minutes| Serves: 4

For the Filling:
non-stick cooking spray
5 ripe peaches
1 cup fresh or frozen blueberries
⅓ cup granulated sugar
1 tablespoon all-purpose flour
1 teaspoon grated lemon zest
For the Topping:
½ cup quick-cooking oatmeal

⅓ cup brown sugar
⅓ cup all-purpose flour
¼ cup blanched slivered almonds
1 teaspoon ground cinnamon
½ teaspoon ground cardamom
Pinch salt
4 tablespoons unsalted butter or vegan margarine

Using cooking spray, coat a square baking pan. Peaches should be peeled and pitted. Cut them in half after slicing them approximately 12 inches thick. About 4 cups of slices should enough. Add the blueberries, sugar, flour, and lemon zest to a medium mixing bowl. Gently toss. Pour onto the baking pan that has been prepared. Combine the oats, brown sugar, flour, almonds, cinnamon, cardamom, and salt for the topping. Cut in the butter with a pastry cutter or a large fork until the mixture is crumbly. Toss the fruit with the topping. Using the control panel, select bake, then adjust the temperature to 350 degrees F and the time to 30 minutes then touch Start. When the display indicates "Add Food", insert cooking tray in the Air Fryer. When done, the top is lightly browned and the peaches are bubbling. Let cool for about 15 minutes before cutting. Serve warm.
Per Serving: Calories 388; Fat 16g; Sodium 87mg; Carbs 61.7g; Fiber 5.9g; Sugar 49.3 g; Protein 5 g

Vanilla Coconut Almond Cookies

Prep time: 10 minutes| Cook time: 25 minutes| Serves: 10

1½ cups coconut flour
1½ cups extra-fine almond flour
½ teaspoon baking powder
⅓ teaspoon baking soda
2 eggs plus an egg yolk, beaten
¾ cup coconut oil, at room temperature
1 cup unsalted pecan nuts,

roughly chopped
¾ cup monk fruit
¼ teaspoon freshly grated nutmeg
⅓ teaspoon ground cloves
½ teaspoon pure vanilla extract
½ teaspoon pure coconut extract
⅛ teaspoon fine sea salt

Use parchment paper to line the perforated pan. In a large mixing basin, combine the coconut flour, almond flour, baking powder, and baking soda. Combine the eggs and coconut oil in a separate mixing dish. Combine the wet and dry ingredients in a mixing bowl. Stir in the rest of the ingredients until a soft dough form. For each cookie, drop roughly 2 tablespoons of dough onto parchment paper and flatten each biscuit until it is 1 inch thick. Using the control panel, select bake, then adjust the temperature to 370 degrees F and the time to 25 minutes then touch Start. When the display indicates "Add Food" insert cooking tray in the Air Fryer. When cooking is complete, the cookies should be golden and firm to the touch. Remove from the oven to a plate. Let the cookies cool to room temperature and serve.

Per Serving: Calories 274; Fat 25.7g; Sodium 69mg; Carbs 8g; Fiber 4g; Sugar 1.6 g; Protein 5.1 g

Oatmeal Crisp with Apple

Prep time: 10 minutes| Cook time: 12 minutes| Serves: 4

2 peaches, peeled, pitted, and chopped	2 tablespoons unsalted butter, at room temperature
1 apple, peeled and chopped	½ cup quick-cooking oatmeal
2 tablespoons honey	⅓ cup whole-wheat pastry flour
3 tablespoons packed brown sugar	½ teaspoon ground cinnamon

Toss the peaches, apple, and honey in a baking pan until everything is well incorporated. In a medium mixing bowl, combine the brown sugar, butter, oats, pastry flour, and cinnamon and stir until crumbly. This mixture should be generously sprinkled on top of the peaches and apples. Using the control panel, select bake, then adjust the temperature to 380 degrees F and the time to 10 minutes then touch Start. When the display indicates "Add Food", insert cooking tray in the Air Fryer. Bake until the fruit is bubbling and the topping is golden brown. Once cooking is complete, remove the pan from the oven and allow cooling for 5 minutes before serving.

Per Serving: Calories 244; Fat 6.7g; Sodium 15mg; Carbs 45.1g; Fiber 4g; Sugar 28.6 g; Protein 3.4 g

Vanilla Almond Walnuts Tart with Cardamom

Prep time: 05 minutes| Cook time: 12 minutes| Serves: 6

1 cup coconut milk	2 eggs
½ cup walnuts, ground	1 teaspoon vanilla essence
½ cup Swerve	¼ teaspoon ground cardamom
½ cup almond flour	¼ teaspoon ground cloves
½ stick butter, at room temperature	Cooking spray

Using cooking spray, coat a baking pan. In a large mixing basin, whisk together all of the ingredients except the oil until well combined. Fill the baking pan halfway with batter. Using the control panel, select bake, then adjust the temperature to 360 degrees F and the time to 13 minutes then touch Start. When the display indicates "Add Food", insert cooking tray in the center position. A toothpick put into the centre of the tart should come out clean once it has finished cooking. Remove from the air fryer and set aside to cool on a wire rack. Serve right away.

Per Serving: Calories 305; Fat 29.3g; Sodium 85mg; Carbs 5.7g; Fiber 2.6g; Sugar 1.6 g; Protein 7.4 g

Cinnamon Berries with Mixed Nuts

Prep time: 05 minutes| Cook time: 17 minutes| Serves: 3

½ cup mixed berries	3 tablespoons almonds, slivered
Cooking spray Topping:	3 tablespoons chopped pecans
1 egg, beaten	

2 tablespoons chopped walnuts	2 tablespoons cold salted butter, cut into pieces
3 tablespoons granulated Swerve	½ teaspoon ground cinnamon

Using cooking spray, lightly coat a baking dish. To make the topping, follow these steps: Stir together the beaten egg, nuts, Swerve, butter, and cinnamon in a medium mixing bowl until well combined. Spread the topping over the top of the mixed berries in the bottom of the baking dish. Using the control panel, select bake, then adjust the temperature to 340 degrees F and the time to 17 minutes then touch Start. When the display indicates "Add Food", insert cooking tray in the Air Fryer. When cooking is complete, the fruit should be bubbly and topping should be golden brown. Allow to cool for 5 to 10 minutes before serving.

Per Serving: Calories 265; Fat 25.3g; Sodium 75mg; Carbs 7.1g; Fiber 3.6g; Sugar 2.6 g; Protein 6.1g

Cinnamon Peach and Blueberry with Lemon

Prep time: 05 minutes| Cook time: 20 minutes| Serves: 6

1-pint blueberries, rinsed and picked through (about 2 cups)	(optional)
2 large peaches or nectarines, peeled and cut into ½-inch slices (about 2 cups)	¼ teaspoon ground allspice or cinnamon
	Pinch kosher or fine salt
⅓ cup plus 2 tablespoons granulated sugar, divided	1 (9-inch) refrigerated piecrust (or use homemade)
2 tablespoons unbleached all-purpose flour	2 teaspoons unsalted butter, cut into pea-size pieces
½ teaspoon grated lemon zest	1 large egg, beaten

In a medium mixing basin, combine the blueberries, peaches, 13 cups sugar, flour, lemon zest (if preferred), spices, and salt. Unroll the crust onto the baking sheet, repairing any tears as needed. Place the fruit in the middle of the crust, leaving approximately 112 inches around the edges. Arrange the butter slices on top of the fruit. Fold the crust's outside edge over the fruit's outer circle, making pleats as needed. Over the crust, brush the egg. Sprinkle the remaining 2 tablespoons of sugar over the crust and fruit. Using the control panel, select bake, then adjust the temperature to 350 degrees F and the time to 20 minutes then touch Start. When the display indicates "Add Food", insert cooking tray in the Air Fryer. After about 15 minutes, check the galette, rotating the pan if the crust is not browning evenly. Continue cooking until the crust is deep golden brown and the fruit is bubbling. When cooking is complete, remove the pan from the oven and allow cooling for 10 minutes before slicing and serving.

Per Serving: Calories 91; Fat 2.5g; Sodium 48mg; Carbs 17.1g; Fiber 2.6g; Sugar 11.6 g; Protein 2.3g

Red Wine Chocolate Cake with Glaze

Prep time: 15 minutes| Cook time: 40 minutes| Serves: 10

For the Cake:	1¾ cups all-purpose flour
7 ounces (198 g) unsalted butter, at room temperature, plus more for the pan	1 teaspoon baking powder
	Pinch of fine sea salt
	½ cup full-bodied red wine (Merlot is perfect here)
5½ ounces (156 g) 70% cocoa solids dark chocolate, broken into pieces	Finely grated zest of 1 orange
	For the Glaze:
1½ cups dark brown sugar	4½ ounces (128 g) 70% cocoa solids dark chocolate, broken into pieces
4 extra-large eggs, at room temperature, lightly beaten	
3 tablespoons cocoa powder	½ cup heavy cream

2 tablespoons port
3 tablespoons confectioners'
sugar, sifted

Line the bottom of a spring form cake pan with parchment paper and butter it. In a heatproof bowl, melt the chocolate over a pan of gently simmering water (the bottom of the basin should not touch the water). Melt the chocolate, stirring occasionally to ensure even melting. Remove the bowl and set it aside to cool. With electric beaters, cream the butter and sugar until light and fluffy. Add the eggs one at a time, beating thoroughly after each addition. Sift together the cocoa, flour, baking powder, and salt in a mixing dish, then stir the ingredients into the batter. The red wine and orange zest are added last, followed by the melted chocolate. Scrape into the pan that has been prepared.

Using the control panel, select bake, then adjust the temperature to 350 degrees F and the time to 40 minutes then touch Start. When the display indicates "Add Food", insert cooking tray in the Air Fryer. A skewer inserted into the centre should come out clean when done. Allow the cake to cool completely in the pan before turning it out onto a wire rack. To make the glaze, melt the chocolate in a heatproof basin as directed. In a separate bowl, whisk together the cream and port until smooth, then add the confectioners' sugar. Allow it to cool somewhat before pouring it over the cake (but not until it has set). Allow the glaze to set for a few minutes before serving.

Per Serving: Calories 631; Fat 18.5g; Sodium 190mg; Carbs 110.1g; Fiber 1.6g; Sugar 77.6 g; Protein 7.3g

Orange Cake with Coconut Orange Frosting

Prep time: 20 minutes| Cook time: 25 minutes| Serves: 6

1 cup applesauce
¼ cup skim milk or low-fat soy milk
1 tablespoon vegetable oil
½ cup brown sugar
1 egg
1½ cups unbleached flour
1 teaspoon baking powder
½ teaspoon baking soda
¼ teaspoon grated nutmeg
½ teaspoon ground cinnamon
½ teaspoon grated orange zest
Salt, to taste

For the Creamy Frosting:
1½ cups confectioners' sugar, sifted
3 tablespoons margarine
1 tablespoon fat-free half-and-half or skim milk
½ teaspoon vanilla extract
Salt, to taste
½ cup sweetened flaked coconut
1 (5-ounce / 142-g) can mandarin oranges, drained well

In a small mixing dish, combine the applesauce, milk, oil, sugar, and egg. Remove from the equation. In a medium mixing bowl, combine the flour, baking powder, nutmeg, cinnamon, orange zest, and salt. Stir in the applesauce mixture thoroughly. Pour the batter into a square baking (cake) pan that has been oiled or non-stick. Using the control panel, select bake, then adjust the temperature to 350 degrees F and the time to 25 minutes then touch Start. When the display indicates "Add Food" insert cooking tray in the Air Fryer. When done, a toothpick inserted in the center should come out clean. Garnish with creamy frosting.

Per Serving: Calories 517; Fat 4.5g; Sodium 154mg; Carbs 105.1g; Fiber 3.6g; Sugar 17.6 g; Protein 13.2g

Chocolate Blueberry Rum Cupcakes

Prep time: 05 minutes| Cook time: 15 minutes| Serves: 6

¾ cup granulated Erythritol
1¼ cups almond flour
1 teaspoon unsweetened baking powder

3 teaspoons cocoa powder
½ teaspoon baking soda
½ teaspoon ground cinnamon
¼ teaspoon grated nutmeg

⅛ teaspoon salt
½ cup milk
1 stick butter, at room temperature

3 eggs, whisked
1 teaspoon pure rum extract
½ cup blueberries
Cooking spray

Using cooking spray, coat a 6-cup muffin pan. Combine the Erythritol, almond flour, baking powder, cocoa powder, baking soda, cinnamon, nutmeg, and salt in a mixing dish and stir well to combine. Mix the milk, butter, egg, and rum extract in a separate mixing bowl until fully blended. Pour the wet liquid into the dry mixture slowly and gently. Add the blueberries and stir to combine. Fill the oiled muffin cups about three-quarters full with the batter. Using the control panel, select bake, then adjust the temperature to 345 degrees F and the time to 15 minutes then touch Start. When the display indicates "Add Food", insert cooking tray in the Air Fryer. When done, the center should be springy and a toothpick inserted in the middle should come out clean. Remove from the oven and place on a wire rack to cool. Serve immediately.

Per Serving: Calories 451; Fat 41.5g; Sodium 222mg; Carbs 44.1g; Fiber 6.2g; Sugar 34 g; Protein 12.2g

Cardamom Pudding with Sour Cherries

Prep time: 10 minutes| Cook time: 45 minutes| Serves: 8

1 cup dried sour cherries
½ cup unsweetened pomegranate juice
1¼ cups heavy cream
1¼ cups whole milk
Pinch of sea salt
Seeds from 2 cardamom pods, ground
3 extra-large eggs, plus 1 extra-large egg yolk generous

½ cup superfine sugar
9 ounces (255 g) brioche loaf
2½ tablespoons unsalted butter, softened
1 teaspoon rose water, or to taste
Squeeze of lemon or lime juice
Confectioners' sugar, to dust

In a small saucepan, combine the dried cherries and just enough pomegranate juice to cover. Bring to a boil, then remove from the heat and set aside to plump up the cherries (they need at least 30 minutes, but longer is fine). In a heavy-bottomed saucepan, bring the cream, milk, and salt to a boil with the cardamom, then remove from the heat and set aside for 15 minutes. Combine the eggs, egg yolk, and sugar in a mixing bowl. Pour the warm milk mixture over it while constantly stirring. Taste the egg and cream mixture after adding a few drops of rose water and a squeeze of lemon or lime juice. You should be able to smell the rose water, but not too strongly. Pour the egg and milk mixture over the layers of bread in a uniform layer. Allow the pudding to settle for 30 minutes to lighten it up. Place the dish in a baking pan and carefully pour boiling water into the pan until it reaches about one-third of the way up the dish's edges. Using the control panel, select bake, then adjust the temperature to 375 degrees F and the time to 45 minutes then touch Start. When the display indicates "Add Food", insert cooking tray in the Air Fryer. The pudding should be fluffy, golden, and just set on top when done. Remove the dish from the oven and set it aside to cool slightly—the pudding will continue to cook in the residual heat—before dusting with confectioners' sugar and serving.

Per Serving: Calories 528; Fat 38.2g; Sodium 217mg; Carbs 39.1g; Fiber 1.2g; Sugar 23.4 g; Protein 8.2g

Vanilla Coconut Chocolate Cake

Prep time: 05 minutes| Cook time: 15 minutes| Serves: 6

½ cup unsweetened chocolate, chopped
½ stick butter, at room

temperature
1 tablespoon liquid stevia
1½ cups coconut flour

2 eggs, whisked
½ teaspoon vanilla extract

A pinch of fine sea salt
Cooking spray

In a microwave-safe bowl, combine the chocolate, butter, and stevia. Microwave for 30 seconds or until completely melted. Allow 5 to 10 minutes for the chocolate mixture to cool. Toss the remaining ingredients into the chocolate mixture in a mixing dish and whisk to combine. Lightly coat a baking pan with cooking spray. Scrape the chocolate mixture into the baking pan that has been prepared. Using the control panel, select Bake, then adjust the temperature to 330 degrees F and the time to 15 minutes then touch Start. When the display indicates "Add Food", insert cooking tray in the Air Fryer. When cooking is complete, the top should spring back lightly when gently pressed with your fingers. Let the cake cool for 5 minutes and serve.
Per Serving: Calories 200; Fat 16.2g; Sodium 144mg; Carbs 10.1g; Fiber 6.2g; Sugar 1.2 g; Protein 5.2g

Coconut Almond Orange Jam Cake

Prep time: 05 minutes| Cook time: 15 minutes| Serves: 6

1 stick butter, melted
¾ cup granulated Swerve
2 eggs, beaten
¾ cup coconut flour
¼ teaspoon salt
⅓ teaspoon grated nutmeg

⅓ cup coconut milk
1¼ cups almond flour
½ teaspoon baking powder
2 tablespoons unsweetened orange jam
Cooking spray

Using cooking spray, coat a baking pan. Remove from the equation. Whisk together the melted butter and granulated Swerve in a large mixing bowl until frothy. Whisk in the beaten eggs until completely smooth. Pour in the coconut milk gradually while stirring in the coconut flour, salt, and nutmeg. Stir in the other ingredients until completely combined. Using a spatula, scrape the batter into the baking pan. Using the control panel, select Bake, then adjust the temperature to 355 degrees F and the time to 17 minutes then touch Start. When the display indicates "Add Food", insert cooking tray in the Air Fryer. When cooking is complete, the top of the cake should spring back when gently pressed with your fingers. Remove from the Air Fryer to a wire rack to cool. Serve chilled.
Per Serving: Calories 490; Fat 46g; Sodium 232mg; Carbs 13.1g; Fiber 6.5g; Sugar 2.2 g; Protein 13.2g

Honey Cinnamon Oatmeal

Prep time: 10 minutes| Cook time: 11 minutes| Serves: 4

1 apple, peeled and chopped
2 peaches, peeled, pitted, and chopped
2 tablespoons honey
½ cup quick-cooking oatmeal
⅓ cup whole-wheat pastry

flour
2 tablespoons unsalted butter, at room temperature
3 tablespoons packed brown sugar
½ teaspoon ground cinnamon

In a baking pan, combine the apple, peaches, and honey until well combined. Blend the oats, pastry flour, butter, brown sugar, and cinnamon in a mixing bowl and stir well to combine. Using a spatula, evenly distribute the mixture over the fruit. Using the control panel, select bake, then adjust the temperature to 380 degrees F and the time to 11 minutes then touch Start. When the display indicates "Add Food", insert cooking tray in the Air Fryer. Once the oven has preheated, place the pan into the air fryer. When cooking is complete, the fruit should be bubbling around the edges and the topping should be golden brown. Remove from the oven and serve warm.
Per Serving: Calories 163; Fat 4.6g; Sodium 32mg; Carbs 30.1g; Fiber 2.5g; Sugar 18.2 g; Protein 2.2g

Sweet Apple Apricots with Cinnamon

Prep time: 05 minutes| Cook time: 15 minutes| Serves: 4

4 large apples, peeled and sliced into 8 wedges
2 tablespoons olive oil

½ cup dried apricots, chopped
1 to 2 tablespoons sugar
½ teaspoon ground cinnamon

In a mixing basin, toss the apple wedges with the olive oil until well coated. In a perforated pan, place the apple wedges. Using the control panel, select Air Fry, then adjust the temperature to 350 degrees F and the time to 17 minutes then touch Start. When the display indicates "Add Food", insert cooking tray in the Air Fryer. Remove the pan from the oven after about 12 minutes. Air Fry for another 3 minutes after adding the dried apricots. Meanwhile, in a small bowl, thoroughly combine the sugar and cinnamon. Transfer the apple wedges to a dish from the air fryer. Serve with the sugar mixture sprinkled on top.
Per Serving: Calories 197; Fat 7.5g; Sodium 2mg; Carbs 36.1g; Fiber 5.9g; Sugar 28 g; Protein 0.9 g

Sweet Buttery Apple Fritters

Prep time:30 minutes| Cook time: 7minutes| Serves: 6

1 cup chopped, peeled Granny Smith apple
½ cup granulated sugar
1 teaspoon ground cinnamon
1 cup all-purpose flour
1 teaspoon baking powder
1 teaspoon salt

2 tablespoons milk
2 tablespoons butter, melted
1 large egg, beaten
Cooking spray
¼ cup confectioners' sugar (optional)

In a small bowl, combine the apple, granulated sugar, and cinnamon. Allow for 30 minutes of resting time. In a medium mixing basin, combine the flour, baking powder, and salt. Stir in the milk, butter, and egg until everything is well combined. Pour the apple mixture into the flour mixture and stir until a dough forms using a spatula. To make the fritters, start by combining all of the ingredients in a large bowl. Divide the dough into 12 equal portions and roll into 1-inch balls on a clean work surface. With your hands, flatten them into patties. Spray the perforated pan with cooking spray and line it with parchment paper. Place the apple fritters on the parchment paper, spacing them equally but not too closely. Using frying spray, coat the fritters. Using the control panel, select Bake, then adjust the temperature to 350 degrees F and the time to 7 minutes then touch Start. When the display indicates "Add Food", insert cooking tray in the Air Fryer. When cooking is complete, the fritters should be lightly browned. Remove from the oven to a plate and serve with the confectioners' sugar sprinkled on top, if desired.
Per Serving: Calories 304; Fat 7.6g; Sodium 645mg; Carbs 55.1g; Fiber 2.4g; Sugar 29.7 g; Protein 5.1 g

Fruit Kebabs with Honey

Prep time:10 minutes| Cook time: 4 minutes| Serves: 4

2 peaches, peeled, pitted, and thickly sliced
3 plums, halved and pitted
3 nectarines, halved and pitted
1 tablespoon honey

½ teaspoon ground cinnamon
¼ teaspoon ground allspice
Pinch cayenne pepper
Special Equipment: 8 metal skewers

Using metal skewers that fit into the oven, alternately thread peaches, plums, and nectarines. In a small bowl, thoroughly blend the honey, cinnamon, allspice, and cayenne. Brush the

glaze generously over the fruit skewers. In the perforated pan, place the fruit skewers. Using the control panel, select Air Fry, then adjust the temperature to 400 degrees F and the time to 4 minutes then touch Start. When the display indicates "Add Food", insert cooking tray in the Air Fryer. When cooking is complete, the fruit should be caramelized. Remove the fruit skewers from the oven and let rest for 5 minutes before serving.
Per Serving: Calories 114; Fat 0.6g; Sodium 0mg; Carbs 28.1g; Fiber 3.4g; Sugar 25 g; Protein 2.3 g

Chocolate Chip Oatmeal Cookies

Prep time: 10 minutes| Cook time: 20 minutes| Serves: 4 dozen

1 cup unsalted butter, at room temperature	2 cups old-fashioned rolled oats
1 cup dark brown sugar	1½ cups all-purpose flour
½ cup granulated sugar	1 teaspoon baking powder
2 large eggs	1 teaspoon baking soda
1 tablespoon vanilla-extract	2 cups chocolate chips
Pinch salt	

In a large mixing basin, cream together the butter, brown sugar, and granulated sugar until creamy and light in colour. One at a time, crack the eggs into the bowl, mixing after each addition. Combine the vanilla and salt in a mixing bowl. In a separate basin, combine the oats, flour, baking powder, and baking soda. Stir the ingredients into the butter mixture until it is thoroughly combined. Add the chocolate chips and mix well. In a uniform layer, spread the dough onto the sheet pan. Using the control panel, select bake, then adjust the temperature to 350 degrees F and the time to 20 minutes then touch Start. When the display indicates "Add Food", insert cooking tray in the Air Fryer. Check the cookie after 15 minutes, moving the pan if the crust is not browning evenly. Cook for another 18 to 20 minutes, or until golden brown. Remove the pan from the air fryer after it's done cooking and let it cool fully before slicing and serving.
Per Serving: Calories 158; Fat 6.5g; Sodium 64mg; Carbs 22.5g; Fiber 1g; Sugar 8.7 g; Protein 2.8 g

Nutmeg Coconut Pound Cake

Prep time:05 minutes| Cook time: 30 minutes| Serves: 8

1 stick butter, at room temperature	½ teaspoon baking powder
1 cup Swerve	¼ teaspoon salt
4 eggs	1 teaspoon vanilla essence
1½ cups coconut flour	A pinch of ground star anise
½ cup buttermilk	A pinch of freshly grated nutmeg
½ teaspoon baking soda	Cooking spray

Using cooking spray, coat a baking pan. Cream the butter and Swerve together with an electric mixer or a hand mixer until smooth. Mix in the eggs one at a time, whisking until frothy. Stir in the other ingredients until completely combined. Place the batter in the baking pan that has been prepared. Using the control panel, select bake, then adjust the temperature to 320 degrees F and the time to 30 minutes then touch Start. When the display indicates "Add Food", insert cooking tray in the Air Fryer. When cooking is complete, the center of the cake should be springy. Allow the cake to cool in the pan for 10 minutes before removing and serving
Per Serving: Calories 247; Fat 20.5g; Sodium 400mg; Carbs 9.7g; Fiber 4.8g; Sugar 2.2 g; Protein 6.8 g

Pineapple Kebabs with Coconut

Prep time:10 minutes| Cook time: 10 minutes| Serves: 4

½ fresh pineapple, cut into sticks	¼ cup desiccated coconut

Place the desiccated coconut on a platter and roll the pineapple sticks in it until they are completely covered in it. In the perforated pan, arrange the pineapple sticks. Using the control panel, select Air Fry, then adjust the temperature to 400 degrees F and the time to 10 minutes then touch Start. When the display indicates "Add Food", insert cooking tray in the Air Fryer. When cooking is complete, the pineapple sticks should be crisp-tender. Serve warm.
Per Serving: Calories 53; Fat 1.2g; Sodium 2mg; Carbs 11.2g; Fiber 1.4g; Sugar 8.3 g; Protein 0.6 g

Luscious Pumpkin Pudding with Vanilla Wafers

Prep time:10 minutes| Cook time: 15 minutes| Serves: 4

1 cup canned no-salt-added pumpkin purée (not pumpkin pie filling)	1 tablespoon unsalted butter, melted
¼ cup packed brown sugar	1 teaspoon pure vanilla extract
3 tablespoons all-purpose flour	4 low-fat vanilla wafers, crumbled
1 egg, whisked	Cooking spray
2 tablespoons milk	

Using cooking spray, coat a baking pan. Remove from the equation. In a medium mixing bowl, whisk together the pumpkin purée, brown sugar, flour, whisked egg, milk, melted butter, and vanilla. Fill the baking pan halfway with the mixture. Using the control panel, select Bake, then adjust the temperature to 350 degrees F and the time to 15 minutes then touch Start. When the display indicates "Add Food", insert cooking tray in the Air Fryer. When the pudding is done cooking, it should be set. Remove the pudding from the oven and set it to cool on a wire rack. Serve the pudding in 4 dishes with a sprinkle of vanilla wafers on top.
Per Serving: Calories 266; Fat 8.5g; Sodium 300mg; Carbs 43.9g; Fiber 2.4g; Sugar 23.4 g; Protein 5 g

Cocoa Bread Pudding

Prep time:10 minutes| Cook time: 10 minutes| Serves: 8

1 egg	2 tablespoons cocoa powder
1 egg yolk	1 teaspoon vanilla
¾ cup chocolate milk	5 slices firm white bread, cubed
3 tablespoons brown sugar	
3 tablespoons peanut butter	non-stick cooking spray

Using non-stick cooking spray, coat a baking pan. Combine the egg, egg yolk, chocolate milk, brown sugar, peanut butter, cocoa powder, and vanilla in a mixing bowl and whisk until smooth. Toss in the bread cubes and toss well to combine. Allow 10 minutes for the bread to soak. Transfer the egg mixture to the prepared baking pan once it's done. Using the control panel, select Bake, then adjust the temperature to 330 degrees F and the time to 10 minutes then touch Start. When the display indicates "Add Food", insert cooking tray in the Air Fryer. When done, the pudding should be just firm to the touch. Serve at room temperature.
Per Serving: Calories 102; Fat 5.4g; Sodium 90mg; Carbs 10.7g; Fiber 1.1g; Sugar 6.4 g; Protein 3.9 g

4-Week Diet Plan

Week-1

<table>
<tr><th colspan="6">Week-1</th></tr>
<tr><th></th><th>Breakfast</th><th>Lunch</th><th>Snack</th><th>Dinner</th><th>Dessert</th></tr>
<tr><td>Day-1</td><td>Biscuits with Smoked Sausage</td><td>Lemony Tuna</td><td>Crispy Sausage Patties</td><td>Buttery Pork Loin</td><td>Simple Pumpkin Tart</td></tr>
<tr><td>Day-2</td><td>Egg Tofu Omelet</td><td>Herbed Lamb Chops</td><td>Cajun Crab Sticks</td><td>Spicy Broccoli</td><td>Nutty Slice with Cinnamon</td></tr>
<tr><td>Day-3</td><td>Mini Pizzas with Smoked Sausage</td><td>Delicious Tomatoes</td><td>Cinnamon Salty Apple Slices</td><td>Mint Flavor Fried Pork Chops</td><td>Luscious Orange cake</td></tr>
<tr><td>Day-4</td><td>Mediterranean-Style Mini Pizza</td><td>Mustard Salmon</td><td>Garlic Chili Sweet Potato Fries</td><td>Spicy Wings</td><td>Apple Lemon Pasty</td></tr>
<tr><td>Day-5</td><td>Classic Cinnamon Fritters</td><td>Chicken Breast with Honey and Mustard</td><td>Tasty Crunchy Peanuts</td><td>Pesto Lamb</td><td>Hemp Seed Brownies</td></tr>
<tr><td>Day-6</td><td>Vanilla Pear Beignets</td><td>Mushrooms with Kale</td><td>Fried Hominy</td><td>Lemon Parmesan Cod</td><td>Tasty Chocolate Coconut Mug Cake</td></tr>
<tr><td>Day-7</td><td>Soft Zucchini Galettes</td><td>Veggies with Italian Sausages</td><td>Garlic Lemon Tofu Popcorns</td><td>Beer Air Fryer Chicken</td><td>Sugary Cinnamon Churros</td></tr>
</table>

Week-2

<table>
<tr><th colspan="6">Week-2</th></tr>
<tr><th></th><th>Breakfast</th><th>Lunch</th><th>Snack</th><th>Dinner</th><th>Dessert</th></tr>
<tr><td>Day-1</td><td>Eggs, Tofu and Mushroom Omelet</td><td>Crispy Pork Scotch Egg</td><td>Sweet Cinnamon Apple Fritters</td><td>Lemon Pepper Sea Bass</td><td>Strawberry Tartar Cake</td></tr>
<tr><td>Day-2</td><td>Vegetable and Sausage Frittata</td><td>Asparagus Wrap with Bacon</td><td>Baked Cheesy Bacon Russet Potatoes</td><td>BBQ Wings of Chicken</td><td>Sugary Cinnamon Chickpeas</td></tr>
<tr><td>Day-3</td><td>Bacon Mini Quiche</td><td>Lemon Garlic Scallops</td><td>Chocolate Banana Pups Crust</td><td>Spiced Lamb Kebabs</td><td>Chocolate Almond Cake</td></tr>
<tr><td>Day-4</td><td>Tomato Frittata</td><td>Tasty Stuffed Potatoes</td><td>Garlic Rosemary Cheese Sticks</td><td>Duck Legs with Full Spices</td><td>Bread with Amaretto Sauce</td></tr>
<tr><td>Day-5</td><td>Salt and black Pepper Polish Naleśniki</td><td>Crispy Drumsticks</td><td>Dijon Beef Quinoa Meatballs</td><td>Tasty Tarragon Beef Shanks</td><td>Almond Coffee Cake</td></tr>
<tr><td>Day-6</td><td>Spinach and Feta Baked Eggs</td><td>Beef Pork Meatballs</td><td>Roasted Almond Garlic Cauliflower Chunks</td><td>Spicy Lemon Garlic Shrimp</td><td>Vanilla Blueberry Pecans Cake</td></tr>
<tr><td>Day-7</td><td>Broccoli Frittata</td><td>Chicken Tenders with Buffalo Sauce</td><td>Honey Coconut Almond Graham Crackers</td><td>Lemon Beef Kebobs with Cream Dip</td><td>Stuffed Apples with Vanilla Sauce</td></tr>
</table>

Week-3

	Breakfast	Lunch	Snack	Dinner	Dessert
			Week-3		
Day-1	Mini Mushroom Frittatas	Spicy Lemon Beef Skewers	Salty Roasted Potatoes	Cheesy Zucchini Chips	Marshmallows S'mores
Day-2	Cheesy Omelet with Scallions	Fried Thyme Lamb Chops	Buffalo Panko Cauliflower	Parmesan Chicken	Orange Sloe Gin
Day-3	Breakfast Muffins with Almonds	Lemon Tilapia with Herbs	Garlic Corn & Beans Fries	Crispy Beef Eggplant Medley	Lime Coconut Cheesecake
Day-4	Mixed Veggies Frittata	Green Beans with Avocado and Tomatoes	Garlic Chili Cheese Toasts with Parsley	Easy Chicken Pie	Delicious Strawberry Danish
Day-5	Salt and black Pepper Greek Tiganite	Chicken Breast with Oregano	Paprika Shrimp with Bacon Bites	Bang Panko Breaded Fried Cod	Spiced Sugary Squash
Day-6	Greek-Style Pita Pizza	Spicy Duck Breast	Fried Tomatoes with Lots of Herbs	Tomatoes and Brussels Sprouts	Cashew Lemon Bars
Day-7	French Toast with Cranberry Jam	Crispy Paprika Fillets	Butter Fried Pecans	Meatballs Made with Turkey	Easy Granola with Apple Pie Spice

Week-4

	Breakfast	Lunch	Snack	Dinner	Dessert
			Week-4		
Day-1	Easy Grilled Breakfast Sausages	Veggies with Mustard	Garlic Paprika Dill Pickles	Tasty Beef Steaks	Coconut Lemon Cookie
Day-2	Pancetta and Spinach Frittata	Tilapia and Salsa	Cheese Cumin Jalapeno Poppers	Crusted Cauliflower Pork Chops	Apple Won Ton with Raisins
Day-3	Favorite Pizza Sandwich	Buttery Fries of Cinnamon	Garlic Cayenne Pickle Slices	Garlic Beef Patties	Cream Cheese Dumplings
Day-4	Chocolate Orange Muffins	Balsamic Flavored Chicken	Paprika Cumin Chickpeas	Tilapia Meniere with Vegetables	Corn Banana Fritters
Day-5	Eggs and Cheese Puffs	Cold Beef Brisket Salad	Vanilla Yogurt Blueberry Muffins	Stir Fried Orange Chicken	Mascarpone Pears and Espresso Cream
Day-6	Sausage Treat	Tuna Stuffed Potatoes	Tilapia Fish Sticks	Pork Neck with Tomato Salad	Sugar Peanut Buttery Biscuit
Day-7	Mexican-Style Quiche	Cheese and Leek Tomato Sauce Chicken	Tasty Vegetable Spring Rolls	Garlicky Herbed Lamb Cutlets	Walnuts Brownie Muffins

Conclusion

The Instant Vortex Air Fryer cooking appliance has six cooking functions: Air Fry, Bake, Roast, Reheat, Dehydrate and Broil. It has user-friendly operating buttons/displays: Time display, Temperature display, cooking status, smart program buttons, dial button, start button and cancel button. The cleaning process of this appliance is pretty simple. It comes with useful accessories like an air fryer basket, cooking tray, cooking chamber, and touch control panel. If you have a problem with your appliance, check the troubleshooting. In this cookbook, you will find delicious recipes. You will find all the useful cooking functions in one pot. I added delicious, mouthwatering, and healthy recipes for you and your family in my cookbook. You didn't need to buy another appliance for cooking food because it has six useful cooking functions in one pot. You can prepare your favorite food on different occasions. Thank you for choosing my book. I hope you love and appreciate my book.

Appendix 1 Measurement Conversion Chart

VOLUME EQUIVALENTS(DRY)

US STANDARD	METRIC (APPROXIMATE)
1/8 teaspoon	0.5 mL
1/4 teaspoon	1 mL
1/2 teaspoon	2 mL
3/4 teaspoon	4 mL
1 teaspoon	5 mL
1 tablespoon	15 mL
1/4 cup	59 mL
1/2 cup	118 mL
3/4 cup	177 mL
1 cup	235 mL
2 cups	475 mL
3 cups	700 mL
4 cups	1 L

VOLUME EQUIVALENTS(LIQUID)

US STANDARD	US STANDARD (OUNCES)	METRIC (APPROXIMATE)
2 tablespoons	1 fl.oz.	30 mL
1/4 cup	2 fl.oz.	60 mL
1/2 cup	4 fl.oz.	120 mL
1 cup	8 fl.oz.	240 mL
1 1/2 cup	12 fl.oz.	355 mL
2 cups or 1 pint	16 fl.oz.	475 mL
4 cups or 1 quart	32 fl.oz.	1 L
1 gallon	128 fl.oz.	4 L

TEMPERATURES EQUIVALENTS

FAHRENHEIT(F)	CELSIUS(C) (APPROXIMATE)
225 °F	107 °C
250 °F	120 °C
275 °F	135 °C
300 °F	150 °C
325 °F	160 °C
350 °F	180 °C
375 °F	190 °C
400 °F	205 °C
425 °F	220 °C
450 °F	235 °C
475 °F	245 °C
500 °F	260 °C

WEIGHT EQUIVALENTS

US STANDARD	METRIC (APPROXIMATE)
1 ounce	28 g
2 ounces	57 g
5 ounces	142 g
10 ounces	284 g
15 ounces	425 g
16 ounces (1 pound)	455 g
1.5 pounds	680 g
2 pounds	907 g

Appendix 2 Recipes Index

Made in United States
Troutdale, OR
03/04/2024

18142968R00123